INDIA'S NEAR EAST

AVINASH PALIWAL

India's Near East

A New History

OXFORD
UNIVERSITY PRESS

Oxford University Press is a department of the
University of Oxford. It furthers the University's objective
of excellence in research, scholarship, and education
by publishing worldwide.

Oxford New York

Auckland   Cape Town   Dar es Salaam   Hong Kong   Karachi
Kuala Lumpur   Madrid   Melbourne   Mexico City   Nairobi
New Delhi   Shanghai   Taipei   Toronto

With offices in

Argentina   Austria   Brazil   Chile   Czech Republic   France   Greece
Guatemala   Hungary   Italy   Japan   Poland   Portugal   Singapore
South Korea   Switzerland   Thailand   Turkey   Ukraine   Vietnam

Oxford is a registered trade mark of Oxford University Press
in the UK and certain other countries.

Published in the United States of America by
Oxford University Press
198 Madison Avenue, New York, NY 10016

Library of Congress Cataloging-in-Publication Data is available.

ISBN: 9780197794692

Printed in Great Britain by Bell & Bain Ltd, Glasgow

To Renate,
for giving strength when it was most needed,
and
Shira Lia,
for asking many beautiful whys / warums / क्यों

"I am the rebel eternal."

Bidrohi by Kazi Nazrul Islam

CONTENTS

Maps   xiii

1. Groundshift: An Introduction   1
    The Making of India's Near East   4
    Partitions, Statecraft, and Geopolitics   7
    Sources and Structure   19

PART I
SOLIDARITY (1947–1970)

2. One Enemy at a Time: Constitutional Survival &   25
    Resistance in Bengal, Assam, and Burma
    Constitutional Survival & Resistance   28
    Revolution or Ruin?   35
    "A Colony of West Pakistan"   42
    Conclusions   52

3. Special Powers, Desperate Acts: Constitutional   55
    Collapse & Militarism in India's Near East
    "Misled"   58
    Windfall   67
    "Contagion"   71
    Himalayan Blunder(s)   74
    Conclusions   79

4. Two and a Half Fronts: War, Borderlands, and   83
    Interventionism after 1962
    Ceasefire   85
    "Maggot"   89
    "Buai"   96
    Line in the Sand   105
    Conclusions   111

PART II
SECURITY (1971–1990)

5. Joy Bangla: The Liberation of Bangladesh & Remaking   117
    of India's Near East
    Rivers of Blood   120
    Secret Wars   127
    Birth of 'Bangabandhu'   135
    Joy Bangla   143
    Conclusions   152

6. Sons of the Soil: Assamese Nationalism and the   155
    Politics of Peacemaking
    Road to Shillong   158
    'Victory is with the God'   165
    Nellie   173
    Sons of the Soil   179
    Conclusions   183

7. Losing the Peace: Famine, Coup, and Countercoup   187
    in Bangladesh
    Second Revolution   189
    Coup, Counter-Coup   200
    Bangladesh Zindabad!   209
    The Last Coup   217
    Conclusions   221

8. Enabling Democracy: Civil-Military Politics in   225
    Rangoon & Dhaka
    8888   227
    Turnaround   233

'The Other Lady'   238
Blowback   245
Conclusions   249

PART III
CONNECTIVITY (1991–2024)

9.   Hard Look East: The Strategic Logic of Authoritarianism   253
'Look East Policy'   256
U-Turn   265
Hasina   268
Narco-Peace   274
Conclusions   280

10. 'Termites': Saffron Geopolitics in the Shadow of   283
China's Rise
Pilkhana   285
Saffron Revolution   292
Act East   297
"Termites"   309
Conclusions   314

Epilogue: Groundswell   317

List of Interviews   329

Acronyms   335

Dramatis personae (select)   339

Acknowledgements   345

Notes   349

Bibliography   423

Index   435

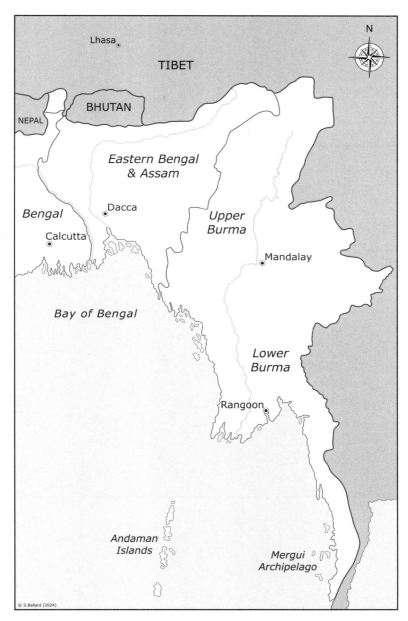

India's Near East Pre-1947

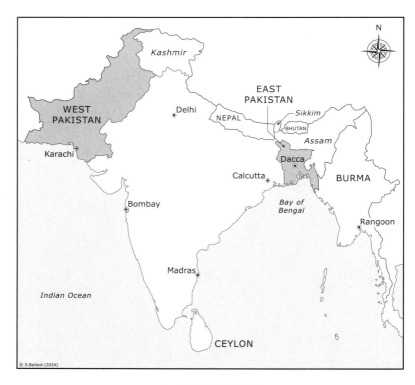

India 1947-1971

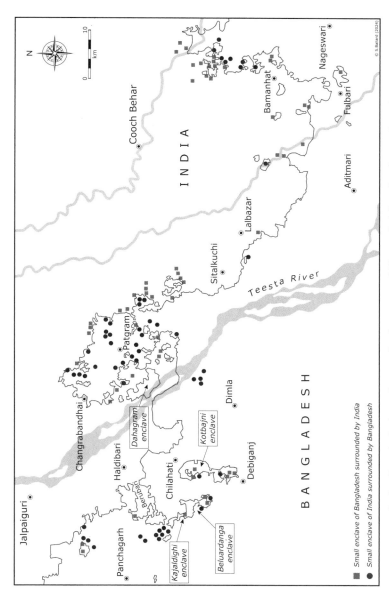

India-Bangladesh enclaves, also known as 'Chitmahals' or 'Pasha enclaves'.

Drug routes connecting the Golden Triangle with India's northeastern states and Bangladesh.

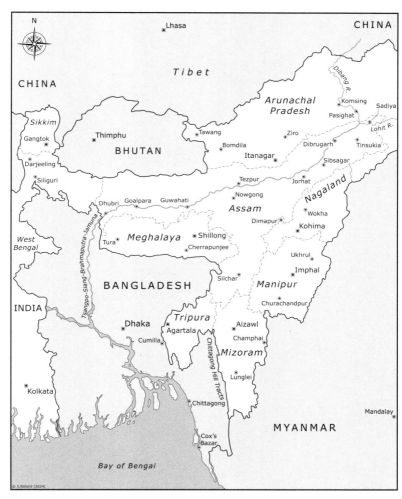

India's northeastern states

1

GROUNDSHIFT
AN INTRODUCTION

'Ten years under Modi govt have been golden era for Northeast'.

Amit Shah, Home Minister of India, January 19, 2024[1]

The mob was agitated. 'If you don't take off your clothes, we'll kill you', it shouted at the two women.[2] Their brother already lynched, these survivors were forcibly paraded naked, molested, and gang-raped. The incident occurred on 4 May 2023, as Manipur imploded into an ethnically-charged civil conflict between the Meitei and Kuki communities. But a police complaint was not filed. After all, the women caught in the maelstrom were allegedly handed over to the mob by the police themselves. The ensuing violence left hundreds dead, thousands injured, and several thousand displaced.[3] Damage to property included destruction of 254 churches and 132 temples.[4] To prevent the conflict from spiraling, New Delhi redeployed multiple battalions of paramilitary and army units, including from the sensitive China border to the small northeastern state bordering Myanmar. They secured a buffer zone between the Meitei-dominated Imphal and the Kuki-dominated hill districts.[5]

Manipur's partition is a grim reality and the government's response to it confounding. The Hindu nationalist Bharatiya Janata Party (BJP)-led state government favoured the majority community.[6] Instead of castigating such partisanship, prime minister Narendra Modi and home minister Amit Shah supported it. Shah visited Manipur but couldn't contain the conflict. Soldiers manning the 'buffer zone' faced hostile units in police uniforms seekings to breach the cordon and enable armed Meitei groups to rampage Kuki areas.[7] When such attempts failed, they lobbed mortars across the 'border'. Kuki groups responded with sniper fire.

Modi's silence spoke the loudest. Had it not been for a video of the mob assault surfacing online and sending shockwaves, India's prime minister probably would never have uttered a word about Manipur. Modi's only Tweet (X) on the northeast in the seventy-plus days before the video leak, celebrated its infrastructural development and connectivity.[8] The fact that a state critical for India's eastward connectivity was partitioned, and that Myanmar traders were dodging bullets and bombs to reach Indian markets to sell wares that few bought, was lost on New Delhi.[9] When pushed to clarify the government's position, Shah blamed displacement from Myanmar and increased drug trafficking since the 2021 Myanmar coup.[10] Instead of fixing apparent governance failures and communal excess, external factors were cited for Manipur's partition.

Such an evasive governmental response brings into sharp relief the tension between India's nation-building and its global ambitions. Driven by electoral concerns and Hindu nationalism, the BJP's majoritarianism feeds division in an ethnically stratified region. It goes against Modi's rhetoric of uniting the northeast (Arunachal Pradesh, Assam, Nagaland, Sikkim, Manipur, Meghalaya, Mizoram, and Tripura) under the BJP's banner. Internationally, it undermines India's quest for connectivity through Myanmar and Bangladesh as enshrined in the 'Act East' policy. Arguably, improved trade and equitable wealth distribution could reduce political violence in the region and increase India's power. For a country invested in the Indo-Pacific and aligned with the United States, Japan, and Australia—the 'Quad'—to counter China, such connectivity is essential.

But India struggles to achieve it. In fact, India's near east is less connected in 2024 than it was in 1947. This book asks why. Carved apart by communal and class violence, this is one of the most intricately partitioned lands anywhere on Earth. India's quest to unite the northeast, and connect it with neighbours, then, goes against the logic of the subcontinent's multiple partitions. The first such partition occurred in 1937 when Burma, a colonial 'province', separated from India.[11] The second took place on 14–15 August 1947; and the third emerged from genocide and war that culminated with Bangladesh's liberation on 16 December 1971. These partitions impart unique centrifugal pressures and centripetal energies on India's statecraft in the northeast and its diplomacy with Bangladesh and Myanmar.

That's why this book is about India's near east. It could have been a treatise primarily on India's northeast, or about India's ties with Bangladesh and Myanmar. But such approaches presuppose national interests and reify binaries between the domestic and the international. Instead, this book argues that India's domestic state-building is inextricably connected to its international diplomacy. It is (geo)political history in inverse and driven by two concerns. The first is a need to shed light on India's statecraft and state-building by turning the lens *outside in*. India's struggle to earn legitimacy and establish a democratic, constitutional contract in the northeast was determined as much by its own errors and accomplishments as it was by cross-border movements and external sponsorship of separatism. From the Naga revolt to the Mizo rebellion, the Assamese insurrection to Meitei discontent, the 'foreign' connection was just as important as domestic sources. Thus, the state remained dominant but never truly triumphed.

The second concern is to unpeel India's diplomacy and foreign policy towards its eastern neighbours *inside out*. From promoting democracy to bolstering authoritarians, arming rebels to waging wars, building ports to granting loans, India has experimented with multiple ideas in this space with limited success. India's struggles with its 'Act East' policy, despite the latter's promise to develop the northeast and counter Beijing, are informed as much by domestic political schisms as they are by strategic rivalry with

3

China and Pakistan. India's decisions to engage the Burmese junta after the 1962 coup, wage war against Pakistan in 1971, aid the democracy movement in 1988-91, and build ambitious cross-border infrastructural projects were often driven by domestic electoral and security calculations.

The Making of India's Near East

This book offers a new history not because it introduces the term India's near east; the claim to novelty lies in its blurring of epistemic lines between the domestic and external, i.e. unpacking the interplay between India's state-building and strategy-making in the *entirety* of its near east. This region encompasses India's northeast, Bangladesh, and Myanmar. The cartography of colonial influence means this region could well include Tibet, China's Yunnan province, and Thailand, if not wider Southeast Asia. But there's a risk here. 'Near East' is a colonial term with problematic colonial and racial connotations. Like the 'Middle East' and the 'Far East', it was created to advance colonial knowledge and interests and has Orientalist underpinnings.[12] Even India's 'northeast' has racial connotations thanks to colonial policies and the unfortunate fact of India's own racially charged politics.[13]

This book doesn't seek to recreate, or even mistakenly endorse, such colonial tropes. India's near east is without a capital 'n' and 'e' in that sense. Used to impart analytical coherence to the geopolitical dynamics of a partitioned land, it denotes a specific geography with diverse demographics, without social insinuation or political meaning. It certainly is not an anthropological term meant to make sense of a people and their 'traits'. India's near east was administratively united *and* communally partitioned by colonialism. This book explores how India dealt with these realties to build a nation and project power.

To be sure, to argue that a country's foreign policies are shaped by domestic politics and vice versa is to state the obvious. But the idea here is not to make new theoretical contributions to the field of international relations. This book goes beyond the obvious by fleshing out the humdrum of India's diplomacy and statecraft towards a region that was once administratively united under colonialism. The partition(s) of this region reframed the postcolonial state's interests and social contract despite certain institutional and territorial continuities from the colonial era.[14] Some of these aspects are valuably covered in existing works.[15] India's northeast, for instance, is studied widely and deeply.

From local politics and history to insurgent warfare and political economies, from centre-state relations to borderland studies, works on India's northeastern states offer rich insights. Similarly, works on Sino-Indian relations and their impact on the security dynamics of India's northeast are burgeoning. China's growing assertiveness also offers context for New Delhi's approach towards Dhaka and Naypyidaw. Cross-disciplinary works on Bangladesh's and Myanmar's politics add further value. On Bangladesh, existing works focus on economics, developmental politics, and the 1971 liberation war. On Myanmar, scholarship is invested in the democracy movement, civil-military ties, religion and the state, the drug trade, and civil wars.[16] These strands of literature on India's near east mostly bypass each other.

This book builds upon these related but unconnected literatures. Myanmar's link to South Asian geopolitics, for instance, is as easily discounted as India's and Bangladesh's impact on Myanmar's politics. This book joins the dots. What makes such a disconnect odd is the fact that Indian policymakers (at least) view the region with more analytical unity than academics. India's foreign ministry has a desk dedicated to Bangladesh and Myanmar. Led by a joint secretary, this desk formulates policies by focusing on interconnections between India's northeast (and West Bengal), Bangladesh, and Myanmar. It could well be India's near east desk. This book's twin concerns about Indian statecraft and nation-building *outside in*, and diplomacy and foreign policy *inside out*, then, makes it a first to break such epistemic barriers.

For that purpose, the book goes into the minutiae of why (and how) India opted for peace, or waged war(s) in its near east. Few works unpack India's decision-making towards the Naga and Mizo movements and the wider northeast by lending focus to what was happening in the erstwhile East Pakistan/Bangladesh and Burma. Even fewer delve into the quality, quantity, timing, and effects of

Pakistan and China's arming of northeastern rebels. To that effect, this book is the first of its kind to offer a detailed story of Indian intelligence and espionage in its near east. There's a reason why India privileges protection of minorities (Hindus), denial of sanctuary to rebels, and support to the Awami League over others in Bangladesh. This book explains how these 'national interests' came into being, and why they've endured.

It also fills silences. Most subcontinental histories overlook India's approach towards East Pakistan *before* 1971. There is literature on the partition of Bengal, the 1943 famine, the 1950 migrant crisis, and the identity politics undergirding the politics of East and West Pakistan.[17] But these works make it seem that India awakened to Bangladesh only after the Pakistani army's genocidal spree. That's not true. India developed deep connections with East Pakistan before liberation. The communal riots in 1960s Bengal, some of the worst in subcontinental history, were decisive in shaping India's approach towards its near east. The impact of these experiences and India's appreciation of anti-West-Pakistan torrents in the east, were on display in 1965 when it decided *not to* invade East Pakistan. Indian policymakers had different ideas about how to solve India's two-and-a-half-front security dilemma, as it became clear in 1971.

There are silences on Burma too. India armed and trained the Burmese army in 1949 to prevent its collapse to ethnic Karen and communist offensives. Shortly after the Maoist victory in China, the spectre of communism in Burma haunted India. India knew that Burma was already a 'modified military dictatorship' when they were arming it in 1949 (long before the 1962 coup). New Delhi's decision to continue engaging with the junta after 1962 was but natural. If anything, Rajiv Gandhi's 1988 support to the democracy movement was a deviation from norm. This history rhymes today. In both Myanmar and Bangladesh, rivalry with China and Pakistan played a significant role in shaping India's approach. But so too did the ruling party's electoral compulsions and ideological bent.

This book is not a complete, comprehensive history. No single volume can do justice to the diversity, size, and importance of this region. The book's vast timeframe obviates coverage of various important aspects. But three aspects stand out. First, there is a significant gap in coverage of environmental shifts and natural disasters. Given how sensitive this region is to floods, tsunamis, earthquakes, and human-made disasters such as famines, one could author a history just around these.[18] Second, the book doesn't cover various identarian movements in the detail they deserve. These include turmoil in Assam's Bodo areas, and the Karbi Anglong and Dima Hasao districts. Similarly, Kuki mobilisation in Manipur and numerous other movements in Meghalaya and Tripura have not been explored in detail.[19] Third, the book sees Sikkim as 'north' more than 'east'. It merits a separate volume.

Partitions, Statecraft, and Geopolitics

The narrative of this book is centred around four interconnected themes that shape India's near east: identity politics, cross-border migration, political economies, and official antinomies. Collectively, they form the substructure of India's near east. From Burma's wartime destruction to Assam's anti-foreigner sentiment, from statist anxieties about communism to acute mass deprivation, India's near east has been riven by insecurities. Unsurprisingly, it birthed extreme nationalism and ideologies. These themes impart coherence to a long history that seeks to turn the lens of diplomacy and statecraft upside down. This raises questions, including: why focus on these themes and not others, how do they relate to each other, and what is their scope? These questions are best answered by unpacking their historical evolution, i.e. how colonial authority and anticolonial resistance, warfare and nationalism, partitions, and postcolonial state-building shaped India's near east. This section focuses on the 1937 separation of Burma and the 1947 partition to explain why these themes are essential, and discusses the scope of these themes in this book.

1937: 'Burma divorces India'[20]

Burma's separation is often viewed as a logical byproduct of colonial oppression. After its defeat in the 1885 Third Anglo-Burmese war, Burma was made a subsidiary province of colonial India.[21] Fought mostly by Indian soldiers under British command, the war generated popular anti-Indian sentiment.[22] Such provincialisation involved destruction of traditional Burman socioeconomic power structures. It aided in fusing anticolonialism with anti-Indian identity politics, which was solidified by the colonial authorities' encouragement of large-scale economic migration of Indians. The number of Indians in Burma increased from 136,504 in 1872 (total population of 2.7 million) to over a million in 1931 (total population of 14.6 million).[23] In Rangoon itself, Indian migrants increased from 87,487 in 1891 to 211,692 in 1931.[24]

Rice cultivation required capital and cheap labour, and Indians offered both. The impact was visible in the acreage of rice cultivation increasing from 354,000 in 1845 to 11,558,000 in 1931.[25] Burmese rice was being cultivated, financed, and consumed by Indians, disenfranchising locals. Profits made by Indians were sent as remittances. Such political economic asymmetry coupled with land alienation deepened social antagonisms, resulting in anti-Indian riots. Burmese nationalism, which gained momentum during the 1920s, categorised Indians as agents of colonialism.[26] In May 1930, labour troubles at the Rangoon docks took a communal turn, resulting in the deaths of nearly 200 Indians and injuries of over 2,000.[27]

Throughout the early 20th century, colonial administrators attempted to abate Burmese nationalism without jeopardising Burma's provincial status. In 1923, the Montague-Chelmsford reforms created dyarchy that allowed limited self-rule.[28] A new 103-member Burma Legislative Council was formed wherein 24 members were appointed by the governor, and 79 were elected on a communal basis, i.e. Indians, Burmans, and other minority communities.[29] Such communal representation sharpened racial and religious divides contributing to the 1930 riots. 'Indians Go Home' became a powerful slogan on Burmese streets.[30]

Matters came to a head in December 1930. A drop in rice prices caused by the Great Depression generated mass unemployment. The ensuing frustration meant that a protest in Rangoon against paying taxes led by Buddhist monk Saya San turned into armed rebellion against colonial rule.[31] In response, apart from using force to crush the revolt, the First India Round Table Conference of 1931 recommended that London accept Burma's separation in principle, ensure protection of minorities in Burma, prepare for a financial settlement between India and Burma, decide for Burma's defence, and transfer all subjects under the viceroy's authority to the Burmese.[32]

The 1935 Government of India Act formalised the separation and set the date for 1 April 1937. But the policy antinomy was that an act meant to neutralise anticolonialism inflamed racial partisanship. Anti-Indian xenophobia deepened in Burma as local lawmakers formulated discriminatory laws. The 1937 Burma Domicile Bill treated all Indians as foreigners.[33] It triggered the worst anti-Indian and anti-Muslim riots in Burmese history.[34] In 1939, the Buddhist Women Special Marriage and Succession Bill sought to discourage marriages between Indian men and Burmese women.[35] Later that year, communal flames were fanned by the introduction of the Registration of Foreigners Bill, which built on the Burma Domicile Bill and, unconstitutionally, treated Indians as foreigners. Similarly, the Burmanisation of Labour Bill discriminated against Indian workers.[36] Though shelved, these bills damaged inter-community relations and triggered a slow, steady, and sizeable displacement of Indians from Burma. The Japanese invasion in December 1941 turned this into a mass exodus.[37]

The impact of 1937 was acutely felt by communities in the India-Burma borderlands. A virtual wall of jungle-clad mountains, these borderlands stretch from the Patkai, the Naga, and the Manipur hills in the north to the Lushai and the Chin Hills in the centre of the frontier region. Narrow and low-heighted, these hills join the Arakan ranges in the south that continue into the maritime sphere and emerge as the Andaman islands in the Bay of Bengal. Demographically, the region is a mélange of linguistic, ethnic, and religious communities. Connected by trade, marriage, history, and culture, these communities had a hierarchical relationship with colonial Britain.

Inhabiting what colonialists considered a 'buffer zone', these communities were allowed to pursue local customs and laws. The ingress of colonial power, often in the form of 'military expeditions, surveys and ethnographies, land and resource expropriations, missionary endeavours, and restrictions on hill-plain interaction' allowed for the framing of geographies of India and Burma by arbitrarily dividing communities and 'fostered ethnicization'.[38] The separation of 1937 appeared less as an 'amiable divorce between two ill-suited partners [and more] as an unfinished and pain-ridden separation' in these borderlands.[39]

Once decided, the separation ignited a drive among Indian and Burmese officials to assert their territorial authority and define citizenship. Such assertion meant regulating hitherto unhindered cross-border interactions. Officials became invested in geolocating the boundary, quibbled over settlement of disputes among villages that lay on opposite sides of the border, and complained about the senselessness of the boundary.[40] During 1937–48, local officials tried to reconfigure the India-Burma boundary in a socially, economically, and topographically sensible manner. But the efforts failed while the boundary was sanctified as a 'historical truth'.

The Second World War transformed these borderlands into a frontline between Britain and Japan.[41] Transregional solidarities forged during the war generated sub-nationalist undercurrents among Naga, Kachin, Chin, and other communities. To counter the Japanese advance, Britain recruited heavily from these communities. Such wartime experience kindled nationalist ('separatist' for the postcolonial state) sentiment among these communities, who viewed themselves as distinct from India, Pakistan, and Burma.[42] Trained in warfare, militarily equipped, and politically conscious, such movements became a threat to independent India, Pakistan, and Burma.

Treatment of Indians, import of rice to a food-strapped India, separatist violence, and 'illegal' cross-border movement came to define India-Burma relations at independence. Article V of the 1951 Treaty of Friendship captured this well. The two states agreed to 'start negotiations for the conclusion of agreements, on a reciprocal basis, relating to trade, customs, cultural relations, communications, extradition of criminals, immigration or repatriation of nationals of each country resident in the other, or of dual nationals of the two countries, and all other matters of common interest to the two countries'.[43] They deliberately overlooked the boundary issue, but asserted the McMahon Line was the official boundary with China—a decision with huge consequences for Asian geopolitics.[44]

Other than anti-colonialism, Indian and Burmese leaders worried about communism. Rangoon was caught in an existential struggle with armed communists. Burma's collapse to a communist onslaught was equally unacceptable to India, who invoked the 'special relationship' to arm and train Burmese army in what became the first act of regional power projection. Burma's separation thus underlined the centrality of identity politics across the region. Mass displacement created a cross-border migration 'problem', but also dislocated regional political economies. A nationalist quest for bounded territorialities made free movement of people and goods at the border illegal, leaving both policymakers and locals unsure about how to deal with such novel uncertainties.[45] Burma's wartime destruction exacerbated such anxieties.

1947: 'Tryst with Destiny' [46]

People, rivers, mountains, irrigation systems, railways, telegraph facilities, military hardware, dusty files, chairs, desks—everything was partitioned. Britain's decision to leave the subcontinent in August 1947 was a seismic event. Divided along Hindu-versus-Muslim lines, Punjab and Bengal bore the brunt of partition violence and displacement. Nearly 15 million were displaced and about a million killed.[47] Multiple authoritative histories of this partition offer insight into the trauma of that moment, and how India, Pakistan, and Burma viewed their relationship with, and responsibilities towards, incoming migrants. Relations between the newly created states were marred by mistrust and, in case of India and Pakistan, war.

This section doesn't re-author these histories. Instead, it underscores the primacy of identity politics and how disruption of regional political economies exacerbated such frictions. Communal strife shaped the subcontinent's nationalisms, social contract, and inter-state relations.[48] Exclusionary ideas such as the Two-Nation theory became potent.[49] In India, a secular leadership, iconised by Nehru, faced challenges from the Hindu right and the communists. Similarly, despite the promise of its founding leader Mohammad Ali Jinnah, Pakistan drifted towards Islamic conservatism and militarism.[50] In Burma, the assassination of Aung San ('father of the nation') in July 1947 drastically reduced the odds of an inclusive union, despite allegedly promising that to ethnic minorities at the February 1947 Panglong conference.[51]

The impact of these competing and often conflicting nationalisms was visible in partition violence and how the postcolonial state dealt with displaced minorities. As Vazira Zamindar demonstrates, Muslims faced systematic persecution in India just as their Hindu and Sikh counterparts faced in Pakistan.[52] To stem cross-border migration, these states required the other to protect minorities.[53] In India's near east, mass displacement between East and West Bengal was key.[54] It brought the two states close to war in 1950 and caused war in 1971.[55]

Bengal was first partitioned along religious lines in 1905 to better facilitate colonial administration.[56] In 1943, when it was forced into a famine killing 3–5 million, the resulting strife had communal overtones.[57] On 16 August 1946, Calcutta was still dealing with the aftereffects of the famine when Hindu-Muslim riots left over 4,000 dead and many more wounded. The 'Great Calcutta Killings' inflamed organised massacres, rapes, and forced conversions leading up to the Noakhali riots in October 1946.[58] Such disturbances and the second partition of Bengal in 1947 triggered mass displacement. The 1951 census of India recorded 2.523 million migrants from East Bengal, 2.061 million of which were settled in West Bengal and the rest in Assam, Tripura, and other states.[59] These numbers swelled over the years.

Unlike Punjab, where institutions were tasked to support migrants, in Bengal, no prior planning went to receive, support, and sustain migrants. Reeling under wartime shortages, such displacement aggravated violence in Assam too. Such was the situation that Assam's Muslim-dominated Sylhet district was offered a referendum in July 1947 in which people voted to join Pakistan. Grounded in colonial authority's role in 'populating' Assam to develop tea plantations, the Sylhet referendum was as much about religious polarisation as it was about Bengali-Assamese linguistic divide.[60] It continues to feed identity politics and cross-border migration, and tie territorial insecurities to communalism.[61]

Burma also developed communal anxieties with Pakistan in Arakan. Rangoon requested that Karachi protect the rights of

Arakanese Buddhists living in Chittagong's coastal town of Cox's Bazar, not arrest Arakanese Buddhists crossing the Naf river (in the middle of which the border lay) to visit family in Cox's Bazar, and discourage people from moving to Arakan's Muslim-dominated Maungdaw and Buthidaung townships.[62] In this communally charged context, the Muslim League government in Bengal supported a suggestion made by the Muslim Chamber of Commerce of Chittagong in 1946 that Buthidaung and Maungdaw could be incorporated into Chittagong, causing 'great indignation' in Burma.[63] Indian officials noted that a section of people in these townships sought separate states like Shan and Kachin. Despite a 'good deal of sympathy' for such causes, India believed that 'Pakistan cannot support such a movement without seriously annoying' Burma.[64]

Jinnah rejected such revisionism.[65] But the idea of Rohingyas seeking separation became stuck, both in Burma and in India.[66] There were colonial antecedents. In April 1942, Britain created the 'Volunteer Force (V-Force)', a guerilla organisation tasked with harassing Japanese troops behind enemy lines in Arakan.[67] Recruited from Muslim communities, members of the V-Force were less effective in targeting Japanese forces, but did destroy Buddhist monasteries.[68] Treated as a problem, the Rohingya faced unceasing state-led assaults after independence.[69] India's reading of the politics of this region developed along similar lines as Rangoon, and contributes towards ongoing antipathy for the plight of the Rohingya.

The second structural problem was economic. India lost vast arable lands during partition.[70] The resulting food shortages were such that they shaped New Delhi's approach towards Burma, its principal supplier of rice and food-grain, as well as the US, which was a critical donor.[71] India also lost access to 75 percent of jute and 40 percent of raw cotton production. Since these were cash crops central to Indian export, such a loss dwindled Delhi's forex reserves. Most of India's jute producing areas went to East Pakistan.[72] Used as packaging material, jute sacks were central to global trade and transportation (the second most widely consumed fibre in the world after cotton) and was mostly produced in Bengal.[73]

In contrast, Pakistan lost infrastructure required to support heavy industry and agricultural processing. It was left without any industrial plant and a small power grid (it inherited a total of 75,000 kwh of electrical power, of which East Bengal received a meagre 15,600 kwh).[74] There was not a single jute processing mill left in east Bengal—all 106 were in Calcutta.[75] Most of this jute was exported through the Calcutta port. To address such imbalances, Pakistan proclaimed an emergency in East Bengal and created the National Bank of Pakistan to ameliorate the loss of Calcutta jute markets. For its part, India began producing more jute, inevitably shrinking land available for rice and cereal production.[76]

India's September 1949 decision to halt coal exports to East Pakistan (despite the latter's dependence on India's 23 million tons of annual production) and devaluation of the rupee aggravated the situation. The devaluation made India the sole processor of Pakistani jute worth £77 million for £60 million.[77] Such friction over jute and coal export expectedly took a communal turn. Failure to reach an understanding led to the February 1949 riots in Khulna and a series of anti-Hindu pogroms in February–March 1950, triggering more displacement. Smuggling of food grains and jute from Pakistan to India (and vice versa for coal) increased as the two countries inched towards war.[78] Forced displacement, poverty and shortages, communalism, and territorial insecurities came to define the 'national interests' for these countries. In the borderlands, such interests became securitised, as 'special' legal provisions enabled impunity.[79]

Thematic Scope

Burma's 1937 separation from India and the 1947 partition underscore the centrality of identity, cross-border migration, political economies, and official antinomies on India's near east. But these are large and complex categories, used with specific intent in this book. Identity politics, for instance, includes different identities, i.e. ethnic, communal, and ideological, around which political (and/ or militant) mobilisation is observable. From Nehruvian secularism and Hindu nationalism at the pan-Indian level, to Naga, Mizo, Meitei, and Assamese nationalisms at the regional level, this category accounts for competing ethnic nationalisms in India's near east. It values indigenous identity politics just as much as it accounts for

Burman-Buddhist and Bengali-secular or Islamic politics in Myanmar and Bangladesh.

The book is careful not to misuse this category when discussing left-wing mobilisation. India's near east is witness to communist movements of varying degrees of militancy and political efficacy. If Burma nearly collapsed to a communist offensive after independence, the Naxalbari movement continues to simmer in parts of India. Such left-wing mobilisation occurred across ethnic lines. But what this history shows is that political alliances, competition, and conflict centred around religious, linguistic, and ethnic identities are paramount in India's near east. The potency of this aspect is demonstrated in multiple events. Examples include the 1950s Naga revolt, Assam's anti-foreigner movement, the Mizo insurgency, the 1971 Bangladesh liberation war, and many more.

These cases indicate that nationalism and postcolonial state-building remain fraught in India's near east. But they pose another challenge: why not foreground India's electoral processes? After all, electoral jockeying is central to Indian politics, and the parliament offers a democratic platform through which identity politics is refracted. This book takes India's electoral politics seriously, both from a domestic and external affairs perspective. Electoral calculations have, at times, directly influenced New Delhi's foreign policy decisions towards neighbours. In fact, this book testifies to how a complex democracy such as India conducts *realpolitik*. But the decision to avoid foregrounding electoral processes is driven by the dual need to maintain analytical and narrative control.

Equally, cross-border migration is a complex theme that is connected to identity politics. This book understands it expansively. Partition-related mass displacement during and after 1947, the exodus of Indians from Burma, and the 1971 Bangladesh refugee crisis feature most prominently in this category. But this narrative deliberately blurs certain lines and includes transborder movement (large or small; legal or illegal; voluntary or forced) of Naga, Mizo, Meitei, and other communities straddling the India-Myanmar-Bangladesh borderlands within this category. This is done to impart narrative ease and analytical coherence, without disrespecting apparent qualitative differences between such cross-border movements.

15

Cross-border movements are central to social, political, and economic life in India's near east. This is visible in India's approach towards Myanmar's refugees after the 2021 military coup and unceasing political mobilisation in Assam around the issue of 'illegal migration' from Bangladesh. As this book shows, New Delhi has developed a complex approach towards cross-border migrants over the decades.[80] Bereft of a refugee policy, (barring the communally partisan Citizenship Amendment Act, 2020), India controls cross-border migration on a selective, bilateral basis in keeping with its domestic political and international strategic priorities.[81] If the 1950 Nehru-Liaquat Pact stemmed the flow of migrants between East Pakistan and India, the 1971 war was triggered for the same reason, i.e. to reverse the influx of over 10 million fleeing Pakistan's genocidal spree.

The third theme undergirding the impact of migration on identity politics of India's near east is the region's political economies. The 1937 and 1947 partitions, as discussed, severely disrupted the economic life of India's near east. Largely agrarian (Assam is 69 percent agrarian, with tea plantations dominating the sector),[82] India's northeast depends heavily on central government loans.[83] Trade with Bangladesh and Myanmar remains suboptimal, thanks to the partition that isolated the northeast from the rest of India and its eastern neighbours. The only land connection is a 21-kilometre corridor through Siliguri. Unsurprisingly, development of its northeast through maritime and overland connectivity to Southeast Asia has been a long-standing Indian objective.

But the flip side of desiring such connectivity for profit is that it brings along insecurities. For a long while, India didn't build roads in its northeast frontier, fearing that they would be used by the Chinese to invade India. This rationale was combined with concerns about the inflow of illicit narcotics, small arms, cattle, gold, betel nuts, and timber.[84] The allure of high-risk, high-profit illicit trade attracts insurgents, officials, politicians, and businesspersons alike. Limited formal connectivity, existence of extractive industries, and a non-uniformly regulated border creates entrenched vested interests.[85]

Attempts to regulate cross-border economic activity and ensure national security ironically fuelled illicit political economies. The loans offered by New Delhi compounded dependencies and discouraged development of local industry. It tied regional economies to centre-state political dynamics, and enabled chronic corruption among local political outfits as well as officials.[86] The northeast's integration with India meant it needed central government financing for public services, but required cash and coercion (offered by militant outfits) to influence elections. Such financing comes from illicit economies that connect India's northeast with southeast Asia.[87] Paradoxically, the most effective, if unfortunate, link that India's northeast has with Bangladesh and Myanmar is illicit in nature.

The Manipuri border town of Moreh handles 99 percent of overland illicit trade with Myanmar.[88] It is a 'convergence point of multiple illicit supply chains' in India's near east where approximately '50,000 people earn their daily income through smuggling'.[89] Across Moreh is Myanmar's trading town of Tamu, which is linked to the opium-producing Golden Triangle at the Laos-Myanmar-Thailand tri-junction, ensuring an unending stream of drugs into India.[90] Such illicit economies exacerbate inequality, instability, and political violence by creating a state-insurgent-smuggler nexus. India's attempt to clamp down on drugs has, for good reason, failed. The trade is too lucrative to disappear and limits the appeal of formal connectivity under India's 'Act East' policy.

Lastly, India's near east experiences tremendous churn thanks to official antinomies. This theme shows how Indian policymakers navigate the socioeconomic diversities of this region in pursuit of state-building and regional power projection. In Naga areas, for instance, India introduced state structures in hitherto quasi-administered spaces without respecting existing village councils led by *gaon-burras* (village elders). The antimony here has been the creation of parallel governance structures, i.e. authority of the state versus the elders. The enduring disconnect between these two sources of power is at the heart of (though not uniformly) this region's poverty, corruption, and violence. It feeds into identity politics, limiting connectivity. Armed separatists straddled this divide, creating a triangulation of power between the state, the village council, and insurgents.[91]

Such contradictions complicate Naga-New Delhi ties. If British rule was considered alien, so too was India's version. This disconnect has long fed resistance, which in turn legitimised coercion by the state. The first manifestation of such coercion was the 1958 Armed Forces (Special Powers) Act, which legalised the use of force in 'disturbed areas'. Meant to counter the Naga movement, AFSPA offered the Indian army legal immunity. Similarly, the North Eastern Council of 1972, which granted statehood to Manipur, Meghalaya, and Tripura, was to ensure national security and regional development. Instead, it undermined the region's politics and autonomy by concentrating power among a handful of officials. Such reorganisation was accompanied by posting retired police, intelligence, and military officers as state governors, who ensured that the state became entrenched in the region and fostered partisan dependencies, without truly resolving political issues.

The Indian constitution allows for such antinomies. Article 244A, for instance, allowed the existence of an autonomous state within Assam with a separate council of ministers and legislatures.[92] This was, in the words of the former home secretary of India, Gopal Krishna Pillai, a shortcut to formal statehood that was eventually granted to Manipur, Meghalaya, and Tripura.[93] It exacerbated identity conflicts. Similarly, Nagaland was granted statehood in 1963. The move was accompanied by the enactment of Article 371(A) that 'no Act of Parliament in respect of (i) religious or social practices of the Nagas, (ii) Naga customary law and procedure, (iii) administration of civil and criminal justice involving decisions according to Naga customary law, (iv) ownership and transfer of land and its resources, shall apply to the State of Nagaland unless the Legislative Assembly of Nagaland by a resolution so decides'.[94] New Delhi was willing to devolve power to Nagas. But the decision didn't address the fact that Nagaland didn't represent all Nagas, lighting long fuses in Manipur and Arunachal Pradesh.

The question of which of these themes is the most causally compelling requires caution. It is difficult, and perhaps counter-productive, to search for monocausality when studying the politics of India's near east. These are inter-related themes that will be unconvincing if studied in isolation. The most enduring of these, of course, is identity politics, as it speaks to primeval forms of social relations. But the evolution of inter-community, and by extension interstate dynamics, cannot be understood by looking solely at collective identities. For such identities are not static, and are strongly conditioned by economic modes of production, interest groups, and the legal structures that govern postcolonial statehood and citizenship. Collectively, these themes form the spirit of this book, its narrative, and its analysis. There could be some places in this book where the reader feels that the 'story' is overpowering thematic analysis, and others where the opposite is true. That is deliberate, for this is a 'new' history, and these themes, even if in the background, form the analytical spirit of this text.

Sources and Structure

Such a history owes much to archival material and the generosity of individuals who agreed to be interviewed. On the archival front, the National Archives of India offered material from the ministries of external, defence, and home affairs, as well as the cabinet office. These documents range from annual and monthly political reports to intelligence assessments. The Nehru Memorial Museum and Library (NMML) offers a trove of private papers that help recreate debates and discussions on issues that animate this history. These documents are supplemented by material from the Mizoram, Assam, and Nagaland state archives, parliamentary debates and resolutions, annual reports of the Narcotics Control Bureau (NCB), and relevant oral histories. Outside India, the International Institute of Social History in Amsterdam opened up various political movements in Bangladesh and Myanmar. In Bangladesh, the rich tradition of oral histories was an asset. It helped piece together memories about the country's birth and post-liberation politics.

The Wilson Center's Cold War collections, along with online libraries of the Foreign Relations of the US and the Central Intelligence Agency (CIA) were important. Colleagues at the Wilson Center helped access otherwise inaccessible documents from the Myanmar National Archives (MNA). Despite attempts, I failed to access the MNA's Yangon collections. Through colleagues who prefer anonymity, I received select Burmese documents on relations with India. To buttress these archives, which thin out as the book closes in on the current moment, I conducted over one hundred interviews in India, Myanmar, Bangladesh, Thailand, the UK, Germany, and the Netherlands. Not all of them are used in the book, but they helped me make sense of the region. These interviews cast a wide net and include retired and serving officials, rebels from different backgrounds, social activists, media persons, and community members. Identities of some interviewees are withheld, and others are disclosed with permission.

The rest of this book is divided into three parts. The first part, *Solidarity*, focuses on the 1947–70 period. It explores how independent India dealt with decolonisation in its near east in the aftermath of partition. For this purpose, chapter two focuses on 1950 to explain how Burma became the linchpin of India's eastward thrust. Against the backdrop of cross-border migration, competing ideologies, and questions about statecraft, India made two critical decisions. First, it offered military support to Rangoon to counter Burmese communists and the Karen rebellion. This was the first time independent India offered military support for a 'friendly' government despite its abhorrence for Cold-War-type military alliances. Second, reeling from the costs of war over Kashmir, New Delhi decided to opt for diplomacy to resolve the East Bengal migrant crisis leading to the 1950 Nehru-Liaquat Pact.

The year 1958 was momentous when a military coup in Pakistan and a military-led 'caretaker government' in Burma ended experiments with democracy. In Pakistan, General Ayub Khan's coup put stress on already strained ties between its western and eastern wings. In Burma, the caretaker government led by General Ne Win was viewed as less chaotic than civilian politics and soon became entrenched. Chapter three details India's approach towards these developments in context of the Naga insurgency, a food crisis, and heating up of the Cold War.

Chapter four explains how defeat in the 1962 war with China birthed India's two-and-a-half front security dilemma, i.e. fighting China and Pakistan simultaneously while tackling insurgent violence in the northeast. The war diminished India's image as a power, and led to a reassessment of its approach towards the near east. Ne Win, in India's calculation, was an ally against Beijing. India's bet on Ne

Win, thanks to the Cultural Revolution, paved the way for the 1967 India-Burma Boundary Agreement. The 1962 defeat also recalibrated Pakistan's approach on Kashmir and laid the foundations for the 1965 war, along with secret support to Mizo and Naga rebels. Militarily bogged, India tried negotiating with the Naga National Council in early 1960s, the failure of which further securitised India's approach.

The second part, *Security*, focuses on the 1971–90 period. Chapter five shows how communalism in the two Bengals during the 1960s shaped India's pursuit to solve its two-and-a-half-front security dilemma. Pakistan's 1965 military misadventure in Kashmir and support to northeast rebels along with China complicated India's options. In this context, the success of the Six-Point movement in East Pakistan led by Sheikh Mujibur Rahman in 1966 whetted India's appetite for interventionism. The road to 1971 was paved in 1965. Chapter six explains how, despite winning the war, India lost the peace in the northeast. Liberation of Bangladesh kickstarted the political reorganisation of the northeast and led to the signing of the Shillong accord with Nagas in 1975 and a lesser known agreement with Mizo rebel leader Laldenga in 1976. But these accords were eclipsed by the outbreak of the Assam agitation in 1979, which was followed by secessionist violence by United Liberation Front of Assam-Independent (ULFA-I) and other communities.

The next two chapters unpack the situation in Bangladesh after liberation, and India's response to democracy movements in Myanmar and Bangladesh after 1988. The bilateral took a sharp nosedive soon after liberation, and became hostile after Zia-ur-Rahman's rise in 1975 following Mujib's assassination. Chapter seven unpacks behind-the-scenes dynamics of the coups and counter-coups that rocked Dhaka and nearly brought the two countries to war in November 1975. Events during this period set the cyclical tone for the future of this relationship, including India's lukewarm response to the 1982 coup. If alignment with military leaders (Ne Win and Hussain Muhammad Ershad) was viewed as a method to secure India's northeast in the 1980s, its failure pushed an electorally challenged Rajiv Gandhi to throw India's weight behind democrats (Aung San Suu Kyi and Sheikh Hasina) just as the Cold War came to a wrap. As chapter eight underscores, the gambit failed.

21

The third part, *Connectivity*, focuses on the 1990–2024 period. Chapters nine and ten unpack the logic and effects of India's 1991 'Look East' policy and its transition to 'Act East' in 2014. From initiating a U-turn on the Myanmar junta to struggling with Khaleda Zia in Dhaka, India reversed most decisions taken during Rajiv's tenure. Two pivotal occurrences in the 1990s were the signing of the Naga ceasefire in 1997 and opening of border trade with Myanmar. Both were half successes. The Naga ceasefire has still not translated into an accord, and while cross-border trade remains limited, India's northeast has become a strategic transshipment hub for drugs from the Golden Triangle. The final chapter expands on the impact of the turbulent 1990s on India's approach towards its near east in the 21st century. It explains why India came close to militarily intervening in Bangladesh in February 2009, and how Hindu nationalism has developed solidarities with Buddhist nationalism in Myanmar. The epilogue shows how identity politics, cross-border migration, political economies, and official antinomies continue to shape India's approach towards its near east today.

PART I

SOLIDARITY (1947–1970)

2

ONE ENEMY AT A TIME
CONSTITUTIONAL SURVIVAL & RESISTANCE IN
BENGAL, ASSAM, AND BURMA

'To my mind the biggest task of the day is this East and
West Bengal matter. It is big, because of the fate of East and
West Bengal and of the tens of millions who inhabit them.
It is even bigger than that, for it overshadows and tends to
overwhelm the whole of India.'

Jawaharlal Nehru to Sardar Vallabhbhai Patel,
February 21, 1950[1]

Jawaharlal Nehru was ready to resign as prime minister. Since
August 1949, a series of attacks on Hindu minorities in East Bengal
pushed nearly one million into West Bengal, Tripura, and Assam.[2]
By January 1950, retaliatory anti-Muslim violence spread across
Calcutta displacing Muslims, who left for East Bengal. According to
the 1951 census, over 27 percent of Calcutta's population was from
East Bengal.[3] To distinguish citizens and 'aliens', the home ministry
prepared a National Register of Citizens (NRC) based on the
census—a document that continues to generate political friction.[4]
Nehru worried that the situation could spiral into full-scale war.
Partition violence in Punjab and the first Kashmir war didn't shake

his faith or threaten his position, but with the two Bengals convulsed in mass bloodshed, Nehru was short on ideas and support. In a telling letter to Louis Mountbatten, the last viceroy of India, Nehru warned that Kashmir was 'secondary' in importance to the situation in Bengal.[5] India lacked the capacity to absorb such high numbers of displaced persons.

On 26 January 1950, the Constitution of India came into effect. India became a republic irrespective of ideological and social violence and a mass of humanity crossing over into its territory. Unless something 'dramatic' occurred, Nehru was convinced that the situation was headed towards 'disaster'.[6] He couldn't rule out full-scale war, and instructed India's military leaders to prepare for it while writing to his Pakistani counterpart, Liaquat Ali Khan, for a diplomatic solution.[7] The scale, intensity, and uncertainty surrounding the crisis was such that within two months (February– March 1950), Nehru considered options from use of force and diplomacy to resignation and visiting Bengal in a private capacity to abate communal passions.

The pressure for action, a 'euphemism for war', from Congress parliamentarians, cabinet ministers, and the Hindu Mahasabha was immense.[8] The party, he believed, was becoming alienated with his politics and methods. The Hindu Mahasabha was pushing the 'Akhand Hindustan' agenda.[9] The passage of the Immigrants (Expulsion from Assam) Act in March 1950 offered parliamentary support for the expulsion of migrants, making the choice of an 'ultimate' sort between war or state collapse in West Bengal and Assam. Forced migration from East Bengal was accompanied by displacement of Burmese Indians.[10] Burma, Bengal, and Assam were riddled with ethnic, communal, and communist violence.

This chapter explores how India's state-building in the northeast was shaped by external pressures, and what impact these domestic processes had on its approach towards Burma and East Bengal (Pakistan). It explains why identity politics, migration, and partitioned economies birthed a sense of constitutional survivalism that guided India's approach towards its near east. For Nehru, and other leaders such as home minister Sardar Vallabhbhai Patel, the sanctity of the constitution, which was a *cordon sanitaire* around

India's political, judicial, and legislative systems, was paramount.[11] Meant to contain Hindutva, ethnic separatism, and communism, the constitution enshrined India's democratic project.[12]

India was not alone in pursuing such survivalism. Burma and Pakistan were equally uncertain about the viability of their states. As historian Pallavi Raghavan argues, a shared sense of survivalism paved the way for unexpected solidarities as these countries decided to keep 'animosity at bay'.[13] India's arming of Burma's army in 1949 and overlooking of Rangoon's anti-Indian xenophobia was driven by survivalism. The Nehru-Liaquat Agreement, signed on 8 April 1950, came into being after Nehru bluntly told Khan to expect war if repatriation did not occur.[14] The Indian army's manoeuvres in western and eastern theaters made this threat credible.

For Nehru, stability in Pakistan and Burma was essential for the survival of India's constitution. Success of militant communists, religious extremists, or ethnic separatists in India's near east could empower similar forces within India. Masked by partisan rhetoric on all sides, such survivalism shaped statist solidarities crucial to prevent war, even if they failed to build peace. It reified the postcolonial state's position as an overarching entity in people's lives, instilled with meaning by nationalist discourses espoused by the Congress. But the antinomies of India's *cordon sanitaire*, especially on the issue of self-determination by ethnic minorities who were expected to accept and abide by the constitution, were left unreconciled.

In four parts, this chapter explains how constitutional survivalism and resistance shaped India's approach towards Bengal, Assam, and Burma. The first section explores how India's struggles to contain communist and communal violence shaped such constitutional survivalism. The second section focuses on India's decision to arm Burma's army to prevent state collapse in 1949. India's support for Nu in Rangoon and lukewarm response to the 1954 land nationalisation that left Burmese Indians landless and stateless is discussed in the third section. The fourth section examines India's response to events in East Bengal during 1952–54, when the language movement began, and the Muslim League was trounced in Pakistan's first-ever elections. It demonstrates why the seeds of war were sowed long before 1971.

Constitutional Survival & Resistance

The influx of conflict-generated migrants from East Bengal and Burma exacerbated ethnic and ideological strains in Bengal and Assam. The scale of displacement was such that it risked state collapse. How India read and responded to such pressures in terms of inward-facing statecraft and outward-facing diplomacy is central to understanding constitutional survivalism. This section animates these aspects in three parts. The first looks at heightened communal and ethnic insecurities in post-partition Bengal and Assam, and how cross-border migration fed into these. This second looks at the state's anxieties of losing legitimacy and losing control to armed communists, especially in the context of a Maoist victory in China. The third section briefly outlines India's diplomatic response to Rangoon and East Bengal, in keeping with such survivalism.

Still reeling from the aftereffects of the 1943 Bengal famine, India lacked the capacity to provide for incoming migrants. The plight of migrants inflamed opinion along communal and class lines in Bengal and Assam. It encouraged Marxist-Leninist ideologues and 'Hindutva-wadis' alike, who either sought to overhaul or overthrow India's constitutional project. Occurring in tandem with the expulsion of Indians from Ceylon—a process that fed the anti-Hindi and communist movements in southern India—the prevention of mass migration became a strategic priority.[15] The Nehru-Liaquat Agreement prevented war and enabled repatriation, but failed to address the source of strife, i.e. communal and ethnic strains.

The politics of partition and condition of religious minorities in East Bengal ensured sympathy for the Hindu-right's narrative. Though Nehru disdained religious politics, he found it difficult to contain. There was support for communism too. But the state's framing of political challenge from the left and the right was different. Hindutva was not viewed as strategic threat, even if it merited containment. But militant communism triggered survivalist anxieties. Indian leaders assessed that the Hindu-right could foment communal violence, but was incapable—or unwilling—to capture state power. In contrast, the communists had the intent to oust governments and, as witnessed in China and Burma, delivered on their promise.

The October 1951 genesis of the Bharatiya Jana Sangh that later became the BJP is linked to events in 1949–50 Bengal (and Assam) and the flourish of conservatives within the Congress. To comprehend the pressure on Nehru, the nature of the challenge to his idea of a social democratic republic enshrined in the constitution requires unpacking. On the ground, sympathy for Hindu and Sikh migrants from Pakistan and East Bengal fed retaliatory violence against Indian Muslims.[16] Soon after riots in Khulna, such violence in Calcutta generated concerns about a rightward lurch of Indian politics. Under pressure from Hindu conservatives such as Syama Prasad Mukherjee to use force, Nehru was concerned that war or state collapse in Bengal could end India's republican aspirations before they took off.

By 1949, Hindu nationalist narratives had strengthened within the Congress. On 11 July 1949, after the Supreme Court of India acquitted the RSS on charges of assassinating Mohandas Karamchand Gandhi, Patel lifted the ban on the organisation and compelled it to pledge allegiance to the constitution.[17] Soon after, the RSS launched the Ram Janmabhoomi movement with support from the Uttar Pradesh Hindu Mahasabha, organised a nine-day recital of the *Ramcharit Manas*, and placed the idols of Rama and Sita inside the Babri Masjid, leading the government to seal the mosque, which lit a long fuse that ultimately exploded with the mosque's destruction in 1992.[18] In 1950, a conservative figure became Congress president with Patel's support and synergised the Hindu right, both within and outside the party.

The East Bengal crisis was conjoined with an upsurge of such Hindu nationalist sentiment, if not political power, across India. Nehru tried mollifying conservative opinion by arguing that India must not encourage the influx of Hindus. A population swap along communal lines, he spuriously counselled, could obviate a potential future merger of East and West Bengal.[19] Given that East Bengal opted for separation along communal lines, such notions of a merger were ill-founded, and Nehru's articulation seemed like a tactic to appease intra-Congress conservatives instead of being official policy. If anything, Nehru wanted India's allies in East Bengal to help rebuild communal harmony and to 'keep up the spirits of the Hindus'.[20] In a letter to West Bengal chief minister, he clarified:

> If the ultimate aim is for the Eastern Pakistan to join West Bengal and the Indian Union, we should not encourage any tendencies or activities which come in the way of this development. Natural forces are working in favour of this change and the only real obstruction to it can come through our own mistakes or over-zealousness.[21]

In effect, India must not get involved barring helping East Bengali Hindus stay where they are. When Patel pressed Nehru to threaten Pakistan that India 'would have no alternative left except to send out Muslims from West Bengal in equal numbers', Nehru resisted.[22] Such a response, Nehru believed, 'would lead to disastrous consequences' by alienating Indian Muslims and harming India's international standing.[23] Thus, his appeal for a diplomatic solution was aimed to prevent war as much as to blunt Hindu nationalists. The agreement triggered the protest resignations of West Bengal parliamentarian Kshitish C Neogy and Mukherjee. In a scathing speech, Mukherjee criticised the agreement for making India and Pakistan 'appear equally guilty, while Pakistan was clearly the aggressor … events have proved that Hindus cannot live in East Bengal on the assurances of security given by Pakistan … [and] the crux of the problem is Pakistan's concept of an Islamic State and the ultra-communal administration based on it'.[24]

Soon after, in December 1950, Patel died. Mukherjee's resignation and Patel's death eased intra-party pressure on Nehru. But public sympathy for Hindu causes didn't abate. Even in Assam, where the secular nature of Assamese identity politics featured anti-Bengali overtones and was undergirded by territorial and resource-related anxieties (thanks to an ill-defined post-partition border and large migrant influx), the structural pull of Hindu nationalist rhetoric remained. With land taxation being a major source of state revenue, Assamese leaders didn't want non-indigenous people to gain access to it.[25]

By the end of the decade, and certainly after 1960, this morphed into a large-scale movement to rid Assam of Bengalis. Such anxieties, especially after the 1947 Sylhet referendum, pushed Assam into adopting a strategy for cultural assimilation.[26] The demand for making Assamese the *only* state language—triggering counter-mobilisation for Bengali recognition—was a case in point. The political knock-on effects of such assimilationism were felt in regions where indigenous communities began resisting Assamese dominance. The seeds of ethnic nationalism and separatism were laid in the early years of independence.

The social appeal—if not political power—of Hindu nationalism became clear when Rajendra Prasad, India's first president, inaugurated the Somnath temple in May 1951, despite Nehru's aversion to mixing politics and religion. Prasad allegedly noted that the temple signified the power of reconstruction was greater than that of destruction, a statement understood as being critical of Muslims.[27] In October that year, Mukherjee launched the Jana Sangh to mobilise Hindus and support Hindu minorities outside India, especially in East Bengal. Despite being politically weak, Hindu activists ceaselessly publicised their cause through, among other ways, celebrating 'Akhand Bharat Diwas'—Greater India Day—on 15 August in Calcutta, inviting diplomatic protests from Pakistan.

But unlike Hindutva, the spectre of communism was viewed with much more concern by the state. On this aspect, the 1949 Chinese communist victory shaped India's threat perception. Equally, communist advances in Burma animated political and policy debates in New Delhi. In a letter to provincial premiers (chief ministers) on 1 April 1949, Nehru noted that the communist victory in China was of 'utmost importance' for India, and would 'affect more and more in the future, not only the entire position in Asia but in the world'.[28] In Burma, he argued, the impact of the 'victory of the Chinese communists and their approach to the Burmese border will make a difference'.[29] He underscored two threats from communism: one, 'continuous tension', and two, 'the raising of communist morale in India', which he assessed as 'relatively low at the present'.[30]

Nehru was open to left-wing ideas on poverty reduction and equitable distribution of resources. But he sought communists to operate *within* constitutional confines. His temperament, shaped as much by an admiration for socialism as by the need to balance conservatives in the Congress, was shared by officials in the ministry of external affairs (which was under his command). But home minister Patel was much more unforgiving towards communists. Such a divergence of views on communism and communalism— even though Patel and Nehru agreed on the paramountcy of the constitution—was visible in Patel's chaperoning the RSS out of the political wilderness in 1949, while empowering the Intelligence Bureau (IB) to intensify reporting on, and targeting of, communists.[31]

India's concerns about communists gaining power in Kerala were mounting when Mao was marching to victory in China, and Burmese communists (and Karen insurgents) were launching offensives against Rangoon.[32] In response, IB director Bhola Nath Mullik prepared detailed dossiers on communist activity along the Assam-Burma border and reported in April 1949 that the Communist International (Comintern) sought Southeast Asian communist parties to plan their activities 'so that they may be able to seize power in the near future'.[33] Based on 'secret and reliable' sources, he claimed that Burmese communists with support from Burmese Indians (Bengali and Tamil) had launched a strong movement.[34] He warned that such elements would start secret work in Assam and 'some members of their party have already infiltrated to Nutanpura Refugee Camp, Chittagong' with the aim of creating 'trouble in Pakistan also'—underlining that communism was a problem that New Delhi and Karachi shared.[35]

The situation in Burma's Chin and Kachin areas was similarly assessed. Communists were preaching that the Chins, Lushais (Mizo), and the Karen being Christian must not fight one another 'but fight with their enemies, the Burmese, and the non-Communists'.[36] If they could capture Lower Burma, then the 'Chin hills will automatically fall into their hands, and it will not be necessary to launch a separate campaign against it'.[37] India's deputy high commissioner in Dacca shared similar reports about communist infiltration into East Bengal 'in the garb of refugees'.[38] Cross-border mobility of communists occurred in parallel with the rising activism of Arakanese Muslim (Rohingya) 'guerillas', who executed attacks against Burma and unfurled the Pakistani flag in Maungdaw and Buthidaung. On this issue, India was on the same page as Pakistan; local Arakan 'Mujahids', though seeking to join Pakistan, were not supported by Karachi as Rangoon alleged.[39] But the communist threat was seen to be real.

The Shillong-based subsidiary intelligence bureau reported in November 1949 that Hamendra Nath Ghoshal, also known as Yebaw Ba Tin, a senior Burmese communist of Bengali heritage, sought the permission of the Communist Party of Burma (CPB) politburo to return to India ('turned down').[40] Known as a 'master theoretician', Ghoshal authored the so-called 'Ghoshal thesis' that was adopted by the CPB during a March 1948 mass meeting in Pyinmana.[41] Burmese communists were believed to be led by Bengalis and tied (ideologically, practically, and historically) to Indian communists.[42] In contact with the Communist Party of India (CPI), in 1948 Ghoshal predicted a 'revolt' against the Government of India 'soon after India Republic is declared'. He sought to connect Burma's 'Democratic Revolution' with India.[43] Unsurprisingly, India viewed Burmese communists as a national security threat that needed to be contained at its source.

In Assam, the communist situation was similarly assessed. In October 1949, the IB reported that communists were planning to make Assam a 'storm centre in the proletarian struggle' and were active in North Cachar Hills with a mixed tribal population of Kacharis, Kukis, and Zemi Nagas, apart from the Bengali population of Cachar district.[44] After infiltrating the region amongst the 'great hordes of labourers being imported' to build the Shillong-Silchar road, the bureau claimed that communists were attempting to undermine the loyalty of the Assam Rifles. Police raids against communists in Assam revealed that the latter had cultivated secret informants within the government and 'knew precisely of the discussions in the West Bengal and Assam Cabinets about actions proposed to be taken against them'.[45]

The IB's two takeaways on communists in Assam were (a) these were largely, if not just, movements led by Bengalis, and (b) they indulged in 'propaganda more on ethnical and racial lines than on Marxist lines'.[46] This is unsurprising given the societal divisions between Assamese and non-Assamese (Bengali, indigenous communities). Communists across India's near east exploited communal and ethnic cleavages to widen their recruitment base, even if their rhetoric was grounded in Marxist-Leninist jargon. It was an acknowledgement of the potency and endurance of ethnic and religious identity politics in Assam, Bengal, and Burma.[47] Such was the IB's fear of communism that it erroneously suspected even nationalist Naga rebels of being communists.[48]

The MEA and Assam government didn't share the IB's concerns on communism.[49] But they couldn't convince the bureau otherwise. In Tripura, the IB assessed that communists were exploiting problems created by cross-border displacement better than even Pakistani agencies.[50] The communists were seen to have weakened only in Manipur between 1948–52. This was due to coercive security measures, and the crossover into Burma and death of founding leader Irabat Singh. Manipur's communist movement began in 1945 under Singh's leadership and sought to expand the 'revolution' from Burma into India with support from the White-band People's Volunteer Organisation, which became the CPB.[51] This was unsuccessful due to lack of communist appeal and outreach among non-Meitei communities north of Imphal and the movement's reliance on 'criminal elements'.[52]

How did India respond to these threats? Driven by constitutional survivalism, New Delhi adopted a three-part strategy. Domestically, it used force. But internationally, it opted for a non-confrontational, even cooperative, stance with Burma and Pakistan. This meant overlooking regime type and limiting criticism of minority discrimination unless it created migrant spillovers or triggered retaliatory communal violence. Indian diplomats reached out to Burmese Indians and Hindus in East Bengal to convince them of staying where they were and becoming citizens.[53] Though sensible insofar as war prevention and constitutional survival went, as following chapters demonstrate, this strategy failed to address underlying causes of political and social turmoil in the region.

India's response to separatist resistance in the northeast is detailed in the next chapter. But the external aspect of its response is discussed in the next sections. They unpack India's response to the 1949 communist and Karen offensives against Rangoon (and, briefly, to land nationalisation), and the language movement and 1954 assembly elections in East Pakistan. In the former, India intervened militarily by arming Rangoon. In the latter, it maintained distance. India wanted stability in its near east for successful state-building in the northeast. These cases, then, underscore how domestic politics shaped the country's diplomacy in the near east. In both cases, violent discrimination against minority communities of Indian origin or Hindus (East Bengal) is a common theme. Karachi viewed Bengali parties' demand for autonomy as treasonous, and fueled by 'enemy agents', an allegation aimed at India.[54] For Rangoon, the line between xenophobic nationalism and decolonisation was thin, and translated into driving the '*kala*'—a racially pejorative term used for Indians—out of Burma. India's diplomatic response on these aspects, in turn, impacted state-building in the northeast.

Revolution or Ruin?

Rangoon faced economic ruin, ethnic separatism, and communist violence in 1949. Communist and Karen offensives in 1948–49 threatened the Burmese state. Such pressures were also fueling concerns about a military takeover in Rangoon and the dislocation of prime minister Nu's government by ambitious generals like Ne Win. If state collapse to communists risked worsening the situation in Bengal and Assam, a military coup could also end Burma's constitutionalism and augment cross-border displacement. For most of 1948, Burmese communists focused their offensives around Pegu (Bago). But Maymyo's fall in February 1949[55] and Mandalay's in March 1949 increased the twin threats of a communist win and military takeover.[56] The collapse of Nu–communist talks in April and Ne Win's appointment as deputy prime minister set off alarm bells.[57] India's ambassador in Rangoon noted that Burma had become a 'modified form of military dictatorship and the army will have greater power as Ne Win will continue in command'.[58] This was an 'extensive retrograde' in Burmese politics.[59]

To arrest Burma's spiraling war and dictatorial drift, Nehru adopted a dual strategy. First, he secretly sanctioned a 'very substantial' cache of weapons supplies for five battalions of Burma's army, with the promise of arming five more battalions; Burma could pay for these arms in cash or rice.[60] It became one of the few 'friendly' countries to whom India supplied weapons.[61] Despite being short on its own defence requirements, India enabled Burma to mount a counter-offensive.[62] Second, on 14 April 1949, Nehru met with Nu and gave him a long letter outlining how to deal with these crises. 'I am not afraid of revolution, but I don't want widespread ruin', he told Nu.[63] Backed by 6 million pounds worth of British financial aid, Nehru insisted that Rangoon pick its battles carefully.[64] This meant conciliation with Karen nationalists (for which Nehru offered 'mediation') but upping the fight against communists.[65]

The nuance of this strategy requires unpacking to understand how constitutional survivalism bound these states in uncomfortable solidarities. India supplied 125 tonnes of military equipment with a capacity of 10,000 cubic feet to Burma in May 1949.[66] This occurred after Nu's urgent visit to New Delhi seeking intervention. The consignment cost over 2.8 million rupees and triggered Burmese requests for more.[67] Nehru was willing to grant these requests but maintained that it 'must be kept completely secret', as India didn't want a military alliance with Burma.[68]

The complexities around the logistics of transporting these weapons and maintenance of secrecy offer unique insights into how survivalist solidarities between newborn states worked in practice. There was a debate in New Delhi and Rangoon on what might be the best transportation route. The sea route via Calcutta was one option wherein India could ask the Scindia Steam Navigation Co. Ltd. To offer a Landing Ship, Tank vessel that could ferry the weapons to Rangoon port wherefrom they could be airlifted to Upper Burma.[69] This was risky given the precarious security situation north of Rangoon and the fact that even Mingaladon airport in Rangoon was unsafe.[70] Expectedly, Rangoon refused and pressed for the other option: a direct airlift to Myitkyina from Calcutta. Given the tonnage of weapons, this meant 50 sorties of a Dakota airplane, which could take 2.5 tonnes per sortie, over Pakistani territory.[71]

The latter option was preferred because it reduced shipment costs, fulfilled India's 'most anxious' desire that supplies did not fall into the hands of communists and Karen insurgents as 'free gifts', and bypassed Burma's air force, which New Delhi believed was incapable of delivering accurate airdrops.[72] But there were different problems with this option. The defence ministry argued that an airlift risked exposing the operation to Pakistan, over whose airspace the sorties would fly. Such exposure could invite 'undesirable' reactions from Pakistan and the foreign press.[73] After some back-and-forth, Burma opted for the sea route, and the weapons were delivered in two installments on 22 and 30 May. Burma's initial indecision on routes and concerns about exposure highlights another aspect underlying the whole affair: secrecy.

New Delhi wanted to keep its support secret to prevent targeting of the 1.1-million strong Burmese Indian community.[74] For this, the Central Board of Revenue was instructed to treat the shipment as 'highly secret' and 'no mention thereof should be made in the trade returns or the Customs House Daily Lists'.[75] But India became wary of Burmese diplomats talking to 'all and sundry' in Calcutta about the shipment. Nu's public declaration of India's 'Top Secret' help (exposing the operation) led to threats against the Indian community.[76] Indian officials dealing with the case thought it best to unilaterally deliver these weapons to prevent exposure.[77]

On the use of Pakistani airspace, New Delhi accepted a counter-intuitive arrangement of forming a committee of Indian, Pakistani, and British ambassadors in Rangoon to coordinate information regarding military and financial assistance to Burma. This obviated concerns about exposure by bringing Pakistan on board.[78] Karachi worked closely, and in secret, with New Delhi and London to ensure Rangoon did not fall to communist and Karen nationalist offensives. Such collaboration occurred despite communal tensions in East Bengal and an uptick in displacement of Hindus to Calcutta and elsewhere in Assam. Pakistan's Inter-Services Intelligence (ISI) and India's IB, otherwise at war, cooperated to ensure Burma's survival. It was an example of statist solidarities emanating from existential anxieties triggered by communism and ethnic separatism. For good measure, Pakistan supplied Burma 1,000 light machine guns and 3,000 rifles of Czech origin to supplement Indian weapons.[79]

The second part of this strategy required Nehru to 'guide' Nu on how to make optimal political use of these weapons. Armed support to Rangoon afforded Nehru leverage over Nu's decision-making, and his advice was simple: divide and conquer.[80] After reassuring Nu that 'the only possible stable government [in Burma] is your government ... the alternative to this is chaos', Nehru recommended conciliation with the Karen National Union (KNU).[81] The Karen, Nehru argued, 'can make for suitable allies' for Rangoon in the future, and any attempt to fight on 'all fronts is not likely to succeed'.[82] In politics, as in warfare, Nehru counselled, 'one takes up one's enemy one by one', and among the many ethnic insurgents, the Karen were worth making peace with.[83] To underline the survivalist logic, Nehru confessed that India's unpopular decision to keep Mountbatten as advisor after independence, maintain draconian colonial policing laws, and join the Commonwealth were meant for state survival. Nehru appreciated that the Karen behaved 'very badly' and there was 'a great deal of ... anger against them', but he advised that 'we cannot judge long-distance policies by present day passions'.[84]

India offered its offices for mediation if agreeable to Nu on the promise that such mediation would not be 'impartial' in that it would not treat the Karen as 'equals' and only strengthen Nu. Nehru worded this aspect carefully given India's 1947 Nine-Point Agreement with Naga nationalists (which did, temporarily, prevent violence).[85] His advice on engaging Karen rebels was based on two considerations. Politically, Nehru viewed ethnic nationalism as less dangerous than communism. The former sought territorial separation, but the latter sought state capture. Indian intelligence suggested the existence of (ineffective) channels between Rangoon and the Karen, and a military stalemate that underscored Rangoon's lack of prowess against the Karen National Defence Organisation (KNDO). The internal displacement of 4,000 Burmese Indians in and around Insein demonstrated that the government was not in control.[86] The Indian embassy blamed the *Sitwundan*, ill-trained Socialist Party levies created by Ne Win, for the 'full scale civil war' with the Karen post-February 1949.[87]

But the real audience of Nehru's letter was not Nu. The Burmese premier appreciated the need to focus political resources on a settlement with Karen rebels and military resources against communists. The message was for fence-sitters, communist sympathisers within Nu's party, and—most importantly—for Ne

Win. Soon after meeting Nu on 13 April 1949, Nehru felt that while Nu was 'impressed by my talk … he seemed to be afraid of his own followers who might desert him and join the Communists or the PVOs if he went too far with the Karens'.[88]

But the security situation was deteriorating quickly. By the end of March, the Kachin state had been cut off from south Burma. To prevent economic collapse, Kachin traders, with support from Indian businessmen and the Indian Trading Corporation, repaired the Stillwell (Ledo) road at 'top-speed' to ensure the export of Burmese rice and other goods to India.[89] If the economic promise of the Stillwell Road was welcomed by some in New Delhi, the fact that thousands of Indians were gathered in Myitkyina to cross over into Assam once the road became motorable raised concerns. India needed Burmese rice, but it did not want more mouths to feed, nor did it want communist infiltration from Burma.

Rangoon's reaction to India's armed support is telling. On 5 May, Nu wrote to Nehru that the letter 'made a great impression on our friends here [a reference to Ne Win]' and promised to write in detail what Rangoon had in mind 'to put an early end to the conflict with the Karens'.[90] In reality, Rangoon only partly followed Nehru's advice about making peace with the Karen while concentrating force against communists. In November 1949, by which time Burma's army reversed the military momentum thanks to Indian arms, Nu again wrote to Nehru. He expressed 'gratitude' for India's 'moral and material support' without which Burma's 'task here would indeed have been a most difficult one'.[91] Throughout April–November 1949, Burma's army had targeted the KNU, while also agreeing to form a separate Karen state. Nu had, in effect, given in to Ne Win's plan to continue targeting Karen nationalists.

Nehru didn't press the case. He understood that Nu's main opponents were not the communists or the Karen, all of whom were surely fighting the state. It was Ne Win, who India held responsible for worsening relations with the Karen. When viewed in this context, Nehru's advice to adopt a conciliatory approach towards the Karen was partly aimed to counter the military's growing political weight. Ne Win was xenophobic, and his ascendancy risked exacerbating ethnic separatism and dislocating Aung San's vision of an inclusive union. The communists were ideological foes, unlike Karen nationalists. To target the former militarily would have, in Nehru's estimation, strengthened Nu's power base not just in relation to the ethnic insurgents, but the military itself.

India's arming of Burma and counsel to Rangoon that it must fight communists was driven by security in Bengal and Assam. India believed that communists were best poised to exploit Assam's troubled identity politics. The fact that Indian and Burmese communist movements were led by Bengalis, and appealed to communities that felt disenfranchised by Assamese dominance or felt neglected in West Bengal, was a cause of concern. Unlike communists, ethnic nationalists such as the Nagas were not militarily resisting India in the early post-independence years. This explains why New Delhi viewed the communist threat as more potent to India, Burma, and Pakistan alike in its near east, and dealt with it accordingly. It was a case of foreign policy being shaped by domestic state-building that dictated the need for solidarities between newborn postcolonial states dealing with transnational left-wing violence.

Constitutional stability in Burma was strategically critical for India, and only Nu could deliver it. This assessment of the Burmese situation became clear in Nehru's lukewarm response to the 1954 Burma Land Nationalization Act and stringent citizenship laws and immigration policies that expelled thousands of Burmese Indians and left many stateless and landless. Rangoon's anti-Indian xenophobia was institutionalised over the decades and was now taking a sharper overtone wherein conditions were being created to push these communities out of the country. Fearful of implications of the same on the exchequer and communist recruitment among displaced Bengalis and Tamils from Burma, Nehru discouraged such migration. But he didn't press Nu on this count. Instead, Indian diplomats were instructed to convince these people to take on Burmese citizenship.[92]

The MEA acknowledged that Rangoon's anti-Indian policies posed a 'knotty' problem and could sour ties with Nu. The best thing would be 'to let sleeping dogs lie' and prevent Burmese Indians from entering India.[93] But without Nehru's intervention with Nu, Indian diplomats could do little. To make sense of Nehru's silence on this issue, there's a need to look beyond financial concerns and the communist threat. Nehru didn't press Nu on this issue because of constitutional survivalism. Nu was an ideological ally who strengthened Nehru's vision of Afro-Asian solidarity, anti-colonialism, and non-alignment. As an Indian assessment of Burma's foreign policy noted, barring the situation of Burmese Indians, there were few 'hiccups' in ties given the 'neutral ideological affinity deriving from parallel independence (sic) movement and lack of dispute or rivalry'.[94]

Nu helped India counter-balance Pakistan when Karachi joined the Southeast Asian Treaty Organisation. He also coordinated Burma's China policy with Nehru. This was visible during the 1950–54 Kuomintang crisis, when nationalist Chinese troops crossed over into Burma. Secretly supported by the US, the Kuomintang undermined Burma's sovereignty, allied themselves with Karen rebels, and even engaged with Naga separatists. India strongly supported Nu. As Krishna Menon, India's representative to the UN, stated in October 1954: 'what hurts Burma, hurts India too', and New Delhi was unwilling to accept a 'state within a state' that could provoke Chinese action.[95] The 1955 Bandung conference was a high point of India-Burma 'teamwork' that pushed an alternative, constitutional vision against Cold War binaries.[96]

Ne Win couldn't offer such constitutional guarantees. If anything, his assertiveness worried India. In 1954, Rangoon claimed a lighthouse on the Table Island, which is part of the Coco Islands chain north of Andaman in the Bay of Bengal. New Delhi obliged but became alarmed at Rangoon's 'alacrity to take over' the lighthouse.[97] In December 1954, Burma announced plans to 'develop the Coco Islands' given its potential for tourism and settle 400 people; in reality, Ne Win was developing high-security prisons for political prisoners.[98] The announcement occurred shortly after Nu's visit to the island. With the land and maritime boundary undemarcated, many in Rangoon believed that Andaman and Nicobar Islands rightfully belonged to Burma. Indian officials cautioned that the Burmese government didn't subscribe to this view, but 'if the volume of opinion is big enough there may be a conflict of interests'.[99]

Rangoon's sudden interest in Coco Islands was seen to be driven by security considerations. For one Indian officer, Burmese activity on the island was acceptable, but 'if at a future date Burma's foreign policy changes, and the Government passes into unfriendly hands, the Coco Islands can present a distinct menace to India; submarine bases can be set up there which would seriously interfere with our shipping in the Bay of Bengal'.[100] The MEA noted that Rangoon must be aware of the strategic significance of these islands, given the Japanese used it during the Second World War and left an airstrip intact. Much of this push came from Ne Win.

Instead of raising the issue with Nu and putting him at odds with Ne Win, the MEA recommended increasing the 'tempo of development and colonisation' in Andaman and Nicobar to obviate Burma making claims on those islands too.[101] In 1953–55, when Ne Win was eyeing Coco Islands and the Burmese Indian community was being systematically targeted, Rangoon's strategic value for India was paramount. To raise this with Nu could have risked waking up 'sleeping dogs', which was best avoided. India had armed Nu and was now doing much to keep him in power. But as next chapters show, Nu's failure to deliver reduced his value as an ally by the early 1960s. Just as non-alignment lost steam and the Sino-Indian boundary dispute took a violent turn, Nu, instead of collaborating with India, turned towards China. The worsening situation in East Bengal during this period made concessions to Nu compelling.

'A Colony of West Pakistan'[102]

An unmarked boundary, land and water disputes, communalism, migration, and divided economies— these issues animated Assamese and Bengali politics, and related to East Bengal's situation.[103] It was to prevent such issues from becoming bigger, and deadlier, that Nehru pressed for a diplomatic solution to the East Bengal migrant crisis in 1950. The Nehru-Liaquat Pact averted war, but the communal situation continued to worsen. In this context, India's decision to *not* interfere in East Bengali politics during the 1950s stands out. Driven by constitutionalism, Nehru desired stability with Pakistan. But Karachi had other plans. The 1954 assembly elections in East Bengal were the first-ever democratic exercise in Pakistan. The turmoil thereafter, when Karachi imposed governor's rule and disrespected the electoral mandate, became an equally powerful watershed. It transformed Nehru's reading of Pakistan and proved Mukherjee correct.

Karachi viewed not only Hindus but even Bengali Muslims with suspicion. India's reaction to the buildup, occurrence, and aftermath of these elections remains unexamined in current literature. This section fills that gap and demonstrates how the 'very extraordinary' events of 1954 sowed the seeds of Bengali separatism. They sparked India's imagination on the regime-type question in Pakistan, just as Nehru began to advocate 'avoiding taking any step which might strengthen an undesirable regime'.[104] If in 1948 he believed that India and Pakistan could resolve their differences, his alienation from Karachi was at an all-time high by 1954. The long road to the 1971 liberation of Bangladesh began being paved in 1954—and it was directly linked to the situation in Assam and Bengal.

India's response to these events developed in three phases. First, Pakistan's Bengali language movement in 1952 (mirroring language politics in Assam and Tamil Nadu) generated concerns that the Nehru-Liaquat Pact would collapse. The language issue began in March 1949 when Liaquat Ali Khan, on Jinnah's cue, stated that 'Pakistan as a Muslim State must have a lingua franca, language of the Muslim nation, and that language can only be Urdu and no other language'.[105] It burst out as street protests in 1952.[106] Second, the victory of Bengali-dominated parties, who were led by the United Front and won 300 out of 309 assembly seats and ousted the Muslim League in 1954, made India optimistic about the emergence of a new political order that might take a softer stance on bilateral disputes including Kashmir. But Karachi's imposition of governor's rule (effectively martial law) and banning of the United Front triggered the third phase wherein optimism gave way to disillusionment.

On 26 January 1952, Pakistani prime minister Khawaja Nazimuddin delivered a speech in Dacca to ameliorate mistrust in the Muslim League. After listing several grants that Karachi offered, he targeted local leaders for being 'frightened of partition and … ready to play with the Hindus'.[107] He particularly blamed the 'traitor' Huseyn Shaheed Suhrawardy for being 'keen on [a] united Bengal and wanting secession of East Bengal from the rest of Pakistan'.[108] In a bid to 'kill Bengali provincialism', Nazimuddin made the cardinal

mistake of reasserting a provocative statement that Jinnah had made
in 1948: 'the state language of Pakistan is going to be Urdu, and no
other language'.[109] The speech, India's deputy high commissioner in
Dacca B K Acharya reported, 'raised a storm of protest and instead
of closing the political ranks' widened the rift.[110] University of Dacca
students led by Maulana Bhashani, known as 'the Red Maulana'[111]
for his left-leaning politics of peasant mobilisation, launched a
movement against the 'Urdu-only' policy and demanded recognition
of Bengali as East Bengal's official language.[112]

The government's coercive response led to several deaths on 21
February 1952. It fueled mass protests.[113] Policymakers in Karachi
viewed Bengali as 'Hinduised' culture requiring 'rectification'.
Instead of accommodating diversity, Pakistan sought to 'unify' the
two wings not just politically but also culturally. Led by Bengali
Hindus and Muslims alike, the language movement birthed the
United Front under the leadership of A K Fazlul Haq, Suhrawardy,
Bhashani, and a charismatic Awami League youth leader named
Sheikh Mujibur Rahman. The United Front introduced the 21-point
programme inspired by the 1940 Lahore Resolution and sought
greater autonomy for East Pakistan *within* the union. This was a key
electoral issue.[114]

For Karachi, it was anathema. Noorul Amin, the chief minister of
East Bengal, viewed it as a joint attempt by communists, Indians, and
other 'malcontents' to undermine Pakistan.[115] As an Indian report
put it:

> The recent student's strike, firing and arrests in East Bengal,
> in connection with the State Language controversy have struck
> terror into the hearts of the minority community. They are afraid
> that communal troubles may follow. In fact, the East Pakistan
> authorities particularly the non-Bengali officials are trying their
> best to give the controversy a communal turn and throw the
> blame for it on India and the Hindus in Pakistan. The relations
> between the non-Bengali and Bengali elements in Sylhet have
> however definitely deteriorated and there is apprehension that
> communal rioting may be encouraged by the officials as an
> escape from present embarrassment.[116]

Soon after, Pakistan introduced a 'passport system' to regulate movement of people between East and West Bengal. Accompanied by rising rhetoric against India and Pakistani Hindus—including by senior officials such as the Director General of Ansars, an East Pakistani paramilitary outfit, who called all Hindus with links to India 'traitors' who should be 'arrested or harassed'—the passport system was viewed as a measure to encourage Hindu exodus. The 'real motive' for ending free movement was to bar 'Hindu migrants who had crossed over to West Bengal and appear now to be returning in a steady stream in spite of the utmost application of the policy of 'squeeze' by the Government of East Bengal', the IB noted.[117]

There was political economic logic to Pakistan's desire to control the movement of people and goods. Devaluation of the Indian rupee in September 1949 halted all formal trade between East Bengal and India. But the dependency between jute production and processing between partitioned Bengal meant that large-scale smuggling ensued. Within the first six months of halting trade, nearly 600,000 bales of jute were smuggled into India.[118] Such smuggling bereaved Pakistan of tax revenues while benefitting Indian business. According to India's trade commissioner in Dacca, jute was being smuggled into Assam from Sylhet and being 'rebooked to Calcutta in bond through Pakistan'.[119] Similarly, Jessore and Khulna, bordering Calcutta, 'gained some notoriety' for being jute smuggling hubs.[120] India did little to prevent such smuggling, just as the economic war intensified and both countries sought decoupling.

Calcutta-based Marwari business families came to dominate the coal and jute industries. Businesspersons such as G.D. Birla, Mungeeram Bangur, Bajoria Bajoria, Badridas Goenka, and Radha Kissen Kanoria bought out European firms trading in jute and coal by the mid-1950s. They dominated the international market.[121] The Bangurs commanded sales of over 7 million rupees and net worth of 6.5 million rupees by the 1980s, making them one of the most powerful Indian business families just behind Dhirubhai Ambani's Reliance during the Congress era.[122] Clampdown on formal trade impacted these businesses adversely, and none shied away from side-stepping legalities. Their entry into the jute and coal industries made Pakistan suspicious about cross-border businesses and their impact on 'anti-national activities'. After all, such smuggling was conducted through black-market transactions where the Pakistani rupee traded at lower value than the official exchange rate on a 'strictly cash basis' or using promissory notes called 'Hundis'.[123] The rate of exchange in this space varied between 100–115 Indian rupees for 100 Pakistani rupees, whereas the official rate was at 144 Indian rupees to 100 Pakistani rupees.[124]

In response, apart from introducing the passport system, Pakistan started seizing India-to-India jute.[125] Karachi worried that East Bengal's Hindu intelligentsia and businessmen could offer strategic leadership to Bengali Muslims (who 'lack leadership') against the Muslim League.[126] Indian intelligence viewed this as the core reason why Pakistan sought to control the movement of Hindus and alienate them from Bengali Muslims. If the passport system helped in achieving the first objective, separate electorates helped in achieving the second. Separation of caste Hindus from scheduled castes, New Delhi assessed, was meant to truly target the *bête noir* of the East Bengal administration. Such targeting of caste Hindus, who could channel dissent against Karachi, was visible in the acquisition of estates worth 11,621,000 rupees, most of which were owned by Hindu landlords, leaving the estates' Hindu employees unemployed for an indefinite period.[127]

The existence of such discrimination was confirmed by the arrest of Indian nationals and Pakistani Hindus on 'false charges' of espionage or fomenting 'trouble' during protests.[128] Concerns about mass influx of migrants were rife in Assam and Bengal in the context of the language movement and crackdown. India was concerned not only about Hindus but also about the mass displacement of disenchanted Muslims as food grain prices soared in East Bengal and the passport system increased anxieties of local Muslims whose daily livelihoods depended on cross-border trade.[129] Such displacement would have fueled the fires of identity politics in Assam, and triggered communal bloodshed in West Bengal, undermining India's state-building goals.

Throughout 1950–52, the IB and MEA reported violence against Hindus. By tapping into migrants entering India and secret cross-border sources, these institutions along with the Assam and West Bengal governments documented many incidents of cattle smuggling, rape, murder, abduction, and police crackdown against Bengali activists (both Muslims and Hindus), as well as trafficking.[130] Apart from the question of minority protection, Nehru had to contend with demands from the West Bengal chief minister, Bidhan Chandra Roy, to intervene with Karachi regarding the detention of Hindu leaders during the language agitation.[131]

Nehru adopted a similar two-part strategy with Pakistan as he did with Burma. He refused to interfere directly. In a 1952 speech in Calcutta, he acknowledged that 'Hindus of East Bengal are living under conditions of great stress'.[132] But to reject demands for intervention, he framed India's options binarily: either using diplomatic channels to build pressure on Karachi, or waging war. 'There is no third alternative. These are the only two methods', he argued.[133] Even a letter to his Pakistani counterpart about the passport system or the detention of prominent Hindus, he argued, was not required as that will 'hardly produce any effect' given that the language controversy has 'rather upset the equilibrium of the East Bengal government'.[134] But there was a contradiction here. If writing letters to his counterpart was considered pointless, then the likelihood of diplomatic pressure to deliver results was even more so.

Instead, Nehru instructed the Indian High Commission to take up the issue with Karachi and the deputy high commission in Dacca to track events and offer consular support to Indians held in East Pakistani prisons.[135] He didn't want to be seen as interfering in Pakistan's internal affairs, and was clear that 'there is no doubt that this was essentially a Muslim agitation', even if Bengali Hindus sympathised with it.[136] He was also clear that India was 'entirely opposed' to the introduction of the passport system but could do little if Pakistan insisted on keeping it.[137] He viewed Karachi's attempts to give a religious tone to the language movement as a failure and one that 'appears to be dying down'. He wanted matters to 'take their course'.[138]

Nehru's non-interference in 1952 was informed by Acharya's assessments and behind-the-scenes activism. Acharya made multiple complaints to his Pakistani counterpart for dragging India and local Hindus into the quagmire. Such objections, he argued, did have an impact. In early March, he noted that Karachi was reducing its anti-India and anti-Hindu propaganda from the 'early days' of the agitation.[139] Instead, Karachi started believing that the language movement was indeed organised by 'imported communists with the help of some leftist professors and students [at] the Dacca University' to 'overthrow the government itself' rather than to get Bengali recognised as an official language.[140] He admitted to Nehru that there was a 'grain of truth' to this assessment because the protest leaflets were full of communist terminologies and spoke freely about toppling the government, and because several communists did arrive in East Bengal from India.[141] In a reference to the language politics in India, Acharya argued that the East Bengal movement 'shows a family resemblance with trouble started elsewhere by communists'.[142] He underlined the communist threat India shared with Pakistan and Burma.

Turmoil over the language agitation came to a head during the 1954 elections. The United Front's landslide electoral victory shocked Karachi. In the first democratic exercise after independence, the party that was pivotal for Pakistan's birth had been trounced. India's reaction to the elections (upended shortly thereafter) is instructive. On 22 March 1954, one of the first leaders Nehru wrote to about the election results was Bakshi Ghulam Mohammad, prime minister of Jammu and Kashmir. The results, according to Nehru, had 'shaken up Pakistan', and it was clear that the 'old order has ended'.[143] The United Front demanded dissolution of the constituent assembly and the formation of a new government considering its electoral gains. Though it was unclear what the 'new order' would look like, Nehru was certain that the Pakistani military was unlikely to 'lead to any major change'.[144] Nehru's letter to Ghulam Mohammad was meant to prepare for a 'more friendly approach' by Pakistan on Kashmir.[145]

The United Front's opposition to America's arming of Pakistan was welcomed in New Delhi, who was trying to prevent Cold War alliances from reshaping the subcontinent's balance of power. Nehru believed that Badshah Khan, the Pashtun leader formerly aligned with the Congress and an opponent of Pakistan in 1947, was likely to play an important role in any new dispensation that came to power in Karachi. Keen on autonomy for Pashtuns within Pakistan, Khan was an ally of Fazlul Haq and supported the recognition of

Urdu, Bengali, and other provincial languages as official languages.[146] Nehru's pre-independence engagement with Khan and Fazlul Haq offered hope that the duo would resolve the Kashmir issue amicably. Nehru's actions at this moment betray his true intent in India's near east; despite framing the East Pakistan question to Congress conservatives in 1948 as one that was to lead towards a merger with West Bengal, he never acted along those lines. The resolution of the Kashmir matter with Bengali and Pashtun leaders at the helm in united Pakistan was preferred.

In a candid admission, Nehru assessed that a Bengali Pakistani leader was likely to be more forthcoming on Kashmir. Here too Nehru's views were informed by Acharya. In the build-up to the elections, Acharya noted, the Muslim League called a 'hartal' against Indian actions in Kashmir after exhausting 'the Islamic State, [and] the fear of a Hindu dominated Government etc., etc.'.[147] But this last-ditch effort to gain popular support 'misfired' when the United Front refused to observe the 'hartal' and called it an 'election stunt' by a party that had 'bungled the Kashmir question for six years'.[148] Unlike in Punjab, Kashmir was not important in East Bengal. Acharya noted the depth of provincial sentiment in East Bengal and ruminated to Nehru that 'it is not in Kashmir alone that Jinnah's two-nation theory is on trial'.[149] The Bengali Hindu, Acharya noted, 'seems to be less disliked in East Bengal today than the Punjabi Muslim … the main reason why the League is finding it difficult to make headway is that the Provincial League leaders are accused of having 'sold' Bengal to West Pakistan'.[150]

Nehru termed the election results 'revolutionary'.[151] Impressed by the rise of young and progressive left-leaning leaders who were 'not communal at all' and fervently 'Bengali', Nehru was positively struck by how East Bengalis sought to claim Rabindranath Tagore and, in 'a spirit of banter', derided West Bengal for becoming too 'Hindi-wallahs'.[152] He was certain that Karachi wouldn't use force, and would accept the electoral fait accompli. His failure to foresee the depth of tensions between West and East Pakistan was paralleled by the sense of shock when Karachi banned the United Front, imposed governor's rule, put Fazlul Haq under house arrest, and jailed Mujibur Rahman, the young corporations minister in the

United Front government. Iskander Mirza became the 'martial' governor of East Bengal on 30 May 1954.

Now, Nehru was livid. 'East Bengal is being treated like a colony of Western Pakistan and a colony under military domination', he complained.[153] The 'unprecedented' situation led to the muzzling of the press, mass arrests, and a blanket ban on public meetings as well as private meetings between elected members of the legislative assembly.[154] Mirza clarified his intent soon after becoming governor. He planned to 'wipe out the Communists to the last man, and if that means stepping on the Hindus toes, then unfortunately it would have to be'.[155] The decision to impose governor's rule was taken after the riots at Karnaphuli Paper and Adamjee Jute mills in Narayanganj.[156] Nehru viewed the riots as 'entirely a Bengali and non-Bengali affair (both Muslims) [where] the Bengali Muslims were shot down ruthlessly by the hundred'.[157]

Haq's detention in Karachi was considered a 'deliberate trap'.[158] In India's reading, Karachi encouraged the *New York Times* journalist James Callahan to conduct an interview with Haq in which the latter allegedly claimed that he sought independence for East Pakistan (Haq denied making the claim).[159] Haq's opposition to Bengal's separation and previous support for partition made Karachi unsure about his politics.[160] A lack of public protest to the martial law, in India's view, was a sign that people were stunned and frightened, though they were harbouring resentment. 'Rebellious spirits', Nehru assessed, 'will go underground and work quietly', as the triumvirate of Bhashani, Haq, and Suhrawardy went missing in action due to temporary exile, detention, and ill health respectively.[161] The arrest of Hindus linked to the Communist Party, the Ganatantra Dal, and the Youth League raised concerns about the impact on the community, but the political shock didn't lead to the feared exodus.

The upending of democracy in 1954, a dress rehearsal for the 1958 coup by General Ayub Khan, was a setback. Keen to ensure territorial and political stability in the subcontinent (far from Pakistani concerns about an Indian plot to undo partition), India developed an understanding with Pakistan on the most pressing subcontinental faultline: the treatment of religious minorities in the postcolonial state. Such an understanding offered space to work out other issues in the east, as witnessed in the conference of chief secretaries from West Bengal, Tripura, Assam, and East Pakistan.[162] But Karachi's paranoia about losing its eastern wing was now getting in the way of sustaining such solidarities.

Events of 1954 altered India's reading of Pakistan. Nehru asked India's diplomats to raise the East Bengal issue 'informally' across world capitals. He instructed India's ambassador to Egypt to inform Cairo that the 'whole business of East Bengal is one of the most shameless incidents of domination and suppression of a people, that you can find anywhere'.[163] The governors of Assam and West Bengal were castigated for replying to Mirza's dishonest request to cooperate in securing minority rights. One of the governors had excitedly responded: 'my government and myself will be only too happy to extend as heretofore our fullest cooperation in settling matters affecting welfare of our respective peoples'.[164] Though conscious of the need for stable ties, Nehru was no longer keen to maintain cordiality. He instructed both governors to keep their responses 'curt' without 'any expression of sympathy' to avoid 'taking any step which might strengthen an undesirable regime'.[165]

The question of what kind of regime India preferred in Pakistan emerged *after* May 1954. Until then, India derided Pakistan's domestic politics but never thought in terms of regime preferences. In April 1953, when Nazimuddin's government was dismissed on spurious charges, Nehru viewed the situation as being 'Gilbertarian' (whimsical humour) and sardonically observed that all there was to Pakistan was 'palace politics and palace intrigues—without a palace'.[166] Quoting Zafrullah Khan, Pakistan's foreign minister, who claimed that Pakistan was part of the Middle East and not the subcontinent, Nehru noted that though that was geographically incorrect, the claim was indeed true as far as Pakistan's politics was concerned: 'the politics of Pakistan are similar to the politics of the Middle-Eastern countries ... a number of unscrupulous persons control the destiny of this unfortunate country'.[167] Indian officials viewed these developments as a sign of increasing 'American influence and a diminution of that of the UK' in Pakistan, but made little of it given Karachi was keen to continue engagement over Kashmir and other issues, and because it didn't truly impact the larger trajectory of India-Pakistan relations.[168]

But unlike the 1953 'coup', India's reaction in 1954 was strong. If imperfect, New Delhi preferred inclusive politics in Pakistan and, on that count, Karachi crossed a line in East Pakistan. Indian officials believed that constitutionalism in Pakistan could stabilise ties. Specifically in East Pakistan, Nehru's brief but welcoming views about the United Front and the rise of Bengali nationalism demonstrated an emerging feature of subcontinental geopolitics, namely that India viewed Punjabi dominance in Pakistan as a hindrance to strategic stability. Nehru's optimism about Bengali-Pashtun leadership being amenable to resolving the Kashmir issue and preemptive efforts to prepare the ground for a breakthrough underlined this aspect.

But Karachi's insecurities ran deep. It wanted to deal with 'disruptive forces and enemy agents who were actively at work in East Pakistan'.[169] Chaudhry Khaliquzzaman, the Bengali governor of East Pakistan before Mirza, presciently warned when declining to continue in office that the dismissal of the United Front will have 'dangerous consequences'.[170] Karachi's charges against Fazlul Haq for inciting violence and advocating secessionism with Indian support proved ironic in the long term. Unlike Nehru, who refused interventionism, Indira Gandhi took a proactive approach when faced with similar problems in 1971. The long road to the liberation of Bangladesh began being paved on 30 May 1954, even if its occurrence was grounded in 'conjuncture and contingency, choice and chance'.[171]

Conclusions

Constitutional survival in the face of resistance from communism and communalism shaped India's approach towards its near east. Mass displacement and religious violence created conditions that could dislodge India's postcolonial state-building project. The near east became a crucible for India's secular democratic constitutional fabric borne out of nationalist solidarities shaped during the anti-colonial movement. The trauma of Punjab's partition and the 1943 Bengal famine was alive when anti-Hindu violence in East Bengal and anti-Indian discrimination in Burma triggered displacement after 1949. Despite being agreeable to a population exchange, Indian leaders quickly realised the political, material, and ideological risks associated with such displacement. Migrants, though in need of support, also created constituencies for outfits opposed to constitutionalism. Such anxieties underscored how India's statecraft was been being shaped by influences from the outside in.

India's decision to find diplomatic solutions, as evidenced in the 1950 Nehru-Liaquat Agreement, was grounded in constitutional survivalism. The inconclusive 1948 Kashmir war made Karachi and New Delhi realise that such endeavours could jeopardise their national projects. New Delhi created a hierarchy of issues that posed an urgent threat to India. In the near east, Hindu nationalism was viewed as a problem, but not an *urgent* threat. Patel's success in convincing the RSS to pledge allegiance to the constitution was a watershed that normalised Hindutva politics in India. Some communists also accepted the primacy of the constitution overtime and joined parliamentary politics. But in West Bengal and Assam, hard-left factions were active. Their aim was to overthrow the constitution and the government just as feared. These forces shaped India's regional diplomacy from the inside out.

Nehru's arming of Rangoon in 1949, overlooking of discrimination against Burmese Indians, and pushback against demands for military action in East Bengal demonstrate how he balanced domestic pressures with foreign policy. His approach towards Burma and East Bengal during the first six years after independence belies the often repeated caricature of an idealist uninterested in military affairs. Nehru saw no other option but to arm Rangoon to prevent state collapse, and then strengthen Nu in whatever way he could to ensure that Burma's polity remained ideologically aligned. India signed a 'Treaty of Peace and Friendship' with Burma on 7 July 1951, making such solidarities a formal interstate partnership.[172] State collapse in Burma would have strengthened transnational communists and threatened India's northeast, but also jeopardised rice imports essential to prevent a lurking famine in India.

Similarly, war in East Pakistan would have drained precious resources and exposed India to Pakistan's claims that Karachi truly represented the interests of Indian Muslims. The Nehru-Liaquat Agreement emphasised minority protection as a domestic imperative of each country (akin to Rangoon being responsible for Burmese

Indians) to arrest the drift of their politics to the religious right. In a demonstration of pragmatism to protect the constitutional *cordon sanitaire*, Nehru used force to counter communism and opted for diplomacy to contain the Hindu right. Far from being uninterested in India's neighbourhood, Nehru was deeply involved in regional geopolitics, even if he viewed these issues as planetary problems that could best be solved at a global level.[173]

Karachi's decision to upend democracy in East Bengal in 1954 was a setback to such postcolonial statist solidarities. It was a point of no return whereafter Nehru harboured no illusions that Pakistan embodied the antithesis of India's republicanism. A prelude to a full-blown military coup in 1958, the 1954 East Pakistan situation forced a recalibration in New Delhi about its Pakistan policy. From then on, the shared perception that communism was the main threat to stability waned. Instead, ethnic nationalism, always present in the background, emerged as the main 'problem' in India's near east—and one on which Karachi and New Delhi had different views depending on who was resisting whom.

India's responses to militant communists and Hindu nationalists set the stage for the next 'threat' in its east: Naga nationalism. Though communist and communal forces continued to the shape regional politics, their salience subsided by the late 1950s. Instead, ethnic separatism became a key problem as the Naga movement went underground in India, Bengali nationalism deepened in Pakistan, and multiple ethnic minorities such as the Kachin, Shan, Chin, Rakhine, Ta'ang, Karenni, and Mon began to agitate against Burman majoritarianism. These movements made these states paranoid enough to assert themselves using force. This became apparent in the collective dissolution of democratic politics and civilian authority in East Pakistan, Burma, and India's northeast in 1958. In September 1958, New Delhi imposed the draconian Armed Forces Special Powers (Assam and Manipur) Act to counter the Naga movement. In October that year, a military 'caretaker government' took charge in Rangoon just as Mirza, now president, abrogated Pakistan's constitution and imposed martial law.

Within a decade, constitutional survivalism gave way to militarism in India's near east.

3

SPECIAL POWERS, DESPERATE ACTS

CONSTITUTIONAL COLLAPSE & MILITARISM IN
INDIA'S NEAR EAST

'No infirm government can function anywhere. Where
there is violence, it has to be dealt with.'

Jawaharlal Nehru on the Armed Forces
(Assam & Manipur) Special Powers Bill, 1958[1]

It came as a 'great shock' to Zapu Phizo, president of the Naga
National Council (NNC) which sought independence from India,
when Pakistani authorities detained him on arrival in Dacca.[2] Ever
since the Naga nationalist movement turned violent, Phizo received
a steady if small flow of arms from Sylhet.[3] Strained relations
between India and Pakistan made him certain that he could count
on the latter's support. Instead of safely facilitating his passage to a
different country, he 'was confined to quarters in the Dhaka police
compound'.[4] General Ayub Khan was Pakistan's defence minister
when Phizo arrived in December 1957. He expected the general
'to be sympathetic' to the Naga cause, especially as Khan had
commanded a battalion in the British Indian Army's Assam Regiment.
But instead of supporting Phizo, Pakistani intelligence pressed him
to acknowledge that Assam belonged to Pakistan. If Phizo accepted

55

that line, he could expect support from Karachi. Burma, as Phizo found out in 1954, was even less cooperative when it came to the use of its territory by Nagas resisting India given Rangoon's ties with New Delhi.

Phizo pleaded with Karachi to let him go. Pakistan was already running secret but small anti-India militant training camps in jungles near Karnaphuli river south of Mizoram. Phizo wanted Naga fighters to receive large-scale, systematic 'guerrilla warfare instruction' in East Pakistan.[5] It was a miscalculation. Not shy in supporting anti-India militants, Pakistan sought commonality of purpose. Karachi wanted to support movements that would help bring Assam into Pakistan's fold and not create new states. On 7 October 1958, ten months into Phizo's detention, Ayub launched a military coup. Apart from ending Pakistan's constitutional experiment, it buried all chances of Karachi supporting an independent Nagaland, even if it had been willing to support the Nagas to harass India.

Ayub's coup occurred less than a month after India passed the Armed Forces Special Powers (Assam and Manipur) Act (AFSPA) on 11 September. An undemocratic and draconian act, AFSPA had colonial origins but passed the parliamentary floor test, and, ironically, found a champion in Nehru, architect of India's democratic constitutional project.[6] Despite opposition, Nehru framed AFSPA as the only viable measure to suppress the Naga rebellion. As often is the case with draconian laws, AFSPA was imposed as a temporary measure to protect Naga areas in Assam and Manipur from 'private groups ... using fascist methods ... to coerce government authorities using organised violence'.[7] It was a geographically limited martial law that undermined India's constitutional mooring in the name of protecting the nation. Ayub's coup also occurred three weeks before Nu stepped down to allow a military-led caretaker government to take charge for a period of six months. Ne Win became prime minister on 28 October.

The constitutional projects that drove solidarities between India, Pakistan, and Burma to counter ideological extremes were simultaneously discarded in India's near east. In all contexts, participatory politics and civil liberties became secondary to postcolonial state-building grounded in insecurities due to an uptick in ethnic armed nationalism. Such crises were not enough—yet—to push these states into open conflict with each other. None of these countries preferred territorial revisionism because secession by one community risked encouraging more such movements. But the fact that ethnic armed politics was not a 'shared' threat—that Naga nationalists were viewed as a threat to India (and limitedly to Burma) but not to Pakistan, or that East Bengalis threatened Pakistan, and their political ambitions were territorially limited—opened space for competitive geopolitics and sponsorship of cross-border rebels.[8]

This chapter demonstrates how Karachi's sponsorship of Naga rebels from East Pakistan—the *outside in* aspect of India's state-building struggles—shaped India's 'firm' response towards the Naga uprising and matter-of-fact acceptance of the military coups in Burma and Pakistan. Equally, China's annexation of Tibet offered a template of how postcolonial states *could* deal with ethnic nationalism. The threat from China along the disputed boundary made India insecure about its northeast. Solidarities grounded in constitutional survivalism against the twin threats of communism and communalism gave way to militarism and constitutional collapse just as threat perception shifted towards territorial insecurity. The imposition of AFSPA, justified from a military standpoint, undermined freedoms that India's constitution afforded citizens. The fact that AFSPA has *never* been fully repealed underscores the tenuousness of India's constitutionalism.

Based on an exposition of developments between 1955–62, this chapter argues that India prioritised security over constitutionalism. Such a shift meant investment in the political, territorial, and administrative unity of the republic at the cost of citizenship rights. The first such development, detailed in section one, was the imposition of AFSPA in September 1958. Justified as a preventive measure, it relegated parts of Assam and Manipur as 'disturbed areas', creating a long-term conflict trap. The second set of developments consisted of Ayub's coup and Ne Win's caretaker government. India accepted these shifts as fait accompli. Though the Pakistan coup had a direct impact on India's security in the northeast, the Ne Win interregnum clarified the limits of the Nehru-Nu partnership and marked an end to constitutional solidarities in India's near east. The third development was China's aggression at the borders with Pakistan, India, and Burma. Instead of uniting the subcontinent, Chinese actions divided it. If this paved the way for the China-Pakistan 'all weather friendship', it also pushed India to formalise its Burma boundary, critical to its state-building endeavours in the northeast.

'Misled'

In principle, India's approach towards the Naga movement was similar to how it dealt with militant communists and the RSS: practice politics (and customs) within India's constitutional framework. But unlike communal and communist violence, Naga separatism didn't take an armed turn until 1955, sporadic instances of localised violence notwithstanding. There were two reasons for this. First, successful diplomacy deferred violence. The 1947 Naga-Akbar Hydari Accord between then-Assam governor Akbar Hydari and NNC representatives carved out space for autonomy in the judicial, executive, legislative, taxation, and territorial domains within the Indian union. Buttressed by the 6th Schedule of the constitution that promised autonomy to district councils in Assam and elsewhere in the northeast, the agreement was meant to be in place for ten years, with the governor of Assam having a 'special responsibility ... to ensure the observance of the agreement'.[9]

At the end of this period, the agreement stated that the NNC 'will be asked whether they required the above agreement to be extended for a further period or a new agreement regarding the future of the Naga people arrived at'.[10] This last clause was read differently by both sides. For India, this was acceptance of the constitution by the NNC, and for the latter, this was India's way of accepting the Naga demand for separation after ten years. As former Dewan of Sikkim, N K Rustomji, informed foreign secretary T N Kaul:

> I do not myself think for a moment that Sir Akbar has any ideas of the Nagas having, under the agreement, the right in independence after the ten year period. The Naga representatives has most probably been putting pressure on Sir Akbar to concede such a right in the agreement, but he intentionally kept the phraseology

vague, in the expectation that, in the course of ten years, the situation would settle down.[11]

Additionally, the 1947 accord split Naga communities on the question of separation versus autonomy and the use of violence. The NNC had a powerful and growing moderate faction led by T Sakhrie, whereas the hardliners were Phizo-led. Nehru's attempts to ameliorate Phizo's position over multiple one-on-one meetings in 1951–52 came to naught. After holding an informal plebiscite in 1952 that New Delhi viewed as an act of coercion, Phizo escaped to Burma in the hope of traveling to Geneva via East Bengal and generating support for Naga independence at the UN.[12] Trailed by Indian spies, he was arrested by Burmese authorities. In January 1953, cognisant of the fact that he couldn't force Rangoon into detaining Phizo indefinitely, Nehru encouraged the Indian ambassador to inform Burma how 'troublesome' Phizo was and that releasing him would complicate the situation on both sides of the border.[13] With a joint Nehru-Nu visit to Naga areas of Assam and the Tuensang Frontier scheduled for March, Nehru sought to politically neutralise Phizo. He was clear that if Phizo 'goes away for a few years, that will do us no harm'.[14]

Once again, the twist came from Ne Win, the general who, in India's reading, transformed Burma into a modified military dictatorship. In early March, three weeks before Nu was scheduled to meet Nehru in Kohima, under pressure from Ne Win, Rangoon decided to release Phizo. The home and external affairs ministries panicked and wanted to prevent the release from coinciding with the Nehru-Nu visit. Certain that his release would complicate the situation, the home ministry sought Assam's opinion whether the latter had enough evidence to detain Phizo under the Preventive Detention Act (PDA) upon his return to India.[15]

Assam wanted more time. As it gathered evidence to book Phizo under the PDA, it asked if Rangoon could book him in breach of immigration rules and prolong imprisonment. If not, then could Burma at least postpone his release by 'a few days ... until tours of Prime Minister and Burmese Prime Minister [is] over'?[16] South Block wrote an urgent telegram to the Rangoon embassy pushing the ambassador to either press Burma to prolong Phizo's detention or, at least, 'repatriate him by sea instead of land so that he is out of the way during Prime Minister's Naga tour'.[17] India succeeded in pushing Phizo's release to June, but that didn't stop him from reaching Tuensang and pursuing secession.

In August 1953, J Carrott, an Anglo-Burman commissioner of Sagaing Division who accompanied Nu during his Naga tour with Nehru, had a long discussion with Assam's governor Jairamdas Doulatram and IB director Mullik. Carrott had interviewed Phizo multiple times during the latter's time in Burmese custody, and warned that the situation on the Indian side of the Naga hills was 'ugly'.[18] Carrott warned Doulatram that within the next three years India would face a serious armed revolt led by the Angamis (an ethnic group within the Naga community to which Phizo belonged).

Doulatram—and Nehru—rejected Carrott's analysis as 'incorrect' and were convinced that the Naga issue will 'simmer' with little chance of a sustained insurgency. It was a miscalculation. In less than three years, Phizo led an armed rebellion that lasted decades.[19] His intentions were not hidden. Soon after his release from Burma and return to Tuensang, he formed the 'Independent Government of Nagaland' or the 'Hongkin Government', and as an Indian backgrounder noted, 'began planning for armed resistance'.[20] The impact of Phizo's return was along expected lines. By October 1954, violence against government employees and people viewed as sympathetic towards the state picked up.[21] The scale, tempo, and intensity of violence increased steadily during 1955 and shaped New Delhi's response.

In the lead up to the imposition of AFSPA in 1958, India adopted a two-part strategy to deal with mounting secessionism. New Delhi and Shillong began to politically engage with moderate NNC leaders such as T Sakhrie and John Bosco Jasokie (who later became the chief minister of Nagaland) to drive a wedge in the Naga movement and isolate Phizo.[22] The strategy worked. Phizo's unilateral decision to launch armed resistance had complicated the NNC's internal dynamics. Though united on the question of independence, the council was divided on the use of violence. Jasokie and Sakhrie had been lobbying within the council and attempting to mobilise non-

Angami Nagas to counter Phizo. In June 1955, to blunt New Delhi's strategy to outmanoeuvre militant Nagas, Phizo and four other Nagas met with Doulatram. Uncompromising on their respective positions, Phizo and Doulatram traded accusations about human rights violations. The meeting ended inconclusively. In a debrief to Nehru, Doulatram assessed that the meeting was Phizo's attempt to 'take the wind out of the sails' of the liberal factions, and that New Delhi should wait for the 'crystallisation of liberal Naga opinion' before making any move.[23]

Phizo's position as president of the council became tenuous after the meeting with Doulatram as Sakhrie-led moderates demanded an end to violence and refused to contribute to the council financially until Phizo resigned.[24] Under political pressure from within the council and military pressure by Indian forces, Phizo decided to target opponents—'traitors'—within the movement in addition to targeting the state. On 18 January 1956, Sakhrie was killed by Phizo's associates (Jasokie escaped). The assassination sent shock waves across Naga communities and marked a decisively violent turn to the movement.

To Bishnuram Medhi, Assam's chief minister, Sakhrie's 'unexpected murder brought about a vital change in the whole situation ... [as] people became demoralised [and] the liberal group of leaders became shaky'.[25] The incident also settled Nehru's mind once and for all on not conceding to Phizo. The resulting violence contributed to serious human rights violations by the insurgents and the state. One week after Sakhrie's assassination, Nehru informed Medhi that 'it has become urgent and essential for immediate action to be taken against Phizo and his new movement ... [and] all possible protection should be given to the moderate elements among the Nagas'.[26] On 31 January, the Naga Hills District and the Tuensang Frontier were declared 'disturbed'.

After killing Sakhrie and intimidating moderates, Phizo organised an all-Naga meeting in March, appointed a 'head of state', 100 'members of parliament', and a cabinet of fifteen ministers, and declared Nagaland an independent state on 22 March 1956.[27] Soon after, the 'Naga Home Guard', armed by weapons available from the Second World War and some offered by Pakistan, made contact with the Indian army. The Naga insurgency was underway. In response, Nehru appointed Maj. Gen. R K Kochar as the General Officer Commanding (GOC) Naga Hills and Tuensang in April, with full control over the police, Assam Rifles, and regular army formations to quell the rebellion.[28] From this moment on, Nehru pushed for a quick military victory. In a letter to Medhi, he was categorical that 'we should hit hard, and swiftly, and in particular gain [battlefield] contact with Phizo's gangs' because slow action will 'prolong our work greatly'.[29] Nehru refused to meet Phizo's emissaries in March, fearing that could empower Phizo further. The emissaries met with home minister Govind Ballabh Pant and some social activists, but failed to make political headway.[30]

The situation worsened in April. In the parliament, Naga legislators such as Rishang Keishing of the Congress, questioned Nehru's coercive response. In a speech that suggests Nehru was misreading the Naga situation and underestimating the negative impact of the army's excesses, Keishing asked the government to issue an appeal to extremist Nagas to 'surrender' and come out of the underground.[31] This, he believed, would have a 'positive' impact and could impart normalcy to a quickly aggravating situation. Nehru welcomed Keishing's speech and asserted that the government treated Nagas as 'friends and fellow countrymen', but refused amnesty to Phizo.[32] The situation deteriorated in May, and so too did criticism of the government. The *Times of India* published a series of columns questioning Nehru's strategy towards the Naga problem. Nehru's decision to not meet Naga emissaries in March was criticised as intransigence at a sensitive moment. Slowly but surely, Nehru began to acknowledge that he might have misjudged certain aspects of the problem, but refused to alter strategy.

On 13 May, Nehru convened a meeting with defence minister K.N. Katju, home minister Pant, top officials from the defence and external affairs ministries, and the chief of army staff, General SM Shrinagesh, to discuss the situation.[33] The meeting recalibrated certain parameters of the government's approach: that the military approach alone is not adequate, (b) that the military approach has to be carried out as effectively as possible to break the back of this resistance, (c) that we have to think of some political approach, but that any obvious move in this direction at the moment may have an adverse effect.[34]

The fact was that Phizo had succeeded in driving a wedge between the Medhi-led Assam government and the MEA's Kaul-led NEFA administration. Behind the scenes, Kaul and Medhi were fighting bureaucratic battles on the question of bringing the entire Tuensang Frontier and Assam's Naga Hills Districts under a singular administration in their respective control[35]—and all this was occurring amidst the NNC's silent support for autonomy-seeking communities in the Garo, Khasi, North Cachar, and Jaintia hills of Assam.[36]

Resentment against Assamese dominance among non-Assamese communities, including the Nagas, was significant. Kaul was aware of and exploiting this sentiment in relation to Medhi, and Nehru understood that these official antinomies and the disenchantment of non-Assamese communities with Medhi's government wouldn't bode well. But Nehru could do little given Medhi's political importance, and the latter's persistence to not 'disturb the present equilibrium' in 'any hill districts' of Assam by acceding to Kaul.[37] The home minister was sympathetic to Kaul but did 'not fully endorse his suggestions' of political shift in the Naga areas, and wanted to focus on military operations.[38] Throughout May–June, Nehru was quizzed about India's handling of the Naga issue by parliamentarians from Assam and West Bengal.[39]

To prevent internal schisms from dislocating state authority in Naga areas and challenge the Congress' political dominance, Nehru upped his divide-and-rule strategy after the 13 May 1956 meeting. In a subtle shift, he started discouraging the use of Phizo's name in official communications to avoid giving him 'too much importance', and undermined the Naga identity by painting it as little more than multiple communities being 'lumped up together' by colonial authorities.[40] It was, in his view, important to distinguish the Angamis, the Semas, the Tangkhuls from the Aos, and so on, to deal with different communities *separately*, thereby strengthening pre-existing cleavages. He also refused to be 'hustled into some action of the political kind' by Kaul and Medhi and 'worried that our nerves seems to be weakening' in Naga areas.[41]

On 15 June, as civil administration in Kohima collapsed, General Shrinagesh sought clearance to use airpower to 'machine-gun hostiles using aircraft' along the Dimapur-Kohima-Imphal road.[42] Nehru was wary of this course of action, which would have been the first time independent India deployed airpower against its own citizens. His concern was *not* the accruing human costs, but the risk it posed to the aircraft. In a letter to the defence secretary, he clarified that 'we cannot afford to have a Harvard struck down by snipers and possibly brought down ... [as] this will greatly increase the morale of the hostiles'.[43] For now, India didn't use airpower, and the military situation remained dismal with no political movement in sight.

Among other issues, the Naga agitation laid bare the contours of anti-Assamese sentiment and desire for autonomy within the union (fuelled by the imposition of Assamese language) by various 'minority' communities in Assam. The creation of Meghalaya in 1972 was a result of anti-Assamese sentiment in Jaintia, Garo, Cachar, and Khasi hills bordering East Pakistan. In this respect, Phizo succeeded in laying the groundwork for the political reorganisation of Assam (as witnessed after 1971), thereby sowing the seeds of Assamese separatism that erupted in the 1980s.

One of India's most undemocratic decisions—apart from regrouping villages to sift out civilians from militants—was creating an irregular militia of Naga volunteers who could fight Phizo's group. Lessons from colonial counterinsurgency in Malaya, Kenya, and Burma shaped India's response. Keen to divide and conquer, Nehru ordered the IB to 'utilise Nagas for this purpose'.[44] The creation of this irregular force, on which little has been written, was a turning point in New Delhi's exploitation of inter-community differences. The testimonies of Nagas on the receiving end of India's counterinsurgency campaign, which included the regrouping of villages, as well as attacks and torture by irregular militias, the police, and the armed forces, demonstrate the brutality of these operations and the scale of violations.[45]

The idea was to raise 'up to 800 rank and file' (cash-strapped, the ministry of finance approved only 400), offer them arms, training, and leadership, a 'basic salary of the Assam Police, namely Rs. 33-p.m. for Constables, Rs. 50-p.m. for Havildars, and Rs. 100-p.m. for

Jamadars', but to 'not take any responsibility of providing ration for this irregular force' and offer them cash for sundry expenditure.[46] Of this group, only 200 militia members were to be armed with rifles and 40,000 rounds of ammunition, and issued a labels-free green uniform that offered camouflage but kept them distinct from the police, paramilitary, and army. The total cost of this operation was estimated to be 454,470 rupees, but the economic pressures to meet the Second Five Year Plan meant that only 266,235 rupees were approved.[47] This force was secretly trained by the Indian army and by 1957 joined combat in Tuensang and northern Manipur. The army favoured this force in areas where it couldn't easily operate.[48] The gambit worked from a military perspective. But it exacerbated intra-community friction, opened room for misappropriation of funds, and set the tone for India's counterinsurgency methods for decades to come.

Against this backdrop, Nehru broke the logjam in September 1956, and invited a delegation of moderate Naga leaders led by Jasokie to New Delhi. In a conversation that lasted two hours, Jasokie and Nehru reached an understanding regarding the need for a separate state carved out of Assam's Naga hills districts and the Tuensang Frontier. They laid the groundwork for the creation of Nagaland in 1963, and further marginalised Phizo.[49] But this meeting was not just triggered by the dismal security situation. On 31 July, as the insurgency raged, multiple detachments of the Chinese People's Liberation Army (PLA) entered 60 miles inside Burmese territory in Wa state, at two points in Kachin state, and at multiple points along the Tibet-Yunnan-Burma border.[50] Rangoon sought India's intervention in the matter. India assured Burma that it was interested in the matter 'both for their own sake and ours' and would take the matter up with China 'in an informal way', but became concerned about the implications of PLA manoeuvres for its own interests. Nehru urgently advised his diplomats to verify possible Chinese ingress at the Burma-India-China trijunction.[51]

The spectre of a military standoff with China over a disputed boundary in conjunction with the insurgency in Naga areas forced New Delhi's hand. The meeting with Jasokie sought to strengthen moderates within the NNC as New Delhi had planned.

Nehru's political appetite for a separate Naga state within the union increased by 1957 and birthed to the so-called Naga Hills-Tuensang Area (NHTA) under the *joint* administration of Assam and the MEA. By this time, the tempo of attacks by armed Nagas had reduced if not halted. In a shift of operational strategy and momentum (and in a controversial decision), the armed forces began to regroup Naga villages as part of NHTA, a strategy utilised by colonial Britain in Malaya, to sift armed Nagas from the rest. A move that scared many, the regrouping and de-grouping of villages did reduce insurgent violence by late 1957. As Nehru informed Kaul on 30 December 1957, 'there has been very little violence and, on the whole, a peaceful atmosphere has prevailed' thanks to the brutal regrouping strategy.[52]

Phizo called it genocide.[53] It was this no-holds-barred use of force and his political marginalisation that forced Phizo to escape to East Pakistan in December 1957. If one goes by the logic of Nehru's own assessment, the situation in NHTA by January–March 1958 was precarious but better than before. The 'Naga Home Guard', according to Indian intelligence, had 'practically ceased to exist' after Phizo's disappearance.[54] Still, pockets of resistance remained, and in combination with an emerging boundary dispute with China and instability at the East Pakistan-Manipur-Assam border, which witnessed routine firing by the forces of both countries, Nehru didn't want to relinquish military control of this sensitive region.[55]

On 22 May 1958, Pant introduced the Armed Forces (Special Powers) Bill in the Lok Sabha, and despite pushback from Bengali and Assamese parliamentarians, the bill was approved and implemented on 11 September.[56] Nehru rubbished concerns about the its negative impact:

> No infirm government can function anywhere. Where there is violence, it has to be dealt with … I do not understand why honourable members opposite should speak in such strong terms as if something very unusual, something extraordinary, was taking place.[57]

The Nagas agitating against India had been, he explained, 'misled'. Democratic functioning and constitutionalism had been laid to rest in the NHTA—with parliamentary approval. Regardless of what Nehru believed, AFSPA only exacerbated the problem.

Windfall

Phizo's arrival in Dhaka was a windfall for Ayub. Concerned that India was stoking anti-Karachi sentiment in East Pakistan, Pakistani security agencies reciprocated by funneling small amounts of weapons through Sylhet to Naga rebels.[58] The first contact between Nagas and Pakistani intelligence occurred in 1956. In August 1957, Mowu Angami, the 'C-in-C' of the Naga Army, was arrested in Cachar District when returning from Sylhet.[59] To pave the way for Phizo's escape, the 'Director of Intelligence' of underground Nagas visited East Pakistan in mid-1957. Throughout this period, according to an Indian defence white paper, 'several small groups [of Naga rebels] visited … East Pakistan for arms and ammunition etc.'.[60] Such support was insufficient to tilt the military balance in Phizo's favour. But his arrival in Dacca, which led Phizo to believe that Ayub would support the Nagas, offered Pakistan leverage against India. An open welcome to Phizo could upset ties when both sides sought to resolve disputes. But detaining him without dislocating the fulcrum of anti-India violence in the NHTA could prove profitable.

Soon after Phizo's arrival in Dacca, Nehru and Firoz Khan Noon, who became Pakistan's prime minister on 16 December 1957, began to focus on resolving the 'pasha enclaves' issue; small territorial enclaves in Cooch Behar lay in East Pakistan, and certain Indian territorial enclaves lay in East Pakistan. A lack of boundary demarcation and existence of such enclaves (in the context of Pakistan's introduction of the passport system and a breakdown of economic ties in 1948–49) often led to firing by security forces on both sides, complicating Assamese and West Bengal politics. After much deliberation, on 12 September 1958, days before Ayub executed the coup, the Nehru-Noon Agreement was signed to reduce tensions in the east, even if the overall relationship remained troubled. To signal its commitment to displaced persons from East Pakistan (and not repatriating them), India launched the 'Dandakaranya Project' under the Ministry of Rehabilitation in Orissa.[61] But communal pressures and displacement were anything but resolved. Shrewdly managing these contradictions and aware that the Naga movement remained alive, the ISI housed Phizo in a Dacca police compound and limited his outside contact.

The ISI's interrogation of Phizo, which involved pushing him to accept Assam as part of Pakistan, was partly to test his commitment to the Naga cause, and partly to gauge how far Karachi could push the envelope in India. Phizo's uncompromising stand on independence impressed the ISI, but also bothered them when it came to the risks associated with such warfare. Until now, for its part, India had done little to fan Bengali separatism. But if India activated its covert assets in East Pakistan *after* Ayub took power, he could arm the Nagas in response. After all, Phizo did want Karachi to train the entire Naga army. But if India accepted the post-coup situation as is, Phizo could be 'cut loose' and could press on with his journey to the UN. On 7 October, the constitution was abrogated, and martial law declared with Ayub as prime minister.

20 days later, Ayub deposed Mirza and took charge as president and chief martial administration. The 'second coup' considerably worsened relations between East and West Pakistan. Leaders like Suhrawardy, who allied himself with Noon's pro-military Republican party to sideline Mirza in 1956 (an alliance that saw Suhrawardy become prime minister), were jailed. The coup raised concerns in India about the impact it would have on bilateral ties. Ayub's inconsistency on Kashmir heightened such concerns. In an interview on 10 October, he emphasised the need for 'friendly' relations with India and promised to respect the Nehru-Noon agreement. But after deposing Mirza, he gave a fiery press briefing claiming that 'should we be forced to take extreme measures, the responsibility will be that of India'.[62] When journalists sought clarification if this meant war, he said, 'yes, certainly'.[63]

As if on cue, one day after this press conference, the 'Prime Minister' of the 'Federal Government of Nagaland (FGN)' wrote a letter to Ayub expressing the gratitude of the Naga underground for his 'sympathetic feelings towards us', and asked Pakistan to give more publicity to the Naga cause.[64] Parallel to an increase in harassment and kidnapping of Indian nationals and border-firing (thirteen incidents in the east, and three incidents in the west *after* the coup, minor cattle-smuggling and criminal activity notwithstanding), the situation in Pakistan worried New Delhi.[65] The brutalisation of a south Indian officer and his wife from India's Assistant High Commission in Rajshahi triggered intense parliamentary criticism of Nehru's recognition of Ayub's regime.

India's official response was to keep calm and carry on. But behind the scenes, there was a recalibration of subcontinental geopolitics. The situation in East Pakistan was explosive and had been building since the ouster of the United Front government in 1954. Suhrawardy's brief premiership (September 1956–October 1957) had done little to assuage it. Instead, his differences with Bhashani created fissures within the United Front as the latter quit formal politics. Ayub's coup crystallised sentiment against Karachi in East Pakistan. Even the US was worried that while Ayub could 'improve' Pakistan's situation—until then ranging between 'the grotesque and macabre'[66]—the 'only real problem would be East Pakistan, which will not be very happy at the prospect of military rule from West Pakistan'.[67]

India keenly followed developments in East Pakistan, with considerable appetite in some sections of the government to exploit it. The bilateral had been on a downward spiral with violence largely focused on the eastern border rather than in the west or over Kashmir. As India's high commissioner to Pakistan noted in April 1959, 'the Kashmir issue was more in the background than in previous years'. The Nehru-Noon agreement's focus on the eastern border was meant to arrest this downturn instead of positively overhauling the relationship.[68] India had, after all, closed its missions in Lahore, Hyderabad, and Comilla in 1958, and Pakistan did the same in Chandigarh, Bombay, and Agartala.[69]

But Nehru refused to fuel the fire in East Pakistan. He was categorical: 'it would be wrong and unwise for us to encourage in any way the leaders or members of the Awami Party or indeed any political or other groups in Pakistan, East or West' to target the new regime because 'we do not interfere with the internal affairs of the country'.[70] Eager to preserve the opening that the Nehru-Noon agreement had created, Nehru worried that even a limited, covertly hostile posture towards Pakistan could have unexpectedly high costs. This is where Phizo came in. If India decided to support Bengali nationalists or resort to excessive border firing, Pakistan could activate substantial support for Naga militants.

The fact that Phizo was not physically harmed, allowed to have visitors, and maintained contact with his group were indications that Ayub was keeping him on a 'retainer' and assessing the extent to which he could utilised to pressure India. The fact that India's counterinsurgency operations were failing to quell the Naga rebellion and that Phizo was still a national security threat indicated Ayub's gambit worked. Nehru not only contained the impulse among Indian security officials to exploit the post-coup sentiment in East Pakistan, but also accepted Ayub's wresting of the presidency without objection. Both sides understood the balance of power and refused to escalate.

Nehru's restraint helped. In less than a year, India and Pakistan signed an agreement regarding 'procedures to end disputes and incidents along the Indo-East Pakistan border areas'.[71] It clarified that the two governments would 're-affirm their determination to implement the Nehru-Noon Agreement in full' and laid out the principles along which the undemarcated sections of the boundary would be demarcated in all sectors, namely East Pakistan's borders with Assam, West Bengal, and Tripura. The river water sharing issue was addressed, and India agreed that it would raise 'no objection' to the development of dams on the Karnaphuli river despite the 'submergence of some areas in India'.[72] Such an attempt to reduce animosity was driven by a mix of Ayub's desire to press forth with economic reforms and playing the cold warrior. As the US informed Nehru, it wanted both countries to jointly counter Soviet and Chinese communism.

Such signaling was reflected in Phizo's ouster from Pakistan in March 1960 and his arrival in Zurich. Met by a man in uniform, Phizo was quietly whisked away without anyone checking his documents. A taxi took him to Hotel Sonnenberg.[73] From here, he had to manage his own affairs. Phizo reached London with help of Reverend Michael Scott (who played an important but controversial role in the India-Naga talks) and David Astor, the owner and editor of the *Observer*, who championed the Naga cause (Nehru found their actions 'not at all commendable').[74] Upon reaching London, Phizo realised that India was unwilling to seek his extradition. For now, Ayub had given up a trump card without cutting the chord with the Naga underground. Nehru's restraint, then, was driven by realpolitik.

'Contagion'

On 28 October, one day after Ayub's coup, Ne Win took power in Rangoon. Both the circumstances and method of Ne Win's takeover were different from Ayub's. After a serious economic slump in the mid-1950s, the Burmese economy was recovering, and communists were surrendering. But factionalism in Nu's party, the Anti-Fascist People's Freedom League (AFPFL), worsened in 1958, and the party formally split into 'Clean AFPFL' led by Nu and 'Stable AFPFL' led by Ba Swe. In a 'modified military dictatorship', as Indian diplomats termed Burma, a split in the main political party invited military intervention. Unlike in Pakistan, where Mirza first abrogated the constitution and was deposed two weeks later, in Rangoon the transfer of power was gradual. Ever since becoming deputy prime minister in 1949, Ne Win had eroded the autonomy and integrity of state institutions. The idea of the Tatmadaw being a vanguard of the nation took root during this period, with support from the Buddhist Sangha. The split in AFPFL, underlining the appeal of stability and anti-corruption rhetoric, offered perfect ground for Ne Win to 'clean up' the system before holding fresh elections.

A democratic India was now mostly surrounded by authoritarian states and monarchies. This had long-term implications for India's near east. On 12 October, when it was clear that Nu would step down for Ne Win to assume power, Nehru braved media queries when pressed to explain his thoughts on the two coups in the region. He rationalised that change of guard in Rangoon was meant to be 'a temporary phase', with elections promised at the end of it, unlike in Pakistan where the coup was honest and total.[75] Given that the transfer of power was deliberate, and had the opposition parties' support, Nehru argued that it was not for him to 'judge'.[76] When pushed about the peculiarity of Ne Win's assumption of power and the whole act being far from democratic, Nehru was evasive: 'it is more democratic than for the president [reference to Mirza] to decide'.[77]

To avoid being cornered, Nehru said that he was unaware of the details of the matter and couldn't say 'what exactly is happening' in Rangoon. But, oddly, he insisted that it was democratic. This was despite knowing that Nu did not relinquish power willingly, and had communicated to India the threat of violence by anti-Nu colonel-level officers under Ne Win's command.[78] Stepping down was Nu's way of 'avoiding violence and bloodshed' after members of his party openly rebuked the military in what he called a 'tactical mistake'.[79] In fact, Indian intelligence observed, Ne Win ordered 'some extraordinary security measures throughout the country' such as the army occupying transport terminals, establishing pickets near public utility services, and increasing checkpoints in large cities.[80] The threat to Nu was real.

Despite signs of coercion, Nu, keen to build bridges with Ne Win instead of letting his opponent lobby the army, asserted that this was a consensual decision, and that 'some misunderstanding had cropped up in the army about his policy and his liberal attitude towards the insurgents [Karen and communists] which had made the situation a little dangerous'.[81] Nu was effectively admitting that Nehru's 1949 advice on reconciling with the Karen and fighting the communists, which he followed only limitedly, had run its course. It was an acknowledgement that Nu himself was willing to depart from constitutionalism to remain in power. This was demonstrated in his electoral programme that promised (a) 'to make Buddhism a state religion, (b) revive the Pyidaungsu (Union) plan, and (c) not to negotiate with the insurgents'—thereby going against almost everything inclusive constitutions stood for. It triggered the Kachin rebellion.[82]

These developments marked an end to the Nehru-Nu ideological partnership. Nehru quickly accepted this reality: 'I have high regard for U Nu's judgement, opinion, and person'.[83] That Ne Win didn't abrogate the constitution gave India something to latch onto, even though Buddhist majoritarianism received a fillip.[84] Ne Win took big decisions during his 1958–60 'military caretaker government', that not only undermined India's efforts to counter China, but also proved disastrous for Burmese Indians. As the Rangoon embassy noted, between January–March 1959, 'the drive against the "economic insurgency" was at its height, and several [Burmese Indian] merchants were summarily arrested and deported'.[85] When asked by a journalist how he planned to stop the 'contagion' of military coups spreading to India, Nehru countered with hope: the 'contagion [of democracy]' from India would spread to these countries instead of the other way round.[86]

India's reluctance to antagonise Ne Win stemmed from its reliance on Burmese rice. His arrival didn't have implications on the Naga insurgency. But a dislocation in ties could stymie India's state-building elsewhere. Large parts of rural India faced acute food shortages in the late 1950s and 1960s. India's national sample surveys showed that nearly 40% of the country's rural population incurred per capita expenditure of 50 paise or less.[87] In some states such as Orissa nearly 68% faced such crises, followed by 57% in Kerala, whereas Andhra Pradesh, Madhya Pradesh, and Madras stood at 47%.[88] As the largest importer of Burmese rice, a food-strapped India could ill afford to downgrade ties with Rangoon. In 1957–58, India imported 385 thousand tonnes of Burmese rice for 166 million kyat. This figure fell to 266 thousand tonnes in 1958–59 for 118 million kyat, only to be reversed to 391 thousand tonnes for 166 million-kyat in 1959–60.[89] Cordial ties with Ne Win, then, were a necessity to prevent famines and droughts and ensure the continuity of rice exports.

Nehru's patience with Ne Win paid off when the two met in Delhi in October 1959 to discuss bilateral ties and relations with China. Nehru was 'much impressed by General Ne Win' who called the former a 'father' like figure who advised Burma 'since Aung San' and was convinced that the general was friendly towards India and 'could be relied upon'.[90] With Pakistan and Burma taking an authoritarian turn, the situation in Naga areas troubled, and relations with China experiencing a downturn, India could not antagonise Karachi and Rangoon given the risk of damaging ties with *all* neighbours.[91] The postcolonial solidarities grounded in constitutional survivalism, as witnessed in the first half of the 1950s, were dead. But shared threat perceptions from ethnic nationalisms and an aggressive China ensured that these countries worked to maintain cordiality and resolve disputes—even as they began to cultivate covert offensive options in relation to each other (especially India and Pakistan). Things seemed under control in October 1959. Then they took a sharp turn south.

Himalayan Blunder(s)

Nehru's carefully calibrated geopolitical balance in India's near east began to crumble after 1959. The push came from China. Peking had been printing maps showing large parts of Kashmir and the North-East Frontier Agency (NEFA) as its territory.[92] In August 1958, the PLA arrested an Indian army reconnaissance party and refused to inform New Delhi. When pressed by New Delhi, China noted that the Indian soldiers were sent back after interrogation, even though multiple search parties failed to locate them.[93] The PLA had also transgressed into Burmese territory and viewed parts of Hunza and Gilgit Baltistan as its own, increasing Pakistani anxieties too. Alarm bells about Chinese coercive intent were ringing in India by now. Arguably, this offered India, Burma, and Pakistan an opportunity to jointly consider their approach. But their failure to do so redefined subcontinental geopolitics.

China's assertiveness and its centrifugal impact on subcontinental geopolitics is deeply tied to India's state-building attempts and diplomacy in its near east. In the northeast, as the following chapters show, India demarcated its boundary with Burma to clarify the state's territorial and political writ central to state-building. But the emergent Sino-Pakistan détente meant that East Pakistan emerged as a staging base for anti-India rebels. These changes are best understood in two phases. The first period (1958–60) saw convergence between these countries on the China question. But ideological differences and mistrust prevented coordination. In the second period (1961–62), Peking exploited India-Pakistan differences and pulled Rangoon away from its Indian embrace. It ended with a border war between China and India.

Domestically, Ayub and Ne Win's post-coup priorities of consolidating control mirrored each other. From banning political parties to declaring hidden wealth worth 1.34 billion rupees, and from reducing prices of daily commodities to setting up a Land Reforms Commission, Ayub promised revolution from above.[94] Similarly, Ne Win promised 'pacification of the country ... holding free and fair elections ... and bringing down the cost of living'.[95] But instead of stepping down in April 1959, Ne Win sought a one-year extension in what India called a 'stage-managed show, constitutionally correct and democratically absolute'.[96] Even though Ne Win was faring poorly in comparison with Ayub, Indian diplomats praised him for 'a soldier's instinct of getting on with the job'.[97]

Internationally, they adopted different courses. Burma was keen to steer clear of great power politics, whereas Pakistan's treaty alliances made it central to the US. These positions were tested in March 1959 when Tibetans rose up against the Chinese army. On 30 March, the Dalai Lama secretly entered India.[98] Burma's reaction was muted. Despite suspicion about Chinese intent and admiration for India's 'bold'[99] stand, Rangoon maintained its silence. China was offering to resolve Rangoon's boundary dispute, and the PLA was secretly evicting Kuomintang remnants from Shan state with Rangoon's approval.[100] India's consulate in Mandalay noted that Burma 'could not afford to annoy the Chinese at the present juncture'.[101]

In contrast, Ayub was livid. Parallel to the Lhasa uprising, Pakistan found that Chinese maps showed parts of north and northeastern Pakistan as Chinese. Aggressive patrolling by the PLA in these areas brought them in contact with Pakistani soldiers, generating friction. Bilateral relations between the two were strained due to Pakistan's alignment with the West and Ayub's anti-communist outlook. On 17 April, Pakistan co-sponsored a UN resolution on Tibet.[102]

In May, Ayub met Indian high commissioner Rajeshwar Dayal to discuss the threat China posed to India and Pakistan. The meeting occurred at the peak of border firing and kidnapping incidents at the East Pakistan-India border.[103] Ayub had an offer: let's resolve our border problems peacefully and undertake 'Joint Defence' against China.[104] Worried that this was a tactic to force India into diluting its position on Kashmir and the canal waters issue, Nehru refused.[105]

Even from an 'opportunist' perspective, solving India-Pakistan disputes was 'desirable', he argued.[106] But a non-aligned India was opposed to military pacts. Nehru suggested a 'no war' pact instead, which Ayub rebuffed.[107]

If 'joint defence' and 'no war' pacts were non-starters, the need to stabilise ties remained pressing. For the worsening of Sino-Indian boundary dispute was paralleled by Pakistan's hosting of the 'Chinese Moslem Haji Mission' from Taiwan in July 1959, earning Chou Enlai's wrath for signalling a 'Two China' policy.[108] In September 1959, thanks to skirmishes between Chinese and Pakistani soldiers, Ayub sealed the border with Xinjiang.[109] Building on his dialogue with Dayal, on 23 October, Indian and Pakistani representatives agreed to abide by the Nehru-Noon agreement.

But on the same day, Ayub announced commencement of boundary talks with China. A lack of progress with India on Kashmir and the brewing Sino-Soviet split were viewed as push and pull factors by Karachi, necessitating dialogue with China. The gamble worked. Peking saw a powerful prospective ally in Ayub and reduced border tensions. The resolution on Tibet co-sponsored by Pakistan was soon lost under an 'all weather friendship'.[110] To be sure, Ayub took the initiative, but it was Chou's masterstroke to resolve issues with India's two neighbours. In January 1960, Ne Win signed a boundary treaty with China, with both sides agreeing to delimit the border along the McMahon Line. This occurred within two months of the Nehru-Ne Win meeting where they agreed to coordinate strategy on boundary demarcation and remain firm on the McMahon Line as a legitimate boundary.[111]

Two years later, after Ne Win ousted Nu in an unpretentious military coup, Chou reminisced that the signing of the agreement 'was done by Ne Win, and not by U Nu, who only signed the agreement at the end … Ne Win is different from U Nu; Ne Win is anti-Indian,' whereas Nu was considered to be in awe of Nehru like a 'student and his teacher'.[112] In retrospect, Chou misread Ne Win's attitude towards India, but his prognosis that there was no ideological alignment between Nehru and the military dictator was accurate. Ne Win did inform Nehru about his talks with Chou and also hinted that not pressing on the term 'McMahon Line', which had colonial connotations, helped Rangoon reduce tensions.[113] Nehru took his point. But with the Dalai Lama in India, the die was cast.

By simultaneously resolving boundary disputes with Burma and Pakistan, China was sending India a message, namely that there would be costs of hosting the Dalai Lama. Peking was convinced that India was secretly arming Tibetans. The irony that it was Pakistan that offered launchpads for anti-Soviet and anti-China operations was lost on Mao.[114] India didn't start training and arming the Tibetans until *after* the 1962 war. By end of 1960, though there had been no movement on the Sino-Pakistan bilateral front, the 'stage had been set' for a border agreement in the future.[115] This held serious implications for India.

Similarly, the Sino-Burmese boundary treaty disturbed India.[116] It amplified Chinese propaganda that the lack of resolution of the boundary disputes was caused by India's intransigence. Arguably, all of India's neighbours like Pakistan, Burma, and Nepal settled their dispute with China peacefully. Then why not India? More worryingly, Burma gave up its claim at the China-Burma-India trijunction, effectively making it a bilateral problem between China and India.[117] On 4 April 1960, Ne Win stepped down and Nu returned as prime minister. Unlike his pre-1958 avatar, Nu was now much more willing to engage with China and didn't require India's support.

To India's annoyance, Nu presented the Sino-Burmese treaty as a format of resolving the Sino-Indian dispute.[118] Ne Win's discrimination against ethnic minorities, which Nu furthered by pushing Buddhism as state religion, triggered the Kachin insurgency adjacent to India's NHTA. In February 1960, the Kachin Independence Organisation (KIO) was formed with Zau Seng as its founding leader and a 27-member army.[119] One year later, in February 1961, the small army expanded to over 100 fighters, and was christened the Kachin Independence Army. Both Ne Win and Nu, in their rush to resolve the border dispute with China and push Buddhist majoritarianism, ended up undermining India's security. The Nagas, expectedly, found a cross-border ally in Kachin rebels.

The 1961–62 period, thus, turned out difficult for India in more than one way. In January 1961, Kennedy became US president and reached out to Nehru to reset bilateral ties. One of his first decisions was to offer India loans over 1 billion USD and food aid worth 1.3 billion USD.[120] Such alignment between India and the US was accompanied by Nehru's 'Forward Policy' along the China border wherein multiple army posts were built in forward areas to counter PLA deployment.[121] In December 1961, in what its adversaries and allies alike viewed as an aggressive move, India used force to liberate Goa.[122] The jubilant effect of Goa's liberation was palpable. These occurrences affirmed Ayub's belief to resolve disputes with Peking.

The brief window of opportunity for an India-Pakistan rapprochement, in Ayub's reading, was lost. Sometime in 1961, under leadership of Maj. Gen. Akbar Khan and Col. Fatah Khan, the ISI launched 'Operation Jim' aimed at offering substantial military and financial support to Phizo's fighters in camps in Sylhet, the Chittagong Hill Tracts (CHT), and near Dacca.[123] In May 1962, Kaito Sema, the 'commander-in-chief' of the Naga army crossed over into East Pakistan with a large contingent and received training in a camp near Dacca until January 1963.[124] Phizo's dream of large-scale training of the Naga fighters in East Pakistan came true. He was called back to Karachi and was flown to Dacca to meet Kaito and his group that month.[125]

Phizo stayed in Pakistan until mid-June and signed an 'agreement' for 'defence cooperation' with Pakistan.[126] Between 1962–65, four large groups of 2,500 Naga fighters received training and arms from Pakistan.[127] The arms and ammunitions included .303 Rifles (168), light machine guns (18), Sten guns (18), Tommy guns (9), medium machine guns (3), 3" mortars (3), 2" mortars (3), pistols (26), grenades (500), a signal pistol, and explosives (6 manloads).[128] Ayub came full circle and exploited the opportunity when India, in his view, was blundering into a border war with China.

In Rangoon, Ne Win, having tasted power, ousted Nu in a military coup on 2 March 1962, without any pretense of constitutionalism and democracy. Having been advised by Ayub and Egypt's Gamal Nasser, whom he met in October 1959 before flying into New Delhi, to not give up power, Ne Win was back for good this time. Nehru, neck-deep in dealing with the Chinese threat, once again, went about dealing with Ne Win as if nothing had happened—much to the detriment of the Burmese Indian community, which experienced the full wrath of state-backed racism and began a painful exodus out of Burma.

Former Indian diplomat Eric Gonsalves, who was posted to Rangoon in the early 1960s, remembers that Nehru was 'hardly there' when it came to the Burmese Indians.[129] In October–November 1962, China militarily humiliated India in a border war to such an extent that Nehru was left asking for an air-defence cover for India from the US and giving up on the defence of Assam and Arunachal Pradesh, eventually dying a broken man in 1964.[130] The 1961–62 period thus changed India and its near east forever.

Conclusions

Postcolonial states privileging security over rights of their citizens was the most consequential shift in India's near east during the late 1950s. Driven by changing threat perceptions, Indian leaders were focused on the political, territorial, and administrative unity of the republic instead of constitutional rights. Economic dislocation caused by the 1947 partition and heightened civil strife in Burma triggered concerns about militant communism and religious partisanship as central threats to independent India in the early 1950s. Such threat perception shifted to armed ethnic nationalism and Chinese aggression by the end of the decade. If the fear of communism brought leaders of India, Pakistan, and Burma together in postcolonial solidarities, armed ethnic nationalism and Chinese aggression triggered interventionism. Cautious, quiet, but increasing desire in Indian policymaking circles to exploit mass alienation in East Pakistan to pressure Karachi was mirrored by Pakistani support for Naga insurgents.

The breakdown of the state-citizen contract as enshrined in the constitutions of India, Pakistan, and Burma—apart from troubled bilateral relations and the sharpening of Cold War bloc politics—triggered competitive cross-border geopolitics in India's near east. Whether done covertly or overtly, systematically or on an ad hoc basis, the fact that people or communities living on the so-called periphery of independent India, Pakistan, and Burma came to be viewed as subversives and anti-nationals who either needed to prove their loyalty to the state or be 'dealt with firmly' (a relic of the colonial age) made them 'exploitable'. Short of achieving actual separation, Pakistan calculated that calibrated, long-term support to Naga separatists would punish India but not push it towards war. As seen in Ayub's initial arrest and eventual activation of armed support for Phizo, Pakistan was playing the proverbial 'Naga card'. China, especially after 1962, and as discussed in next chapters, picked up on this covert threat from Pakistan in 1965.

By 1962, India's near east became a space where postcolonial republics needed to earn their presence using force, even at the cost of legitimacy. The threat of ethnic nationalism *internally* and Chinese coercion *externally* impacted how the state functioned in these regions. China's invasion of Tibet was part of an authoritarian trend that was panning out in India's near east during this period. Countering Chinese communists required ideological commitment to the territoriality and constitution of India. The desire to make India's constitution the *only* acceptable, even sacred, document to which everyone needed to owe allegiance reached fever pitch in Naga areas during this period. Nehru's justification to use force against armed Nagas, even as he advocated patience with the larger Naga community, was done in the name of the constitution. That there were excesses from both sides on the ground was understood but overlooked.

The imposition of AFSPA in Assam and Manipur and creation of local irregular forces to counter Phizo was an admission that Nehru's constitutionally-minded India was failing to convince all Nagas about its benign intent. It later became a template for counterinsurgency in Kashmir and Chhattisgarh where the state created local militias to counter separatist and Naxalite militants. Such practices not only failed but led to more violations and created conflict traps. Unlike advocates of Hindutva or even communists, both of whom accepted operating (largely) within constitutional confines, Naga nationalism was opposed to the very idea of India.

The fact that AFSPA has not been fully repealed and has found advocates for its forever imposition reveals the depth of damage done to India's constitutionalism in the initial years of the Naga insurgency. The idea that short-term use of force could help build a long-term democratic union in the Naga areas never ultimately proved true. Even though Nagaland became a separate state in in 1963, its politics, along with that of other northeastern states, became intimately attuned to separatist violence, ethnic polarisation, and illicit cross-border trade networks.

The result of such constitutional damage is visible in the deeply corrupt electoral system in the northeast wherein violence continues to simmer. In that sense, the state, despite being the more powerful entity in these regions in a military sense, never truly triumphed over separatist and ideological violence. The outbreak of the Mizo nationalist movement in 1966, the ultra-left wing Naxalbari movement in West Bengal in 1967, the Kachin insurgency in Burma coupled with armed politics of the Communist Party of Burma (CPB), and the 'six-point' movement in East Pakistan leading up to the 1969 mass uprising and the liberation war in 1971 underscore how a shift away from democracy, participatory politics, and inclusion, in the direction of authoritarianism, shook the foundations of the postcolonial state in the 1960s.

A less appreciated impact of authoritarianism and armed ethnic politics in the near east was their shaping of Pakistan's miscalculation of a similarly strong separatist sentiment among Kashmiris. Ayub's support for Phizo after 1961 was ultimately meant to tie India down in the east while Pakistan wrested Kashmir. Unfortunately for Pakistan, the 1965 war over Kashmir and proxy warfare in the northeast tilted Indian decision-making in favour of interventionism in Pakistan's eastern flank. Unlike Nehru, Lal Bahadur Shastri, who became prime minister after Nehru's demise, and Indira Gandhi, who took office in January 1966, opted for coercion in dealing with external threats. The age of postcolonial solidarities came to a slow but decisive end in the 1960s. India's near east, more than Kashmir, was the centre of gravity of such shifts. The violent processes in this region, as the next chapters demonstrate, not only shaped India's relations with its neighbours, but remade India itself.

4

TWO AND A HALF FRONTS
WAR, BORDERLANDS, AND INTERVENTIONISM
AFTER 1962

'Ministry of Defence have prepared a draft White Paper ...
to show the common efforts of two of our neighbouring
countries, China, a revolutionary power seeking ideological
and spatial expansion, and Pakistan with all its hostile moods
and designs in fomenting and sustaining tribal insurgency in
north eastern India with the intention of disintegrating and
weakening India'.[1]

S Loveraj, Director (North East),
Ministry of Home Affairs, 26 June 1972

India faced two adversaries after 1962. Ayub didn't exploit the
situation immediately but laid the ground for an offensive in
Kashmir. Unimpressed by American arms supply to India, Pakistan
began talking to China. On 12 October 1962, as Indian and Chinese
forces made contact, Pakistani and Chinese diplomats began secret
boundary negotiations. On 2 March 1963, the two sides signed a
border agreement, cementing alignment.[2] Under pressure from the
US to resolve Kashmir, Nehru reluctantly entered talks with Ayub.[3]
He noted that 'Pakistan authorities tended to regard the crisis in Sino-

Indian relations as an opportunity to press India to make all sorts of concessions'.[4] The talks lasted six rounds, but failed. Throughout this period, Nehru's health deteriorated. At 2pm on 27 May 1964, the union steel minister announced in the parliament: 'the light is out'—Nehru had succumbed to a severe heart attack.[5]

Convinced that humiliation in 1962 followed by Nehru's death dealt a crippling blow, Ayub probed India's military capabilities in the Rann of Kutch and Dahagram in Bengal between January–April 1965.[6] Tactical successes in Kutch buttressed Pakistan's confidence to execute a larger operation to wrest Kashmir. In August 1965, it launched Operation Gibraltar followed by Operation Grand Slam in September.[7] The 1965 India-Pakistan war was underway. It was based on Pakistan's ill-founded assumption that a full-scale attack would trigger a rebellion in Kashmir. India's counter-escalation in Punjab and near-capture of Lahore combined with the absence of an anti-India uprising in Kashmir wrecked Ayub's plans.[8] China's siding with Pakistan and even threatening intervention reified the 'two-and-a-half-front' war perception in India. The eventual military stalemate and 1966 Tashkent agreement only sharpened regional faultlines.

This chapter argues that the political, military, and economic environment in India's near east in context of the 1962 Sino-Indian and 1965 India-Pakistan wars strengthened ethnic separatism, and opened space for covert and overt interventionism. It strengthened India's resolve to assert its authority in the northeast even if necessitated using force outside India's borders. Far from post-independence solidarities and 1950s militarism, the 1960s witnessed interstate hostilities. To explain this, the first section unpacks the impact of Pakistan's support for Nagas on India's decision to declare a ceasefire and create Nagaland as a separate state within the union in 1963. The second section looks at India's relatively muted response to Ne Win's 1962 coup and the consequent mass exodus of Burmese Indians. India couldn't afford another adversary in its neighbourhood. Both these sections underscore the continuing centrality of identity, cross-border migration, and official antinomies in shaping India's diplomacy and statecraft in its near east.

The third section delves into the Mizo insurgency in Assam's Lushai hills that broke out in 1966. New Delhi responded with force and pressed ahead with the demarcation of its boundary with Burma to assert its writ over a restive population. Instead of offering a linear history of the Mizo movement, this section lends focus to cross-border connections with China and Pakistan. The Mizo movement received covert state sponsorship, but also developed rebel solidarities with ethnic nationalists in Burma. The fourth section unpacks India's push to formalise the boundary with Burma to aid its political and military response to the Naga and Mizo movements. Left unattended in 1947, India's decision to clarify the Burma boundary was triggered by war, displacement, and interventionism.

Ceasefire

The 1962 defeat sharpened India's desire to deepen its administrative and political writ in the northeast. This was visible in the creation of Nagaland with support from liberal Naga factions in 1963 and the signing of the 1964 ceasefire agreement. Apart from Ladakh, the war saw heavy fighting in the North-East Frontier Agency (NEFA) including at the Burma trijunction where Rangoon de-staked its claims in 1961. Shocked, Indian policymakers sought to consolidate administrative control. The aftermath of 1962 in India's near east was felt along two axes: first was the emergence of the two-and-a-half front threat scenario wherein India needed to fight China, Pakistan, and ethnic separatism simultaneously. Pakistan's appetite for coercion, leading to the 1965 war, and support for the Nagas, Mizos, and other rebel groups compelled India to enter a ceasefire with Phizo. The second was India's acceptance of Ne Win's coup and the mass exodus of Burmese Indians, one of the largest in Asian history at the time, as fait accompli. The desire to maintain friendly ties with Rangoon was powerful enough to make Nehru overlook the situation of Burmese Indians. This section unpacks the first point, and the one thereafter focuses on India's response to the 1962 coup in Burma.

Phizo's visit to Pakistan in June 1962 earmarked the onset of large-scale Pakistani support. It began with a Kaito Sema-led contingent. Driven by a breakdown of Sino-Indian relations and increasing alignment between the US and India, Pakistan sought to pressure New Delhi. The 1962 defeat and failure of Nehru-Ayub talks increased the appeal for coercion to settle Kashmir. From that point until the 1965 war, Pakistan trained nearly 2,500 Naga fighters in East Pakistan.[9] In December 1963, after Sema's group was re-inducted, another 277 Naga fighters crossed over into East Pakistan led by their 'commander-in-chief' Lt. Gen. Mowu Angami.[10] The four-week course included physical training, drills, weapons handling, and maintenance in relation to rifles, Sten guns, Tommy guns, light machine guns, medium machine guns, 3" mortars, and explosives. The instructors included 10 West Pakistani intelligence operatives led by 'Maj. Alam'. Of the 277, some 30 fighters were taken to Chittagong for firing practice in February 1964 and supplied with arms and ammunition.[11]

Pakistan's expansion of support to Naga rebels occurred during heightened violence in the northeast. Under military pressure, the Naga movement had been operating from bases in Burma. In August 1960, an Indian air force Dakota DC-3 crashed during a sortie meant to drop supplies for an outlying post. All nine airmen including Capt. Anand Singha were captured and arrested by Sema's group and kept in camps near the Burma border at Purr.[12] In response, the Indian Air Force (IAF), which was not allowed to undertake airstrikes in 1956 for fear of losing a fighter jet, undertook independent India's first targeted airstrikes for counterinsurgency purposes in September 1960. Nehru was satisfied that the total 'hostile casualties' were 'between 60 and 100'.[13] The strafing prevented Sema from killing Indian airmen fearing more airstrikes, but also prevented the IAF from undertaking more raids to obviate guaranteed killing of its personnel.[14] Instead, the army launched a bigger operation, which led to the infamous Matikhrü massacre.[15]

The stalemate on captured airmen continued through 1961 as Sino-Indian border clashes spiked. R S Mani, India's ambassador in Rangoon noted in May 1961 that the Burmese, though sympathetic to Indian requests to target these Nagas, were unable to 'translate their good intentions into effective action' due to limited resources and difficult terrain.[16] Mani clarified that the Naga fighters had 'a few friends' in Burma even though the major AFPFL factions 'have been unresponsive to their appeals for sympathy and help'.[17]

Frustrated, on 31 January 1962, Nehru requested that Nu permit the Indian army 'to cross the border a little to deal with these hostile Nagas' as 'it could prevent them from using Burmese territory as a refuge'.[18] Nehru reminded Nu of previous similar asks and pressed his counterpart to deliver. If required, India was willing to draw a line 'a few miles from the international border' inside Burma that Indian forces would not cross.[19] To ensure that specifics were not lost, Nehru recommended a line from Somra (in Burma) to Teera, and a 'slight extension' of the line parallel to the international boundary. Such an understanding required Burmese police and army posts in Somra, Pensat, Layshi, Konkalion, and Teera, all within a radius of three to five miles, to remain alert and inactive. India intended to execute operations in mid-February without resorting to 'indiscriminate bombing'.[20]

The IAF offered air cover to ground forces and, from India's perspective, clearing of this 'broad belt of jungle' was the only way to address the situation. Nehru noted that 'any assistance given to us by your [Burmese] police posts nearby would be greatly appreciated'.[21] The pressure worked. By March 1962, bases of Kaito-led 'hostiles' in Burma were 'cleared'.[22] Most insurgents found themselves in East Pakistan within weeks of escaping Burmese jungles. In September 1962, after cross-border operations in Burma and before the war with China, Indian parliament passed the State of Nagaland Act.

The Act was developed in coordination with the liberal Nagas who signed a 16-point resolution with Nehru in 1960. New Delhi had agreed to grant statehood in August 1960. On 1 December 1963, Nagaland became the 16th state of India. Its territorial boundaries, consisting of Assam's Naga districts but excluding Naga areas of NEFA and Manipur, reflected Naga grievances in relation to Assam and favoured those communities that accepted autonomy within India. But it sharpened intra-Naga fissures and inflamed separatist sentiment that wanted all Naga areas under greater Nagaland.

These issues manifested in renewed violence in January 1964 when the first Nagaland state assembly elections occurred. Separatists, now trained and armed by Pakistan, targeted leaders viewed as pro-India, just as the latter engaged in counterattacks with support of the Indian army. P Shilu Ao, member of the Naga People's

Convention (NPC) that signed the 16-point resolution, won the elections and became Nagaland's first chief minister. But statehood didn't quell separatism, and India's administrative and military reach remained uneven.

Expectedly, the 1962 war and Pakistani aid buoyed the morale of Naga militants. But nearly a decade of violence, fatigue, and displacement created room for dialogue. Just as violence during elections peaked, Longri Ao and Kenneth Kerhuo, senior missionaries of the Nagaland Baptist church, demanded the creation of a 'Peace Mission'. Accepted by all sides, Jayprakash Narayan (JP), a national leader, Bimala Prasad Chaliha, the Assam chief minister, and Michael Scott, the Anglican missionary who helped Phizo escape to London (and thus had his confidence) formed the mission.[23]

The peace mission succeeded in securing a ceasefire on 23 May, four days before Nehru's death, that was formally declared on 6 September.[24] On 23 September, the Nagaland Peace Talks began. According to JP, there were two preconditions for a peaceful settlement. First, that 'both sides should renounce the use of armed force for achieving their political objectives'; and second, 'both sides should realise that a peaceful settlement in Nagaland has to be of the nature of a compromise'.[25] The mission outlined a four-part plan wherein New Delhi would lay out its force strength by 15 November, and then offer a withdrawal plan. This would be paralleled by the Federal Government of Nagaland (FGN), which would list and deposit all arms and ammunition in its control to the mission. Following disarmament, a joint meeting was planned by the end of the year to create a trust that would curate a peace treaty.[26] Operational details about what both sides could and could not do were laid out in detail.[27]

Despite goodwill for the mission on both sides, the plan collapsed. New Delhi wanted the Nagas to disarm *before* de-induction of the army, wanted the state government to remain responsible for security, and wanted the Indian army to be present in border areas. Though the military footprint aimed at China was accepted, the other two demands were in contravention to the mission's principles. Similarly, the FGN demanded that foreign observers supervise the withdrawal of Indian forces. This demand was unacceptable to New Delhi as it would amount to external interference in domestic affairs. The FGN's success at having Michael Scott on the mission was considered a concession 'under special circumstances', and further internationalisation was anathema. Concerned that disarming would undermine their aims, Naga fighters, JP noted, 'rebelled against the proposal and threatened to arrest the Naga delegates to Peace talks'.[28]

But, with support from the Baptist church, the ceasefire held. Pakistan's support to the Nagas, in the context of India's defeat from China, added weight to the FGN's logic of not giving up weapons. It is unclear whether Ayub's decision to increase support for the movement was linked to his predilection of using force in Kashmir to bog down India's military resources. But it did shape India's thinking of its regional security environment in terms of the 'two-and-a-half-front threat' scenario, which would involve simultaneously fighting China, Pakistan, and ethnic insurgencies. Had the peace mission failed to secure a ceasefire, the possibility of such a scenario could have become reality. The Chinese forces, for instance, entered Ladakh and elsewhere during the 1965 war, increasing Indian anxiety of a joint Sino-Pakistani offensive. It was the first aftershock of 1962 and left a deep imprint on India's security planning.

'Maggot'

A nosedive in Sino-Indian relations and concerns about a two-and-a-half front conflict were accompanied by a massive exodus of Indians from Burma after 1962. On 2 March 1962, Ne Win ousted Nu in a coup with little pretense for constitutionalism. At 2 am, the Burmese prime minister was roughly woken up and arrested by soldiers shouting, 'we caught the maggot' and frog-marching Nu to jail.[29] India's reaction was muted. Instead of criticising Ne Win, India accepted the change of guard and quickly recognised the new government. On 6 March, four days after the coup, Nehru wrote a letter to Ne Win seeking coordination and policy continuity on a forthcoming international conference on disarmament. But the letter ended reaffirming India's desire for uninterrupted engagement with Rangoon:

May I add that our Ambassador in Rangoon has transmitted to us your declaration of policy of positive neutrality and your desire to maintain and strengthen friendly relations with all countries. We have asked our Ambassador to inform you that we entirely reciprocate these feelings and shall endeavour to strengthen our friendly relations with Burma with whom our contacts have always been intimate and cordial.[30]

Nehru deliberately avoided asking Ne Win about Nu's health and safety. Such questions, he thought, could irk Ne Win, and undermine ties when India could ill-afford it. Ne Win executed the coup precisely when Indian troops were undertaking combing operations inside Burmese territory against Naga militants. Nehru couldn't risk angering Ne Win for fear of losing military support from Rangoon. Nehru understood the costs of engaging with the junta which included distress and exodus of the Burmese Indians. But he had made up his mind on this issue even *before* the coup. Three days before Nu was ousted, he refused to ask Burma not to nationalise its import and export policies.[31] Instead, he wanted India to prepare for a mass influx of Burmese Indians.

This decision was taken despite parliamentary criticism about 'wholesale arrests, raids on premises and other administrative harassment' of Indians in Burma due to a 'lack' of immigration agreements between the two countries.[32] Nehru was clear that 'as for Indians who return to India following the closure of their business, we may take up this matter with the Ministries concerned here'.[33] The decision to not intervene—and to not be seen as intervening— was consistent with India's position on 1954 land nationalisation. But to prepare for influx was novel. Unlike earlier when the threat of communist infiltration shaped India's response to migration from Burma, by 1962, such concerns became marginal.

To make sense of the coup's impact on India's near east, it is essential to unpack the causes and consequences of India's reaction. Apart from the obvious need to maintain strong ties with Burma, India's response was shaped by interpersonal and situational factors. Nu's premiership for the 1960–62 period was lackluster. With the domestic and external political agendas set by Ne Win during the 'caretaker' period, Nu pushed Buddhist nationalism. Despite strains in India's own constitutional credentials in the northeast, the ideological alienation between Nehru and Nu was complete thanks to Nu's communalism.

Nu's inability to target Naga rebels sheltering in Burmese territory without Ne Win's approval further undermined his value. But what lubricated India's alienation from Nu was the related fact that during his two-year stint as premier in 1960–62, Burma's rice exports to India fell drastically. In 1959–60, India procured 391 thousand tonnes of Burmese rice worth 166 million kyat, whereas in 1960–61 this figure was reduced to 151 thousand tonnes worth 65 million kyat.[34] Such a downturn in rice trade had less to do with India's dwindling forex reserves, and more to do with supply-side shortages thanks to Rangoon's economic mismanagement.

Even Pakistan's rice imports (the second largest importer of Burmese rice after India) fell from 256 thousand tonnes in 1959–60 to 158 thousand tonnes in 1960–61. But unlike Pakistan, which was able to maintain its overall momentum of rice imports from Burma (in 1961–62, it imported 204 thousand tonnes compared with India's 214 thousand tonnes), India's consumption of Burmese rice never returned to the 1958–59 levels in the early 1960s, while its demand for rice and food grain exploded with droughts and famine-like situations in multiple central Indian states.[35] Nu's inability to govern and reliance on religion risked undermining India's food security. Instead, in Ne Win, Nehru found an ideologically opposed but strong leader who could make independent decisions and implement them.

India could do business with Ne Win. The other reason for India's lukewarm response to Nu's ouster was the zeal with which he embraced China during his final stint in power. Though Ne Win was pivotal in signing the Sino-Burmese boundary agreement in January 1960, it was Nu who celebrated it. Public mood in Rangoon in December 1960 during Chou Enlai's visit was 'strikingly different' from January when Ne Win visited Peking.[36] 'Deep rooted suspicion and resentment of Chinese evasiveness in negotiation gave way to enthusiastic orgies of welcome', Indian Ambassador Mani noted.[37]

To this effect, China had 'active support from both the retiring and the incoming Prime Ministers of Burma [Ne Win and Nu respectively]'.[38] For Mani, China made the best of the boundary agreement and was successful in its deliberate policy of improving relations with India's neighbours, 'if necessary by a special display of sweet reasonableness'.[39] Nu's return to power, as opposed to Ba Swe, who remained circumspect of China, was 'lucky' for Peking. Nu's 'frenzied drive to organise mass enthusiasm for the new entente cordiale' despite widespread suspicion about Chinese intent didn't go down well in India.[40]

India worried that the Sino-Burmese boundary treaty left the point of the China-Burma-India trijunction undefined. The primary purpose of Nu's January visit to India was to discuss specificities of this trijunction. In a move that left India feeling 'most unsatisfactory', Nu gave up Burma's claim on where this trijunction lay, making it a Sino-Indian bilateral issue. In an address to the parliament, Nu explained that 'if and when China settled their boundary question it should happen that where the agreed boundary is not at the Dhipuk [Diphu] Pass but at some other point' then then treaty would need to be altered and the maps updated.[41] Nu explained the specificities of the agreement to Nehru and confessed that his team failed to mark the trijunction 10 miles north of Diphu Pass. In August 1960, Nehru warned Nu that Sino-Indian relations were marred by deep 'resentment and distrust', that Indian sentiment was 'greatly shocked' by Chinese actions in Tibet, and that he was finding it difficult to 'restrain' such feelings.[42]

Indian diplomats presciently warned that Burma's acceptance of a 400-million-kyat interest-free loan from China in 1961, a 'mana from heaven', 'places China in a strong position of infiltrating the Burmese economic life'.[43] India issued diplomatic protests to China on the boundary issue in this context, generating a strong response from Peking in August 1961:

> The Indian government continues to insist in its Note on its misinterpretation of the Sino-Burmese Boundary Treaty and the attached maps, arbitrarily asserting that the Treaty and the attached maps had defined Diphu Pass as the Western extremity of the Sino-Burmese boundary. An exhaustive answer to this was already made by the Chinese Government in its memorandum

of February 21, 1961, and its Note of May 4, 1961, pointing out clearly that the Sino-Burmese Treaty had not defined the location of the western extremity, i.e., the tri-junction of China, Burma, and India and that this was because China and India still differ in their understanding of the eastern section of the Sino-Indian boundary and a settlement through negotiations was yet to be achieved.[44]

Nu's—and Ne Win's—decision to keep Burma out of the Sino-Indian boundary dispute, while seeking Chinese support to counter Kuomintang remnants and accept Chinese loans, was to India's disadvantage. The boundary treaty was criticised in parliament with the opposition seeking explanations about why Nu failed to respect Indian concerns. India's response was two-fold. Internally, Nehru and other officials grew critical of Nu. For Mani, however much India welcomed Nu's statements on the trijunction, it needed to recognise: '(a) that the map in part of the treaty and has been referred in the treaty, and (b) that U Nu's general statements are one-sided and there is no indication that they are corroborated by the Chinese'.[45]

Nehru didn't initiate talks about the boundary issue with Nu during the latter's India visit in January 1962. But when Nu passed on China's message for a meeting with Nehru to 'negotiate' the Sino-Indian boundary issue, Nehru shot down the idea. His response was firm: '... negotiations could only take place if there was some helpful approach made by the Chinese government. Merely talking vaguely about negotiations was not helpful', and if Nu so wished, he could convey this to Chou.[46]

However, in public, Nehru mounted a defence of Nu's predicament and argued that the terms of agreement were 'fixed when General Ne Win as Prime Minister visited Peking', thereby shifting blame.[47] On the trijunction, Nehru confessed that Rangoon made it clear to New Delhi before and after signing the agreement that they didn't accept the interpretation of the map where the trijunction remained undefined. He endorsed Nu's argument that the trijunction was indeed a Sino-Indian issue and 'none of their [Burmese] business'.[48]

Such public defence of Nu stood in contrast with what Indian officials thought in private. Nu's show of enthusiasm in welcoming

Chou coupled with the embassy's reading that his opponent would have been less inclined to such a tilt left its mark. Even before Nehru wrote his letter of support to Ne Win four days after the coup, Eric Goncalves, a young Indian diplomat in Rangoon noted that 'we were fairly confident that the Generals were going to remain and there would be no return to the democratic set up'.[49] Nehru was clear that India must go ahead and give the military regime a formal note of recognition—making it the first country to do so—and not overburden the situation with sentimentality.[50]

The decision had far-reaching consequences. As Goncalves, posted in Rangoon one month before the coup, recollects, the decision to recognise the junta was 'mature' but, 'ironically, this got us little benefit'.[51] Ne Win welcomed Indian recognition but didn't address Indian concerns on most counts. The situation along the India-Burma borderlands remained uncertain. Though India could undertake cross-border operations, Naga fighters developed solidarities with the newfound KIO and took shelter in areas that were beyond Rangoon's control. If Ne Win was okay with India undertaking cross-border operations, secessionism in Kachin state complicated such manoeuvres.

Additionally, in total disregard for the rights of Burmese Indians, Ne Win nationalised all enterprises and import-export businesses, disenfranchising an already marginalised community. The so-called 'Burmese Way to Socialism' drove the country into geopolitical and geo-economic isolation and became the last nail in the coffin of colonial attempts to administratively unite India and Burma. The separation that began in 1935 finally culminated in a true and tectonic rupture in bilateral economic, if not political, relations between India and Burma in 1962.

It triggered the largest exodus of people the subcontinent had seen since partition. Over 300,000 Burmese Indians were forced to flee or were detained after 1962.[52] Despite the pressures this generated, India accepted the situation as fait accompli. New Delhi acknowledged that Ne Win's policies were driven by majoritarian views of seeing foreigners (especially Indians) as 'economic exploiters', and that he was implementing a deliberate policy of 'squeezing' Indians out.[53] Throughout 1962–64, the situation of

Burmese Indian steadily worsened, undermining bilateral ties. Two weeks before his death, Nehru beseeched 'friend' Ne Win that those Indians wanting to leave must be allowed 'to come home with at least part of their assets to enable them to start afresh in India'.[54]

The appeal didn't work. Oddly, the Rangoon embassy noted that Ne Win's reticence was grounded in his belief that Nehru 'disapproved of him for the rather drastic way he ousted U Nu and his Government' and refused to stop raising the matter of Burmese Indians.[55] Despite Nehru's acceptance of Ne Win's coup and recognition of his regime, the dictator sought more respect, and targeting Burmese Indians was a way of making demands from New Delhi. Unsurprisingly, India-Burma relations were 'bitterest' when Nehru died.[56]

But in December 1964, Indira Gandhi visited Rangoon as a 'personal guest of General and Mrs. Ne Win' and laid the foundation for what became a strong interpersonal bond like the one that existed between Nehru and Nu.[57] Ne Win paid a reciprocal visit to New Delhi in February 1965. During the 1965 India-Pakistan war, Rangoon maintained neutrality and appreciated that the trouble in Kashmir 'was started by Pakistan'.[58] Rangoon didn't believe that China would militarily intervene unless the war spread to East Pakistan, or if Pakistan performed poorly. In this context, India's desire to keep Rangoon aligned in relation to China and Pakistan triumphed over its preference for democracy or even supporting Burmese Indians.

In mid-1965, Indian Prime Minister Lal Bahadur Shastri's private secretary visited Burma to purchase 80,000 tons of rice as a 'gesture of friendship'.[59] In December, Shastri himself visited Rangoon. Focused on the conditions of Burmese Indians, he secured unconvincing assurances from Ne Win that 'resident foreigners, who could play a useful role in the new social order that Burma is building, would be given facilities to enable them to live and to work in Burma as citizens should they desire'.[60] Shastri deliberately avoided the boundary issue, didn't bring up the Naga situation even though armed Nagas were routinely crossing over into Burmese territory despite the ceasefire, and bypassed another problem of armed Mizos crossing the border. These were India's 'internal matters', not worthy of being raised with Rangoon.[61] The strategy worked.

95

India signed a boundary agreement with Burma in January 1967 at the peak of the Sino-Burmese fallout, shortly after Gandhi became prime minister upon Shastri's untimely demise in January 1966.[62] Chou, speaking to an Albanian communist delegation in June 1962, acknowledged that Nu's departure was good news for China as he was a 'pro-India element'.[63] But he was farsighted enough to realise that Ne Win would create problems in the long term. Ne Win's xenophobia was not limited to Indians alone, but encompassed ethnic Chinese too. Just because he signed the boundary treaty, didn't mean the general was beholden to China. The outbreak of the 1966 Mizo insurgency after a preventable famine in 1960, a movement with roots in postcolonial discontentment among communities residing in Assam, made India's outreach to Burma strategically compelling.

'Buai'

Pakistan's bid to wrest Kashmir failed in 1965. But Ayub's bet on a man named Laldenga succeeded. Laldenga led a powerful movement for an independent Mizoram in Assam's Lushai Hills. Like Naga and other communities unhappy with Assamese dominance and the neglect of border regions, the Mizos felt that decolonisation of the subcontinent had been unfair. There were multiple views about whether to remain independent, join the co-ethnic Chins in Burma, or remain in India. But the Mizos were not given options.[64] Unlike Naga nationalism that took a violent turn in mid-1950s, Mizo nationalism didn't have a trigger until 1960.

Mizo communities had been warning the government since 1958 of an impending bamboo famine called *Mau Tam*. A huge number of rats, feeding on bamboo, destroyed the region's food stocks. Panicked, the Assam government made urgent requests to Burma for 10,000 tons of rice through Chin state, requested that East Pakistan allow this rice to be shipped through the Karnaphuli river (and offer more rice if it could), and explored the possibility of Rangoon airdropping a few thousand tons to 'meet immediate need'.[65] Burma agreed to supply a 'suitable stock of rice' and Pakistan agreed to its transit.[66] But the measures were too little, and too late.

The *Mau Tam* sharpened secessionist sentiment and birthed the Mizoram National Famine Front (MNFF) led by Laldenga.[67] Disillusioned by government's failure to address a predicted famine, the MNFF took a political turn and became the Mizo National Front (MNF) in October 1961. It took the MNF another five years to launch armed rebellion in Aizawl in an operation called 'Jericho', and to trigger a two-decades-long separatist insurgency. This section does not offer a detailed history of the Mizo movement.[68] Instead, it focuses on the cross-border connections Mizo nationalists forged with Pakistan, China, and ethnic nationalists in Burma (the KIO and the Arakan National Liberation Front, ANLF), India's reaction thereto, and the impact of this movement in India's near east. Mizo secessionism coupled with Naga nationalism fed Indian security planners' concerns about a two-and-a-half-front conflict and pushed them to recalibrate their security strategy in the near east (having secured status quo ante in the western front during the 1965 war).

Before delving into the Mizo revolt, it is essential to offer wider context. During the 1950s and '60s, there was discontentment with postcolonial Indian nationalism, and perceived Assamese dominance among many communities. But not all of it turned violent. Naga nationalists, despite the 1964 ceasefire, were trying to galvanise revulsion against India among Mizos, Baites, Paites, Hmar, Kuki, and Meiteis to varying degrees of success. For Manipur's chief commissioner in 1964, India's problems in that area could be divided into three 'major heads': (a) to 'contain hostile activities' within the Nagas of north Manipur; (b) to 'insulate' non-Naga 'tribes' (Meitei, Kuki, Zomi, Hmar, Paite, and Baite among others) from outreach by armed Nagas and prevent them from joining the NNC's ranks; and (c) to 'strengthen' India's security apparatus to prevent an outbreak of insurgent violence.[69] Manipur's history with militant left-wing movements (infused with nationalist overtones) and inadequacy of armed personnel made the commissioner seek an increment in the size and equipment of the Manipur Rifles and the Home Guard.[70] The Nagas were also supporting the MNF by this point, but the situation in the hitherto peaceful Lushai Hills, unlike Manipur, remained off India's political radar.

India's humiliation in 1962 and the stalemate in 1965 ignited Mizo ambitions. Weakened and stretched, the Indian army, Laldenga assessed, could be bogged down. Aware of Kaito's visit to East Pakistan and the ISI's support for the Nagas, the MNF contacted Pakistan's Assistant High Commissioner (AHC) in Shillong in July 1962, before the outbreak of war. India had considered shutting this consulate down earlier, but concerns about Pakistan's retaliatory closure of India's AHCs in East Pakistan prevented this. The Pakistani AHC was supportive of the MNF and in November 1963 facilitated Laldenga's visit to Dacca along with Lalnunmawia, the MNF's 'Vice President'.[71] Like the Nagas, the Mizos wanted financial and military support. Pakistan promised all of that and more. Laldenga received cash-in-hand and three revolvers. But upon his return, he was captured by Assam police and put in Silchar jail along with Lalnunmawia.[72] However with Assam Congress leaders distracted by the Naga issue, and pressure from the MNF's elected members of the state assembly (and a written undertaking by Laldenga of being a 'good citizen'), the police released the duo in February 1964.

Unlike the Assam government which underestimated Laldenga's appeal and the MNF's radicalism, the Burmese government became increasingly concerned. Under pressure from multiple ethnic outfits and cross-border movement of Naga rebels, Burmese intelligence watched ethnic mobilisation in the Chin hills, south of which was Rakhine state where the ANLF was active, with alarm. Rangoon launched the 'Ma Ma Operation' in April 1963 to administratively integrate the Chin hills with Burma and was using proactive bureaucratic and military mechanisms to assert authority in what it considered its territory. It wanted to prevent the MNF from allying with Chins and demanding an independent Mizoland.[73] Burma's activism in border areas equally heightened the risk of targeting Indian citizens. But with its resources focused on the Naga issue, the China border, and an increasingly hostile Pakistan, India couldn't dedicate the kind of resources in Mizo hills that the situation demanded.

In October 1964, the MNF's 'defence minister' visited Dacca to organise training for rebels and the procurement of arms and ammunition. In November, the first batch of Mizo fighters were trained by Pakistani instructors in camps near Mymensingh,

Rangamati, and eventually at a location 40 miles from Dacca.[74] From using basic weaponry to the use of explosives, mines, and booby traps, they were taught musketry, how to engage in unarmed combat, use signals, and fight at night and in jungles. This batch returned in March 1965 with arms and other forms of aid that the ISI offered.

On 20 October 1965, as a forewarning, Laldenga submitted a memorandum to Shastri offering a 'last chance' for peaceful separation and threatening 'whether the Mizo nation should shed tears in joy, to establish firm and lasting friendship with India in War and in Peace, or in sorrow and in Anger, is upto the Government of India to decide'.[75] To generate international support, and aware of strained Delhi-Jakarta relations (Jakarta mobilised its navy to pressure India during the 1965 war), Laldenga authored a letter to Indonesian president Sukarno on 20 January 1966.[76] After elucidating Mizo history, Laldenga appealed for Indonesian support for the 'freedom fighters of Mizoram and to give support in politics and in material for the realisation of their just demand'.[77]

On 1 March 1966, a few minutes past midnight, Laldenga announced Mizoram's independence and launched multiple attacks on government buildings and military installations.[78] The treasury in Aizawl fell, along with army outposts in Champhai and Lunglei districts. Four months later, in July 1966, senior Mizo commanders left for East Pakistan along with a group of 300 fighters to collect arms.[79] Operation Jericho, as the MNF termed its first salvo against India, surprised and shocked Delhi. The MNF failed to gain control of the district, but its declaration resonated with locals and undermined India's efforts to integrate the northeast.

The cadre of Pakistan-trained Mizo fighters helped sustain the movement against a strong Indian counterattack.[80] Laldenga shifted his family and staff to Dacca, but Jericho burnished his credentials as rebel leader. This also allowed Ayub to pursue covert interventionism despite having failed to wrest Kashmir. Soon after, the MNF reached out to Chinese intelligence in Dacca. In the throes of the Cultural Revolution, China was keen to support anti-Indian insurgents.[81] China's offensive strategies were paying dividends in Burma where militant communists were, once again, challenging Ne Win.

The MNF's representatives met with Chinese spies at least nine times before Laldenga visited the Chinese consulate in Dacca on 27 March 1967. He received confirmation of support—with Pakistan's blessings—and the Chinese consulate worked as the 'channel for Chinese financial aid', propaganda material, and 'Maoist literature for indoctrination'.[82] Soon after the 'Director General of the Mizo intelligence' visited China with a 'shopping list for arms and equipment'.[83] In January 1968, the first batch of Mizo rebels— purportedly 'special forces'—left for China.

Laldenga made his first visit to Peking in September 1968, along with 'foreign minister' Lalthangliana (who stayed in China until February 1969), and met with Chou. In an 'almost midnight' meeting at the Great Hall, Chou 'spoke softly and sympathetically' to Mizo rebels.[84] In the middle of the conversation, Chou told Lalthangliana: 'you're too young to be a foreign minister', who quickly responded: 'Your excellency, you'll never know the situation we're in. In our place to be a Foreign Minister you have to run v-e-r-y fast!'.[85] The room burst out with laughter, and the meeting ended with Chou promising to equip a standing Mizo army of 3,000 combatants and financial aid of 500,000 yuan.[86]

The new ethnic faultline in Assam's Mizo district was set to burn for a long time, despite Indian crackdown. The Indian army's General Officer Commanding, Eastern Command, Lt. Gen. Sam Manekshaw, who rose to fame in the 1971 Bangladesh liberation war, explained how he saw the situation to the press corps in Calcutta: 'we were caught with our pants down'.[87] Under direction from Indira Gandhi and legal aid of AFSPA, the Indian forces intensified the crackdown. On 5 March, just days after the MNF declared independence, four fighter jets of the Indian air force (French 'Toofanis' and British Hunters) took off from Tezpur, Kumbigram, and Jorhat in Assam, and bombed Aizawl.[88]

At first these jets used machine guns, but from day two, they began using incendiary bombs on civilian targets. The aerial bombing pushed most civilians to the hills and MNF cadres to hideouts in Burma and East Pakistan. Until March 1966, there were approximately 1,000 rebels that operated from across the border. This figure increased substantially after May–June 1966.[89] Mizo communities were shocked by New Delhi's use of airpower that lasted until 13 March. It was combined with 'village grouping' that was used in Naga areas and dislocated nearly 80% of people into military-controlled settlements.[90]

Buai, or 'troubles' in the Mizo language, had begun. According to a witness, the fact that New Delhi used the air force in Aizawl but not against China in 1962 was telling: 'they hit the heart of Mizoram, but not the Mizo spirit'.[91] This meant that Pakistan and China had a recruitment windfall.[92] If the Mizos and Nagas could jointly counter India, it could heighten the risk of secession. As the next section shows, Pakistan, frustrated by its failure in 1965, and China, buoyed by its victory in 1962 coupled with the onset of the Cultural Revolution, did just that: it launched joint support for *all* ethnic nationalist and militant left-wing movements in India. Discontent was brewing among Zo-Kuki and Meitei communities in Manipur too, and secessionists in Kachin and Arakan offered moral, political, and military inspiration. All China and Pakistan had to do was offer these groups guns, sanctuary, and money.[93]

After 1965, even Nagas received large-scale military and financial support from China. During 1966–68, about 1,650 Nagas went to China for training and arming.[94] One of these rebels was Thiungaleng Muivah, a young fighter who went on to lead the movement.[95] With support from Burmese Nagas and the KIO (which provided them shelter, ration, and guides), Naga rebels such as Muivah crossed over into China. Senior Naga leaders were allowed to observe firing demonstrations by a unit in the 93rd division of the PLA just outside Peking and met with Burmese communists to improve the Naga-communist compact.[96] Peking wanted the Nagas to join the Communist Party of India (Marxist), CPI(M), to form a United Front against 'Indian imperialists'.[97]

In Ten-chung, the Nagas were given ideological education (daily lectures on Maoist thought, Mao's theory of guerilla tactics, serving the people, and mobilising the masses, the People's Army, and the Chinese revolution); practical skills (handling personal as well as automatic weapons, using wireless sets for communications, and armour and mortar training); and other skills such as swimming and first aid.[98] They were also offered caches of light and heavy weaponry.[99] In 1968, Nagas operating from East Pakistan remained in touch with the Chinese consul and returned to China in August 1969 on a Pakistan International Airlines flight. This time they were given three months of training at the Nanking Military Academy. They returned to India in March–April 1970.[100] Throughout this period, the ISI, KIO, and Burmese Nagas facilitated connections between Indian Nagas and Chinese intelligence.

The Tashkent Declaration, signed in January 1966, raised concerns in China that Pakistan could resolve bilateral disputes with India diplomatically. To blunt such a possibility (unfounded in reality), China dispatched Chairman Liu Shaoqi and Second Foreign Minister Chen Yi to Dacca and Karachi in April. The visit reified India's perception of the two-and-a-half-front war scenario even though the visit itself was 'remarkably bare' and over which unofficial enthusiasm demonstrated by Pakistani officials 'deflated very quickly' according to India's deputy high commissioner in Dacca.[101]

New Delhi assessed that the visit was intended to 'bolster and stiffen Pakistan's stand against India' by strengthening radicals over moderate elements within the Pakistani government.[102] India noted that China was also offering unqualified support for Kashmir's right to 'self-determination' but would aid Pakistan only if the latter offered resolute resistance to India.[103] The signal, as received in India, was that if Pakistan stopped supporting secessionist elements in Kashmir, then China could 'independently encourage the struggle for so-called national self-determination'.[104]

In Dacca, Chen Yi was categorical about 'national unity' in Pakistan, signaling that it did not support the Bengali movement. This aspect coupled with Pakistani foreign minister Zulfiqar Ali Bhutto's statement that Pakistan sought to consolidate relations with Sikkim and Bhutan ('as if they were independent sovereign states', Indians noted with unsubtle paternalism) were viewed as signs that Pakistan and China had a common policy of 'promoting subversion' in India's border areas.[105]

Though there was no evidence, New Delhi didn't rule out a common military alliance or, at least, an understanding regarding the defence of East Pakistan between its two adversaries. Without fail, in June 1966, the IB authored a paper on 'Chinese offensive capabilities against India'. It assessed that while Chinese capabilities for a full offensive were limited due to Tibet's uncompromising terrain, if Peking were to attack India, the maximum pressure was to be felt in Ladakh, Chumbi Valley, Tawang, and the Walong sector. Walong is where the disputed China-Burma-India trijunction lay.[106]

The possibility of a two-and-a-half-front war was real in India's mind. Just as India followed these developments and measured its options, the MNF shifted tactics towards protracted war from bases in Burma and East Pakistan.[107] To ensure that the rebellion endured, the MNF moved its headquarters to Vancheng, southeast of Aizawl and closer to Champhai and Tedim (in Burma) in December 1967. When this proved onerous under counterinsurgency pressures, it relocated to Sajek Valley, Mahmuam, in East Pakistan in 1969.[108]

The MNF received most of its weapons through the Chittagong port and delivered it to its cadre in Ruma Bazaar. The other location where a large consignment of arms was received in January 1966 was the East Pakistan Rifle's Chittagong Cantonment. From here the weapons were brought in trucks to Kaptai and sent to the Mizoram border using boats on the Karnaphuli.[109] This specific weapons consignment (2" mortars, LMGs, Sten guns, Tommy guns, automatic rifles, hand grenades, high explosives/detonating fuses) was to be divided between the Paites, Baites, and the Mizos.[110] Pakistan also allowed the MNF to use its territory for contacting other Burmese armed groups.

Throughout 1966–69, the MNF tried establishing a cooperative relationship with the KIO, the ANLF, and Chins to create 'Greater Mizoram' separate from India and Burma. Senior MNF officer Vanlalngaia led the outreach to the KIO with China's encouragement. In Rakhine, another Mizo emissary met with ANLF's president in February 1968. The KIO offered military training for Mizo cadres and a transit route to China in return for payment, whereas the ANLF sought guns for sanctuary.[111] Vanlalngaia stayed in Kachin for four months and trekked over into China at the peak of the Cultural Revolution and an ongoing struggle between the 'White Flag' Burmese communists who were trying to infiltrate the KIO and the Kachin nationalists.[112] This experience taught him and KIO leaders something essential—there was little synergy between their ethnic nationalisms, undergirded by Christianity and Maoism. 'I went through Mao's philosophy no less than five times', Vanlalngaia conceded later, 'but I was disillusioned by Communism as a philosophy. I realised that it ran contrary to my beliefs'.[113]

In May 1968, unbeknownst to Laldenga, the Mizo army launched 'Operation Chin Hills'. The idea was to capture four Burmese towns in Chin state and signal to Rangoon and New Delhi that their 'arbitrary international demarcations were only a figment of their own imagination'.[114] The operation succeeded as Tedim fell along with a Tatmadaw outpost, replenishing the MNA's stocks with 3 LMGs, 16 Sten guns, 122 rifles, 3 US carbines, 19 .38 pistols, and approximately 103 'local arms'.[115] The Mizo army contingent that targeted the Chin state treasury found 23,287 kyat (approximately 500,000 rupees).[116] Rangoon was in a panic as Chin hills had been relatively peaceful and integrated after Operation Ma Ma. In response, the Tatmadaw dispatched counterinsurgency special forces units, which included highly trained Chin soldiers, to retake territory. Aware of the strength and tactics of these units, Mizo rebels preemptively vacated captured locations. But the trick worked. Operation Chin Hills tied down Tatmadaw's resources in Chin, while allowing 800 Mizo cadres to cross over into China through Kachin.

In October 1970, Laldenga again visited Peking and met with Chou and the Director of the Asian Affairs Department.[117] By now Chou was asking Laldenga to actively coordinate with the Naga movement, the KIO, and the Burmese and Indian communists— all of whom were receiving Chinese sponsorship. After this trip, China supplied the MNF with clothing and equipment (500 sets), duplicators (5), Pakistani currency (350,000 rupees), and Indian currency (551,250 rupees).[118] Similarly, Indian intelligence estimated that during 1964–71, Pakistan's total financial aid to the Mizos amounted to 413,000 rupees.[119] When openly challenged by India about such support, Ayub expectedly responded with denial. This was, according to Indian parliamentarians, a 'defensive act' that did nothing to placate a worsening dynamic.[120]

By 1971, apart from pressuring India, the MNF began supporting the Pakistani army against Bengali nationalists. The ISI offered free rations, a cash allowance of 1.43 rupees per head per day, and a pocket allowance of 15 rupees per month to all Mizo fighters in 1971 to counter India-backed Bengali nationalists. Both ethnic separatism and inter-state interventionism (covert and overt) were in full swing in India's near east during the 1960s. As the next chapter shows, India was far from being a mute spectator.

Soon after the 1962 war, India collaborated with US intelligence to train and arm the Tibetan Mustang Resistance Force.[121] This covert US-India support for Tibetans went on until 1973. Indian army officers also created something called the Establishment 22, a highly trained secret force of Tibetans. This force was rechristened as the Special Frontier Force (SFF), which was meant to conduct special operations along the Tibet-India frontier against the PLA. After the 1965 war, India's interaction with, if not substantial support for, Bengali nationalists in East Pakistan also increased. For India's security planners, the China-Pakistan nexus required a response—with support from the US if needed.[122]

Line in the Sand[123]

Operation Chin Hill's objective to show New Delhi and Rangoon that the boundary demarcations were 'arbitrary' and pointless had context. In 1966, soon after Operation Jericho and India's coercive response thereto, India's leadership sought to demarcate the India-Burma boundary. The idea was to impart administrative clarity to the borderlands. On 28 March 1966, a few weeks after Jericho, Foreign Minister Swaran Singh briefed parliamentarians that the MNF's actions undermined India's security, made Rangoon 'unhappy', and 'may create some problem for our friendly neighbour Burma with whom we will co-operate fully for taking suitable steps to cope with this act of the Mizos'.[124] On 2 August 1966, Indian parliamentarians called the attention of the house to 'a matter of urgent public importance'.[125] Burmese forces had shot at Manipuri people near Moreh, killing one and injuring several in two separate incidents. Burma claimed that these people had entered their territory and did not surrender when challenged.

Home Minister Gulzarilal Nanda faced tough questions regarding the incidents, why they occurred, and what help Burma was offering

India. Nanda was emphatic that Burma supported India by capturing and returning Naga and Mizo 'hostiles' but failed to explain why it viewed certain parts of Indian territory as its own. When asked whether the boundary was demarcated with pillars, Nanda responded: 'It has been demarcated'.[126] Given that no formal process had begun, this was a 'soft lie' to ensure space to manoeuvre. The incident indicated that Burmese support on Naga and Mizo issues, though important, was not adequate to resolve outstanding border issues. It also highlighted that the occurrence of such incidents came with political costs and risked tarring India as a weak state.

On 1 October 1966, the Joint Intelligence Committee (JIC), operating within the 'Intelligence Wing' of the Cabinet Secretariat, soberly assessed the border situation. It emphasised that India's eastern and north-eastern frontiers were strategically and politically 'very sensitive'.[127] In particular, the three major movements for an independent Nagaland, a sovereign Mizoland, and a greater Chinland were 'threats to the territorial integrity of India'.[128] It forewarned that the MNF had gained influence since the start of the year and was likely to turn violent, as it already had. The chairman of the JIC argued that there were indications of 'transborder tribal unity' among the Burmese and India Nagas as well as the Mizos and the Chins.[129]

The JIC was confident that countermeasures by the Burmese military would weaken Chin insurgents and reduce the strength of the Mizo–Chin alliance. The Naga ceasefire, which was due to be over on 15 October, could get extended despite visible strains. The 'embarrassment' of Naga 'hostiles' in Tuensang, where followers of 'Rani Guidaillu', leader of the Zeliangrong Nagas, surrendered to Indian forces, and the loss of control in Ukhrul were blows to the Naga movement.[130] This was despite Paite, Baite, and 'extremist factions' from the Kuki communities in Manipur joining the Nagas, and the Mizos receiving cross-border training.[131] In Assam, the 'threat of direct action' by the All Party Hill Leaders Conference, which was seeking a separate state in the Khasi and Jaintia hills and received covert support from Pakistan, was 'viewed with concern'.[132] To tackle these simultaneous movements, New Delhi needed to collaborate with Burma. The JIC ended on a sombre note:

The paragraphs above show that the situation in the Eastern and North Eastern tribal areas of India is more serious than when the JIC made its previous assessment in February, 1966. Unless quick and effective action is taken, violent movements are likely to develop on a larger scale. Both Pakistan and China will encourage and assist such movements against the integrity and security of India.[133]

But for such collaboration to occur, the two sides needed clarity about their boundaries. By late 1966, the need to demarcate the boundary had become pressing because a variety of issues became aligned: (a) the need to assert statehood and territorial limits on a dissenting populace (at a time when India's domestic borders were also being reorganised), (b) India demonstrating that it could provide livelihood and security to its citizens living at border areas, and (c) ironically, the securing of support from Burma to contain the Naga and Mizo insurgencies. There was also the added propaganda benefit of formalising the boundary to demonstrate to Peking that India too could peacefully resolve issues with its neighbours.

On 29 December 1966, the MEA pitched the boundary agreement to the 'Secretaries' Committee on Foreign Affairs' for clearance. It was approved within four days. Cabinet Secretary D S Joshi, who had been forewarned about the situation, concurred that while the Indo-Burma border did not present any serious challenge 'at present,' it was a good idea to 'have the border demarcated in agreement with the Burmese government as early as possible so that it may not in future become a crisis'.[134] The committee wanted to seize the moment in view of Ne Win's 'very friendly attitude towards India,' a fact that could change any moment given how top-down decision-making was in Rangoon.

The committee noted Burma's anxieties about external interference in domestic affairs and suggested caution. Joshi was emphatic that the Indian team should not 'rush the Burmese who have natural suspicion of undertaking formal obligations'.[135] To impress the other side about the usefulness and advantage of demarcating the border, the Cabinet Secretary took pains to highlight the 'way forward'. As a first step, an informal approach was recommended, 'preferably in the course of discussions on other issues'.[136] This was to be done by any officer accompanying the foreign minister in the latter's forthcoming visit to Indonesia, wherein the officer could return 'via Rangoon'.[137] As this was an international boundary, there was no mention of consulting state-level stakeholders.

In January 1967, instead of sending a mid-level diplomat, the newly appointed external affairs minister M C Chagla himself visited Burma.[138] Joshi and Chagla's tactics underlined India's appreciation of Burmese anxieties and the importance of demarcating the boundary. R D Katari, India's ambassador in Rangoon, noted that despite 'excellent' discussions, 'in deference to Burmese susceptibilities', no joint communique was issued after Chagla's visit.[139] What was more important, Katari said, was that 'it became evident (as indeed we had suspected all along) that Ne Win's main concern in the foreign field at the moment is to utilise the growing USSR–USA pressure on China'.[140] As Sino–Burmese relations soured, Rangoon welcomed Indian overtures.

India's strong desire to strike an agreement was underscored by its willingness to cede territory if required. For a country that lost territory in 1962 and saw it as a national shame, this was a bold step. Indira Gandhi's confidante and private secretary P N Haksar too suggested that India accept the Burmese point of view on this issue and 'not worry unduly about the reactions in Manipur' even though the 'possibility of Chinese fishing in troubled waters' of the region remained.[141]

If such planned territorial concessions risked national outcry, they guaranteed pushback from the states. In his secret letter to the MEA, Joshi noted that 'India should be prepared, in keeping with our friendly relations with Burma, to show a sense of accommodation and if necessary, give in on small demands that might be put forward by Burma during the course of the negotiations'.[142] When quizzed by the opposition in June 1967 on whether India did lose territory to Burma, Chagla denied the suggestion.[143] Technically he was correct because the two sides reached an agreement without demarcating the boundary. In February, an Indian delegation consisting of members from the ministries of defence, external affairs, home, and education, and the Survey of India, reached Rangoon to start formal negotiations.[144]

Both sides agreed that there was no 'dispute' regarding the border. Then, a map was drawn and initialled and the boundary drawn and accepted. Such boundary-making proceeded on two bases: there were some sectors in which recent official notifications between the two sides solidified the boundary. In other sectors, it remained undefined.[145] These sectors were to be jointly patrolled and delimited by the Joint Boundary Commission. The 906-mile-long border was divided into five main sectors, most of which had two or more subsectors. These were sector A–B signifying the boundary at the Mizo District, sector B–D in Manipur, sector D–F in Nagaland, sector F–J in the Tirap Frontier Division and the Burmese Naga Hills District, and sector J–K between Lohit Frontier Division and the Myitkyina District.[146] All these sectors were to be demarcated using numbered boundary pillars.

On 10 March 1967, India and Burma signed the boundary agreement. It was ratified on 30 May. Expectedly, 'difficulty' arose between the two sides regarding the northernmost J–K sector at the China–Burma–India trijunction. India wanted Burma to identify the trijunction five miles north of the Diphu Pass in the Talu Pass area. For Rangoon, such a position risked becoming embroiled in a raging Sino-Indian boundary dispute, and it insisted on keeping the trijunction undescribed. Burma had already given up its claim on this stretch during the 1961 boundary agreement with China. Despite Indian demands, Rangoon kept the language of the agreement vague on the exact location of the trijunction and didn't highlight it on their maps.

China was irate, and its state-controlled media blamed Ne Win for being a 'cat's paw of Indian reactionaries', threatening action against the conspiracy to 'occupy ... large tracts of Chinese territory'.[147] The tactic worked. The two sides agreed to show the trijunction at Diphu Pass as shown on Chinese maps. The *buai* meant that India not only used force to assert state authority in Assam's Mizo district, but also formalised the boundary with Burma, incensing local opinion which saw the agreement as a postcolonial version of an illogical imperialist artefact that divided communities.[148]

Such state-building measures were coupled with addressing what Indian policymakers viewed as the root cause of the Mizo uprising—namely economic failure. Long before it became a central pillar of India's Look East policy after the 1990s, on 18 March 1968, Indira Gandhi's Burma-born information advisor Boobli G Verghese offered a solution. New Delhi should propose to Ne Win, who was then in India on a 'private' visit, that India would develop a road-river link between Mizo Hills District and Akyab (Sittwe).

Surprised that since independence India never broached the idea of an economic link through Chittagong port with Pakistan—the 'natural outlet for the Southern half of what is today the North-Eastern region of India'—Verghese noted that the loss of the East Pakistani market and access to Chittagong port severely impacted the economy of India's far eastern region.[149] Though acknowledging that an outlet to the sea from Belonia railway station in Tripura via Fenny to Chittagong and from Demagiri in Mizo district down the Karnaphuli to Chittagong would be a 'much more attractive outlet', Verghese pressed Gandhi to not allow political impediments with Pakistan to stop India from building (at the cost of over 1,200,00 rupees per mile) the road connecting Lawngtlai in Mizo district with Akyab.[150]

The economic and strategic benefits of such connectivity outweighed financial costs. To assuage Burmese concerns that the road would infringe on its sovereignty or augment Indian hegemony, Verghese recommended handing it over to Rangoon on completion, using local labour to build it in the first place, offering free maintenance for five years, and steering clear of anything like a territorial lease or a 'corridor' through Burma.[151] In fact, India should even reach out to Karachi to access the Chittagong port and offer Pakistan railway transit facilities through Indian territory to connect its two wings. After all, Pakistan's cost of shipping between Karachi and Chittagong ports was far less than the cost India incurred to ensure transit of goods between the northeast and rest of the country. Verghese's proposal became the first to advocate economic connectivity as a solution to India's security woes in its near east. As he put it, 'both links would justify themselves in view of our very high political stakes in the development, stability, and ultimate security of the north-eastern region of India'.[152] But nothing came of it. Isolationist in its outlook, Rangoon heard Indian proposals but didn't act. As for Pakistan, it soon found itself at war with India once again.

Conclusions

India's wars with China and Pakistan in 1962 and 1965 reshaped the geopolitical dynamics of its near east. They strengthened the resolve of ethnic nationalists to use force to achieve self-determination. Deprived of economic opportunities, adequate representation in Indian political life, and bereft of state support during the 1960 famine, Mizo communities opted for violence. The postcolonial state's paradoxical use of indiscriminate force to ostensibly preserve India's constitutional integrity and concomitant struggle to effectively counter Naga separatism emboldened other communities to explore similar pathways.

Identity politics defined India's northeast during the 1960s. Such movements received fillip from cross-border sponsorship in East Pakistan and China. The violent turn the Mizo movement took was cultivated in the hill tracts of Chittagong and military cantonments and rebel training camps across East Pakistan after 1960. Burma didn't offer support to such movements but struggled to deny them access. Regardless, at war with Pakistan and China, India could ill afford to spoil relations with Rangoon. Such compulsions, shaped by the limits of the postcolonial state to persuade northeastern communities about the merits of India's constitutional experiment, as well as ongoing conflicts with China and Pakistan, made New Delhi treat a military coup and subsequent exodus of Burmese Indians after 1962 as fait accompli.

These wars and ethnic movements increased the state's resolve to tighten its administrative grip in the northeast. Gandhi's push to formalise the India-Burma boundary, accommodate Burmese Indians without complaining about their fate, and use force, including airpower, against civilians and insurgent Mizos alike marked a militant turn in the state's commitment to its territorial integrity. China's humiliation of India and Pakistan's adventurism sharpened concerns around a two-and-a-half-front conflict situation. Such nightmarish scenarios, which continue to animate Indian security considerations and practices, made India compromise on citizens' rights and freedoms in the northeast, which became increasingly militarised under AFSPA. The logic of securing India's territorial integrity and administrative reach in its northeastern peripheries overrode the constitutional logic that guided the republic's domestic and foreign policies in the early years of independence.

The seeds for structural reorganisation of India's northeast were now sowed. Ideas about how to quell the fires of identity politics were actively discussed in New Delhi. The 1971 liberation of Bangladesh offered an opportunity to implement some such ideas. On 16 December 1971, the Pakistani army signed the instrument of surrender with India, and on 30 December, the government of India passed the North-Eastern Council Act.[153] The idea was to reorganise the northeast and divide Assam by offering statehood to agitating communities. But one other shift that occurred in the security bureaucracy was the decision to create a separate external intelligence agency. This institution would offer early warnings about developing threats in the region and beyond. In November 1967, Gandhi ordered the recruitment of a suitable officer who could create and lead such an institution. Rameshwar Nath Kao, who earlier created Ghana's external intelligence agency in 1958–60, was hired for the job.[154]

The Research & Analysis Wing (R&AW) was born. Gandhi's instructions to Kao were not to make an intelligence agency like the IB that would be 'old wine in new bottle'.[155] He was to develop a modern intelligence agency after studying similar outfits elsewhere. Apart from India's intelligence failures during 1962 and 1965, it was New Delhi's failure to foresee the Mizo and 1967 Naxal uprising that triggered a rethink and R&AW's creation. Joint Chinese-Pakistani support for secessionists and communists was the final straw. Kao knew that his role was not just defensive in nature but had an offensive element too—especially in East Pakistan.[156] Though the idea of Bangladesh's liberation was not a priority, Indian security planners were willing to support Bengali nationalism.

If the 1965 war excited Mizo nationalists' separatist ambitions in India, it had a similar effect in East Pakistan, where the Bengali language movement took a sharper turn in the direction of greater autonomy under the leadership of Sheikh Mujibur Rahman. The Six-Point Movement, as it came to be known, sought greater agency for East Pakistan and refused to accept Urdu as Pakistan's national language. The following chapter explains how India's concern about simultaneous conflict with China and Pakistan laid the groundwork for Bangladesh's liberation in 1971.

PART II

SECURITY (1971–1990)

5

JOY BANGLA
THE LIBERATION OF BANGLADESH & REMAKING OF INDIA'S NEAR EAST

'What we have to plan for is not an immediate defeat of the … superior military machine of West Pakistan; we have to create the whole of East Bengal into a bottomless ditch which will suck the strength and the resources of West Pakistan.'[1]

Durga Prasad Dhar,
Indian envoy to Soviet Union, 18 April 1971

How could a two-and-a-half-front conflict be avoided? This question guided India's approach in the 1960s. Given the power differential with China and stalemate with Pakistan, India sought a solution in its near east. Building on Raghavan's argument that Bangladesh's liberation was 'the product of conjuncture and contingency, choice and chance', this chapter argues that India's commitment to reset the regional balance of power had deeper underpinnings.[2] It was needed to protect India's territorial integrity and secure the northeast. India didn't proactively seek to break Pakistan—but with the situation in Assam and West Bengal worsening, Pakistan's dismemberment became a serious, viable option.

Such considerations were driven by India's desire to address two national security 'red lines'. First, migrant flows from East Pakistan had to cease. This was critical to assuage the inflamed identity politics and communal tensions in Assam and West Bengal respectively. It required Pakistan to safeguard Hindus. Displacement in the 1960s was different from the influxes of 1949 and 1971, but thousands entered India daily. The Nehru-Liaquat pact became obsolete as communalism and displacement became a strategic drain.

Second, India became committed to denying sanctuary to northeast rebels in East Pakistan. Something had to give in India's near east to reduce the half of the two-and-a-half-front threat. Stable ties with Burma allowed for a focus on East Pakistan. From New Delhi's standpoint, Pakistan's military was using its eastern wing as a staging base for operations against India, encouraging anti-Hindu violence, and discriminating against Bengalis. In contrast, Pakistan's Bengali leaders were viewed as less hostile and willing to resolve disputes amicably.

There were two ways India could address this: a change of guard in Pakistan, or dismemberment. The end of Pakistan's constitutional experiment in 1958 and rising militarism only worsened relations. For India, Ayub needed to go. The debate was on how and when this could happen. Indian leaders were split on this question until the final moments before Bangladesh's liberation. This chapter unpacks India's foreign policymaking debates and practices *inside out* on the East Pakistan question for the pre-1971 period.

Indian policymakers, especially in the MEA, believed that the Bengalis could gain power electorally and resolve the Kashmir issue diplomatically. Such thinking went back to 1954 when Nehru believed a Bengali-Pashtun leadership was in India's interest. But conservative segments in India's security apparatus were unconvinced that a Bengali would be allowed to lead Pakistan and alter its Kashmir policy. This debate was settled in favour of supporting the liberation movement to the hilt once it became clear that the military was unwilling to concede ground despite the Awami League sweeping the 1970 elections.

This chapter examines how cross-border migration, identity politics, political economies, and official antinomies increased the appetite for interventionism in East Pakistan. There was systematic anti-Hindu violence in East Pakistan and tit-for-tat anti-Muslim violence in India in the early 1960s. Almost always resulting in the displacement of minorities, such communalism undermined Nehru's belief in Pakistan, and strengthened the All India Hindu Mahasabha's logic and appeal. Accompanied by border firing and cross-border movement of Naga and Mizo rebels, the early 1960s made a deep imprint on India's security planning.

The first section of this chapter explains how India perceived and responded to such communalism, firing by the East Pakistan Rifles (EPR) units at the Assam and West Bengal border, and mass displacement during 1959–65. This period is critical in making sense of India's approach towards East Pakistan. Tensions with China didn't distract India from the situation in its east. If anything, Assamese nationalist pushback against Bengalis had consolidated by 1960. Such sentiment was paramount in the context of anxiety about being left undefended in the face of a Chinese invasion in 1962. In West Bengal, cross-border movement of Bengali Muslims instilled fears of migrants being enemy agents who would side with Pakistan in the event of war.

The second section explains how India responded to these issues. It opted for covert interventionism in Pakistan and China—but not Burma—by supporting Bengali and Tibetan nationalists. In East Pakistan, India found an ally in Sheikh Mujibur Rahman of the East Pakistan Awami League (EPAL). The Awami League's secularism was viewed an antidote to communal politics.[3] For good reason, this made Mujib anathema with West Pakistani leaders, who viewed him as an 'Indian agent'.[4]

Instead of offering a blow-by-blow account of the liberation war, the third section focuses on the antinomies created by India's investment in Mujib.[5] Primarily a populist, Mujib's organisational skills, unlike Tajuddin Ahmed, the AL's general secretary, were limited. India's support to the Mukti Bahini was paralleled by the creation of a smaller, better trained and equipped force called the Mujib Bahini. Viewed as insurance if the Muktis took a communist, communal, or otherwise anti-India turn, the Mujib Bahini sowed the seeds of discord within and outside Bangladesh even before liberation. One of the least known aspects of this episode is that India's security planners, including Kao, held reservations about Mujib's capability to govern Bangladesh inclusively. But spelling out these fears risked dislocating India's relations with the one figure it had invested in.

Rivers of Blood

India and Pakistan reaffirmed their commitment to the Nehru-Noon pact regarding procedures to end disputes along the India-East Pakistan border in October 1959. But the ground had shifted. Strain between East and West Pakistan and the displacement of Hindus marked a reversal of gains made by the pact. The coup undermined Nehru's argument that supporting Pakistan's constitutionalism helped India. Communal tensions in East Pakistan were coupled with the EPR's resort to force along the India border, and, in some instances, occupying tracts of land in Tripura. Between November 1958–October 1959, the EPR dramatically increased the arrests and harassment of Indian fishermen.[6] Such acts coupled with Pakistan's desire to control limestone quarries in Berubari[7] and seizure of land-tracts in Tukergram didn't help.[8] India protested diplomatically and beefed up security at the Rajshahi border.[9] But the EPR's strength at the Assam border stood at 5,000 troops matched by only 1,900 Indian soldiers.[10] The balance of forces in West Bengal was worse due to India's focus on northern and western frontiers.

Ever since the coup, India and Pakistan were engaged in a propaganda war. The All India Radio's Calcutta station insisted that East Pakistan had become a 'colony of west Pakistan' (a view Nehru held, which resonated across East Pakistan), whereas Pakistani propaganda painted local Hindus as traitors.[11] The result was an expected displacement of minorities on both sides (larger in scale from East Pakistan than in reverse). India tried settling displaced persons at the Dandakaranya camps, but the situation worsened.[12] In 1960, 8,791[13] Hindus crossed over into India according to official estimates, and 'half a million in the last few years' according to media reports.[14]

The situation exploded in May–June 1961 with anti-Hindu violence in Gopalganj, near Dacca. Over 500 people from the Namasudra community were killed with alleged facilitation of local police and the EPR.[15] Nehru came under immense pressure to respond. Communist parliamentarians and Hindu Mahasabha leader N C Chatterjee alike pushed him to protect Hindus in East Pakistan.[16] Incoming migrants were staking claims on properties of Indian Muslims, complicating the situation in West Bengal.[17]

In June 1961, the IB warned that the Hindu Mahasabha sought to kill '20,000' Muslims if they didn't condemn the killing of Pakistani Hindus.[18] Anti-Muslim massacres rocked Orissa, Bihar, and West Bengal, internally displacing Muslims and forcing many to leave for East Pakistan. Pakistan further angered India by not letting the Indian Deputy High Commission in Dacca prepare an honest report on Gopalganj.[19] Keen to 'put an end to this … mischief', Nehru ordered the MEA to issue strong but carefully worded protests to Pakistan.[20] The 1962 Sino-Indian war overshadowed some of the worst communal violence in India's near east.

On 22 March 1962, riots broke out between the Santhal community in West Bengal's Malda district and local Muslims.[21] The Pakistani Deputy High Commissioner (DHC) in Calcutta was allowed to visit the riot-struck areas, but tit-for-tat restrictions were imposed on him like those faced by the Indian DHC visiting Gopalganj in 1961.[22] Unsurprisingly, his statements on Malda and Pakistani propaganda triggered large anti-Hindu massacres in Rajshahi (and some in Dacca) in April 1962. By July, over 9,000 Pakistani Santhals crossed over into India, and about 1,000 Muslims (over 5,000 according to Pakistani figures) migrated to East Pakistan.[23] West Bengal chief minister Prafulla Sen worried about more anti-Muslim violence in West Bengal.[24]

Nehru became increasingly convinced that anti-Hindu violence was 'deliberately whipped up by Pakistan authorities'.[25] In August 1962, anti-Hindu violence rocked Noakhali. To replicate Gandhi's 1946 Noakhali tour after pre-partition riots, Vinoba Bhave, a Gandhian activist, embarked on a similar journey. In Nehru's view, Bhave's visit 'will do a lot of good' for the people, even if government-to-government relations were strained.[26] It didn't. Mass displacement of Pakistani Hindus against the backdrop of worsening ties with China became a national threat.[27]

India responded by expelling Pakistani Muslims from West Bengal, Assam, and Tripura ('Project PIP' put 'illegal' migrants in detention camps). State governments were forcibly repatriating Pakistani Muslims (not Hindus) after 1961. That month, shortly before a meeting between India's Commonwealth Secretary Y.D. Gundevia and Ayub Khan in London, Nehru asked Home Minister Lal Bahadur Shastri to 'proceed very cautiously' and not to encourage such expulsion.[28] For this, Ayub expressed 'gratitude' because returnees from Tripura and Assam were inflaming local communal opinion.[29] By 1964, Nehru sought the full closure of detention camps, much to the chagrin of state governments and the IB who viewed the expulsion as successful and needed.[30]

India's 1962 defeat had a deleterious impact on the communal situation in its near east. Pakistan became increasingly critical of Nehru, refusing to compromise. In March 1963, hundreds of Chakma and Hajong families left the Chittagong Hill Tracts (CHT) for Assam and Tripura due to 'insecurity', 'personal molestation', and 'economic depression'.[31] This became a trend by October wherein deliberate targeting of the CHT's indigenous communities became Pakistan's policy, adding to India's insecurities.[32] In January 1964, Hindus were massacred in Khulna, Dacca, Narayanganj, Rajshahi, Sylhet, and Mymensingh. This time, it was in response to the alleged theft of the Prophet's hair from the Hazratbal shrine in Jammu and Kashmir.[33] 'Blood will flow down the rivers of Sylhet' claimed firebrand speakers in Sylhet where troubles started in February.[34] The Hindu exodus, already significant, increased exponentially after these massacres.

Pakistan was not only pushing India on Kashmir, but also training northeast rebels and weaponising migration. All this, as events of 1965 demonstrated, was a build-up towards the use of force to wrest Kashmir. In Assam, mass displacement aggravated identity politics, which turned violent in the 1970s. In West Bengal, communalism was dire enough for Congress leaders to worry about the loyalty of Muslims towards India in the event of war with Pakistan. Two examples are worthy of note. In July 1960, when significant numbers entered Assam and 'language riots' rocked the state, West Bengal governor Padmaja Naidu took a three-day Assam tour along with Indira Gandhi.[35]

Naidu authored a note on violence between Assamese and Bengali migrants regarding language politics, resource-sharing, and employment.[36] Migration from East Pakistan, she argued, sowed the seeds of long-term problems in Assam. Though she was unconvinced that the '*Bongal Kheda Andolan*' (drive out the Bengalis) had picked up, Naidu acknowledged a 'subconscious desire' to that effect.[37] Apparently, people believed that 95% of jobs were going to Bengalis and that the government was being partial to Bengali Muslims. The most disturbing fact, she informed Nehru, was that the students in Assam 'are out of hand and imagine that they have to rescue Assam and mould it after their own wishes'.[38]

It was a prescient forewarning about the All Assam Student's Union (AASU) that was created in 1967 and led the 'Assam Movement' (1979–85) against 'illegal migration' from Bangladesh typified by violence. It led to the 1983 Nellie massacre that saw the killing of over 2,100 Bengali Muslims (unofficial figures are higher).[39] Gandhi, who accompanied Naidu and became prime minister seven years later, entered with a different mindset than her father—who avoided escalation—when it came to how to deal with India's security issues in the near east. Gandhi's exposure to the birth of anti-foreigner agitation in Assam in 1960 paved the way for the use force in 1971.

The 1961 census assessed that 220,691 migrants entered Assam illegally.[40] In response, the Assam government launched a concerted drive in 1962 to 'detect and deport such infiltrants'.[41] By mid-1964, four foreigners tribunals were setup across Assam, and the National Register of Citizens (NRC), created in 1951, was used to identify foreigners.[42] Illegal settlers were issued 'quit India' notices, detained, and deported to East Pakistan. Such deportations using augmented police and intelligence mechanisms were called 'Project PIP': 'Prevention of Infiltration into India of Pakistani Nationals'.[43] According to an Assam government 'white paper on the foreigner's issue', 178,952 'infiltrants' were deported during 1961–66, but nearly 40,000 remained.[44] The PIP was discontinued in 1969.

But the issue of updating the NRC and a widely held belief that many migrants never returned ensured that the issue remained politically sensitive.

On 16 June 1965, the home ministry issued a secret letter (no. 4/366/63-IC) instructing Assam's chief secretary

> that those migrants (whether they came with or without migration certificates or travel documents) as have severed ties and connections with Pakistan and have settled in service, trade, and profession in India, may be registered as Indian citizens under section 5(1) (A) of the Citizenship Act 1955, provided they fulfil conditions laid down in Section 9 of the Indian Citizenship Rules, 1956.[45]

Any individual who resided in India for seven years was eligible for citizenship as per section 5(1) (A) of the Citizenship Act 1955.

The letter built upon Nehru's desire to halt forcible expulsion of Pakistani Muslims, and was opposed by Assam.[46] In December 1965, after the war, the home minister advised the Assamese government to distinguish between migrants from East Pakistan based on security risks.[47] In a move underscoring deep communal fissures, the state police detained and harassed even Indian Muslims, fearing disloyalty.[48] Senior Assamese Muslim Congress leaders such as Fakhruddin Ali Ahmed had to threaten resignation to get the party to understand the damage 'Project PIP' was doing to communal harmony in the state.[49]

In West Bengal, the situation was such that the chief minister requested that the home minister create a 'Hindu belt in West Bengal' because he couldn't trust the patriotism of Indian Muslims.[50] Citing the inclusion of Muslim-dominated pockets in West Bengal (Islampur subdivision of West Dinajpur) during post-partition reorganisation, he claimed that if Pakistan were to make a military push together with China, these Muslim communities could turn hostile. Bengali Muslims, Sen outlined, were mostly Shersabadia Muslims coming in from East Dinajpur.

Islampur was not far from the east Nepal border, and 'threatened' the Siliguri corridor. To address this 'problem', Sen proposed that vacant lands in Goalphokar, Chopra, and Islampur police station areas should be requisitioned and 'Santhals, East Bengal refugees, and other Hindus of the West Dinajpur district be settled there' because 'this will create a strong belt of dependable and loyal individuals right on a vital stretch of Indo-Pakistan border'.[51] The idea was not to settle Hindus in and around Islampur in lieu of failing to relocate them elsewhere, but entirely for security reasons—namely, to protect the border.[52]

By the time Pakistan attacked in 1965, displacement in the eastern sector took a qualitatively different turn. Communalism and displacement were not about localised inter-community violence. These were strategic threats that could further inflame India's communal fabric. A response to these problems was to be sought beyond diplomatic protests. On 22 May 1964, five days before his death, Nehru acknowledged that nearly 3,000 conflict-generated migrants were entering India daily.[53] Physically weak and politically exhausted after the China war, Nehru became disillusioned with Pakistan.

Nehru started routinely writing to the Hindu Mahasabha's Chatterjee and Bengali communists about how 'distressed' he was with the situation in East Pakistan.[54] On 13 April 1964, in his last parliamentary debate on external affairs, Nehru alerted his opponents that communal violence and displacement occurred on both sides,[55] something that Ayub didn't miss any opportunity to remind Indians about.[56] During this debate, Nehru was under pressure from Hem Barua of the Praja Socialist Party to act decisively. He left an ominous warning for Pakistan's leadership:

I would have hoped that India and Pakistan would be able to come together much closer, even constitutionally closer … But I believe a new generation is rising up in Pakistan which looks different at this problem than the older generations. I believe in East Pakistan specially, there are all kinds of movements which do not like these old methods. It is, therefore, particularly unfortunate that East Pakistan is a particularly weak spot in the Pakistan chain and possibly this is one of the reasons why the Pakistani authorities have made East Pakistan the special place where these atrocities have occurred as to get East Pakistan tied up with these atrocities and to move their thinking away from the other trends of thought …[57]

Nehru didn't initiate military action. But his views on a new generation of East Pakistani leaders seeking autonomy and independence (an unsubtle hint to Mujib) were matched by a new generation of leaders emerging within India. Indira Gandhi, who had a ringside view of these developments and enjoyed the pride of place in the Congress as Nehru's daughter, empathised with Mujib much more than Nehru did.

In August 1965, before launching an invasion of Kashmir, Pakistan tested India's military resolve. In March–April, when India intensified patrolling in the Tin Bigha corridor, a stretch of Indian territory between Dahagram (the largest East Pakistani enclave in India) and the East Pakistani mainland at the West Bengal border, locals in Dahagram fled after 'staging widespread looting and arson' (in an Indian reading of events).[58] Pakistan falsely claimed that India had occupied the enclave and intensified border firing. The Dahagram incident inflamed opinion in both sides of Bengal, and a ceasefire was reached after the Indian and Pakistani High Commissioners met in Dacca followed by a meeting of Chief Secretaries on 9–10 April 1965. According to Indian officials, the events in Dahagram, followed by Pakistani incursions in the Rann of Kutch, offered a 'foretaste of what was to come in August and September'.[59] India's national security red lines in relation to its east were now set.

The 1958 coup confirmed Nehru's apprehensions about Pakistan's disinterest in constitutionalism, and appetised India to address its security problems with its neigbour 'for good'. The shock defeat against China imparted logic and urgency to remove threats in India's near east. As the next section shows, despite Nehru's restraint, India's decision-making fulcrum on its eastern front shifted decisively during the 1959–65 period. Pakistan upping the ante in the northeast and encouraging virulent anti-Hindu and anti-Bengali propaganda in East Pakistan pressed India to explore coercive options. Imprisonment of East Pakistani leaders after 1958 should have made it difficult for India to establish contact with Bengali figures. But Ayub's push for 'one unit' entailing one economy, one language, and one religion fuelled the desire for separation among Bengalis to such an extent that gauging the intensity of local views, if not exploiting them, became easy. The IB, embedded in India's missions in Dacca and Rajshahi, generated considerable intelligence.

It amounted to a consequential decision during the 1965 war: to *not* attack East Pakistan.

Secret Wars

'It was a masterstroke'.[60] This is how Gowher Rizvi, International Affairs Advisor to the Prime Minister and a senior Awami League leader, remembers India's decision to not attack East Pakistan in 1965. 'It launched the Six-Points Movement', he says.[61] To mount such an offensive in East Pakistan would have required a major reorientation of India's force posture, but it was not impossible.[62] As India's 'red lines' became clear, New Delhi adopted a nuanced two-part strategy to secure relations with Burma, and a people-centric approach in East Pakistan. In addition to accepting the Burma coup as fait accompli, India refused to support Kachin rebels when they came asking in 1964–65.[63] Such denial of support to Kachin rebels was coupled with collaboration with the US to train the Tibetan Mustang Resistance Force and allow CIA flights from the Charbatia airbase.[64]

The Establishment-22, known as the Special Frontier Force (SFF), a secret battalion of highly trained Tibetan paratroopers who could undertake subversive action behind Chinese lines, was established. Similarly, the Special Service Bureau (SSB), later renamed Sashastra Seema Bal, was created in 1963 to support the IB's foreign intelligence arm.[65] Kao noted that the SSB was to 'function as a clandestine resistance organisation, if the Chinese attacked again, and meantime, to counteract any espionage and subversive activities'.[66] Instead, the SFF and SSB became pivotal to India's East Pakistan strategy.

Soon after its creation, the SSB posted its units in north Bengal, Tripura, and Assam.[67] They developed 46 intelligence outposts on all sides of the border, generated intelligence, cultivated dissidents, undertook covert action, and later trained the Mukti Bahini in guerrilla warfare.[68] These organisations undertook operations inside East Pakistan along with the SFF in the lead-up to the 1971 war.[69] As IB's armed wing and later R&AW's, the SSB was pivotal in setting up the secret infrastructure for a sustained insurgency *before* the convulsions of 1970–71. It is in this context that an Indian intelligence officer posted in Dacca urged New Delhi to intervene in March 1971 when a military crackdown was imminent: 'If we can gain gratitude of Bangla Desh by showing slightest good gesture, our Naga and Mizo problems would be settled fully and Kashmir problem fifty percent'.[70]

On this aspect, Raghavan argues that Bangladesh's liberation was not inevitable—that is correct. But a deeper exploration of the 1960s shows that India was invested in increasing Pakistan's security costs even if liberation itself was not preferred or planned. As Rizvi remembers, 'R&AW started training and arming Awami League cadres in 1969, much before the situation worsened', as there were fears that the military wouldn't allow elections to be held.[71] Though the 1970 elections and subsequent upheaval in East Pakistan took India's covert support to a different level, the intent to pressure Pakistan had existed before.

To make sense of India's approach towards East Pakistan before 1971, there is a need to revisit events in the immediate aftermath of the 1958 coup as much as the period from 1959-65. With memory of the 1954 martial law fresh, and a good grasp of anti-military sentiment in East Pakistan, the 1958 coup raised two questions in India. First, what did '*mukti*', or liberation, truly mean for those seeking it? There was no appetite in India to support a movement seeking a united Bengal (an idea Nehru entertained in 1948). The trauma of communalism was too deep and the risk of territorial revision too high for India to undo partition. A liberation movement was only worth supporting if it halted the targeting and displacement of Hindu minorities.

Second, who among the East Pakistani Bengali leaders—arrested, exiled, or free—could lead such a movement? It was essential that the movement had popular legitimacy, the leadership was not divided, and it could withstand military pushback. Most of the AL guard was old and frail (Fazlul Haque), pro-China (Bhashani), or of 'unsavoury character' (Suhrawardy).[72] Sheikh Mujibur 'Mujib' Rahman stood out. Moreover, competition between different East Pakistani parties was so intense that it led to violence in the assembly chambers and death of the deputy speaker, which triggered martial law.[73] For India, the situation in 1959 was not conducive to a mass movement.

The answer to these questions was written on the wall in 1966 when the Six-Points movement started: secular Bengali nationalism grounded in language politics, driven by the AL with grassroots support and Congress-type organisational structures, under the leadership of Mujib and Tajuddin. But it took India seven years to commit to Mujib. The process began in 1959. In August that year, at the peak of border firings, senior parliamentarian and future Indian education minister Humayun Kabir went to East Pakistan on a 'private visit'. Hardly of the kind, the visit entailed meetings with Fazlul Haque, governor Zakir Hussain, the chief secretary, the chief martial law administrator, and a broad range of others. Upon his return, Kabir submitted a report to Nehru assessing the ground situation and how India should approach it.

Three faultlines were sharpening in East Pakistan since the coup. First, the Bengali versus non-Bengali divide (more than the Hindu-Muslim divide) was most inflamed. The majority of senior civil servants posted in East Pakistan were non-Bengalis who didn't want to be there and 'looked down upon the people of Bengal'.[74] The Punjabi officers, Kabir was told, 'were the worst in that respect', but even officers from Bihar and Uttar Pradesh (from pre-partition India) held similar views, didn't like the bonds between the two Bengals, and deliberately inflamed communal tensions. The governor, who was close to Ayub and secure in his position, often sought help from senior Bengali police officers to undertake civil tasks that non-Bengali officers were unwilling to do. Such anti-Bengali racism made people feel like they were being treated as a 'colony', and had little say in their own fate and culture.[75]

The second faultline was between the civil and military bureaucracy that oversaw the martial law. The civilian governor didn't agree with the chief martial law administrator (an army officer) on how people were being treated. But the third and most important assessment Kabir made was the 'sharp difference between the Government and the people in their attitude towards India'.[76] The people of East Pakistan sought good relations with India. But they also preferred a separate state and didn't want the reunification of the two Bengals—something non-Bengalis were actively propagating to India. On this, Kabir clarified to his interlocutors: 'even if East Bengal wanted such a Union [of both Bengals], the people of West Bengal would resist the move'.[77]

Such divergence between the government and people on India, coupled with regime clampdown, increased 'subterranean political activities', with many turning towards the Communist Party.[78] Kabir reported that many people thought that 'unless there is early improvement of relations with India and free flow of trade between East and West Bengal, the communists might come to power there'.[79] Martial law meant that the people's voices were not being heard, but 'there is little doubt that popular will cannot be long suppressed', Kabir noted.[80] India must do 'everything possible for maintaining and indeed strengthening the cultural bonds between the two Bengals, and help as far as we can to restore normal economic and trade relations with them'.[81] Though not advocating subversion, Kabir's point of distinguishing between the government and people in East Pakistan made impact.

Evolution of a people-centric strategy was visible in Nehru's approval of 10,000 units of cholera and typhoid vaccines to be despatched as medical relief on 3 November 1960, after a powerful cyclone hit East Pakistan.[82] Given India's struggle to effectively respond to an ongoing famine in Assam's Mizo district and Pakistan's refusal to send supplies citing shortages, India's medical aid to East Pakistan, even if symbolic, was targeted to ensure good people-to-people relations. The aid package was organised and delivered by the People's Relief Committee, Calcutta, and was not to be seen as a government initiative. The Information Service of India pushed Bengali films and literature into East Pakistan and organised cultural events when possible.[83]

The harder edge of this people-centric strategy involved aggressive propaganda by the All India Radio (AIR) pushing the line that East Pakistan was a 'colony' of the West, increasing anger against the regime and making both the chief secretary and martial law administrator in East Pakistan jittery.[84] An even sharper edge of India's approach, namely engagement with the East Pakistani underground, came to the fore on 4 April 1961 when Lt. Col. Gunnindra Lal Bhattacharya, Assistant Director-Intelligence, was shot at and captured—on Indian territory—by his Pakistani counterpart Capt. Mumtaz Malik from the Pakistani army's 614 Field Intelligence Unit posted in Jessore.[85]

Bhattacharya was captured by Malik when he was to meet a Bengali agent at the Jessore border to collect sensitive military documents.[86] Instead of handling it with care, New Delhi muddled basic details about the circumstances under which Bhattacharya was arrested to the point of spuriously claiming that he was not a serving officer—a classic tactic when a spy is disowned.[87] But the case became high-profile and was making headlines, and the fact that Bhattacharya was being tried for espionage under martial law rocked the Indian parliament. Under pressure, India offered consular, legal, and financial support to Bhattacharya. Soon, requests for spy swaps and to have Bhattacharya interviewed by India's DHC Sourja Kumar Choudhury became routine.[88]

The case and the publicity it received demonstrate that India was engaged in aggressive intelligence gathering, and that the DHC-Dacca was critical for this. The closure of India's mission in Comilla and reciprocal closure of Pakistan's mission in Agartala after the 1958 coup meant that India's mission in Dacca and Rajshahi held increased espionage responsibilities. This became clear in Nehru's rejection of the Assam chief minister's April 1962 request to shut down Pakistan's mission in Shillong. Both the MEA and IB were opposed to the move.

Why? Because, as Nehru noted, activities 'of the Pakistan office in Shillong are well-known to us and in fact they give us a good deal of useful information about Pakistan attempts to keep in touch with the Nagas and others'.[89] To shut Pakistan's consulate could dry up India's intelligence on Nagas rebels in East Pakistan. In retaliation, Pakistan could shut Indian outposts in Dacca and Rajshahi, undermining Indian operations, which would 'not have good consequences'.[90] With the 'new situation arising in East Pakistan this would be particularly harmful to us', Nehru said, and he clarified that in 'balance' India had an upper hand on Pakistan on this front.[91]

What was the new situation? The creation of the Swadhin Bangla Biplobi Parishad (SBPP, or Free Bangla Revolutionary Council) in 1961 under Mujib's leadership along with committed student firebrands Serajul Alam Khan, Abdur Razzak, and Kazi Aref Ahmed.[92] The Parishad created a political arm called Bangladesh Liberation Front (BLF) and began underground activity aimed at securing independence. The IB, through Choudhury, established contact with BLF. In February 1962, two months before the Assam chief minister sought the closure of Pakistan's Shillong outpost, Mujib secretly crossed over into Agartala.

In Agartala, he met with senior Congress leader and soon-to-be Tripura chief minister, Sachindra Lal Singh ('Sachin-da'), and, using him as an interlocutor, sought Nehru's support for armed insurgency. 'Only my mother, I and other siblings knew about it. No one else was supposed to know. One of the two people who helped him reaching Agartala also knew', remembers Sheikh Hasina, Mujib's daughter and current Bangladeshi prime minister.[93] Cautious about taking a decision that could worsen India's security situation, Nehru sympathised with Mujib but was non-committal. He sought patience and 'no haste' from Mujib.[94]

Hasina concurs: 'after failing to get much response from him [Nehru] for some reason, Bangabandhu returned home'.[95] Pakistani intelligence agents became 'crazy' as they could not trace him for four to five days and 'tried to trace him by quizzing us repeatedly'.[96] On 6 February 1962, on his return from Agartala, Mujib was booked under the Public Security Act (PSA), and the military started building a case against him—culminating in the 1968 Agartala Conspiracy Case—for working with India to dismember Pakistan.[97] The fact was that Mujib was handed over to Pakistani border police by Indian security officials unaware of the purpose of his visit and without coordination with New Delhi. When Gundevia informed Nehru about Mujib's arrest, the latter was unhappy. On 16 March 1962, in response to Gundevia about how India should deal with the East Pakistan situation and what happened to Mujib, Nehru noted:

> I agree with you. We should function in a neutral manner in this matter. It is unfortunate that Mujibur Rahman was handed over to the Pakistani authorities. If anyone from East Pakistan comes to India and seeks refuge, we should certainly give it. But

otherwise, we should not play any part which might be construed as encouraging one party or the other.[98]

India's decision to remain 'neutral' in East Pakistan itself was a change. Nehru didn't support the BLF, but didn't seek to undermine its cause either. It remains unclear whether handing Mujib to Pakistan was a considered tactic to protect his family from ISI harassment, a genuine mistake, or a deliberate snub to Mujib. He was released on 18 June 1962, and received a congratulatory message from the Dacca-based Indian press attaché R M Maitre for organising a large rally in July.[99]

There's also a counter-narrative that Nehru's refusal scarred Mujib to such an extent that he refused to cross the border in 1971. Mujib's demand for autonomy didn't dampen his secessionist aspirations. Just after midnight on 25 December 1962, he, along with Manik Mia, editor of *Daily Ittefaq*, secretly met with a political officer in India's DHC-Dacca.[100] Mujib handed the officer a 'top-secret' letter for Nehru seeking long-term 'moral, political, financial, and material support' for Bangladesh's liberation struggle. The letter went into logistical details, and expressed Mujib's desire to announce Bangladesh's independence on 1 February 1963 (or latest 1 March) from exile in London.[101]

Mujib was informed that the letter would also be read by DHC Choudhury, the IB station chief in Dacca Col. Sailendra C Ghosh (with whom Mujib had first met under house arrest in 1960), the foreign secretary, and the DIB.[102] Indian officials held two follow-up meetings with Mujib and Manik Mia in 1963, but nothing came of them. Mujib was recommended patience, to build a mass base, and to focus on secular Bengali nationalism. For the ISI, Mujib's outreach to India made him anathema. The situation came to a head in November 1963. Concerned about the depth and breadth of India's covert activities, Pakistan ordered the closure of India's mission in Rajshahi. The complaint was that India used the mission to push anti-Pakistan propaganda and encourage Hindu migration, even if that was against India's desire to limit migrants.[103]

Nehru rejected Pakistan's 'unusual' and 'serious' charges, and noted that in such cases the officer under suspicion is asked to leave at most.[104] Given that Indian missions in Pakistan were under heavy surveillance, surrounded by guards, and that the Assistant High Commissioner (AHC) was not even 'allowed to move out of his residence, except under mobile police escort', it was 'fantastic', that Pakistan would make such allegations.[105] The opposition wanted to know if India was planning reciprocal action. The most logical response was to shut Pakistan's Shillong mission, something the Assam government was demanding. But it didn't. When the US ambassador asked about 'Pakistan's obvious attempts to … provoke' India, Nehru highlighted his restraint and the need to 'watch developments'.[106] The IB had penetrated Pakistan's Shillong consulate thoroughly, and India's mission in Dacca was of critical importance.

Organisational details of India's mission in Dacca in 1964 demonstrate the investment New Delhi made in gathering intelligence. The DHC was supported by three first secretaries: political and head of chancery, consular, and information.[107] The political and consular desks were dedicated to intelligence purposes. The highest expenditure the mission incurred was not for trade, information services, real estate, or salaries, but 'other expenditures' under the chancery and visa section. This figure amounted to 634,079 rupees in 1964–65 (from a total of 1,751,106 rupees) and included payment to informants among other activities. In comparison, India spent 154,186 rupees on the Information Service of India and 107,332 rupees on the trade wing in 1964–65.[108]

Just before the 1965 war, India undertook a change of guard in Dacca when the station chief Col. Ghosh was replaced by IB's P N Ojha on 15 April 1965. Ojha's real name was P N Banerjee, also known as 'Nath Babu'. He was a critical intelligence personality in the lead-up to the 1971 war.[109] Banerjee maintained a channel with Mujib and followed the pulse of public opinion in East Pakistan. Mujib's persistent demand for Indian support, advocacy for secular nationalism, and revival of the AL in 1964 after Suhrawardy's death in December 1963 made him both the chosen and the *only* Indian ally in East Pakistan. He sought autonomy, but merged the SBPP with the AL's student body thereby creating a pro-liberation clique within the party that was fiercely loyal to Mujib, and became his personal vanguard.

India's nuanced understanding of the situation allowed it to withstand the hiatus that Nehru's death and Pakistan's aggression brought with them. Indian officers and their families in Dacca were subject to 'inhuman treatment, insult, and indignity'.[110] The 458 members of all Indian missions combined were herded into seven houses without facilities or medical aid, the chancery was seized, and the DHC's house was locked by the police, effectively making it a 'house arrest' during the course of the war.[111] India could have attacked East Pakistan if it wanted to in 1965—but it didn't.

This was partly because the move would require military mobilisation in the eastern sector, which meant reduced focus on the northern and western sectors. China was already warning India not to invade East Pakistan.[112] But the most pressing reason why India opted to open a 'fourth front' in Punjab was because of a 'lack of popular Bengali support for any Indian military action ... and no tangible gains from an advance into monsoon-affected terrain'.[113] India would have lost the goodwill it enjoyed in East Pakistan. As A K Ray, India's DHC-Dacca, noted in 1966, 'the fact that India deliberately decided to spare East Pakistan, coupled with a growing knowledge about the horrors of war brought the feeling [that the whole manoeuvre by Ayub was "unjustifiable ab initio"] to the surface'.[114]

The situation was paradoxical for Ayub, who faced pushback from Dacca for leaving the eastern wing undefended, but received support for the Tashkent declaration that sought resolution of bilateral disputes. Such support for the declaration ostensibly went against the belief in West Pakistan that Bengalis harboured 'secessionist tendencies'.[115] India's decision to not intervene was a masterstroke because it allowed Mujib to launch the Six-Point Movement and become the mass leader India always wanted him to be. It was the beginning of Pakistan's end as a country with two separate geographies.

Birth of 'Bangabandhu'

Mujib criticised 'Indian aggression' in 1965.[116] When Indian airplanes strafed the eastern sector, Mujib asked people to 'sacrifice' their lives and stand up to Indian aggression.[117] But he was more critical of Ayub's contention that the 'strategic defence of East Pakistan lay in West Pakistan'.[118] Pakistan's failure to wrest Kashmir emboldened Mujib to push for autonomy. Insecurities of war, exacerbated by brief aerial combat in the eastern sector, fed into the popular perception of being colonised by West Pakistan.

Mujib was the first to strike, and raised the following six points: (a) federation for Pakistan as per the Lahore resolution with parliamentary democracy, (b) the federal government should only deal with defence and foreign affairs, (c) two separate but freely convertible currencies, and guaranteeing no flight of capital from east to west, (d) taxation and revenue collection should be within the jurisdiction of the federal units and not the central government, (e) two separate accounts for foreign exchange earnings, and (f) East Pakistan should have a separate military or paramilitary force, and the naval headquarters should be located there.[119] The last demand had its origins in the 1962 Sino-Indian war when Suhrawardy advocated that Pakistan must raise a Bengali-only force of 30,000 soldiers, and make conscription compulsory in East Pakistan because the 'Chinese are near Assam'.[120]

Mujib's timing and ideological determination towards autonomy (or liberation, if autonomy failed), made him an ally for India. Though not an institution-builder, he became a mass leader, professed Bengali nationalism without seeking a united Bengal, and challenged the military as well as civilian leaders such as Zulfiqar Ali Bhutto. With the question of what *mukti* (liberation) meant and who could lead a mass movement sorted, India began assessing the situation along two lines. First, could civilian political parties opposed to military rule overcome internal rivalries and the east-west divide? Aware that the military would not resolve the Kashmir dispute diplomatically, India hoped that civilian leadership might offer a solution.

But who among the civilian leaders could deliver? This question was grounded in Nehru's belief that a Bengali leadership would be willing to resolve the Kashmir issue. Until March 1971, when the Pakistani army began a campaign of genocide and mass rape codenamed Operation Searchlight, India was willing to use covert tools to pressure Pakistan, but didn't bet on secession, much less intervening militarily itself.[121] Indian assessments from Dacca during the 1966–70 period offer insights into these two aspects.

Throughout 1966, Indian officials lauded Mujib for capturing people's imagination. Conservative parties such as the Council Muslim League, the Jamaat-e-Islami, and the Nizam-e-Islam were viewed as lacking in organisational calibre and popular appeal. The personality politics of the National Democratic Front and ideological split between pro-Moscow and pro-Peking factions in the National Awami Party (NAP) were also noted. The former was led by Prof. Muzaffar Ahmed, as NAP-M, and the latter by Bhashani, as NAP-B. The NAP-B's stock was on the rise after 1965 when China supported Pakistan.[122] Indian officials noted how the NAP-M 'felt concerned at the mounting popular feelings in support of the six-point programme and at the march which the Awami League had clearly stolen over the other Opposition elements in East Pakistan by launching the movement for the six-points'.[123]

India's bet on Mujib looked promising in 1966. Ayub reached a similar assessment and believed that Mujib's momentum needed slowing. He started targeting the 'autonomists' as 'enemy agents', and used West Pakistani parties to create splits in the AL.[124] The first part involved blaming 'alien' Bengali culture (works of Rabindranath Tagore) in fomenting secessionism.[125] This was a direct reference to India using its soft power to fan Pakistan's dismemberment. Slander against the six-point programme took a sharp turn on 17 April 1967. Mujib and Manik Mia were imprisoned along with other Leaguers. Most East Pakistani parties issued 'cautious and lukewarm condemnations' instead of supporting the programme.[126] The only serious response to these arrests came from student leaders who declared 7 June as '*Mukti Dibas*' (Liberation Day).[127] A lack of cohesion among East Pakistani parties was apparent.

Such intra-Bengali disunity strengthened India's belief in Mujib as the only leader who could deliver. But his arrest meant that the AL was susceptible to pressure and manipulations. The Pakistan Democratic Movement (PDM), launched by former chief minister of West Punjab Mian Mumtaz Mohammad Daultana in May 1967, did exactly that. Aimed at developing a minimum programme 'for wresting the democratic rights of the people from unwilling hands',[128] the PDM sought to unite all opposition parties in East and West Pakistan against Ayub.[129] It launched its own eight-point programme, which was 'not radical enough' and failed to entice the AL.[130]

Riddled with ideological contradictions and competing interests, the PDM became a theatre of the absurd with mud-slinging between top leaders. With Mujib in prison, it laid bare differences between moderates and hardliners on the six-point programme. Ostensibly over joining the PDM or not, the long-apprehended split in the AL occurred in August when 14 pro-PDM members left the working committee, and were joined by 150 (of 950) councillors.[131] For India, 'the threat posed to the party by the pro-PDM does not seem to be great', but that this was the fourth split since the AL's inception in 1949 was worrisome.[132]

The Indian DHC noted: 'after this split in the East Pakistan Awami League it becomes painfully evident that so far as East Pakistan is concerned the PDM has, instead of forging unity in the Opposition camp, brought about greater disunity and dissensions'.[133] Daultana succeeded where Ayub, with all his power, patronage, and repression, failed. India wondered whether Daultana had an 'understanding' with Ayub, and if curating this split would bring him rewards. Nawab Nasrallah Khan, president of the Pakistan Awami League (the national version of the EPAL), who was also the PDM chief keen to moderate the six-point programme, announced the EPAL's dissolution, leaving 'pro-Six Pointers' no option but to retaliate. The NAP was also not immune to such pressures, and split in October over the question of joining the PDM or allying with EPAL. The NAP-M sought cooperation with the AL's 'six-point group'.[134]

To India's detriment, the AL's split in Mujib's absence reoriented its political resolutions. To bring itself closer to the NAP-M, the Awami League (six-point group) called for the dissolution of the One-Unit scheme, but compromised on Kashmir. In an echo of the NAP-M, the EPAL's revised resolution clarified that it sought to extend 'all-out help and cooperation to the Kashmiri freedom fighters in their struggle from liberation of the motherland'.[135] India was now concerned about chronic disunity, and the regime's success in splitting both the NAP, and the 'most popular, and potentially the most dangerous party', the AL.[136]

This is when Ayub erred. In January 1968, the regime charged Mujib alongside other Leaguers with treason for collaborating with India to break Pakistan. They used Mujib's secret visit to Agartala in 1962, contacts with Ojha (Banerjee), and two Indian intelligence officers named 'Maj. Menon' (K Sankaran Nair, future R&AW chief) and 'Lt. Col. Mishra' (real name unknown) to imprison Mujib and his allies. Ojha was declared *persona non grata* and left Dacca on 7 January.[137] For a former student leader who fought during the war, 'all this [seeking India support] started in late-1950s when Ayub Khan disenfranchised the Bengalis'.[138] It was a blunder.

Meant to keep Mujib out of politics for a prolonged period, or sentencing him to death, the Agartala Conspiracy Case backfired. Instead of marginalising Mujib, it consolidated his mass appeal and forced other East Pakistani parties to join the cause of securing his release. In its desperation to keep Mujib isolated, the regime missed political signals that even Bhutto, Mujib's adversary, was sending. In October 1967, Bhutto 'reconnoitred' East Pakistan to placate Bengali opinion. Conscious that he wouldn't be able to make much headway without Mujib's support, Bhutto began to regret that 'a national leader like Sheikh Mujib who sacrificed a lot for the achievement of independence and did much for the people, has been labelled a disruptionist and put behind the bar'.[139] He opined that the six points were not a 'secessionist move', and banning Tagore's work was senseless. Bhutto's U-turn was so blunt and opportunistic, that few took it at face value. But for the regime, it meant that the need to keep Mujib imprisoned was never greater.

Years later in June 1974, Subimal Dutt, India's high commissioner to Dacca, articulated his 'horrible suspicion' that after 1971 Mujib remained skeptical of Indian intentions because of his past experience.[140] During the 1960s, Mujib's contact with the DHC was populated by requests for assistance of various kinds to 'subvert the Pakistan Government's authority in East Pakistan'.[141] Dutt 'was told' that the Agartala conspiracy alleged against 'at least some' was 'not entirely baseless'.[142] Shawkat Ali, one of the accused, stated decades later that the charges were correct.[143] There is little doubt that Mujib was working with India to pressure Pakistan and seek autonomy or liberation.

But India's support began in the mid-1960s, even if it didn't translate into results until 1971. The situation in 1968 deteriorated to such an extent that the longer Ayub kept Mujib behind bars, the more it increased the latter's stature. Throughout 1968, as the trial went on, political violence in East Pakistan increased, and so did harassment of Indian nationals, especially those working at the mission. In October, India complained that the ISI was undertaking large-scale forgeries of Indian visas in Dacca, and blamed Pakistan for not protecting Indian diplomats against a 'large number of thefts and burglaries' at the 'residence of members' of the mission.[144] Locally recruited Hindu staff too began 'pressing hard' for help with migrating to India, and quit their jobs.[145] Furthermore, Ojha's ouster meant the mission didn't have a cypher specialist for most of 1968, undermining communications secrecy.

In January 1969, when 'complete lawlessness prevailed' in parts of Dacca and public anger against the 'one unit' policy boiled over across the country, all opposition parties formed the Democratic Action Committee. The committee sought a return to democracy, full autonomy for East Pakistan, the establishment of sub-federal units in West Pakistan offering full autonomy to Balochistan, Northwest Frontier Province (NWFP), and Sindh, and 'abandonment of the Agartala Conspiracy Case'.[146] The regime responded by introducing multiple 24-hour curfews, which made people more restive.[147] Indian diplomats were impressed by Bengali students who, in their view, 'have added a new chapter to the history of East Pakistan's struggle against the Ayub regime'.[148] Worried about the turn the situation was taking, Ayub dropped all charges against Mujib and others accused in the Agartala Conspiracy case in February 1969.

On 22 February, the day Mujib was released, the students organised a 'mammoth public reception' and conferred on him the title of 'Bangabandhu' (Friend of Bengal).[149] But at the moment he was christened as the uncrowned king of East Pakistan, the students also 'warned' him that if he 'faltered' in his leadership or compromised, he would be 'branded' a traitor.[150] Mujib's predicament was sealed that day. There were limits to what he could and couldn't do, and those limits were being shaped by radical student bodies. This moment marked a turning point.

Mujib had built what Nehru wanted him to: mass support in favour of secular Bengali nationalism typified by the popular slogan 'Joy Bangla'. He burnished his credentials as a mass leader, but took a populist turn. He had a mass base, a coterie of loyalists, but he was no institution- and consensus-builder. Mujib's meteoric rise was marked by his inability to bring together competing groups. His release from prison was the last blow for Ayub, who quit office on 26 March 1969, and handed over power to Gen. Yahya Khan.

The military crackdown in 1971 was a foregone conclusion. Two days before leaving office, Ayub wrote a farewell letter to Yahya in which he made it abundantly clear that Mujib and his 'allies':

> acting under cover of a mass movement, struck blow after blow at the very root of the country during the last few months ... I have exhausted all possible civil and constitutional means to resolve the present crisis ... It is beyond the capacity of the civil government to deal with the present complex situation and the Defence forces must step in.[151]

Given that Pakistan was already under military rule, the call for the defence forces to step in was Ayub's way of calling for a severe crackdown to prevent Pakistan from disintegrating. This was his last mistake. Because Yahya did exactly that and made Bangladesh's liberation inevitable.

But before the crackdown, Pakistan geared up for elections in 1970. Indian officials watching the manifestos and promises of all political parties noticed one difference between AL and others. Nearly all parties supported the liberation of Jammu and Kashmir, but not the AL. Mujib had diluted the clause on the AL's support for Kashmir's liberation from India. In September 1969, Mujib had openly questioned the regime's sincerity given 'they did not allow the Kashmir dispute to come in the way of solving the problems of the Indus Basin and the Rann of Kutch' as it did in the case of flood control in East Pakistan for which 'India's cooperation is a must'.[152] India found it 'noteworthy' that Mujib didn't raise Farakka barrage and Ganga river water sharing issues in rallies.[153]

Mujib's decision to turn the Kashmir question on its head to pressure the regime instead of becoming hemmed in convinced India that Mujib would solve the dispute amicably and end cross-border Naga and Mizo activism. From being critical of India's Kashmir policy (and, at times, refusing to meet the Indian consul for that reason),[154] Mujib had come a long way to India's satisfaction.[155] In December 1969, he made regional autonomy an election issue, and student leaders demanded that East Pakistan be renamed 'Bangladesh'.[156] If there was any doubt about who held the political momentum in East Pakistan, Cyclone Bhola, which hit during 7–13 November 1970, settled the debate. The regime's failure to respond worsened its public image.[157] Even though it would have happened without Bhola, the Awami League swept the 1970 elections and won 160 (+7) seats in the national assembly whereas Bhutto won 81(+5).[158]

On 3 January 1971, the R&AW presented a 25-page top-secret report on East Pakistan. Its two main points were: 'an impressive increase in Pakistan's armed might since her confrontation with India in 1965' and the possibility that Pakistan might start 'fomenting violent agitation' in Jammu and Kashmir 'followed by extensive infiltration'.[159] Kao was keen to ensure that Gandhi understood that though the Pakistani army may make 'temporary successes in Bangla Desh', it would fail to crush the liberation movement.[160] The longer the underground movement lasted, the higher the chances were of radical pro-China communists capturing it 'greatly to India's disadvantage'.[161]

Haksar, Gandhi's Principal Secretary and confidante, asserted that

> with the overwhelming victory of East Pakistan Wing, the solution of internal problems of Pakistan have become infinitely more difficult ... I think that the time has come when our Armed forces need to make a very realistic assessment both of Pakistan's capability and our response. I have a feeling that there are many weak spots in our defence capabilities. These need to be remedied without loss of time.[162]

Haksar advised Gandhi to have a meeting with the three chiefs of staff, defence secretary, and the defence minister 'and share with them her anxieties ... without any publicity'.[163] Despite seeking a quick end to the conflict, the R&AW mobilised SSB and SFF units along the East Pakistan border to train a large number of village volunteers, and prepare the ground for a long insurgency against Pakistan.[164] The scene was set for a showdown.

Joy Bangla

The people of East Pakistan fought back. On 26 March 1971, Mujib declared independence. One day later, the declaration was broadcast from the secret *Swadhin Bangla Betar Kendra* (Free Bengal Radio Centre) by an obscure Maj. Ziaur-Rahman who omitted any reference to Mujib.[165] Mujib's victory meant that the six-point programme had electoral support. Bhutto and Yahya's failure to accept this mandate meant the demand for autonomy translated into a crackdown. The consequent Bengali pushback ended with Bangladesh's liberation on 16 December 1971, the day Pakistani forces signed the instrument of surrender with attacking Indian forces.

A history of the war is beyond this book's scope. Instead, this section focuses on the contradictions that shaped India's approach towards warfighting and the Mujibnagar government. Aware of the fractious nature of East Pakistani politics coupled with Mujib's cult, working with diverse sections of Bengalis united in their desire for liberation—but ideologically divided—was challenging. Who would credit for liberation became a fractious issue. The need to manage fissures in Bangladesh's body politic was as important as ensuring India's military preparedness with Soviet support and diplomatic mobilisation against Pakistan's genocide.

The job fell on the shoulders of Durga Prasad Dhar—popularly known as 'DP'. India's envoy to the Soviet Union, Dhar played a critical role in the signing of the 1971 Indo-Soviet Friendship Treaty. Haksar appointed the quick-witted and charming DP as chairman of the MEA's policy planning committee to coordinate and lead the war effort as he himself was 'physically, and mentally, stretched beyond the breaking point'.[166] On 19 August 1971, DP was formally appointed to lead the 'one-man committee' to coordinate wartime political communications and intelligence liaison.[167] Gandhi was 'anxious' that liaison with leaders of the Bangladesh movement should be centralised and maintained 'by the clandestine agency and the secret channels of R&AW'.[168]

If Kao commanded R&AW's special kinetic operations, DP was to command its special political operations. This meant working with all factions in the Bangladesh government, and channelling their capabilities towards liberation. For this, if needed, DP was to coax radical elements to toe the Bangladeshi government's line, and fight under the Mukti Fauj. To make sense of his appointment and approach, it's essential to unpack the ideas DP had on how to manage these issues while he was still in Moscow.

On 7 April, a few days after the launch of Operation Searchlight, he received a letter from Haksar. Gandhi's principal secretary wanted to know if 'India and Soviet Union and perhaps others do anything to bring the conflict to an early end, or to sustain the truly nationalist forces in East Pakistan so that, politically speaking, they continue to command the respect and loyalty of the vast majority of the people'.[169] Gandhi was concerned that she couldn't withstand domestic pressures, especially from the Jana Sangh, to recognise Bangladesh as a separate country after a point, and that there were thousands of people from West Bengal who were volunteering to fight in East Pakistan.

The 1967 Naxalite uprising, known connections between Indian and Bangladeshi Naxals, China's ideological and material support to these groups, and the recent outbreak of a communist uprising in Ceylon worried New Delhi that the resistance in East Pakistan could 'slip out of the hands of these [nationalistic] elements into the hands of pro-Chinese factions'.[170] This 'was bound to affect the whole of India and endanger its stability', she believed.[171] Haksar warned DP that R&AW was receiving reports of 'beginning of rumblings' that 'the leadership of Mujibur Rahman and his colleagues has failed the people' and the East Pakistani counterpart of 'our Naxalites alone can deliver the goods'.[172] In India's reading, China was playing a classic 'double-faced game' by publicly supporting West Pakistan, but 'working clandestinely to increase its influence in East Pakistan'.[173]

India received a sympathetic but noncommittal response from Moscow through a 'disappointed' DP.[174] On 18 April, a few days after noting his disappointment with the Soviets, DP authored an optimistic and considered note to Haksar. He argued that Moscow was more forthcoming and sympathetic in reality than its written notes reflect, and recommended that India consolidate its position both in the 'East Pakistani people's mind and in the assessment made of our motives and our attitude in the different countries of the world'.[175] He noted that Moscow was willing to depart from its policy of discouraging secessionism in light of Pakistan's crackdown against Bengali nationalism, which 'is secessionist in essence'.[176]

Moscow informed DP that it guided the Communist Party of India (CPI) to utilise its channels to help the 'politically correct groups in East Pakistan', namely the NAP-M and the Communist Party of Bangladesh. Moscow also advised the CPI to suspend its rivalry with CPI(M) for the conflict's duration.[177] The situation in West Bengal in 1970–71 was precarious.[178] After meeting CPI's Rajeshwar Rao and CPI(M)'s Bhupesh Gupta in Moscow, DP was convinced that Soviet influence was working on Indian communists.

But most of all for DP, the month preceding the onset of Pakistan's crackdown demonstrated 'to the delighted surprise of all us that the East Bengalis have it in them'.[179] There had been apprehensions among Indian officials about the stamina and commitment of the Bengali people to resist Pakistan.[180] DP did not want New Delhi to seek an immediate defeat of the Pakistani army, but to 'create the whole of East Bengal into a bottomless ditch which will suck the strength and the resources of West Pakistan'.[181] India had to think in terms of one or two years, not a week or two, and wage a long-term covert campaign inside East Pakistan instead of using overt military force, he suggested. His advocacy had support in New Delhi. K Subrahmanyam, director of the Institute for Defence Studies and Analyses, argued that India should intervene to 'save the majority population in a country from genocide by a military oligarchy',[182] and that such an act 'will be in the spirit of the action India has been demanding' from the UN and the West against oppressive 'white minority regime[s]' in South Africa and Rhodesia.[183]

In July, on his return to India, DP met with Bhashani and Tajuddin, and presented a seventeen-page assessment to Gandhi that explained how to manage the fractious politics of East Pakistan in keeping with India's interests.[184] His basic point was to caution Gandhi against total war despite the risk of an insurgency becoming a 'festering wound', and to 'use the Bengali human material and the Bengali terrain to launch a comprehensive war of liberation'.[185] Somewhat derogatorily, DP continued that India's efforts to train and arm Bengali guerrillas were woefully small and the R&AW should 'convert every potential beggar—because anyone who lives on doles for a long time loses initiative and becomes a beggar—into a committed liberation fighter.'[186] Once these 'steeled fighters' could operate with greater speed and gain territory, it was likely that the situation may escalate to war between India and Pakistan.

He went on: 'of such a possibility we need not be unduly afraid. If war comes in this manner, well, let it come and we should not avoid it. As a matter of fact, I discern a ring of inevitability about an Indo Pak war'.[187] But how could internal differences be managed in the liberation movement? DP drew from past experiences, including the world wars, to build a case for a disciplined vanguard within the movement. He was clear that 'it will be nothing short of a miracle that no bickering should arise amongst the constituents of Bangladesh ... the list of differences and complaints against the Government of India and their functionaries is also likely to become fatter and fatter'.[188]

To manage the AL-dominated Mujibnagar government's internal issues and create a united front, DP recommended forging battlefield unity among fighters (instead of creating 'manifesto-borne-unity'), like in the Spanish civil war.[189] His biggest worry was the AL leadership turning 'wishy washy ... leading to endless argument and quarrels', and creating grounds for the movement's leadership passing into the hands of 'sober or the extreme communist'.[190] India had to 'identify the really liberal, democratic and brave elements amongst the cross section of the leadership of the East Bengalis. This would become the hard core around whom we could build an edifice which could at once be dependable and stable'.[191] Though sensible to keep the liberation movement united, DP's approach had its antinomies. The nationalist vanguard he had in mind was suited to India's interests, but militated against participatory politics. The other contradiction lay in how India viewed and dealt with communists.

The 'sober' left, DP argued, could be supported through Indian communists, but the Naxals must not be alienated either. This became a controversial decision with future ramifications. The 'left of the left' in East Bengal mustn't 'be driven to the wall', DP argued.[192] This was to prevent NAP(B) from seeking support from Peking, and Chinese agents and the CIA from exploiting friction to dislocate the liberation movement. 'If that happens, everything is lost in East Bengal', he warned.[193]

Gandhi apprised Soviet foreign minister Andrei Gromyko in August that the 'Naxalites had expressed their support for President Yahya Khan, and were accusing India and the USSR of having caused the present situation in Bangla Desh'.[194] But one wing of Naxals didn't support Yahya's crackdown and was, by corollary, to be engaged with and supported. This specific Naxalite wing planned to fight against Pakistan, unlike others who fought the Mukti Bahini.[195]

Iqbal Hassan Mahmood, the State Minister for Power (2001–06) who was involved in the Naxalite movement during his student days, says: 'the radical left wanted to fight both the class war and the nationalist war', but circumstances and factionalism made that impossible, and parts of the Naxal factions became more invested in national liberation than fighting against fellow Bangladeshis.[196] The problem was that a quick end to the war was desired because India felt that the Mukti Bahini could fall into Naxal hands. But support to even a select faction of Naxals could, and did, anger the liberal vanguard about India's intentions.

Operation Searchlight forced figures from across East Pakistan's political spectrum to shelter in India. Mujib was arrested on the night of 25 March.[197] Why he opted for arrest over retreat remains unclear. But it's clear that until 14 March 1971, Mujib was 'dissatisfied' with India's support and felt that Pakistan was able to move two and a half divisions from Quetta to East Pakistan because India reduced its forces along the western border.[198] He wanted India to intercept Pakistani troops, ships, and aircraft in March itself. R&AW officers posted in Dacca urgently requested that 'India's decision in this regard be communicated immediately so that Mujib can decide his next move'.[199] If India refused armed support, R&AW warned that Mujib would accept an offer by the US ambassador Joseph Farland to 'ensure withdrawal of Pakistan army from East Pakistan on condition of leasing of a bay island for seven years'.[200]

Unsure of India's decision-making, Mujib played a high-stakes game with Gandhi. It is unclear how India responded to this specific top-secret request, but whatever transpired in the interim ten days, Mujib felt safer to remain in Dacca and court arrest instead of moving to India. Instead, Tajuddin Ahmed and Amirul Islam, two senior leaguers, crossed over into India and ran the Mujibnagar government with Mujib as president-in-absentia and Syed Nazrul Islam as acting president.[201] Before entering India, Ahmed and Islam sought Gandhi's agreement to 'receive them as officials of independent Bangladesh, not as asylum seekers', Islam remembers.[202] Gandhi obliged.

Bhashani too was in India. He was put up in a hill resort in Ranikhet,[203] and received privileged treatment with a monthly allowance of 2,000 rupees and a free car.[204] Despite his pro-China stance, Bhashani was not spared by Lt. Gen. Tikka Khan, Yahya's man in East Pakistan. Instead of declaring independence unilaterally, Bhashani informed India that he appreciated the 'utmost necessity of unity' with the AL.[205] But he demanded help to set up his HQ near Dhubri in Assam to execute armed action in Mymensingh, publish a weekly bulletin 'to keep up the morale of the people', establish 'training facilities for guerrilla warfare', secure arms and ammunition, and meets with Tajuddin and other AL leaders.[206]

Mercurial and 'unpredictable', Bhashani proposed 'forming a confederation of India and Bangladesh'.[207] His idea was to rebuild a united Assam and Bengal across caste and religious lines. Though the idea of a merger held some emotional value in 1948, including with Nehru, it was not desirable in 1971. Such advocacy of a confederation made a 'nervous' India ensure that Bhashani was kept away from journalists.[208] Bhashani confessed that before 1968, he routinely met with CIA agents to seek support 'for creation of an independent state comprising of Assam, East Pakistan, and West Bengal'.[209] It took India months to convince him against both ideas. But his authority among left elements meant that neither India nor Tajuddin could isolate him.

On the other hand, student leaders involved in the erstwhile SBPP, who had nurtured and carried forward Bengali nationalism and the idea of independence since 1961, demanded 'the government to be dissolved and be replaced with a Liberation Front or War Council in which they could play a major role'.[210] Serajul Alam, Abdur Razzak, and Kazi Aref Ahmed, now joined by Tofael Ahmed from the *Chattro Sangram Parishad* and Mujib's first cousin Sheikh Fazlul Hoque Moni, formed the nucleus of Mujib loyalists and wanted to lead the struggle for Bangladesh's liberation similar to Bhashani and his Maoist supporters.

They were the nucleus DP was referring to in his note to Gandhi. Apparently, before his arrest, Mujib secretly informed India that he trusted these 'khalifas', and wanted them to lead the armed movement.[211] Suspicious of Tajuddin's intent, the khalifas, especially Moni, refused to follow him or to fight under the Mukti Bahini,. They sought a force of their own, the 'Mujib Bahini'. Most members of the Mujib Bahini came from the *Chattra League* and opposed the communists.

This was the problem DP had warned about. Fissures in the liberation movement risked undermining the effort. It could dislocate the movement by leading to disjointed tactical battles with little strategic effect, and undermine India's aim of reversing the 10-million-strong refugee crisis. India had to bring these competing, and conflicting, groups together, and DP was to do that. Tajuddin understood these issues, and was reluctant to lift the mantle in Mujib's absence.[212] But he was counselled by Rehman Sobhan, a young political economist with access to Haksar and Prithvi Nath Dhar, another confidante of Gandhi, to drop self-doubt and take charge. In a short span, Tajuddin developed a strong equation with Gandhi and gained her confidence.[213] Ironically, though India convinced Bhashani about the futility of fighting separately, it struggled to convince the Mujib Bahini to accept Tajuddin's leadership.

Trained and led by Maj. Gen. Sujan Singh Uban, the SFF commanding officer, the Mujib Bahini was better equipped and separately trained than the Mukti Fauj. But it experienced less combat, and when it did (in Chittagong), it was not allowed to own it—the Mukti Bahini took credit. This incensed the khalifas.[214] Mujib Bahini was viewed as insurance in case the Muktis fell into Naxal hands. India's decision to raise these groups, though paradoxical, was meant to ensure control over the movement. Such control was maintained by making India the dominant weapons supplier, and embedding Indian soldiers and spies in its ranks.[215] Tajuddin and Bhashani knew this. Aware of how little the khalifas trusted him, and the fact that Mujib and the Mukti Bahini cadre occasionally clashed, this 'training-in-silos' arrangement suited Tajuddin.

India's support to select Naxalites came to light when Mujib Bahini's men accidentally saw Indian spies meeting these communists in luxurious hotels.[216] Uban himself didn't know that R&AW was training and arming some Naxals. When he took the matter to Kao, the spymaster confirmed that this was done to counter-balance the Mujib Bahini.[217] Uban's protests that such an arrangement was unacceptable to the Mujib Bahini led to an angry outburst by an overworked Kao who said that the Mujib Bahini could 'go to hell' if they couldn't accept the reality that India treats them as an 'important wing of the overall project' but 'not as an independent political authority'.[218] Tajuddin, Kao told Uban, 'regards Bhashani's men as a great asset against Pakistan ... how can we ignore their advice?'.[219]

This was despite Kao receiving reports from PN Banerjee from Calcutta in July that Tajuddin had no acceptance in the AL.[220] Banerjee reported that on 25 March, after leaving Mujib's residence, Tajuddin, Islam, and Kamal Hossain held a separate meeting before leaving for India.[221] Their decision to secure recognition from India for the Mujibnagar government with Tajuddin as prime minister was viewed with suspicion.[222] The khalifas and certain cabinet members opposed Tajuddin.[223] But, 'Mujib refused to go underground that night with us, he preferred arrest', says Islam.[224] Mujib isolated himself from the war when both time and his presence were of the essence.

Tajuddin was seen as a capable organiser.[225] He communicated AL's demands to New Delhi: 'this is our war, not your war, but we need your support' and 'the relationship between the first government of Bangladesh and the Indian government must be of equals'.[226] There were concerns that India might refuse to support Mujib the way it did in 1962.[227]

Tajuddin's moves, though far-sighted, left the khalifas seething.[228] Anxious about the impact this would have on the movement, Tajuddin lamented: 'Mujib bhai depended too heavily on the student leaders and the younger members in the party and relied on their tall talks of what they could do and how well they were prepared to meet the army'.[229] He confided to his aide that Bangladesh, 'will be free, but it will not be liveable'.[230] Unable to resolve differences among Bengali politicians, India segregated them into silos. The tactic backfired.

The khalifas blamed DP, among others, for their isolation, limited combat exposure, and failure to receive credit where it was due. Moni believed that this was a communist ploy to keep Bengali nationalists (including Mujib, whose fate was unknown) on the margins. DP was viewed as a pro-Soviet communist conspiring against them. Had Mujib died in a Pakistani prison, the Mujib Bahini would have become rudderless and Tajuddin would have emerged as the leader of liberated Bangladesh. But India's invasion in December 1971 helped secure his release and return to a hero's welcome in January 1972.

This meant that Mujib, who had not witnessed combat, inherited a well-trained, well-equipped, loyal force whose leaders grudged DP and Tajuddin. Despite his advocacy for a democratic Bangladesh, Mujib used the outfit for political purposes. On 1 February 1972, the Mujib Bahini was refashioned as the Jatiya Rakkhi Bahini (National Defence Force; JRB), a paramilitary unit meant to fight insurgencies and maintain law and order. In reality it became what a journalist called 'a gang of hoodlums little different from the Nazi Brown Shirts'.[231]

The JRB was separate from Bangladesh's armed forces constituting former EPR soldiers who fought as 'freedom fighters', and those repatriate soldiers who were jailed in West Pakistan. It was an explosive situation. 'It's difficult for me to articulate on this issue. But just look at how it [Mujib Bahini] was used later', says Islam.[232] From March onwards, these young people who formed the Mujib Bahini just wanted to fight Pakistan, 'and not worry about governance and not act as a government … but we were able to persuade them', he says.[233]

The ground for a Mujib-Tajuddin split was thus laid even before Bangladesh's liberation. When it did occur upon Mujib's release, India became both cause and casualty. In a twist few saw coming, Mujib complained that 'Tajuddin had sold the country to India', whereas Tajuddin believed that Mujib was (mistakenly) beholden to the US 'for saving his life'.[234] This split is the most seminal, seismic event in Bangladeshi history. The mass leader who didn't participate in the war fell out with the institutional genius who ran Bangladesh's wartime cabinet. The split, among other wartime traumas, shaped Bangladeshi politics along authoritarian lines since birth. The one Indian official who faced the brunt of these problems and the contradictions of India's approach was DP himself.

During his visit to Dacca in 1972, DP became the only Indian to be greeted by 'black flags'.[235]

Conclusions

The 1960s was a long decade in India's near east. From coups, wars, ethnic secessionism, and left-wing movements to famines and cyclones, the region experienced acute turmoil. Bangladesh's liberation was, in many ways, the culmination, if not the end, of pressures India faced during this decade. Worried about having to fight a two-and-a-half-front conflict, Indian policymakers were keen find a solution in the near east. With the prospect of constitutionalist solidarities and Nehru himself both relics of the past, India was less wary of using force. To counter Pakistan's support for northeastern rebels, India encouraged the Bengali underground in East Pakistan. Pressures of state-building domestically made it go to war externally in East Pakistan. As India's tumultuous engagement with East Pakistan before 1971 shows, identity politics, political economies, official antinomies, and cross-border migration came together to change South Asia's political geography.

Fueled by New Delhi's economic and political neglect, the armed turn of the Mizo movement and India's coercive response marked a low point in its constitutional dream. The Mizo insurgency whetted the Indian security establishment's appetite to use force in East Pakistan—even at the risk of dismembering Pakistan—to resolve the two-and-a-half-front security dilemma. Critically, it occurred in parallel to rising communist violence. Throughout Bengal, students from across class and caste lines were embracing communism to challenge the idea of India. The Naxalbari uprising, wherein a few hundred peasants in Siliguri rose against local landlords and authorities, was led by upper-caste leaders.[236] In this context, to ensure that the Mukti Bahini's nationalism didn't encompass both Bengals, the first flag of liberated Bangladesh came with a territorial map of East Pakistan on it.[237]

The Naxalbari uprising and the 1971 communist revolt in Sri Lanka helped Indian officials convince Gandhi and the Soviet Union that the real threat in East Pakistan was from Naxalites. Communist militancy with Chinese support reached a new high in Burma during the Cultural Revolution, culminating in anti-Chinese riots in June 1967.[238] China dubbed the Naxal uprising as 'spring thunder over India'.[239] It also offered support to Indian Naxals.[240] But as a senior Indian Marxist says, 'even the Chinese knew that there's no serious take for revolution in India despite all the rhetoric'.[241] In East Pakistan, China understood that 'this was a nationalist question and not a revolutionary issue'.[242] But the complexity of ideas and identities pushed New Delhi to opt for a 'hard core' of secular Bengalis under Mujib as their preferred allies.

The limits of this solution became apparent when contradictions in India's approach burst into the open. The notion of a vanguard around Mujib went against the idea of a democratic republic. Driven by strategic concerns, India came to view East Pakistan—and Bangladesh—as a playground for great power politics. Even if the success of such a wartime strategy was in liberation, its failure in peacetime, as detailed in the seventh chapter, became equally clear. India's struggle to reconcile its constitutionalism with use of force in Assam played out just as much in Bangladesh, where it sought a democratic government—but only unless it was secular, liberal, and pro-India. It's no surprise that Mujib's populism quickly morphed into anti-Indianism. As a conservative Bangladeshi lawyer once asked an Indian diplomat, 'why do [you] want to have servants in Bangladesh when you can have so many friends?'—the Indian diplomat didn't respond, but according to the lawyer, 'he got the point'.[243] This sense that India opted to 'put all its egg in one basket' in the Awami League continues to agitate Bangladeshi politics.[244]

India's preference for democracy in Bangladesh was at odds with its state-building processes and security concerns in the northeast.

Bangladesh's liberation and India's engagement with the Burmese junta (which had 'misgivings' [245] about 1971, sheltered 20,000 Bengalis during the war, and opened its airfields for the Pakistani air force)[246] were intended to address security concerns. The goal was to stem the flow of minorities fleeing persecution and deny rebel sanctuaries in East Pakistan and Burma. India temporarily succeeded on both counts. But the weight of contradictions between its political preferences and security concerns was such that neither independent Bangladesh, nor engagement with the junta brought peace. The next chapters show how India won the war, but lost the peace.

6

SONS OF THE SOIL
ASSAMESE NATIONALISM AND THE
POLITICS OF PEACEMAKING

'I trust my strong insistence on a common Governor [of Northeast] will not be construed as an exercise in empire-building. I am too lazy to want to be an Emperor; and if I wanted an Empire I would choose a less primitive one.'[1]

Braj Kumar Nehru, Governor of Assam,
on North-East Council (NEC), October 1970

The second part of solving India's two-and-a-half-front security puzzle was to reorganise the northeast. Peace with Burma and Bangladesh's liberation were coupled with Assam's restructuring. Gandhi's 1960 Assam tour and witnessing of anti-Bengali violence left an imprint. Assam's vulnerability to China in 1962 and the Mizo insurgency forced Gandhi into action. With the Burma boundary formalised, it was time to carve out new states from Assam. Twin logics were at play here. Statehood within the union was expected to allay identity politics, make administration easy, and increase regional economic dependence on and loyalty towards New Delhi. It could enhance the Congress' electoral fortunes. Even before 1971, statehood for Tripura, Meghalaya, and Manipur were seen

155

as consolidating the Congress' political grip by taking 'the wind out of the sails of the CPM, CPI, and other parties'.[2] This, in turn, could strengthen the state's grip in the northeast, reduce Assamese dominance, and demonstrate the success of Indian federalism while limiting China's scope for exploiting domestic faultlines.[3]

But there was a problem. In an apparent official antinomy, India passed the North-East Council (NEC) Act on 30 December 1971, two weeks after Pakistan's surrender in Dacca. Assam stood divided, but instead of enjoying federal empowerment, all states were put under a 'common governorship' scheme. Baruah terms it 'cosmetic federalism' wherein neither were the political aspirations of people inhabiting these states met, nor their developmental needs catered to.[4] The Indian state did yield power, but as a patron who paid bills rather than a partner facilitating development. Listed as 'special category states' with few revenue-generation sources, these states sustained themselves on central government packages that consisted of 90% grants and 10% loans.[5] Such dependence, as former home secretary Pillai argues, encouraged 'systemic' corruption.[6] Coupled with unceasing migration from Bangladesh, this restructuring triggered a violent 'sons of the soil' movement in Assam. Under the leadership of Paresh Baruah and Arabinda Rajkhowa, the United Liberation Front of Asom (ULFA) launched armed rebellion against India.

The hope that Bangladesh's liberation would solve the Naga and Mizo issues was just that—hope. The situation in northeast worsened *despite* 1971. Assam's restructuring, economic dependence on New Delhi, and state-led crackdown under AFSPA and the Unlawful Activities (Prevention) Act 1967 (UAPA) increased violence and corruption. In November 1975, India signed the Shillong Accord with the Naga National Council (NNC). The accord formalised the 1964 ceasefire and mainstreamed moderate factions. Phizo, who was now a British citizen but commanded respect in the Naga movement, rejected the accord.

In less than five years, on 31 January 1980, the National Socialist Council of Nagaland (NSCN) was born with a Phizo-inspired tripartite alliance between Isak Chishi Swu, a Sumi from Nagaland ('a statesman'), Thuingaleng Muivah, a Tangkhul from Manipur ('an ideologue'), and Shagwang S Khaplang, a Burma-based Hemi Naga.[7] The Naga movement morphed but didn't end. To worsen matters, multiple armed outfits like the People's Liberation Army of Manipur (PLA-M), the People's Revolutionary Party of Kangleipak (PREPAK), and the Kangleipak Communist Party (KCP) emerged in Manipur's Imphal Valley during 1977–80, inviting the imposition of AFSPA in September 1980. It led previously unarmed outfits such as the United National Liberation Front (UNLF) to also take up arms during the 1980s.[8]

To contain the Assam movement, India signed a Memorandum of Settlement, known as the Assam Accord, on 15 August 1985 with the AASU. The Citizenship Act was amended in 1986 to identify 'illegal' Bangladeshis who entered Assam *after* 25 March 1971, the first night of Pakistani crackdown in erstwhile East Pakistan. The accord failed to deliver, and, apart from fueling anti-state violence, triggered similar movements by Bodo communities after 1986. The Karbi Anglong movement for a separate state in North Cachar Hills and Karbi Anglong too gained momentum. In 1989, a smaller movement against Bangladeshi migrants began in Tripura under the aegis of the National Liberation Front of Tripura (NLFT). China and Pakistan now had more options to harass India. The only movement that India succeeded to make peace with was the Mizos. The MNF began a long reconciliation process after 1971 that culminated in the Mizoram Accord in 1986.

Despite such accords, India lost the peace in its northeast. This chapter maintains focus on the themes shaping India's *outside in* state-building in the northeast. The first section explores the NEC's contradictions that centralised power under Braj Kumar Nehru, a cousin of India's first prime minister. The second section delves into politics of peacebuilding in Mizoram and how the 1975 change of guard in Bangladesh influenced it. The third section covers the Assam movement and making of the 1985 accord that, ironically, ignited full-scale secessionism in Assam. The final section explains how India's post-Emergency politics, and the success of Naga, Mizo, and Assamese nationalists deepened regional conflict economies, giving many people, including in Manipur and Tripura, a reason to pick up arms and engage in cross-border drug trade for both survival and ambition.

Road to Shillong

For Braj Kumar 'Bijju' Nehru, India's northeast was a socially primitive and politically backward place that needed New Delhi's paternal management to experience true freedom and 20th century modernity. Only he could deliver this, Nehru believed. Appointed governor of Assam and Nagaland in 1968 after his ambassadorship in Washington, D.C., and around the time Naga and Mizo fighters were returning from China, Nehru became Gandhi's point-person in Shillong. Nehru's rise typified the Congress split. Congress (I), where 'I' stood for 'Indira', emerged after Gandhi undermined inner-party democracy.[9] Nehru was an ally in this transition, and advocated the imposition of Emergency in 1975.

Driven by colonial understandings of local cultures in the northeast, postcolonial hubris, a hardline attitude, and frustration over the endurance of Naga and Mizo movements, Nehru made two consequential recommendations. First, he sought the creation of NEC with himself as the 'common governor' of all northeastern states including administering the Mizo union territory. This contrasted with the MHA push for separate governors: one for Assam and Meghalaya, and another for Manipur, Tripura, and Nagaland.[10] Second, Nehru wanted to halt negotiations with the Naga and Mizo underground. The only entity New Delhi should engage with, he believed, was the chief minister of Nagaland who represented the people, and only through the 'common governor'. Gandhi accepted both demands.

Nehru demanded common governorship to make administration effective. Not only did he want to become the governor of all states, administrator of union territories, and NEC chairman, but he also wanted the central government to stay away from the day-to-day running of states. Instead, New Delhi should 'retain their distance and superior control through the Governor'.[11] To impart administrative unity to the region, Nehru advocated a common High Court, one Public Service Commission, and a single cadre of the All-India Service from the region. Even the Director-IB, whom Nehru believed was playing a 'lone hand' with groups belonging to Ao communities, must 'at least' inform him.[12]

The impracticality and political unfeasibility of his recommendations birthed the two-governorship idea, but Nehru insisted he could handle the job. The foreseeable problem of streamlining communications within the region and between New Delhi and Shillong could be solved by appointing adequate Joint Secretary-level officers, strengthening wireless and telecom connectivity, and having a helicopter at his disposal for free travel to any state.[13] The real reason for Nehru's drive for overarching powers was political. He believed that people of the region were in need of direction and modernity, and that only India, through him, could offer that.

Nehru's annual republic day speeches as governor were peppered with colonial tropes. In January 1971, he claimed that 'it is only since the independence of India including Nagaland and the breaking down of our isolation that the benefits of modern civilisation have been brought to us [a reference to Naga communities] in appreciable measure'.[14] He argued that 'for the last few years since peace has been restored the pace of development in Nagaland has been truly remarkable. Thanks to the fact that we receive very much more financial assistance from the Govt. of India than any other State of the Union we are progressing very fast.'[15]

That his views typified the hegemony many detested and resisted was lost on him. Cognisant of risks, the home ministry pushed back. Just one high court for the entire region, the ministry argued, was insufficient. The single civil service cadre idea was similarly shot down because candidates from Nagaland and Mizo areas would not be able to travel with ease to Guwahati if there was only one entrance examination centre.[16] The MHA also opposed Nehru's demand for NEC chairmanship and instead recommended a cabinet minister holding the portfolio with Nehru as vice-chairman. Such an arrangement risked the NEC chairman being away from the region for long periods, but it was better than having a potential spat between Nehru and a chief minister that could lead to a crisis.[17]

The idea of common governorship was most sensitive. Apart from Meghalaya, and Assam chief minister B.P. Chaliha agreeing to it in August 1969 (the latter viewed common governorship as a proxy to retain Assam's dominance), most others opposed it.[18] The fact that a non-elected official wielded such power was not acceptable. The lieutenant governor of Manipur indicated that local political parties sought two governors, and wanted the Mizo union territory to be put under the charge of the governor of Manipur, Nagaland, and Tripura, instead of Assam and Meghalaya.[19] The lieutenant governor of Tripura went so far as to demanding three governors, whereas Nagaland couldn't care about the number of governors until they had a separate governor ('not conceded').[20]

Nagaland was opposed to any arrangement that brought it back into Assam's fold when the two states were sparring over disputed border, and the administrative fate of the Naga-dominated Tuensang frontier was unclear. Foreign secretary Kaul was skeptical of Nagaland accepting common governorship with concerns that Nehru's 'viceregal' presence could worsen the security situation, despite—or because of—the latter's preference for heightened use of force. Nehru's demands even risked decreasing the MEA's writ in the northeast that it commanded since independence.

Nehru took Chaliha in confidence, and rubbished Nagaland's concerns. He conceded that the NEC Bill must not be introduced in the parliament simultaneously with the Assam Reorganisation Bill to respect Assamese sensitivities. But in a letter to the home minister, he asserted that 'Nagaland should be included whether it agrees or not'.[21] If Nagaland didn't join, New Delhi should leave a seat available for it to join whenever it wants to do so in future, Nehru argued. To make it work, he added, the Council 'must be seen to have a fairly good stock of carrots and a reasonably sized stick'.[22] Specifically, Nehru sought control over the 4-billion-rupees budget for the northeastern region to use it as 'investment in any of the council units on the advice of the Council'.[23] In a hint of bribing Naga communities with cash, Nehru held that the Nagas 'who are a very practical people, might wish to reconsider their stand'.[24] What Nehru wouldn't permit as 'douceur being offered' was an 'eventual special constitutional benefit for the State of Nagaland as "a final settlement of the Naga problem" if they agree to join the Council.'[25] If they still refused to accept, then Gandhi had to pressure deputy minister S C Jamir and the Nagaland Chief minister to 'fall in line'.[26]

On 6 July 1971, as India prepared for war with Pakistan, Gandhi greenlighted Nehru's demands. He became the sole governor of all northeastern states and, as a compromise, the Council's chairpersonship went to a cabinet minister. Blamed of empire-building, Nehru flippantly told the home minister that 'I am too lazy to want to be an Emperor; and if I wanted an Empire, I would choose a less primitive one'.[27] In his view, the region's core problems emanated from Nagaland. Not only did the Naga underground need a stiff response, but even mainstream politicians required tough handling.

Nehru's strained relationships with Jamir, who led negotiations for Nagaland's statehood in 1960, and former member of the Naga peace mission JP Narayan are instructive. Soon after becoming governor, Nehru complained that Jamir was too critical of army operations. Jamir claimed that such ops breached the 1964 ceasefire, were conducted without the chief minister's permission thereby undermining civil government, that the 'army always tell lies', and if such operations didn't cease, 'we Nagas will all unite once again against the Indian government'.[28] As a Naga leader, Jamir maintained contact with the underground and sought political resolution. He often criticised Nehru[29] who advocated liberal use of force under AFSPA.[30]

JP Narayan left the Naga peace mission in 1967 after Gandhi became prime minister and when she appointed Nehru governor. But his advocacy for reconciliation earned him respect in Naga society. After two years, JP visited Nagaland on 1-4 August 1969. During his stay, where he met Naga leaders across the spectrum, Kohima witnessed violence by armed Nagas that cost several lives. In response, JP appealed for peace, ruled out independence, and proposed more talks with the underground.[31]

For Nehru, JP's utterances 'set back the political climate' and ignited feelings that if the underground used force, it could bring New Delhi to the negotiations table (again).[32] This was unacceptable for Nehru. His position on talks was clear: 'we are not anxious to have any more talks with anybody ... and that we are not prepared, in any event, to go beyond the 1960 agreement' that led to statehood for Nagaland.[33] He sought 'complete liquidation' of the

Naga underground, and noted that negotiations could only be held among equals.[34] The Naga movement, he argued, was desperate and divided, as reflected by their attacks during JP's visit. But more than the attacks, it was JP's advocacy for talks that rankled Nehru.

JP's Nagaland visit occurred during a windfall for the Indian forces. On 11 April 1969, Dusoi Chakesang, a 'Lt. Gen.' and Commander-in-Chief of the Naga army in 1960, and deputy chief in 1958–60, was captured along with 75 fighters and handed over to India by Burma.[35] 'Dignified' and 'highly intelligent', Chakesang offered critical intelligence. 'The local Burmese commanders who were usually paid some cash, co-operated and sometimes, actually provided them with guides', Chakesang revealed.[36] But Rangoon's desire to improve ties with India, and Tatmadaw's belief that Indian Nagas were inciting and arming Burmese Nagas ('not correct') made them take action.[37]

Unlike the Indian army, Dusoi noted, Burmese troops were 'inhuman' and 'fond of looting'.[38] When being marched to jail, the Burmese army escort shot dead three Naga prisoners 'in cold blood', and took wrist watches, personal belongings, and 14,000 rupees in cash after the group's surrender.[39] Dusoi informed Indian interrogators that the Nagas and Chinese were 'poles' apart and the former will 'never accept the communist way of life'.[40] He underscored that though the time was 'ripe' for a peaceful settlement, 'there can be no settlement without Phizo'.[41] Chakesang supported JP's conciliatory pitch.

But for Nehru, Phizo's group was 'microscopic' with 'no more people than can be counted on the fingers of two hands', all of whom were 'freebooters whose capacity for productive work is limited'.[42] Instead of New Delhi talking to Phizo, the Nagas should be grateful to India for defending against Chinese aggression and offering them money for development 'and generally to play about with'.[43] Nehru believed that JP belonged to a 'historical' school of thought that dealt with the Naga issue since its inception and believed in dialogue. Such a conciliatory approach undermined the Nagaland state government, often rubbished as an Indian 'puppet'.[44] Instead, Nehru saw himself as belonging to the 'normalisation' school that sought to deal with Nagaland like other Indian state 'except for certain privileges it enjoys because of the primitive nature of its tribal population'.[45] If anything, Nehru preferred that the Indian media stop giving 'as much prominence' to Nagaland, as it gave 'psychological aid and comfort' to separatists.[46] Gandhi agreed with him.

But Nehru's hardline approach was as much a failure as JP's push for dialogue. In 1973, Nehru was posted to London as India's high commissioner. He was replaced by Lallan Prasad Singh, a career bureaucrat who reversed Nehru's hardline policies. There was realisation in the system, which was also dealing with Mizo rebels, that Nehru's tactics drove the Naga 'movement more underground and strengthened the hands of the extremist factions'.[47] After their initial setback, the Naga rebels recovered and 'started hitting back at the Security Forces'.[48] Protests by regional stakeholders and a worsening security situation ensured that the NEC was watered down. Chief ministers retained political authority, and secret talks with the Naga and Mizo rebels picked up.

Singh's efforts led to the signing of the Shillong Accord on 11 November 1975, shortly after the Emergency was imposed. In a letter to Nehru on 12 April 1976, Singh noted that though the future may prove him wrong—as it shortly did—he believed that India had entered an 'era of peace' in Nagaland.[49] There was a problem though. Singh ensured that Phizo, a foreign national, was not permitted join the talks with the Liaison Committee of the Naga Peace Committee (NPC) led by Kenneth Kerhuo.[50] But Phizo's repudiation of the accord coupled with the escape to China of underground leaders Isak Swu and Th. Muivah in 1974/75 risked undermining the effort.[51] Even though the Burma army 'mauled' some of these groups, Muivah and Swu's fighters sheltered in Kachin territory, and all of them were ardent Phizo-supporters.

Indian intelligence kept a close eye on these relationships. Phizo held several secret meetings with Swu, Muivah, Mowu Angami, other supporters and even Mizo leader Laldenga in Paris during 1968–72. Indian spies noted that after Kathmandu, 'Paris has become a centre where tribal insurgent leaders have been meeting Phizo'.[52] Muivah left for China in 1966 but remained abroad since. In 1970 he moved to Tirana, Albania, where he lived for a few months, and from there he traveled to France. In January 1971, before the crackdown in East

Pakistan, Phizo, along with an ISI Liaison Officer, met with Muivah and Swu in Paris. Here, Phizo ordered the airlift of 77 Naga rebels (out of about 230) undergoing guerilla training in East Pakistan to training camps in Yunnan, China. The disbandment of Pakistan's Guerilla Warfare Training Centre in East Pakistan necessitated the move. Muivah was entrusted with the job.[53] By June 1971, Phizo decided that whereas open support to Pakistan 'would not be viewed with favour in any democratic country', the Federal Government of Nagaland (FGN) should avoid 'hurt[ing] the feelings of Pakistan', which was the first country to support them.[54] In 1971's aftermath, most Naga fighters began to operate from Yunnan and from Kachin territory.[55]

Even though Indian intelligence assessed that Phizo was frustrated by his inability to garner support at the UN, he continued to command respect among Naga fighters.[56] These fighters termed the NPC 'arch-traitors' and promised to fight with Chinese and Kachin support. This was a problem.[57] The NPC recommended travelling to London, where Phizo lived, and convincing Phizo of accepting the accord. But for such a visit to happen, Nehru's support was critical. Unimpressed, Nehru advised L P Singh not to bank on Phizo changing his mind. But he did send a London-based *Hindustan Times* journalist to contact Phizo on behalf of the Indian government.[58] Initially reluctant, Phizo met the journalist at his Bromley residence and emphasised that 'any day' he'll meet the prime minister of India 'in India or elsewhere without any conditions' and was open to accepting the Indian constitution.[59] The journalist noted that Phizo wanted to build his legacy as the greatest Naga leader who settled the problem. Nehru viewed this as Phizo's intransigence and warned against sending NPC's 'wild men' to London.[60]

But the situation in Nagaland was turbulent enough, despite the accord, for Gandhi to approve the visit in February 1977. The NPC tried convincing Phizo for a month in vain.[61] Phizo didn't change his demand of meeting Gandhi personally, and they told her as much in a letter from London.[62] Now, Nehru felt vindicated. Not only did India's outreach to Phizo fail, Muivah and Swu were planning a long insurgency. Just as the Naga delegates were trying to convince Phizo, R&AW intercepted communications from the Muivah and Swu group in Burma claiming that they didn't have direct channel with Phizo, but were following his guidelines offered during their stay in China to use eastern Naga areas as a staging base for operations.[63]

A batch of 200 fighters had left for China with Muivah, but the Burma-based groups were struggling due to the 'arrival of 300 Burmese commando troops'.[64] The R&AW station chief in London, who coordinated and monitored the visit, authored a top-secret note in March 1977 explaining how Phizo fell out with the NPC, and that the delegate's demand for staying in London to receive Gandhi's response to meet Phizo was 'ridiculous'.[65] Nehru was triumphant, and offered unsolicited advice to New Delhi that none of the returning NPC members should be 'received by any person of consequence in New Delhi'.[66] In January 1980, Swu, Muivah, and Khaplang formed the National Socialist Council of Nagaland (NSCN), and continued anti-state violence. The road to Shillong was circular, and the Naga conflict, unending.

'Victory is with the God'

Laldenga was torn about the way forward. Should he enter peace talks with India, or continue armed struggle? India's anti-MNF operations in Bangladesh after 1971 dislocated Mizo rebels to Arakan. At one point, SFF units almost captured Laldenga.[67] In Burma, the Tatmadaw conducted operations in Chin state to deny sanctuary and space.[68] But presence of multiple other groups including Burmese communists, the Arakan Independence Army, the ANLF, and Mujahids (Rohingyas) offered about 1,000 MNF cadre space and time to reconsider strategy (even though nearly 2,400 cadre surrendered to India's 'liberalized offer' of amnesty until early 1972).[69] By mid-1972 the Arakan-based Mizo rebels were jointly fighting with communists against the junta.[70] Later that year, they supported the anti-Dacca Muslim Bangla Movement in Chittagong. India's high commissioner in Dacca clarified the 'hard fact' that 'anti-Bangladesh elements in Arakan have been reinforced by the dissident Mizo and Chakma malcontents'.[71]

Creation of the clandestine Muslim Bangla Radio by the Akyab (Sittwe)-based Pakistani consul, the presence of *Razakars* (paramilitary

165

outfits created during Operation Searchlight), and reports of CIA-supplied arms and ammunitions for such groups had the potential to destabilise the Mujib government and empower Mizo activism.[72] Indian intelligence suggested that the US ship 'Manhattan', meant to deliver food and anchored 40 miles off Chittagong was, in reality, a 'center for CIA espionage activities', and that the Americans were active not only in Arakan, but also in the Sundarbans.[73]

There was a kernel of truth to Indian concerns about Pakistani activism in Arakan. In April 1972, the ISI flew Laldenga and his colleague Zoramthanga from Arakan to Rangoon (escaping detection by Rangoon) and took them to Karachi to meet with Zulfiqar Ali Bhutto. Here, Laldenga erred. He sought asylum in Pakistan to the Pakistani prime minister's disappointment. Worried that his presence on Pakistani soil could derail talks with India and Bangladesh on the prisoners of war issue, Bhutto confined the Mizos to a small compound outside Rawalpindi without amenities.[74] Laldenga's hands were tied.

In September 1973, with few allies left, Laldenga ordered Zoramthanga to travel to Afghanistan after the ISI cleared the visit. He was to meet the Indian defence attaché and R&AW station chief in Kabul.[75] Inspired by Gandhi's talks with Sheikh Abdullah in Kashmir and with NPC in Nagaland, Laldenga wanted Zoramthanga to develop a direct, secret line with New Delhi.[76] This occurred parallel to the rise of the Mizo Union in local elections and its merger with the Indian National Congress. The 'Kabul channel' helped both sides manage turbulence in Mizoram and paved the long, tortuous road to the 1986 accord.

There are three reasons why it took 15 years to sign the accord, and why it continues to endure. First, though Laldenga reconsidered strategy after 1971, it took him time to develop consensus within MNF to accept talks. On this count, the emergence of the Brig. T Sailo-led Mizo People's Conference (MPC) in 1975 complicated local politics. It occurred in parallel to mass displacement of Chakma and Hajong communities from Bangladesh to Mizoram. This made Laldenga's job to convince hardline MNF cadres to talk with New Delhi onerous. Second, the situation in Arakan exploded in 1978, with the junta targeting Rohingyas and entering a tense standoff with

Bangladesh. This made Arakan unsafe as a staging base for the MNF. Third, the accord endured thanks to the social cohesiveness of Mizos (unlike intra-community differences among Nagas), wherein once a consensus emerged, it was easier to deliver.

Why did Laldenga opt for a channel with India through Kabul? The outreach was meant to pave the way for a settlement. Bhutto's 1973 cold shoulder to Laldenga was followed by a series of assassinations of Indian officials including a failed attempt against India's Lt. Gov. in Mizo hills on 10 March 1974. This heightened New Delhi's threat perception of the MNF. For the next three years, despite MNF's depleting strength and increasing isolation, the security situation remained tense. The 'Kabul channel' ensured that each side was aware of the other's intention and prevented indiscriminate violence.

To monitor the situation in Burma, R&AW opened a consulate in Chiang Mai, Thailand in 1972. The sole purpose of this consulate was, and still is, to monitor political and military developments in Burma with an eye on China and the Golden Triangle. In the 1970s and 1980s, the Chiang Mai consulate with support from the Bangkok embassy opened channels with Burmese rebels including Arakan-based outfits who were helping the MNF. Chiang Mai became a frontline outpost to operationalise the Kabul channel. As an official put it, Chiang Mai is as important for India as Beirut is for Western intelligence agencies.[77]

Such an intelligence-led channel with MNF after Bangladesh's liberation was accompanied by the Assam chief secretary's demand to declare the MNF 'unlawful' under the UAPA (1967).[78] Former governor Nehru declared the outfit unlawful in 1968 but didn't extend it after 1970. For the chief secretary, the killing of government officials by the MNF in 1973–74, meant to 'pressurize and demoralize the Government servants', was having the desired effect.[79] The MNF, he believed, was using a policy of 'carrots and rods' to win over the people of Mizoram as well as government servants to achieve full secession.[80] Leaflets issued by the MNF in 1973 (falsely) declared that in secret talks India sought peace only after declaring the Mizo 'a downtrodden people'.[81] The leaflets were signed: 'victory is with the God'.[82] On 11 March 1974, the Indian army sought early imposition of UAPA to effectively contain the situation. Agreeable, the chief secretary offered land in Shillong to jail detainees whose numbers were expected to rise.[83] Even surrendered MNF cadre, the official claimed, were misusing their freedom to undertake violence.[84]

But the IB shot down the idea of reimposing UAPA. Such a move, it argued, apart from offering 'short term tactical advantage … may not in the long run be conducive to tackling the overall insurgency situation in Mizoram'.[85] The IB cautioned that the Lt. Governor attack was done without Laldenga's approval, by elements who wanted to push India into taking a hardline approach to scuttle talks, give the MNF undue 'importance', and place them 'at par with the Naga Federal Government, which is far more well-organized and well-equipped'.[86]

Given that most MNF cadre were Arakan-based, declaring MNF unlawful would not affect most fighters, and risked pushing surrendered militants to the underground. Leaders of the Mizo Union and Mizoram Pradesh Congress, the IB noted, held talks with the MNF. Even though the outcome of these talks was uncertain, declaring the MNF unlawful could derail such efforts. There was also a risk that Mizo authorities, not on board with the chief secretary and the army's demand for a hardline policy, could resist UAPA just like the Nagaland government did.[87]

In this context, Laldenga once again dispatched Zoramthanga to Kabul from where the latter flew to Bangkok.[88] With talks between the Naga underground and New Delhi pressing forward, Laldenga was determined to leave Pakistan. In Thailand, Zoramthanga finalised details of a meeting between Laldenga and Indian intelligence officials in a third country. On 20 August, travelling on a Pakistani passport without fully briefing the ISI, Laldenga flew to Geneva and stayed in a hotel under the alias 'Peter Lee'. In a series of clandestine meetings with a R&AW officer Laldenga agreed to author a note for Gandhi to formally iterate his desire for peaceful negotiations and agreed that 'the solution of the Mizoram political problem will have to be achieved within the Constitution of India'.[89] He wanted Gandhi to help him escape Pakistan 'for good', return to India, enable contact with his underground fighters, and give him time to convince them to give up arms. 'I am confident and can assure you that I would succeed in bringing them over to my line of thinking for a settlement of the problem', he promised Gandhi.[90] Gandhi greenlighted the operation. Soon after, R&AW gave the MNF 15,000 USD to leave Pakistan.[91]

On 24 January 1976, Laldenga landed in New Delhi. He was put up in a bungalow in Gulmohar Park with his family and received top intelligence officers and ministers to build the momentum for an accord. After some back-and-forth, Laldenga held an MNF convention in Calcutta in April to bring the entire MNF underground to the mainstream and sign an accord whose details were hammered out in February. The convention was partly successful and led to the signing of the agreement on 1 July wherein the MNF agreed that 'Mizoram is an integral part of India'.[92] The only thing left now was to end violence. This took another ten years. Though Laldenga succeeded in signing the accord in 1976, his presence in New Delhi raised suspicion among Mizo hardliners. Like the Shillong accord signed just a few months prior, the so-called 'February Accord' failed to deliver results. Stuck in Gulmohur Park, Laldenga struggled to get his comrades to disarm. Fissures in the movement deepened.

Laldenga's logic of suing for peace was clear. But why did New Delhi invest in him? Because the MPC emerged as a third political force in Mizoram under Sailo. A decorated Indian army officer, Sailo mobilised Mizo opinion by formally complaining to Gandhi about the use of excessive force and grouping of villages. His advocacy, within India's constitutional fabric, aroused public support, offering the MPC political wings. But Sailo's timing was inopportune. The MPC undermined MNF's advocacy of secession and threatened Congress' electoral base.[93] On 3 June 1976, before the agreement was formalised with Laldenga, Sailo was arrested under the Maintenance of Internal Security Act for undermining the peace process. 'If I had joined the Congress in the beginning, everything would've been completely different', he remarked.[94]

The failure of the 1976 agreement to reduce violence, Laldenga's isolation in New Delhi, and an uptick in Chakma and Hajong displacement after a coup in Dacca in 1975 (next chapter) stymied the Congress' hold in Mizoram. In June 1978, Sailo became chief minister for six months followed by president's rule but returned to power in 1979 and completed a full term until 1984. Sailo's electoral appeal, built on anti-Chakma sentiment across Mizoram (R&AW was arming sections of Chakma communities in Tripura to target post-coup Bangladesh) and the promise of service delivery, challenged Laldenga and Gandhi alike. Gandhi's ouster in 1977 enabled Sailo's rise.

Talks with Laldenga collapsed in March 1978, creating a 'vertical split' in the MNF with half of the outfit—figures who Laldenga sought to bring on board—walking away from pro-Laldenga loyalists.[95] The MNF-MPC rivalry intensified with attacks by the former reigniting requests from Mizoram-based officers and Sailo in March 1979: (a) 'Orders for Suspension of operations by the Security Forces should be immediately revoked', (b) 'MNF be declared unlawful' under UAPA, and (c) 'Army strength in Mizoram be increased to the 1975 level'.[96] Opposed to the Gandhi-Laldenga 'understanding', Desai agreed to Sailo's request. On 8 July 1979, MNF was declared unlawful and Laldenga was arrested by the Delhi police from Gulmohur Park.[97] In a role reversal, the home ministry now blamed Laldenga for scuttling peace 'for his own personal motive'.[98]

The MNF's 'Quit Mizoram Order' in June 1979 offered a trigger to impose UAPA. The order demanded non-Mizos leave the state before 1 July, and declared that:

Killing of non-Mizos in Mizoram is permissible. Seizure and destruction of their goods and properties are also permissible. Any non-Mizo still remaining behind is to be killed. Don't hesitate to kill non-Mizos save the person under the employ of Churches.[99]

The R&AW and IB also witnessed renewed Chinese support to the MNF's 108-fighters strong faction. This group visited China between 28 July 1975–3 January 1976, received military, political, wireless communications, and medical training, was paid 36,407 USD and 91,000 Burmese kyat, and received an assortment of Chinese arms and ammunition.[100] Another group received an assortment of weapons, 32,000 USD, 62,000 Burmese kyat, and 50 gold chains weighing 1 'tola' each.[101] For New Delhi, this was unacceptable. The idea of a settlement with Sailo, not Laldenga, took root in the Desai government.

The MNF blamed three individuals for fomenting disunity: Sailo, Biakchhunga, the Mizo Army Chief who sought to replace Laldenga with Sailo's support, and the Subsidiary Intelligence Bureau's Assistant Director Ajit K. Doval, who did the actual scheming.[102] Doval, who went on to become DIB (2004–05) and National Security Advisor (2014–ongoing), seeded confusion between Laldenga and Biakchhunga, whereas Sailo authorized the army to ambush China-backed factions in the hope that it would marginalise Laldenga, strengthen a compromised Biakchhunga, and help New Delhi curate peace on its terms.[103] The only problem was that the Indian army couldn't contain China-backed Mizos, a failure that strengthened Laldenga. Unsurprisingly, Biakchhunga was ousted. Such failure ensured that when Gandhi returned to power in 1980, Laldenga's position in Mizo politics remained strong despite Sailo's rise. Keen to keep the MPC under check, the Congress struck a deal with MNF. This was a pattern that Gandhi followed elsewhere too. In Punjab, Gandhi aligned with separatists to outflank the Sikh conservative Shiromani Akali Dal only to ignite an insurgency. In Mizoram, such politicking brought peace dividends.

Changes in the regional geopolitical environment also necessitated rapprochement. In 1978, Bangladeshi strongman Zia-ur-Rahman restarted support for the MNF. As detailed in the next chapter, for the first time since their 1972 ouster from Bangladesh, armed Mizos found shelter closer to Mizoram and a state sponsor. Doval's push to sow discord within MNF with Sailo's support, then, was not just to buttress a new political compact between the non-Congress central and state governments, but also to blunt cross-border sponsorship. Peeved at India's support to Chakma-dominated Shanti Bahini that was inflicting casualties on the Bangladesh army, Zia-ur-Rahman sought leverage by rearming Mizos and Nagas. Such support was to counter India, and fight Chakma rebels who were also at odds with the MNF.

Often entering India from the Tripura and Mizoram border, the predominantly Buddhist Chakmas were not welcome in Mizoram. That they sought rehabilitation and requested that Gandhi create a separate administrative unit in west Mizoram stoked inter-community and inter-insurgent tensions. On 15 November 1971, two weeks before India went to war with Pakistan, local Chakma leaders associated with the Congress wrote a letter to Gandhi and the home and defence ministers to seek support against Bangladeshi persecution and Mizo anger.[104] There was sympathy for their cause in New Delhi in the 1970s. To counter such trends, Zia supported MNF factions that sought to fight with or without Laldenga. Problematically, Zia sponsored Mizo rebels despite reaching an understanding with Desai to cut such support. The move instilled enduring mistrust in New Delhi about his motives.

The other complicating factor was a brewing crisis between Bangladesh and Burma. Ne Win's policies pushed over 150,000 Rohingyas from northern Arakan to Chittagong.[105] According to Nurul Islam, chairman of the Arakan Rohingya National Organisation, who took up activism in 1974, 'the situation in 1978 was dire. Ne Win was pushing us hard and killing people indiscriminately … even though there was relatively more solidarity among Rakhine Buddhists and our people then than there was later'.[106] As 'guests', Arakan-based Mizo rebels often arbitered conflict between the Mujahids and Rakhine-Buddhists—even if that meant using force.[107] In 1975, after Zia's takeover, Indian intelligence assessed that Dacca would arm Rohingyas in Burma. Distracted by domestic issues, Zia didn't do this. But in 1978, when thousands of Rohingyas crossed over, Zia threatened Rangoon with war if it didn't accept repatriation.[108] One Bangladeshi official was candid:

> If a peaceful solution isn't found quickly, the only possible solution will be war … the best way for us to cope with the problem will be to arm the refugees and help them form a liberation front … [to] fight for their homes and their language and their dignity. I'm sure Rangoon will understand that.[109]

Zia's threat was credible. If he could arm anti-India rebels, doing the same with Burma was easier. Bangladesh's warning to Ne Win, coupled with Burma's self-imposed isolation, paved the way for the 1978 repatriation agreement in July. The agreement confirmed that Burma recognised the Rohingya as legal residents of Burma.[110] But for India the crisis raised a different problem. Zia relocated the MNF to CHT. Settled in power and now leading the newly formed

Bangladesh Nationalist Party (BNP) with close ties to the US, Pakistan, and China, in Indian eyes Zia was trying to exert more power than subcontinental realities permitted.

If Dacca armed Rohingyas, it could complicate India's position in Rangoon, especially if NeWin sought Indian intervention with Dacca. During Gandhi's tenure, despite operational underperformance and corruption in its officer corps, the Burma army did help secure parts of Chin territory against the MNF and Naga outfits. Gandhi wanted to ensure that India-Burma relations didn't turn hostile, and to that effect, in 1973 offered to deny former prime minister Nu asylum if that irritated Ne Win. Nu had been leading an armed struggle against Ne Win from the Thai-border. Ne Win didn't object to Gandhi offering Nu asylum insofar as Nu didn't get politically active from his abode in Bihar.[111] It worked. Years later, New Delhi noted that Nu's rebellion became 'more an irritant than a threat' after the latter's arrival to India.[112]

The 1978 Burma-Bangladesh agreement heightened India's worries about Zia's ambitions. Zia's 1981 assassination, his successor's reduction of support to the MNF, and Sailo's rise in Aizawl paved the way for reconciliation between Laldenga and Gandhi. On 30 June 1986, the Mizoram Peace Accord was signed. On 21 August 1986, Laldenga won the elections and became chief minister, putting an end to the 'buai'. But elsewhere, the situation was worsening. Punjab was reeling with Sikh radicalism and violence, and so was Assam. In their focus on the Naga and Mizo insurgencies, India's leaders overlooked how their decisions to end violence in these regions bolstered Assamese nationalism. In 1979, parallel to the Mizo movement taking a violent turn and the Shillong accord failing to deliver, an anti-foreigner sons-of-the-soil uprising broke out in Assam.

Nellie

Gandhi's partisan peacemaking in Mizo and Naga areas was informed by the twin logics of expanding the state's writ and deepening the Congress' electoral hold in the northeast. In Assam, such partisanship led to the massacre of Bengali Muslims in Nellie followed by an insurgency under the popular slogan of '*Joi Aai Axom*' ('Glory to Mother Assam').[113] On 18 February 1983, sixteen villages in Nagaon district witnessed a six-hour massacre of people believed to be Bangladeshi Muslim migrants. Officially, over 2,000 were killed, but unofficial estimates stand at 10,000.[114] Apart from underscoring the anti-foreigner tumult brewing since 1960, Nellie demonstrated that Bangladesh's liberation didn't solve India's woes. The realities and myth of migration from Bangladesh in combination with creating new states, and alleged inclusion of Muslim 'foreigners' into the electoral roll by the Congress, triggered an agitation in 1979. The 1983 massacre, then, occurred in the lead-up to the 1983 state elections that Gandhi announced despite lack of popular desire for them (termed a 'gory farce' by a police officer then posted in Assam).[115]

There were portents of these troubles long before 1971. Soon after the 'Project PIP' ended in 1969 and the foreigners tribunals were shut down, B.K. Nehru explained to the president of India how the situation remained volatile. Though Naxalite activity in Bengali-dominated areas of Cachar and Goalpara came to a 'full stop', an increase in the state's population was a problem.[116] Nehru assessed:

> Our density of population is still comparatively low, but we are, of course, trying hard to destroy that advantage by doing nothing about birth control. We are also unwillingly adding to our population through migration from East Pakistan of both Hindus and Moslems. The influx of Pakistani Moslems has, it is generally held, been reduced but there is really no means of telling at what rate they are coming in, for since the change in policy last year and the abolition of the Foreigners Tribunals, there is no means of detecting or deporting any Pakistanis who succeed in reaching the interior.[117]

The note underscored Nehru's sympathy towards Assamese concerns and explains why he pushed for a stronger NEC with Chaliha agreeable to the idea. Though the scale of migration in Assam was 'fairly small compared to what is happening in West Bengal', Nehru claimed that the 'loud clamour that was raised when Pakistani Moslems were being evicted from Assam' did not strengthen 'communal harmony' that the government sought.[118] Such political trends deepened by the end of the decade in context of the 1971 war and post-Emergency politics.

Leaders of the 'Assam movement', especially Prafulla Kumar Mahanta and Bhrigu Phukan, sought to prevent enfranchisement of 'foreigners'.[119] This meant identifying and deporting people who entered Assam after partition. In their first meeting with Gandhi in February 1980, AASU leaders and the newly formed All Assam Gana Sangram Parishad asked New Delhi to detect and delete names of those who illegally entered Assam based on the 1951 census dateline.[120] This demand contradicted the understanding reached according to the Nehru-Liaquat Pact and Gandhi's agreement with Mujib that anyone who entered India before 24 March 1971 will not be considered Bangladeshi.[121]

Even Nepali migrants whose numbers spiked from 350,000 in 1971 to nearly 500,000 in 1980 were unwelcome, deadlocking AASU-Gandhi talks.[122] This saga evolved against the backdrop of electoral competition between Assamese parties, Congress, communists, and the Janata coalition with the Bharatiya Jana Sangh—BJP in 1977—at its forefront.[123] Paranoid about external interference, Gandhi and the communists blamed the 'foreign hand' in stoking separatism and the BJP for communal politicking. Gandhi and Mahanta held three rounds of talks between February–April 1980 followed by formal meetings between AASU and Governor LP Singh in 1981, but the deadlock remained.

The Assam movement was marked by heightened violence. Between March 1978, when the Janata party candidate Golap Borbora became chief minister, and March 1983, days after the Nellie massacre when Congress' Hiteshwar Saikia came to power, there were long hauls of president's rule in Assam riddled with anti-foreigner violence, punctuated by short periods of elected leadership.[124] The massacre occurring in context of the 1983 elections, with allegations that a politicised state police deliberately let the incidents occur. Decades later, former Assam police chief Kanwar Pal Singh Gill claimed that the police were not partisan, and he did issue orders to prevent the massacre.[125]

There is a concrete bridge on River Kopili in Nellie. It is a choking point for Nellie. I was constantly on the move that day but placed a CRPF [Central Reserve Police Force] platoon on that bridge. But the SP, Nagaon, thought he was a wiser man, moved it from there. That was a blunder.[126]

Gill blames Borbora for 'using' the agitating students to take Muslims off the electoral list to obviate the Congress' return in Assam, thereby intensifying communal divide that led to the massacre.[127] Four days after the massacre, Gandhi visited Nellie. Just before she landed, the state police and paramilitary allegedly sanitised the massacre site by hurriedly covering a ditch full of dead bodies with mud.[128] When pressed by the *New York Times* on whether she accepted moral responsibility for the massacre, Gandhi shot back: 'Why should we? It is the agitators who are responsible. They may not like the elections, but do they have the right to stop them?'.[129] Could the killings have been prevented if she didn't call for elections in the middle of the agitation? 'It has been happening since 1980', she responded.[130] Later, in an interview with the *Financial Times*, she made a more candid and controversial claim underscoring the brutal realpolitik of Indian politics: 'one has to let such events take their course before stepping in'.[131] The massacre's causes are so sensitive that the TP Tewary Commission Report, created to investigate the incident and list measures to prevent its recurrence, has never been published. Instead, the Congress was back in power with Saikia as chief minister days after the massacre.

But the long-term political beneficiary of the massacre were Hindu nationalists, carefully biding their time and building organisational strength across the northeast. The 1968 Karimganj riots helped the BJP deepen its footprint in Assam. Wary of Muslim 'infiltrators' but supportive of Hindu 'refugees' from East Pakistan/Bangladesh (something the BJP and AASU disagreed on at an ideological level), the BJP supported AASU during the agitation.[132] In 1982, the Vishwa Hindu Parishad organised the 'Purvanchal Hindu Sammelan' that mobilised 8,000 supporters from across the region. The massacre and its aftereffects strengthened the BJP's anti-infiltration politics.[133] As Shekhar Gupta, an Indian journalist who covered the massacre noted, 'thanks to the lack of political pragmatism among the AASU leadership, the RSS elements have been able to operate at a different and more political level, succeeding in solely influencing some of the leaders in mofussil towns'.[134]

So, when the Congress introduced the Illegal Migrants (Determination by Tribunals) Act (IMDT) in December 1983, which listed procedures to detect and evict illegal migrants from Assam, the BJP was able to shape the politics around it. Parliamentary debates demonstrate how contested the issue of cut-off year for deportation was. Though government cited international law to establish 1971 as the cut-off year, the BJP resisted and sought to treat anyone who entered India illegally before or after 1971 as such. BJP parliamentarian Ram Jethmalani opposed the bill on sovereign and legal grounds: 'What right has any Foreign Minister to say that million persons who occupied our territory illegally will continue to occupy that territory illegally?'.[135] Such advocacy encouraged Assamese nationalism and communalism alike.

The communists allied with Congress. Rajshahi-born CPI(M) leader Arun K. Roy, representing Dhanbad, Jharkhand, acerbically countered:

> I would like to ask the BJP people who are now in the forefront: what is their concept of 'Akhand Bharat'? Do we consider a Bangladeshi as a foreigner, seriously, even if he comes with a passport? Let us ask our soul: have we reconciled ourselves to the partition of India in such a way that we consider the Bangladeshi as a Foreigner even to the extent of thinking that his entry is detrimental to our country? There should be a limit to everything.[136]

For decades, RSS mouthpieces such as the *Organiser,* and Assam-based *Aalok* increased anxieties around Muslim 'infiltration' into West Bengal and Assam.[137] The IMDT became a piece of legislation around which the BJP could organise political resistance.

Gandhi's assassination in 1984 changed the calculus. Her son Rajiv was keen to find a solution in Assam and not cede ground to the Hindu-right. Despite Saikia's removal being a key AASU demand, Rajiv went ahead with negotiations.[138] He agreed to remove Saikia and paved the way for Mahanta to become chief minister in December 1985.[139] Charges against 'agitators' for igniting the massacre were dropped.[140] In return, the Asom Gana Parishad (AGP), Mahanta's party, accepted 1966 as baseline for granting citizenship with the provision for disenfranchisement of those who entered Assam in 1966–71.[141] Given that migration peaked during 1963–65 when the Shastri government issued a couple of secret orders to settle migrants in Assam, this was a deal Mahanta could build consensus around. Such compromises with figures previously deemed anti-India meant that the Congress understood the limits of its influence.

But unlike the Mizoram Accord, the Assam Accord did not deliver peace. In fact, Indian concerns about a dormant separatist streak within the Assam agitation, came to the fore *after* the accord. Whereas Laldenga succeeded in keeping the MNF's internal politicking in check, the AGP crumbled under its contradictions as Mahanta and Phukan turned form being allies in agitation to rivals in power.[142] As state home minister, Phukan secretly supported ULFA, led by a young footballer named Paresh Baruah and his ally Arabinda Rajkhowa.[143] The ULFA's origins are obscure with some claiming that it was founded in 1979 and others pinning its creation and rise to after 1983.[144] But what's certain is that ULFA briefly became the best organised and lethal insurgent outfit in entire South and Southeast Asia. Supported by the National Socialist Council of Nagaland-Isak Muivah (NSCN-IM), ULFA cadres were trained by Kachin rebels. The first batch, led by Baruah, crossed over to KIO territory in 1986 followed by another group under the Rajkhowa's leadership.[145]

Phukan's link with ULFA was meant to outflank Mahanta within the AGP and seek a better deal from the Congress. His power play was combined with New Delhi's own pressures against Mahanta. Ousted from power, the Assam Congress under Saikia was keen to make a comeback. In an interview with Sangeeta Barooah Pisharoty, Mahanta blamed the Congress for misusing R&AW (again) to exploit grievances among the Bodo communities seeking autonomy.[146] Pisharoty argues that senior Congress leaders claimed to have seen evidence of R&AW's creation of the Bodo Security Force (trained in army camps in Tezpur) to weaken the AGP.[147] Bodo communities protested two clauses of the Assam Accord: clause 6 that protected

'Assamese identity', and the clause to evict 'foreigners' that led to the eviction of some Bodos, sparking both identarian anxieties and anger over loss of land.[148] Bodo rebels capitalised on such grievances to seek 'sovereignty', but settled for a council within the union.[149]

Throughout the Assam movement and post-accord turmoil, ULFA operated from Kachin territory and opened outposts in Bhutan. A hard-pressed Mahanta allegedly resorted to extrajudicial methods of letting state police target family members of ULFA leaders, including Baruah, but failed to contain the insurgency. By 1988, Assam was reeling with full-scale separatism like Kashmir and Punjab. Congress' populism and electoral excesses coupled with the imposition of AFSPA in most of Assam and president's rule by 1990 meant that when the Cold War ended, New Delhi struggled to keep the country united. Apart from communalism and separatism, the Assam situation birthed multiple armed movements across the northeast. Far from being secure, the northeast became more divided after 1971.

Sons of the Soil

Political upheaval in Assam, occurring against the backdrop of Mizo and Naga insurgencies reignited existing nationalist and sub-nationalist movements across the region. Demand for autonomy by Bodos was echoed by communities in the Karbi Anglong district in central Assam. Concerned about Assamese domination, the Bodos sought administrative autonomy. Preexisting social grievances in Assam took a turn towards armed politics after the 1985 accord. For Mahanta, this was a Congress ploy to keep the AGP off balance after caving into their demands and accepting dissolution of the Saikia government. But such identity politics, with accompanying competition over financial resources and administrative power, was not the only reason why such movements took an armed turn. The weakening of India's democratic fabric during the Emergency, the rise of Hindutva, a struggling economy, and Bangladesh's openness to hosting anti-India insurgents with Pakistani and Chinese support meant there was both an opportunity to take up arms, and a promise that the Indian state would buckle under pressure.

Though promising a political solution to long-running (or newly emerging) insurgencies, such accords had a flip side of encouraging the use of organised violence by groups who sought to pressure New Delhi. In Punjab, the 1985 Rajiv-Longowal accord that sought to contain the Khalistan movement by giving into demands of the Shiromani Akali Dal, against whom the Congress supported radicals such as Bhindrawale, added to such precedents. Like in Assam, the Sikh insurgency picked up after 1985. Elsewhere, in 1987, the compromise of assembly elections ignited the Kashmir insurgency, which received cross-border support. The 1980s, in that sense, was a decade that marked a peculiar moment in the history of India with the outbreak of multiple insurgencies from the east to the west, and with the risk of the same in the south with polarisation and violence between Sri Lankan Tamils and Sinhalese communities spilling over into Tamil Nadu, a state with a history of language riots and identity-based mobilisation.

It is difficult to do justice to the myriad of armed movements that emerged in India's northeast during the 1980s, but the core dynamic was two-fold: a continuing push for autonomy or independence by Assamese, Nagas, Mizos, and Meitei communities fed into sub-nationalist movements that saw their struggle in relation to regional majorities. The demand for an independent Bodoland is a case in point. Concerned about discrimination by the AGP, radical elements of the All Bodo Students Union resorted to arms and created the Bodo Security Force that later became the National Democratic Front of Bodoland (NDFB).[150] In a tactical alliance with Naga and other outfits operating from Burma and Bhutan, the NDFB compounded India's security woes. Similarly, Karbi communities demanded a separate state for similar reasons. In 1979, just when the Assam movement took off, the Karbi Anglong People's Conference declared that they needed a separate state (within the union) in Karbi Anglong and North Cachar Hills.[151] The Karbi movement took a violent turn in the 1990s.

Cross-border migration and state-sponsorship, an ever-powerful factor in the politics of India's east, triggered similar anxieties in Tripura. Assam's experience and the success of the Mizo movement inspired an anti-foreigner movement against Bangladeshi migrants in

Tripura. In 1989, the National Liberation Front of Tripura (NLFT), a small but impactful militant group, began to shape state politics along exclusionary ethnic lines. Though ironic in light of its anti-Bangladeshi Muslim politics, the NLFT received covert support from sections of Bangladeshi intelligence. India's support for the Shanti Bahini continued to afford a tit-for-tat logic to Bangladesh's limited yet sustained support for such groups.[152]

Similar dynamics unfolded in Manipur. With a rich history of armed politics and powerful Meitei nationalism, Manipuri politics became divided (not neatly) along Meitei versus non-Meitei lines. The Naga hills of north Manipur were aligned with the Naga movement, whereas the southern Manipur belt was aligned with Zo-Kuki, Chin, and Mizo politics. These communities were at odds with the Meitei-dominated Imphal Valley and mobilised to unite to prevent discrimination from local majorities. As per a 1971 IB report on 'Separatist Tendencies amongst non-Naga Tribals of Manipur and their Unification Movement', the Kukis 'apprehended that the majority community i.e., the Meiteis might do [to them] what the Assamese did to the Nagas', and 'being afraid of exploitation and inferior status, these enlightened [Kuki] leaders started a movement to unify the non-Naga group of people under one banner'.[153]

The IB reported that the identification of Kukis with Mizos, especially after 1966 and the MNF's support to Kuki leaders, was a 'turning point in tribal politics in this region', with Kukis toying with the idea of a joint Kuki-Mizo union and accepting Churachandpur, Jiribam, Sadar Hills, and parts of Tamenglong being termed the 'Runbung area of Mizoram State'.[154] The problem for Kuki mobilisation was intra-community fissures. Hmars, for instance, sought more power in Kuki affairs, complicating relations with competing community members such as the Kipgens, Paites, and Baites.[155] Kuki groups had links with Burma-based outfits, and remained active during the 1980s. But the unification drive eroded after the Mizoram accord. In 1994, clashes between Naga and Kuki groups claimed hundreds of lives, where intra-community differences resulted in Kuki-Baite violence in 1997 led by the Kuki National Front and the Zo Revolutionary Army. Fought over land resources, including control over important narcotics trade routes, such inter-insurgent rivalry, and its exploitation by a dominant state, became routine in the northeast.[156]

Other movements that received a fillip in the late 1970s thanks to the post-Emergency political churn were Meitei-dominated groups in Manipur. Infused with left-wing political rhetoric, armed groups such as PREPAK, PLA-M, and KCP emerged in October 1977, September 1978, and April 1980 respectively. The PLA-M built upon the legacy of Irabat Singh, one of the first Manipuri communists to challenge the state of India in 1948–52 with Burmese communist support. The difference in the 1980s was that the left-wing rhetoric of such groups was infused with Meitei nationalism.[157] The term *Kangleipak* means 'dry land' in reference to Manipur's historical name.

Incensed by statehood to Nagaland, Manipuri identity politics centered around territorial integrity in relation to Nagaland. Expectedly, anti-state violence in Manipur led to the imposition of AFSPA in September 1980. Far from being a special measure to be applied selectively and for as short a period as possible, AFSPA became omnipresent in the northeast. For Pillai, who dealt with Manipuri politics both as home secretary and New Delhi's chief interlocutor with NSCN-IM, 'settlement of the Naga issue is key to peace in Manipur'.[158] But India's northeast became embroiled in armed politics and illicit finance.

The outburst of ethnically charged armed movements underscored the impact of cross-border migration, official antinomies, and regional political economies. Just as in Nagaland and Mizoram, where the politics of peacemaking was linked to the Congress' electoral strategies, or in Assam where manipulation of electoral rolls complicated state politics, Manipuri armed groups and their political fortunes became linked to those of the mainstream parties they secretly allied with and their ability to generate illicit profit via cross-border drug trade. Important in garnering votes using coercion or securing kinship alliances, Meitei armed groups engaged with the Manipur branch of the Congress or the BJP.[159] 'Don't go by the ideological rhetoric of these groups and parties, they'll partner with whoever is willing to offer them more money' says Pillai.[160]

Patronage from the ruling party in the state (who would ideally be in power in New Delhi too) is critical to ensure the logistical lines of illicit trade such groups engage in. Manipuri groups, for instance, moonlight as drug cartels while being card-carrying ideologues wanting to rid the state of 'drug vice' during the day.[161] Like cartels anywhere, their relationship with the state is marked by an uncomfortable but logical symbiosis of violence, threats, and unaccounted funds. Cross-border capabilities of such groups assist politicians in maintaining cash flows for individual and party-political purposes. In return, these groups receive patronage and protection, including the promise of suspension of operation agreements with the armed forces when their mainstream allies come to power. The irony of such illicit political economies (not limited to Manipur) is that in a perverse way, they make secessionists otherwise open to support from China, Pakistan, or Bangladesh structurally dependent on India's complicated democracy.

Conclusions

India launched Operation Bajrang against ULFA in November 1990 followed by Operation Rhino in September 1991. Rajiv Gandhi's attempt to contain separatism in Assam by co-opting student leaders, and his simultaneous attempt to undermine them after 1985 by encouraging non-Assamese communities to resist, created contradictory pressures that fueled violence instead of abating it. The final compromise that led to the signing of the Assam accord earmarked the baseline date for deporting migrants as 24 March 1971, but the baseline for conferring citizenship was agreed to be 1966 when migration peaked due to communal violence in Bengal and Assam. This allowed India to keep its promise to Bangladesh on returnees and demonstrates how migration influenced the domestic and international politics of India's near east.

But the accord's failure to contain violent separatism underscored the antinomies of Indian politics. Unlike the Nehru-era Congress that worked with regional powerbrokers, Indira and Rajiv opted for aggressive populisms, including tactical deals with religious radicals which undermined these accords. The bottom line of such politics was to confer respect and power to regional powerbrokers on the premise that they would respect the Constitution of India. That didn't happen.

Herein, success of the Mizoram Accord is instructive. On 17 September 1988, months after Laldenga became chief minister, New Delhi imposed the president's rule in Mizoram. The move was accompanied by the fostering of a split within the MNF by state Congress representatives and leaders.[162] The reason for this was linked to Rajiv's electoral ambitions, and associated insecurities in neighbouring Assam and Nagaland where insurgencies raged. The move not only took Laldenga by surprise, but generated cross-spectrum Mizo criticism. The fact that the decision came days after Laldenga openly stated that 'I'm a Rajiv loyalist' (and politically too weak to take on the Congress) riled people up enough to start a campaign across Aizawl with the warning: 'Rajiv don't force us back to the jungles'.[163] Saikia, ousted as Assam's chief minister and made Mizoram governor, defended Rajiv's decision on spurious grounds that president's rule was imposed because no single party could have commanded a majority in the Mizoram assembly.

Despite knowing that Laldenga's appeal was declining, and that the Congress could have won state elections on its own merit (as it did after the president's rule was lifted in 1989), New Delhi felt the need to press ahead with dissolving an elected government. Former Mizoram chief minister Zoramthanga, who led the Kabul channel in the 1970s, claims that the reason for imposing president's rule in 1988 'still remains unknown'.[164] But the Congress' electoral politics and concerns that its electoral base in Mizoram would be dislocated were it to cede ground to regional politics in the wake of peace accords were key motives. The situation in Nagaland was similarly paradoxical. Despite genuine Indian attempts to bring Phizo on board, the Shillong accord failed to convince both the Naga overground and underground about its viability. The effect was periods of president's rule punctuated by short-lived, unstable governments. The NSCN-IM, which emerged as a powerful insurgent, allied with the ULFA in the 1980s, complicating India's challenges and laying the ground for Operations Bajrang and Rhino.

The rise of ULFA and NSCN-IM along with the proliferation of armed outfits raised questions about the efficacy of Burma and

Bangladesh in delivering on counterinsurgency and connectivity. Ne Win shared a rapport with Gandhi and delivered, even if limitedly and unevenly so, on denying space to the MNF and the Naga underground. But the junta's patchy counterinsurgency record along with its isolationist streak made it impossible for India to push through on its developmental projects that were proposed in 1968. Neither did Dacca eliminate NSCN-IM, MNF, or ULFA bases in Bangladesh. The choice of operating from Burmese soil under the control of insurgent allies such as the KIO and coordinating armed activity through Burmese migrant camps in Thailand (Mae Sot, Chiang Rai, and Chiang Mai) that offered access to drug supplies from the Golden Triangle was preferred by most northeast rebels. India's northeast remained unstable after 1971. And as the next chapter shows, India was struggling just as much in independent Bangladesh.

7

LOSING THE PEACE
FAMINE, COUP, AND COUNTERCOUP
IN BANGLADESH

'Our approach should be to maintain correct rather
than enthusiastic or friendly relations with the present
government of Bangladesh. Our attitude on matters of
tangible bilateral interest like Farakka, exploration of oil in
the Bay of Bengal, border security and border trade, etc.
should not be as conciliatory and accommodating as it was
during Sheikh Mujib's tenure in power.'

Jyotindra Nath Dixit, India's Deputy High Commissioner
in Dacca, 1972–75, 10 October 1975[1]

It was a pyrrhic victory. India lost the peace after 1971—but as is
often charged, not in Kashmir.[2] The Simla Agreement, signed on
2 July 1972, created an 'imperfect peace' and ushered temporary
calm in Kashmir.[3] But in the near east, where it sought a solution
to the two-and-a-half-front conflict problem, India lost out. The
decision to wage war was driven by India's need to reverse mass
displacement, contain communal violence, and deny sanctuary to
northeast rebels. The way India fought the war signalled its desire to
marginalise Indian Naxalites umbilically tied to China. Things were

187

going Gandhi's way. In Dacca, India became Mujib's 'closest ally and leading benefactor' and signed the Treaty of Friendship, Cooperation, and Peace on 19 March 1972.[4] Both the Naga and Mizo underground sought talks with India. But then the situation took a turn for worse.

On 25 June 1975, Gandhi imposed the Emergency, and on 15 August, Mujib was assassinated. On 7 November, another coup rocked Bangladesh, generating concerns in India about violence and a Hindu exodus. The new regime, led by Maj. Gen. Zia-ur-Rahman was perceived as pro-Pakistan, and by 1978 most anti-India insurgents who were pushed out in 1972 returned to Bangladesh with Zia's support. To explain why India lost the peace *despite* winning the war, this chapter focuses on post-1971 developments. Invested in the *inside out* aspect of India's diplomacy, it shows how identity politics, official antinomies, economic woes, and fears of mass displacement from Bangladesh and its potential impact on India's state-building shaped its response towards Bangladesh.

The first section explores India's reading of and approach towards Bangladesh in 1972–75. Forged in the proverbial trenches of 1971, anti-India sentiment overlapped with much that went wrong during Mujib's time in power. Despite appreciating growing anti-Indianism (that replaced anti-Pakistan sentiments due to the populist structures of Bangladeshi politics), New Delhi failed to gauge the depths of disaffection with Mujib within the army. Keen to preserve an ally, India overlooked Mujib's authoritarianism, inability to contain corruption, and failure to uplift the economy or acknowledge the contribution of others in Bangladesh's liberation.[5] The 1974 famine tilted the scales against Mujib.[6]

Based on untapped Indian intelligence reports, the second section unpacks India's response to Mujib's killing. Indian policymakers adopted a business-as-usual approach but decided against showing enthusiasm towards the new government. Between 15 August and 7 November 1975, New Delhi debated how to regain influence in Dacca. Did it have to stick to diplomacy, or should it try coercion? The third section explains how the November coup tilted the balance towards coercion.. The Indian army was ready to enter Bangladesh if needed.[7] The coup worried India that its security 'red lines' of preventing a Hindu exodus and use of Bangladeshi soil by rebels could be breached (again).[8] India armed elements opposed Zia until Gandhi was in power. Even the Janata Dal interregnum didn't fully stabilise ties. The fourth section unpacks the March 1982 coup by Lt. Gen. Hussain Muhammad Ershad, and why India accepted him.

Second Revolution

In the early hours of 15 August 1975, a group of soldiers led by Maj. Shariful Haque Dalim entered Mujib's Dhanmondi residence and killed the Bangabandhu with all his family members and their personal guard. The assassins then dashed to the radio station and announced Khandkar Moshtaque Ahmed as president. Around two hundred people were killed that day after a nationwide curfew was imposed.[9] The youngest was Sheikh Russel, Mujib's 10-year-old son.

The killings marked a dangerous turn in regional geopolitics. Informed about these developments just before her Independence Day speech at the Red Fort, Gandhi was shaken. It fuelled her paranoia about what her own enemies could do—a fear that developed in parallel with India's rise as a paramount subcontinental power after 1971 and led to the imposition of Emergency in June 1975.[10] She used Mujib's assassination to justify the imposition and continuation of the Emergency.[11] In four years of liberation, India lost an ally in Dacca, and R&AW, the Machiavellian architect of Bangladesh's liberation, stood humiliated. India saw Mujib's assassination as Pakistan 'striking back'.[12]

New Delhi had feared for Mujib's life. Ten days before the assassination, Kao visited Dacca to warn Mujib about such threats and requested he shift his residence to 'Bangabhaban'.[13] Mujib refused.[14] But now that Mujib was dead, New Delhi engaged with the new regime. It debated the merits of such engagement and also considered arming pro-Mujib figures. To understand India's actions after Mujib's death, it's critical to understand how it viewed Bangladesh's economic and political situation before the act.

Bangladesh felt the real force of the 1947 partition's economic disconnect from India *after* liberation.[15] Pakistan's half-hearted attempts to augment jute and textile production and exports from East Pakistan, failure to enhance industrial and infrastructure capacities, and inability to manage unionism meant that economic disenfranchisement with West Pakistan drove Bengali separatism as much as language politics. During Operation Searchlight, Bangladesh's human capital received a further blow as its educated and business elite were targeted.

Inheritance of such a troubled economy ensured that feeding all Bangladeshis and stabilising the economy were pressing concerns for Mujib. Unfortunately, he failed to develop systems that could prevent famine. Food grain production was not the problem; lack of distribution capacities coupled with corruption and instability was. Bangladeshi leadership's failure to overcome internal fissures helped create the 1974 famine. Mujib's 'drastic' response to ban political parties and create a one-party system known as the Bangladesh Krishak Sramik Awami League (Baksal)—a Moscow-backed idea that Mujib termed a 'second revolution'[16]—topped the list of structural causes for his assassination in India's reading.[17]

As someone who lived through the famine remembers, 'during 1974 all we used to eat was rice water, and my mother owned just two *sarees*'.[18] For an economist, it was '1943 re-enacted'.[19] The traumas of the 1974 famine, which occurred after the flooding of river Padma, are documented in *The Unfashionable Tragedy* by filmmaker John Pilger. He notes that it was 'possibly the greatest famine in recorded history'.[20] The official death estimate stands at 27,000, but unofficial estimates range between 1 to 1.5 million.[21] Indian officials noted that the famine led to another spurt in cross-border displacement and the BSF 'intercepted about 50,000 Bangladesh nationals' between August 1974 and July 1975.[22] Most were 'pushed back'.[23]

Mujib needed to urgently augment food production and streamline distribution. But to fill the gap, food donations from India and the US were critical. The US food aid, as part of the PL480 programme, helped preventing famine *before* 1974.[24] But it was contingent on Cold War geopolitics. Washington, D.C. cancelled two large shipments scheduled for delivery in September 1974. Why? Because the aid came with a clause that recipients must not trade with countries blacklisted by the US (Cuba in this case). Indian food aid itself had stopped in July 1972 due to drought in Andhra Pradesh, Bihar, and West Bengal.[25] Bangladesh's tiny forex reserve, and a global food grain price hike in the early 1970s worsened the situation.[26] India offered to rebuild destroyed infrastructure and improve bilateral trade as solutions. But that counted for little.

The speed and scale of Bangladesh's economic collapse meant that India was first in line for people's fury. Propaganda blaming India for destroying the Hardinge bridge and Indian engineers who repaired it for stealing Bangladeshi property was pervasive.[27] Bilateral ties tensed over Ganga river water sharing. The existence of Farakka barrage and hitherto abortive talks with Pakistan meant that 'India is drying us up' became a popular refrain.[28] In April 1972, India offered 40,000 cusecs of water, as opposed to Mujib's demand for 35,000 cusecs, to subside the issue.[29]

But a popular feeling that India was exploiting Bangladesh took root. Worried that Indian private interests were encouraging smuggling, Dacca demanded government-to-government economic interactions only.[30] This meant that big businesses such as the Scindia Steam Navigation Co. led by Sumati Morarjee, the first woman leader in Indian shipping, who wanted to 'serve Bangla Desh by establishing its trade and commerce with the rest of the world', were asked not to enter the field.[31] The idea of an India-Bangladesh Economic Community was also shot down. It could make 'third countries ... inimical to India and Bangla Desh' argue that India was 'trying to exploit Bangla Desh and are treating it as a satellite country'.[32]

On 5 July 1973, months before famine hit, India and Bangladesh signed a trade agreement that came into effect on 28 September.[33] It introduced a Balanced Trade Payments Arrangement (BTPA) for a three-year period with the clause of planning annual trade deals. Trade plans for 1973–74 allowed India to import Bangladeshi jute and newsprint at international prices but sell coal at a domestic price of 82 rupees per tonne when the international price was 364 rupees.[34]

Expectedly, none of these arrangements or post-war relief prevented the famine that began in March 1974 due to flooding, state incapacity, and corruption.[35] The government opened 4,300 langar-khana (feeding camps) that fed nearly 6 million people by October–November 1974.[36] But even here, the hoarding of supplies undermined efforts. Itself banking on PL480,[37] India viewed the BTPA as unsustainable and increased coal prices by 50% mid-famine.[38] The Indian Red Cross did offer 500,000 rupees (65,000 USD) worth of relief, and Gandhi sanctioned another 5.5 million rupees (700,000 USD) in assistance, but clarified that India couldn't offer more.[39]

Indian diplomats felt that Mujib's 1975 emergency measures were too little, too late. From Dacca, Jyotindra Nath Dixit, India's ambitious deputy high commissioner, reported that Mujib's plan to shift the 'centre of gravity from the District headquarters to the Taluk headquarters' was done in the 'pious hope' of shifting the state's distributive capacities in rural Bangladesh.[40] Instead, it alienated elites, and 'did nothing to remove the burden on ordinary Bangla citizens'.[41] Though Mujib was still popular, Baksal's failure could 'result in his elimination from the political affairs'.[42] The authoritarian anticipations on Mujib's part had come true.[43]

As Amartya Sen notes in his seminal 1981 study, Bangladesh's food grain production in 1974 was higher than in previous years.[44] It was post-Emergency measures, including the creation of Baksal, that were ineffectual. Bangladesh was played a bad economic hand in 1971, and there were limits to what any government could have done. But Mujib made the situation worse, and many people believe that he paid the price for it with his life.[45] A week after his assassination, Indian officials noted the 'deep scepticism of Mujib's capacity to improve matters' tilted the balance against Bangabandhu.[46]

As India, Pakistan, and Bangladesh negotiated on the prisoners of war issue, diplomatic recognition, and repatriation, two official antinomies emerged—and caused political collapse.

The first antinomy was Bangladesh's reliance on India. Coupled with a troubled experience of joint warfighting and tensions over water-sharing, trade, migration, and smuggling, such reliance became a liability for Mujib. This antinomy turned Bangladeshi opinion against India. The notion that India treated 1971 as a conflict with Pakistan instead of a people's war continues to rankle Bangladeshis. Leaders such as Bhashani, who received Indian support during the war, returned to anti-India politics. Equally, the NAP-B, along with the 'best organised of all'[47] left-wing Jatiya Samajtantrik Dal (JSD) led by former freedom fighter and India critic Md. Abdul Jalil, claimed that India was encouraging smuggling (a long-time

Pakistani allegation).[48] They criticised Calcutta-based Marwari businesspersons for dumping sub-standard products and stealing Bangladeshi wealth.[49]

Such campaigns fed popular beliefs that India was looting Bangladesh and wanted to make it a semi-colony.[50] Public sentiments were on display when people blocked the train in which Indian engineers who repaired the Hardinge bridge were returning. Under impression that their equipment was Bangladeshi, protesters allowed the engine and the engineers to leave, but confiscated the wagons and goods.[51]

The charge that India was stealing Bangladeshi wealth had to do with the Indian army's behaviour after the war. As Maj. Gen. B N Sarkar, India's defence attaché in Dacca, informed Subimal Dutt, India's first high commissioner, the Indian army openly removed sizeable quantities of Pakistani arms 'even from stocks' as trophies before returning three months after liberation.[52] To worsen matters, the Commander-in-Chief of Bangladeshi Forces, Gen. MAG Osmany, 'was deliberately slighted by our army bosses', with Manekshaw adopting a 'condescending attitude'.[53] Osmany became a fervent India critic.

The silence around Indian army's behaviour in Bangladesh becomes pressing because most 1971 war records were destroyed.[54] Frictions between Indian and Bangladeshi forces, about which DP presciently forewarned, undermined bilateral ties. 'We criticised the Indian business community and its malpractices openly but didn't criticise the army given the sensitivities around that', says a Bangladeshi politician.[55] Herein, India's assessment that Mujib's failure to discourage 'chronic anti-Indian feeling' offered 'pro-Muslim groups' the confidence to kill him was misplaced.[56] It suited Mujib to encourage anti-India rhetoric because that prevented his opponents from criticising governance failures.[57] Dutt was convinced that Bhashani and Mujib had a 'secret understanding' that the former would use anti-Indianism as a pressure point during the 1973 elections, but would 'fall sick' before elections (as he did) to ensure that votes didn't get split to Mujib's disadvantage.[58]

Mujib marginalised pro-India figures such as Tajuddin Ahmed and foreign minister Abdus Samad. Pro-US figures such as Kamal

Hossain (whom Dutt didn't trust) were promoted. It showed Mujib's balancing act between anti-Indianism and the need to maintain ties with Gandhi.[59] Tajuddin earned India's respect for leading the wartime government. His estrangement from Mujib reflects the discomfort Mujib felt from peers who demonstrated political calibre and organisational skill. India didn't complain about Tajuddin's sidelining. Dixit noted that the euphoria characterising Indo-Bangladesh ties in 1972 'completely disappeared in 1973' because 'the influence of the Mujibnagar group of politicians [Tajuddin] as well as civil servants in national affairs came to an end'.[60]

Tajuddin routinely voiced concerns to Dutt about Mujib's dalliance with Bhashani,[61] openness to the US, and support of anti-Indianism to remain 'popular with the entire people'.[62] Dutt was certain 'that Tajuddin will not abuse our confidence' if India confidentially advised him on how to manage Mujib.[63] It is ironic that an estranged Tajuddin stood by Mujib until the end whereas Moshtaque, whom Mujib trusted, ousted him. Moshtaque was 'a Trojan horse in Mujib's camp' according to Indian officials.[64] Tajuddin and wartime acting president Syed Nazrul Islam were imprisoned after Mujib's assassination. Ultimately, it was Tajuddin's murder along with other AL leaders that shook India more than Mujib's killing itself.

The second antinomy was in the civil-military sphere. Bangladesh struggled to reconcile the freedom fighters' demand for plum positions in the army and the pushback against such perks by repatriate officers.[65] This tussle, which turned violent and led to Mujib's assassination, had a logic of its own. But it was not bereft of an Indian imprint. India trained and equipped the Mujib Bahini (later JRB) as insurance if the Mukti Bahini went rogue. This proved accurate when militant communists such as Siraj Sikder targeted the government *after* liberation. The JRB captured and extrajudicially executed Sikder.

In January 1974, to ensure that Bangladeshi Maoists were neutralised, Dacca-based Indian diplomat Chandrashekhar Dasgupta advocated imparting 'anti-insurgency training' to the Bangladesh Armed Forces and the Rakkhi Bahini.[66] Dasgupta underscored that the 'Rakkhi Bahini is likely to play a particularly significant role in this sphere'.[67] But the JRB didn't just target communists;

it targeted everyone, including the army. This made many officers view the JRB as Mujib's personal vanguard meant to keep the army in check. Handsome budgetary allocations to the JRB heightened fears. Indian officials acknowledged that the 'petty bullying by the Rakhi Bahini strong troopers' generated fierce resentment among 'uncommitted people'.[68]

But they noted that

the more shrewd among Mujib's opponents realised that ... if he was given the time to establish the new Governor system and develop the Rakhi Bahini as a huge para-military force, about one-and-half lakh strong with an Indian-trained officer corps and with memories of India's help to Bangladesh and fanatic personal loyalty to Mujib. Given two or three years, this militia would have successfully neutralized the Army's power.[69]

This is why the assassins acted while Mujib's unpopularity was high, 'before the result of his reforms was beginning to be felt'.[70] The date of murder, 15 August, India believed, was 'chosen primarily because it is India's Independence Day when we could be caught off-guard', and because of the symbolic significance as the 'Independence Day of original Pakistan'.[71]

India was less worried about Mujib's failure as a democrat, but did worry about Mujib's failure as an autocrat. It is possible that Indian assessments sought to placate Gandhi's undemocratic instincts during the Emergency. But India's reaction to the November coup demonstrates that it truly intended to support Mujib loyalists at the cost of Bangladesh's democratic promise, imparting credit to the belief that India prefers AL over others.[72] This is reflective in Indian denials when addressing rising anti-Indianism before 1975. Welcomed by black flags in Dacca, DP, still the chairman of the Policy Planning Committee in 1972, instructed Dixit to brief Indian journalists 'to depict a more hospitable and less gloomy picture of the returning evacuees' and 'not to be unduly critical of Sheikh Mujibur Rahman or his government'.[73]

DP argued that 'objective judgement must not receive preference over our national interests'.[74] Dutt and Dixit made efforts to ensure that journalists from the *Statesman,* the *Times of India*, and the

Ananda Bazar Patrika didn't report on Mujib's excesses, economic mismanagement, and dishonesty.[75] On the last aspect, Dutt noted how the editor of *Janapad* who 'takes down dictation of Sheikh's memoirs by Sheikh himself' maintained that though Mujib gave the call for independence on 7 March, it was Major Zia-ur-Rahman who declared war on 25 March.[76] But Mujib falsely took credit for that.[77] Such lies damaged Bangladeshi politics and turned Zia against Mujib and India. To this effect, India's Counsellor (Economic) in Dacca offered a sharp assessment of Mujib in January 1973:

> I do not think he has any ideology or intellectual comprehension of the development of political forces within and outside his country. If history is any guide, one would venture to think that he can be unscrupulous, undemocratic, and even communal, if that suits his political interests. But one cannot doubt his nationalism or his consciousness of his image as a great popular mass leader.[78]

Mujib would remain a friend if he believed 'that India is not and will not be against him personally', the counsellor argued.[79] Similarly, Dixit noted that Mujib was capable of transcending parties and ideologies given his hold over people who don't lack judgement 'but lack the political sophistication to match the needs of the country by demanding the requisite leader'.[80] Mujib had 'no basic ideological framework for his national policies' and 'not a sufficiently strong conviction' when it came to secularism as reflected in his 'lack of any effort' to stop communalism.[81]

People were disillusioned because of the ideological corrosion of their leaders. 'The result is politics is devoid of idealism ... and a government devoid of any ideological base, capable of inspiring the people', argued Dixit.[82] The media was unable to offer effective and timely criticism, and Mujib's advisors couldn't offer him needed advice. Dutt was more willing to give Mujib's secularism the benefit of the doubt, but noted that his detractors, including those who knew him well, noted that 'the Sheikh, who had his training in communal politics in the forties, is not as secular as he professes to be'.[83] But his permission for Indian operations against Mizo rebels and support for returnees meant that he delivered on the two red lines that mattered most to India. Persecution of Bangladeshi Hindus was a problem, but not until it led to mass exodus.

Mujib's secularism had limits, and so did his trust in India. Soon after liberation, one of the first things he did was reduce India's intelligence footprint in Bangladesh. He didn't want R&AW to cultivate links with his opponents, especially the JSD. Mujib's ties with Indian intelligence in the 1960s to subvert Pakistan worried him that New Delhi could adopt a similar strategy against him.[84] There was truth to this because Banerjee, R&AW's point-person on Bangladesh, was indeed engaging with Mujib's critics in the Chattra League who joined the JSD. In September 1972, Dutt warned that while he had 'no knowledge whatsoever of R&AW's activities in Bangladesh', he hoped that Banerjee didn't offer money to 'Ganakantha' (a newspaper run by Mujib's critics), which many believed was the case.[85] Undoubtedly, R&AW was furious that it 'lost' Bangladesh less than four years after 1971.[86]

Here, it's critical to underscore how India viewed the role of external powers in Mujib's assassination. India's first reading shows that it saw the killing as a Pakistani plot with an indirect British connection.[87] In a political sense, Indian officials felt that Bhutto and Pakistan were 'merely pegs on which anti-Mujib groups wanted to hang their coat on [and] Pakistan could very well be exaggerating its influence or responsibility'.[88] Given that neither Pakistan nor China were physically present in Bangladesh, India sought to 'avoid jumping to conclusions about actual physical interference by their agencies' because 'there is all the difference in the world between diffuse sympathy and actual conspiracy'.[89] But in a practical sense, the real villain of the piece in New Delhi's eyes was the Bangladeshi community in the UK that housed 'a highly organised pro-Pakistan anti-Mujib movement' with Pakistani support.[90]

India concluded that the 'necessary details of the actual coup, the courier arrangements etc. must have been the work of conspiracy between anti-Mujib Bangladesh bureaucrats and Army officers in the U.K. with the Pakistan government'.[91] The belief in a British link to the conspiracy was strengthened by the fact that a 'crucial military intelligence figure' returned to Dacca from London on 12 August, indicating that the 'manner of the coup' was decided abroad.[92] India was not blaming London for the coup, but such aspects deepened India's concerns that the Pakistani and British Bangladeshi diaspora was inimical to India.

On the role of the US, Indian officials were unsure whether the CIA was involved and assessed that 'in the absence of hard evidence, it would be unwise to distribute responsibility over too wide an area'.[93] Given the turbulent underbelly of India's relations with Mujib, his assassination shocked Gandhi and humiliated the R&AW, but India's overall reaction was measured. A K Damodaran, Joint Secretary (Public Policy) at the MEA, who followed the situation closely with Jagdish Ajmani, JS (Bangladesh), identified four areas where India's interests could face direct consequences.

The first was the 'possible revival of Mizo rebellion'. The second was an uptick in Naxalite activity in the border areas, and 'recrudescence' of ultra-leftist groups in the Sunderbans. The third was an attempt to 'reactivate the small Muslim minority movement in the Arakan district of Burma', namely the arming of Rohingyas.[94] Finally, Bangladesh could call itself an Islamic Republic, leading to another Hindu exodus.[95] None of these issues required drastic measures. India dealt with Moshtaque with caution but not panic.

Damodaran recommended that having expressed 'unequivocal regret' at Mujib's death, India must return to 'business as usual'.[96] This was done when the Bangladeshi high commissioner to India called foreign secretary Kewal Singh four days after the killing and clarified that there would be no change in Dacca's foreign policy.[97] Singh welcomed continuity, regretted that the Indian high commission's telephones were disconnected, and signalled that New Delhi sought normalisation between Pakistan and Bangladesh.[98] In fact, the MEA recommended that Samar Sen, India's high commissioner in Dacca who'd recently replaced Dutt (was in India on the day of the killing), must return to Bangladesh sooner rather than later to avoid indicating 'India's coolness or even displeasure towards the new government'.[99]

India's aid commitment must not increase but should be 'purposeful and efficient', and the security forces must create a *cordon sanitaire* along the borders to 'prevent population transfers and smuggling'.[100] On Farraka, India should insist on the observance of the interim agreement, and stress continuity between the two governments given 'Khondkar's Mujibnagar past and presence of some pro-Indian Ministers'.[101] On publicity and cultural matters, Damodaran recommended maintaining a low profile, operating on the assumption that

> ... anyone not overtly anti-Indian is for us and not the other way round. We have to be extremely subtle and delicate to the point of hypocrisy in attributing to most Bangladeshi bureaucrats and politicians a virtue they may not possess. This is what Pakistanis are now doing. We should assume that Bangla population continues to be grateful to us and would be with us if only their major economic ills are overcome.[102]

Then came the kicker. To justify this approach as if nothing had happened, Damodaran counselled, and others agreed, that India 'should recall the converse fact that at no moment did Mujib or his colleagues make any basic concessions because of his being 'pro-India".[103] In agreement with Damodaran, Dixit forewarned that Moshtaque 'himself may be replaced by a more authoritarian political leader or officer from the Bangladesh armed forces'.[104] He advocated that India had to maintain its

> extensive contacts in the army and para-military forces whom we should continue to cultivate to the extent possible. Our overall objective should be to encourage the re-emergence of a government which would be friendly to India, and which is dedicated to the ideas of policies which motivated the liberation struggle of Bangladesh.[105]

India's relations with Mujib were troubled, but he was essential to Indian interests. Unsurprisingly, the Indian army's eastern command including GOC-in-C Lt. Gen. Jack F R Jacob, who fought in 1971, was 'relaxed and unconcerned' on the day Mujib died.[106] But this changed in November. On 3 November, Tajuddin, India's actual ally, was murdered in Dacca Central Jail along with three AL stalwarts: Syed Nazrul Islam, AHM Qamaruzzaman, and Md. Mansur Ali. Four days later, another coup—a countercoup, in fact—rocked Dacca. Tajuddin was killed by Dalim and his comrades just before they flew to Bangkok to ensure that R&AW stood no chance of re-installing pro-India figures in Dacca. Now India panicked.

Coup, Counter-Coup

Unlike the day of Mujib's killing when he was unconcerned, Jacob ordered his troops along the Bangladesh border to be on full alert on 7 November.[107] The BSF and myriad units of SFF and SSB—pivotal during the war—too were put on alert. The BSF had 239 border posts in West Bengal; 114 in Assam, Meghalaya, and Mizoram combined; and 58 in Tripura.[108] About 400 Indian troops were already operating 'a few miles over the border into Bangladesh in the northern and north-western sectors' near Islampur as a preparatory measure in case an invasion was ordered.[109]

An Indian Air Force aircraft allegedly 'deliberately' violated Bangladeshi airspace that day.[110] In addition to the army, the home ministry too issued plans to Assam, West Bengal, and Tripura on how to manage a mass influx.[111] Closely following these developments, senior Bangladeshi officers in New Delhi—military attaché Brig. M A Manzur and future strongman Maj. Gen. Ershad—warned their US counterpart that if Tajuddin's and Mujib's killers returned to Dacca, 'the likelihood of Indian intervention will increase markedly'.[112] They believed that despite it being 'foolhardy', Indian intervention couldn't be ruled out.[113]

India worried about a Hindu exodus and warned that it would 'intervene if Bangladesh proclaimed itself an Islamic state'.[114] In an urgent report on India's military capabilities, an interagency intelligence committee in Washington, D.C. assessed that New Delhi could commence full-scale military operations within three days of a decision. India could also commit 'over 150,000 men without significantly weakening its defenses against China and Pakistan'.[115] The US concluded that 'India would establish full control over the government of Bangladesh and all urban and administrative centers within a maximum of two weeks—probably much sooner' even if guerrilla warfare against the Indians continued for longer.[116] The chances of Indian success were high also because the best months for such operation were December through April.

Why and how did India's reaction shift from calibrated nonchalance to coercion? After deciding on a business-as-usual manner, Indian officials, expecting the situation to deteriorate, debated options and implications of engaging with Moshtaque. The R&AW wanted to retaliate. Though open to the idea, the MEA advised caution. In Samar Sen's absence, the most senior official in Bangladesh was the acting high commissioner A K Das. His cables coupled with secret intelligence telegrams offered a fuller picture of the killing. At 4pm on 14 August, during a meeting at Ganabhaban, Mujib sought to replace Bangladesh Rifles units from border posts with Jatiya Rakkhi Bahini (JRB). This decision, combined with false propaganda that Mujib was planning a 'merger of Bangladesh with India', got many army personnel 'excited'.[117]

Soon after, Dalim reached Ganabhaban and sought Mujib's resignation, leading to a scuffle and Dalim's forcible removal.[118] Forewarned about the threat to his life, Mujib now called Tofael Ahmad, the JRB leader and one of the five 'khalifas' he trusted, to handle Dalim and his coterie. In the absence of Brig. Nuruzzaman, the Director General of JRB, Tofael was the only person who could get Rakkhi Bahini to act. But he didn't.

Instead, Tofael took shelter in the house of a close friend named Anwar Hossain Manju, owner of the *Daily Ittefaq*, a pro-AL newspaper.[119] Das noted that it was 'fairly evident' that Tofael had been 'a snake in the grass' and betrayed Mujib when Bangabandhu needed him most.[120] If there were doubts about Tofael's betrayal, Cochran, a 'known CIA official' informed Indian diplomats that 'Tofael would not be tried or punished by the new government'.[121] Mujib had alienated Tofael—an arch-loyalist who coined the term Bangabandhu—by elevating Moshtaque. Das retrospectively called this 'another instance of Sheikh Mujib's oversight'.[122] In Baksal, Mujib distanced himself from Tofael and became dependent on Moni. It was a mistake.

As Indian officials had presciently forewarned in 1973, Mujib's lack of foresight and preference for show of force could make him support Moni over Tofael. But Mujib's shrewd sense of self-interest, Indian officials hoped, would make him realise that the 'predominance of Sheikh Moni and his group may act as Frankenstein's Monster'.[123]

Perhaps without realising the import of his actions, Mujib's preference for Moni became the most important reason that led to the breakup of the khalifas and the implosion of the Chattra League itself. Mujib failed to grasp the fatal impact of such politicking. India's foreign minister and foreign secretary received similar assessments in September 1975 when they met the new foreign minister Abu Syed Chaudhury on the sidelines of the Non-Aligned Summit in Peru.

'Stunned' by Mujib's killing, Chaudhury was 'greatly worried' that he too would be arrested.[124] Instead, Moshtaque offered him a cabinet position. Chaudhury noted that Mujib had lost much of his charisma 'over the last three years'.[125] The emergency measures as part of the one-party state were 'arbitrary' and put Mujib above the constitution, which was a 'great mistake'.[126] Corruption in the system was rampant, and it was 'well known' that a number of Mujib's close relations 'amassed fortunes through illegal means'.[127] Younger officers strongly believed that Mujib was deliberately keeping the army weak 'on the advice of India'.[128] Such rumours received currency by Mujib's talk of calling on the Indian army 'in case of difficulty'.[129] Plus, an 'overconfident' Mujib rubbished warnings of mounting discontent.[130]

Apart from Moshtaque, Maj. Gen. Ziaur Rahman's significance was evident. India didn't believe that Zia was directly involved in the killing.[131] His rise to power seemed to indicate that he might be the 'true leader' of the killing. He appointed Maj. Gen. Khaliur Rahman as Chief of Defence Staff and promoted Brig. Hussain M. Ershad, then in India, as deputy chief.[132] Gen. Osmany was appointed defence advisor. The only thing in common between Osmany and Moshtaque was that they 'developed anti-India feelings during the course of the liberation struggle'.[133] These changes belied the Indian expectation that 'there are so many desperate elements within the armed forces that it is hard to imagine that a strong and unified leadership within the Armed Forces would emerge easily'.[134]

But the situation remained in flux. Despite promising continuity, Moshtaque was settling scores, 'witch-hunting', purging the administration and appointing loyalists 'well known for their sympathies for Pakistan', and wasting cabinet meetings on 'national dress and national headgear'.[135] Moshtaque did nothing to discipline the officers who killed Mujib. Instead, he promulgated an indemnity without parliamentary approval. It offered Mujib's killers legal immunity.

Shortly after the assassination, India realised that the Bangladeshi army established border posts at the Khowai border between Agartala and Brahmanbaria.[136] Then, it sealed these borders, and no one, including passport and visa holders, was allowed to enter or leave Bangladesh. The JRB was disbanded, and its cadres disarmed within days. JRB and AL offices were being 'guarded' by the army, photos of Mujib were being 'forcibly' removed, and people were told not to discuss Mujib or listen to the All India Radio.[137] To win sympathy, the army released old stocks of rice to 'abnormally' reduce the price, with informal surveys indicating that '90 percent off people of Sylhet are happy with the present government'.[138] Hindus were threatened, allegedly, by 'pro Pak' groups, making the community 'panicky'.[139] Gandhi Ashram officials in Noakhali corroborated such incidents.

On 3 September, Das met with Moshtaque. Protection to Hindus topped the agenda. Moshtaque agreed that some 'Mullahs taught communalism' and promised action in Noakhali, but 'did not make any commitment' on the overall situation.[140] When Das complained about increased police and military surveillance against the high commission, Moshtaque displayed understanding and asked Das to bring 'any specific complaint' to his attention.[141] On JRB's future, Moshtaque was blunt. The checks and balances against the JRB 'could never work', but he had not made up his mind on how best to integrate its cadre in the military and paramilitary.[142]

In September–October, the situation clarified itself for India to reconsider the approach. Appointments of India critics and Pakistan sympathisers were coupled with enthusiastic welcome of the new regime by Pakistan, China, and Saudi Arabia. This increased Indian anxiety about losing Bangladesh for good. Bhutto quickly shipped large quantities of food grain to Dacca after the coup, just as Indian officials in Peking noted China's reaction of 'approbation punctuated with caution'.[143] Chinese media reportage of Moshtaque was positive throughout. But trouble came when Riyadh sent a congratulatory telegram to Moshtaque of the 'Islamic Republic of Bangladesh' on

17 August.[144] Editorials in Arabic and English Saudi newspapers eulogised Islamic unity and hoped for closer ties between Pakistan and Bangladesh.[145]

India's caution didn't win it allies. The decision to not formally recognise the new regime drew suspicion, with even senior Hindu leaders informing India that people viewed the silence as 'having a deeper meaning'.[146] On 9 October, Bangladeshi law minister Manoranjan Dhar visited Calcutta. He debriefed Indian officials that while army officers were not interfering in day-to-day governance, they were sitting in policymaking committees.[147] Pro-Pakistan elements were 'jubilant' at Mujib's death and 'stirring up communal and anti-India propaganda'.[148]

Deeply religious, Moshtaque opened his office to clerics, which never happened under Mujib. Dhar believed that the secret of Moshtaque's presidency lay in the 'balancing trick' between intra-army factions. But the opening of Pakistani and Chinese embassies, he warned, could give anti-India elements an upper hand and the Hindus could 'suffer'.[149] Regardless of whether such reports were curated for an Indian audience or reflective of what ministers truly thought, the emergent theme was that the anti-India, pro-Pakistan lobbies had strengthened in Dacca.

By now, resistance against the coup was brewing both inside and outside the army. Within days of Mujib's killing, Indian intelligence reported that student leaders of the Baksal-sponsored Jatiya Chhatra League held a secret meeting in Brahmanbaria, near the Tripura border. The students decided to 'oust the present KHANDAKAR govt', and were convinced that pro-Pakistan Moshtaque got Mujib killed.[150] Baksal student units reached Brahmanbaria despite army firing on 18–20 August.[151] Disbanded Baksal central committee members who had escaped arrest went underground. India expected that most rebels would 'come to Agartala for shelter'.[152] Shortly after this meeting, posters and wall writings demanding punishment for Mujib's killers appeared in several places in Brahmanbaria.[153] The Chhatra League was making its presence felt.

In the Mymensingh-Tangail region, a pro-Mujib militia led by Kader 'Tiger' Siddique was active.[154] The core of this militia, R&AW assessed, stood between 1,000 and 3,000, with the lower figure being more realistic, from its erstwhile maximum strength of 17,000 in 1971.[155] Though not a force that could withstand pressure from the army, the Kader Bahini tied down sections of 72nd brigade from Rangpur and the Tangail-based 77th brigade.[156] Siddique was joined by the former operations chief of JRB who fled four days before Mujib's assassination, and Chittaranjan Suttar, a Hindu parliamentarian close to Mujib and India.[157] Suttar had been in solitary confinement in a cell opposite Mujib's when both were imprisoned in the 1950s. Shanti Bahini, the militant wing of the Parbatya Chattagram Jana Samhati Samiti (PCJSS), also intensified recruitment and training.[158] Created in 1972 to represent the Chittagong Hill Tracts' (CHT) indigenous communities, the PCJSS is still active.

These aspects were coupled with unease in the army with the turn of events and implications for institutional discipline. Baksal dissidents realised that several officers of the Bangladesh Rifles (BDR) and the Reserve Police were willing to offer clandestine or open support to the resistance. Dissenters who were in touch with R&AW informed that they expected an 'armed revolution'.[159] Some BDR and JRB personnel planned a 'surprise raid on' Moshtaque himself.[160]

It was against the backdrop of this evolving situation that Das met a 'depressed' Manju. The *Ittefaq* editor argued that the coup-makers and their supporters in the army didn't amount to more than 200 persons, and 'could be easily disciplined if a determined effort was made'.[161] When Das countered that the coup-makers had tanks in their possession, Manju responded: 'tanks could be captured at night or destroyed by the Air Force'.[162] Manju fed into New Delhi's debate on whether and how to use force to arrest Dacca's slide away from India. The Bangladeshi foreign minister hinted in Peru about the 'uncertainty of the stability of the new regime', and concerns of whether he was too quick to join government sharpened this debate.[163]

Two options emerged. The first was to activate large-scale covert military and financial support for anti-regime dissidents seeking refuge in India and those still inside Bangladesh. The second was to continue with the low-risk policy of diplomatic engagement in the hope that Dacca would not cross India's red lines by becoming an Islamic republic, entering into defence pacts with China and Pakistan, or systematically persecuting minorities.[164]

The R&AW wanted to opt for coercive option. According to fleeing Awami Leaguers, thousands of pro-Mujiib leaders and workers sought Indian support for a 'democratic national government'.[165] Nasim Ali, former prime minister Mansur Ali's son (Mansur was killed with Tajuddin) recreated the 'Mujib Bahini 2.0' and wanted support to carry out 'commando style armed operations'.[166] But the MEA, in a top-secret assessment three days before the jail killings, cautioned against coercion. Ajmani was categorical that India must not drag itself 'into a situation which is not of our choosing, by political refugees some of whom may be coming to India only for personal safety, abandoning their colleagues and cause'.[167] He worried that coercion could embarrass India, without much to show for impact by commando raids by an assortment of guerrillas. There were enough arms in Bangladesh to launch an insurgency without outside support.

The key to power in Bangladesh lay with the army, Ajmani argued. If the army was united, 'guerrilla movements are unlikely to make much headway.'[168] India would undermine its influence if it openly identified with the Bangladeshi underground, for 'nothing remains secret where a large number of political émigré's is involved'.[169] In an echo of Dixit's advocacy to support the re-emergence of a pro-India dispensation, Ajmani (considered a 'hardliner' by the US)[170] wanted these guerrillas to operate 'within the Bangladesh Armed Forces'.[171] If they were on Indian soil, these guerrillas had to be disarmed and deported.

Ajmani further argued that India must bide its time, let the regime collapse under its contradictions, and respond to Dacca's unfriendliness in a graduated manner by using 'other weapons in our diplomatic armoury, viz. economic, political, and psychological etc.'.[172] In reference to Manju's point that the coup-makers could be disciplined, the MEA preferred to 'encourage and support the pro-Indian groups in the Army to establish their supremacy'.[173] If India were to intervene, it should do so at a time of its choosing, and on behalf of a strong faction in the army supported by popular forces outside. 'We should strive to impress upon the Bangladesh

Government the folly and danger of confrontation with India', Ajmani clarified.[174]

On 3 November, two days after this top-secret report, a 'pro-India' Brig. Gen. Khaled Mosharraf, who 'thoroughly disliked Sheikh Moni' and JRB, launched a countercoup.[175] It occurred with support from the Bangladeshi air chief, who, along with Mosharraf, allowed Dalim and other killers of Mujib to leave Dacca. Mosharraf and Zia differed on how to deal with Mujib's killers. So, Mosharraf put Zia under house arrest during his operation. There is no archival or forensic evidence that India supported Mosharraf, even though his family members organised a pro-Mujib (and pro-India) rally in Dacca on the day.[176] Had he succeeded, India could have welcomed Mosharraf. But, according to a 'top-secret' R&AW source, Dalim killed the four top-level political detainees in Dacca Central Jail allegedly on Moshtaque's orders.

Four days later, Mosharraf himself was killed in what India called a JSD-led 'sepoy mutiny'. Indian newspapers, such as the Calcutta-based *Patriot*, termed Mosharraf's attempt disastrous and the man 'either a fool or a knave'.[177] Underestimating the JSD's infiltration of the Bangladeshi soldiery and anti-India propaganda therein, Mosharraf went against the mood in the army. But, according to another 'top-secret' left-wing R&AW source, the more disastrous aspect of that 'debauche' Mosharraf's countercoup was his reliance on Inayatullah Khan.[178] A leading critic of Mujib and editor of *Holiday*, a left-wing weekly, Khan was aligned with China and the US rather than with India. Khan worked Mosharraf's ambition while leaking the latter's plans to the government—who then 'hatched' the jail killings, making Moshtaque the 'actual murderer of the four leaders in jail'—thereby making Mosharraf 'willing prey to the wiles of his brother-in-law'.[179] It was Khan who convinced Mosharraf to let Dalim leave for Bangkok.

Whatever the origin of Mosharraf's venture, his premature action 'destroyed the possibility of a real change' that India sought in Bangladesh's armed forces—namely, a true counterforce to Zia. Instead, it led to violent backlash by JSD-inspired troops who killed officers loyal to both Mosharraf and Zia. 'Not a single Pakistani repatriate officer was killed', whereas all Hindu and pro-Mujib officers were picked up and killed.[180] The 1975 JSD-led 'sepoy mutiny' against the officers scarred India's view of Bangladesh's civil-military politics and influenced its reaction to a different but equally powerful BDR mutiny in 2009.

Ironically, apart from Abdul Jalil, the other leader of JSD was Serajul Alam Khan, creator of the *Swadhin Bangla Biplobi Parishad* in 1961 that Mujib aligned with, who was the only JSD figure to support Baksal.[181] Considered a communist with 'Trotskyite persuasion', Alam, along with Jalil, were believed to be 'in the payroll of the US' by R&AW.[182] The narrative among rebelling troops was that Mosharraf was 'purchased' by Samar Sen 'with four lakh takas'.[183] A few days after the coup, Sen survived an attack by gunmen.[184] The mutiny was anti-India, and New Delhi wondered whether Khan truly played 'Iago to Khalid's Othello'.[185]

Events in early November heightened the risk of Bangladesh becoming an Islamic republic. On 15 November, armed men kidnapped the Superintendent of the Ramna Gurudwara, and ten days later three men in military uniform threatened the priest of the Dhakeshwari Temple in Dacca and decamped with the idols of Dhakeshwari, Kali, and Vasudeva.[186] The following day Sen was attacked. Ajmani had urged his US counterparts on 25 October to warn Dacca that its proclamation of an Islamic republic will turn relations with India hostile.[187] Convinced that Tajuddin and others 'would wear the crown of martyrs' and Mosharraf's (who showed 'reverence for Mujib's memory') overthrow was 'another blow by the killers of Mujib', Ajmani wanted to impress upon Zia the danger of confronting India.[188] His warnings had the desired effect. The CIA accurately assessed that 'movement of refugees into India, would force New Delhi to intervene regardless of the consequences'.[189]

The debate on whether India should support the resistance settled in favour of covert support, and if needed, overt action. Whether it was a bluff against Zia (Moshtaque stepped down as president on 6 November) or mobilisation with the true intent of invading Bangladesh remains unclear. But it worked. Soon after consolidating power after Mosharraf's abortive attempt, Zia reached out to Das to placate tensions and withdrew an article he authored for the liberation day that pitched 1975 as the real year of Bangladeshi liberation.[190] He didn't declare Bangladesh an Islamic republic and didn't target Hindus. If anything, within a month, Indian officials 'very tentatively' concluded that 'in the absence of anyone else' Zia was their 'best bet'.[191] His 'anti-Pakistani, not pro-American, and perhaps not anti-Indian or anti-Mujib' sensibilities were tolerable, and his pro-China tilt was to be monitored.[192] Jacob's men could now stand down. But as Deb Mukharji, India's political counsellor to Dacca in 1977 and later ambassador to Bangladesh (1995–2000) remembers, 'Zia altered the secular Bengali fabric to conservative Bangladeshi nationalism that reintroduced a powerful Pakistan glue'.[193] It was a tectonic shift.

Bangladesh, Zindabad!

In his brief presidency, Moshtaque changed the national slogan of Bangladesh from *Joy Bangla* to *Bangladesh, Zindabad* (Long live, Bangladesh). It offered an ideological counterpoise to secular Bengali nationalism. Instead of making Bangladeshi identity primarily about being Bengali, which connoted an affinity with India, the new slogan sought to distance India.[194] The idea became concretised with creation of the Bangladesh Nationalist Party (BNP) on 1 September 1978, under Zia's founding leadership.[195] In a 19-point programme, the BNP promised to 'protect the country's independence, total integrity, and sovereignty', and 'build friendships with all foreign countries and to tie up strong relations with Muslim countries'.[196] Former Minister of Commerce (2001–04) and BNP leader Amir Khasru Mahmud Chowdhury says, 'we are secular in the truest sense as our nationalism is grounded in pluralism and an inclusive Bangladeshi identity that respects ethnic and religious minorities a lot more than the Awami League, whose focus is on Bengali nationalism that undermined and alienates others'.[197]

Bangladesh didn't become an Islamic republic, but it tilted in that direction. The Jamaat-e-Islami, and other groups such as Al Badar, Council Muslim League, and the Nizam-e-Islam became powerful.[198] Zia furthered a process that Moshtaque started by allowing clerics access to the presidential palace. In the BNP's worldview, this was reflective of local realities, and attracted both the radical right and left to the party. The most controversial decision Zia took was to rehabilitate Mujib's and Tajuddin's killers. The Indemnity Ordinance gave Mujib's assassins legal immunity. Zia didn't overturn the ordinance. 'He could've distanced himself from the whole affair. But instead he added legal weight to the ordinance by turning it into a constitutional amendment. So for a time ours was perhaps the only constitution in the world that protected self-proclaimed killers', says Mahfuz Anam, editor-in-chief of the *Daily Star*.[199] Zia's request for US weapons also worried India—so much so that an angry Jacob warned US diplomats: 'don't play with fire over there'.[200] Jacob's warnings were rubbished as 'schizophrenia about Bangladesh', and by October 1976, Washington, D.C. was pushing for military supplies to be sent to Dacca.[201] The situation was expected to worsen.

India believed that Zia's restraint was 'an act for our benefit'.[202] The lessons Indian policymakers learnt after these shocks, and the approach they adopted until Gandhi's 1977 ouster demonstrates how the vocabulary of being pro- or anti-India became entrenched. India mourned its failure to support pro-India elements rather than helping Bangladesh build resilient and inclusive political systems. In a 'confidential' MEA note titled 'For a New Policy Orientation Towards Bangladesh', officials noted that their biggest failure was the inability 'to retain the hard core of pro-India elements there'.[203] This highlighted Tajuddin's loss. That India failed to support an inclusive system or contain Mujib's authoritarian instincts was overlooked. Bangladesh was a theatre where big powers played games, and India's failure meant that it was now left with no friends in power.

It all began, the report noted, with DP's 'inept' handling of Bangladeshi politics.[204] His push for an alliance between AL, the National Awami Party-Muzaffar (NAP-M), and the Communist Party of Burma (CPB) made Mujib 'suspicious'.[205] Separate training to the Mujib Bahini was also criticised. The JRB, New Delhi acknowledged, created 'mental scars' that affected the situation.[206] Appointment of 'old man' Dutt 'was a mistake', and a younger, dynamic high commissioner would have been a better fit.[207] Even the Joint Secretary who took charge of Bangladesh after liberation had the 'most fatalistic' attitude and was 'devoid of any imagination and drive'.[208] The pervasive attitude among Indian officials was that they had done enough for Bangladesh, and that Dacca must behave nicely or 'we will put them at their proper place at the right moment' showed complacency.[209]

In an admission of guilt, the note highlighted what Bangladeshi politicians still blame India for, i.e. it was true that the Indian army dismantled entire arms factories and took them away. This was done 'with the encouragement and active connivance of Marwari businessmen', but no one was punished.[210] Indian businessmen, along with 'unprincipled' Bangladeshi businessmen and with 'active support of security forces on the Indian side', engaged in large-scale smuggling.[211] The high commission's denial about such smuggling had little credibility and lowered Dutt's prestige.

An activity that wreaked economic and political 'havoc' in Bangladesh, the lure of easy money 'corrupted an important section of the leadership of the Awami League and blackened its image in the popular mind'.[212] The charge that India was dumping sub-standard products was also correct. The State Trading Corporation of India was sending 'utterly rejected material' to Bangladesh.[213] In such a situation, it was natural that Bangladeshis believed that India was 'crippling' the Bangladeshi economy. When R&AW befriended some of the 'brilliant and active youth leaders' of the JSD in Calcutta, Mujib suspected that India was undermining him.

Lastly, statements by Suttar that he rejected the 'Mountbatten plan', implying that he sought a merger of India and Bangladesh, 'alienated' even the most pro-India elements.[214] Suttar routinely met with Dutt to debrief him on AL's inner politics. He complained that Hindus had no future in Bangladesh given Mujib's appeasement of the Muslim Bangla Movement.[215] When encouraged by Dutt to raise the issue with Mujib, Suttar claimed that Hindu parliamentarians can't complain as it would make them pariahs. Instead, he suggested that if 'there will be serious repercussion across the border and Muslims within India will be under pressure, then the Muslims would not dare to do anything against the Hindus in Bangladesh'.[216] The 1964 communal riot, Suttar argued, was evidence such tactics worked.

The killing of Muslims in West Bengal, in Suttar's view, sobered the then East Pakistani authorities' behaviour towards Hindus.[217]

211

Though Dutt rejected Suttar's 'absurd' suggestions, the latter pushed Dutt to ensure that

> Sheikh [Mujib] should not have the feeling that whatever he does the Government of India will stand by him … [and] that the Sheikh should have a healthy fear of Indian intervention if life is made intolerable for the minorities here and hundreds and thousands of refugees once more trek to India.[218]

Suttar's public statements and private requests alienated Mujib from India, the note argued. It was a scathing self-indictment.

But India continued to make the same mistakes. Officials reaffirmed their faith in India's central aims in Bangladesh after 1975: prevent anti-Indian powers from using Bangladesh as an ops base against India, and prevent Hindu exodus. But the prescription was more of the same, i.e. to have a 'friendly government' in Dacca and forge 'mutually advantageous links' as Bangladesh became 'more and more involved with India'.[219] It was an acknowledgement that India still viewed Bangladesh as a dependency.

Why was there a difference between theory and practice? This is where India's hegemonic ambitions and domestic insecurities come into view. The self-critical note offered a patronising psychological analysis of Bangladesh. First, 'intense anti-India and anti-Hindu propaganda' before 1971 left a 'residue' in the subconscious Muslim minds.[220] Second, the disconnect between East Pakistan and India meant that Bangladeshis didn't understand India and believed all propaganda (despite the report acknowledging that Bangladeshi charges against India after 1971 were accurate). Third, being a small new nation, Bangladesh had a 'natural sense of inferiority, which every 'aided' nation resents'.[221]

The note advocated a 'mature' long-term approach that aimed to strengthen pro-India lobbies, and sought a 'cultural conquest' that would expose Bangladeshis to Indian secularism and ally with the Soviets to forestall the US-China-Pakistan nexus.[222] Anything that undermined India's 'unipolarity in Bangladesh' in the long term must be avoided.[223] But in the near future, New Delhi had to convince Zia not to confront India. On 2 January 1976, R&AW Joint Secretary N Framji Suntook, who became chief of R&AW a year later, authored a top-secret note on the strengths and weaknesses of the Bangladeshi government and the opposition groups such as the JSD and Kader Bahini. He noted that 'emphasis on Islamic identity by the majority community' coupled with the rise of China and Pakistan was bad for India.[224] Suntook listed what Pakistan's mission would do in Bangladesh and how India must 'counteract'.[225]

In R&AW's reading, Pakistan was planning to post 100–150 personnel in Dacca and open a consulate in Chittagong. Such a footprint would allow the ISI to exploit the 'old boys network', and have pervasive influence in Bangladeshi ministries. It risked exposing India's problems with Bangladesh 'from A to Z' making Pakistan the 'invisible third party exercising influence' in bilateral negotiations on boundary settlement and water sharing.[226] Pakistan could infiltrate Bangladeshi media and educational institutions to foment pro-Islamic, pro-Pakistani feelings, and encourage anti-India and anti-Hindu sentiments.

Once things started going their way, 'Pakistan may promote the idea of a confederation' with Bangladesh.[227] Why? Because Bhutto viewed Bangladesh's proximity to India's northeast as a strategic advantage and believed this region 'had the potential of developing into another Viet Nam'.[228] True to style, Bhutto met with Mizo rebel leader Laldenga in 1973 to reassess Pakistan's support after the 1971 setback.[229] Suntook believed that Pakistan would also support Naxalites and fuel disaffection against India in Nepal. Zia's conservative nationalism, viewed from this perspective, was anathema.

Suntook recommended an aggressive campaign. For starters, India needed to broaden and deepen its intelligence gathering system to track Pakistani operations. Such measures included cross-governmental coordination with the State Trading Corporation, Aid, Shipping, Coal Board, and so on who dealt with Bangladesh. Suntook proposed maintaining 'steady pressure' on Dacca about Pakistani activities, and to 'make it clear to the leaders of Bengla Desh that their alignment with Pakistan would pose a threat to our security and would not be acceptable beyond a point'.[230] Close cultural ties that 'keep the memories of the freedom struggle' and the 'atrocities committed by Pakistan alive' were also recommended.[231] For this, the scale of India's cultural activities needed to be on a scale 'comparable to that of the Americans and the Russians in India'.[232] But there was a sharper edge to R&AW's strategy. After mapping out the who's who that could target Zia', Suntook recommended all 'feasible measures' to 'soften up areas which are contiguous to Indian territories'.[233] In security parlance, this meant arming the Shanti and Kader Bahinis, and AL rebels such as Suttar (known to R&AW as 'Chittu babu').[234]

Then came Suntook's final blow:

> ...serious thought should be given to the idea of providing strong support to anti-Pakistani activities in NWFP, and Baluchistan now being carried on from bases in Afghanistan. To relieve Pakistani pressure on India through Bengla Desh, it may be necessary to intensify pressure on Pakistan through Afghanistan to the extent that it is feasible to do so.[235]

Suntook's recommendations echoed bureaucratic consensus and became policy until Gandhi lost power in March 1977.[236] Zia came to believe that R&AW was after his life. After coming to power, he prevented an Indian intervention by not declaring Bangladesh an Islamic republic. But he faced intense pressure by anti-regime elements, all of whom received covert Indian support.[237] Officially, India communicated to the US that it was 'calm and cool' about Bangladesh and acknowledged that large-scale persecution of Hindus was not happening.[238] Unofficially, it pressured Zia.

US intelligence noted that the BSF opened more training camps after November 1975 for anti-Zia rebels. By August 1976, India helped an estimated 'two to three thousand' such elements to cross over into Bangladesh.[239] Cross-border violence by India-trained rebels became routine in 1976. Such kinetic support to the Shanti Bahni was accompanied by relocation of Chakma refugees to Arunachal Pradesh.[240] To augment infiltration, the BSF launched a big operation on 20 April 1976 at the Bandarkata border post in Mymensingh.[241] Sylhet and the Meghalaya-Tangail/Mymensigh border areas were specific points where India increased pressure. Many of these India-trained 'miscreants' created 'instability' with the 'ultimate objective of overthrowing the existing government'.[242]

214

Certain members of the Gono Bahini, the JSD's armed wing, joined the Kader Bahini.[243] By May 1976, India had trained the first batch of Shanti Bahini fighters in Dehradun and Haflong, Assam.[244] By 1979, 700 Chakma fighters received training and most of the 150,000 displaced Chakmas were relocated. Just before Gandhi lost power, R&AW asked the Shanti Bahini for a 'big push forward' with the promise of expanding its cadre to 15,000.[245] For his part, Suttar intensified the *Bangabhumi* movement for a separate Hindu state in Bangladesh.[246] Little understood, the *Bangabhumi* movement resonated with Bangladeshi Hindus. 'Our relationship with Suttar was very benign' and the operational understanding 'deep' says an Indian intelligence officer with knowledge of these matters.[247]

On ganga water sharing, both sides negotiated in September 1976, but failed to reach an agreement. India refused to budge on Bangladeshi demands to maintain similar levels of water flow as was happening until mid-1975 (40,000 cusecs), and Bangladesh refused to entertain Indian demands on the Haldia-Calcutta port question or support a Ganga-Brahmaputra link. Reflective of bilateral acrimony, the Indian delegation noted that 'Bangladesh proposals meant that India should be starved of the waters of Ganga. While India was prepared to negotiate, it was not prepared to be dictated to'.[248] In turn, Zia internationalised the issue by raising it at the Non-Aligned Movement conference to India's displeasure.[249] Zia's hardball with India and Gandhi's counter-pressure worsened ties. In June 1976, the Director General-BDR stated that 'in 1971 we fought for independence and 1976 is the year of protecting and safeguarding our independence'.[250] Zia responded to Indian pressure by crossing the latter's red lines. He created thousands of Village Defence Parties and reopened Bangladesh to Mizo rebels and other insurgents who were on the run since 1972.

The situation changed only marginally after Morarji Desai became prime minister in March 1977. The opposition's harassment during the Emergency meant Desai sympathised with Zia. One of the first acts Desai did was undercut R&AW's offensive ops, including in Bangladesh.[251] Suntook was forced to reduce the scale of India's support to Bangladeshi rebels. The impact of this shift was visible in September 1977, when soldiers of the 22nd East Bengal Regiment mutinied in Bogra before a failed coup on 2 October.[252] Forewarned by Egypt, Zia prevented the coup, empowering him in talks with India.[253] On 7 November 1977, an agreement on Ganga water sharing was signed.[254] India allowed the flow of 37.5% (20,800 cusecs) and 62.5% (34,700 cusecs) of the minimum flow of 55,000 cusecs at Farakka during the lean season.[255] Having understood Desai's lack of desire to pushback, Zia ordered the execution of 561 mutineers in February 1978.[256] The event triggered the 'Mayer Kanna' movement by family members of slain soldiers seeking justice. It still haunts the BNP.

More than the November agreement, Zia's first visit to India on 17–20 December 1977 offered him clarity about Desai's intent. In defiance of protocol, Zia was received at the airport by both Desai and Sanjiva Reddy, the Indian president.[257] The process that culminated in Zia's visit and signing of the Ganga water sharing agreement began after the Janata Dal came power. In April 1977, India's young external affairs minister, Atal Bihari Vajpayee, met with Zia's foreign affairs advisor and scheduled an impromptu meeting with Desai. When the officer asked Desai why he stopped Bangladesh's 'rightful share of the waters of the Ganges', Desai shot back: 'I did not do that. That woman did'.[258] In June, Desai and Zia met in London. Here, Desai promised Zia that he would not support Bangladeshi rebels.[259] Zia didn't reciprocate the favour. Cognisant of Desai's politically infirmity, Zia restarted support for Mizo rebels in 1978. Desai's 1979 ouster and Gandhi's return proved Zia's calculus accurate, but fatal.

When Gandhi returned to power, the geopolitical situation was radically different. The Soviet invasion of Afghanistan intensified regional rivalries. On 21 January 1980, Zia travelled to India for the 3rd summit of the United Nations Industrial Development Organisation along with his wife Khaleda Zia and met Gandhi for the first time. The 45-minute meeting was 'cordial', even though its details are sketchy. But it didn't fill Zia with confidence that Gandhi's views about him had changed.[260] The Farakka agreement was the first casualty. As Narasimha Rao put it, despite 'constructive dialogue' on the land and maritime boundary dispute, illegal cross-border movements, railway transit, and trade, the Joint Rivers

Commission, which met in January 1981, couldn't tackle 'the toughest of the problems, Farakka'.[261] The 1977 agreement, Rao argued, 'did not safeguard the principal purpose of the Farakka barrage', which was to ensure adequate supply of water to Calcutta port (and inland industries in UP and Bihar), and neither did it ensure a time-bound programme for the overall utilisation of the Ganga basin water.[262]

Bangladesh's argument that its dependence on Ganga was 'total' and that it 'abnormally' received 'a quantum much below the normal flows' between 24 January–26 April 1980 (after Gandhi's return) reflected the political nature of the problem.[263] What Gandhi and Mujib could achieve, and Desai and Zia could resolve, didn't work between Gandhi and Zia. In an acknowledgement of the complexities of water sharing, and noting the fact that Bangladesh could legitimately not take any loss of supply 'lightly', Rao noted in April 1981 that resolving the dispute required political will and statesmanship.[264] Zia was seen to be punching above Bangladesh's regional weight. In the end, though Zia pivoted Bangladesh to the conservative right, he failed to contain intra-party friction. On 30 May 1981, he travelled to Chittagong when a group of army officers stormed the Circuit House and shot him dead.[265]

The Last Coup

On 24 March 1982, Gen. Hussain Muhammad Ershad, the chief of army staff, deposed the civilian government and imposed martial law. Unlike 1975 when India panicked about Zia's rise to power, which included promoting Ershad as deputy chief while he was attending the National Defence College in New Delhi, India's reaction to Ershad's coup was almost positive. In a note prepared by R&AW in April 1982 titled 'Coup in Bangladesh', India's assessment was 'mixed'.[266] Ershad didn't have a 'special anti-India record' and was a 'fairly happy officer in the NDC' when Mujib was killed.[267] Though outspoken about political differences with his Indian colleagues, Ershad was a professional soldier 'anxious to develop an efficient professional army'.[268] Under the 'special circumstances' of Bangladesh's recent history, the R&AW found

Ershad's position 'reasonably coherent'—he wanted 'the army to play a constitutionally legitimate role in spheres outside the purely professional field'.[269] Ershad's championing of freedom fighters, R&AW noted, widened his support without undermining the loyalty of repatriate officers (being a repatriate himself). India could do business with Ershad and assessed that he would not 'completely side' with Islamic conservatives.[270]

Far from being disappointed by the suspension of the Constitution, Rao informed the parliament that the situation in Bangladesh was 'under control', all Indian personnel 'safe', that the coup was an internal matter, 'and it is our expectation that nothing will happen which will affect our bilateral relations adversely'.[271] In his first acts, Ershad invited Rao to Dacca to ensure continuity and stability in ties. On 23 May 1982, New Delhi and Dacca issued a joint statement iterating a desire to 'expeditiously' find a 'mutually acceptable solution' to the myriad problems ailing the bilateral, and especially the river water sharing agreement.[272]

In August 1982, the Joint Rivers Commission met again, and unlike in 1981, 'achieved a greater measure of understanding on the elements to be taken into account for finding an equitable solution of the problem'.[273] In October, Ershad visited India, and was felicitated by Gandhi as such: 'you are no stranger to India [and] may this visit be the starting point of a new chapter of trust and co-operation between our two countries'.[274] Ershad's response was swift: 'I am convinced that we must be friends. I mean, good friends, and it is in this spirit that I have come to Delhi, quite confident that, by the Grace of God, we will find honourable and equitable solutions to our problems'.[275] The negotiations restarted.

India's welcoming attitude made many believe that Ershad was the true 'mastermind' of Zia's killing, and 'worked towards that goal since his stint at the NDC' in India.[276] The Indian intelligence officer at the Bangladesh desk when Zia was killed remembers:

In the last week of May 1981, we were overcome by events … we had received a source report from an untested source, a junior or mid-level military officer in Bangladesh, after examining which, our military analysis branch warned in an

internal note that disgruntled officers might try to kill Zia ...
but we weren't convinced.[277]

The officer rejects that India propped Ershad against Zia, because
'Ershad was a weak leader, and couldn't be trusted with such acts'.[278]
R&AW was of the view that Zia's murder by Maj. Gen. Md.
Abul Manzoor and his group evolved from Zia's turbulent relations
with the next top three officers, namely Ershad, Mir Shaukat Ali,
and Manzoor himself.[279] Though India's troubles didn't end with
the coup, as repatriate factions in the army continued to harbour
some (not all) anti-India rebels, Ershad's presence reduced friction.
To make sense of why India reacted the way it did, it's important to
explore the June 1981–March 1982 period after Zia's assassination.

From an Indian perspective, three problems emerged: one,
dissension in the BNP; two, factionalism in AL; and three, Moshtaque's
return to political life. All these issues emerged when anti-India
sentiment was high, food supplies were low, prices of essentials were
lofty, and the Soviet-Afghan war sharpened regional faultlines. Plus,
intra-BNP troubles took on new life after Zia's assassination.

Ruthless against dissenters and staunchly nationalist, Zia struggled
to build institutional cohesion in the army and the party. Soon after
his assassination, Vice President Abdus Sattar took charge as acting
president and proclaimed Emergency. Presidential elections were
scheduled for November 1981.[280] Sattar won a 'genuine' majority
in the elections according to R&AW even though the process was
far from perfect with all sides accusing the other of malpractice.[281]
But formation of the government laid bare factionalism. Both right-
wing and left-wing figures were unimpressed by Sattar's cabinet. The
situation worsened when Khaleda Zia, Zia's widow, to whom Sattar
promised but never delivered party presidency, demanded a more
'balanced' cabinet.[282] Such factionalism led to clashes over control
of the party office.[283]

The army cooperated with Sattar, but civil-military ties became
strained when he rejected Ershad's request to participate in the
government. Ershad wanted a Presidential Advisory Group, whereas
Sattar created a National Security Council wherein the service
chiefs were in minority. Ershad's rejection of this council created

a stalemate. Eventually Sattar gave in and reduced the cabinet to eighteen members and replaced the NSC with a new six-member advisory body consisting of three service chiefs, the president, the vice president, and the prime minister. Some argued that Sattar had 'at the last moment, averted an army takeover' in February 1982.[284] But that was not the case. Divisions in the BNP, and Ershad's ambitions meant that a showdown was imminent. For India, Sattar's error was giving in to the 'old reactionary Muslim League wing of the BNP' against the 'centrist Begum Zia' or the leftist group.[285]

The BNP's house was divided. So was the AL's. On 17 May 1981, two weeks before Zia's killing, Sheikh Hasina, Mujib's daughter who took asylum in India after the assassination, returned to Dacca. Hasina was in Germany when the assassination occurred. Supported by Yugoslavian leader Joseph Broz Tito and Gandhi, Hasina returned to a heavily guarded safe house on Pandara Road in New Delhi with her husband and children. She lived under the name of 'Mrs. Talukdar'. Gandhi had personally informed Hasina on 24 August 1975 that all her family members had been killed.[286] During her six years in India, Hasina steered clear of politics, and developed close ties with Congress leader Pranab Mukherjee.

Hasina's return to Dacca worried the BNP, who blamed India for interfering in Bangladeshi politics.[287] Despite such propaganda, Indian officials noted with satisfaction that Hasina 'was accorded an extra-ordinary and emotion-charged reception … mammoth crowds also greeted'.[288] Her foremost demand was to bring Mujib's killers to justice. Ironically, by September, as elections approached, Hasina's criticism of the BNP was that 'the present Government had sold Bangladesh's interests to India' in a reference to the 1977 Ganga water sharing agreement (which expired in 1982 and was not renewed) and other agreements that Zia had reached with Desai.[289]

Hasina's return occurred when the two countries were embroiled in a naval face-off at the New Moore Island, known as South Talpatti, just off the Sundarban coast. On 11 May 1981, Bangladesh protested the presence of an Indian survey vessel near the island, ordered its navy to halt the vessel, and directed its soldiers to land on the island.[290] India ordered a counter mobilisation and began planning for a permanent BSF presence.[291] The stand-off led to resolutions in the Bangladeshi parliament, and Dacca aimed 'strong resentment and condemnation' against India.[292] Though eventually resolved, the BNP ensured that it clubbed the naval stand-off with Hasina's return and painted it as Indian interference. With elections approaching, such tensions went in the BNP's favour. But they also complicated Hasina's position, who needed to be seen as independent from India.

Dr. Kamal Hossain, former foreign minister whom many Indian officials didn't trust, curated Hasina's return in 1981. He says that she was not satisfied with India's support during her time in New Delhi. 'She used to complain that India didn't offer her amenities such as a car and driver', limiting her mobility.[293] Gowher Rizvi says that 'Hasina believes India didn't do enough after Mujib's assassination to counter Zia-ur-Rahman and help the democratic forces in Bangladesh'.[294] Indian intelligence officers who dealt with Hasina agree that New Delhi refused some of Hasina's 'excessive demands'.[295]

More than personal dissatisfaction, Hasina's compulsion to feign distance from India was critical. Her criticism of the BNP for not pushing a harder bargain on water sharing, trade, and land boundary, was directed towards the Zia-Morarji understanding, not Gandhi. But she was still 'too young' to stand for office, so Hossain became AL's candidate. Worried that India was interfering through Hasina, Sattar increased surveillance on the Indian high commissioner leading to protests by a livid Gandhi.[296] Sattar's political mishandling and harassment of the IHC offered Moshtaque an opportunity to call fresh elections. Ershad had other plans.

Conclusions

India lost the peace in Bangladesh because it became obsessed with security. Instead of strengthening democratic institutions, India limited its Bangladesh policy to preventing Hindu exodus and denying space to Pakistan, China, the US, and northeast rebels. Whoever could deliver on these was considered pro-India. India's failure to achieve security in its near east was testament to an acute failure of imagination on how to treat a smaller neighbour and deliver on democratic constitutionalism. It took the killing of Mujib for Indian policymakers to reflect on their errors. They still failed to adapt their approach to supporting institutional integrity in Dacca and better securing Indian interests, instead of allying with a single party or individual. Zia's support to Mizo rebels in 1978 showed how deeply India's regional hegemony was resented in Dacca.

India's wars with China and Pakistan played a major role in securitising Gandhi's regional approach. The 1971 Bangladesh liberation war was *both* a culmination of anger against the Pakistani military among Bengalis, and India's regional insecurities and ambitions. The irony of Bangladesh's liberation was that it strengthened India's security-centric vision, making New Delhi a victim of its own success. Driven by fears of mass migration that could fuel communal fires and the presence of guerrillas demanding separate homelands, India developed a contradictory approach towards Bangladesh. It didn't want to interfere in Bangladesh, but had good reason to—and did so regularly. The strengthening of constitutionalism was a lesser ideal than security, and for that, India accepted Mujib's errors and excesses.

Gandhi's failure to secure India's near east, where it sought to solve its two-and-a-half-front dilemma, underscored official antinomies. India supported Bangladesh's liberation on the premise that Pakistan was undermining Mujib's democratic mandate that should have seen him become prime minister of a united Pakistan—a development India would have welcomed in the belief that it could resolve Kashmir. But both Mujib and India undermined those very principles after 1971, despite enshrining them in the 1972 constitution. Ultimately, the fear of Hindu exodus is what led India to shed the pretence of non-interference and prepare for military intervention in November 1975. The idea that Bangladesh could become an Islamic republic and partner with China and Pakistan militated against India's security red-lines.

Newly declassified documents demonstrate how prevalent the belief to intervene in Bangladesh truly was in India during the 1970s. This is not surprising given the resurgence of the Mizo and Naga movements, outbreak of the Assamese agitation, and tumult among various indigenous communities in India's northeast. To settle these insurgencies and undertake state-building at home, India needed allies. From concerns around mass migration that could sharpen identity politics in Assam and Bengal, and apparent official antinomies, Bangladesh's liberation and India's failure to capitalise on it shows what can, and did, go wrong in India's near east. The 1980s were a testament to these struggles. It was in this context, and that of Congress' electoral losses, that pro-democracy protests rocked Rangoon and Dhaka—offering India an opportunity.

8

ENABLING DEMOCRACY
CIVIL-MILITARY POLITICS IN
RANGOON & DHAKA

'We have noted the undaunted resolve of the Burmese
people to establish a fully democratic structure in their
country. This aspiration fully accords with India's firm
commitment to democracy.'[1]

Official Spokesperson's Statement, MEA,
September 10, 1988

Rajiv Gandhi inherited the consequences of Indira's misjudgements.
He urgently needed to address growing communalism and ethnic
separatism, and arrest economic decline. He adopted a dual-strategy.
Thanks to a massive electoral mandate, he sought reconciliation
with Sikh and Assamese separatists, made compromises to religious
conservatives, and tried stabilising ties with neighbours.[2] Next, he
pressed ahead with economic liberalisation. The first step could
assuage domestic and regional faultlines, whereas the latter could
reshape India's political economy. In India's near east this meant
urging allies in Rangoon and Dhaka to deliver on counterinsurgency
promises and economic connectivity. The former could stabilise
domestic politics, and latter could limit China's influence by

kickstarting India's business and trade links with Southeast Asia. But such strategies birthed severe antinomies that defined the country's domestic and regional predicament during the 1980s.

A detailed analysis of Rajiv Gandhi's tenure is beyond the scope of this book.[3] Instead, this chapter focuses on the links that bound India's regional geopolitics to state-building processes during this period. It explains why Rajiv's outreach to Burma and Bangladesh failed, and what made him explore coercive strategies towards India's eastern neighbours. In Rangoon, India went from engaging with Ne Win to supporting a disjointed anti-junta rebellion by ethnic armed organisations and pro-democracy activists. Caught in institutional stasis, the Tatmadaw failed to recognise Rajiv's intent during his December 1987 Rangoon visit. Rajiv wanted Burma to open itself for business and deliver on counterinsurgency. Instead, he was admonished by an ageing dictator.

In Bangladesh, India continued to sponsor the Shanti Bahini and support the Awami League that sought a return to power through elections. To gain legitimacy, Ershad shed his uniform and founded the Jatiya Party in 1986. But instead of convincing people, he came under criticism from the AL, BNP, and his officer corps alike. When democracy protests reverberated across continents, symbolised by events at Tiananmen Square in Beijing and the fall of the Berlin Wall in 1989, anti-military agitations in Burma and Bangladesh seemed to be part of a global trend. Arch-rivals Hasina and Khaleda jointly pressured Ershad, despite attempting to outbid each other. In both countries, India viewed its security strategic interests to be better served by inclusive, democratic, and federal (in Burma) political systems. Aung San Suu Kyi's rise as a democrat and Hasina's doggedness promised alternatives to entrenched juntas. These two women were considered allies who could help abate India's insurgencies and contain Chinese influence.

The first section explains why India supported the democracy movement and ethnic rebels in Burma. From buttressing the Tatmadaw against ethnic insurgents and communists in 1949, India now intervened against the junta. The second section unearths the secret history of India's arming of Kachin and Chin rebels. Unlike 1965 when India rebuffed the KIO to prevent dislocation of ties with

Ne Win, in 1988 New Delhi supported the outfit—and more—to deny Naga and Assamese rebels sanctuary and support in Kachin territory. Based on a miscalculation that the Burmese junta was about to collapse, such state-rebel alliances, though temporarily successful, collapsed shortly thereafter.

The third section explains how India dealt with turmoil in Bangladesh. Unlike Zia, Ershad was less hostile towards India. But pro-Pakistan elements in the army continued supporting anti-India rebels. India urged Ershad to stand down, thereby paving the way for elections. The assumption was that democratic participation could help check Chinese influence in both countries, and address India's security woes in the northeast. These desires were on par with India's activism in Sri Lanka where it sought provincial elections in Tamil areas and helped usher in the 13th Amendment to the Sri Lankan constitution that recognised Tamil as an official language.[4] The strategic considerations to limit third-party involvement in India's neighbourhood, secure its northeast, and counter China's footprint were paramount in pushing this democratic agenda.

Unfortunately for India, neither Hasina nor Suu Kyi gained power. Hasina's electoral loss in 1991 to Khaleda Zia heightened India's insecurities. In Burma, Suu Kyi's National League for Democracy (NLD) won the 1990 elections, but the junta refused to recognise the results. Unlike their Bangladeshi counterparts, Burmese generals were unwilling to relinquish power. The fourth section unpacks the blowback of India's regional interventionism and the Congress' electoral insecurities. This was a testament to the fact that India was pursuing hope, not strategy. New Delhi's support to Burmese rebels and Hasina was predicated on the assumption that they would succeed in marginalising anti-India civil or military constellations. It backfired, and Rajiv's 1991 assassination marked a violent end to an expensive experiment.

8888

Ne Win rankled Rajiv Gandhi. The Indian prime minister couldn't understand why the general was digressing to his relations with Indira Gandhi and Jawaharlal Nehru instead of focusing on Rajiv's economic connectivity pitch. Rajiv had picked up pre-existing proposals to connect India's northeast to Southeast Asia through Burma and Bangladesh. From here emerged the 'Look East' concept that became foreign economic policy after 1991.[5] If Ne Win allowed India access, Look East could succeed. Instead, Ne Win rejected all of Rajiv's suggestions in an 'avuncular' manner and failed to improve ties.[6] This was not unexpected. Ne Win enjoyed good rapport with Gandhi despite a patchy counterinsurgency record and xenophobia. So, after Gandhi's assassination, he advised Rajiv 'not to bulldoze his way forward in his youthful zeal, for India is also an ancient land where the elders must also be respected even though they might appear to him to be slow and out of date'.[7]

Burma's isolationism peaked during the 1970s, limiting Rangoon's concern with China to the latter's support for the CPB, and little more than interpersonal warmth between Indira Gandhi and Ne Win in India's case. In 1976, the Indian ambassador in Rangoon noted that bilateral ties were friendly, and Ne Win's approach towards Naga and Mizo rebels had undergone 'great change' with increased intelligence sharing.[8] Such support was better than in the past when Burma 'refused to get involved' in these operations and didn't share any intelligence.[9] The situation of Burmese Indians became less acute with large scale repatriations halted in 1974, even though Burmese xenophobia was at a 'peak'.[10]

Rangoon's decision to offer the Water and Power Consultancy Services (India), WAPCOS, a 600,000 USD contract in 1976 to participate in the Rangoon Water Supply Project (overall cost 31 million USD) was a highlight on the commercial front.[11] Instead, what caught Indian attention was an uptick in Burma's drug trade and increased burning of opium across the country. Linked to Burma's insurgent landscape and systemic governmental corruption, an increase in regional narcotics distribution was reshaping the political economy of India's northeast as much as that of Burma.

Ne Win's India visit in November 1980, and Indian external affairs minister Narasimha Rao's Burma visit in October 1981, did little more than reaffirm cordiality in ties. In a secret 1983 report on the 'present situation and future trends in Burma', the MEA noted that despite insurgent and communist threats to the regime, and an intra-junta coup attempt in 1976, Ne Win was 'firmly ensconced' in power.[12] The ethnic rebellions, which denied the junta 40% of the total land area ('though a much smaller percentage of the population'), were considered more 'serious', if territorially limited.[13] The 1982 Burma Citizenship Act that transformed Burmese Indians into 'guest' citizens confirmed India's assessment that Burma was going through another 'transition'. But such was New Delhi's disinterest that it didn't make a single Burma-specific statement that year.[14] As a former deputy chief of mission to Rangoon put it, Burma's lack of interest became a source of 'frustration', as India could do 'nothing ... on the political side'.[15]

In 1985, a young diplomat named Ranjan Mathai (later foreign secretary) was appointed deputy secretary in MEA's Bangladesh-Sri Lanka-Burma desk. He says,

> Rajiv Gandhi took a fresh approach and felt we needed to work on economic cooperation, which held good potential, starting with the Northeast, but extending more generally to the rest of India ... that it was an area where we should take up opportunities to build influence and strong ties before everybody else got in.[16]

The 1985 visit of former US president Richard Nixon to Burma, accompanied by former Treasury Secretary who was known for links to oil industry, piqued Mathai's interest. Though few details could be ascertained, he flagged the information, and it received some high-level attention.[17] Mathai notes,

> At that point in time there was no sense as to just how entrenched China was going to become but it was evident that China, Japan, and the US continued to take an interest in Burma despite the fact that Burma maintained this withdrawn, almost isolationist kind of stance ... that is what motivated him [Rajiv].[18]
>
> 'Oil was important for our security' and Burma had reserves that India could access.[19]

Mao's death and Deng Xiaoping's 1978 Burma visit improved Sino-Burmese ties. Deng's 'open door' policy to foreign trade and investment and development of Special Economic Zones in Yunnan increased trade with Burma from 10–20 million USD in 1978 to over

440 million USD by 1984–85.[20] The Deng-Ne Win rapprochement didn't yet raise concern in India about Rangoon's China tilt. But it did generate limited criticism by parliamentarians such as George Gilbert Swell from Meghalaya who blamed New Delhi for not giving enough attention to Burma, and treating bilateral ties like a 'fire brigade'.[21]

Just as Indian diplomats prepared the groundwork to break the impasse with Ne Win, in December 1985, on India's request, Rangoon launched an operation against Naga rebels. To monitor the operation, India's Chief of Army Staff visited Rangoon in 1986 and offered military assistance. He was turned down. The Burmese offensive failed as Naga rebels either countered the Tatmadaw or escaped to KIO-controlled territory. Such failure buttressed the confidence of Assamese, Manipuri, and Bodo outfits to deepen their alliance with the KIO, making the latter pivotal to India's security dynamics. But the idea to shore up ties with the junta developed in New Delhi despite such setbacks. In 1986, India sent Swell on a formal visit to Rangoon, only to have his views reconfirmed. When the government pitched his visit as a sign of cordial ties with Rangoon, he called it 'the biggest joke of the century'.[22] When countered by the foreign minister that if relations have not grown then 'we are not responsible for it…on our part we want to build friendly relations with Burma', Swell quoted the junta's views on India: 'Burma is saying we have no cognitive thinking'.[23]

The Maritime Boundary Delimitation Agreement in December 1986 settled the dormant dispute about ownership of the Coco Islands, and offered an opportunity to explore a prime ministerial visit to Rangoon.[24] Burmese foreign minister Ye Guong's September 1987 New Delhi visit finally paved the way for Rajiv's visit. To please the junta, Rajiv presented them manuscripts of Maha Bandoola, a 19th-century Burmese general who expanded Burmese kingdoms in Manipur and Assam but died in the 1825 First Anglo-Burman War.[25] The manuscripts were brought to Calcutta by the British, and Rajiv's gesture was meant to capitalise on the junta's Burman nationalism. Rajiv even invited Burma to join SAARC.[26] None of it worked. Ne Win's rejection of India's outreach wouldn't have generated a strong reaction had it not been for a steadily worsening political and security situation in the northeast.

Congress-AGP tensions in Assam were increasing when Rajiv returned from Rangoon. Armed skirmishes with NSCN in Nagaland and Manipur coupled with electoral insecurities in Mizoram led to the imposition of president's rule in Nagaland and Mizoram in August and September 1988 respectively. Frustrated with Ne Win, Rajiv directed the R&AW chief to engage with the KIO, who in turn ordered Bibhuti Bhushan Nandy, his station chief in Bangkok, to act on the channel R&AW maintained with KIO through Thailand. Nandy, along with Rajinder Khanna, India's consul in Chiang Mai (who later became R&AW chief and deputy NSA) cultivated KIO leader Maran Brang Seng. Like in Sri Lanka where India supported Tamil militants to influence Colombo, and in Bangladesh where it supported Chakma rebels to influence Dhaka, in Burma it supported the KIO and other outfits to pressure Rangoon.

More than concerns about Chinese ingress in a neutralist Burma, India's domestic politics and Ne Win's non-cooperation created ground for a turnaround in India's approach, i.e. from deepening ties with the junta to a pro-democracy posture. The shift had little to do with idealism, even if the belief that a democratic Burma was in India's interest was widely held. The sequence of actions after Rajiv's Rangoon visit impart clarity on this aspect. Rajiv's visit occurred after Ne Win demonetised 25-, 35-, and 75-kyat notes in September 1987 and introduced 45- and 90-kyat bills because of his astrological fixation on number '9'. The streets of Rangoon were reeling with protests and violence due to economic hardship when Rajiv was spelling out connectivity plans to Ne Win.

In February 1988, a Burmese delegation (including army officers with economic interests)[27] visited India as a follow-up to increase trade (then at 346.2 million Indian rupees, i.e. approximately 28 million USD)[28] and promised more rice exports for various imports from India.[29] Going by optics, India was committed to the junta well into 1988 despite public protests. On 5 April 1988, both sides agreed on the 'strengthening of bilateral cultural relations', cooperation in Information and Broadcasting, and controlling drug trafficking.[30] But Aung San Suu Kyi's return to Rangoon from Oxford in April, Ne Win's resignation in July, and around half a million people flooding downtown Rangoon in protest on 8 August 1988 (8-8-88) (in the belief that the number '8' was an astrological counterpoise to Ne Win's '9') shifted India's policy line.

On 10 September 1988, India issued a statement in support of democracy protesters:

> We have been watching the recent developments in Burma with particular attention. We have noted the undaunted resolve of the Burmese people to establish a fully democratic structure in their country. This aspiration fully accords with India's firm commitment to democracy. It is our hope that the Burmese people will be able to fulfil their legitimate democratic aspirations for a representative government. The need of the hour is for the unity and consensus of democratic forces for a peaceful and orderly transition to permit free and fair elections.[31]

It was a half-baked turning point, and India's appeal to democracy was performative and not substantial. Based on a miscalculation that the junta was collapsing, India criticised the regime without investing sufficient resources to ensure that the collapse did occur. Diplomatic ties were downgraded, the ambassador was recalled, and Lalthlamuong Keivom, a diplomat from Manipur, was asked to run the embassy as chargé d'affaires. During initial crackdowns, the Indian embassy offered medical care to the wounded on humanitarian grounds. This incensed the military, who viewed it as intervention in domestic affairs. The Tatmadaw cordoned the embassy to prevent locals from entering, and heightened surveillance of Indian officials and citizens alike.

Girish Gupta, a trader who imported books from Rangoon, remembers vividly how the junta would clean the streets of blood after each crackdown.[32] 'The military fenced the Indian embassy from all sides, and checked anyone who entered and exited', he remembers.[33] Given a Rangoon-only visa, Gupta regularly reported his presence to the police. '*Bahut dikkat thi* (it was very inconvenient)', he remembers.[34] Those Burmese Indians who helped Gupta (many of whom were diehard Suu Kyi supporters) received Hindu religious artefacts such as '*ganga-jal*' (holy water from the Ganges) and *Hanuman Chalisa* and 'put their lives on the line to help' him.[35]

Turnaround

India adopted a two-pronged approach against the junta. Politically, its diplomatic tone became sharper. After Ne Win's resignation, Sr. Gen. Saw Maung took control and became Chairman of the State Law and Order Restoration Council (SLORC) with Vice Sr. Gen. Than Shwe as deputy. Indian diplomats lobbied international opinion against SLORC and opened the door to those fleeing the regime.[36] Unlike 1973, when Gandhi almost refused Nu asylum to keep Ne Win happy, in 1988 India supported the former Burmese prime minister's abortive initiative to become the node of political coordination within the democracy movement.

Nu's daughter, Than Than Nu, held a job in the AIR's Burmese-language vertical and broadcasted strong-worded anti-junta segments.[37] The Congress passed a resolution that 'unambiguously' supported the democracy movement.[38] From Rangoon, Keivom reported the scale of unrest. In contact with the democracy movement's leadership on a '24-hour basis', Keivom was supported by four intelligence officers, one each from R&AW, IB, military intelligence, and the NCB.[39] 'I met with Suu Kyi many times and collected information', he says, and had reservations about her willingness to accommodate minorities.[40]

Treatment of Burmese Indians was a case in point. 'I said it decades ago that Suu Kyi is a Burmese nationalist', and that the 'Burmese are Burmese, they hate the Indians more than the Chinese due to colonial legacies', he notes.[41] In a reference to the ethnic cleansing of the Rohingya in northern Rakhine, Keivom says that the issue existed to a lesser extent even during Rajiv's time. 'I sent a lot of reports on this issue during my time in Rangoon', he says, and notes that Suu Kyi was aware but did nothing about it.[42] She felt 'that Muslim penetration is a problem' and didn't bother to include the Rohingya in the democracy movement.[43] Posted in Rangoon until 1990, Keivom used his position to convince ethnic minorities, especially the Chin, to participate in elections as that would make them Myanmar citizens.

The second aspect of India's interventionism was of the military nature. India began arming ethnic armed outfits and pro-democracy rebels in Burma, and offered military training in former MNF camps in Parwa and Champhai. Meant to deny sanctuary and support to India-centric rebels, such arming of cross-border rebels was buttressed by the assumption that the junta was collapsing anyway. Brutal crackdown by the Tatmadaw's 22nd, 44th, and 77th Light Infantry Divisions that killed over 3,000 unarmed civilians had pushed many Burmese students to join hands with ethnic armed organisations.[44] In this context, the '8888' movement, and the sympathy it evoked in India, imparted a political dimension to such ops—somewhat confusing ends and means.

The timing of India's outreach to the KIO and the scale of support offer clues. India's channel with the KIO existed since 1972 when it opened the Chiang Mai consulate. Since 1975, Thailand-based Indian intelligence officers maintained links with the KIO's Col. James Lum Dau. In 1985, shortly before the Mizoram accord was signed, Indian intelligence officers sought Lum Dau's insight on why New Delhi was struggling to get the MNF to sign the accord despite Laldenga's willingness to engage. By now the R&AW-KIO channel was ten years old, and R&AW trusted Lum Dau enough to debrief him on India-MNF talks.

Lum Dau's response was categorical:

> I would like to talk to you like an old friend. I think it seems to me that your representatives treated the revolutionary group like a 'cat' watching or staring at a 'mouse' from a higher level. The talks will not be successful when one party does not feel that they are equal in status. The situation is similar to the talks between the Burmese authority and the revolutionary groups in Burma.[45]

Lum Dau was treated as state guest by Mizoram government after 1986 and invited to Aizawl on three occasions for lunches and dinners with Laldenga.[46] The decision to elevate this channel into an alliance occurred after Rajiv's Rangoon visit but *before* 8 August 1988, when democracy protests rocked Rangoon.

On 11 December 1988, Brang Seng landed in New Delhi and met with top security and political figures.[47] Thus began a five-year-long secret engagement wherein New Delhi offered the KIO political and armed support. To operationalise the relationship, R&AW's Nandy coordinated with counterparts in the IB and the military intelligence.[48] The KIO was given a safe house in East Delhi,[49] promised to establish and expand jade trade in India, offered free education to some Kachin students, and delivered weapons.[50] India's only ask from Brang Seng was that ties were cut with ULFA and NSCN-IM.[51]

The decision to airdrop the first round of weapons and rations for the KIO in April 1990 was a result of this denial strategy.[52] India's help at a moment when the KIO was struggling to keep up its momentum was effective. In July 1990, the KIO announced an end to its decades-long relationship with the NSCN-IM, and with ULFA. Brang Seng halted training for these groups and asked them to leave 'with a heavy heart'.[53] Though the Nagas comprising the former left quickly in April,[54] the ULFA 'was the last to leave in October 1990'.[55] Enabled by the KIO's denial of access and support, the Indian army launched Operation Bajrang to target ULFA in November.[56]

Successful execution of Operation Bajrang augmented the KIO's strategic value for India. New Delhi elevated the relationship, and on 27 January 1991, one day after India's 41st Republic Day, Brang Seng met with India's prime minister Chandra Shekhar. In this thirty-minute meeting, Chandra Shekhar agreed to fund a media station and allow the opening of a Representative Office of Kachin Affairs in New Delhi for the Democratic Alliance of Burma (DAB), a cross-ethnic alliance of 23 armed groups of which Brang Seng was the founding vice-chairman.[57] For the KIO itself, Chandra Shekhar instructed R&AW to discuss 'in detail … other aid'.[58]

The KIO didn't have alternatives. Its traditional patron Beijing had thrown its weight behind the Tatmadaw. Even erstwhile allies such as the CPB didn't receive succor from China.[59] Consequently, in early 1989, the CPB, which had been an uncomfortable ally for the KIO, imploded, exacerbating the latter's vulnerability. Factional infighting and other losses compounded such challenges.[60] The plan to open an office near the India border, then, was both an ambitious geopolitical bet and survivalism. To prevent the KIO from collapsing militarily, the Indian army had secretly airdropped between '700–900 assault rifles, light machine guns, carbines, grenades', assorted ammunition, and daily rations in April 1990.[61]

On 15 September 1991, the Indian army launched Operation Rhino in Assam and Arunachal Pradesh, with the KIO blocking ULFA's escape routes. Shortly after, India promised Brang Seng another tranche of 6,000 used small-arms.[62] Between 13 May–5 June 1991, these weapons were lifted from Calcutta's Dumdum airport and helidropped in 4–5 rounds at the KIO's Wungau camp near the Indian army's airstrip in Vijayanagar. Brang Seng paid 12,000 USD to the Government of India for the use of helicopters.

Support from India ensured that the KIO cut its relations with Pakistan before the death of its president Zia-ul-Haq in 1988. Keen to mobilise and incorporate armed Rohingyas in the democracy movement, Brang Seng had deputed Lum Dau to seek Rawalpindi's support. The ISI connected Brang Seng with Afghan Islamist Gulbuddin Hekmatyar, who hosted a KIO delegation for three days in Peshawar in April 1988 and offered weapons. In return, Zia-ul-Haq sought Brang Seng to support Khalistani militants in Punjab. This nexus didn't materialise due to Zia-ul-Haq's untimely death and R&AW's outreach to the KIO.

The other group that received Indian attention was the Chin National Front (CNF). Modelled along the lines of KIO, the CNF was created on 20 March 1988 under the chairmanship of No Than Kap. Trained by Kachin militants, the CNF had a small armed wing, which was launched in November 1988.[63] With support from the Zo Reunification Organisation, led by former Mizoram chief minister Sailo, and operating from Aizawl, No Than Kap acquired an Indian passport, and operated under the cover name of 'John Khaw Kim Thang'.[64] With the Mizo rebellion quelled in 1986, the CNF sought to join the Indian Union along with other Zo-Chin groups.[65] They saw brighter prospects in India than in Myanmar.[66] In July 1989, the IB's 'Dr. Surinder Das' (also in contact with Brang Seng) visited Aizawl and met with Sailo and No Than Kap.[67] Das clarified that India was not interested in 'even an inch of your [Chin] area', but promised to offer financial support, access to the Indian Air Force airstrip in Vijaynagar, and training in Champhai.

'Rajiv Gandhi was a man with a vision, and the way I see it, he wanted the whole Chin Hill area as an India-managed semi-independent buffer state', No Than Kap says.[68] He was tasked with coordinating the CNF's cash flows through Sailo.[69] In August 1989, Das gave 600,000 Indian rupees to No Than Kap, and promised another 1 million Indian rupees via Sailo. But the money never came. 'Sailo was thinking of using the funds together, but we could not let him do that. Instead, he used the funds for his local party in Mizoram … I made a huge mistake by trusting him', remembers No Than Kap.[70] For his part, Sailo informed the CNF that 'India wants the Chin parties to unite and have one leader and one voice. India wants the strongest party to stand and other parties should join them'.[71] The CNF never emerged from internal rivalries, and No Than Kap was ousted in a putsch in 1992. On weapons supplies, instead of delivering them directly, India asked the CNF to procure them from KIO, chaperoning a four-year 'very close' relationship between the two outfits.[72] The KIO trained over 80 CNF in 1989–91.

Instead of help construct a buffer state, the CNF was a small player that became a cog in India's counterinsurgency strategy in the northeast. Given its access to the NSCN-IM and ULFA, the CNF could offer valuable intelligence. But as No Than Kap recollects:

> [The] Indian army wanted to ambush them [Nagas] and asked us for help, but we never gave the Indian army the true locations of NSCN-IM. It was very difficult to deal with both sides … but I managed to help the Nagas and maintain good relations with the Indian army at the same time. This way the CNA got some weapons too.[73]

The CNF's infighting and No Than Kap's double-game cost the outfit Indian support after 1992. Indian agencies ensured that Burmese outfits received just enough support to keep them afloat when Chinese support was shrinking, but not become powerful enough to topple the junta or turn against India. New Delhi's decision to not arm rebels far from the India border (Mon, Shan, Karenni, Wa, and others) highlights defensive intent, i.e. it was meant to obviate space and sancutuary for Indian rebels in Burmese rebel territory and not undermine Rangoon, even if it looked like India sought regime change. The next section explains why India's coercion failed.

'The Other Lady'

Bangladeshi strongman Zia-ur-Rahman's death, Ershad's coup, and Hasina's return reduced bilateral acrimony with Dhaka. But this was optics, not substance. To abate factionalism in the army, Ershad accommodated the freedom fighters, and to prevent dislocation of loyalties among repatriate officers and India critics, he let the Directorate General of Forces Intelligence (DGFI) support anti-India rebels, if at a smaller scale. Despite tilting towards India, Ershad needed to have 'good relations with Pakistan, otherwise we would have been seen as being too pro-India, that had its own costs', according to Shafi, a former senior minister in Ershad's cabinet.[74] 'His army was very anti-India' even if he didn't see New Delhi as such, notes another Jatiya parliamentarian.[75] Effective management of intra-army rivalries was critical for regime survival, and there were powerful pro-Zia lobbies in the officer corps. The Ershad years (1982–90) were typified by his inability to contain anti-India impulses in Bangladesh. Instead, he struck a bargain with pro-Pakistan elements while promising India to limit, if not eliminate, their activities.

Ershad's bargain involved the promise of democratisation, returning the military to the barracks, and resolving long-standing disputes with India. By the time he was ousted in 1990, Ershad failed to deliver on all aspects. The military refused to support him, both Hasina and Khaleda Zia launched protests, and India-Bangladesh ties returned to being fraught. The initial welcome that Ershad received in India dissipated. Though formal relations, as Rajiv told parliamentarians, were 'very cordial and stable', differences continued to shape the bilateral.[76] Indira Gandhi's desire for the two countries to 'concentrate on what is common between us and try to enlarge its area' was not panning out that way after her assassination.[77]

Three specific issues continued to undermine relations: river water sharing, boundary demarcation, and displacement of Chakmas to India. These were all central to India's state-building project and held tremendous political salience at the state and national level. By 1990, the domestic situation for Ershad worsened to such an extent that his attempts to resolve problems became remote. India's ability to shape Bangladesh's politics also reached an all-time low during this period due to internal tumult.

On river water sharing, Rajiv and Ershad decided to engage. To address Bangladeshi concerns, India requested that Dhaka provide a link-canal from the Brahmaputra river to increase water flows. A Memorandum of Understanding to this effect was signed on 22 November 1985.[78] But for this to happen, storage reservoirs were needed upstream in Nepal, for which neither India, Nepal, nor Bangladesh had the resources or political will. In April 1987, external affairs minister Narayan Dutt Tiwari informed the parliament that though the focus was on 'augmenting' water flows to Bangladesh with Nepalese support, 'all this is a very, very remote possibility, as of now'.[79]

In August 1987, the Ministry of Water Resources prepared a report termed 'India, Nepal, and Bangladesh: Approach to Water Resources Development' that listed all relevant technical and geological aspects. It noted that 'mobilisation of adequate financial resources is a persistent and recurring problem in the case of large-scale multi-purpose projects'.[80] Instead of resolving the issue, both sides talked about it and formed task forces without much to show. Shafi blames the failure of talks on the obduracy of Indian bureaucrats who prevented Rajiv from proceeding on Farakka.[81] The affair became a diplomatic dance wherein both sides understood that no progress would be made, but the appearance of cordiality to fend off domestic opponents was important.

Shafi remembers that Farakka was both a rallying cry that fed anti-Indianism and 'a cheap slogan'.[82] He states:

When Ershad came to power, he had an understanding [with New Delhi] … we were receiving 55,000 cusecs of water, and we wanted to continue that amount. So a few consultants were hired to see what was feasible. But to get 55,000, we realised that there was a need to develop dams upstream in Nepal. We didn't have the money for it and doing anything with Nepal and India together was almost impossible. We also realised that 55,000 was not possible on a sustained basis without augmenting water upstream. 25,000 cusecs were considered feasible. Incidentally, this was the amount that had been understood between Morarji and Zia too. We asked the Indians to guarantee that they'll continue to allow 25,000 cusecs to ensure the bare minimum. Political leaders like Rajiv Gandhi, Narasimha Rao, and Gujral were all on board to do it and find a long-term solution. But the bureaucracy was not on board. They kept coming up with some sort of problem or another.[83]

The need to continue failing diplomatic parleys around the river water sharing, then, became a political necessity as much as lack of resolution became a geopolitical reality.

Apart from the politics of resource sharing, cross-border insurgencies stymied the relationship. In 1983, concerns resurfaced about DGFI supporting the Tripura National Volunteers (TNV), initially known as the Tribal National Volunteers, a Christian separatist movement that started in 1978 with support from the MNF. The TNV undermined security in CPI(M)-ruled Tripura. When the communists raised the matter in parliament, the Congress evaded the issue by claiming that Dhaka denied the existence of sanctuaries.[84] It was classic deniability when all parties understood the nature of the conflict, but neither wanted to own it. Parliamentarians such as Chitta Basu of the Forward Bloc and CPI(M)'s Somnath Chatterjee pressed the government on Bangladesh. In December 1983, they raised concerns when Dhaka decided to auction or dispose properties of Indian nationals held as 'enemy property' since the 1965 war.[85] This could lead to losses for Indians and Indian-owned companies. But New Delhi didn't budge.[86] Such issues fed into debates on 'illegal migration' from Bangladesh as the Assam agitation raged.

Cross-border smuggling, lack of progress on land boundary demarcation, and displacement of Chakmas became equally problematic. From gold to watches, opium to livestock, and Pakistani currency to vehicles, the scale of cross-border smuggling on the India-Bangladesh border for the six-month period ending in December 1982 stood at 15.5 million rupees, and was steadily increasing.[87] This added to the need for border controls, and explains why Rajiv agreed to continue supporting R&AW covert operations in Bangladesh that Indira Gandhi had started.[88] In 1984, after the Nellie massacre and the ongoing Assam agitation, India decided to fence the Bangladesh border. Until September 1985, New Delhi spent 755,000 rupees on a Central Public Works Department (CPWD) survey on a barbed wire fence and border road, with costs estimated at an additional 2.07 billion rupees to be completed in five years.[89]

Bangladesh responded adversely to the fencing, which was supposed to be 50 meters inside Indian territory. The Bangladesh Rifles (BDR) began erecting multiple watchtowers (16 new towers were sanctioned, as opposed to 105 watchtowers of the BSF on the Indian side), and incidents of cross-border firing and killings increased.[90] India was forced to halt the fencing, triggering fierce parliamentary debates. Swell from Meghalaya, who kept close tabs on India's ties with eastern neighbours, complained that people living close to the border routinely faced harassment from 'unruly' Bangladeshis who entered India to steal limestone, betel leaves, forest produce, and other goods to sell in local markets.[91] The government grudgingly acknowledged that not only fencing, but even survey work for the fencing didn't progress. This was because four people were killed in 1984 due to BDR firing on a CPWD survey team.

In response, India rushed 27 BSF battalions with 500 personnel each to the border in Tripura, West Bengal, Meghalaya, and Assam.[92] Assam Rifles contingents were reinforced and equipped to treat the border as troubled. Home minister Shankarrao B. Chavan admitted that 'Bangladeshis are trying to threaten any activity on our side of either construction of road or going in for fencing of the area'.[93] Chavan warned that Bangladeshi forces were offering military training to people in border villages to sabotage fencing. He promised that the foreign secretary would take up the matter at the highest levels in Dhaka. As a result, by 1987, the border (including riverine crossings) became heavily militarised, and the BSF apprehended 18,895 'infiltrators' that year (157 in Assam, 85 in Meghalaya, 2,826 in Tripura, 15,804 in West Bengal, and 23 in Mizoram).[94] New Delhi noted that unlike most of these (Muslim) 'infiltrators', it was allowing 'temporary shelter' to a 'large number of tribal refugees', i.e. Chakma (Buddhist) and Hajong (Hindu) communities, who crossed over into Tripura.[95]

By March 1990, official figures of tribal migrants in Tripura stood at 64,955, of which 52,733 were Chakmas.[96] It cost the exchequer 253.6 million rupees during 1986–91, and another 77.5 million rupees were allocated for 1991–92.[97] India allowed Chakma migrants to protest outside Bangladesh's visa office in Agartala.[98] In November 1990, when Indian high commissioner to Dhaka, Krishnan Srinivasan, offered Dhaka to send IG-BSF from Agartala to discuss the Shanti Bahini issue with GOC-Chittagong (while raising ULFA's presence in Sylhet), the latter demurred because the BSF was not 'army'.[99] A glimpse into the archives of the PCJSS offers insight into how the Chakma movement operated from Agartala. Shafi notes that 'Rajiv Gandhi didn't deliver on the Shanti Bahini' (Srinivasan did reach a repatriation deal despite R&AW's reservations),[100] though he acknowledged that the Bangladeshi army 'had its own agenda in that area and was supporting anti-India rebels'.[101] But India's support to Chakmas, Shafi concurs, 'was to pressurise the army … as these things were beyond the foreign ministry's ambit'.[102]

Such turbulence was matched by Rajiv's and Ershad's political desperation. Rajiv was struggling to maintain his electoral fortunes, and Ershad his legitimacy. In retrospect, Ershad's downfall began in March 1985 when he held a sham referendum on military rule despite thousands marching against the exercise. In January 1986 he created the Jatiya party and announced general elections that were held in May. Boycotted by the BNP, the AL contested the elections but lost to a simple majority favouring Jatiya, making Hasina cry foul about irregularities. To protect Ershad, the Jatiya government passed the 7th Amendment Bill in November 1986, giving the dictator legal immunity before lifting martial law. Instead of strengthening his position, the 1986 elections and lifting of martial law united Hasina and Khaleda Zia against Ershad. By June 1987, the opposition crippled Jatiya to such an extent that Ershad announced elections in 1988. This time, all parties boycotted them.

Ershad's twin failures to settle issues with India and inability to gain popularity amidst an onslaught by BNP and AL made his government shaky as the decade ended. One of the many outcomes of his desperation was to adopt populist anti-India rhetoric even though formal relations remained acceptable. Tariq Karim, who was posted to New Delhi as Bangladesh's deputy high commissioner during this period, remembers:

> Rajiv had developed a personal rapport with Ershad, and the both of them got along well ... but under pressure to have elections and to restore democracy, Ershad decided to play the India card ... as I viewed it from New Delhi, Rajiv felt that Ershad had stabbed him in the back, and then India turned increasingly hostile.[103]

Dissolution of the Bangladeshi parliament and fall of the Ershad-led cabinet due to protests in December 1987 led to the political smearing of India by the Jatiya party. The party's secretary-general and serving deputy prime minister claimed that anti-government agitation was fuelled by India because Dhaka refused transit facilities for Indian troops (India and China were caught in the Sumdorong Chu standoff). India reacted strongly:

> We are amazed to see the statement ... The assertion is blatantly false. If the insinuation is that such facilities are required to engage China, with which India is improving its relations, it is clearly the product of a fevered imagination ... It is an old ruse, but one which is patently ill-founded.[104]

Ershad's relations with India hit rock bottom. After 1988, though the BNP and AL jointly countered Ershad, Khaleda Zia criticised Hasina for letting the regime survive at India's behest.[105] Such populism increased the BNP's popularity.[106] During this period, Ershad's anti-India rhetoric sharpened. In April 1989, to appease Islamic conservatives, he introduced the Bill on Islamisation, generating concern about the increased 'sense of insecurity' among Hindu minorities.[107] By November 1990, the communal situation was so fragile that a false rumour about the demolition of the Babri Masjid triggered 'the worst communal outbreak' in Bangladesh.[108] When Srinivasan raised these issues with Ershad, the latter promised 'winning' the Hindus back within a month, but failed to protect the community.[109]

Ershad declared Emergency in November 1990. Without mentioning India's name, he claimed the action was necessary to prevent a 'foreign power' from conducting a 'campaign to create political and economic chaos'.[110] Once again, India denied involvement and claimed that 'such insinuations in no way help building good neighbourly relations'.[111] The scale of street protests and political violence in Bangladesh peaked during this period. As Srinivasan puts it, anti-Ershad forces seemed 'more determined than ever to mobilize forces against him, curfew or no curfew'.[112]

Privately, Srinivasan already doubted Ershad's survivability, when the latter resigned on 5 December 1990. His decision to reshuffle the military's top brass, inability to handle intra-army pressures, and forcing unelected army officers to sit in local administrative units meant that he had few supporters left both within and outside the army. 'Ershad and I took the decision', says Shafi.[113] 'I pushed him to relinquish power because public safety and our security was becoming an issue'.[114] For Srinivasan, it was a 'momentous week' with many calling Ershad's abrupt collapse a 'revolution'.[115]

India welcomed Ershad's resignation: 'which we hope would pave the way for free and fair elections, under conditions acceptable to all political parties'.[116] Ershad was rankling the Congress, and his decision to return four Indian Air Force MI-8 helicopters meant for flood relief was viewed as an 'affront' to Rajiv.[117] Where India erred was in calculating that Hasina could win elections after Ershad. Instead, the BNP won the February 1991 elections, making Khaleda Zia, known as 'the other lady' in India's power corridors,[118] Bangladesh's first female prime minister.[119] Srinivasan blamed it on Hasina's overconfidence and inability to keep her alliance intact.[120] Hasina's push to remove Islam from the Bangladeshi constitution and 'shrill attacks on Khaleda, Zia-ur-Rahman, and Ershad proved counter-productive'.[121] India's pre-election assessment that the AL could win half the seats in Chittagong also proved inaccurate.[122] 'We didn't expect to win in 1991, but when the results came even young unknown candidates that the party fielded in Chittagong won', says a Chittagong-based BNP-linked businessman.[123]

Hasina was in shock. Soon after the electoral loss, her party experienced another split when Kamal Hossain, Mujib's one-time confidante, formed the Gono Forum in 1992. Years later, Hossain claims that he 'underestimated the importance of dynastic politics in Bangladesh' when the Gono Forum failed to fly.[124] But his departure increased Hasina's struggles. The situation in 1991 was different from 1986, when Hasina contested the elections that BNP boycotted. The undercurrents then were in Hasina's favour, making Ershad anxious to seek a backroom deal. This context made many, including India, believe that Hasina stood a chance in 1991. Instead, of the 300 seats, BNP won 140, AL 88, and Jatiya was reduced to 35.

The BNP's return meant that India's security situation in the east was to worsen. On 28 February, shortly after the elections, MEA issued a terse statement: 'We welcome the return of democracy in Bangladesh following the elections. We look forward to working with the new Government for the benefit of both our countries'.[125] Within a week, the *Indian Express* reported that bilateral relations were likely to be 'correct but cool', eliciting clarifications from South Block that it had 'no reason to expect any change in the quality of the State relationship between our two countries'.[126]

When Srinivasan met with Khaleda and sought the 'laconic' BNP supremo's support to 'remove the impression that the BNP was anti-India', she didn't jump at the idea.[127] Her response 'did not do much to reduce our national apprehensions', writes Srinivasan, who notes that other BNP leaders were warm and welcoming.[128] Though negotiations on river water sharing and other forms of cooperation continued, bilateral ties took a nosedive. To make sense of the BNP's rise and India's options, Srinivasan met with many AL stalwarts from 1971. They all warned about Khaleda Zia's preference for a presidential system over parliamentary democracy.[129]

But the most 'thought-provoking' input came as a secret note from Manju, editor of *Daily Ittefaq* who offered India insider intelligence after Mujib's assassination. Having gone into hiding after BNP's victory, Manju advised Srinivasan that India should either firmly oppose the BNP 'or do nothing at all'.[130] Srinivasan concurred. Shortly thereafter, the NSCN-IM and ULFA, ousted from Kachin territory, found themselves in DGFI safe houses in Dhaka.

Blowback

On 20 March 1991, Khaleda Zia was sworn in as the prime minister of Bangladesh. The *New York Times* praised her victory in glowing terms: 'Khaleda Zia, who transformed herself in less than a decade from the self-effacing wife of a powerful general to a formidable political leader in her own right, today emerged the winner of the freest national election in this country's history'.[131] But for India, the fact was that Khaleda Zia held a grudge against New Delhi for supporting her opponents.[132] One of her first decisions, with encouragement from India critics in the DGFI, was to resume covert support to anti-Indian rebels. She also appointed loyalists to leading positions in the National Security Intelligence (NSI), Dhaka's civilian intelligence agency.[133] Jointly, the DGFI and NSI opened support for Naga and Assamese rebels.

In mid-1991, the NSCN-IM ordered its officer in Bangkok to shift to Dhaka. In charge of the group's 'Alee Command', this officer was responsible for its foreign relationships. The NSCN-IM developed a network of camps and safe houses across Bangladesh, including in the CHT near the India border.[134] Named Goshen, Bethel, and Zion, these camps were supported by an office in Chittagong city.[135] According to a charge sheet prepared by India's National Investigation Agency, 'these camps are being used for ground preparation, storage, and transportation of arms and ammunition consignment illegally procured through Cox's Bazar' to the various NSCN-IM camps within India.[136]

On losing KIO's support, the NSCN-IM opened channels with Rakhine insurgents active at the Bangladesh-Myanmar border and procured illegal arms worth 2 million Thai bhat (approximately 61,000 USD). Codenamed Operation Jordon, these weapons were stored at a transit camp in Alikadam, south of Cox's Bazar.[137] The NSCN-IM's pivot to Dhaka undermined New Delhi's attempts to deny it arms and international access through Myanmar. The ULFA continued to struggle in the face of the Indian army's counterinsurgency operations, but found space to regroup and rebuild from Bangladesh.

By the end of 1991, Rajiv was assassinated, India's economy was collapsing, the Myanmar junta was resilient, Dhaka was hostile, the northeast remained unstable, and Chinese influence in the region expanded. Similar to the 1971 war that was expected to solve India's security problems in its east, New Delhi's support for democracy in Burma and Bangladesh was supposed to do the same in 1988–90. Both strategies failed.

Blowback against interventionism from Indira and Rajiv Gandhi was so severe that both were assassinated, and the backfiring was not restricted to these assassinations. China benefited from India's miscalculations. Beijing had long adopted a conciliatory posture towards Myanmar. The 1988 pro-democracy protests and 1989 Tiananmen Square massacre strengthened this relationship. India's pro-democracy tilt was in line with Western countries celebrating liberal uprisings the world over. But as former Myanmar ambassador to India Wynn Lwin put it, India 'pushed us into the arms of China'.[138]

One of the most visible aspects of China's foothold in Myanmar was the fact that despite ULFA bases being cleared of Kachin territory, Chinese weapons were finding their way to ULFA cadre. Though taking note of such concerns, Beijing explained to Indian diplomats 'that China's relationship with Burma did not imply Chinese approval of the domestic situation in Myanmar' and 'as compared to the past, the level of relationship between China and Myanmar had come down considerably' with a drop in bilateral visits.[139] In a quip that Indian policymakers themselves began to adopt, Beijing noted that the need to contain cross-border drug smuggling without dislocating trade (a centrepiece of Deng's reforms) is what 'impelled' China to engage SLORC.[140] This two-track Chinese policy of limiting bilateral visits but deepening cross-border ties was pivotal in denying India influence in Myanmar. As the next chapter shows, India's strategic backsliding in Myanmar triggered a policy rethink wherein India silently built bridges with the junta even though public opinion supported Suu Kyi.

Mathai argues that India 'went a bit overboard' because 'there was a very personal element in Rajiv Gandhi's feeling to Suu Kyi [and] the military's suspicion of our embassy supporting the protesters was directly linked to that'.[141] Wynn Lwin offers a similar assessment: 'the leadership changed, and things changed. No more General Ne Win and no more Indira Gandhi ... but Suu Kyi went to Lady Sri Ram College in Delhi and then to Oxford [and] was very close to Sonia and Rajiv Gandhi'.[142] In addition to such personal equations, and the Congress' electoral compulsions, there was another feature that made this miscalculation inevitable. India's pro-democracy tilt meant reduced access with the junta. Keivom, who was based in Rangoon and was in touch with the NLD, could offer excellent inputs on the state of protests, but say little on what was transpiring within the Tatmadaw. It was a blind spot that strengthened an already dominant belief that India must support the democracy movement *because* the junta was about to collapse.

Fatally, India overlooked the CPB's collapse in 1989. 'We didn't focus on the CPB because that was an internal matter of Burma' notes Keivom, despite India caring about other Burmese internal matters.[143] To be sure, R&AW officials engaging with Brang Seng did understand that Beijing was pulling the plug on the CPB and the KIO in favour of the junta. But such assessments didn't initiate a rethink about how the collapse of the most powerful armed outfit in Burma would shape its civil-military politics. During 1988–92, India was arming Burmese rebels when China was cutting such support. But India didn't arm these groups enough to help them turn the tide against the junta. Such half-baked endeavours cornered India in Myanmar wherein its civilian democratic allies were jailed, and its ethnic armed allies didn't have the capacity to create a federal democratic republic.

In retrospect, a closer look at official Indian statements underscores the limited nature of India's support to the CNF and KIO. In December 1988, Rao mentioned that cross-border insurgencies in relation to Burma were a 'constant', and 'existed for many, many years'.[144] This meant that support to such groups didn't mean that India sought territorial revisions—even if it vied for political revisions in Rangoon. When parliamentarians such as George Fernandes quizzed the government about what the junta was doing to support India's security concerns, the response often was: 'They have assured us that it is not their policy to support insurgent groups against a neighbouring country and indicated their willingness to cooperate in monitoring insurgent activity. On this basis, border commanders of the two countries maintain contacts with each other'.[145] Myanmar could monitor Indian insurgents, but not execute area-denial measures. From failed attempts to engage the junta to losing Myanmar to Beijing without success of the democracy movement, India's Myanmar policy lay in tatters.

Similarly, when the BNP came to power in Dhaka, a consensus developed there to cultivate ties with China. Though it was Zia-ur-Rahman who opened Bangladesh's doors to Beijing to counterbalance India, Ershad continued the process, making five official visits to Beijing between 1982 and 1990. As Sreeradha Datta notes, Sino-Bangladeshi relations (embraced even by AL to offset its pro-India image) were facilitated by geography and domestic politics.[146] China routinely sided with Bangladesh on issues such as Ganga water sharing.[147] To India's consternation, much of the Chinese-made weapons that ULFA and NSCN-IM found access to came from maritime routes connecting Chinese ports to Chittagong. Even though India's influence in Bangladesh remained wide in scale and scope relative to Myanmar, the BNP's rise and willingness to push back heightened the risk of secessionism in India's near east.

Conclusions

India's pro-democracy tilt towards Burma and, to an extent, Bangladesh under Rajiv Gandhi is often ascribed to strategic overreach by a young idealist. As this chapter shows, Rajiv was neither an ideologue driven by democracy promotion, nor was he attempting overreach in a territorial and political sense. The source of his failure is grounded in the fact that he was neither of the two. If his pro-democracy tilt was lubricated by familial ties with Suu Kyi, it was driven by frustration that the junta was unwilling or unable to deliver on economic connectivity critical for India's growth, and counterinsurgency essential for national security and Congress' electoral dominance. This is highlighted in the suddenness of Rajiv's shift towards Burma. Until April 1988, both Rao and Rajiv were advocating strong ties, despite Ne Win's reluctance. This changed when Suu Kyi entered the equation. What made this shift fatal was its incoherence. India's support for democracy was based on a false calculation that the junta was crumbling, and that all India had to do was nudge it.

Never truly supportive of territorial revisionism, India's engagement with Burmese ethnic outfits was to deny ULFA and NSCN-

IM sanctuary in Myanmar. In fact, India resented the KIO's decision to use India-supplied weapons against the Tatmadaw in 1992. Such open criticism of the junta and support to Suu Kyi but limited arming of the pro-democracy rebels left India in the worst of all worlds. India's failure demonstrated the junta's resilience with Chinese support, and underscored how New Delhi blinded itself of intelligence about tumult within the Tatmadaw after Ne Win's resignation. Pressures within the junta led to an internal coup in April 1992 by a hardline Than Shwe, who blamed Saw Maung for allowing the 1990 elections and letting Suu Kyi nearly dislocate the army's interests.

In Bangladesh, the story was worse. The BNP rose to power democratically using anti-India rhetoric. Anti-India undercurrents in Bangladesh were powerful and exploitable enough that Hasina's and Ershad's pro-India images became both a geopolitical asset and a domestic liability for these leaders. Equally, the BNP's anti-Indianism became an electoral asset but strategic liability for New Delhi. The central themes influencing such dynamics were the same as before, i.e. cross-border migration and its impact on local electoral politics. Rajiv's failure in Bangladesh lay less in his desire to resolve disputes, and more in his advisory setup that disabled him from exploring pathways to conflict resolution with Dhaka. Ershad's own failures compounded such problems.

The Congress' electoral, economic, and geostrategic compulsions were such that the party went from winning the largest electoral mandate in independent India to being ousted within five years, and then losing Rajiv to a Sri Lankan Tamil assassin. The geopolitical trajectory of India in these seven years that coincided with the end of the Cold War is so momentous that it'll take a lot more scholarship to make sense of the changes it wrought on 21st century India. For most leaders of the time, it was fashionable to term Rajiv a 21st century leader who envisioned India as a digital superpower. But Rajiv's regional excesses and economic mismanagement complicated India's rise. Rightly praised for breaking the deadlock in Sino-Indian relations, Rajiv also broke the deadlock for China in India's neighbourhood by pushing Bangladesh, Burma, and other South Asian states in China's direction. As the final part of this book shows, it took longer than a decade to pedal back from Rajiv's errors.

PART III

CONNECTIVITY (1991–2024)

9

HARD LOOK EAST
THE STRATEGIC LOGIC OF AUTHORITARIANISM

'Your appointment is the culmination of a long saga of toil
and sacrifice for the people of Bangladesh [and] am confident
that India and Bangladesh would develop relations of great
cordiality, friendship and cooperation, to the mutual benefit
of both our countries, while you are at the helm of affairs.'[1]

I.K. Gujral, External Affairs Minister of India to
Sheikh Hasina, 25 June 1996

To restrain and reorient India, Prime Minister P.V. Narasimha
Rao tethered New Delhi's post-Cold War foreign policy to its
economic interests. He then pursued nuclear weapons testing to
alleviate India's territorial anxieties and augment national prestige.[2]
Previously external affairs minister, Rao understood the causes and
consequences of New Delhi's regional excesses. With this in mind,
and in the context of the Soviet collapse, assassinations of two Indian
prime ministers, an impending debt default, separatist violence
from Kashmir and Punjab to Assam, and as the leader of a minority
government, Rao decided to overhaul India's domestic and foreign
policy architecture. In India's near east, this meant taking a hard look
at the reality of soured ties with both Myanmar and Bangladesh. To

achieve economic connectivity and national security, Rao returned to the pre-1988 approach of engagement. Such reversal required acceptance of India's overtures by an unfriendly Dhaka, an angry Yangon, and an Indian elite that remained committed to supporting Suu Kyi and Hasina.

It took India all of the 1990s to execute this U-turn. Grounded in the politics of identity, regional political economies, official antinomies, and cross-border migration, the decade marked a dual pivot in India's approach towards its near east. First, religious nationalisms, typified by Hindutva in India, Buddhist nationalism in Myanmar, and Islamic conservatism in Bangladesh became salient in this triangular dynamic. The Babri Masjid's demolition in 1992 undermined India's secularism and angered Bangladesh. But Myanmar didn't raise an objection, allowing New Delhi to rebuild ties with Yangon using religious diplomacy. Second, the 1991 economic collapse and consequent opening of the Indian economy tied its foreign policy to domestic economic interests. Such an economics-driven approach liberated India from any pretence to promote democracy in the region. This pivot was not novel to India's foreign policy, but such was the power of India's democracy rhetoric that dealing with authoritarians in Yangon and Dhaka came to incorrectly be viewed as an amoralistic anomaly.

To balance national interests that required engagement with unfriendly regimes, Rao launched the 'Look East Policy' (LEP). Framed in geo-economic terms and covering the entirety of India's east up to Japan, the LEP afforded New Delhi a cover to undertake two readjustments. First, it enabled a U-turn on India's Myanmar policy. Criticism of the junta was halted and support to democracy activists reduced. The first casualties of this 'Two Track' approach were ethnic armed outfits. For the next decade, Indian agencies executed support termination operations to neutralise Burmese militants in lieu of Yangon's support against anti-Indian militants. The second casualty was the democracy movement. Despite conferring the Nehru Award of International Understanding in 1995 to Suu Kyi—without Rao's approval—India reduced support for the NLD.

The second readjustment was with Bangladesh. The LEP wanted India to engage with Dhaka to deepen multi-modal connectivity. This is reflected in Rao's April 1993 Dhaka visit for the SAARC summit, and bagging of road-building contracts shortly after the Bangladeshi parliament passed a resolution criticising the Babri demolition.[3] But R&AW continued to arm the Shanti Bahini. It was ironic. India was at odds with a democratically elected government in Dhaka and keen to build bridges with the junta. The LEP, in this sense, underscored the limits of India's power in its region, and imparted strategic logic to authoritarianism in its near east. With Ne Win gone, New Delhi could influence the Tatmadaw's India policy. Than Shwe's April 1992 coup offered an opening. But India couldn't convince Khaleda Zia to limit anti-India populism. Hasina's 1996 victory is what made India see light in its near east and led to the signing of the Ganges Water Treaty followed by an India-facilitated accord between Dhaka and the Shanti Bahini.

Such experiences birthed a consensus in New Delhi that friendly regional authoritarians were better than adversarial populists. This idea continues to guide India's regional approach and has become orthodoxy. But the endurance of such a consensus lies elsewhere. China's expanding strategic imprint in India's near east coupled with the explosion of illicit cross-border trade with Myanmar (even though formal trade is limited) after 1991 strengthened this consensus. Beijing's engagement with SLORC necessitated India's pursuit of similar ties. But it is the conversion of illicit cash flows from the Golden Triangle-linked drug trade into electoral finance in the northeast that makes the junta palatable. On this aspect, the 1994 opening of Moreh-Tamu border-crossing played a role. Though India's desire of inclusive growth in the northeast remains unfulfilled, Moreh is a transshipment hub for regional drugs.[4]

The infusion of drugs, arms, and insurgents into an electoral system undergirded by corruption and fueled by ethnic politics redefined India's northeast. The 1990s witnessed a transformation of separatist groups into drug cartels invested in profit over welfare and representative politics. The drug trade doesn't employ at scale, making it easier for the state to target groups at will.[5] This created dynamics wherein outfits seeking separation during the day moonlit as drug cartels to pay off politicians for protection. Such a nexus between crime and politics is deep-rooted in India's democracy and offers a counterintuitive fix to secessionism by tying separatists to Indian politics.[6] The exclusionary and illegal nature of such interactions make ceasefires appealing but conflict resolution and political integration undesirable. The dichotomy of this aspect is visible in the 1997 ceasefire between the NSCN-IM and New Delhi, which came into effect after secret talks between Rao and Naga rebels in Paris in 1995.[7] The ceasefire holds, but the accord is elusive. The following sections elaborate the LEP and India's Myanmar U-turn, followed by troubles in Bangladesh. The final section discusses Nagaland's ceasefire politics.

'Look East Policy'

India's economic and political turmoil before Rajiv's assassination pushed Rao into recrafting India's foreign policy and tying it to an economic reform agenda. In words of a former official who was Secretary (East) in the MEA in 1991 when LEP was launched, the policy was meant to 'forge new bonds with South East Asia, mend ties with China ... look at Japan differently than as an ally of one superpower ... and help establish a world order more just than the one offered by the post-world war institutions'.[8] But a closer look at policy practice shows humility as much as ambition. India's relations were troubled with almost *all* its neighbours. To stabilise ties, Rao needed to accept the limits of India's power. In the near east, this meant accepting the reality of the junta's endurance and the BNP's grip in Dhaka. After introducing the LEP, the MEA undertook a classified Myanmar policy review.[9] It 'really spelled out the need for a more balanced approach', remembers Mathai.[10] But this was to be done 'very carefully' given pro-Suu Kyi sentiments in India.[11] An Indian diplomat on the Bangladesh-Myanmar desk during that period notes that the Indian media played a big role in pressing the pro-democracy line, making outreach to the junta tough.[12]

India operated along dual tracks in both Bangladesh and Myanmar. In Dhaka, it opted for economic engagement, but informally pressured Khaleda Zia by supporting the Shanti Bahini. In Yangon, it opened channels with the junta without shaking the perception back home about this shift. Such duality, wherein New Delhi sought to contain Khaleda Zia's populism and cushion itself from a domestic push of a pro-democracy line in Yangon, imparted a strategic logic to dealing with—and tacitly encouraging—authoritarianism in India's near east. Indian policymakers accepted that supporting regional democrats may not yield results. A lack of resources to impose a democratic order meant that New Delhi desired friendly authoritarians. The Bangladeshi case was telling. Khaleda Zia's democratic credentials were strong, but so was the BNP's alliance with the illiberal clergy. In a move that worried New Delhi, Khaleda Zia appointed the majors responsible for Mujib's assassination in her government. Regardless, Rao pressed ahead with the economic agenda, and made SAARC the platform of choice. Myanmar's insurgent violence and Bangladesh's political fragility honed India's appetite to accept whosoever was in power, as long as they respected Indian interests.

In 1990, India appointed Preet Malik ambassador to Myanmar. Afforded a 'restrictive' mandate, Malik was instructed not to meet with Myanmar's intelligence czar, Khin Nyunt.[13] The AIR's anti-junta broadcasts equally complicated his situation.[14] Led by Than Than Nu (Nu's daughter), these broadcasts were viewed as state propaganda in Myanmar. The army chief, Saw Maung, who, unlike Ne Win, was open to deepening engagement with India, told Malik as much when the latter presented his credentials. Saw Maung believed that Rajiv's return to power in 1991 would mean more pressure, making him seek guarantees from Beijing.[15] Expectedly, Rajiv's assassination led to a collective 'sigh of relief' in Yangon.[16] Soon after, the AIR broadcasts were halted.[17] 'One day the government came and told us to stop broadcasting', so we needed to comply, remembers Than Than Nu.[18] But it took Saw Maung's forced ouster by Than Shwe in April 1992 and a reassessment in the MEA for bilateral ties to improve. Chaperoned by foreign secretary JN Dixit and Rao's principal secretary AN Verma, the first step of this U-turn was a go-ahead to Malik to meet with Khin Nyunt.

In this meeting, Malik secured the Tatmadaw's support against NSCN-K in return for reduced support for the democracy movement. In January 1992, the Tatmadaw launched an operation against Burmese Naga rebels, paving the way for formal talks with

New Delhi in February. The DG-Department of Political Affairs in Myanmar's foreign office met with Dixit to take the conversation forward. They put in place the building blocks of a rapprochement.[19] Rao's, Verma's, and Dixit's turnaround led to the Myanmar president's India visit in August 1992. Than Shwe's political and economic impulse, India reasoned, could help balance China. Beijing had already offered a 1.2-billion-USD defence assistance package to Yangon after 1988.[20] In the first inter-ministerial delegation meeting, both sides focused on the two things that mattered most: halting cross-border insurgencies and fostering cross-border trade.

In March 1993, Dixit visited Yangon. He held discussions with Khin Nyunt, whom India identified as the 'person with whom we had to do business'.[21] He impressed on Khin Nyunt that Myanmar's China-tilt and allowance of Chinese navy basing facilities in the Bay of Bengal and the Andaman Sea, i.e. the Coco islands, would be 'unacceptable'.[22] Khin Nyunt responded positively, leading to a breakthrough in January 1994. The two sides signed a border trade agreement and opened the Moreh-Tamu crossing.[23] It was a small step that overhauled the northeast's political economy. Hidden in the official spokesperson's stoic note that the agreement 'represents the continuing and sincere endeavours by the two countries to improve and strengthen their bilateral relations particularly in the sphere of trade and commerce without allowing extraneous obstacles to mar their growth' was India's and Myanmar's desire to stabilise ties.[24] Than Shwe and Khin Nyunt, though dependent on China, were not tied to it, and saw value in links with India.

In August 1995, Myanmar's deputy home minister Col. Tin Hlaing visited India to discuss security and economic cooperation. His visit convinced the Indian home minister enough to note: 'Myanmar would extend its full cooperation in foiling the activities of some negative elements involving smuggling of arms, narco-trade etc. across the borders. Such a cooperation will give a proper signal to all negative elements indulging in insurgent and militant activities that they will be dealt with firmly'.[25] Tin Hlaing's visit was important because in May, India conferred the Nehru Award of International Understanding to Suu Kyi. Given without Rao's approval, the award disrupted an ongoing joint operation called 'Golden Bird' by the Indian army and the Tatmadaw. Meant to intercept a large consignment of arms for ULFA-I, NDFB, NSCN-IM, and Manipuri militants entering Mizoram through Bangladeshi territory, the Tatmadaw's support was critical. Tin Hlaing's visit occurred after India handed over India-based Burmese rebels to the Tatmadaw. The need for Golden Bird and India's efforts to warm up to the junta underscored that other than countering China, Myanmar's support was essential to balance Bangladesh.

Myanmar's support was so urgent thanks to Dhaka's adversarial approach that Indian forces terminated support for most Myanmar militants that R&AW cultivated during 1988–92. Detailed in the following sections, India's containment of Chin, Kachin, and Arakanese outfits helped the Tatmadaw enter ceasefires and dominate Myanmar's insurgent landscape. Speaking about Wynn Lwin and other Myanmar officials who dealt with India, Mathai notes that they were 'hard-nosed' and realised that neither was pro-Suu Kyi sentiment dying in India, nor were pro-democracy protests disappearing in Myanmar, where lots of people expected India's support.[26] Instead of letting these realities obstruct state-to-state relations, these officers deepened ties.

V Balachandran, then R&AW's deputy chief covering the neighbourhood, notes: 'we had a pragmatic relationship with Myanmar because of trade and other things'.[27] The surest way of doing this was to develop influence over, if not full control of, licit and illicit cross-border movements. The existence of AFSPA made the army a key interlocutor. In a demonstration of India's defence diplomacy, outreach to the Tatmadaw was dominated by defence attachés and army officers posted at the border. A former officer with knowledge of the operation says that Golden Bird 'was not an operational success, and the Myanmar army wasn't very efficient even though they wanted to support us'.[28] So when the op failed, it 'didn't undermine the Indian army's engagement with Tatmadaw'.[29]

Mathai notes: 'They [the junta] themselves realised that depending solely on China was a serious problem and were already throwing in ASEAN membership as a balancer, and wanted India included in their diversified relationships'.[30] In July 1997, Myanmar joined the Association of Southeast Asian Nations (ASEAN), and in

December 1997 it joined the sub-regional BIMSTEC that included India, Bangladesh, Sri Lanka, and Thailand. G Parthasarthy, India's ambassador to Myanmar (1992–95) offers insight into how India managed this transition. 'We were becoming concerned about China's footprint, including in the Coco Islands', and realised that Myanmar was also concerned about this.[31] With the border agreement signed, Parthasarthy worked with the junta to contain narcotics flows and develop a line between the NCB and their Myanmar counterparts.[32] The border opening had augmented the smuggling of prohibited goods, especially Indian pharmaceutical products that were required for drug processing in Myanmar.[33]

To manage domestic pushback against such moves, India engaged with the junta without fanfare. 'We did it very quietly; all this happened with minimum publicity', says Parthasarthy.[34] The Nehru Award to Suu Kyi created some setbacks, but didn't derail the process. When Gujral became prime minister in 1997, he introduced more accommodative policies under the so-called 'Gujral doctrine', which pressed forward engagement with Myanmar. But a more committed—and overt—overhaul of India's Myanmar policy occurred after 1998 under the BJP. Not only was India keen to tame narcotics, increase formal trade, and limit insurgencies to counter China, it also sought to stake a claim in the oil fields of the Bay of Bengal that lay in Myanmar's waters. The 1995 agreement recognising the maritime trijunction with Thailand laid the ground for such conversations. By 2002, the state-owned Oil and Natural Gas Ltd. Videsh (ONGC) acquired a 20% stake in a 2,129-square-kilometre block off the Rakhine coast known as Shwe gas.[35] By this point, the bilateral was strong enough for the Myanmar army's vice chief Maung Aye (considered 'pro-India') to offer to fly Indian delegates to Coco Islands to reduce Indian fears about Chinese encirclement.[36]

India was having a hard look at its near east. Unlike Myanmar, the Bangladeshi situation was different. In August 1991, Rao had a long conversation with Srinivasan, India's envoy in Dhaka. The idea was to reassess India's approach towards Bangladesh in light Dhaka's renewal of support to anti-India militants. Rao felt that the BNP had no intention of being friendly given their anti-India rhetoric and alliance with Islamic conservatives. If anything, in

April 1992, the Bangladesh chapter of the Harkat-ul-Jihad-al-Islami (HUJI-B) was launched.[37] But Rao was willing to give the 'benefit of the doubt since it was a proxy struggle between India and Pakistan for the hearts and minds of the second most populated Muslim country in the world'.[38] In an acceptance of India's miscalculation on Bangladesh, Rao noted that the animus against Bangladesh in India was due to the 'unrealistic expectations' that many Indians harboured in 1971 that the two-nation theory had been laid to rest once and for all: this was 'wishful thinking'.[39] Rao was open to a one-sided relationship to keep 'emotional temperatures' low, and told Srinivasan as much.[40]

Shortly thereafter, Srinivasan met with Bangladesh's chief of general staff who requested that India 'give democracy a chance'.[41] Srinivasan viewed this as possibly his plea for the BNP due to apprehension that Hasina could take to streets again, or fears about potential 'Bonapartism on the part of [chief of army staff] Nuruddin or some other generals'.[42] Either way, Srinivasan noted that Khaleda Zia was not astute in thwarting Mujib's commemoration ceremonies, or failing to condemn physical attacks on or making an active 'Pakistani collaborator in 1971' the president of Bangladesh.[43] With this in mind, New Delhi adopted a dual approach wherein it sought economic connectivity and improved people-to-people relations with Bangladesh. But behind the scenes, it piled on insurgent pressure.

There were a series of talks between India and Bangladesh during the 1992–96 BNP rule. On Rao's invitation, Khaleda Zia paid an official visit to India on 26 May 1992. To pave the way for her visit, Rao agreed to reach an understanding on the Tin Bigha corridor that allowed Bangladesh access to Dahagram and Angarpota enclaves.[44] This arrangement was grounded in the 1974 land boundary agreement, which was renewed in 1982, and again in 1992. In contrast to Rao's concerns that the CPI(M) would jettison the Tin Bigha offer, the West Bengal chief minister Jyoti Basu agreed to the arrangement.[45] During the visit, Rao extolled the virtues of Kazi Nazrul Islam, Tagore, Fakhir Lallan Shah, and Jasimuddin, to evoke the shared cultural bonds between the two countries and asserted his open-mindedness to resolve disputes.[46]

From Chakma repatriation to river water sharing (both sides acknowledged this would be 'slow and gradual'), Dhaka and New Delhi left few aspects unaddressed.[47] Rao praised Bangladesh's leadership of SAARC and underscored the importance of the association for regional connectivity. All this occurred despite Dhaka hosting NSCN-IM and ULFA, and India sheltering the Shanti Bahini. In fact, by 1993, both sides agreed on Chakma repatriation.[48] Dhaka's success in repatriating Rohingyas in 1991/92 left little room to deny the same for some, if not all, Chakmas.

The schizophrenic character of this bilateral was on full display. Official visits focused on economic ties despite little to show. In 1993, for instance, the Indian Railway Construction Co. (IRCON), a public sector undertaking, bagged a contract worth 230 million rupees (8 million USD) under a project funded by the World Bank to build the Nagarbari-Pabna highway.[49] In May 1993, the Bangladeshi communications minister paid a seven-day visit to discuss trade, and encouraged India to supply boulders and stones worth 100 million USD for the Jamuna River Bridge construction.[50] In June that year, the Bangladeshi foreign minister visited India to take stock of bilateral ties and focus on the South Asian Preferential Trade Agreement.[51]

Even as these visits occurred, the bilateral took a nosedive. Dhaka correctly blamed India for not sharing the promised amount of Ganga water, i.e. 30,000 cusecs. Srinivasan found India's growing water needs in Calcutta and inability to make concessions to Dhaka 'disturbing'.[52] But the demolition of the Babri Masjid in Ayodhya by Hindu natinoalists on 6 December 1992 sent shock waves across the Muslim world. Bangladesh had already witnessed anti-Hindu riots when rumours of Babri's demolition stoked majoritarian fires. But this time it was real, and the fallout was immediate.

Within hours, 97 Hindu temples were destroyed, 340 houses and 100 shops belonging to Indians (or Bangladeshi Hindus) were burnt down, and the Indian High Commission and the Indian Airlines office in Dhaka came under attack.[53] These were official Indian estimates. Unofficial figures of human and material costs of organised anti-Hindu and anti-India violence across Bangladesh are higher. As is common in South Asia, such violence often has tacit government sanctioning, and New Delhi admitted that BNP leaders encouraged and participated in 'mob attacks'.[54] In January 1993, calls to organise a 'long march' to Ayodhya by Bangladeshi parliamentarians made New Delhi threaten armed action if people entered India 'illegally'.[55] When the Bangladeshi parliament passed a resolution against the demolition, India took the gloves off: 'we take strong exception to the fact that the ruling party BNP in Bangladesh has thought it fit to indulge in public denunciation of our policies and actions and also to arrogate to itself the right to advise us on matters in which it has no locus standi whatsoever'.[56] Communal violence against Bangladeshi Hindus, New Delhi argued, shows that the 'attempt to present Bangladesh as a model of communal harmony cannot be taken seriously'.[57] Such events deepened mistrust between India and the BNP. Rao's suspicion that the BNP wouldn't forgo anti-Indianism was proving right, and Hindu nationalism fed this dynamic.

This is when Khaleda Zia made another move. Angered by India's lack of supply of Ganga water, she raised the Farakka barrage issue at the UNGA on 1 October 1993. The idea was to pressure India when its international reputation took a hit due to Babri's demolition. India noted 'considerable regret' at her statement, and Rao's decision to offer the BNP benefit of the doubt was now a thing of the past.[58] There was already a marked uptick in NSCN-IM, NDFB, and ULFA attacks from bases in Bangladesh. In 1994, India was tipped off about a large arms consignment arriving through Bangladesh by rebels belonging to the National United Party of Arakan (NUPA). Overseen by Bangladesh's intelligence, these arms were meant for multiple insurgent groups and were to enter through Tripura. To counter this consignment, India needed the Tatmadaw's support, and thus emerged Operation Golden Bird. The more Dhaka went against India, the more India relied on Yangon.

Bangladesh's response to Babri reaffirmed India's belief that the BNP could not be trusted, and that anti-India populism in Bangladesh was deep-rooted. The 1991 elections were free and fair, and voted an anti-India party into power precisely for that reason. In alliance with the Jamaat-e-Islami, and harbouring radical Islamists apart from promoting Mujib's killers, the BNP had a visible pro-Pakistan tilt. Its rise reignited concerns in India about a reversal to the 1960s' tit-for-tat geopolitical communal violence. Such communalism was reflected in a resolution proposed by BJP parliamentarian R.S. Rawat in March 1996 criticising the government's 'appeasement' of Bangladeshi Muslim 'intruders' for 'vote bank politics'.[59]

Citing data from the 1991 census, Rawat noted that despite national population growth being 36.83% in 1981–91, Muslim communities in Arunachal Pradesh grew by 135.01%, in Manipur by 29.5%, in Mizoram by 105.08%, in Nagaland by 74.84%, in Tripura by 41.84%, in West Bengal by 36.79%, and in Orissa by 36.03%.[60] When countered by left-wing parliamentarians that the census doesn't offer figures based on nationality, or by the Congress' young and fiery leader Mamata Banerjee that such communalism was 'wrong', Rawat hit back that illicit migration increased ISI activities and economic discontent in India.[61] The rise of Hindutva coincided with growing communalism in Bangladesh and sharpened narratives on global Islamist terrorism.

This is why, when a caretaker government came to power in Dhaka in 1996, New Delhi sent its best wishes for carrying out 'the great responsibilities with which it is entrusted', i.e. to hold free and fair elections.[62] When Hasina won the 1996 elections in June, New Delhi couldn't have been more relieved. Gurjal noted:

> Your appointment is the culmination of a long saga of toil and sacrifice for the people of Bangladesh [and] am confident that India and Bangladesh would develop relations of great cordiality, friendship and cooperation, to the mutual benefit of both our countries, while you are at the helm of affairs.[63]

As for India's desire for transit facilities over Bangladeshi soil to its northeast, Gujral bluntly noted that the 'Government of India have been interested in securing multi-modal transit facilities through Bangladesh territory to the North Eastern States and have taken the matter with the Government of Bangladesh on a number of occasions', but the latter 'have not yet reacted positively to our proposals'.[64] If anything, BDR firing in January 1996 against India's construction of a customs office at the Dawki Tamabil border crossing connecting Sylhet and Shillong had halted cross-border trade.[65]

U-Turn

To lubricate its outreach to Yangon, India not only promised Than Shwe access to Indian market, but also clamped down on Myanmar rebels operating from India. The KIO's failed operations against the junta and lack of jade demand in India (unlike China) put an end to Brang Seng's plans for federal autonomy. He made a last trip to India in 1993, and with no support forthcoming, entered a ceasefire with Than Shwe in February 1994.[66] India didn't need to use coercion or deception to contain the KIO. But with other groups, India executed a violent U-Turn. By late 1993, the Assam Rifles in Manipur and Mizoram began to target the CNF.[67] In April 1995, more CNF leaders and soldiers were arrested, and two died in custody.[68] No Than Kap, who was ousted from CNF in 1992, sought a comeback after intra-CNF rivals failed to kill him in December 1995, and the Mizoram state government offered medical support and police security. It is in this context that he received a Burmese-speaking visitor from the Indian army. 'I don't know how he came to know about my plans, but [Lt. Col. V.S.] Grewal turned up under the cover name of Col. Saathi (partner), and promised that India would give me 100-rifles', he says.[69]

Grewal invited No Than Kap to the Assam Rifles' camp in Vairengte to meet senior officers and pick up guns. Instead, in September 1996, the former CNF supremo was arrested and handed over to the Tatmadaw.[70] Such operations continued, and in January 1999 another CNF member was arrested and handed over as a goodwill gesture.[71] Similar arrests were made in October 2000 and afterwards until the CNF signed the Nationwide Ceasefire Agreement (NCA) in 2011.[72] Grewal participated in most such operations, codenamed 'Friend', 'Sunrise', and 'Leech', and directly coordinated with Khin Nyunt.[73] Conducted outside the public view, such support termination ops were central to India's strategy to rebuild ties with Myanmar. The media leak of Leech in 1998 blew the cover of these ops. Painted as a corrupt double-agent on the junta's payroll, Grewal was forced to retire prematurely from the army. But Leech was not aimed at the CNF; it was targeting NUPA, which supported India's intelligence gathering to enable Golden Bird in collaboration with the Tatmadaw.

The onset of India's support for the Arakanese (Rakhine) groups, especially NUPA, which was created in 1994, stands out for its timing: by then, New Delhi had begun terminating support for other groups. The exercise itself was not new, and Indian agencies allowed the Arakan National Liberation Party (ANLP) (which merged with other Arakan communist and nationalist parties to form NUPA) to operate from Parva at the Mizoram-Bangladesh border in 1970s.[74] The BSF provided ANLP with uniforms, medicine, and daily rations.[75] But support was abruptly halted, forcing Arakanese rebels to relocate to Thailand. The democracy movement triggered Arakan nationalists to shift to Bangladesh. With DGFI's support, the Arakan Army (AA), part of NUPA, undertook operations inside Rakhine.[76] In 1993, the AA once again returned to Parva. The R&AW's Nandy orchestrated AA's relocation to India and subsequent creation of NUPA, plus its sustenance for the next four years from New Delhi.[77] On the field, Grewal managed this relationship.

Similar to CNF, India asked NUPA to offer intelligence on Naga and Assamese rebels, and on Chinese activities in the Indian Ocean Region (IOR) and the Coco Islands, where Beijing was rumoured to have established a radar station.[78] Unlike the KIO and CNF, NUPA operated in the Bay of Bengal and had knowledge of the illicit arms networks linked to Thailand and Cambodia. Its theatre of operations at the India-Myanmar-Bangladesh trijunction, links with the Karen insurgents who were active in the China-Myanmar border areas, and marine capabilities made NUPA important. Grewal's inroads with NUPA helped the army execute counterinsurgency operations. An amalgam of Rakhine Buddhists and Muslims, including senior Rohingya leaders, NUPA's support was critical to keep tabs inside Bangladesh and in Rakhine. But Hasina's victory in 1996 and the 1997 Dhaka-Shanti Bahini accord reduced NUPA's value. It was now open to exploitation by its Indian handlers.[79] Grewal promised NUPA access to the Landfall Island in north Andaman as a staging area for ops, and sought heavy bribes in return.[80]

To add weight to his operations, Grewal feigned contact with India's Cabinet Secretary and the Chief of Army Staff and asked NUPA to reach Landfall in January 1998. When the rebels reached the island, six of their leaders were shot dead, and the rest were arrested.[81] Details of Operation Leech leaked out in the media, and a senior human rights lawyer, Nandita Haksar, took over the case. 'Initially I was not sure about the case, but the more I focused on it, the more it became apparent that India betrayed Burmese freedom fighters', says Haksar.[82] Nandy, who initiated support, criticised the army for targeting NUPA.[83] There was pressure on the army and the Ministry of Defence to launch an official inquiry into the incident and take action against Grewal, who came to be known as a rogue agent.[84] Instead, Grewal was promoted to Colonel, and asked to take early retirement with full honours.

India's senior military leaders with knowledge of the case are clear that Grewal 'was just following orders'.[85] He was in touch with Khin Nyunt throughout the decade.[86] Such outreach is not possible without superior approval and was part of India's strategy to allow the army to stabilise ties with Yangon. The Indian army developed a strong relationship with its Myanmar counterpart, and Indian defence attachés enjoyed considerable access to the junta. As Lt. Gen. (r) Shakti Gurung notes, 'during my three-year tenure (2000–03) as defence attaché, we had a total of 38 delegation exchanges—the largest till then. A number of these were at the top level'.[87]

The Kaladan Multi-Modal Transit Transport Project was introduced in 1999–2000 to connect Mizoram to the Sittwe port by road. It was the same idea that Verghese first proposed in 1968. While the army paved the way to implement the LEP by neutralising Myanmar rebels, Indian diplomats overtly worked on economic connectivity and religious diplomacy to reopen political doors in Yangon. In this context, the more Bangladesh went against India's interests, the more India warmed up to Myanmar. Outfits such as CNF, KIO, and NUPA became pawns in India's strategy to stabilise its northeast and realise the LEP. Rao buried Rajiv's experiment of supporting the democratic resistance in Myanmar. Even George Fernandes, India's pro-Suu Kyi defence minister in March 1998–2001 (and October 2001–May 2004), who even sheltered democracy activists at his home, didn't halt India's U-Turn towards the junta, to NUPA's 'disappointment'.[88] The strategic logic of authoritarianism, as long as it was pro-India, was apparent.

Hasina

It is the pace at which India resolved outstanding issues with Bangladesh after Hasina's arrival that demonstrates the quality of bilateral mistrust with the BNP. On 12 December 1996, i.e. within six months of Hasina's rise, the two countries signed a historic 30-year water sharing agreement, and on 2 December 1997, thanks to Indian facilitation, the Shanti Bahini signed the CHT accord.[89] Tariq Karim, who was now posted to India as high commissioner, attributes this to an 'alignment of stars' wherein he worked with Indian officials with whom he enjoyed trust and similar worldviews.[90] Bangladesh was offered the 'most favoured nation' status to augment trade. In a statement on the Ganga Water Treaty, India's prime minister H.D. Deve Gowda noted that this 'new relationship should be of immense benefit to India in the long term in all areas of bilateral relations including security, trade, and other areas'.[91] Celebrated by all parties, a short parliamentary discussion on the treaty saw the opposition point that China was eyeing Chittagong and India must not implement the agreement if it meant a loss of water supply to the Calcutta port.[92] India's relations with Bangladesh during 1996–2001, despite visible successes, were wrought with contradiction.

For India, illegal migration from Bangladesh, the DGFI's continuing support to northeast rebels, and little progress on connectivity were problems on which Hasina failed to deliver. For Hasina, the alliance with India was a domestic hurdle that needed balancing. As a first-time prime minister, she couldn't get the DGFI to curb support for anti-India rebels, despite India's help in containing the Chakma insurgency. To make sense of this period, it is critical to focus on Hasina's positionality. After boycotting general elections in February 1996, Hasina agreed to fight the June elections under a caretaker government. During the campaigning period, a military coup was thwarted. Though Hasina won thanks to anti-incumbency, she won 146 seats out of 300 and a 37% vote-share as opposed to the BNP's 34%.[93] She allied with Ershad—who was jailed on corruption charges—to become prime minister, and entered a four-point agreement with the BNP, a powerful opposition, to smoothly run the government. Alliance with Ershad and understanding with BNP limited Hasina's space to manoeuvre.

Engaged in fire-fighting, Hasina faced opposition walk-outs in the parliament and street violence as the understanding with the BNP broke down in 1997. Her inability to deliver economic stability generated protests. Hamstrung, she sought to capitalise on the Ganga water treaty and the CHT accord as achievements that the BNP failed to deliver on. But instead, the agility with which she signed the water treaty with India opened Hasina to criticism by both the BNP and the Jatiya. 'In 1996 the Awami League went for an agreement without minimum guarantees. It worked, but negotiations stopped after that,' says Shafi, one of Ershad's negotiators on water sharing in the 1980s.[94] The BNP levelled similar charges that the treaty was skewed in India's favour. In a political blow in September 1997, Ershad, who secured his released from jail after aligning with Hasina, pulled the plug on the alliance and joined hands with the BNP.[95] Apart from securing landmark deals with India, Hasina pursued what the BNP did during 1991–96. i.e. erasing symbols commemorating Zia-ur-Rahman, just like the BNP and Ershad did with Mujib after 1975.[96] This tactic, in the light of her fragile electoral agenda, backfired.

Now leading a minority government, Hasina's turnaround on the Ganga water treaty and the Chakma accord collapsed politically. Hasina's struggles to alleviate poverty and target anti-India insurgents eroded popular appeal and frustrated New Delhi. According to A. Mathur, a R&AW officer posted in Dhaka during this period, 'Hasina was very cautious in her relations with the military [and] Begum Zia had a stronghold in the army'.[97] This meant that Hasina 'had to defer to the *uttar para* [reference to the army cantonment in north Dhaka] even though she was very sensitive to our needs'.[98] The DGFI maintained links with Pakistan and 'Hasina didn't want to defy them' when the Bangladeshi intelligence refused to hand over 'these boys, even if they were not allowed a free run'.[99]

One key figure who relocated from Thailand to Bangladesh in mid-1991 was Anthony Shimray. Promoted within NSCN-IM, Shimray was its chief arms procurer, held multiple Bangladeshi passports, and led NSCN-IM's overseas 'Alee command'. He set up base in the Goran area of Dhaka and contacted Arakanese rebels to

procure arms in an operation codenamed Jordon.[100] Dhaka allowed
him to open camps named Goshen, Bethel, and Zion. He was the
reason why India needed Myanmar's support in Operation Golden
Bird, and why R&AW recruited NUPA. Dhaka didn't extradite
Shimray to India until 2010.

But more than Shimray, for India entered a ceasefire with NSCN-
IM in 1997, it was the presence of ULFA-I General Secretary Anup
Chetia in Bangladesh that troubled India. Ever since their 1991 ouster
from Kachin state, the ULFA-I relocated to camps in Bhutan to the
Bhutanese king's displeasure. On 21 December 1997, less than three
weeks after signing of the CHT accord, and in a quid pro quo with
India, Chetia was arrested in Mohammadpur, Dhaka, along with
two associates.[101] But when India demanded his extradition, Hasina
demurred. 'She couldn't send him to India because the BNP made
it a nationalist issue', remembers Mathur.[102] He admits that the lack
of an extradition treaty didn't prevent India from 'picking up' minor
NSCM-IM and ULFA-I cadre, but Hasina couldn't deliver on big
actors such as Shimray and Chetia.[103] In June 1998, when the foreign
secretary visited Dhaka, Indian press reported that he reassured
Hasina that New Delhi would not press for Chetia's extradition
given the pressure she was under. The MEA quickly clarified: 'This is
baseless and untrue. India has reiterated its demand for the handing
over of Chetia'.[104]

In August 1998, CPI leader Indrajit Gupta, who served as India's
home minister (June 1996–March 1998) in Deve Gowda's cabinet,
raised the issue of Hasina's struggles on India's security demands:

> I do not doubt her faith. She had assured, at the Government
> to Government level and at the Prime Minister's level to us
> some time ago that she would not like the Bangladesh soil to be
> used by any of these insurgent groups from India to go and take
> refuge there, to establish bases there and to carry out anti-India
> activities from Bangladesh. It is very easy for them to cross the
> border. They are doing it all the time. But later on, we got some
> disquieting reports that for some reason or the other, Bangladesh
> authorities were not very successful in checking these people
> and controlling their activities ... They have got some weakness
> in their administrative setup and so on.[105]

Gupta pressed the recently elected BJP government to pressure Dhaka for Chetia's extradition. But India went easy on Hasina on the condition that Chetia must remain imprisoned. On this, Hasina could, and did, deliver.

There was little movement on economic connectivity. In June 1997, Bangladesh, India, Sri Lanka, and Thailand launched a subregional economic grouping BIST-EC (Economic Connectivity). Myanmar joined the initiative in December 1997, and Nepal and Bhutan joined a few years later, creating the Bay of Bengal Initiative for Multi-Sectoral Technical and Economic Cooperation (BIMSTEC). The initiative held its second meeting in Dhaka in December 1998, but other than conceptualising its core goal and creating working groups, it did little else. In fact, the railway lines connecting India to erstwhile East Pakistan destroyed during the 1965 war were still awaiting reconstruction. Despite IRCON's interest in Bangladesh's railway sector and bagging some contracts, the company did little to enhance connectivity during Hasina's tenure. As an Indian official notes, 'we focused on the Sittwe port and pushed for the Kaladan multi-modal project in Myanmar, because things were not moving with Bangladesh'.[106] This was despite the fact that Chittagong was more important for India's northeast than the Sittwe port.

But geopolitical pressures trumped geo-economics, and Hasina's premiership remained unproductive. Turmoil in Dhaka was such that the MEA calculated it would be easier to change Than Shwe's mind on rapprochement and develop the Kaladan project than expect Hasina to deliver, or to change Khaleda Zia's mind on India. This was despite the fact that Myanmar's trade with India was at a dismal 1.18 billion rupees in 1992–93 (67.9 million rupees in exports and 1.12 billion rupees in imports) and increased only to 1.32 billion rupees in 1996–97 (0.27 billion rupees in export, and 1.05 billion rupees in imports).[107] In contrast, trade between India and Bangladesh grew from 10.7 billion rupees in 1992–93 (10.3 billion rupees export, and 0.36 billion rupees imports, creating a trade deficit for Dhaka) to 28.9 billion rupees in 1996–97 (26.2 billion rupees in export, and 1.9 billion rupees worth of imports). India also offered Bangladesh minimum tariff concessions of 50% during SAARC negotiations for nearly half of the tradeable products basket.[108] But when external affairs minister and BJP stalwart Jaswant Singh was asked in March 1999 on whether Bangladesh allowed India transit for goods and persons, his response was the same as his predecessor: 'Government has made repeated proposals to the Government of Bangladesh for overland transit facilities for passenger and freight traffic. Bangladesh has not agreed to these proposals'.[109]

The communal politics undergirding illegal migration from Bangladesh added to Hasina's woes. India had taken a Hindu nationalist turn, and illegal migration of Bangladeshi Muslims became ever more sensitive and central. When Hasina visited India on 27–29 January 1999, New Delhi's main ask was to control migration. Singh specifically conveyed to Hasina the 'seriousness and magnitude of the problem of infiltration and illegal migration', and she assured him of stronger preventive measures.[110] Such pressure on Dhaka only grew over the years. In February 1997, the BJP introduced a Lok Sabha resolution condemning illegal migration. It argued that there were 'approximately two and half crore Bangladeshis in India' and the problem was that they were Muslims.[111] Unlike Buddhist Chakmas and Bangladeshi Hindus, Muslims were viewed with suspicion. They criticised the Illegal Migrants (Determination and Tribunals) Act (IMDT), 1983, as 'good for nothing' and called for its scrapping.[112] The 25 March 1971 cut-off and the fact that IMDT was in force only in Assam, even though it was meant for the entire country, was unacceptable to the BJP.

The issue of illegal migration was ideologically important and had electoral salience for the BJP. To make inroads in Assam, it needed to mobilise around an issue that distinguished it from the Congress without alienating the AGP. The BJP imparted clarity on this by urging the government to maintain a national register of citizens (NRC), and to seal the entire India-Bangladesh border.[113] This eechod the AGP's core demands. The BJP blamed communal tensions in Mumbai (which witnessed rioting after Babri's demolition) and 'anarchy' as being the 'handiwork' of 'these infiltrators only'.[114] In May 1997, as these debates raged, the Indian Union Muslim League (IUML) countered that of the 287,000 complaints referred to the migrants tribunal, only 8,000 cases were identified as illegal migrants.[115]

In contrast to the AGP's and BJP's argument that these illegal migrants were used to expand Congress' vote bank (going back to the 1978 Mangaldoi constituency case), the IUML claimed that Assam's electoral roll increased from 1,18,73,952 in 1991 to 1,25,87,659 voters in 1996: 'So what is the increase? You talk about large scale infiltration. You talk about millions coming in and getting registered as electors, as voters ... but then, what is the percentage rise in the electoral roll?', the IUML parliamentarians argued.[116] They lamented that the issue had become so communalised that 'non-Muslims coming from Bangladesh were called refugees and the Muslims coming from Bangladesh were called infiltrators'.[117]

In a demonstration of the communalism undergirding this issue, the Shiv Sena-BJP alliance in Maharashtra launched a drive in August 1998 to deport 'illegal Bangladeshi migrants'. The Mumbai police arrested 38 *Zari* workers and put them on a train to West Bengal for deportation to Bangladesh. When the train reached Uluberia, near Howrah, a 9,000-strong CPI(M)-led mob armed with sticks 'rescued' the 38 persons.[118] The communists argued that these people were Indian Muslims, whereas the BJP called them Bangladeshis. As *India Today* eloquently put it: 'In India's thriving democracy, political battles are a dime a dozen. But rarely has the country witnessed the curious spectacle of two state governments, without even a common border, slugging it out over another country.'[119]

The deportation drive became a parliamentary spat between the BJP and the Left Front, and witnessed action in West Bengal where the communists did all they could to scuttle the deportation. CPI(M) leaders from West Bengal shot letters to the home minister to intervene, pressed that '...we see a constant confusion between Bangla-speaking [Muslims] and citizens of Bangladesh', and clarified that the CPI(M) didn't encourage illegal migration from Bangladesh.[120] They argued that these persons were not the 'real culprits', and even if India wanted to deport someone, it must be done humanely. 'After all, the foreigner is also a human being not an animal ... we should deport him properly. As we had already done in the case of Chakmas'.[121]

Communalism in India was matched by the BNP's anti-India rhetoric, and the Jamaat-e-Islami's conservatism in Bangladesh.

These political forces manifested in a major standoff between the BDR and BSF on 16 April 2001, when a large BDR contingent crossed the Indian border at East Khasi Hills in Meghalaya, detained a BSF patrol, and killed 16 personnel.[122] Shortly after, cross-border BDR-BSF firing spread to Assam. The entire saga, known as the 'Rowmari incident' lasted for four days before prime ministerial interventions. But the damage was done. Photos of tortured bodies of Indian soldiers made it to the front pages of Bangladeshi newspapers.

India's *Pioneer* newspaper termed the BDR 'barbarians' while the leader of the opposition, Sonia Gandhi, noted that 'the indignities perpetrated on them even as the bodies were being returned have shocked and shaken every one of us, every Indian'.[123] The Shiv Sena asked the government to 'teach Pakistan and Bangladesh a lesson'.[124] Aware that it was an election year in Dhaka and strong Indian response could undermine the AL, Jaswant Singh tried calming temperatures by saying that Hasina was 'deeply saddened' and promised an investigation.[125] But the incident triggered widespread anti-India nationalism in Bangladesh helping the BNP return to power in an alliance with the Jamaat-e-Islami in October 2001.

Narco-Peace

Hope came from unexpected quarters. At 9pm on 25 June 1995, Rao held a secret 30-minute meeting with top NSCM-IM leaders Th. Muivah and Isak Chishi Swu in a suite at Hôtel de Crillon on Place de la Concorde in Paris. Kept out of the loop, both the Indian embassy in Paris and French authorities were unaware that Rao had agreed to a face-to-face meeting with the rebels.[126] Logistics of the meeting were curated by R&AW's deputy chief Balachandran. He established a channel between an unknown interlocutor who convinced Rao to meet the Nagas, Rao's principal secretary Verma, and a R&AW officer despatched to Paris to manage the meeting. Given the history of Naga presence in Paris, France was a logical place for such outreach. Muivah and Swu wanted to keep it secret from their cross-border counterpart Khaplang, worried that the latter would kill them if he got wind of it. Balachandran notes that it was a 'positive' meeting followed by similar endeavours between

Verma and the Nagas in Bangkok and Europe.[127] Even though Rao's term ended in 1996, the Paris 'breakthrough' set the stage for a ceasefire on 25 July 1997 under Deve Gowda.[128]

Amidst India's struggles to improve ties with Myanmar, manage Bangladesh, and deal with communalism, the NSCN-IM and New Delhi sued for peace. For India, this was success. 'The NSCN-IM was in a leadership position' in the northeast, argues Balachandran.[129] Rao's 'sincere' outreach went a long way, making Muivah and Swu note in September 1997 that 'among the prime ministers of India, he stands out because he alone recognised that the Naga problem could be solved through political means'.[130] On 3 February 1997, Deve Gowda too met the Nagas in Zurich paving the way for ceasefire and setting the tone for future prime ministers, all of whom met Muivah and Swu in person to ensure that the ceasefire holds. Though a peace accord remains elusive, the ceasefire endures. This raises the counterfactual of had Indira and Rajiv Gandhi met with Phizo earlier, would a ceasefire have come into effect sooner? There's no guarantee. Nehru's meetings with Phizo in 1951–52 didn't yield results. Phizo's 'irreconcilable and diehard' attitude made Nehru view him as 'slippery' and unreliable even in 1960 when he was in the throes of pursuing engagement and agreed to grant Nagaland statehood within the union.[131] As is often the case, the context in which such meetings take place is more critical.

The 1997 ceasefire occurred due to a confluence of three factors: one, a mutually painful military stalemate; two, positive economic prospects; and three, Rao's accommodation of NSCN-IM when New Delhi was building bridges on fronts internal and external. From a military perspective, India had used every tactic from airpower and re-grouping of Naga villages to exploiting intra-community fissures to break the Naga movement. None of them worked. But the outbreak of the Assam insurgency and R&AW's co-opting of KIO to deny ULFA-I and NSCN-IM sanctuary affected NSCN-IM's operability more than ULFA-I's. Shimray could procure arms through Bangladesh and transfer them to his cadre, but developing military momentum without bases in Myanmar limited the outfit's ability to deliver violence. Whereas ULFA-I could operate from Bhutan, the only cross-border access NSCN-IM had was via Myanmar.

The 1988 NSCN split between Isak and Muivah (IM) and Khaplang (NSCN-K) further undermined NSCN-IM's access to Myanmar. The KIO pulling the plug in 1991 was an additional blow, and so was R&AW's infiltration of Arakan-based groups, who tipped off India about Shimray's plans. But the more India's relations with the junta deepened, the better it could convince Myanmar to target NSCN-K, thereby creating the conditions for a ceasefire with the NSCN-IM. In 2000, when the chief of the Indian army, Gen. V.P. Malik, met with Vice Sr. Gen. Maung Aye in Mandalay and the latter reciprocated with a visit to Shillong, India offered intelligence on NSCN-K hideouts that led to a Tatmadaw operation against the outfit.[132]

The NSCN-IM's shrinking ability to deliver violence—it could still, and did, disrupt routine life—challenged its leadership among groups in the northeast. The ULFA-I, though in tactical alliance with the Nagas, was becoming a competitor over limited resources. Baruah and Chetia had developed enough access in Bhutan and Bangladesh and links with Chinese and Pakistani intelligence to be able to challenge NSCN-IM's dominance over such networks. Sustenance of kinetic action in such onerous conditions gave NSCN-IM an impetus to cease fire even if a solution was not to be reached. Preparations for the Paris meeting started in January 1995, before Golden Bird occurred. Though India's decision to confer the Nehru award to Suu Kyi halted the operation, its success in thwarting the arms consignment complicated Swu's and Muivah's positions. Balachandran argues that the date of the Paris meeting was determined by Rao's official travel plans.[133] But the fact that Golden Bird occurred (April–May 1995) just before the June meeting ensured that Swu and Muivah had little illusion about Rao's intentions and India's capabilities. In that sense, Golden Bird succeeded.

The political economy of the ceasefire is noteworthy. Just before the Paris meeting, Balachandran held long conversations with a Delhi-based Naga leader who 'revealed staggering facts' about NSCN-IM's shadow influence in Nagaland, 'technically under Congress rule'.[134] Most local newspapers were coerced into publishing NSCN-IM's political bulletins on the front page, and nearly everyone had to pay 'taxes' to the parallel government.[135] The ceasefire promised continuity on this front and was a tacit recognition by New Delhi of its inability to bring peace without the NSCN-IM. 'After the 1997 ceasefire, we function openly. We have been running the government in 26 regions … All disputes: village, individuals, all courts are Naga. No one goes to India. We settle the disputes', noted NSCN-IM's *Kilo Kilonser* (home minister) in 2016 to scholars Shalaka Thakur and Rajesh Venugopal.[136] But in 1997, apart from promising peaceful coexistence, the ceasefire promised rewards from the growing drug trade between the northeast and the Golden Triangle. Not that illegal cross-border trade needed formal opening of the India-Myanmar border, but the 1994 agreement improved cross-border trade. The NSCN-IM could now become involved in businesses and sustain and grow its profit. Done without accountability, such economic prospects also promised to reverse NSCN-IM's relative decline in relation to ULFA-I.

In February 1997, shortly after Rao agreed to meet the Nagas, the Ministry of Finance offered an estimate of heroin smuggled into India from the Golden Triangle in response to a parliamentary query. It was telling. Though acknowledging that the northeast was 'sensitive to drug trafficking', the ministry had 'no precise valuation of drugs, which are often of indeterminate strength and composition and are liable for destruction, can be made. Hence the value of heroin smuggled into the country through these routes cannot be estimated'.[137] The ministry listed the measures it took to keep tabs on the drug trade, including quarterly meetings with NCB, and highlighted 12 different routes through which Southeast Asian heroin entered India. Unsurprisingly, on the top of the list was the Tamu-Moreh crossing leading to Imphal, followed by a panoply of routes that illicitly connected the entire northeast with Myanmar and Bangladesh.[138]

It is a two-way trade. Chemicals needed to manufacture heroin and codeine-based Phensedyl came from India's pharmaceutical industry. The finished narcotics then re-entered India from Myanmar using these routes. It is no surprise that in 1992, when junta officials met Dixit, they proposed to limit poppy cultivation in Myanmar but wanted India to clamp down on illicit exports of chemicals needed to process opium into heroin.[139] The Moreh-Tamu crossing became a transhipment hub for drugs. The NSCN-IM and other Manipur-based insurgents intended to capture illicit market share. It is unsurprising that access to land and control over drug trade routes became a huge flashpoint between Naga and Kuki armed groups, leading to violent clashes and killings in 1994. Access to illicit resources became a key source of livelihood (admittedly, for some and not many) in a region bereft of economic progress.[140]

Narcotics smuggling from Myanmar and gold from Bangladesh had picked up in 1980s when the northeast witnessed an explosion of armed outfits. In 1985, the Congress introduced 'The [Prevention of Illicit Traffic in] Narcotic Drugs and Psychotropic Substances Act (NDPS)' that sought to contain drug smuggling on the eastern and western borders.[141] Concerned that India was becoming a centre of gravity for shipment of heroin produced in the Golden Crescent (Afghanistan, Pakistan, Iran) and the Golden Triangle (Myanmar, Laos, Thailand), New Delhi addressed the issue legally. Government agencies were witnessing a spike in heroin and cannabis seizures: in 1984, 138.7 kilograms of heroin were seized.[142] Cannabis seizures rose from 1,017 kilograms in 1983 to 2811 kilograms by 1985 (tip of the iceberg).[143] When the NDPS failed to make an impact, more stringent measures were incorporated in 1988, after Rajiv issued a '14-point directive … constituted a Cabinet Sub-Committee under the Home Minister to oversee and coordinate working of different Ministries to combat trafficking and abuse'.[144]

The problem in Burma was India's limited intelligence on traffickers and routes.[145] Government data underscored how little heroin sourced from Burma was being seized: a meagre 3.025 kilograms in 1990–91, 6.234 kilograms in 1991–92, and 6.37 kilograms in 1992–93.[146] As for the full estimate of the drug trade, the government surreally argued: 'since smuggling is a clandestine activity, it is not possible to say whether smuggling of gold and heroin into the north-eastern States of the country from neighbouring Myanmar and Bangladesh is on the rise or otherwise'.[147] Over the decades, Manipur became the largest source of cannabis with seizures in 2002 at 93.447 tonnes, and in 2020 at 560 tonnes.[148] If one goes by the 2020 price estimate of cannabis in India of 175.41 USD per kilogram as per the United Nations Office on Drugs and Crimes (UNODC), the value of seized marijuana stood at over

98.2 million USD.[149] Most of it came from the northeast, and it is just one of the many drug types smuggled in and from the region.

These figures indicate that the overall drug economy in the northeast is a multi-billion-dollar trade. Between January–April 2023, 164 kilograms of heroin were seized in Manipur.[150] If one uses the UNODC's 2021 pricing of heroine in India at 33,901 USD per kilogram, it shows a seizure worth 5.5 million USD in 2023 (the actual pricing for 2023 is likely higher).[151] The amount of drugs that slip through the NCB's net in the northeast is likely to be a lot higher than the seized amounts. What afforded sufficiency to the political compromise in 1997 was Rao's openness to a 'live-and-let-live' arrangement with NSCN-IM and other insurgent outfits. In return for drug profits, they were expected to reduce violence. Problematic in terms of upholding India's constitutional values, the ceasefire was extended multiple times (indefinitely in 2007) and did lead to a reduction in political violence in Manipur, Nagaland, and adjoining Naga-dominated areas. But the drug and arms trade became a source of easy, high-risk finance for insurgents and politicians alike. This often led to understandings between local politics and insurgents doubling as cartels. It fed inter-insurgent and inter-community strife.

As scholar Sanjib Baruah notes, 'I'm amazed how close some government officials and politicians are with these so-called insurgents in the northeast', indicating a classic crime-politics-bureaucracy nexus central to Indian politics.[152] Pillai is more scathing: 'it's all about money power there; whichever party can offer more money will attract local leaders and votes. Earlier it was the Congress, today it is the BJP'.[153] For a senior retired military officer who has served in the Assam Rifles, the nexus between insurgents and politicians is 'huge'.[154] He says, 'This is the main thing and it'll continue. Each group has their favourite politician who can get them released on arrest. They all play the game, and they all contribute to the ecosystem'.[155] Cash flows from central government and cross-border drug trade are key sources of electoral finance, and both are deeply entrenched in the northeast.

Neither are the local police and armed forces immune to such corruption.[156] There have been multiple cases of armed forces personnel being charged for smuggling gold and drugs.[157] The retired officer notes that such insurgent-politician links make their jobs 'extremely difficult, because you don't know where and who you're going to be dealing with'.[158] He echoes Pillai when unpacking state elections: 'There's no ideology, it's all about money ... and there's enough cash coming in from the central government'.[159] Such systemic corruption limits the scope for political resolution of outstanding issues, given how lucrative the drugs-infused homicidal ecologies are. The other problem with the regional drug trade is that it is not labour-intensive. This means it remains concentrated among a limited set of armed state and non-state actors who enjoy a complicated, complicit relationship. While consequential for local political economies, the drug trade doesn't have redistributive power, making it susceptible to exploitation whenever officials see fit, thus entrenching a perverse social contract, shorn of accountability, and prone to excesses by government and insurgents alike. The depths of such corruption and violence in the northeast came to light in 2016 when a sharpshooter of the Manipur police Thounaojam Herojit outed corruption cases and extrajudicial killings he had himself executed.[160]

Rao did achieve a political breakthrough with the Nagas. But it didn't settle the region's politics.

Conclusions

Heightened communalism and primacy of geo-economics became core features of India's domestic and international politics. Rao was a reformist on economy, but conservative in politics. In India's near east, this meant accepting the BNP's rise and seeking connectivity through Chittagong. In Myanmar, it meant rebuilding ties with the junta and seeking access to Sittwe. These were complicated tasks in light of the BNP's anti-India politics, the junta's reluctant re-embrace, and China's growing interest in both countries. None of these ideas were new. Rao was pushing the geo-economics agenda Rajiv christened but failed to deliver on. The Look East Policy, in essence, rebranded old ideas and masked the failure of Rajiv's interventionism and electoral insecurities as new, bold, geo-economics to counter Chinese influence.

Babri's demolition hugely impacted India's near east. In Dhaka, it reignited communal violence, bringing back memories of 1960s riots. In Yangon, though there was no perceptible shift in how the junta viewed India, the rise of Hindu nationalism and its undergirding anti-Muslim and anti-Christian beliefs sat well with Myanmar's xenophobic Buddhist nationalism. If anything, Wynn Lwin openly noted to the Indian press: 'Did you ever hear anything from us about Ayodhya? That is Myanmar's way of behaving with other countries. We do not interfere in the internal affairs of anyone and we feel our neighbours should do the same'.[161] The reality was that the Myanmar army had brutally killed Rohingyas in 1991, leading to a mass exodus into Bangladesh. Like Zia-ur-Rahman in 1978, Khaleda Zia adopted a strong stance and succeeded in securing repatriation. But on minorities within Bangladesh, the BNP and Jamaat's targeting of Bangladeshi Hindus demonstrated the endurance of communalism in subcontinental geopolitics. Similarly, the BJP's communalisation of Bangladeshi migrants helped it develop electoral appeal. Parliamentary debates on 'illegal' migration and efforts to repulse this demography continue to shape Indian politics. As the next chapter shows, the demand to maintain the NRC and (re)define citizenship along communal lines became central to India with the introduction of the Citizenship Amendment Act (2020).

Rao's economic reforms and political conservatism imparted a strategic logic to authoritarianism in India's near east. New Delhi worried about the BNP's anti-India populism, and felt the need to have Hasina in power during 1991–96. In Myanmar, India gave up on the democracy movement even if it continued to couch its policy in liberal terms. If Than Shwe could deliver on India's counterinsurgency requirements and economic aspirations, there was no need to support Suu Kyi. The junta's engagement with India could help counter China, check separatism, and balance an unfriendly Bangladesh. If this meant accepting limited levels of cross-border drug trade that helps fill the pockets of corrupt officials on both sides, and offers ethnic armed outfits access to profits while degrading their military capabilities—it was acceptable.

The US-led so-called Global War on Terrorism after 9/11 exacerbated these processes. With a global power focused on transnational Islamists and militarily invading Afghanistan (2001) and Iraq (2003), the political vocabulary and practice of India's near east shifted in the 21st century. In Bangladesh, the BNP-Jamaat coalition, which returned to power in 2001, (re)complicated India's security dynamics so profoundly that when Hasina rose to power in 2009 after brief period of a military-led 'caretaker' government (2007-09), India ensured that she became the arch-authoritarian ally it always sought in Dhaka.

Ever since, not only has Hasina targeted those associated with Bangladesh's Islamic right to actual hardcore Islamists in the name of countering terror, she also 'influenced' two general elections in 2014 and 2018 to ensure the BNP doesn't return to power.[162] In Myanmar, a series of protests by Buddhist monks shook the foundations of the junta ushering in constitutional reforms aimed at political liberalisation in 2008. But when this experiment with electoral politics ended with the February 2021 coup that ousted Suu Kyi from power (again), unlike 1988, India didn't utter a single word of criticism.

10

'TERMITES'
SAFFRON GEOPOLITICS IN THE
SHADOW OF CHINA'S RISE

'Infiltrators are like termites in the soil of Bengal.'[1]

Amit Shah, BJP party president and
later Home Minister of India, 11 April 2019

Before they fell apart, things were falling into place. In May 2008, Myanmar ratified its third constitution that re-ushered electoral politics. It was hailed as a step towards democratisation. In December 2008, Hasina returned to power after a two-year hiatus of a military-led caretaker government. These events were windfalls for India. Political and economic reforms could check China's influence by mobilising deep-rooted, popular anti-China sentiment across Myanmar. In Bangladesh, Hasina's return could check cross-border violence, contain the BNP-Jamaat alliance, and limit China's footprint. The 2001–06 BNP-Jamaat rule was marked by turbulence in ties. The 26/11 Mumbai attacks made these developments especially auspicious. Calm in the near east could help India focus on its west. Though not liberal, these developments marked the deepening of democratic politics. This promised to obviate the strategic logic of authoritarianism if there could be friendly democrats in power.

But the optimism was relatively short-lived. In February 2021, the junta ended the post-2008 constitutional order by executing a coup against Suu Kyi. The post-2021 junta, under the leadership of Sr. Gen. Min Aung Hlaing, is brutal, embattled, and severely dependent on Chinese and Russian support. By 2023, anti-Hasina sentiment in Bangladesh had become pervasive. Worst of all for India, in the intervening period, China's influence deepened in both countries. Even though separatist violence in the northeast decreased, the hope to economically connect the region through Bangladesh and Myanmar remains unfulfilled. This chapter asks why India continues to struggle in this region despite purported allies in Dhaka and Yangon. The answer lies in the aspects that have always shaped India's approach: politics of identity, cross-border migration, official antinomies, and political economies.

Far from the constitutionalist solidarities of the post-independence years or the militarism of the intervening decades, New Delhi's approach towards its near east in the 21st century is determined by strategic competition with China and Hindutva. These aspects mark a deepening of processes that gained momentum after 1991, i.e. the strengthening of religious nationalisms and focus on connectivity without thought for its redistributive potential and environmental impact. On the first count, the US-led Global War on Terrorism proved to be a force-multiplier for Hindu and Buddhist nationalisms, while feeding global Islamist violence. On the second aspect, China's assertiveness under the rubric of the Belt and Road Initiative (BRI) risked undermining India. If connectivity through Bangladesh didn't proceed during the 2001–06 BNP-Jamaat rule for political reasons, it failed in Myanmar due to bureaucratic delays. In effect, the long U-turn on the junta succeeded in opening doors in Naypyidaw, but India failed to deliver.

This chapter doesn't offer a detailed political history of these two decades. Instead, it focuses on two specific moments that were pivotal in shaping the geopolitics of India's near east. First was the February 2009 BDR revolt and India's response. This incident and how India tackled it explains why and how Hasina took an authoritarian turn to counter religious radicalism and her civilian opponents. Concerned about Hasina's physical safety and political survival, India almost militarily intervened in Bangladesh in 2009. Based on primary interviews, this section recreates this moment and outlines why India responded with such urgency and anxiety. The second section unpacks India's response to the '2007–08 Saffron Revolution' in Myanmar when Buddhist monks protested against the junta, attracting crackdown. Unlike Bangladesh, where India threatened intervention, New Delhi did nothing in Myanmar. The 2008 reforms vindicated India's decision (falsely, in retrospect) to opt for restraint towards Naypyidaw.

The third section unpacks India's response to China's growing power and presence in its near east. Rechristened 'Act East', India's policy towards this region has been underscored by its desire for improved economic connectivity and geopolitical conservatism. If the former is visible in the push by the Reliance and Adani group of industries, the latter is apparent in India's subdued response to the Rohingya genocide, and continuing support for an increasingly authoritarian Hasina. The final section returns to India's northeast, and shows how communal politics impacts the region. From the BJP's president (and later home minister) calling Bangladeshi Muslim migrants 'termites',[2] to the RSS allegedly stalling talks with NSCN-IM, India's approach towards this region lays bare the contradictions of its 'Act East' policy: it seeks strategic unity while fostering societal divisions. It underscores how the partition continues to shape India's near east.

Pilkhana

Maj. Kamaldeep Singh Sandhu of the 6th Battalion of the Parachute Regiment was on 'spearhead' duties that day. It was 5pm on 26 February 2009 when the orders came. An emergency code had been activated, and the vanguard companies of the paratrooper's spearhead were to mobilise. A battalion strength strike force alert 24/7 for emergency deployments, the spearhead is central to India's power projection. A similar emergency code was activated and rescinded the night before. But when the order came again, accompanied by 'five or six' IL-76 aircrafts and AN-32s, Sandhu knew something big was happening.[3] Two and a half hours later, over 1,000 Indian paratroopers found themselves at the Kalaikunda Air Force Station in West Bengal. Settled for the night, Sandhu's commanding officer gave instructions. The BDR had mutinied and were killing Bangladeshi officers and their families. The recently elected prime minister Hasina, who also held the defence portfolio, felt threatened and couldn't count on the army's support. 'She asked India for help ... and that's why we were there', awaiting orders and 'preparing for all eventualities when we touch down in Dhaka', remembers Sandhu.[4] New Delhi worried about the safety of Indian diplomats in Dhaka, who could well come under fire if violence escalated.

The worst massacre of army officers in Bangladeshi history was underway.[5] Shortly after the killings began, Hasina called her closest ally in New Delhi, top Congress leader and recently appointed finance minister Pranab Mukherjee. Upon hearing what was going on, Mukherjee promised 'to be responsive'.[6] The 'SOS' from Dhaka triggered the mobilisation of paratroopers, and prompted foreign secretary Shivshankar Menon to urgently engage with American, British, Japanese, and Chinese envoys to lobby support for Hasina.[7] Apart from Kalaikunda, paratroopers were mobilised in Jorhat and Agartala.[8] If the order came, Indian troops would enter Bangladesh from all three sides. The aim was to secure the Zia International Airport (renamed Hazrat Shahjalal International Airport) and the Tejgaon airport. Subsequently, the paratroopers would wrest control of Ganabhaban, prime minister's residence, and evacuate Hasina to safety. The Brigade commander overseeing the operation began distributing 'first line' ammunition meant for use during active combat. A 'very unusual' act, it underscored the severity of the moment.[9] The Bangladeshi army's reaction was a concern. If Bangladeshi generals turned against Hasina, they would resist Indian soldiers. 'If it came to that, we have a whole corps in the east' which would have sent reinforcements, says Sandhu.[10]

India *almost* intervened militarily in Bangladesh on 27 February. But the orders never came. Pinak Ranjan Chakravarty, India's high commissioner to Dhaka (2007–10) who has family origins in Bangladesh and called Hasina 'Aapa' (elder sister) out of respect, says that 'we did put some forces on alert, and conveyed to Hasina that we're worried about her safety'.[11] Why? Because India 'didn't know how far this'll go'.[12] In Dhaka, the mutineers murdered their director-general and his wife at the BDR-HQ called 'Pilkhana' (stable for elephants), igniting similar attacks against officers across Bangladesh. Pressure on the army chief, Gen. Moeen Uddin Ahmed, to act against the mutineers was tremendous. But if he initiated such action, it could lead to a bloodbath and heighten instability, risking Hasina's political and personal well-being. She could be killed by the mutineers, by angry officers, or be ousted in a coup. She had been arrested once before in 2007, and that could happen again.[13] India couldn't take chances, so it did what it felt was needed. It threatened Moeen against the use of force.

'I was told by those who were closer to power that Gen. Moeen was asked not to use force otherwise [Indian] paratroopers will drop in Dhaka within one hour', says Touhid Hussain, then Bangladesh's foreign secretary.[14] India was not bluffing. 'It was all real … we would've intervened if required', confirms a top Indian official who was part of foreign and security decision-making.[15] The final orders didn't come because Moeen stepped back from the brink. 'The Prime Minister directed that the crisis should be solved politically and it has been resolved in that manner', announced then Brig. Gen. Mahmud Hossain, the Director of Military Intelligence.[16] 'He should've given orders and allowed the military to address the situation', says Lt. Gen. (r) Mahfuzur Rahman who was commanding a brigade at Bandarban.[17]

There were ripple effects of the mutiny in local BDR outfits across the country over the next two days. 'It was not political, and as a military crisis situation, my understanding was that the military should have been allowed to respond within set Rules of Engagement, but that didn't happen', Rahman notes.[18] India's intervention in 2009 would have altered the subcontinent's history. But its non-occurrence was an equally powerful turning point. By threatening to employ the use of force to protect Hasina, India blunted the Bangladeshi army to such an extent that it freed Hasina's hand to counter opponents with impunity. Unlike her first tenure, Hasina was now liberated from pressures emanating from a politicised military, thanks to India.

Why did New Delhi react this way? After all, intervention would have undermined Bangladesh's sovereignty, and worsened India's reputation as a hegemon. It might have saved Hasina's life, but risked ending her career condemning her as an Indian 'stooge', an allegation she already struggles with. Instead, India witnessed a proactive Hasina who believed that the mutiny was meant to destabilise her government and acted as such. 'She took security measures too, but realised that the mutiny has to be dealt with politically and she went and met the officers' whose families and colleagues were murdered, says Chakravarty.[19] Abused and heckled by officers, Hasina held her ground, heard them out, and acted against the mutineers. 'It was appropriate that she did that, because it had a calming effect', argues Hussain.[20] The mutiny's end—about 200 were arrested after the army entered Pilkhana with tanks under the home ministry's 'supervision'—and Moeen's restraint cleared the field for Hasina to consolidate power.[21] Every officer who misbehaved eventually lost his job, and the BDR was disbanded. 'She handled it very boldly and bravely, a courageous woman with a lot of steel in her', Chakravarty notes in hindsight.[22]

But that the situation came down to India considering force exposed the fragility of its near east. To understand India's insecurities when the mutiny occurred, it is essential to focus on the turbulence in ties during the 2001–06 BNP-Jamaat government in Dhaka and the 26/11 Mumbai attacks. Still reeling from the shock of 26/11, New Delhi viewed the mutiny from a Pakistan-centric lens and as a national security threat. In addition to the BDR rank and file's grievances, Indian policymakers were worried about the mutiny's ideological composition. 'During the BNP-Jamaat rule a lot of Jamaatis were recruited into the BDR as rank and file so they were used apparently by Pakistan', says Chakravarty.[23] Just as relations with Pakistan hit the lowest ebb after a surge of optimism during the composite dialogue (2004–07), New Delhi could ill afford instability or an adversarial regime in Dhaka. Even though the mutiny and its international linkages generated much rumour and insinuation, the stakes for New Delhi were too high. With Indian general elections due in May, and the Sri Lankan civil war entering its final stages, Indian policymakers could ill afford Hasina's dislocation in Bangladesh. Menon informed the US that India was concerned that if anything happened to Hasina, the Jamaat and Harkat-ul-

Jihad-al Islami Bangladesh (HuJI-B) would execute attacks in India from Bangladesh.[24]

On this count, BNP parliamentarian Salahuddin Quader Chowdhury attracted attention. A powerful shipping magnate with access to the Chittagong port, Chowdhury was Khaleda Zia's advisor and considered an ISI agent since 1971.[25] Just as the mutiny unfolded, the India affiliate of the US-based CNN news network alleged that Chowdhury instigated the mutiny on Pakistan's behalf. Livid, Chowdhury threatened to sue the channel and noted that Khaleda Zia would not cooperate with Hasina.[26] On 8 March, a week after the mutiny, he triumphantly informed Western diplomats that the AL's mishandling of the situation created deep and wide pockets of anger against Hasina among junior and mid-ranking officers, most of who supported the BNP.[27] Chowdhury's role around the mutiny and the fact that CNN India blamed him even before investigations began indicate a complicated history. Despite continuing formal consultations on issues such as water sharing and economic connectivity, bilateral ties had become frosty after the BNP-Jamaat rose to power in October 2001, and Chowdhury had a role to play.

India's national security advisor Brajesh Mishra was the first foreign dignitary to congratulate Khaleda Zia in 2001. He visited Dhaka on 26–27 October two weeks after she took office.[28] But this time her son Tarique Rahman, who was a teenager when his father was assassinated in 1981, influenced government decisions and the party more than Khaleda Zia. According to Mathur, who developed a rapport with Tarique, 'he was well-disposed towards India and didn't let his personal biases come in the way of improved bilateral ties'.[29] But this didn't lead to improved relations. The two 'red lines' India held with Bangladesh—cut support to northeast rebels and protect Hindu minorities—were both undermined during this period. Mishra conveyed these concerns to Dhaka. But soon after elections, members of Hindu communities in Bhola and Jessore districts came under attack by ruling party members and the Jamaat. Killed, gang raped, and their properties destroyed, local Hindus were traumatised and displaced.[30]

Similarly, Bangladesh's support for northeast insurgents 'received vigour' during this period.[31] It came to the fore on 1 April

2004, when ten trucks full of weapons were caught in Chittagong. The largest arms haul in Bangladeshi history, this consignment was meant for the northeast, and the operation was monitored by the ULFA-I chief Paresh Baruah from a Dhaka safe house. The weapons were trans-shipped to trucks from a larger vessel moored at the St. Martin's Island, Bangladesh's southernmost point, and then positioned at the government-owned Chittagong Urea Fertilizer Co. Ltd.'s docks. The vessel at St. Martin's was owned by none other than Chowdhury who, India believed, was working at Pakistan's behest and with Tarique's approval. 'That overambitious son of Khaleda Zia took over a lot of power and began pushing arms and ammunition', says Chakravarty.[32] Shortly after, India provided a list of 148 camps in CHT to Dhaka in coordination with the US agencies. 'They would come back to us saying no, no, we've checked and these camps are not there ... making it a game of cat and mouse', remembers Chakravarty.

Dhaka denied the existence of such camps, but an unconvinced India responded by initiating covert operations against them.[33] Tarique's relations with India took a downturn during this period, and have not recovered since. Mathur admits that Tarique gravitated towards Pakistan, despite the former's attempt to keep him close to India.[34] Such estrangement was driven by unrealised expectations on the granting of duty-free goods access, which was an emotive issue in Bangladesh. 'He became disillusioned about support from New Delhi. Despite efforts to convince him otherwise, he succumbed to pressure from anti-India lobby within the party to nudge him in Pakistan's direction', adds Mathur.[35] People like Chowdhury, along with Pakistan-supported Islamists, were part of such intra-BNP lobbies pitched against India.

Chowdhury's alleged role in the August 2004 Dhaka grenade attack that nearly killed Hasina further complicated the situation. 'There are serious question marks about Pakistani involvement in the 2004 grenade attack', notes Pankaj Saran, India's ambassador in Dhaka (2012–15) and former deputy national security advisor (2018–21).[36] Chowdhury's involvement in the 2004 Chittagong arms haul and alleged facilitation of the grenade attack fed Hasina's belief that her opponents sought to eliminate her—just like her father—and sharpened India's insecurities. Saran puts it eloquently: 'Hasina being alive is an accident of history. She herself says she would've died that day, and it's a miracle she's alive. Plus, she cannot get over that event in August 1975'.[37]

In this context, when a military-led caretaker government took power on 11 January 2007 under the leadership of Fakhruddin Ahmed and Moeen, India saw an opportunity. New Delhi wanted to ensure that Hasina returned to power, and found an ally in Moeen. 'People often talk about our failure, and not about our successes ... but I know how we engaged with the military to pave the way for elections and Hasina's return. That was a success', Chakravarty claims.[38] In what became known as the 'Minus-Two' formula wherein the Bangladeshi military charged Hasina (arrested in July 2007) and Khaleda Zia (exiled) for corruption, and arrested Tarique in March 2007 (tortured), India initiated closed-door diplomacy to shape the endgame. Worried about empowering Jamaat, Hizb-ut-Tahrir, and other jihadist groups such as the HuJI-B and the Jamaat-ul-Mujahideen Bangladesh (JMB), New Delhi sought to obviate the BNP's return. Moeen's engagement with Mukherjee convinced India that unlike Pakistan, the Bangladeshi army was uninterested in holding power indefinitely. The promptness with which Moeen arrested and executed Siddique ul-Islam, 'Bangla Bhai', the JMB's leader in 2007, strengthened such beliefs.

Later, when the mutiny occurred, Indian intelligence officials noted that apart from grievances around living conditions and pay scales, the execution of Bangla Bhai fanned enduring anti-officer grievances among BDR personnel, many of whom were associated with the Jamaat and Hizb-ut-Tahrir.[39] India worried that political dislocation of Hasina and re-strengthening of conservatives would worsen its security. There were already multiple blasts in India during the 2000s, most of which were initiated by Pakistan-linked outfits. Such blasts fuelled anti-Pakistan, anti-Bangladesh, and anti-Muslim rhetoric, and concretised the Indian view that the BNP was a pro-Pakistan party. On 1 October 2008, for instance, four people were killed in Agartala. Three weeks later, blasts in Imphal killed 17 people and left over 40 injured. Shortly after, serial blasts in Guwahati killed 81 and injured nearly 500.

To add insult to injury, just after 26/11, multiple bombs went off in Guwahati before home minister P. Chidambaram's visit on 1 January 2009. These incidents shook the parliament with many blaming Dhaka for hosting anti-India insurgents 'just like Pakistan'.[40] Kiren Rijiju, a BJP parliamentarian from Arunachal Pradesh, claimed, 'If we were to go to the root of the incident which took place in the North Eastern Region I cannot stop but have to point a finger to Bangladesh'.[41] Dhaka's hosting of north-eastern rebels coupled with unchecked migration into Assam, were understood as the root cause of such blasts.

The 2009 mutiny occurred in a context of heightened religious radicalism, political violence, and India's and Pakistan's failure to resolve disputes as the Global War on Terrorism raged in Afghanistan. For India, the mutiny could have dislodged Hasina, undermined its security, and put paid to India's efforts to curate her rise. In the run-up to the 2008 elections, for example, Mukherjee guaranteed Fakhruddin Ahmed that Hasina would not harass him when in power.[42] In February 2008, when Moeen undertook a six-day India tour and received a red carpet welcome, he met Mukherjee at the latter's residence and the two discussed elections, cross-border rail transit, and rice supplies to a food-strapped Bangladesh. 'That was a good trip', says Moeen.[43] He was keen to preserve the army's interests, and if India could guarantee protection from whoever came to power next, that was acceptable. Mukherjee did just that: like Fakhruddin Ali, he promised Moeen that Hasina would not target him if she became prime minister.[44] India trusted Hasina. This was not just because of mistrust with the BNP and opposition to the Jamaat. It was because the AL was, at least in principle, secular, and Hasina was close to the Gandhi family. As Chakravarty put it, 'we wanted to help Hasina, and gave her the space to rework the bilateral'.[45] Uncertainty about Hasina's physical and political survival was unacceptable.

Saffron Revolution

In September 2007 when Buddhist monks across Myanmar took to the streets in protest against the junta and were gunned down, New

Delhi supported Than Shwe. India's outreach to the junta was paying off. The junta regularly engaged with India, kept it informed about Chinese activities, and supported New Delhi's drive to counter north-eastern insurgencies. Unlike 1988, when India underestimated the junta's resilience, in 2007 it was clear that the monk-led 'Saffron Revolution' and Suu Kyi's supporters would not topple the regime. Than Shwe was an ally. Menon, then India's foreign secretary, notes that the Naga peace process 'was one very big determining factor'.[46] Myanmar's denial of sanctuary to Naga rebels became effective during this period. In 2001, such support helped secure a ceasefire with the Myanmar-based NSCN-K.[47] Occurring four years after the NSCN-IM ceasefire, this was a big breakthrough. In April 2007, the NSCN-K ceasefire was extended by a year, and in July 2007 the ceasefire with NSCN-IM was extended indefinitely.[48]

Criticism of the junta could have undermined such ceasefires. Plus, dislocation in ties with Myanmar could offer rebels cross-border sanctuaries to restart violence while ensuring arms supplies via Bangladesh. Apart from NSCN-K, the BLT also announced a ceasefire in 1999.[49] In 2003, the BLT signed a peace accord and settled for a Bodo Territorial Council wherein it received autonomy on 36 subjects ranging from agriculture to various other industries.[50] Additionally, other than India desiring support from Myanmar, most Myanmar-centric rebels were 'divided', says Menon.[51] 'They were not quite sure where they stood ... nor were they serious about coming to the table', he notes. When the 1994 KIO ceasefire broke down in 2011, Menon was India's NSA. 'The Myanmar army became key to each of these things ... and they knew it. People tend to disregard this and say they're very weak, totally dependent on the Chinese and isolated. That was not really true'.[52] Indian policy planners concluded that seeking support from Myanmar's ethnic outfits was not conducive to sustainability of the Naga process.

In October 2004, Than Shwe undertook a six-day India visit, a first in twenty-five years. It was hailed as 'historic', and reciprocated by India's president in 2006.[53] The visit was significant because of its timing. It occurred shortly after the Chittagong arms haul and the grenade attack against Hasina, and signaled that India could bypass Dhaka to strengthen relations with its other eastern neighbour.

Myanmar's ambassador to India, Brig. Gen. Kyi Thein, notes that India was keen to enter Myanmar's hydrocarbon space, import petroleum, develop road connectivity, and facilitate the entry of Tata Motors.[54] New Delhi 'didn't talk too much about Suu Kyi, and focused on bilateral trade, which reached the 1-billion-USD mark by 2008', says Kyi Thein.[55] On insurgents, India often shared intelligence with Kyi Thein. 'During my tenure these problems were not very big … because our army did not accept the presence of anti-India insurgents, and both sides agreed to fight these insurgencies together', he claims.[56]

The other aspect driving India's approach towards the junta was its 'goal to bring Myanmar back into our fold' in relation to China, as Menon puts it.[57] Under US-led sanctions, Myanmar was termed an 'outpost of tyranny' by the US Secretary of State Condoleezza Rice in 2005, and faced similar censure from the EU.[58] During his New Delhi visit, US President Barack Obama 'lectured' India that it wasn't being 'hard enough' on Myanmar without acknowledging the argument that Thein Sein was liberalising the country.[59] Concerned that the EU and the US were 'treating Myanmar as some rogue state and dragging them into the arms of the Chinese', New Delhi was eager to pursue an autonomous path. India's belief was buttressed by the fact that Than Shwe was keen to limit Myanmar's reliance on China. This was visible in the fact that he allowed India to open a consulate in Mandalay despite Chinese protests.[60]

But the 'Saffron Revolution' along with Western sanctions put significant pressure on the junta. Led by monks associated with the State Sangha Maha Nayaka Committee, known as the Mahana, the protests sent shockwaves throughout the military that sought religious legitimacy. Coupled with Western pressure and underlying discomfort about its reliance on China, the monk-led protests compelled Than Shwe to expedite reforms. He responded by introducing a new constitution in 2008 that reintroduced elections, opened civil society space, and silently co-opted the Mahana. The junta announced elections in 2010 (boycotted by the NLD) that ensured the rise of reformist insiders such as Thein Sein and Soe Thane (former navy chief) on the plank of pro-junta Union Solidarity and Development Party (USDP). Thein Sein implemented the 2008 constitution in 2011. But it reserved 25% parliamentary seats for the army, and mandated a 75%+ majority for the enactment of amendments.[61] The military, thus, continued to dominate politics even if, as noted by Suu Kyi's education advisor, it 'didn't interfere in matters of routine governance and non-military sectors'.[62]

India's decision to overlook Myanmar's civil-military relations for strategic reasons, propensity to congratulate itself for nudging the junta towards reform, and the conviction that Myanmar could be weaned away from China proved illusory. The only thing reforms ensured was the strengthening of exclusionary Buddhist nationalism, as false hopes of democratisation surged the world over.[63] The elusive peace process with ethnic armed outfits, the 21st century Panglong process (initially launched by Thein Sein to get most outfits to sign the NCA), remained stuck, and the Rohingya crisis exploded in 2017. Tapping into latent mistrust of the Rohingya, all political parties including the NLD found it convenient, even desirable, to hone their nationalist credentials by encouraging anti-Rohingya politics. The post-2007 transition paved the ground for the Rohingya genocide.

The significance of extremist Buddhist monks such as Ashin Wirathu, once called the 'Osama bin Laden of Myanmar' underlined a trend in Myanmar that few countries wanted to confront. In a 2013 statement, Wirathu said: 'You can be full of kindness and love, but you can't sleep next to a mad dog … I am proud to be called a radical Buddhist. If we are weak, our land will become Muslim.'[64] Reminiscent of the dehumanisation of Jews in Nazi Germany or of Tutsis in 1994 Rwanda, the anti-Rohingya discourse reached fever pitch in 2015, making the situation ripe for exploitation by both Islamists belonging to the Arakan Rohingya Salvation Army (ARSA) and the junta. As Soe Thane, former navy chief, considered a reformer before he backed the 2021 coup, claimed, 'the Myanmar people are worried about losing territory in the west, next to Bangladesh … if you go to Maungdaw, you will see these people, they're just like Bangladeshis…'[65] Similar sentiments were heard from almost everyone this author spoke with in Yangon and Mandalay in 2018. Violent religious politics became the norm in India's near east.

When she rose to power in 2015, Suu Kyi embraced three big agendas. First, she embraced religious populism to shore up popularity while attempting to dislocate the military's power. This dynamic played out in Rakhine where anti-Rohingya crackdown generated international condemnation. Cognisant of the salience of this issue among the Burman majorities, Suu Kyi backed genocidal acts while taking umbrage at ARSA's violence. Instead of reassuring the junta, Suu Kyi's decision to compromise her global reputation as an icon of democracy worried Min Aung Hlaing. He feared her as a politician. Suu Kyi also sought to undercut the military's veto in the parliament and campaigned to dilute either the 25% reservation of seats for army personnel or the need of over 75% of votes to pass a bill or amendment.

Second, such jockeying was coupled with Suu Kyi's parleys with ethnic outfits, with whom she continued the process that Thein Sein started. For this to succeed, she needed to bypass constituents cultivated using majoritarian nationalism. The idea of compromising with Christian minorities didn't fit with Suu Kyi's politics. Inevitably, the entire effort failed. In 2018, when this author interviewed members of the Peace-Talks Creation Group in Myitkyina who tried finding middle ground between the KIO and Naypyidaw, they noted their frustration at Suu Kyi's lack of interest. Thein Sein, they argued, was more invested in bringing peace than Suu Kyi.[66] Chin negotiators shared similar concerns.[67]

The UN reached a similar assessment. Vijay Nambiar, the UN Secretary General's special envoy to Myanmar (2010–16) and at one time India's deputy national security advisor, says:

> It was in 2013 when the UN first became involved in the peace process. This was a time when violence in Kachin state spilled over into China and prompted Beijing to bring the two sides to the negotiating table under their auspices. I was in Myanmar then, and Maj. Gen. Aung Min [Minister of the President's Office of Myanmar, 2012–16] was leading the peace process on the government side in Ruili within China. On his return after the talks in China, I had the occasion to join him on his aircraft from Lashio to Naypyidaw, and it was then that he mentioned that while they had problems with the Kachin, they were not comfortable with having peace talks with their 'own' people in

a foreign country. Eventually, the peace talks were resumed in Myitkyina. The Kachin wanted other countries as observers, and not just China but also India, US, and the UK—this was even though China was not keen on it and had initially even refused to participate in the first round of talks.[68]

Thein Sein's decision to negotiate with the KIO in 2013 with Aung Min leading the charge and support from Soe Thane received pushback from hardliners within the military. But he remained firm and pushed for a peaceful settlement without China dictating the terms of talks or dominating the process. When in 2013 China proposed a tripartite format of negotiations between Naypyidaw, the KIO, and Beijing, both the Myanmar government and Kachin rebels demurred. Suu Kyi buried Thein Sein's conflict resolution strategies as soon as she came to power. 'Suu Kyi was not willing to accept discussing the issue of federalism, and while the UN left the process, the Chinese became more entrenched in the peace talks', says Nambiar.[69] Beijing effectively became the only arbiter in Myanmar's conflict with the KIO and other ethnic outfits. 'The idea that the Chinese were unpopular among the Myanmar military and their influence will thus go down is untrue', adds Nambiar.[70]

Suu Kyi's politics militated against her imperative of bringing all ethnic outfits on board to sign the NCA that was key to finding a solution to multiple ethnic conflicts. But on all these aspects, Suu Kyi needed China's support, and her tilt towards Beijing, demonstrated in Xi Jinping's January 2020 Myanmar visit, became the proverbial straw that broke the camel's back. Suu Kyi was more popular than Min Aung Hlaing and was conducting successful international diplomacy. This was unacceptable. Min Aung Hlaing responded by ousting her in a coup on 1 February 2021.

Act East

In 2014, India's newly elected prime minister Narendra Modi rechristened 'Look East' to 'Act East'. Intended to signal determination to deliver on infrastructure projects in India's near east, the renaming was done to underscore failures of the Congress-led United Progressive Alliance (UPA) government (2004–14). Still, ten years later, India's eastern connectivity remains limited. To understand the transition from 'look' to 'act east', it's critical to focus on both external and domestic triggers. More than to spite the Congress, the idea to act east became central to India's strategic planning after 2013 thanks to China's infrastructural push as part of its BRI. The China-Myanmar Economic Corridor, an approximately 20-billion-USD project, sought to connect Rakhine with Yunnan.[71] In Bangladesh, Beijing sought to develop the Sonadia port[72] and enter other sectors such as the Dhaka metro rail project.[73] To make sense of the 'long 2010s' in India's near east, this section unpacks India's economic and political approach towards Myanmar and Bangladesh as captured by its 'Act East policy'.

The BRI increased India's sense of strategic encirclement by China. In Myanmar, it fuelled the need to deliver on the Kaladan multi-modal transit project and develop the trilateral India-Myanmar-Thailand highway. As Kyi Thein put it, 'between Thailand and Myanmar it was ok, but between India and Myanmar there were issues [and] unfortunately we couldn't achieve it'.[74] Stymied by bureaucratic delays and instability in border areas, India failed to build strategically significant projects. For Aung Tun Thet, who was a member of the Myanmar Investment Commission and the president's economic advisor, 'the Indians were not quick enough' to invest after Myanmar opened its financial sector.[75] The Tata group became central to developing connectivity. Tata International, Tata Motors, Jaguar Land Rover, Tata Power, Titan, and the Tata Consultancy Services all opened offices in Yangon.[76] But apart from the Tatas, 'I don't see many other Indian companies coming in', Aung Tun Thet noted in 2018.[77] Singaporean banks, Japanese aid, and Chinese capital were outcompeting Indian capital and governmental aid during Myanmar's experiment with democratisation.

The Modi government decided to reinvent India's presence in Myanmar. Though it encouraged Tatas to expand operations, by 2019 Modi's preferred corporate ally, Gujarati industrialist Gautam Adani, became the key arbiter of India's 'Act East'. In 2019, the Adani group was granted permission by Naypyidaw to build and operate a container terminal at the Yangon port.[78] Such connectivity could have been more successful than building roads through regions prone to insurgency. But the 2021 coup and consequent sanctions against the junta jeopardised these plans, forcing Adani to divest. In contrast, Chinese capital flowed unhindered. As Aung Tun Thet put it, there were concerns in Naypyidaw about Myanmar's dependence on China, but when 'the Chinese come in big with investments', it became difficult to say no.[79]

To improve border connectivity, India and Myanmar developed the Free Movement Regime (FMR). The FMR allows visa-free movement across the border for a 16-kilometre stretch (this varies from state to state on the Indian side).[80] India's developmental budget for Myanmar stood at 50 million USD in 2021, and it built the Sittwe port in Rakhine.[81] This was coupled with exporting defence equipment such as coastal radars. By 2021, nearly 50% of India's defence exports were channelled to Myanmar.[82] Despite such initiatives, New Delhi struggled to make its presence felt in Naypyidaw, underscoring the antinomies of India's approach. The Sittwe port has been built, but the road that must connect it to Mizoram has not. Even if the road is constructed, there is little clarity about the business potential in such a region.

Similarly, the FMR fosters social and limited economic connectivity, but also augments security concerns about movement of insurgents. As the former director general of India's defence intelligence agency, put it: 'because of the freedom of movement, which is on both sides, the insurgents take full advantage of moving closer to the border. They have camps close to the border … and because the armed forces don't cross like this, they have an inherent advantage'.[83] Equally, India's failure to rebuild the Stilwell Road despite pitching it and then not doing it when the offer was on the table exacerbated such issues. The road could connect Arunachal Pradesh to China through Myanmar.[84] Pillai, who served as India's commerce secretary as well, notes that India's inability to deliver on this was a 'big strategic mistake'.[85]

In Bangladesh, by contrast, India capitalised on its alliance with Hasina, and bilateral trade reached nearly 18.2 billion USD in 2021–22.[86] But Dhaka's concerns about a burgeoning trade deficit

(Indian exports were 16.2 billion USD and Bangladeshi exports were 2 billion USD) and India's failure to resolve Teesta gave Dhaka reason to diversify ties with China. Soon after securing her base after 2009, Hasina visited India in January 2010 and signed agreements for duty-free access of Bangladeshi goods in Indian markets, enhanced railway and waterway connectivity, easier transit to Nepal and Bhutan, and received a 1-billion-USD line of credit.[87] But in March 2010, she visited Beijing and received investments worth 2.2 billion USD, followed by Russian entry into Bangladesh to develop the Roopur nuclear power plant worth 13.5 billion USD.[88] In June 2011, China cancelled all pre-2008 Bangladeshi debt, but when Indian prime minister Manmohan Singh made his first trip to Dhaka after a twelve-year gap in September, the two sides struggled to sign an agreement on Teesta thanks to opposition by the West Bengal government.

China's 2014 plans to develop the Sonadia port under the BRI were shelved in 2015. Pressure from India and Japan played a role in its rollback. Instead, the Japan International Cooperation Agency was offered to develop the Matarbari port. Similarly, Dhaka issued a tender for the development of the Payra port over which there was a geopolitical scramble between Beijing, Tokyo, and New Delhi. Such struggles came to a head in October 2016 when Xi Jinping made a landmark visit to Dhaka and signed agreements worth over 24 billion USD for 27 developmental projects, and promised to deliver two refurbished Chinese Ming-class submarines.[89] To blunt the import of Dhaka's turn to China, Hasina visited New Delhi in April 2017, one month after the two Chinese submarines were delivered, and signed 22 agreements on defence, nuclear energy, cyber security, and media with India extending two more lines of credit, including 4.5 billion USD for development and infrastructural projects.[90] By 2020, accumulated BRI investments in Bangladesh stood at 38 billion USD, whereas India's line of credits reached 10 billion USD.[91]

But unlike Myanmar where the Tatas were trying to gain a foothold, India's big corporate shied away from Bangladesh. In 2004, Tatas proposed to the BNP-led government a 3-billion-USD investment to develop four large projects including a 2.4-million-tonne steel plant, a 1-million-tonne urea plant, a 1,000-megawatt power plant, and a 6-million-tonne coal mining project.[92] These were in addition to Tata International's and Tata Motor's existing operations. But after a three-year deadlock over pricing of natural gas that Dhaka was to supply for these industries, the deal collapsed in 2008.[93] Though bilateral trade grew, the next big investment offered by Indian firms came in June 2015 after the announcement of India's 'Act East' policy and during a two-day visit by Modi. The Adani and Reliance groups offered a combined investment of 5.5 billion USD to set up power projects in Bangladesh. The Mukesh Ambani-led Reliance Power sought to develop a 3,000-megawatt gas-based power-plant for 3 billion USD, and Adani promised a 1,600-megawatt 2.5-billion-USD coal-powered plant.[94] The catch for Adani's plant was that it is based in Godda, Jharkhand, and supplies power across the border.

Beginning to supply power to the Bangladesh Power Development Board in March 2023, Adani charges Dhaka a monthly 423 million USD, i.e. a capacity charge of 11 billion USD over the plant's lifetime.[95] A high price to pay, the deal raised questions about why Hasina agreed to such biased terms. As it became clear, this was because Modi enjoys considerable leverage over Hasina.[96] When New York-based short-seller Hindenburg Research charged Adani for executing the 'largest con in corporate history' by allying with the BJP and undertaking debt-soaked expansion, Hasina tried to re-negotiate the deal. Adani simply refused.[97] The saga shows Hasina's political dependence on India. On the economic front, it is Japanese, not Indian, development of Matarbari that could overhaul the Bangladeshi economy.[98] Even in Myanmar, Tokyo, not New Delhi, has played the role of conciliator between the junta and the Arakan army to limit conflict in Rakhine state.[99] A cautionary tale of India's response to Chinese presence in Myanmar and Bangladesh, it underscores the limits of India's geo-economic power.

India's political response to instability and authoritarianism in its near east is telling. In Myanmar, after the constitution came into effect in 2011, India engaged with both civilian and military leaders. Keen to limit China's influence, Naypyidaw was courting global investment and political capital and riding the narrative of democratisation. Thein Sein's government (2011–15) cancelled

China's bid to develop the Myitsone Dam in Kachin state, which could have dislocated local populations and ecologies, generated civil resistance, and threatened the Irrawaddy's ecosystem. He pushed the ethnic peace process and drafted the NCA. On 15 October 2015, nearly ten ethnic armed outfits signed the agreement. These included the KNU, the ALP, the Restoration Council of Shan State, and the CNF, among others. It was a landmark agreement despite the breakdown of the 1994 KIO ceasefire and failure to get the United Wa State Party on board.

A senior minister in Suu Kyi's cabinet, says it was 'strategically very important' for Myanmar to 'work closely with India on defence cooperation to contain cross-border insurgent and illegal drugs movement' and other aspects such as strengthening federalism.[100] Though he maintained that the solution to Myanmar's ethnic conflicts could only emerge from within, India could share its 'constitutional experience' and help with peacebuilding. The Indian constitution, he noted, could offer a 'very good framework for asymmetric federalism' in Myanmar.[101] Indian officials in Yangon often delivered talks on constitutionalism, without becoming involved in the minutiae of the peace process (India had observer status).[102]

Though unsure about India's ability to influence the KIO to sign the NCA, Suu Kyi's senior minister was open to the idea of India leveraging Kachin rebels to bring them to the negotiating table. The R&AW did have contacts with KIO leaders but couldn't use such access to foster amity.[103] Pillai explains that India has been 'funding the Chin and Kachin insurgents groups just to keep a foothold in that area ... it gives us information about what is happening inside Myanmar'.[104] The R&AW's contacts with Myanmar rebels was not meant to build the peace process.

By 2014, India began posting army officers to Myanmar's Defence Services Academy. On two-year stints, these officers often have command and combat experience in the northeast. Their formal charter is to teach English, but they also help India better understand the military's internal dynamics. Critical to maintain intelligence about China's activities in Myanmar, such engagements are essential for India. In New Delhi, Zin Yaw, Myanmar's ambassador (2012–14) remembers being asked by Menon on several occasions to ensure 'cooperation between the two countries' security apparatus [because] they were concerned about insurgency in the northeast, and tried to get our consent to not get involved with [India-centric] insurgent groups'.[105] When in June 2015 the Indian army undertook an operation inside Myanmar in response to an ambush in Manipur, access in Naypyidaw contained diplomatic damage. The operation itself was not a problem, but its celebration as a sign of Modi's '56-inch chest' (signifying muscularity) raised questions.[106]

The cross-border raid caught Gautam Mukhopadhaya, India's ambassador in Yangon, off guard. Uninformed about the raid in advance, Mukhopadhaya emphasised the text of New Delhi's official aide memoir to underscore that the operation occurred 'along' and not 'across' the border to his Myanmar interlocutors.[107] But the next day, he was confronted by deputy foreign minister Thant Kyaw, who cited Indian media reports saying that the operation was inside Myanmar's territory. 'Myanmar had a problem with chest-thumping … but they were still very discrete in their criticism', Mukhopadhaya says.[108] Thant Kyaw concurs: 'we didn't make it a political issue, and didn't even let it become big in Myanmar media'.[109] Suu Kyi hadn't come to power when the raid took place. But Suu Kyi's senior minister, who followed these developments, says that internally 'people got very angry and … this is interference with the sovereignty of our country'.[110] He adds, 'The Myanmar military lost face. If we have to make some defence cooperation along the border, it must not be publicised, and should be very quiet'.[111]

Charismatic and resourceful, Mukhopadhaya developed access in Naypyidaw and met with Min Aung Hlaing on several occasions. Well-travelled in Myanmar and with deep knowledge of India's northeast, he developed a rapport with Aung Min, Min Aung Hlaing's confidante and Thein Sein's point-person for the peace process. Apart from the raid, the sharper balancing act for Mukhopadhaya was between Min Aung Hlaing and Suu Kyi. Unlike the 2011 elections boycott, Suu Kyi contested the 2015 polls and was keen to signal to Myanmar's neighbours that she was coming to power. Her message to Mukhopadhaya was 'we're going to win, so don't make a mistake' of solely siding with the junta.[112] Her ability to outmanoeuvre the military and build a strong political base by adopting ethno-religious populism made Min Aung Hlaing insecure. He worried about losing his edge for good if Suu Kyi returned to power with another mandate in 2021—as she did—and altered the constitution to the benefit of civilian parties. Mukhopadhaya ensured that Suu Kyi received a red carpet welcome in New Delhi.

But under the public radar, the politics of the India-Myanmar bilateral underwent a huge shift. The mainstreaming of Hindu nationalism in India and potency of Buddhist nationalism in Myanmar offered a unique, often understated, majoritarian glue. It went back to Myanmar's silence on the Babri demolition. The politics of Hindu and Buddhist majoritarianism pinned separatism in the borderlands on the spread of Islam and Christianity. If Western missionaries had not uprooted animist customs of local populations straddling the border, there would be no separatism in these regions, in their worldviews.[113] A telling explication of such undercurrents came from an unlikely source: an RSS *pracharak* posted to Yangon as liaison with the Sanatan Dharma Swayamsevak Sangh (SDSS). Though unwilling to be identified, this *pracharak* not only blames China for fomenting violence in India, but equally blames the West. In his version, the 'church and England work together in Myanmar, northeast, and other parts of the subcontinent to spread Christianity and capture business'.[114]

The Hindu-Buddhist compact in this context is both safe and desirable. On the question of the relationship between Buddhist nationalism and Hindutva, both the SDSS chief Ram Niwas and the RSS *pracharak* were clear that they accept Buddhist hegemony in Myanmar.[115] As someone who spent years in Mumbai, Niwas is a trusted RSS inspired ally in Yangon. He has acted as translator for visiting Indian leaders including former vice president Bhairon Singh Shekhawat and Prime Minister Modi. Connected to the All Myanmar Hindu Central Council, an umbrella body for all Hindus in Myanmar, Niwas ensures that the Hindu community continues to be accepted and supported by the junta. 'In India the RSS has *rashtravaad* (nationalism), but here we're trying to make our people good citizens of Myanmar with full *nishtha* (devotion), and the [Myanmar] government trusts us', he says.[116] This compact is different from how Hindutva views itself in relation to other religions with territorial sources in the subcontinent (Sikhism, Buddhism, Jainism, etc.).

India's response to the Rohingya crisis demonstrates how communalism shapes geopolitics. There are two elements here. From a foreign policy perspective, the Rohingya crisis tested India's relations with Bangladesh. Dhaka wanted New Delhi to pressure Naypyidaw to halt the exodus. Karim, Bangladesh's envoy to India, sought New Delhi's support but realised this was futile.[117] Rohingya influx to Bangladesh began long before 2017, when, Karim notes, 'the dam burst'.[118] Dhaka could have started to 'scream high heaven' sooner given its inability to undertake military action against Naypyidaw, he notes.[119] Mahfuzur Rahman concurs:

> The Myanmar army undertook several military operations starting from 2016 and early 2017 before launching a full scale attack against the Rohingyas. These operations were meant to test how Dhaka and international community would respond. Neither Dhaka nor the international community responded in a way to deter Myanmar, and Naypyidaw saw that as an opportunity or green-light for a larger operational drive in north Rakhine.[120]

Instead of pressing Suu Kyi to contain the exodus, India launched Operation Insaniyat (humanity) to offer relief to those who crossed over into Cox's Bazar.[121]

In Rakhine, New Delhi offered tents and other relief material, rationalising it from a humanitarian perspective. Even when Beijing became involved and Myanmar suggested a four-way dialogue between China, India, Bangladesh, and Myanmar, India distanced itself.[122] Aung Tun Thet, former economic advisor appointed chief coordinator of the Union Enterprise for Humanitarian, Resettlement, and Development in Rakhine in 2017, clarifies that India was more 'understanding' of Myanmar's response to the worsening security situation in Rakhine.[123] Firm in his belief that India understood the complexity of the Rohingya issue, he maintains that India's approach was appreciated in Naypyidaw. But, adding with candour and 'mischief', he argues that India's actions against Bengali Muslim migrants in Assam 'helped us … if India could get rid of three million citizens in Assam then don't come and talk to us about citizenship of 700,000. It gave us a cover, that look if the world's largest democracy can do it then …'.[124] Fear of regional Islamists in the context of the 25 August 2017 attack against the Myanmar army and police by the ARSA (an incident Aung Tun Thet was investigating), featured largely in his views.

Parallel to India's limited response to anti-Rohingya violence was communalisation at home. On 9 August 2017, Rijiju, then Minister of State for home affairs, notified the parliament that the central government ordered all state governments to identify and expel Rohingyas residing illegally in India, including the 16,500 registered with the United Nations High Commissioner for Refugees.[125] Rohingyas living in slums of Jammu, New Delhi, and Hyderabad became a target of Hindu-right propaganda and attacks. Branded 'terrorists-in-making', the Rohingya became essential to Indian communalism. Despite the fact that most Rohingyas in India arrived before 2017, their situation became so precarious that by 2022, many left for camps in Bangladesh, becoming twice displaced.[126] Communalisation of the Rohingya issue helped the BJP mobilise electoral support. The impact was such that even avowedly secular parties such as the Aam Aadmi Party targeted Rohingyas to outbid the BJP's religious majoritarianism.[127]

India's response to this crisis underscores another contradiction in its 'Act East' policy. New Delhi wants to develop infrastructural connectivity, but limit cross-border mobility, largely because of communal politics. Though communal undercurrents existed even before, the BJP's rise ensured that the Rohingya issue was viewed primarily from a communal angle. The Rohingyas living in India for decades suddenly found themselves to be unwelcome.[128] India's response has historical precedent and deeper ideological roots: it has *always* shared Myanmar's perspective on this issue. In 1949, Indian officials worried about unceasing movement of Pakistani Muslims into Arakan and the violent methods of the Mujahid Party (a mid-20th-century precursor to ARSA). Five years later, in November 1954, when Rangoon claimed that it killed 128, wounded 103, and captured 23 Mujahids in an operation against 400 Mujahids, the Indian defence attaché considered the claims 'grossly exaggerated' but admitted that 'this operation provided one of the very few really contested engagements that have taken place with the insurgents. As a result, the Mujahid menace was at least temporarily completely liquidated. Some 100–150 were reported to have escaped to East Pakistan'.[129] In 1958, when the Mujahids revived the insurgency under the 'notorious … ring leader' named 'Cassim' and 'Abdul Raschid', Indian officials noted that Pakistan 'encouraged and aided' their 'depredations'.[130]

In 1968, Indian intelligence reported that 4,000 Pakistanis (Rohingyas) 'entered Arakan [and] since most of them know Burmese and also have connections in the area, it has proved difficult to detect them'.[131] It was noted that these migrants, along with armed Mujahids, engaged in large-scale rice and timber smuggling from Arakan to East Pakistan. The focus and tenor of India's reports on the Rohingya issue didn't change after 1971. In 1976, India noted that Burma-Bangladesh relations were marred by a 'degree of distrust and fear', due to 'illicit influx of Bangladeshis into Arakan and from there to places all over Burma'.[132] Such migration from Chittagong coupled with 'separatist rebel movement of the Muslims in Arakan' complicated the situation. What made it worse was Libya's interest in this movement, and Muammar Gaddafi's sponsorship of rebel 'camps on Bangladesh territory, just across the border from Burma, where Burmese Muslims are kept ready to move when the time comes.'[133] Such Indian assessments—that the Rohingyas seek separation and groups such as ARSA enjoy links with Pakistan and Pakistan-tilting governments in Dhaka—continue to inform India's reluctance to support the Rohingya.

But such a response generated friction between Dhaka and New Delhi. To be clear, Hasina's rise has brought strategic dividends for India. Her targeting of opponents in the International Crimes Tribunal, giving in to the 2013 Shahbag movement's demand to execute radical Jamaat-e-Islami preacher Abdul Quader Mollah, and counter-terrorism operations fit with India's objectives. Hasina's response during the 2009 BDR mutiny was worthy enough for India to back her again in 2014 when the opposition boycotted elections that were compromised. Soon after, in 2015, India received a breakthrough on the extradition of ULFA-I leader Anup Chetia, something it had sought since Chetia's 1997 arrest.[134] Post-2009

Hasina put a lid on northeast insurgents operating from Bangladesh. Saran says: 'Hasina has a great sense of history. In 1996–2001, she wasn't her own boss … during 2008–2013, she was consolidating herself, and strengthening relations with India. But after 2013, she really went for the trials' of the 1971 war criminals.[135] Expectedly, in 2018, when the opposition did participate in elections only to find they were compromised, India continued to support Hasina.

But just as India-Myanmar ties deepened, India-Bangladesh relations came under stress despite healthy trade and Dhaka's economic rise. After all, Hindu majoritarianism does not fit with New Delhi's preference for a secular Hasina. Explaining Hasina's dependence on a Hindu nationalist India to the Bangladeshi public has become difficult for the AL. Matters came to a head when the BJP introduced the Citizenship (Amendments) Act in 2020 promising to offer citizenship to Hindus and Sikhs persecuted in Bangladesh, Afghanistan, and Pakistan. In combination with NRC, which sought to identify and expel 'illegal' 'infiltrators' from Assam, the CAA-NRC generated pushback from Dhaka. In a rare criticism, Hasina questioned the decision: 'we don't understand why [India] did it. It [CAA] was not necessary'. On the question of people leaving India for Bangladesh, she clarified, 'there is no reverse migration from India', and said that 'within India, people are facing many problems'.[136] Karim was blunt: 'don't expect Bangladesh to remain an island of secularism surrounded by a vast ocean of majoritarianism'.[137]

India's concern is what if Hasina takes a pro-Islamic tilt while engaging with China? Under pressure from the West to hold free and fair elections, with reduced capacity to raise electoral finance, and facing widespread disgruntlement against her authoritarianism and corruption, Hasina has good reason to engage with the Hefazat-e-Islam and the Jamaat-e-Islami to remain in power. Dislocation of Bangladesh's macro-economic growth story due to COVID-19 and Russia's invasion of Ukraine that reduced its forex reserves and revenue-generation capacities has further eroded Hasina's appeal. Additionally, targeted attacks against Hindus across Bangladesh, especially during the 13–19 October 2021 Durga Puja celebrations, became worrisome. Though such attacks imparted political logic to the CAA-NRC, the fact that they occurred after and possibly because of the CAA-NRC shows how communalism feeds geopolitics. Hindu nationalism simultaneously become an unstoppable electoral force and a hindrance to enduring peace.

'Termites'

In April 2019, during a rally in West Bengal, the then-BJP party president and current home minister, Amit Shah, promised to push illegal migrants into the Bay of Bengal. To clarify, he explained that Bengali Muslim 'infiltrators are like termites in the soil of Bengal'.[138] This one speech defines the BJP's approach towards Muslims and the northeast. Delivered before the introduction of the CAA, it dehumanised Bengali Muslims.[139] The domestic feature of India's Act East under the BJP was the political consolidation of the latter's electoral base across eastern India. Though the Trinamool Congress, led by Mamata Banerjee who remains in power in Kolkata, the BJP has succeeded in gaining power in most northeastern states. Often in alliance with local sub-nationalists, the BJP is in power in Assam, Manipur, Meghalaya, Nagaland, Sikkim, and Tripura. In Mizoram, the ruling MNF is an uncomfortable ally. Once again, the antinomy here is that India seeks to integrate a region, but in practice, fosters social and political division.

The BJP's communalism fits with Assam's anti-foreigner and Manipur's anti-minority, anti-migrant politics. Himanta Biswa Sarma, an erstwhile Congress leader in Guwahati joined the BJP in 2015 to become chief minister in 2021. He routinely engages in communal partisanship. A long-time advocate of anti-foreigner sentiment for religious (not linguistic) reasons, the BJP succeeded in coming to power in 2016 and co-opted Congress candidates frustrated at their party's inability to distribute patronage. The BJP's rise in Assam coincided with the reframing of the Act East policy and Chetia's extradition. Apart from dislocating the Congress, communal partisanship coupled with the use of force against Paresh Baruah and Chetia's allies helped Sarma undermine ULFA-I. Even if the political sentiment of ULFA-I, i.e. secular Assamese nationalism, holds sway in certain quarters, the outfit remains marginal. If anything, there have been failed attempts by Sarma to repatriate Baruah from his hideout in China and sign a peace accord.

The depths of communalism in Assam is visible with the Rashtriya Bajrang Dal, a branch of the Vishwa Hindu Parishad, holding militant training camps for Hindu youth in Dhubri, 250 kilometres from Guwahati.[140] Launched in 2019, the aim of the group according to one of its members is 'to prepare for the dangers from the rapidly increasing population of Bengali origin Muslims and to thwart their plan of capturing political power in Assam'.[141] When juxtaposed with statements by Sarma that 'madrasas should disappear, and Muslims are originally Hindus', Assam's trajectory seems at odds with New Delhi's idea to connect Bangladesh with India.[142] Not just anti-Muslim, the RSS-affiliated Janajati Dharma-Sanskriti Suraksha Manch demands the amendment of Article 342A to de-list tribal communities who have undergone conversion from the Schedule Tribe (ST) status to 'foreign religions' such as Christianity or Islam.[143] Originally taken up by Congress parliamentarians in the 1960s, the idea is to limit the ability of these communities to accrue 'double benefit' of reservations by using both their lower caste and religious minority status.[144] Often targeting Christian-dominated Nagaland and Meghalaya, such groups openly practice communal politics.

The historical cord that binds the politics of present-day Assam goes back to the 1950 Nehru-Liaquat Pact that birthed the Jana Sangha. The subsequent rise of the anti-foreigner movement in the 1950s, and its transformation into the Assam agitation until the 1985 accord was signed, continues to inform Assamese politics. The fractious question of defining citizens and foreigners in this context received a fillip when the BJP-led government amended the Act in 2003. In what was viewed to be the first step in the BJP's journey to clarify the contours of India's citizenship landscape and mandate the government to (re)construct and maintain the NRC, the CAA-2003 was a precursor to the CAA-2020. Had the BJP returned to power in 2004, there's a chance that it would have acted on CAA-NRC earlier. But even after Modi's rise in 2014, it took the momentous victory of 2019 to deliver on three ideologically central issues: abrogating Article 370 from Jammu and Kashmir, the Ram Mandir issue, and

CAA-NRC. Implementation of the Uniform Civil Code is the only promise yet to be delivered.

The other explanation of the BJP's rise in Assam relates to the region's political economy. During 2004–14, the Congress lost control over its finances. Corrupt, inefficient, and unable to manage intra-party fissures, it became a shadow of its former self unable to contain growing ambitions of regional leaders demanding top posts. Sarma's departure is one of many such defections. The BJP not only promises power, but also offers money to promising candidates who are willing to join the party regardless of its ideological fixations. In Manipur, the Meitei-Naga divide and the state's dependence on central government subsidies helped the BJP catapult to power in 2017, and again in 2022. After being in power for 15 years (2002–17), the Congress lost out thanks to the BJP's control of resources in New Delhi. The fact that dominant Meitei communities in Imphal are mostly Vaishnava Hindus helped ease the BJP's rhetoric. In Manipur's Naga hills, the Hindu right found allies in Zeliangrong communities who refused to convert to Christianity and remain at odds with Naga separatists.

But there are limits to such societal overlaps. If the BJP was able to attract the Meitei and Zeliangrong communities in 2017, it developed a complicated relationship with the Nagas. The contradictions of Hindu nationalism are visible in Christian-dominated states such as Mizoram, Meghalaya, and Nagaland, where the church is powerful. In Mizoram, the BJP continues to remain a weak political force in relation to the MNF. But in November 2022, the two formed a coalition to stake claim in the Mara Autonomous District Council (MADC) in south Mizoram that disrupted the Congress-MNF coalition.[145] Though ideologically dissimilar, the MNF finds it convenient to use its heft in Mizoram to shape relations with New Delhi and ensure continuing financial and political support. One of the many reasons it allied with the BJP to oust the Congress in MADC was to ensure that New Delhi doesn't halt movement of Chin migrants fleeing Myanmar after the 2021 coup. There is sympathy for Chin refugees in Mizoram. To shut Aizawl's doors on these people could risk dislocating the MNF's electoral base. Driven by this calculus, Mizoram chief minister Zoramthanga struck a deal with the BJP to obviate obstruction to his support for Chin migrants in return for an upshot in the BJP's local seat tally.

The most under-appreciated but critical impact of Hindu nationalist politics in the northeast has been on the Naga peace process. In July 2022, the NSCN-IM issued a statement that held the RSS responsible for obstructing the accord. The key sticking points are the latter's demand for a separate constitution and flag. Despite the government respecting these demands in a 2015 framework agreement, the RSS continues to oppose it. Cornered and convinced by Sardar Patel in 1950 to drop its own flag and constitution in favour of the Indian constitution, the RSS is unwilling to compromise to the Nagas.

In a statement, the NSCN-IM noted that

the irony is that this matter was already resolved long back but the RSS factor came in between, questioning how there can be two flags and two constitutions ... the manifesto of the RSS/ Hindutva sharply contradicted the principal agreement of the FA [Framework agreement]. The actual point of delay started from here'.[146]

When challenged by the RSS that such an arrangement would go against the spirit of Indian nationalism, the NSCM-IM countered that 'these two arrangements are parallel in nature, one is within the Indian Constitution and the other is outside the purview of the Indian Constitution', effectively claiming that a separate Naga constitution and flag was not at odds with India.[147] But interlocutors and observers of the process note the religious undercurrent to the RSS's obstruction of peace with a Baptist armed outfit.

The contradiction here is that the two sides came close to a resolution in 2015 when they signed the framework agreement. Since the 1997 ceasefire, parallel governance systems were maintained while respecting ceasefire protocols. Modi's 2014 victory and Swu's terminal illness (he was in the ICU when signing the framework agreement) created a window to translate the ceasefire into an accord while Swu was still alive.[148] 'The NSCN-IM were desperate', notes Pillai.[149] With Tangkhuls, represented by Muivah, located in Manipur, the NSCN-IM needed a foothold in Nagaland after Swu's death. The framework agreement offered that. There was little new in it and 'the NSCN-IM had agreed to everything' when Pillai was home secretary (2009–11).[150] Muivah agreed to end the movement if Tangkhuls were granted autonomy in Manipur to decide on the appointment of district collectors and superintendents of police.[151] But Imphal refused. Despite being 'hogwash', in Pillai's words, the framework agreement created an impression that resolution of the conflict was on the anvil.[152] It was to scuttle the possibility of such rapprochement that NSCN-K ambushed an Indian army convoy in Manipur, triggering the June 2015 cross-border operation. The promise of a settlement with India-based Nagas ended the ceasefire with alienated Myanmar-based Nagas. The framework agreement ensured that Nagaland remained peaceful when Swu died in June 2016, and his loyalists either accepted Muivah's leadership or became part of the Naga National Political Groups (NNPG) that accepted the terms and conditions as set by New Delhi.

India successfully manipulated Naga factions, even though it desired a centralising figure who could arbiter lasting peace. The notable aspect here was India's manipulation of NSCN-K's internal power struggle in coordination with Naypyidaw after Khaplang's death in June 2017. By January 2019, the Khango Konyak-led faction of the NSCN-K joined the NNPG, thereby strengthening New Delhi's position in relation to Muivah, who continues to press for a separate constitution and flag.[153] One month after Konyak joined the peace talks, the Myanmar military took control of NSCN-K's headquarters in Ta Ga in Nanyun township of the Naga Self-Administered Zone of Sagaing. It was a forced but bloodless takeover given the NSCN-K's informal truce with the Tatmadaw since 2012.[154] Accommodation of the Swu-led faction in Nagaland and Khaplang-led faction in Myanmar after the death of their leaders instilled faith in New Delhi that waiting for leadership change in the Muivah-led faction might be the best way forward.

This calculation explains why Indian interlocutors, especially former governor RN Ravi who received sharp criticism from Muivah for negotiating in bad faith, are not finalising the accord. The argument that the RSS' pushback is the sole reason for such delay misses the point that the internal balance of power between Modi and the RSS favours the former. If Modi wants, he can bypass the RSS to sign the accord. But that's not happening because Indian agencies are convinced that they can shape post-Muivah politics of NSCN-IM and get an accord that favours India. Whether Muivah's ouster will usher in peace or worsen the situation is yet to be seen. But one thing is certain: 75 years after independence, the demand for autonomy has decreased in Naga society. As Kohima-based scholar K Yhome says, 'the Naga society has changed, for better or for the worse', and the political appeal of Naga political movement 'is low among the younger generations'.[155] Few people in Nagaland, east Arunachal Pradesh, or north Manipur want to pay 'taxes' for the NSCN-IM in 2024. All New Delhi needs to do is wait for Muivah to die.

Conclusions

The 'long 2010s' demonstrate how India's domestic state-building is inextricably linked to its international diplomacy. The promise of connectivity with Myanmar and Bangladesh to counter China's influence and the rise of Hindu nationalism in the northeast are the hallmarks of India's near east during the 21st century. If the former remains unfulfilled, the latter has succeeded to a considerable extent. Shaped by the turbulent history of cross-border migration, contemporary politics of citizenship in India has emerged along religious lines. Given that the Jana Sangha came into being in response to persecution of Hindus in East Bengal, the CAA-NRC remains ideologically central to the BJP. Once its dominance in Indian politics was confirmed after the 2019 general elections, the party quickly delivered on its manifesto promises to amend the CAA and update the NRC. Done in addition to the abrogation of Article 370 and the Ram Mandir verdict, this is an assertion of India's rightward turn. Even though Hindutva is at odds with India's desire to better connect (demographically) with Christian- and Muslim-dominated parts of its near east, the fact that such nationalism has become dominant is unsurprising.

The electoral unity of northeastern states, almost all of whom have a BJP or BJP-allied government, betrays the political flexibility of both ethnic nationalists and the Hindu right which adapts itself to local realities. But the true strategic import of such religious nationalism is witnessed in Myanmar where the Hindu right has accepted a minor position in relation to the Buddhist Sangha. More than the rich theological connect between Hinduism and Buddhism, it is the shared hatred for Muslims and Christians that has come to shape this relationship. To be clear, there were powerful ethnic and religious undercurrents in the relationship even before the BJP came to power. Given that Indian diplomats used Bodh Gaya to reconnect with Than Shwe during Congress-led governments, and that Nehru himself held reservations about missionaries and their role in fomenting centrifugal politics demonstrates how deep-rooted these features truly are. In the more recent context, it explains why India prevented the Rohingya from entering India and never criticised Myanmar. It also explains why Indian policymakers desire a secular regime in a Muslim-dominated Bangladesh. These trends will define India's near east for decades to come.

Fear of Chinese encirclement is a feature of India's approach towards its near east. Unlike the wider IOR where India finds it easy to ally with the US and its Quad allies, there is little meeting of minds in its near east. Though the US and the EU criticise Hasina's authoritarianism and demand free and fair elections while wanting to counter Chinese ingress, New Delhi is unwilling to easily part with its arch-ally in Dhaka even at the cost of alienating Bangladeshi public opinion. The difference in Indian and American approaches towards Bangladesh has often been on display during elections (2014 and 2018) and itself is a relic of the past, going all the way back to 1971 when New Delhi and Washington, D.C. found themselves at odds on the question of liberation. On Myanmar, India scoffs at the US for adopting the moral high ground and a human-rights-driven policy without doing much for Myanmar's people. Despite being aware of Chinese entrenchment in Myanmar, New Delhi criticises the West's hypocrisy more than China's exploitative practices. This is visible in US engagement with the National Unity Government (NUG) that is resisting the junta and India's reluctance to do so despite Mizoram hosting NUG parliamentarians.

The most notable aspect of Modi's method to counter Chinese capital in India's near east is his favouritism for Adani. The fact that

Adani Power Jharkhand Ltd. won the contract to supply power to Bangladesh at highly inflated rates in 2015 and won the 2020 bid to develop a terminal at the Yangon port reflects how India's Act East operates. In both these countries, Adani won contracts due to his proximity to the BJP.[156] This intimate marriage between Hindu nationalist politics and Gujarat-centric capital—itself not new or unique, but in this case centralised and unaccounted for on both fronts—has been central to India's geo-economic response to China's financial and infrastructural push across the subcontinent. Curiously, just as the long 2010s come to an end in India's near east, so too does its connectivity story. The 2021 coup dislocated Adani's plans to develop the Yangon port, forcing the group to divest. In Bangladesh, Hasina's loss of power could jeopardise the Godda project.

EPILOGUE
GROUNDSWELL

Months after Manipur's partition, India came full circle in its near east. In September–October 2023, the National Investigation Agency arrested operatives belonging to Meitei and Kuki armed groups active in the regional drug trade. It blamed a 'transnational conspiracy by Myanmar and Bangladesh based leadership of terror outfits to wage war against India by exploiting' the ethnic unrest in Manipur.[1] The Free Movement Regime (FMR) with Myanmar, critical to India's Act East Policy, was ended in January 2024.[2] Instead, New Delhi vowed to fence the entire Myanmar border. Expectedly, there has been no accountability for the excesses by the state government. If anything, in a direct affront to the legitimacy of the state, in January 2024, a Meitei radical group, Arambai Tenggol, summoned all Meitei Members of Legislative Assembly to take an oath to protect Manipur under the group's aegis.[3]

These developments underscore the core argument of this book: India's domestic state-building and international diplomacy are inextricably connected in its near east. A lack of accountability and sourcing domestic insecurities to external forces is central to this region. Unsurprisingly, Manipur's situation will continue to lubricate India's engagement with the Myanmar junta and explain its doubling down on support for Sheikh Hasina (again) in Dhaka. It underscores how identity politics, official antinomies, cross-border

317

migration, and political economies impart continuity to India's approach towards its near east.

From developing constitutional solidarities after independence to achieving security after the 1962 war, and aspiring to attain connectivity in the last three decades, India's success in its near east is suboptimal. Despite the aspirational rhetoric of connectivity and realities of India's regional power, there are limits to what New Delhi can do to reshape the strategic environment in this region. In Myanmar, three years after the coup, the junta holds little to no control of multiple parts of the country.[4] In fact, Operation 1027, launched by the Three Brotherhood Alliance, severely undermined the junta in Shan, Chin, Kokang, and Rakhine states.[5] Such a loss of control prevented Naypyidaw from holding elections or fostering an environment conducive to economic growth. In a candid interview to a Hong Kong-based broadcaster in May 2021, Min Aung Hlaing admitted that he didn't expect such pushback.[6] In November 2023, Myanmar's president went further and claimed that the country risked breaking apart.[7] Anger from Suu Kyi's loyalists was expected. But what occurred was a groundswell of people's resistance. Even those ethnic outfits that previously signed the NCA resumed fighting. Chin state went from being a sleepy peripheral border state to ground zero for anti-junta resistance.

To India's peril, Min Aung Hlaing misread his country. Though brief, the so-called 'democratic deviation' had a deep impact on the aspirations of Myanmar youth. The coup undermined these possibilities. For India, which decided to engage with the junta for fear of losing to China, the coup has been a liability. Manipur's situation is, partly, a testament to this. After having convinced themselves that Myanmar generals were wary of China and that resistance is fragmented, Indian officials refuse to engage with the resistance. But the geopolitical ramifications of the coup are such that today, a broken Myanmar is more dependent on China than ever before. It proves Vijay Nambiar, the UN's former special envoy to Myanmar, correct. He warned that India's assessment of the junta being pro-India and anti-China 'is wishful thinking'.[8] Myanmar's realities are such that Naypyidaw will remain dependent on China regardless of how its military feels about this fact. No amount of dealing with the junta will alter that for India. In truth, New Delhi was forced to fruitlessly confront Naypyidaw in April 2023—just before Manipur imploded—about China's military infrastructure in Coco Islands, reigniting old fears.[9]

India's connectivity push, crumbling under the weight of bureaucratic inertia, has become even more stuck with the culling of the FMR. The road meant to connect Mizoram with Sittwe crosses territory under control of the resistance. The Chin National Front and the Arakan Army are in active conflict with the junta in these areas, with big towns such as Paletwa under rebel control. Their support is critical not just in building the road, but also in making it operational. The current state of civil war in Rakhine and Chin states ensure that such projects, even if completed, are unlikely to generate profit. Instead of enriching its economy by facilitating roadbuilding, the coup put pressure on Mizoram's limited resources by displacing over 20,000 people.[10] Such displacement is grudgingly accepted by New Delhi thanks to the Mizoram's support for ethnic kin.[11] The BJP-led Manipur government, which has been witnessing smaller but surer movement of war-displaced people, has been unforgiving. It still blames migrants for unrest in the state. Apart from securing the well-being of Burmese Hindus and ensuring limited access in Naypyidaw, India's engagement with the junta has offered little else.

Instead of targeting them, the junta hired Manipur rebels sheltering in Myanmar to kill civilians.[12] It is not surprising that the People's Liberation Army of Manipur (PLA-M) emerged as the junta's sword-arm in Sagaing. Emboldened by new realities of an unstable Myanmar and a spike in Golden Triangle-linked drug trade, the PLA-M killed an Indian army officer and his family in south Manipur in November 2021, before actively participating in the 2023 civil unrest.[13] Formerly posted in Mizoram, the army officer was targeting the regional drug trade. Critical for the sustenance of the junta's power, drug production increased by 33% after the coup according to the United Nations Office on Drugs and Crime.[14] Specifically, there was an uptick in opium production across the border in south Manipur (in northern Chin state) where the officer was killed. This is one of the few belts in Chin state that is under the junta's control.[15] Given the history of the junta's involvement in drug trade, and its growing illicit empire, one wonders why New Delhi doesn't confront Naypyidaw on this.

A similar question remains on India's approach towards Bangladesh. Why does India not diversify ties despite Hasina's unpopularity? Ever since India backed Hasina in 2009, the two became acutely inter-dependent. Hasina's crackdown against civilian opponents and Islamists alike, 'management' of elections, denying sanctuary to anti-India rebels, enabling limited cross-border connectivity, and rewriting Bangladesh's growth story indicated that she succeeded where her father failed: as an effective autocrat.[16] The 2024 elections, rigged (again) to maintain Hasina's rule and boycotted by the opposition, underscore this aspect. Such civilian autocratic success suits India's interests and ensures New Delhi's unstinting support for Hasina despite democratic decline. India's own tryst with Hindu majoritarianism means that supporting democracy in Bangladesh is not on the agenda. But Hasina's problems with India have worsened with Hindutva's rise. To brush it aside as India's domestic problem, as Hasina tried, has complicated her situation. Even if rhetorical, secular nationalism in India is more desirable for Hasina as it allows her to contain communal passions at home.

Such communal tensions surfaced during Modi's visit in March 2021 to celebrate the 50th anniversary of Bangladesh's liberation. People associated with the Hefazat-e-Islam and the Islami Andolan Bangladesh staged protests in Chittagong, inviting police action.[17] By the time the situation subsided, 17 were dead and nearly 500 injured.[18] The incident laid bare the contradictions of India's approach towards Bangladesh, and underscored Hasina's missteps and dilemmas. Hindu nationalism has empowered Islamic conservatives in Bangladesh. It has pushed Hasina into appeasing conservatives by compromising with Hefazat and Jamaat.[19] Communalism is accompanied by economic troubles. In 2022, Bangladesh's economic miracle lost its shine. Dhaka's forex reserves are at a meagre 21 billion USD and falling, whereas revenues from readymade garment exports and remittances couldn't meet growing costs to exchequer.[20] The pandemic and the war in Ukraine worsened these woes, pushing Dhaka to seek loans from the International Monetary Fund.[21] These issues betrayed the darker underbelly of Bangladesh's growth model.

Bangladesh's rise has been predicated on Hasina's authoritarian control of institutions, and an alliance with select business groups. These businesses dominate Bangladesh's private sector and became what they did thanks to massive loans from public sector banks. A shock came in November 2022 when the S Alam group, which holds stakes in multiple Bangladeshi banks, took out a series of excessive loans and invested in Singapore.[22] These loans are so big that if the investments fail, it could wreck Bangladesh's financial system. Undoubtedly, the government launched an investigation into why such loans were granted. But given S Alam's stature as Hasina's key financier, it is unlikely that the group will be held accountable. Such a marriage between politics and capital is not new to the subcontinent, as is seen in the BJP's alliance with the Adani Group. But in Bangladesh the stakes are higher than in India. If S Alam's investments fail, the people of Bangladesh will be the main losers.

Chronic corruption is intimately related to such marriage between politics and capital. Critical to doling out patronage, corruption cuts across Bangladesh's political and bureaucratic spectrum. The Rooppur Nuclear Power Plant deal with Russia is a glaring example. Bangladesh owes Russia 13.5 billion USD for building a plant that cost India 3 billion USD.[23] The Padma Bridge, for which Dhaka paid from its pocket, was dropped by the World Bank in 2012, which cited corruption.[24] To be clear, leakage of public funds is a global problem. But the scale of corruption in Bangladesh is such that it limits Dhaka's ability to redistribute wealth. Curiously, the mainstay of Bangladesh's success in human development and poverty reduction is the non-governmental sector, part of which is the micro-finance movement led by Nobel Laureate Dr Muhammad Yunus. But the politics of micro-finance and macro-growth are at odds with each other. For micro-finance to deliver at scale, banks need stronger government intervention. Corruption in public sector banks is so entrenched that it limits the government's ability to intervene without risking leakage of funds that belong to the poorest Bangladeshis. In this respect, the political—and increasingly personal—fallout between Yunus and Hasina demonstrates the antinomies in Bangladesh's growth.[25]

Hasina could well experience a groundswell of protests moving forward. The staggeringly low voter turnout in the 2024 general elections, and the need to jail nearly 20,000 BNP activists and leaders in the run-up to the elections, signals serious anti-incumbency. Even allies such as the Jatiya party are frustrated with political stifling. For Shameem Haider Patwary, a Jatiya parliamentarian who lost his seat in 2024, 'it is a very critical situation for the Jatiya party as we've supported the Awami League … but are not part of their corruption and torture and are trying to find an identity of our own'.[26] The widespread belief that the BNP became defunct with an ailing Khaleda Zia, and exiled Tarique Rahman proved inaccurate. Ironically, despite centralisation of power in an exiled figure, the BNP demonstrated operational leadership when mobilising for protests. Not surprisingly, its key ask has been to have free and fair elections without Hasina's oversight. Hasina sought the same in 1996.

The BNP's mobilisation ability unsettled Hasina and complicated India's choices. Apart from the memory of the 2004 arms haul, and sheltering anti-India rebels, India's problem is that unlike the AL it has little leverage over the BNP. Despite concerns that Hasina could wreck Bangladesh's gains to remain in power, India has embraced the costs of Hasina's errors, just as Hasina has accepted the costs of her dependence on India. Such mutual dependencies, which go against India's rhetoric of a people-centric approach, are strong enough for New Delhi to not engage with the BNP. From India's perspective, such engagement could compromise Hasina's position. India's mistrust of the BNP runs deep, but a one-sided approach increases the risk of long-term political dislocation. If that happens, India will be facing a situation where most of its neighbours are experiencing acute crises, while China sits on Indian territory and continues to deepen its footprint in South Asia. Beijing's intent was on display when its ambassador in Dhaka visited the Teesta barrage days after New Delhi refused to resolve it in September 2022.[27] India risks losing regardless of who comes to power in 2024.

***

The more things change, the more they stay the same. During the 1950s, India privileged stability with Pakistan and China over economic opportunity. Couched in constitutional terms, the 1950 Nehru-Liaquat Pact was an admission by India and Pakistan of their limits when it came to containing communalism. The fact that the two states couldn't overcome differences to build mutually beneficial economic ties or return to pre-partition levels of connectivity demonstrates the actual value attached to such connectivity. It is telling that the first serious proposal to connect India's northeast to Chittagong and Sittwe emerged in 1968, two decades after independence. But it never became reality thanks to Burma's isolationism and Bangladesh's reluctance. The former turned inwards, but Dhaka's reluctance emerged from the memory of being manipulated by India which took large weapons stockpiles as rewards and dumped substandard products in Bangladesh. The logic that both sides will gain by enhancing trade continues to hit a historically informed glass-ceiling in Dhaka. Bangladesh's burgeoning trade deficit with India only feeds this aspect.

The political economies of India's near east continue to inform these processes. Limited connectivity augments illegal cross-border trade in drugs and other items. The irony of India's near east is that it is best connected by illicit trade such as the smuggling of humans to cattle, drugs to weapons, and safety pins to rice. Such illicit connectivity fuels discontentment and organised violence. If the largely unregulated jade trade was the mainstay of both junta-sponsored militias and the KIO in Kachin state, illegal rare earth mining has replaced that today.[28] Another fact is that Myanmar's myriad ethnic outfits who are fighting for a federal union also engage in criminal activities, disrespect human rights, and find succor in drug economies. How can economic interactions be legalised when local businesses and political outfits are versed in violence, and find profits from illicit trade more attractive than whatever formal trade could offer? Unless such contradictions are addressed, the aspiration of improved connectivity shall remain just that—an aspiration.

The dominance of religious politics and long-standing ethnic nationalisms feeds such contradictions. If the BJP views India's northeast as important to Hindutva, there will be limits to how much connectivity will be socially and politically desirable. To understand the import of this aspect, one needs to look at Indira Gandhi's discomfort with Bhashani's idea of a confederation in 1971. Given the history of communalism in West Bengal and East Pakistan, and the anti-foreigners movement in Assam, even a soft merger is unacceptable. These aspects have become more pronounced today. Though Bangladesh has emerged as the largest source destination for tourism to India, cross-border movement remains securitised and monitored. In Assam, a detention centre for 'illegal migrants' was opened in January 2023.[29] Euphemistically termed 'transition camp', the question of how illegal migrants will be identified and where they'll be sent remains unanswered. What opening of such centres clarifies is that Assam is recreating the communal atmosphere of the 1960s. Just before the state's partition, Imphal too was demanding the application of NRC in Manipur and withdrawing from ceasefires with Kuki groups—to disastrous results.[30]

Communal politics not only undermines connectivity, but also wrecks hard-earned ceasefires in the northeast. Even though AFSPA was lifted from various parts of Nagaland, Assam, and Manipur in 2023, immunity for soldiers who have committed excesses remain.[31] If the RSS obstructs peace with NSCN-IM because Nagas are Christians and such compromises would be seen to undermine the constitution and Hindu pride, there's a chance that these fissures could dislocate whatever little peace the northeast has experienced in recent decades. The recent rekindling of Khalistan politics in Punjab is a warning that communal disharmony doesn't bode well. Myanmar houses some of the longest running ethno-religious movements in the world for the same reason. Mistrust of Christian minorities explains why Myanmar remains torn by civil strife. Instead of learning lessons from the past, the junta doubled down on its xenophobia.

Ideological camaraderie between Hindutva and Buddhist nationalism in Myanmar doesn't instill hope on connectivity. Even if institutional arbiters of religious nationalism such as the Mahana-junta and the BJP-RSS compacts may contain internal differences, they are exclusionary in nature and will foster division more than harmony. Here, the warning about not expecting Bangladesh to be an island of secularism could prove accurate. Even if Hasina remains in power, she's unlikely to be able—or willing—to protect Hindus or Buddhists. Her conservative tilt might require compromise on these aspects wherein targeting Hindus becomes a proxy of standing up to 'Hindu India'. The sad part of such a potential political turn is that India's near east has witnessed all of it in the past.

Exclusionary nationalisms and illicit political economies create pressures that complicate the geopolitics of India's near east. The BJP's push for the Uniform Civil Code (UCC) that seeks to formulate and implement personal laws that apply to all citizens regardless of religion, gender, and sexual orientation not only generates anxiety among Muslims, but is also being resisted by Christians. In February 2023, the Mizoram state assembly adopted a resolution to oppose any move by the BJP to implement the UCC in India.[32] According to the then-home minister of Mizoram, if enacted the UCC 'would disintegrate the country as it was an attempt to terminate the religious or social practices, customary laws, cultures and traditions of the religious minorities, including the Mizos'.[33] The more New Delhi tries to homogenise the ethos of a diverse country, the more it is likely to encounter resistance.

Other antinomies relate to constitutional amendments that are loaded with communal intent akin to the CAA-NRC. India's decision to abrogate Article 370 and revoke Jammu and Kashmir's statehood in 2019 impacted negotiations with NSCN-IM. New Delhi did it without approval from the J&K assembly as required by the constitution and put the sitting chief minister Mehbooba Mufti and other senior politicians under house arrest.[34] J&K was divided into two Union Territories without any democratic representation. This meant that the Kashmiri flag and constitution were also done away with. Expectedly, the move riled up the NSCN-IM, who began to view New Delhi as negotiating in bad faith. If the BJP could abrogate Article 370 and revoke J&K's statehood, could it not do the same to Article 371A that gave constitutional privileges to Nagaland? In an October 2020 media interview, Muivah noted that the J&K move impacted the Naga talks, and that 'there can be no solution without a flag and a constitution' of the Naga issue.[35]

Such agitation in India's near east, which remains a crucible of India's postcolonial state-building, is marked by unending movement of people. From voluntary movements to sudden conflict-triggered mass displacements, cross-border migration is a constant in India's near east. Between November 2022–February 2023, hundreds of Bawm people residing in the CHT escaped to Mizoram thanks to Bangladeshi military operations.[36] But unlike the Chin from Myanmar, Bangladesh's Bawm communities don't find Aizawl welcoming. In fact, with support from the MNF, New Delhi ramped up border security measures in this sector to prevent them from entering Mizoram. Similarly, 2,000–3,000 Rohingya fled to Bangladesh in 2022, and many more went 'underground' due to the growing hostility of the Indian state and society, making them twice displaced.[37]

***

India's approach towards its near east is a cautionary tale. Humbled by strife within its borders, limited by suspicion in the Bangladeshi public mind, and hindered by the Myanmar junta's self-sabotage, there are limits to what India can do in its near east without incurring costs. New Delhi's decisions to over-invest in the junta and Hasina, driven by a conservative strategic logic, undermine its objective of connectivity that requires diversification of social and political ties. Policies that feed India's image as a junta-enabler and the blame it gets for Hasina's authoritarianism militate against India's desire to shape regional geopolitics in its favour. Such antinomies explain why, despite the 'Act East', regional connectivity grew by a mere 5% during 1996–2016, intra-subcontinental trade fell from 18% in 1948 to 5% in 2018, and the logistical costs of connectivity in the subcontinent are the highest in the world at 14%.[38] The simple, persistent reason for such a dismal state of affairs is the fact that New Delhi privileges partisan political stability over risk-ridden economic opportunity.

This is what makes China's economic presence and assertiveness a challenge to India's great power aspirations on a subcontinental—even global—scale. Beijing tied India's political hands and limited material resources by forcing it to militarise the Sino-Indian boundary on a permanent basis. The 2017 Doklam standoff and the 2020 Galwan clash have been game-changers. For starters, the Ladakh standoff re-triggered long-standing anxieties of a two-front war, the historical roots of which lie in India's near east.[39] India diverted battalions of Assam Rifles away from COIN duties in the northeast and the Myanmar border to strengthen defences along the China border. The ensuing gaps led to a spike in movement of drugs, arms, and people—and was reversed in May 2023 when Manipur imploded. The 57th mountain division, meant to secure the China border, is aiding efforts to secure the 'buffer zone' between Meitei and Kuki areas in Manipur. In this context, the risk of collapse of the Naga ceasefire is real. But such dislocation will occur due to India's own political, ideological excesses, rather than Chinese or Pakistani interventionism.

On that count, it is important to remember that China still hosts anti-India figures belonging to the NSCN-IM and ULFA-I. The organisational cohesion and military strength of these outfits is vastly reduced, but the ideas they embody continue to simmer. That Beijing has not cut its ties with these entities, arguably in response to India hosting the Dalai Lama, is a sign of where things stand. China has historically trained, financed, and armed separatist movements in India's northeast, and these sinews are not entirely broken. The arms meant for ULFA-I and other rebels caught during the Chittagong arms haul, for instance, came from China's Beihai port.[40] In addition to economic dominance represented by the large trade deficit India accrues to China, the unilateral alteration of the Line of Actual Control, and regular probing of Indian defences in Arunachal Pradesh, the possibility of renewed Chinese support for ethnic violence is real.

The more India alienates its minorities, the more it becomes vulnerable. Communal disharmony can help win elections but is harmful to India's national security. India's founding leaders including Sardar Patel, often lionised by the Hindu right, understood this aspect when insisting on a secular constitution. After all, communalism runs so deep in the subcontinent that fanning these flames for tactical purposes could ignite uncontrollable fires. The scars of 1960s riots in Bengal, or sub-nationalist backlash against 'illegal migration' in Assam, or dynamics of inter-state wars, insurgencies, and interventionism throughout the last seven decades should give New Delhi pause. For the BJP, a party that emerged in response to the persecution of Hindus in East Bengal and elsewhere, religious politicking has long crossed the threshold of just being an electoral tactic. It is an ideological quest to make India a *Hindu Rashtra*. But communal passions are easy to spark and difficult to contain. If there is one lesson to be learnt from the geopolitics of India's near east, it is this.

LIST OF INTERVIEWS

Interview 1: Lalthlamuong Keivom, India's chargé d'affaires in Rangoon (1986–89), New Delhi, 21 May 2019

Interview 2: Lt. Gen. (r) Gauri Zau Seng, Former Vice Chairman of the Kachin Independence Organisation (KIO), Chiang Mai, 18 June 2019

Interview 3: Retired top Indian foreign and security official, Skype, 3 May 2023

Interview 4: Vappala Balachandran, Special Secretary, Research & Analysis Wing (R&AW) (1995–97), Telephone, 18 May 2019

Interview 5: Chin National Front negotiator in the peace process, Yangon, 20 August 2018

Interview 6: Vijay Nambiar, UN Secretary General's Special Advisor on Myanmar (2010–16), and India's Former Deputy National Security Advisor, Telephone, 20 November 2020

Interview 7: Col (r) VS Grewal, Indian army, military intelligence (1992–99), WhatsApp, 28 June 2021

Interview 8: No Than Kap, Founding chairperson of the Chin National Front (CNF), Yangon, 21 August 2018

Interview 9: Preet Malik, Indian ambassador to Myanmar (1990–1992), New Delhi, 28 May 2018

Interview 10: Indian diplomat with experience on Myanmar, New Delhi, 18 May 2018

Interview 11: Confidential interview with a former director general of India's Defence Intelligence Agency, New Delhi, 18 May 2018

Interview 12: Peace-talks Creation Group, Kachin State Peace Council, Myitkyina, 28 August 2018

Interview 13: Confidential interview with a former senior minister in Aun San Suu Kyi's cabinet, Skype, 25 September 2018

Interview 14: Confidential interview with top Indian army official, Telephone, 30 June 2018

Interview 15: Shivshankar Menon, National Security Advisor of India (2010–14), New Delhi, 15 May 2019

Interview 16: Gautam Mukhopadhaya, India's ambassador to Myanmar (2013–15), New Delhi, 28 May 2018

Interview 17: Lt Gen (r) Md. Mahfuzur Rahman, Principal Staff Officer of the Armed Forces Division (2016–2020), Dhaka, 13 May 2022

Interview 18: Pinak Ranjan Chakravarty, India's high commissioner to Bangladesh (2007–09), New Delhi, 30 May 2018

Interview 19: Deb Mukharji, Indian ambassador to Bangladesh (1995–2000), Telephone, 15 June 2021

Interview 20: Tariq Ahmed Karim, Bangladesh's ambassador to India (2009–2014), Telephone, Part I (21 June 2021); Part II (5 July 2021)

Interview 21: Confidential interview with senior Indian army officer, Telephone, Part I (31 October 2019); Part II (5 November 2019)

Interview 22: Kyi Thein, Myanmar ambassador to India (2003–10), Yangon, 31 August 2018

Interview 23: Pracharak of the Rashtriya Swayamsevak Sangh, Yangon, 18 August 2018

Interview 24: Gopal Krishna Pillai, Home Secretary of India (2009–11), Telephone, 8 December 2020

Interview 25: Lt. Gen. (r) Shakti Gurung, India's defence attaché to Yangon (2000–03), Email, 12 September 2018

Interview 26: Sanjib Baruah, Professor of Political Studies, Bard College, Skype, 28 November 2020

Interview 27: Confidential interview with Indian army officer, 2018

Interview 28: Ram Niwas, Head, Sanatan Dharma Swayamsevak Sangh, Yangon, 18 August 2018

Interview 29: Eric Gonsalves, Indian diplomat in Rangoon (1962), Telephone, 31 May 2018

Interview 30: Gowher Rizvi, International Affairs advisor to Bangladesh prime minister Sheikh Hasina (2009), Oxford, 2 June 2022

Interview 31: Habibul Alam, Bir Protik, Dhaka, 8 May 2022

Interview 32: Amirul Islam, Lawyer and freedom fighter (Mujibnagar government), Food Minister (1974), Dhaka, 10 May 2022

Interview 33: Iqbal Hassan Mahmood Tuku, State Minister of Power and Agriculture (2001–06), Bangladesh Nationalist Party (BNP), Dhaka, 10 May 2022

Interview 34: Central Committee Member, Communist Party of India (Marxist), New Delhi, 2 April 2022

Interview 35: Bangladeshi politician, Amar Bangladesh Party, Dhaka, 9 May 2022

Interview 36: Shamim Haider Patwary, Former Member of Parliament, Jatiya Party, Dhaka, 15 May 2022

Interview 37: Amir Khasru Mahmud Chowdhury, Minister of Commerce (2001–04), BNP, Dhaka, 9 May 2022

Interview 38: 'Shafi' (name changed), former senior minister in General H M Ershad's cabinet, Jatiya Party, Dhaka, 17 May 2022

Interview 39: Zin Yaw, Deputy Foreign Minister of Myanmar (2012–14), Yangon, 2 September 2018

Interview 40: Bangladeshi Journalist, Dhaka, 5 May 2022

Interview 41: Mahfuz Anam, Editor-in-Chief, *The Daily Star*, London, 30 June 2022

Interview 42: Pankaj Saran, Indian High Commissioner in Bangladesh (2012–15), Deputy National Security Advisor (2018–21), New Delhi, 19 May 2022

Interview 43: Khriezo Yhome, Indian academic of Naga heritage, New Delhi, 16 May 2018

Interview 44: Confidential interview with former senior education advisor to Aung San Suu Kyi, Yangon, 1 September 2018

Interview 45: A. Mathur, Head of the Aviation Research Centre, R&AW, Telephone, 21 April 2022

Interview 46: Kamal Hossain, Law Minister (1972–73), Foreign Minister (1973–75), Former Awami League and currently Gono Forum, Dhaka, 10 May 2022

Interview 47: Chittagong-based businessman, BNP, Chittagong, 11–12 May 2022

Interview 48: Confidential interview with former R&AW official, 23 April 2023

Interview 49: Confidential interview with Indian diplomat, 2018

Interview 50: Nurul Islam, Chairman, Arakan Rohingya National Organisation, London, 28 August 2022

Interview 51: Aung Tun Thet, Chief Coordinator, Union Enterprise for Humanitarian Assistance & Development in Rakhine State, Yangon, 4 September 2018

Interview 52: Ranjan Mathai, Foreign Secretary of India (2011–13), New Delhi, 20 May 2019

Interview 53: Girish Gupta, Indian businessman with links to Rangoon in 1988, New Delhi, 22 December 2016

Interview 54: Wynn Lwin, Myanmar ambassador to India (1992–99), Yangon, 17 August 2018

Interview 55: Than Than Nu, daughter of former Burmese prime minister U Nu and former All India Radio officer, Yangon, 21 August 2018

Interview 56: Nandita Haksar, Human Rights Lawyer, New Delhi, 22 December 2016

Interview 57: Thant Kyaw, Deputy Foreign Minister of Myanmar (2012–16), Yangon, 21 September 2018

Interview 58: G Parthasarthy, Indian ambassador to Myanmar (1992–95), Telephone, 14 July 2019

Interview 59: Confidential interview with senior Indian army officer, Telephone, 10 August 2018

Interview 60: Confidential interviews with Indian diplomat, New Delhi, 2019

Interview 61: Confidential interview with senior Indian military official, Telephone, 29 May 2018

Interview 62: Soe Thane, Minister of President's Office of Myanmar (2012–ongoing) and former navy chief, Yangon, 6 September 2018

Interview 63: Md. Touhid Hussain, Foreign Secretary of Bangladesh (2008–09), Dhaka, 9 May 2022

Interview 64: Maj. (r) Kamaldeep Singh Sandhu, Former Indian army paratrooper, London, 12 June 2018

ACRONYMS

AA	Arakan Army
AASU	All Assam Student's Union
AFPFL	Anti-Fascist People's Freedom League
AFSPA	Armed Forces Special Powers Act
AGP	Asom Gana Parishad
AHC	Assistant High Commission
AIR	All India Radio
AL	Awami League
ANLF	Arakan National Liberation Front
ANLP	Arakan National Liberation Party
ARSA	Arakan Rohingya Salvation Army
BAKSAL	Bangladesh Krishak Sramik Awami League
BDR	Bangladesh Rifles
BIMSTEC	Bay of Bengal Initiative for Multi-Sectoral Technical and Economic Cooperation
BJP	Bharatiya Janata Party
BLF	Bangladesh Liberation Front
BLT	Bodo Liberation Tigers
BNP	Bangladesh Nationalist Party
BRI	Belt and Road Initiative
BSF	Border Security Force
BTPA	Balanced Trade Payments Arrangement
CAA	Citizenship Amendment Act
CHT	Chittagong Hill Tracts

CIA	Central Intelligence Agency
CNF	Chin National Front
CPB	Communist Party of Burma
CPI	Communist Party of India
CPI(M)	Communist Party of India (Marxist)
CPWD	Central Public Works Department
CRPF	Central Reserve Police Force
DAB	Democratic Alliance of Burma
DGFI	Directorate General of Forces Intelligence
DHC	Deputy High Commission
EPAL	East Pakistan Awami League
EPR	East Pakistan Rifles
EU	European Union
FA	Framework Agreement
FGN	Federal Government of Nagaland
FMR	Free Movement Regime
GOC	General Officer Commanding
GOI	Government of India
HQ	Headquarters
HUJI-B	Harkat-ul-Jihad-al-Islami-Bangladesh
IAF	Indian Air Force
IB	Intelligence Bureau
ICU	Intensive Care Unit
IMDT	Illegal Migrants (Determination by Tribunals) Act
IOR	Indian Ocean Region
IRCON	Indian Railway Construction Co.
ISI	Inter-Services Intelligence
IUML	Indian Union Muslim League
J&K	Jammu & Kashmir
JIC	Joint Intelligence Committee
JMB	Jamaat-ul-Mujahideen Bangladesh
JRB	Jatiya Rakkhi Bahini
JSD	Jatiya Samajtantrik Dal
KCP	Kangleipak Communist Party
KIO	Kachin Independence Organisation
KNDO	Karen National Defence Organisation
KNU	Karen National Union

LEP	Look East Policy
LMG	Light Machine Gun
MADC	Mara Autonomous District Council
MEA	Ministry of External Affairs
MHA	Ministry of Home Affairs
MMG	Medium Machine Gun
MNA	Myanmar National Archives
MNF	Mizo National Front
MNFF	Mizoram National Famine Front
MPC	Mizo People's Conference
NAP	National Awami Party
NAP-B	National Awami Party (Bhashani)
NAP-M	National Awami Party (Muzaffar)
NCA	Nationwide Ceasefire Agreement
NCB	Narcotics Control Bureau
NDFB	National Democratic Front of Bodoland
NDPS	Narcotic Drugs and Psychotropic Substances Act
NEC	North East Council
NEFA	Northeast Frontier Administration
NLD	National League for Democracy
NLFT	National Liberation Front of Tripura
NHTA	Naga Hills-Tuensang Area
NNC	Naga National Council
NNPG	Naga National Political Groups
NPC	Naga People's Convention
NRC	National Register of Citizens
NSCN	National Socialist Council of Nagaland
NSI	National Security Intelligence
NUG	National Unity Government
NUPA	National United Party of Arakan
NWFP	Northwest Frontier Province
PCJSS	Parbatya Chattagram Jana Samhati Samiti
PDA	Preventive Detention Act
PDM	Pakistan Democratic Movement
PIP	Prevention of Infiltration into India of Pakistani Nationals
PLA	People's Liberation Army

PLA-M	People's Liberation Army of Manipur
PREPAK	People's Revolutionary Party of Kangleipak
PSA	Public Security Act
PVO	People's Volunteer Organisation
R&AW	Research & Analysis Wing
RSS	Rashtriya Swayamsevak Sangh
SAARC	South Asian Association for Regional Cooperation
SBPP	Swadhin Bangla Biplobi Parishad
SDSS	Sanatan Dharma Swayamsevak Sangh
SFF	Special Frontier Force
SLORC	State Law and Order Restoration Council
SSB	Special Service Bureau
ST	Scheduled Tribes
TNV	Tripura National Volunteers
UAPA	Unlawful Activities (Prevention) Act
UCC	Uniform Civil Code
ULFA	United Liberation Front of Asom
UK	United Kingdom
UN	United Nations
UNGA	United Nations General Assembly
UNLF	United National Liberation Front
UNODC	United Nations Office on Drugs and Crimes
UPA	United Progressive Alliance
US	United States
USDP	Union Solidarity and Development Party
USSR	Union of Soviet Socialist Republics
WAPCOS	Water and Power Consultancy Services (India)

DRAMATIS PERSONAE (SELECT)

India

Jawaharlal Nehru	Prime Minister (1947–64)
Vallabhbhai Patel	Deputy Prime Minister (1947–50)
Narendra Modi	Prime Minister (2014–current)
Amit Shah	Home Minister (2019–current)
Rajiv Gandhi	Prime Minister (1984–89)
Gopal Krishna Pillai	Home Secretary (2009–11)
Syama Prasad Mukherjee	Founding President of the Bharatiya Jana Sangh (1951–52)
Bhola Nath Mullik	Director, Intelligence Bureau (1950–64)
Indira Gandhi	Prime Minister (1967–77; 1980–84)
Triloki Nath Kaul	Foreign Secretary (1968–72)
Jayprakash Narayan	Senior Political Leader (1950s–70s)
Gulzarilal Nanda	Home Minister (1963–66); Interim Prime Minister (1966)
P N Haksar	Principal Secretary to the Prime Minister (1971–73)
Rameshwar Nath Kao	Chief of R&AW (1968–77)
Durga Prasad Dhar	Indian ambassador to the Soviet Union (1969–71)
Y D Gundevia	Foreign Secretary (1963–65)

Lal Bahadur Shastri	Prime Minister (1964–66)
P N Banerjee	Commissioner (Eastern Zone), R&AW (Special Bureau)
Subimal Dutt	Foreign Secretary (1955–61)
Braj Kumar Nehru	Governor of Assam (1968–73), Nagaland (1968–73), Meghalaya (1970–73), Manipur (1972–73)
Morarji Desai	Prime Minister (1977–79)
Jyotindra Nath Dixit	Foreign Secretary of India (1991–94)
P V Narasimha Rao	Prime Minister (1991–96)
Pranab Mukherjee	President (2012–17)
Krishnan Srinivasan	Foreign Secretary (1994–95)
Inder Kumar Gujral	Prime Minister (1997–98)
Jagdish Ajmani	Joint Secretary (Bangladesh), MEA, 1975
A K Damodaran	Joint Secretary (Public Policy), MEA, 1975
Laldenga	Chief Minister of Mizoram (1986–88)
Zapu Phizo	President, Naga National Council (NNC)
John Bosko Jasokie	Chief Minister of Nagaland (1975; 1980–82)
Bishnuram Medhi	Chief Minister of Assam (1950–57)
Rishang Keishing	Chief Minister of Manipur (1994–97)
Kaito Sema	'Commander in Chief', Naga Army (1960s)
Bimala Prasad Chaliha	Chief Minister of Assam (1957–70)
Thiungaleng Muivah	General Secretary, NSCN-IM (1988–current)
Prafulla Chandra Sen	Chief Minister of West Bengal (1962–67)
Hem Barua	Lok Sabha Parliamentarian from Assam; Praja Socialist Party (1957–72)

Paresh Baruah	Co-Founder, ULFA-I
Arabinda Rajkhowa	Co-Founder, ULFA-I
Isak Chishi Swu	Foreign Secretary, Federal Government of Nagaland
S C Jamir	Chief Minister of Nagaland (1993–96)
T Sailo	Chief Minister of Mizoram (1979–84)
Hiteshwar Saikia	Chief Minister of Assam (1991–96)

East Pakistan / Bangladesh

Sheikh Mujibur Rahman	President (1971–72); Prime Minister (1972–75)
Gen. Zia-ur-Rahman	President (1977–81)
Gen. Hussain Md. Ershad	President (1983–90)
Khaleda Zia	Prime Minister (1991–96; 2001–06)
Sheikh Hasina	Prime Minister (1996–2001; 2009–current)
Huseyn Shaheed Suhrawardy	Prime Minister of Pakistan (1956–57)
A H K 'Maulana' Bhashani	Member of Parliament and senior politician
A K Fazlul Haq	Governor of East Pakistan (1956–58)
Tajuddin Ahmed	(Wartime) Prime Minister (1971–72)
M Amirul Islam	State Minister of Food (1973–74)
Tofael Ahmed	Minister of Commerce (2014–19)
Sheikh Fazlul Hoque Moni	Founder, Mujib Bahini
Kamal Hossain	Foreign Affairs Minister (1973–75); Law Minister (1972–73)
Khandkar Moshtaque Ahmed	President (1975)
Anwar Hossain Manju	Editor and Publisher, *The Daily Ittefaq* (1972–2007)
Chittaranjan Suttar	Member of Parliament

Gen. Khaled Mosharraf	Chief of Army Staff (1975)
Abdus Sattar	President (1981–82)
Gen. Moeen Uddin Ahmed	Chief of Army Staff (2005–09)

Burma, Pakistan, China

Aung San	President, AFPFL (1945–47)
Gen. Ne Win	Chairman of Union Revolutionary Council (1962–74), President (1974–81), Chairman of the Burma Socialist Programme Party (1962–88)
Nu	Prime Minister of Burma (1960–62; 1948–58)
Aung San Suu Kyi	State Counsellor of Myanmar (2016–21), General Secretary of NLD (1988–current)
Shagwang S Khaplang	Leader of NSCN-K
Maran Brang Seng	Chairman of the Kachin Independence Organisation
Sr. Gen. Than Shwe	Chairman of the SLORC, Myanmar (1992–2011)
Wynn Lwin	Myanmar ambassador to India (1992–99)
Gen. Khin Nyunt	Prime Minister of Myanmar (2003–04)
Vice Sr. Gen. Maung Aye	Vice Chairman of the State Peace and Development Council (1993–2011)
Soe Thane	Minister of the President's Office of Myanmar (2012–current)
Sr. Gen. Min Aung Hlaing	Chairman of State Administration Council (2021–current), Myanmar
Mohammad Ali Jinnah	Governor General of Pakistan (1947–48)
Gen. Md. Ayub Khan	President of Pakistan (1958–69)
Liaquat Ali Khan	Prime Minister of Pakistan (1947–51)

DRAMATIS PERSONAE (SELECT)

Iskander A. Mirza	President of Pakistan (1956–58)
Firoz Khan Noon	Prime Minister of Pakistan (1957–58)
Zulfiqar Ali Bhutto	Prime Minister of Pakistan (1973–77)
Gen. Yahya Khan	President of Pakistan & Chief Martial Law Administrator (1969–71)
Gen. Md. Zia-ul-Haq	President of Pakistan (1978–88)
Mao Zedong	Chairman of the Communist Party of China (1943–76)
Chou Enlai	Premier of the People's Republic of China (1954–76)
Deng Xiaoping	Chairman of the Central Advisory Commission (1982–87)

ACKNOWLEDGEMENTS

I was forewarned by friends that the second book is more challenging to write. Unlike the first that emerged from a doctorate, there is no thesis to revert to when in doubt. What I did not appreciate was how demanding it would be, both intellectually and personally. This project began as a history of India's approach towards Myanmar. To unpack this 'less explored' Indian neighbour made sense. The aim was to tell India's story using Myanmar as a springboard. But India's entanglements with Myanmar, both real and imaginary, are so dense that making sense of these required a wider canvas. This seemingly obvious but practically overwhelming realisation birthed 'India's near east'. The choice was to either write a history of the entire region covering India's northeastern states, Bangladesh, and Myanmar, or to cull the project. This dilemma was compounded by the birth of our daughter in 2020 during the first lockdown. To balance the personal and professional is challenging on a good day, and here we were in the middle of a once-a-generation pandemic.

Though I like to think so at times, expanding the scope of this project was not an intellectual decision. It emerged from a need to escape the realities of pandemic parenting—a particularly unique experience for first generation migrants. In hindsight, I am glad it happened. The book felt more worthy of authorship, and gave clarity and energy in coping with, and strengthening, the personal. None of this would be possible without the support of family, friends, colleagues, students, mentors, and the many interlocutors who shared their thoughts, experiences, and time with me. For starters, the Centre for International Studies and Diplomacy, the Department of Politics and International Studies, and the Research and Knowledge Exchange at the SOAS University of London afforded me time and money to undertake long, expensive travels and hire research support. More than that, SOAS has offered a home full of highly knowledgeable, kind, and caring colleagues.

Early on in this project, Mandy Sadan introduced me to Kachin affairs and Somnath Batabyal to Assam in his own novel way. Hanns Kendel and Adeeba Khan were kind guides on and gracious hosts in Dhaka. Srinath Raghavan shaped this book from the outset. Asmita Mahajan, Subhadeep Chowdhury, Paridhi Gupta, Sam Pongener, Shounak Sett, Khin Thet San, Khushi Singh Rathore, and Vanlalhmangaiha offered stellar support at the archives in New Delhi, Kohima, London, and Aizawl. Eef Vermiej helped me access previously unexplored documents at the International Institute of Social History, Amsterdam. Gautam Mukhopadhaya and Constantino Xavier, highly knowledgeable on the region, guided me during fieldwork in Myanmar. Smita Pant's insights on the region and support during my travels to Bangladesh and Thailand kept me excellent stead. In (and on) Myanmar, Kyaw Minn Htin, Shweta Singh, Khin Zaw Win, and other colleagues who prefer anonymity guided me through the country's politics. In Myitkyina, Dan Seng Lawn and the Kachinland Research Centre's team, especially Lamai Nawthun and Jacintar, offered tremendous support.

In Bangladesh, Shafiqul Alam, Konstantina Loup, Humayun Chowdhury, Humaiun Kobir, Shirin Lira, and Shafqat Munir helped open my mind, and many doors. In Chiang Mai, Bertil Lintner and Gauri Zau Seng offered deep insight into the history of India's approach towards Myanmar and the Kachin national movement in particular. In Manipur, Indrajit and Rajni Singh were generous hosts, and Kamaldeep Singh Sandhu a true friend. Over the years, I have learnt a lot from my engagement with serving and retired allies within the Government of India. You know who you are, and I am grateful for your support.

Whether it was reading parts of the book, translating documents, brainstorming ideas, offering a platform, or enabling access, I am thankful (in no particular order) to: Harsh Pant, Hugo Meijer, Elisabeth Leake, Hans Steinmuller, Abhishek Choudhary, Mushtaq Khan, David Brenner, Martin Smith, Jo Allchin, Ashfaque Ronnie, Nicolas Blarel, Claire Yorke, Sandra Destradi, Vineet Thakur, Manjeet Pardesi, Swapna Kona Nayudu, Yogesh Joshi, Kaustav Chakrabarti, Devesh Kapur, Alexandre Pereira, Paul Staniland, Daniel Markey, Asfandyar Mir, Sunil Pun, Abhijan Das, Edward Simpson, Jairam Ramesh, Shivshankar Menon, Shirish Jain, Sarvinder Singh, Hkanpha Sadan, Happymon Jacob, Vijay Nambiar, Rana Banerjee, Surya Valliappan Krishna, Medha Chaturvedi, Deep Pal, the late Joyeeta Bhattacharjee, the late Shakti Sinha, Chandan Nandy, Swati Chawla, Dheeraj Paramesha Chaya, Sriparna Pathak, Pawan Gupta, Kapil Gupta, the late Mukul Arya, Devjyot Ghoshal, Rajeev Bhattacharyya, Narayani Basu, Golan Naulak, Angshuman Choudhury, Prashant Jha, Rudra Chaudhuri, and Pallavi Raghavan.

Aryaman Bhatnagar and Johann Chacko read the first cut of this manuscript and helped develop it in style and substance. But once the manuscript was deemed presentable, it was put to test at a SOAS book workshop in July 2023. The feedback I received was immense, and I am in debt to all who took time to read and comment—Rohan Mukherjee, Pradyumna Jairam, Samah Rafiq, Shirin Rai, Saskia Wilven, Daniel Haines, Hanns Kendel (again), Pallavi Roy, Phil Clark, Fiona Adamson, and Martin Bayly. At Hurst, Michael Dwyer patiently guided me and ensured that I didn't get sidetracked. The two anonymous reviewers helped sharpen the size and shape of the book, Victoria Jones' sharp editing imparted flow to this text, and Daisy Leitch was of great help during the production phase. My parents, Vimal Paliwal and Renu Sharma, as always, are a source of encouragement. My wife, Nina Kaysser, is my rock and has given much more than I deserve. This book is dedicated to my mother-in-law, Renate Kaysser, who gave us strength when it was most needed, and to our daughter Shira Lia, for asking many beautiful why/warum/क्यों and introducing us to a whole new dimension of happiness.

NOTES

1. GROUNDSHIFT

1. '10 years under Modi govt have been golden era for Northeast', says Amit Shah, *Hindustan Times*, 19/01/2024, https://www.hindustantimes.com/india-news/10-years-under-modi-govt-have-been-golden-era-for-northeast-says-amit-shah-101705673436529.html

2. Arunabh Saikia, 'If you don't take off your clothes, we will kill you': Kuki women paraded naked in Manipur', *Scroll.in*, 19 July 2023, https://scroll.in/article/1052938/video-shows-kuki-women-being-paraded-naked-by-a-mob-manipur-police-confirm-fir-filed.

3. 'Three people killed, houses set ablaze in fresh violence in India's Manipur state', *Reuters*, 5 August 2023, https://www.reuters.com/world/india/three-people-killed-houses-set-ablaze-fresh-violence-indias-manipur-state-2023-08-05/; 'Manipur violence: Over 50,000 displaced people staying in 349 relief camps', *The Economic Times*, 11 June 2023, https://economictimes.indiatimes.com/news/india/manipur-violence-over-50000-displaced-people-staying-in-349-relief-camps/articleshow/100912307.cms?from=mdr.

4. Nagen Singh, '96 dead bodies still unclaimed: Manipur government releases data of death and destruction after 4-months of violence', *The Times of India*, 16 September 2023, https://timesofindia.indiatimes.com/videos/toi-original/96-dead-bodies-still-unclaimed-manipur-government-releases-data-of-death-and-destruction-after-4-months-of-manipur-violence/videoshow/103715544.cms.

5. Deeptiman Tiwary, 'New Manipur security strategy: One force, one area', *Indian Express*, 1 July 2023, https://indianexpress.com/article/india/new-manipur-security-strategy-one-force-one-area-8695103/.

6. Suhasini Raj and Alex Travelli, 'A Rising India Is Also, in One Remote Pocket, a Blood-Soaked War Zone', *The New York Times*, 09/06/2023: https://www.nytimes.com/2023/06/09/world/asia/india-manipur-conflict.html

7. Vijaita Singh, 'In Manipur, Army and paramilitary forces face a constant challenge—armed men in police uniforms', *The Hindu*, 10/09/2023: https://www.thehindu.com/news/national/other-states/in-manipur-army-and-paramilitary-forces-face-a-constant-challenge-armed-men-in-police-uniforms/article67292272.ece

8. Narendra Modi, 'Northeast the Growth Engine', *X*, 13/06/2023: https://x.com/narendramodi/status/1668481578841014272?s=20

9. Karishma Hasnat, 'Myanmar traders dodge bullets & bombs to sell in Manipur's Moreh market. But no one's buying', *The Print*, 28 August 2023, https://theprint.in/ground-reports/myanmar-traders-dodge-bullets-bombs-to-sell-in-manipurs-moreh-market-but-no-ones-buying/1733917/.

10. Abhinay Lakshman, 'Home minister's remarks draw sharp reactions from Kuki groups in India, Myanmar', *The Hindu*, 10 August 2023, https://www.thehindu.com/news/national/home-ministers-remarks-draw-sharp-reactions-from-kuki-groups-in-india-myanmar/article67180812.ece.

11. Berenice Guyot-Réchard, 'Tangled Lands: Burma and India's unfinished separation, 1937-1948', *Journal of Asian Studies*, 80 (2), May 2021, pp. 293–315.

12. Arwa Syed, 'The Middle East: An Orientalist Creation', *E-IR*, 25 February 2021, https://www.e-ir.info/2021/02/25/the-middle-east-an-orientalist-creation/.

13. Yuimirin Kapai, 'Spatial Organisation of Northeast Inia: Colonial Politics, Power Structure, and Hills-Plains Relationship', *Indian Historical Review*, 47(1), 2020, pp. 150–169.

14. Martin Bayly, Elisabeth Leake, Avinash Paliwal, and Pallavi Raghavan eds. 'The Limits of Decolonisation in India's International Thought and Practice: An Introduction', *The International History Review*, 44(4), 2022; Ted Svensson, *Production of Postcolonial India and Pakistan: Meaning of Partition* (London: Routledge, 2013).

15. Jelle Wouters, Tanka Subba eds., *The Routledge Companion to Northeast India* (London: Routledge, 2023); Sajal Nag, 'Nehru and the Nagas: Minority Nationalism and the Post-Colonial State', *Economic and Political Weekly*, 44 (49), 5–11 December 2009; Sanjib Baruah, *In the Name of the Nation: India and its Northeast* (Stanford: Stanford University Press, 2020); Samrat Choudhury, *Northeast India: A Political History* (London: Hurst Publishers, 2023); Sanjoy Hazarika, *Strangers No More: New Narratives from India's Northeast* (New Delhi: Aleph Books, 2018); Namrata Goswami, *The Naga Ethnic Movement for a Separate Homeland* (New Delhi: Oxford University Press, 2020); Willem van Schendel, 'A War Within a War: Mizo Rebels and the Bangladesh Liberation Struggle', *Modern Asian Studies*, 50 (1), 2015, pp. 75–117; Thongkholal Haokip, *India's Look East Policy and the Northeast* (New Delhi: Sage Publishers, 2015); Sreeradha Datta, *Act East Policy and Northeast India* (New Delhi: Vitasta Publishers, 2021); Lydia Walker, 'Decolonization in the 1960s: On Legitimate and Illegitimate Nationalist Claims-making', *Past & Present*, 242(1), Feb. 2019, pp. 227–264; Berenice Guyot-Réchard, 'When Legions Thunder Past: The Second World War and India's Northeastern Frontier', *War in History*, 25(3), 2018, pp. 328–360;

NOTES

Sangeeta B. Pisharoty, *Assam: The Accord, The Discord* (New Delhi: Penguin India, 2019); Rajeev Bhattacharya, *Rendezvous with Rebels: Journey to Meet India's Most Wanted Men* (New Delhi: HarperCollins India, 2014); John Thomas, *Evangelising the Nation: Religion and the Formation of Naga Political Identity* (London: Routledge, 2015); Malini Sur, *Jungle Passports: Fences, Mobility, and Citizenship at the Northeast India-Bangladesh Border* (Pennsylvania: University of Pennsylvania Press, 2021); Joy Pachuau, *Being Mizo: Identity and Belonging in Northeast India* (Oxford: Oxford University Press, 2014); Sahana Ghosh, *A Thousand Tiny Cuts: Mobility and Security across the Bangladesh-India Borderlands* (California: University of California Press, 2023); Reeju Ray, *Placing the Frontier in British North-East India: Law, Custom, and Knowledge* (New Delhi: Oxford University Press, 2023); Sanjay Barbora, *Homeland Insecurities: Autonomy, Conflict, and Migration in Assam* (Oxford: Oxford University Press, 2022).

16. Bertil Lintner, *Great Game East: India, China, and the Struggle for Asia's Most Volatile Frontier* (New Delhi: HarperCollins India, 2016); Melissa Crouch ed. *Islam and the State in Myanmar: Muslim-Buddhist Relations and the Politics of Belonging* (New York: Oxford University Press, 2016); Michael Charney, *A History of Modern Burma* (Cambridge: Cambridge University Press, 2009); Edith Mirante, *Down the Rat Hole: Adventures Underground on Burma's Frontiers* (Hong Kong: Orchid Press, 2006); Thant Myint-U, *The River of Lost Footsteps: A Personal History of Burma* (London: Faber & Faber, 2008); Matthew J Walton, *Buddhism and the Political: Organisation and Participation in the Theravada Moral Universe* (London: Hurst Publishers, 2019); Mary Callahan, *Making Enemies: War and State Building in Burma* (Ithaca: Cornell University Press, 2005); Jurgen Haacke, *Myanmar's Foreign Policy: Domestic Influences and International Implications* (Singapore: IISS Press, 2017); David Steinberg, Hongwei Fan, *Modern China-Myanmar Relations: Dilemmas of Mutual Dependence* (Singapore: NIAS Press, 2012); Maung Aung Myoe, *In the name of Pauk-Phaw: Myanmar's China Policy Since 1948* (Singapore: ISEAS Publications, 2011); Diana S. Kim, *Empires of Vice: The Rise of Opium Prohibition across Southeast Asia* (New Jersey: Princeton University Press, 2020); Pierre-Arnaud Chouvy, *Opium: Uncovering the Politics of Poppy* (London: I B Tauris, 2009); David Brenner, *Rebel Politics: A Political Sociology of Armed Struggle in Myanmar's Borderlands* (Ithaca: Cornell University Press, 2019).

17. Neeti Nair, *Hurt Sentiments: Secularism and Belonging in South Asia* (Cambridge, MA: Harvard University Press, 2023) pp. 198–240.

18. For more, see Kasia Paprocki, *Threatening Dystopias: The Global Politics of Climate Change Adaptation in Bangladesh* (Ithaca: Cornell University Press, 2021); Camelia Dewan, *Misreading the Bengal Delta: Climate Change, Development, and Livelihoods in Coastal Bangladesh* (Washington, D.C.: University of Washington Press, 2022).

19. For more on these, see Choudhury, *Northeast India, 2023*.

20. John L Christian, 'Burma Divorces India', *Current History*, 46(1), pp. 82–86, 1937.

21. Thant Myint U, *The Making of Modern Burma* (Cambridge: Cambridge University Press, 2001).

22. Nalini R Chakravarti, *The Indian Minority in Burma: The Rise and Decline of an Immigrant Community* (London: Oxford University Press, 1971) p. 96.

23. Richard Kozicki, *India and Burma, 1937-1957: A Study in International Relations* (unpublished PhD thesis, University of Pennsylvania, 1959) p. 61.

24. Bertie R. Pearn, *The Indian in Burma* (Le Play House Press, 1946) p. 8.

25. J R Andrus, *Burmese Economic Life* (Stanford: Stanford University Press, 1948) p. 18.

26. Rajashree Mazumder, 'Illegal Border Crossers and Unruly Citizens: Burma-Pakistan-Indian borderlands from the nineteenth to the mid-twentieth centuries', *Modern Asian Studies*, 53 (4), July 2019, p. 1173.

27. Matthew Browser, 'Partners in Empire? Co-colonialism and the Rise of Anti-Indian Nationalism in Burma, 1930–1938', *The Journal of Imperial and Commonwealth History*, 49 (1), 2021, pp.118–47.

28. Chakravarti, *The Indian Minority in Burma,* p. 117.

29. Ibid., p. 117.

30. Ibid., p. 170.

31. Robert L Solomon, *Saya San Rebellion* (Washington, D.C.: Rand Corporation, 1969).

32. Kozicki, *India and Burma, 1937–1957*, p. 98.

33. Chakravarti, *The Indian Minority in Burma*, p. 157.

34. Browser, 'Partners in Empire?', pp. 118–147.

35. Rajashree Mazumder, '"I don't envy you": Mixed marriages and immigration debates in the 1920s and 1930s Rangoon, Burma', *The Indian Economic and Social History Review*, 51 (4), 2014, pp. 497–527.

36. Chakravarti, *The Indian Minority in Burma,* pp. 163–164.

37. For more on these campaigns see: Chris Bayly and Tim Harper, *Forgotten Armies: Britain's Asian Empire &War with Japan* (London: Penguin, 2005); Srinath Raghavan, *India's War: The Making of Modern South Asia, 1939–1945* (London: Allen Lane, 2016).

38. Réchard, 'Tangled Lands', p. 297.

39. Ibid., p. 295.

40. Ibid., p. 295.

41. Guyot-Réchard, 'When Legions Thunder Past', pp. 328–360.

42. Martin Smith, *Burma: Insurgency and the Politics of Ethnicity* (New York: Zed Books, 1999) pp. 60–64; Japan's training and equipping of the Burma National Army (BNA), akin to the Indian National Army (INA), which was fighting colonial Britain, sharpened ethnic divisions as most of its recruitment was from Burman communities.

43. Government of India (GoI), 'Treaty of Peace and Friendship between India and the Union of Burma', 7 July 1951, http://mea.gov.in/bilateral-documents.htm?dtl/6645/Treaty+of+Peace+and+Friendship.

44. Gardner, *Frontier Complex*, Introduction; Menon, *India and Asian Geopolitics*, pp. 1–85; John Garver, *Protracted Contest: Sino-Indian Rivalry in the Twentieth Century* (Perth: UWA Press, 2002); Tanvi Madan, *Fateful Triangle: How China Shaped US-*

India Relations During the Cold War (Washington, D.C.: Brookings Institution Press, 2020).

45. Mazumder, 'Illegal Border Crossers and Unruly Citizens', pp. 1144–1182.
46. Jawaharlal Nehru, *A Tryst with Destiny*, full speech: https://www.files.ethz.ch/isn/125396/1154_trystnehru.pdf.
47. William Dalrymple, 'The Great Divide: The Violent Legacy of Indian Partition', *The New Yorker*, 22 June 2015.
48. On how Indian leaders envisioned the state-citizen contract, see Jawaharlal Nehru, *The Discovery of India* (London: Penguin Books, 2004); K M Panikkar, *State and Citizen* (Asia Publishing House, 1960).
49. Mushirul Hasan, 'Memories of a Fragmented Nation: Rewriting the Histories of India's Partition', *Economic and Political Weekly*, 10–16 October 1998, 33 (41), pp. 2662–2668.
50. Ayesha Jalal, *The Sole Spokesman: Jinnah, the Muslim League, and the Demand for Pakistan* (Cambridge: Cambridge University Press, 1994); Farzana Shaikh, *Making Sense of Pakistan* (London: Hurst Publishers, 2018); Mariam Mufti, Sahar Shafqat, Niloufer Siddiqui eds. *Pakistan's Political Parties: Surviving between Dictatorship and Democracy* (Washington, D.C.: Georgetown University Press, 2020).
51. Matthew J Walton, 'Ethnicity, Conflict, and History in Burma: The Myths of Panglong', Asian Survey, 48 (6), 2008, pp. 889–910; Smith, *Burma*, Introduction; Mandy Sadan ed., *War and Peace in the Borderlands of Myanmar: The Kachin Ceasefire 1994–2011* (Singapore: NIAS Press, 2016).
52. Vazira Fazila-Yaccobali Zamindar, *The Long Partition and the Making of Modern South Asia: Refugees, Boundaries, Histories* (New York: Columbia University Press, 2010).
53. Pallavi Raghavan, *Animosity at Bay: An Alternative History of the India-Pakistan Relationship, 1947–1952* (London: Hurst, 2020), pp. 23–78.
54. Md. Mahbubar Rahman and Willem van Schendel, 'I am not a Refugee': Rethinking Partition Migration', *Modern Asian Studies*, 37 (3), July 2003, pp. 551–584.
55. Antara Datta, *Refugees and Borders in South Asia: The Great Exodus of 1971* (London: Routledge, 2013).
56. David Ludden, 'Spatial Inequity and National Territory: Remapping 1905 in Bengal and Assam', *Modern Asian Studies*, 46(3), 2012, pp. 483–525.
57. Janam Mukherjee, *Hungry Bengal: War, Famine, and the End of Empire* (Oxford: Oxford University Press, 2011).
58. Anwesha Roy, *Making Peace, Making Riots: Communalism and Communal Violence, Bengal 1940–1947* (Cambridge: Cambridge University Press, 2018) pp. 184–213.
59. GoI, Census of India, 1951: http://piketty.pse.ens.fr/files/ideologie/data/CensusIndia/CensusIndia1951/CensusIndia1951AllIndiaPartIb.pdf
60. Sanjib Baruah, 'The Politics of Language in Assam', *The India Forum*, 9 June 2012, https://www.theindiaforum.in/article/politics-language-assam.
61. Ashfaque Hossain, 'The Making and Unmaking of Assam-Bengal Borders and the Sylhet Referendum', *Modern Asian Studies*, 47 (1), 2013, pp. 250–287.

62. Mazumder, 'Illegal Border Crossers and Unruly Citizens', pp. 1170–73.

63. GoI, 'Reports regarding the political situation and incidents on the borders of Burma—activities of Muslim guerillas', *MEA*, 3-2/49-UN-II, SECRET, 1949, p. 9.

64. Ibid., p. 10.

65. Jayita Sarkar, 'Rohigyas and the Unfinished Business of Partition', *The Diplomat*, 16 January 2018.

66. Mazumder, 'Illegal Border Crossers and Unruly Citizens', p. 1173.

67. Bayly and Harper, *Forgotten Armies*, pp. 383–384.

68. Aye Chan, 'The Development of a Muslim Enclave in Arakan (Rakhine) State of Burma (Myanmar)', *SOAS Bulletin of Burma Research*, 3 (2), Autumn 2005, pp. 396–420.

69. Sarkar, 'Rohingyas and the Unfinished Business of Partition', 2018; A K M Ahsan Ullah, 'Rohingya Refugees to Bangladesh: Historical Exclusions and Contemporary Marginalisation', *Journal of Immigrant and Refugee Studies*, 9 (2), 2011, p. 139–161; A K M Ahsan Ullah, 'Rohingya Crisis in Myanmar: Seeking Justice for the "Stateless"', *Journal of Contemporary Criminal Justice*, 32 (3), 2016, pp. 285–301.

70. Wayne Wilcox, 'The Economic Consequences of Partition: India and Pakistan', *Journal of International Affairs*, 18(2), 1964, pp. 188–97; Joya Chatterji, *The Spoils of Partition: Bengal and India, 1947–1967* (Cambridge: Cambridge University Press, 2007); Anwesha Sengupta, 'Breaking Up: Dividing Assets between India and Pakistan in times of partition', *The Indian Economic and Social History Review*, 51 (4), 2014, pp. 529–548.

71. David C Engerman, *The Price of Aid: The Economic Cold War in India* (Cambridge, MA: Harvard University Press, 2018).

72. Anwesha Sengupta, 'Unthreading Partition: The Politics of Jute Sharing between Two Bengals', *Economic and Political Weekly*, 53(4), January 27, 2018, pp. 43–49.

73. Tariq Omar Ali, *A Local History of Global Capitalism: Jute and Peasant Life in the Bengal Delta* (New Jersey: Princeton University Press, 2018).

74. Wilcox, 'The Economic Consequences of Partition', p. 195.

75. Sengupta, 'Unthreading Partition', p. 43.

76. Wilcox, 'The Economic Consequences of Partition', p. 194; Chatterji, *The Spoils of Partition*, pp. 45–48.

77. Ibid., p. 194.

78. Ali, *A Local History of Global Capital*, pp. 185–88.

79. K. S. Subramaniam, *State, Policy, and Conflicts in Northeast India* (London: Routledge, 2015).

80. 'Illegal immigrants are like termites, will throw them out if BJP comes back to power: Amit Shah', *India Today*, 11 April 2019.

81. Avinash Paliwal, 'Politics, Strategy, and State Responses to Conflict Generated Migration', *Journal of Global Security Studies*, 7(1), 2022.

82. On Assam's tea plantations see Jayeeta Sharma, *Empire's Garden: Assam and the Making of India* (Durham: Duke University Press, 2011); Nitin Verma ed. *Coolies*

of Capitalism: Assam Tea and the Making of Coolie Labour (Oldenbourg: De Gruyter, 2018); Deepak Mishra, Vandana Upadhyay, & Atul Sarma, *Unfolding Crisis in Assam's Tea Plantations: Employment and Occupational Mobility* (London: Routledge, 2012); Andrew B. Liu, *Tea War: A History of Capitalism in China and India* (Yale: Yale University Press, 2020).

83. Rakhee Bhattacharjee, *Development Disparities in Northeast India*, New Delhi: Cambridge University Press, 2011; Namrata Goswami, 'Drugs and the Golden Triangle: Concerns for Northeast India', *IDSA Comment,* 10 February 2014, https://idsa.in/idsacomments/DrugsandtheGoldenTriangle_ngoswami_100214.

84. Tara Kartha, *Tools of Terror: Light Weapons and India's Security* (New Delhi: IDSA, 1999); Binalakshmi Nepram, *South Asia's Fractured Frontier: Armed Conflict, Narcotics, and Smalls Arms Proliferation in India's Northeast* (New Delhi: Mittal Publishers, 2002).

85. For a general overview of such complexities in the northeast, see Anubha Bhonsle, *Mother, Where's My Country?: Looking for Light in the Darkness of Manipur* (New Delhi: Speaking Tiger Publishers, 2016); Dolly Kikon, *Living with Oil and Coal: Resource Politics and Militarization in Notheast India* (Washington, D.C.: University of Washington Press, 2019).

86. Interview 24.

87. For more on India's political economy, see Devesh Kapur and Milan Vaishnav eds. *Costs of Democracy: Political Finance in India* (New Delhi: Oxford University Press, 2018); Milan Vaishnav, *When Crime Pays: Money and Muscle in Indian Politics* (New Haven: Yale University Press, 2017); Barbara Harriss-White, 'South Asian Criminal Economies', in Barbara Harriss-White & Lucia Michelutti eds. *The Wild East: Criminal Political Economies in South Asia* (London: UCL Press, 2019) pp. 322–351.

88. The other town in Manipur that is an entrepot of drugs into India is Behiang, in Churachandpur, south Manipur. Plus, Kamjong in north Manipur near Nagaland. Prem Mahadevan, 'Crossing the Line: Geopolitics and Criminality at the India-Myanmar Border', *Global Initiative against Transnational Organized Crime Research Report,* November 2020, pp. 1–21.

89. Ibid., p. 14.

90. Mahadevan, 'Crossing the Line', p. 16.

91. Interview 24.

92. Article 244A: https://indiankanoon.org/doc/1371525/.

93. Interview 24.

94. Article 371a: https://indiankanoon.org/doc/371998/.

2. ONE ENEMY AT A TIME

1. Nehru to Patel, *SWJN*, 21/02/1950, p. 50.

2. Kali Prasad Mukhopadhyay, *Partition, Bengal and After: The Great Tragedy of India* (Reference Press, 2007).

3. GoI, Census of India, 1951: http://piketty.pse.ens.fr/files/ideologie/data/CensusIndia/CensusIndia1951/CensusIndia1951AllIndiaPartIb.pdf.

4. Government of Assam, 'White Paper on Foreigner's Issue', *Home & Political Department*, 20 October 2012, p. 7.

5. Nehru to Mountbatten, 5 March 1950, 14(1), *Selected Works of Jawaharlal Nehru (SWJN)*, p. 91.

6. Nehru to Rajaji, 20 March 1950, 14(1), *SWJN*.

7. Nehru to Rajaji, 16 March 1950, *SWJN*, 14(1), p. 128.

8. Nehru to Rajaji, 16 March 1950, *SWJN*, 14(1), p. 126.

9. 'The Situation in Bengal', 23 March 1950, *SWJN*, 14(1), pp. 141–44.

10. Ian Brown, *Burma's Economy in the Twentieth Century* (Cambridge: Cambridge University Press, 2013) pp. 96–102.

11. Pradeep K Chibber and Rahul Verma, *Ideology, and Identity: The Changing Party Systems of India* (New York: Oxford University Press, 2018).

12. Sunil Khilnani, *The Idea of India* (New York: Farrar, Straus, & Giroux, 1997); Madhav Khosla, *India's Founding Moment: The Constitution of a Most Surprising Democracy* (Cambridge, MA: Harvard University Press, 2020); Pratap Bhanu Mehta, *The Burden of Democracy* (New Delhi: Penguin Random House India, 2017).

13. Raghavan, *Animosity at Bay*, pp. 1–23.

14. Nehru to Liaquat Ali Khan, *SWJN*, 17 February 1950, 2(14), pp. 41–42.

15. Raphaelle Khan and Taylor C Sherman, 'India and overseas Indians in Ceylon and Burma, 1946–1965: Experiments in post-imperial sovereignty', *Modern Asian Studies*, 56(46), 2021, pp. 1153–1182; Sumathi Ramaswamy, *Passions of the Tongue: Language Devotion in Tamil India, 1891–1970* (LA: University of California Press, 1997).

16. Zamindar, *The Long Partition*, pp. 12–45.

17. Christophe Jaffrelot, *The Hindu Nationalist Movement and Indian Politics: 1925 to the 1990s* (New Delhi: Penguin Books, 1993) p. 88.

18. Ibid., p. 88.

19. GoI, Nehru to BC Roy, SECRET, 22/03/1948, *Jawaharlal Nehru (JLN) Papers*, FN 7, Nehru Memorial Museum and Library (NMML), p. 185.

20. Ibid., p. 185.

21. Ibid., p. 185.

22. Nehru to Patel, *SWJN*, 27 October 1948, 2(8), October-December 1948, p. 286.

23. Ibid., p. 286.

24. GoI, 'Statement by Dr. S P Mookerjee on his Resignation as Minister of Industry and Supply', *LSD*, Proceedings other than Questions and Answers, 19 April 1950.

25. Arupjyoti Saikia, *The Quest for Modern Assam: A History, 1942–2000* (New Delhi: Penguin India, 2023) pp. 102–05.

26. Ibid., pp. 211–257.

27. Romila Thapar, *Somnatha: The Many Voices of a History* (London: Verso Books, 2005) pp. 199–201.

28. GoI, Nehru to Provincial Premiers, 01/04/1949, SECRET, *JLN Papers*, NMML, p. 11

29. Ibid., p. 10.

30. Ibid., p. 9.

31. This led to an anti-communist impulse within India's intelligence community, which Mullik and T Sanjeevi Pillai were keen to develop in an intelligence partnership with London, which, for its part, was keen to contain communism within the Commonwealth. Avinash Paliwal, 'Colonial Sinews of Postcolonial Espionage—India and the Making of Ghana's External Intelligence Agency, 1958–61', *The International History Review*, 44(4), 2022, pp. 914–934.

32. GoI, 'Participation of the members of the Cochin Ruling family in Communist activities', *Ministry of States*, SECRET, 5(37)-P/50, 1950.

33. GoI, 'Intelligence reports regarding Communist activities in Burma and on the Indo-Burma border', *MEA*, SECRET, 3-1/49-0.3II, 1949, National Archives of India (NAI), p. 7.

34. Ibid., p. 2.

35. Ibid., p. 2.

36. Ibid., p. 2.

37. Ibid., p. 10.

38. Ibid., pp. 28–34.

39. GoI, 'Reports regarding the political situation and incidents on the borders of Burma—activities of Muslim guerillas', p. 11.

40. GoI, 'Intelligence reports regarding Communist activities in Burma and on the Indo-Burma border', *MEA*, SECRET, 3-1/49-0.3II, 1949, NAI, p. 43.

41. Bertil Lintner, *The Rise and Fall of the Communist Party of Burma (CPB)* (Ithaca: Cornell Southeast Asia Program, 1991), pp. 3–25; Robert H. Taylor, 'The Burmese Communist Movement and Its Indian Connection: Formation and Factionalism', *Journal of Southeast Asian Studies*, 14 (1), March 1983, pp. 95–108.

42. Taylor, 'The Burmese Communist Movement and Its Indian Connection', p. 99.

43. GoI, 'Intelligence reports regarding Communist activities in Burma and on the Indo-Burma border', *MEA*, SECRET, 3-1/49-0.3II, 1949, NAI, p. 43.

44. GoI, 'Reports on communist activities on Assam-Burma Frontier and in the Tribal areas of Assam', *MEA*, SECRET, 143-NEF/49, 1949, NAI, pp. 9–12.

45. Ibid., p. 10.

46. Ibid., p. 10.

47. GoI, 'Note by Mr. H V R Iyenger, Secretary Ministry of Home Affairs, regarding situation on the Indo-Burma border in Assam', *MEA*, SECRET, 46-291/49-BCI (B), 1949, NAI, p. 5.

48. GoI, 'Reports on communist activities on Assam-Burma Frontier and in the Tribal areas of Assam', *MEA*, SECRET, 143-NEF/49, 1949, NAI, p. 13.

49. GoI, 'Intelligence reports regarding Communist activities in Burma and on the Indo-Burma border', *MEA*, SECRET, 3-1/49-0.3II, 1949, NAI, p. 3.

50. GoI, 'Note recorded by Shri. B N Mullik, Director Intelligence Bureau on the situation in Tripura with special reference to the activities of Communists', Ministry of States, SECRET, 21(32)-PA/51, 1951, NAI, p. 12.

51. GoI, 'A Note recorded by the D.I.B. on the Communist situation in Manipur. Judgement delivered in the Manipur Communist Conspiracy Case', Ministry of States, SECRET, 11(19)-PA/52, NAI, p. 2.

52. Ibid., p. 5.

53. This two-part strategy was tied to India's decision of not signing the 1951 Geneva Convention on Refugees. Pia Oberoi, *Exile and Belonging: Refugees and State Policy in South Asia* (New Delhi: Oxford University Press, 2006); Ria Kapoor, *Making Refugees in India* (Oxford: Oxford University Press, 2021).

54. Layli Uddin, '"Enemy Agents at Work": A Microhistory of the 1954 Adamjee and Karnaphuli riots in East Pakistan', *Modern Asian Studies*, 55 (2), 2021, pp. 629–664.

55. GOI, 'Political Situation in Burma-Karen Rebellion', *MEA*, SECRET, 1949, NAI, p. 64.

56. Lintner, *The Rise and Fall of the CPB*, p. 15.

57. Rangoon to New Delhi, Telegram CCB No. 4176 (Immediate), TOP SECRET, 2 April 1949, *JLN Papers*, NMML, p. 12.

58. Ibid., p. 12.

59. Ibid., p. 12.

60. Or in iron or steel scrap. GoI, 'Agreement between the Premiers of India and Burma on Supply of Arms and Ammunition to Burma', *MEA*, TOP SECRET, F24-3/49-BI, 1949, NAI, p. 41.

61. Prime Minister's Secretariat, Nehru to Defence Secretary, *JLN Papers*, SECRET, 09/03/1953, NMML, p. 187.

62. GoI, 'Agreement between the Premiers of India and Burma on Supply of Arms and Ammunition to Burma', *MEA*, TOP SECRET, F24-3/49-BI, 1949, NAI, p. 43.

63. Nehru to Nu, *SWJN*, 14 April 1949 2 (10), February–April 1949.

64. Nehru to Rauf, *SWJN*, 28 April 1949, 2 (10), February–April 1949, p. 419.

65. Ibid., pp. 410–416.

66. GoI, 'Agreement between the Premiers of India and Burma on Supply of Arms and Ammunition to Burma', *MEA*, TOP SECRET, F24-3/49-BI, 1949, NAI, p. 13.

67. Included 65 light-machine guns (Bren Guns), 3,000 rifles, 5,000 grenades, 250 pistols, and 450,000 (later increased to 750,000) rounds of ammunition for the rifles and LMGs. Ibid., p. 5; GoI, 'Agreement between the Premiers of India and Burma on Supply of Arms and Ammunition to Burma', *MEA*, TOP SECRET, F24-3/49-BI, 1949, NAI, p. 59.

68. Nehru to Rauf, *SWJN*, 15 April 1949, 2 (10), February–April 1949, p. 415.

69. Ibid., p. 9.

70. According to a 1949 report on Burma by the Joint Intelligence Committee, 'the Burma Air Force is very small in size, the effective strength being equal to hardly more than three flights. Very little effort is being made to recruit personnel or

otherwise to expand the Force'. The report also highlighted the air force's lack of organisation, even though it was being used to machine-gun and drop small bombs against insurgents. Burma's air force could not, it was assessed, undertake complex operations. GoI, 'Joint Intelligence Sub-Committee's Report No. 12(49) on Burma', *MEA*, SECRET, 3-31/49-BI, 1949, NAI, p. 21.

71. GoI, 'Agreement between the Premiers of India and Burma on Supply of Arms and Ammunition to Burma', *MEA*, TOP SECRET, F24-3/49-BI, 1949, NAI, p. 9.

72. Ibid., p. 78.

73. Ibid., p. 9.

74. Renaud Egreteau, 'Burmese Indians in contemporary Burma: heritage, influence, and perceptions since 1988', *Asian Ethnicity*, 12(1), pp. 33–54.

75. GoI, 'Agreement between the Premiers of India and Burma on Supply of Arms and Ammunition to Burma', *MEA*, TOP SECRET, F24-3/49-BI, 1949, NAI, p. 51.

76. GOI, 'Political Situation in Burma-Karen Rebellion', *MEA*, SECRET, 1949, NAI, p. 126.

77. GoI, 'Agreement between the Premiers of India and Burma on Supply of Arms and Ammunition to Burma', *MEA*, TOP SECRET, F24-3/49-BI, 1949, NAI, p. 20.

78. This didn't mean that India lowered its guard when it came to Pakistan's intent to strengthen relations with Rangoon. Ever since independence, New Delhi has been, accurately or otherwise, wary of Pakistan's engagement with Burma/ Myanmar. Even when agreeing to form a joint committee of ambassadors to coordinate the supply of military and financial aid to Burma and prevent the fall of Rangoon, India mandated its embassy in Rangoon to keep a check on Pakistan's attempts of creating misunderstanding between India and Burma. GoI, 'Report of the Indian ambassador on Burma's Attitude towards India and Pakistan', *MEA*, SECRET, 3-26/49-BCI (B), 1949, NAI.

79. GoI, 'Agreement between the Premiers of India and Burma on Supply of Arms and Ammunition to Burma', *MEA*, TOP SECRET, F24-3/49-BI, 1949, NAI, p. 5.

80. Attlee to Nehru, Telegram CCB No. 3558, 13/04/1949, TOP SECRET, *JLN Papers*, NMML, p. 178.

81. Nehru to Nu, *Selected Works of Jawaharlal Nehru (SWJN)*, 14 April 1949, 2 (10), February–April 1949, pp. 410–416.

82. Ibid., pp. 410–416.

83. Ibid., pp. 410-416.

84. Ibid., pp. 410-416.

85. Ibid., p. 416.

86. GOI, 'Political Situation in Burma-Karen Rebellion', *MEA*, SECRET, 1949, NAI, pp. 28–30.

87. Ibid., p. 31.

88. Nehru to Rauf, *SWJN*, 15 April 1949, 2 (10), February–April 1949.

89. GoI, 'Migration of Indians from Burma to India through Stillwell Road on account of disturbances in Burma', *MEA*, SECRET, 1949, pp. 19–21.

90. In the same letter, Nu proposed that India, Burma, Ceylon, and Pakistan create a joint defence and economic pact—this was rebuffed by Nehru as 'premature'. Nu to Nehru, 5 May 1949, SECRET & PERSONAL, *JLN Papers*, NMML, p. 75; On Nehru's polite rejection of the idea to enter a defence and economic pact with Pakistan: Nehru to Nu, 10 May 1949, SECRET & PERSONAL, *JLN Papers*, NMML, p. 76.

91. GoI, 'Protection to the Zeyawaddy Sugar Factory: Question of supply of arms and recruitment of Gurkhas in India to work as guards at the factory', *MEA*, SECRET, F3-34/49-BI, 1949, NAI, p. 17.

92. Ibid., p. 6.

93. GoI, 'Disabilities of People of Indian Origin in Burma – Policy', *Ministry of External Affairs*, 1955, 48-2/55-BC, SECRET, NAI.

94. GoI, 'Special report from Burma and Ceylon on the evolution of their foreign policy', *MEA*, SECRET, B/54/1333/4-5, NAI, p. 51.

95. GoI, 'KMT forces aggression into Burma; Burma's complaint to the UN', *MEA*, SECRET, B/54/1412/4, 1954, NAI, p. 166. For more discussion on this issue, see Uma Shankar Singh; *Burma and India, 1948–1962: A Study in the Foreign Policies of Burma and India, and Burma's Policies Towards India* (Oxford: IB&H Publishers, 1979), pp. 121–143.

96. Singh; *Burma and India*, pp. 83–154.

97. GoI, 'Coco Island-Development Plans of the Govt. of Burma', *MEA*, SECRET, B/54/99147/4, 1954, NAI, p. 8.

98. Ibid., p. 2. For history of the Coco Islands, see Andrew Selth, 'Burma's Mythical Isle', *Australia Quarterly*, 80 (6), November–December 2008, pp. 24–40.

99. Ibid., p. 7.

100. Ibid., p. 6.

101. Ibid., p. 6.

102. Nehru to Chief Ministers, 15 June 1954, *SWJN*, 2(26), p. 546.

103. Saikia, *The Quest for Modern Assam*, pp. 79–115.

104. Nehru to Jairamdas Doulatram, 7 July 1954, *SWJN*, 2 (26), p. 460.

105. GoI, 'Chronology of Principal Events in Bangla Desh', *MEA*, SECRET, HI/121(1)/71, NAI, p. 4.

106. For more on East Pakistan's language movement, see Nair, *Hurt Sentiments*, pp. 149–183; Alyssa Ayres, *Speaking Like a State: Language and Nationalism in Pakistan* (Cambridge: Cambridge University Press, 2009); Saadia Toor, *The State of Islam: Culture and Cold War Politics in Pakistan* (Chicago, US: Pluto Press, 2011); Sufia M Uddin, *Constructing Bangladesh: Religion, Ethnicity, and Language in an Islamic Nation* (Chapel Hill, NC: UNC Press, 2006).

107. GoI, 'Fortnightly Reports from the Deputy High Commissioner for India in Pakistan, Dacca', *MEA*, SECRET, L/52/1321/202, 1952, NAI, p. 27.

108. Ibid., p. 27.

109. Ibid., pp. 27–28.

110. Ibid., pp. 27–28.

111. Layli Uddin, 'Red Maulanas: Revisiting Islam and the Left in twentieth-century South Asia', *History Compass*, October 2023, https://compass.onlinelibrary.wiley.com/doi/full/10.1111/hic3.12787.

112. Uddin, *Constructing Bangladesh*, pp. 11–154.

113. Ibid., pp. 11–154.

114. GoI, 'Chronology of Principal Events in Bangla Desh' *MEA*, SECRET, HI/121(1)/71, NAI, p. 7.

115. GoI, 'Reports from West Bengal, Assam, and Tripura regarding the condition of Hindus in East Bengal', *MEA*, L/52/1322/202, SECRET, 1952, NAI, p. 19.

116. Ibid., pp. 27–28.

117. Ibid., p. 28.

118. Ali, *A Local History of Global Capital,* p. 185.

119. GoI, 'P. Das Gupta, Asst Indian Govt, Trade Commissioner in Eastern Pak, Dacca to C.C. Desai, Secy, GoI, Commerce Ministry', *Cabinet Secretariat* [Economic Wing]/ECC, 15(108)-P/49, 14/12/1949, NAI.

120. Ibid.

121. Omkar Goswami, 'Sahibs, Babus, and Banias: Changes in Industrial Control in Eastern India', *The Journal of Asian Studies*, 48 (2), May 1989, pp. 289–309.

122. P K Mathai, Kamaljeet Rattan, 'Premier business family Bangurs split its properties', *India Today*, 15 January 1988, https://www.indiatoday.in/magazine/economy/story/19880115-premier-business-family-bangurs-split-its-properties-796841-1988-01-14.

123. Quoted in Ali, *A Local History of Global Capital,* p. 186.

124. Ibid., p. 186.

125. Sengupta, 'Unthreading Partition', pp. 43–45.

126. GoI, 'Reports from West Bengal, Assam, and Tripura regarding the condition of Hindus in East Bengal', *MEA*, L/52/1322/202, SECRET, 1952, NAI, p. 28.

127. Ibid., p. 28.

128. GoI, 'Indian nationals detained as security prisoners in East Bengal', *MEA*, L/52/66320/202, SECRET, 1952, NAI.

129. GoI, 'Reports from West Bengal, Assam, and Tripura regarding the condition of Hindus in East Bengal', NAI, p. 25.

130. GoI, 'Reports from West Bengal, Assam, and Tripura regarding the condition of Hindus in East Bengal', NAI; GoI, 'Frontier Incidents in the Assam-East Bengal Border', *MEA*, L/52/193/5/202, SECRET, 1952, NAI; GoI, 'Frontier Incidents on the borders of Nadia (W Bengal) and Kushtia (E Bengal) Districts', *MEA*, 1952, L/52/1936/202, NAI.

131. Nehru to CD Deshmukh, *SWJN*, 26 March 1952, 2 (17), November 1951–March 1952, pp. 486-487.

132. 'Pledge to Build a New India', Nehru's Speech in Calcutta, 1 January 1952, All India Radio Tapes, *SWJN*, 2 (17), November 1951–March 1952, pp. 74–75.

133. Ibid., p. 75.

134. Nehru to B C Roy, 26 March 1952, *SWJN*, 2 (17), November 1951–March 1952, pp. 484-485.

135. GoI, 'Indian nationals detained as security prisoners in East Bengal', NAI.

136. Nehru to Deshmukh, *SWJN*, p. 487.

137. Nehru to Secretary, Commonwealth Relations, *SWJN*, p. 484.

138. Nehru to Secretary, Commonwealth Relations, 16 March 1952, *SWJN*, 2 (17), November 1951–March 1952, p. 484.

139. GoI, 'Fortnightly Reports from the Deputy High Commissioner for India in Pakistan, Dacca', *MEA*, SECRET, L/52/1321/202, 1952, NAI, pp. 50–52.

140. Ibid., pp. 50–52.

141. Ibid., pp. 50–52.

142. Ibid., pp. 50–52.

143. Nehru to Bakshi Ghulam Mohammad, *SWJN*, 22 March 1954, 2 (25), February–May 1954, pp. 323–325.

144. Ibid., p. 324.

145. Ibid., p. 324.

146. GoI, 'Chronology of Principal Events in Bangla Desh', *MEA*, SECRET, HI/121(1)/71, NAI, p. 8.

147. GoI, 'Situation Report from Dacca', *MEA*, SECRET, 45-RM154, 1954, NAI, p. 17.

148. Ibid., p. 17.

149. Ibid., p. 19.

150. Ibid., p. 19.

151. Nehru to Chief Ministers, 26 April 1954, *SWJN*, 2 (25), February–May 1954, pp. 561–562.

152. Ibid., p. 562.

153. Nehru to Chief Ministers, *SWJN*, 15 June 1954, 2(26), June–September 1954, pp. 545–546.

154. Ibid., pp. 545–546.

155. 'American Consul, Dacca, Pakistan, 1 June 1954, 'Political developments in East Pakistan', Record Group 84, United States National Archives and Records Administration (NARA).

156. Uddin, 'Enemy Agents at Work', pp. 629–664.

157. Nehru to Ali Yavar Jung, *SWJN*, 7 June 1954, 2 (26), June–September 1954, p. 458.

158. Nehru to Chief Ministers, *SWJN*, 15 June 1954.

159. Ibid.

160. Nari, Hurt Sentiments, p. 165–66; Semanti Ghosh, *Different Nationalisms: Bengal, 1905–1947* (New Delhi: Oxford University Press, 2017).

161. Nehru to Chief Ministers, *SWJN*, 15 June 1954, p. 546.

162. GoI, 'Proceedings of Chief Secretaries' Conference', *MEA*, L/54/6612/202, UNCLASSIFIED, 1954, NAI.

163. Nehru to Jung, *SWJN*, p. 459.

164. Nehru to Jairamdas Doulatram, *SWJN*, 7 June 1954, 2 (26), June–September 1954, p. 460.

165. Ibid., p. 460.

166. Nehru to Mountbatten, *SWJN*, 19 April 1953, 2 (22), April–June 1953, pp. 316-317.

167. Ibid., p. 317.

168. Conference of Heads of Missions in Europe and the USA, Switzerland, *SWJN*, 2 (22), April–June 1953, p. 523.

169. The Takeover: PM', *Dawn*, 31 May 1954, quoted in Uddin, 'Enemy Agents at Work', p. 631.

170. Nehru to Chief Ministers, *SWJN*, 15 June 1954.

171. Raghavan, *1971*, p. 8.

172. GoI, 'Treaty of Peace and Friendship between India and the Union of Burma', *MEA*, 7 July 1951: https://www.mea.gov.in/bilateral-documents.htm?dtl/6645/Treaty.

173. Manu Bhagavan, *The Peacemakers: India and the Quest for One World* (New Delhi: HarperCollins India, 2012).

3. SPECIAL POWERS, DESPERATE ACTS

1. 'GoI', 'Armed Forces (Assam & Manipur) Special Powers Bill', SWJN, July-August 1958, p. 298.

2. Steyn, *Zapuphizo,* p. 101.

3. Ibid., p. 101.

4. Ibid., p. 101.

5. Ibid., p. 102.

6. Vivek Chadha ed. *Armed Forces Special Powers Act:The Debate* (New Delhi: Manohar Parrikar Institute for Defence Studies and Analyses, 2012) pp. 10–14.

7. 'Armed Forces (Assam and Manipur) Special Powers Bill', 28 August 1958, *SelectedWorks of Jawaharlal Nehru (SWJN)*, 2(43), p. 300.

8. Avinash Paliwal and Paul Staniland, 'Strategy, Secrecy, and External Support for Insurgent Groups', *International Studies Quarterly, 67(1)*, March 2023.

9. Text of the 6th Schedule of the Constitution of India: https://www.mea.gov.in/Images/pdf1/S6.pdf, Text of Agreement: https://peacemaker.un.org/sites/peacemaker.un.org/files/IN_470628_Naga-Akbar%20Hydari%20Accord.pdf; the NNC represented Western and Eastern Angami, Kukis, Kacha Nagas, Rengma, Sema, Lotha, Ao, Sangtam, and Chan Naga communities.

10. Ibid.

11. Rustomji to Triloki Nath Kaul, TOP SECRET, 31 May 1956, *Rustomji Papers*, Nehru Memorial Museum and Library (NMML), p. 125.

12. GoI, 'Background note on Angami Zapu Phizo and Rev. Michael Scott prepared by US (Naga) in April 1970', *MEA*, CONFIDENTIAL, NI102(42)/70, 13 March 1970, National Archives of India (NAI), p. 5.

13. GoI, Nehru to Secretary General Prime Minister's Secretariat, 5 January 1953, *Jawahalru Nehru (JLN) Papers*, SECRET, NMML, p. 216.

14. GoI, Nehru to Doulatram, *JLN Papers*, 5 January 1953, SECRET, NMML, p. 215.

15. GoI, New Delhi to Shillong, Telegram, CCB No. 1206, TOP SECRET, 11 March 1953, *JLN Papers*, NMML, p. 278.

16. GoI, Shillong to New Delhi, Telegram, CCB No.2411, 14 March 1953, *JLN Papers*, NMML, p. 206.

17. GoI, New Delhi to Rangoon, Telegram, CCB No.1258, 14 March 1953, *JLN Papers*, NMML, p. 237.

18. GoI, 'Summary of Conversation with Mr. J Carrott. Commissioner of Sagaing Division', *JLN Papers*, SECRET, 29 August1953, NMML, pp. 328–9.

19. GoI, 'Summary of Conversation with Mr. J Carrott. Commissioner of Sagaing Division', *JLN Papers*, SECRET, 29 August 1953, NMML, pp. 328–9.

20. GoI, 'Background note on Angami Zapu Phizo and Rev. Michael Scott prepared by US (Naga) in April 1970', *MEA*, CONFIDENTIAL, NI102(42)/70, 13 March 1970, NAI, p. 6.

21. GoI, 'Naga-Phizo: Note by T N Kaul', *MEA*, SECRET, CG/133/61, 4 November 1961, NAI, p. 4.

22. The Governor of Assam was trying to break the Ao away from the hardline Sema and Angami Nagas. Government of Nagaland (GoN), 'Negotiations initiated by the Governor with Ao Hostile Leaders for their surrender', *Confidential Department*, SECRET, PR 948, 1957, Nagaland State Archives (NSA), pp. 1–52.

23. Doulatram to Nehru, 1 June 1955, *JLN Papers*, SECRET & PERSONAL, NMML, p. 353.

24. Nehru to Medhi, *SWJN*, 2(31), November 1955–January 1956, p. 142.

25. Medhi to Nehru, TOP SECRET & PERSONAL, *Bishnuram Medhi Papers*, 1, 190(LL), 25 May 1956, p. 24.

26. Ibid., p. 24.

27. GoI, 'Background note on Angami Zapu Phizo and Rev. Michael Scott prepared by US (Naga) in April 1970', *MEA*, CONFIDENTIAL, NI102(42)/70, 13 March 1970, NAI, p. 6.

28. Nehru to Medhi, *SWJN*, 21 March 1956, 2(32), p. 121.

29. Nehru to Medhi, *SWJN*, 28 February 1956, 2(32), p. 118.

30. Nehru to UN Dhebar, *SWJN*, 30 March 1956, 2(32), p. 124.

31. Nehru to Keishing, *SWJN*, 12 April 1956, 2(32), pp. 127–8.

32. Ibid., pp. 127–128.

33. Nehru to Medhi, *SWJN*, 13 March 1956, 2(33), p. 171.

34. Nehru to Kaul, *SWJN*, 13 May 1956, 2(33), pp. 174–5.

35. Medhi opposed such centralisation and argued that the fact that the parallel Naga government was created in Tuensang Frontier, and not Assam, demonstrated that central authorities were incapable of dealing with the problem. Government of Nagaland (GoN), Medhi to Nehru, *Confidential Department*, 22 May 1957, PR-946, TOP SECRET & PERSONAL, Nagaland State Archives (NSA), pp. 6–7.

36. SM Dutt, deputy director of IB, wrote to S K Datta, Chief Secretary to the Assam government, advocating central government control over all Naga areas because '90 percent of the Nagas are determined to get out of the Assam Government … this is not a matter of opinion but a statement of hard fact whatever few stooges

[of the Assam government] may say'. He warned about the threat of other communities in Assam seeking autonomy from Assam turning into separatist movements if the Naga issue was not resolved quickly. GoN, Deputy Director Intelligence Bureau to Chief Secretary, Assam, 11 July 1957, *Confidential Department*, SECRET, NSA, pp. 5–10.

37. Medhi to Nehru, TOP SECRET & PERSONAL, *Medhi Papers*, 1, 190(LL), 25 May 1956, p. 30.

38. Home Minister to Nehru, TOP SECRET, 22 May 1956, *V K Krishna Menon Papers*, NMML.

39. 'The Naga Resistance and Government Actions', *SWJN*, 30 May 1956, 2(35), pp. 185–190.

40. 'Appraisal of the Naga situation', *SWJN*, 2(33), 19 May 1956, pp. 178–179.

41. Nehru to Home Minister, *SWJN*, 2(33), 21 May 1956, p. 181.

42. Nehru to Defence Secretary, *SWJN*, 2(33), 15 June 1956, p. 198.

43. Ibid., p. 198.

44. GoN, 'Raising of Naga militia', *Confidential Department*, SECRET, 1956, PR-904, p. 2.

45. Nandita Haksar and Sebastian M Hongray, *Kuknalim, Naga Armed Resistance: Testimonies of Leaders, Pastors, Healers, and Soldiers* (New Delhi: Speaking Tiger, 2019).

46. GoN, 'Raising of Naga militia', *Confidential Department*, SECRET, 1956, PR-904, pp. 3–10.

47. Ibid., p. 5–6.

48. Ibid., pp. 28–29.

49. 'Talks with Naga Leaders', *SWJN*, 15 September 1956, 2(35), pp. 142–147.

50. 'Chinese incursions into Myanmar', *SWJN*, 26 August 1956, 2(34), pp. 385–6.

51. Ibid., p. 386.

52. Nehru to Foreign Secretary, *SWJN*, 30 December 1957, 2(40), pp. 403–404.

53. Steyn, *Zapuphizo*, pp. 110–116.

54. Role of Army in NHTA, *SWJN*, 16 January 1958, 2(41), pp. 501–2.

55. 'The Assam-Pakistan Border Situation: Cabinet Ministers Meeting', 10 June 1958, *SWJN*, 2(42), p. 422.

56. 'Armed Forces (Assam and Manipur) Special Powers Bill', *SWJN*, 2(43), July–August 1958, p. 298.

57. Ibid., pp. 298–300.

58. Steyn, *Zapuphizo*, p. 101.

59. GoI, 'Foreign involvement in insurgency in North-Eastern India' *Ministry of Home Affairs (MHA)*, SECRET, NII/102(33)/72, 1972, NAI, p. 45.

60. Ibid., p. 45.

61. Uditi Sen, *Citizen Refugee: Forging the Indian Nation After Partition* (Cambridge: Cambridge University Press, 2018) pp. 54–58; K Maudood Elahi, 'Refugees in Dandakaranya', *The International Migration Review*, 15 (1/2), Spring-Summer 1981, pp. 219–225.

62. Quoted in 'India and the World', Nehru's Press Conference on 7 November 1958, *SWJN*, 2(45), p. 207, fn. 181.

63. Ibid., p. 181.
64. GoI, 'Foreign involvement in insurgency in North-Eastern India' *MHA*, SECRET, NII/102(33)/72, 1972, NAI, p. 45.
65. Lakshmi Menon statement in Lok Sabha, *SWJN*, 20 November 1958, 2(45), p. 690.
66. Quoted Wilcox, 'The Pakistan Coup d'état of 1958', pp. 142–163.
67. 384th meeting of the National Security Council of the United States, 30 October 1958, *Foreign Relations of the US* (FRUS), https://history.state.gov/historicaldocuments/frus1958-60v15/d332.
68. GoI, 'Annual Report for 1958 from Karachi', *MEA*, SECRET, 1959, 3(10)-RI/59, NAI, p. 43.
69. Ibid., p. 43.
70. Nehru to Desai, *SWJN*, 2(44), 15 October 1958, p. 564.
71. Text of Agreement: https://peacemaker.un.org/indiapakistan-enddisputeseast-border59.
72. Ibid.
73. Steyn, *Zapuphizo*, p. 106.
74. GoI, Nehru to Pandit, 24 June 1960, Pvt. & Confidential, *Vijaya Lakshmi Pandit Papers*, File No. 61, NMML, pp. 304–305.
75. Press Briefing-II, *SWJN*, 2(44), 12/10/1958, pp. 131–132.
76. Ibid., pp. 131–132.
77. Ibid., pp. 131–132.
78. Government of Burma (GoB), Nu to Nehru, 1 October 1958 SECRET, AG-12/3, Myanmar National Archives (MNA), p. 35.
79. GoI, 'Annual Reports for 1958 from Rangoon', *MEA*, SECRET, 3(12), R&I-59-I, 1959, NAI, p. 47.
80. GoI, 'Reports (other than annual) from Burma', *MEA*, B(12)-Rt9/58, SECRET, NAI, pp. 109–110.
81. Ibid., p. 110.
82. GoI, 'Annual reports from Rangoon', *MEA*, SECRET, 3(12), R&I/60, NAI, p. 95.
83. Press Briefing-II, *SWJN*, 2(44), 12 October 1958, pp. 131–132.
84. Robert H Taylor, *General Ne Win: A Political Biography* (Singapore: ISEAS Press, 2015) pp. 232–233.
85. GoI, 'Annual reports from Rangoon', *MEA*, SECRET, 3(12), R&I/60, NAI, p. 101.
86. Press Briefing-II, *SWJN*, 2(44), 12 October 1958, p. 132.
87. Cited in SS Madalgi, 'Hunger in Rural India: 1960–61 to 1964–65', *Economic & Political Weekly*, 3(1/2), Jan. 1968, pp. 61–68.
88. Ibid., p. 61.
89. GoB, *Economic Survey of Burma, 1963*, Superintendent, Government Print, 1963, p. 67.
90. Nehru to MEA, 'Burma-China Relations', *SWJN*, 2(53), 9 October 1959, pp. 510–512.

91. In fact, Nehru even tried to build bridges with Nu's opponent Ba Swe, who thought that the Indian leader 'didn't like him', by instructing the Indian ambassador to dispel such notions. Nehru to Lalji Mehrotra, *SWJN*, 2(45), November–December 1958, p. 761.

92. On Panchsheel, see text of agreement: http://www.commonlii.org/in/other/treaties/INTSer/1954/5.html. For an appraisal of the boundary dispute, see Srinath Raghavan, 'Sino-Indian Boundary Dispute, 1948–60: A Reappraisal', *Economic and Political Weekly*, 41(36), September 9–15, 2006, pp. 3882–3892.

93. Nehru to Dutt, *SWJN*, 2(45), 4 November 1958, pp. 697–698.

94. GoI, 'Annual Report for 1958 from Karachi', *MEA*, SECRET, 3(10)R&I/59-I, 1960, NAI, pp. 38–39.

95. GoI, 'Reports (other than annual) from Burma', *MEA*, SECRET, 6(12)-R&I 9/58, 1958, NAI, p. 132.

96. GoI, Reports (other than annual) from Rangoon (Burma), *MEA*, SECRET, 6(12) R&I/59, 1959, NAI, p. 32.

97. GoI, 'Annual reports from Rangoon', *MEA*, SECRET, 3(12),-R&I/60, NAI, pp. 93–94.

98. Shakya, *The Dragon in the Land of Snows,* pp. 185–236.

99. GoI, 'Reports (other than annual) from Mandalay (Burma)', *MEA*, SECRET, 2 May 1959, 6(81)R&I/59, NAI.

100. GoI, 'Annual reports from Rangoon', *MEA*, SECRET, 3(12)R&I/60, 1960, NAI, p. 101.

101. GoI, 'Reports (other than annual) from Mandalay (Burma)', *MEA*, SECRET, 2 May 1959, 6(81)R&I/59, NAI.

102. Rasul Baksh Rais, *China and Pakistan: A Political Analysis of Mutual Relations* (Lahore: Progressive Publishers, 1977), p. 10.

103. 'Lok Sabha: Border Incidents with Pakistan', SWJN, 2(47), 12 March 1959, pp. 499–504.

104. Nehru to Dayal, 'Joint Defence with Pakistan', *SWJN*, 2(49), 26 May 1959, pp. 527–528.

105. Dixit, *India-Pakistan in War and Peace,* p. 138.

106. Nehru to Dayal, *SWJN*, 2(49), 26 May 1959, p. 528.

107. Bruce Riedel, *JFK's Forgotten Crisis: Tibet, the CIA, and the Sino-Indian War* (Washington, D.C.: Brookings Institution Press, 2017) p. 39.

108. Rudra Chaudhuri, 'The Making of an All Weather Friendship, Pakistan, China, and the History of a Border Agreement: 1949–1963', *The International History Review*, 40(1), 2018, pp. 41-64.

109. Rais, *China and Pakistan,* p. 10.

110. Chaudhuri, 'The Making of an All Weather Friendship', pp. 47–49.

111. William Johnstone, *Burma's Foreign Policy: A Study in Neutralism* (Cambridge: Harvard University Press, 1963), p. 147.

112. 5th Official Meeting Between the Delegation of the Albanian Labor Party and the Delegation of the Chinese Communist Party, 19 June 1962, *Wilson Center*

Digital Archive: https://digitalarchive.wilsoncenter.org/document/110806. pdf?v=1550651706b85ae905446e24cb29e6af.

113. Nehru to MEA, 'Burma-China Relations', *SWJN*, 2(53), 9 October 1959, pp. 510–512.

114. Kenneth Conboy and James Morrison, *The CIA's Secret War in Tibet* (Kansas: University of Kansas, 2011).

115. Chaudhuri, 'The Making of an All Weather Friendship', p. 49.

116. B Pakem, *India-Burma Relations* (New Delhi: Omsons Publishers, 1992) p. 97; Avinash Paliwal, 'A Cat's Paw of Indian Reactionaries? Strategic Rivalry and Domestic Politics at the India-China-Myanmar Trijunction', *Asian Security*, 16(1), 2020, pp. 10–11.

117. Paliwal, 'A Cat's Paw of Indian Reactionaries?' pp. 9–11.

118. Ibid., p. 8.

119. Mandy Sadan, *Being and Becoming Kachin: Histories Beyond the State in the Borderlands of Burma* (Oxford: Oxford University Press, 2013).

120. Madan, *Fateful Triangle*, p. 133; Robert McMahon, The Cold War on the Periphery: The United States, India, and Pakistan (New York: Columbia University Press, 1996); Rudra Chaudhuri, *Forged in Crisis: India and the United States since 1947* (London: Hurst Publishers, 2014).

121. On forward policy, see, Raghavan, *War and Peace in Modern India*, pp. 267–310.

122. Paul McGarr, *The Cold War in South Asia: Britain, the United States, and the Indian Subcontinent, 1945–1965* (Cambridge: Cambridge University Press, 2013) pp. 119–148; P N Khera, Operation Vijay: *The Liberation of Goa and Other Portuguese Colonies in India, 1961* (New Delhi: Ministry of Defence of India, 1974).

123. GoI, 'Foreign involvement in insurgency in North-Eastern India' *MHA*, SECRET, NII/102(33)/72, 1972, NAI, p. 30.

124. Ibid., p. 46.

125. Ibid., p. 46.

126. Ibid., p. 47.

127. Ibid., p. 30.

128. Ibid., p. 31.

129. Interview 29; also quoted in Constantino Xavier, *From Inaction to Intervention: India's Strategic Culture of Regional Involvement (Nepal, Sri Lanka, and Myanmar, 1950s–2000s)*, PhD thesis, Johns Hopkins University, July 2016, p. 138 (fn. 322).

130. For a history of the 1962 war, see Raghavan, *War and Peace in Modern India, 2010*; Arjun Subramaniam, *India's Wars: A Military History, 1947–1971* (New Delhi: HarperCollins India, 2017); John Dalvi, *Himalayan Blunder: The Curtain-Raiser to the Sino-Indian War of 1962* (Bombay: Thacker Publishers, 1968).

4. TWO AND A HALF FRONTS

1. GoI, 'Foreign involvement in insurgency in North-Eastern India' *MHA*, SECRET, NII/102(33)/72, 1972, National Archives of India (NAI), p. 1.

2. Text of the agreement: 'People's Republic of China-Pakistan Agreement on the Boundary Between China's Sinkiang and the Contiguous Areas, March 02, 1963', *The American Journal of International Law*, 57 (3), July, 1963, pp. 713–716.
3. Chaudhuri, 'The Making of an All Weather Friendship', pp. 52–54.
4. Jawaharlal Nehru, 'Changing India', *Foreign Affairs*, 41 (3), April 1963, pp. 453–465.
5. Anirudh Dhanda, 'The day Nehru died', *Tribune India*, 29 May 2021: https://www.tribuneindia.com/news/musings/the-day-nehru-died-260065.
6. Farooq Bajwa, *From Kutch to Tashkent: The Indo-Pakistan War of 1965* (London: Hurst Publishers, 2013) pp. 65–96.
7. Ibid., pp. 97–160.
8. Arzan Tarapore, 'Defence without deterrence: India's strategy in the 1965 war', *Journal of Strategic Studies*, 2019, pp. 1–30.
9. GoI, 'Foreign involvement in insurgency in North-Eastern India' *MHA*, SECRET, NII/102(33)/72, 1972, NAI, p. 16.
10. Ibid., p. 17.
11. Other groups led by Dusoi Chakesang, Yeveto Sema, and Zuheto Sema received similar training and support. Ibid., pp. 17–19.
12. Prime Minister's Secretariat, Nehru to FS, SECRET, 12 September 1960, *Jawahalru Nehru (JLN) Papers*, NAI, p. 193.
13. Ibid., p. 193.
14. Ibid., p. 193.
15. Gavin Young, *Indo-Naga War* (Pennsylvania: American Baptist Historical Society, 1961) pp. 29–30.
16. GoI, 'Rangoon to Delhi', *MEA,* 6(12)-R&I/61, NAI, pp. 49–84.
17. GoI, 'Annual Political Report for 1960 for Burma', *MEA*, 1102(1)-SD/61, SECRET, 1961, NAI, p. 9.
18. GoI, Nehru to Nu, 13 January 1962, SECRET, 148-PMH/62, *JLN Papers*, NAI, pp. 353–354.
19. Ibid., p. 354.
20. Ibid., p. 354.
21. Ibid., p. 354.
22. Prime Minister's Secretariat, Nehru to JS (East), 14 March 1962, SECRET, 731Pt-II, *JLN Papers*, p. 243.
23. Nibedon, *Nagaland*, pp. 109–88.
24. Peace Mission's Proposals: https://www.satp.org/satporgtp/countries/india/states/nagaland/documents/papers/text_the_peace_mission.htm.
25. Underlined in original. 'Statement on Peace-Making in Nagaland', *JP Narayan Papers*, 4 September 1966 Serial No. 34, NAI, p. 3-5.
26. Ibid., pp. 8–10.
27. For instance, the Indian security forces were not to undertake jungle operations, raid camps of the 'underground', patrol beyond 100 yards of security posts, search villages, take aerial actions, make arrests, or impose punishment. Similarly, the FGN and the Naga army was to refrain from sniping

and ambushing, imposing fines, kidnapping, recruiting, sabotaging, raiding and firing on security posts, moving with arms and uniform in towns, or approaching within 1,000 yards of the security posts. No arms or ammunition were to be imported from outside Nagaland, and so on. Terms of Cease Fire Agreement (July 1964), Appendix B to Joint Intelligence Committee Paper No. 8(66), 16 February 1966, *Gulzarilal Nanda Papers*, Nehru Memorial Museum and Library (NMML), p. 68.

28. Ibid., p. 10.

29. U Nu, *U Nu: Saturday's Son* (New Haven: Yale University Press, 1975) p. 236.

30. GoI, Nehru to Ne Win, SECRET, 06 March 1962, File 731(I), *JLN Papers*, NAI, pp. 137–138.

31. GoI, Nehru to Commonwealth Secretary, 730 (II), SECRET, *JLN Papers*, NAI, p. 180.

32. GoI, 'LSQ 6960 re. harassment of Indians in Burma', *MEA*, SECRET, 3001(26)-SD/60, 1 March 1960, NAI, p. 3.

33. GoI, Nehru to Commonwealth Secretary, 730 (II), SECRET, *JLN Papers*, NAI, p. 180.

34. Government of Burma (GoB), *Economic Survey of Burma, 1963*, Superintendent, Government Print, 1963, p. 67.

35. Ibid., p . 67.

36. GoI, 'Annual Political Report for 1960 from Burma', *MEA*, 1102(1)-SD/61, SECRET, 1961, NAI, p. 6.

37. Ibid., p. 6.

38. Ibid., p. 6.

39. Ibid., p. 6.

40. Ibid., p. 6, underlined as in original.

41. Ibid., p. 7.

42. Prime Minister's Secretariat, Nehru to Nu, 19 August 1960, 706(III), CONFIDENTIAL, *JLN Papers*, NAI, p. 464.

43. GoI, 'Burma: Annual Report for the year 1961', *MEA*, 15 March 1962, SECRET, NAI, p. 17.

44. 4th LSD, 2nd Session, 'Statement re. India-Burma Boundary Agreement', 13 June 1967; quoted by EAM Chagla in the parliament.

45. GoI, 'Annual Political Report for 1960 from Burma', *MEA*, 1102(1)-SD/61, SECRET, 1961, NAI, p. 7.

46. Prime Minister's Secretariat, Nehru to Foreign Secretary, 13 January 1962, TOP SECRET, 729(I), *JLN Papers*, NAI, p. 96.

47. Parliament of India, 'Prime Minister's Statement on Foreign Affairs', 24 February 1961, 715, *JLN Papers*, NAI, pp. 122–23.

48. Ibid., pp.122–123.

49. Oral History Record, 'Ambassador Eric Goncalves', *Indian Council of World Affairs*, (ICWA), 2010, p. 33.

50. Ibid., p. 33.

51. Ibid., p. 33.

52. Kalpana Sunder, 'Why memories of Burma live on in Chennai', *The Juggernaut*, 12 April 2021: https://www.thejuggernaut.com/why-memories-of-burma-live-on-in-chennai.

53. GoI, 'LSQ 6960 re. harassment of Indians in Burma', *MEA*, 3001(26)-SD/60, 1 March 1960, NAI, p. 6.

54. Government of Burma (GoB), Nehru to Ne Win, SECRET, 13 May 1964, Myanmar National Archives (MNA).

55. GoI, 'Annual Report from Rangoon for the year 1964', *MEA*, 1965, SECRET, HI-1011(12)65, NAI, p. 16.

56. Ibid., p. 16.

57. Ibid., p. 16.

58. GoI, 'Political Reports (other than annual) from Rangoon', *MEA*, SECRET, 07 October 1965, HI/1012(12)/65, NAI, p. 74.

59. GoI, 'Visit to Burma by the Secretary to the Prime Minister', 3rd LSD, 15th Session, 8 August 1966.

60. 'Sardar Swaran Singh's Statement on late Prime Minister Shastri's visit to Burma', MEA, 1 February 1966, FAR 1966.

61. 3rd Rajya Sabha Debate (RSD), 'Statement by Minister re Visit of Late PM Lal Bahadur to Burma', 1 March 1966.

62. Paliwal, 'A Cat's Paw of Indian Reactionaries', pp. 73–89.

63. Fifth Official Meeting Between the Delegation of the Albanian Labor Party and the Delegation of the Chinese Communist Party, 19 June 1962, *Wilson Center Digital Archive*, https://digitalarchive.wilsoncenter.org/document/110806.

64. Schendel, 'A War Within a War', pp. 75–117.

65. GoI, 'Mizo district of Assam—damage to crops—Procurement of rice from Burma', *MEA*, SECRET, 1406(13)0-SD60, 1960, NAI, p. 4-B.

66. Ibid., p. 7.

67. For more on the famine, see Sajal Nag, 'Tribals, Famine, Rats, State and the Nation', *Economic and Political Weekly*, 36(1), 24 March 2001, p. 1029; Nirmal Nibedon, *Mizoram: The Dagger Brigade* (New Delhi: Lancer Publishers, 1980) pp. 22–54.

68. For this see Nibedon, *Mizoram* (1980); Pachuau, *Being Mizo* J V Hluna and Rini Tochhawng, *The Mizo Uprising: Assam Assembly Debates on the Mizo Movement, 1966–1971* (Newcastle upon Tyne: Cambridge Scholars Publishing, 2012); C G Verghese and R L Thanzawna, *A History of the Mizos-Volume I* (New Delhi: Vikas Publishing House, 1997).

69. GoI, 'Note Recorded by Chief Commissioner, Manipur', SECRET, *Nanda Papers*, NMML, pp. 46–49.

70. Ibid., pp. 46–49.

71. GoI, 'Foreign involvement in insurgency in North-Eastern India' *MHA*, SECRET, NII/102(33)/72, 1972, NAI, p. 68.

72. Nibedon, *Mizoram*, p. 45.

73. Ibid., pp. 46–47.

74. GoI, 'Foreign involvement in insurgency in North-Eastern India' *MHA*, SECRET, NII/102(33)/72, 1972, NAI, p. 68.

75. Mizo National Front (MNF), 'Memorandum Submitted to the Prime Minister of India', 20 October 1965, *Nanda Papers*, NMML, pp. 3–8.

76. Justin Paul George, 'When Indian Navy worried Indonesia would send submarines to aid Pakistan in 1965', *The Week*, 26 April 2021: https://www.theweek.in/news/india/2021/04/26/when-indian-navy-worried-indonesia-would-send-submarines-to-aid-pakistan-in-1965.html.

77. MNF, Laldenga to Sukarno, 20 January 1966, *Nanda Papers*, NMML, p. 12.

78. GoI, 'MNF: The Mizo Uprising', *Ministry of Information and Broadcasting*: https://www.mib.gov.in/filmsdivisionvideo/mnf-mizo-uprising.

79. GoI, 'Foreign involvement in insurgency in North-Eastern India' *MHA*, SECRET, NII/102(33)/72, 1972, NAI, p. 22.

80. Nibedon, *Mizoram*, p. 133.

81. GoI, 'Foreign involvement in insurgency in North-Eastern India' *MHA*, SECRET, NII/102(33)/72, 1972, NAI, p. 69.

82. Ibid., p. 69.

83. Ibid., p. 23.

84. Nibedon, *Mizoram*, p. 154.

85. Interview with Lalthangliana quoted in ibid.

86. Ibid.; Nibedon, *Mizoram*, p. 154.

87. Quoted in Subir Bhaumik, *Insurgent Crossfire: North-East India* (New Delhi: Lancer Publishers, 1996) p. 151.

88. David Buhrill, '50 years ago today, Indira Gandhi got the Indian Air Force to bomb its own people', *Scroll.in*, 5 March 2016: https://scroll.in/article/804555/50-years-ago-today-indira-gandhi-got-the-indian-air-force-to-bomb-its-own-people.

89. 3rd LSD, 14th Session, 'Mizo Refugees in Burma', 28 March 1966

90. C Nunthara, *Impact of the Introduction of Grouping of Villages in Mizoram* (Delhi: Omsons Publications, 1989); Nandini Sundar, 'Interning Insurgent Populations: The Buried Histories of Indian Democracy', *Economic and Political Weekly*, 46(6), 2011, p. 47.

91. Buhrill, '50 years ago today', Scroll.in.

92. J V Hluna, 'MNF Relations with Foreign Powers', in R N Prasad ed. *Autonomy Movements in Mizoram* (New Delhi: Vikas Publishers, 1994) p. 190; Bhaumik, *Insurgent Crossfire*, pp. 145–149.

93. JIC, 'Assistance given by Pakistan and China to the Nagas, Mizos, and Other Tribes', SECRET, 16 June 1966, *Nanda Papers*, NMML, pp. 73–76.

94. GoI, 'Foreign involvement in insurgency in North-Eastern India' *MHA*, SECRET, NII/102(33)/72, 1972, NAI, p. 17.

95. GoI, 'Tribal Affairs: Paris—a Centre of contact and coordination of Indian tribal insurgents', SECRET, *MHA-Intelligence Bureau*, 21 October 1971, NAI, p. 72.

96. GoI, 'Foreign involvement in insurgency in North-Eastern India' *MHA*, SECRET, NII/102(33)/72, 1972, NAI, p. 18.

97. Ibid., p. 18.

98. Ibid., p. 18.

99. Ibid. These weapons included 76 SL Rifles, 30 SMGs with 25,000 rounds of ammunition, 3 60-mm mortars with 240 bombs, 3 LMGs with 3,000 rounds of ammunition, 3 40-mm RLs with 80 rockets, 10 Pistols with 800 rounds, 1 signal pistol with 40 cartridges, 250 hand grenades, 100 mines, 2 wireless sets, and 60,000 kyat.

100. Ibid., p. 21.

101. GoI, 'Annual Report for the year 1966 from the Dy. High Commission, Dacca', *MEA*, SECRET, HI/1011/91/6, NAI, p. 9.

102. JIC, 'Implications of the visit of Chinese leaders, Liu Shao Chi and Chen Yi to Pakistan in March/April 1966', SECRET, *Nanda Papers*, NMML, pp. 89–90.

103. Ibid., pp. 89–90.

104. Ibid., pp. 89–90.

105. Ibid., pp. 89–90.

106. JIC, 'Chinese Offensive Capabilities against India', SECRET, 27 June 1966 *Nanda Papers*, NMML, pp. 93–94.

107. JIC, 'Future Tactics of the Mizo National Front', SECRET, Paper No. 16(66), 12 April 1966, *Nanda Papers*, NMML, pp. 95–99

108. Mizo camps were operational in Roma Bazaar, Kuagrashri, Ruma, Rangtlang, Rangamati, Rangkhtanu, and Thanchi. Ibid., p. 77; for more, see Lalthakima, 'Insurgency in Mizoram: A Study of its Origin, Growth, and Dimension', PhD thesis, Mizoram University, 2008; available: https://shodhganga.inflibnet. ac.in/handle/10603/1202.

109. Ibid., p. 78.

110. Ibid., p. 78.

111. Nibedon, *Mizoram*, pp. 125–133. The details of these meetings and their timelines are confirmed in GoI, 'Foreign involvement in insurgency in North-Eastern India' *MHA*, SECRET, NII/102(33)/72, 1972, NAI, pp. 25–26.

112. Nibedon, *Mizoram*, p. 132.

113. Quoted in ibid, p. 132.

114. Ibid., p. 133.

115. Ibid., p. 134.

116. Ibid., p. 134.

117. GoI, 'Foreign involvement in insurgency in North-Eastern India' *MHA*, SECRET, NII/102(33)/72, 1972, NAI, p. 69.

118. Conservative estimates of military aid during this period amounted to 781 rifles (with 7,000 rounds of ammunition), 37 LMGs, 107 Stens/TMCs/Berettas (with 55,000 rounds of ammunition), 43 pistols/revolvers (with 1,200 rounds of ammunition), 30 2" mortars, 22 rocket launchers, 111 hand grenades, and 160 'unspecified Chinese arms given in 1971'. Ibid., pp. 24–25.

119. Ibid., p. 25.

120. GoI, 'Pakistan's Hand in Training Mizos', 3rd LSD, 15th Session, 29 August 1966.

121. A S Bhasin, *Nehru, Tibet, and China* (New Delhi: India Viking, 2021), Chapter 1.

122. Madan, *Fateful Triangle*, pp. 7–9.

123. This section draws upon Paliwal, 'A Cat's Paw of Indian Reactionaries?', pp. 1–20.

124. 3rd LSD, 14th Session, 'Mizo Refugees in Burma', 28 March 1966.

125. 3rd LSD, 15th Session, 'Firing by Burmese Customs Personnel on Indian Baite Tribesmen', 2 August 1966.

126. Ibid.

127. Joint Intelligence Committee (JIC), 'Developments Among the Tribes of Nagaland, Manipur, and Assam since February 1966', Cabinet Secretariat (Intelligence Wing), TOP SECRET, Paper Number 41(66), 1 October 1966, *Nanda Papers*, NMML.

128. Ibid.

129. Ibid.

130. On Rani Gaidinliu see Longkumer, *The Greater India Experiment*, pp. 190–229.

131. JIC, 'Developments Among the Tribes of Nagaland, Manipur, and Assam since February 1966', Cabinet Secretariat (Intelligence Wing), TOP SECRET, Paper Number 41(66), 1 October 1966, *Nanda Papers*, NMML, p. 11.

132. Ibid. For more see BK Bhattacharyya, 'A Separate Assam Hills State: What Does it Mean?', *Economic and Political Weekly*, 2(9), 4 March 1967, pp. 491–494, Esther M Tariang, *Glimpses on Political Developments in Meghalaya* (Chennai: Notion Press, 2022).

133. JIC, 'Developments Among the Tribes of Nagaland, Manipur, and Assam since February 1966', Cabinet Secretariat (Intelligence Wing), TOP SECRET, Paper Number 41(66), 1 October 1966, *Nanda Papers*, NMML, p. 11.

134. Cabinet Secretariat, SECRET, 'Demarcation of Indo-Burma Border', Joshi to MEA, SECRET, 4 January 1967, NAI.

135. Ibid.

136. Ibid.

137. Ibid.

138. 4th LSD, 2nd Session, 'Statement re. India-Burma Boundary Agreement', 13 June 1967.

139. GOI, Rangoon, SECRET, 'Political Report for the Month of January 1967', 3 February 1967, D713/R1/67, NAI.

140. Ibid.

141. Haksar to Gandhi, *Prime Minister's Secretariat*, TOP SECRET, 17 September 1970, *P N Haksar Papers*, Instalment I, Subject File (SF) 46, NMML, pp. 7–8.

142. Cabinet Secretariat, 'Demarcation of Indo-Burma Border', Joshi to MEA, SECRET, 04/01/1967, NAI.

143. 4th LSD, 2nd Session, 'Statement re. India-Burma Boundary Agreement', 13 June 1967.

144. GoI, 'India-Burma Boundary Agreement', MEA, SECRET, 3 September 1974, D1760/DDHDIII/74, NAI.

145. 4th LSD, 2nd Session, 'Statement re. India-Burma Boundary Agreement', 13 June 1967.

146. GoI, 'India-Burma Boundary Agreement', MEA, SECRET, 3 September 1974, D1760/DDHDIII/74, NAI.

147. Quoted in Pakem, *India-Burma Relations*, p. 113.
148. This had long been a discussion topic since the separation of the two countries in 1937 but could not be achieved due to the Second World War, and India's other troubles in Kashmir and Naga areas after 1947. Guyot-Réchard, 'Tangled Lands', pp. 293–300.
149. 'Proposal for a Road-River link from the Mizo Hills District to Akyab in Burma', Prime Minister's Secretariat, SECRET, 18 March 1968, *Haksar Papers*, 1ˢᵗ Instalment, SF36, pp. 241–246.
150. Ibid., p. 242.
151. Ibid., p. 242.
152. Ibid., p. 245.
153. Leake, 'Where National and International Meet', pp. 4–10.
154. Paliwal, 'Colonial Sinews of Postcolonial Espionage', pp. 914–923.
155. R K Yadav, *Mission R&AW* (New Delhi: Manas Publishers, 2014) p. 28.
156. B Raman, *The Kaoboys of R&AW: Down Memory Lane* (New Delhi: Lancer Publishers, 2009) pp. 8–12.

5. JOY BANGLA

1. GoI, Dhar to Haksar, 18/04/1971, TOP SECRET, MOS/AMB/461/71, *Haksar Papers*, 3rd Installment, SF 89, NMML, p.33.
2. Raghavan, *1971*, p. 8.
3. Nair, *Hurt Sentiments*, p. 93–100.
4. Maj. Gen. S S Uban, *Phantoms of Chittagong: The 'Fifth Army' in Bangladesh* (New Delhi: Allied Publishers, 1985), pp. 4–5.
5. On the war itself, see Anam Zakaria, *1971: A People's History from Bangladesh, Pakistan, and India* (London: Vintage, 2019); Richard Sisson and Leo E. Rose, *War and Secession: Pakistan, India, and the Creation of Bangladesh* (California: University of California Press, 1991).
6. Nehru to BC Roy, *Selected Works of Jawaharlal Nehru (SWJN)*, 2(47), 7 March 1959, pp. 261–262.
7. Desai to Nehru, *SWJN*, 2(61), June–July 1960, pp. 821–823.
8. 'In Lok Sabha: Reply to questions on Indo-Pakistan border demarcation', *SWJN*, 2(47), 16 March 1959, pp. 502–504.
9. Ibid., pp. 502–504.
10. Nehru to MEA, 'Border Incidents with East Pakistan', SWJN, 2(47), 12 March 1959, p. 498.
11. Nehru to M J Desai, *SWJN* 2 (46), January–February 1959, p. 362; Tridevi to M J Desai, *SWJN*, March–April 1960, pp. 462–463.
12. 'Rehabilitation of Displaced Persons', *SWJN*, 2(61), 17 June 1960, pp. 511–515.
13. 'Lok Sabha: Arrival of Hindus from East Pakistan', *SWJN*, 2(65), 21 December 1960, p. 522.
14. 'Press Conference', *SWJN*, 2(69), 30 June 1961, p. 50.
15. Ibid., p. 47.

16. Ibid., p. 391.
17. 'At the plenary session: Panchayati Raj', *SWJN*, 2(66), 7 January 1961, pp. 221–222.
18. 'From the Intelligence Bureau: Hindu Mahasabha Plans', *SWJN*, 2 (69), 15 June 1961, pp. 747–748.
19. Ibid., p. 381.
20. Nehru to Desai: Gopalganj Riots, *SWJN*, 2 (69), 12 June 1961, pp. 389–390.
21. Keesing's Contemporary Archives, https://web.stanford.edu/group/tomzgroup/pmwiki/uploads/1310-1962-xx-xx-KS-a-JZW.pdf.
22. BC Roy to Nehru: Pakistan Officials Visit Malda, *SWJN*, 2 (76), 25 April 1962, pp. 630–632.
23. Prafulla Sen to Nehru: Santhal Influx from East Pakistan, *SWJN*, 2(78), 23 July 1962, pp. 112–113.
24. Ibid., pp. 112–113.
25. Nehru to Nkrumah: Kashmir Problem, *SWJN* 2(78), 25 July 1962, p. 559.
26. 'In Lok Sabha: Hindus in Noakhali', *SWJN* 2(78), 9 August 1962, pp. 122–125.
27. 'From Rajya Sabha: Minority Community Migration from East Pakistan to West Bengal', *SWJN*, 2(78), June–July 1962, pp. 303–306.
28. 'To Lal Bahadur Shastri: Expelling Muslims from Northeast', *SWJN* 2(78), 12 September 1962, p. 126.
29. 'Gundevia to Nehru: Meeting with Ayub Khan', *SWJN* 2(78), 12 September 1962, p. 125.
30. Sangeet Barooah Pisharoty, 'Cop and Class', *The Hindu*, 6 December 2013, https://www.thehindu.com/features/metroplus/cop-and-class/article5429660.ece.
31. 'In Lok Sabha: Hindus in East Pakistan', *SWJN* 2(81), 3 April 1963, pp. 324–326.
32. 'In the Lok Sabha: On the President's Address', *SWJN* 2(83), 27/02/1963, pp. 210–14.
33. Mukhopadhyay, *Partition, Bengal, and After*, pp. 48–51.
34. 'Recurrent Exodus of Minorities from East Pakistan and Disturbances in India', A Report to The Indian Commission of Jurists by its Committee of Enquiry', *The Indian Commission of Jurists*, 1965, p. 377.
35. On the language riots see Baruah, *India Against Itself*, p. 105.
36. 'Impression of Visit to Assam', *SWJN*, 2(61), 20 July 1960, pp. 356–363.
37. Ibid., p. 361.
38. Ibid., p. 362.
39. Monirul Hussain, 'State, Identity Movements, and Internal Displacement in the North East', *Economic and Political Weekly*, 35(51), 16–22 December 2000, pp. 4519–4523.
40. Government of Assam, 'White Paper on the Foreigner's Issue', p. 8.
41. Ibid., p. 8.
42. Ibid., p. 8.
43. Ibid., p. 9.

44. Ibid., p. 8.

45. 'Forty Years Ago: Secret Letter, *Indian Express*, 9 March 2022, https://indianexpress.com/article/opinion/editorials/march-9-1982-forty-years-ago-secret-letter-7807484/.

46. Pisharoty, *Assam*, p. 60.

47. Ibid., p. 61.

48. Monirul Hussain, *The Assam Movement: Class, Ideology, and Identity* (New Delhi: Manak Publishers, 1993) pp. 214–17.

49. Ibid., pp. 217–18.

50. 'From PC Sen: Creating a Hindu Belt in West Bengal', *SWJN*, 2(83), 21 August 1963, pp. 800–803.

51. Ibid., p. 801.

52. Ibid., p. 801.

53. 'Press Conference', *SWJN*, 2(85), 22/05/1964, p. 25

54. Nehru to Chatterjee, *SWJN*, 2(85), 15/02/1964, pp.2–3.

55. 'In Lok Sabha: External Affairs, *SWJN*, 2(85), 13/04/1964, pp. 217–224.

56. 'From Ayub Khan: East Pakistan Refugees', *SWJN*, 2(85) 23/03/1964, pp. 367–368.

57. 'In Lok Sabha: External Affairs', *SWJN*, 2(85), 13/04/1964, p. 219.

58. GoI, 'Annual Reports from Dacca for 1965', *MEA*, SECRET, N1/1011 (10)/66-II, 1965, National Archives of India (NAI), p. 92.

59. Ibid., p. 92.

60. Interview 30.

61. Ibid.

62. Most railway tracks connecting India and East Pakistan were destroyed in 1965 to prevent the movement of Indian troops. The Indian Air Force sought to destroy the only squadron of Pakistan Air Force (PAF) Sabre Jets, but had such terrible military intelligence that it targeted multiple airbases including in Kurmitola and Chittagong but not Tejgaon where the squadron was in fact positioned. It triggered a strong response from the PAF which attacked the IAF Central Air Command's Kalaikunda airbase in West Bengal, destroying eight combat aircrafts and losing two Sabres of its own in dogfights over Kharagpur. Subramaniam, *India's Wars*, pp. 322–323.

63. GoI, 'Political Developments among the tribes on the Indo-Burma-Pakistan Border', Joint Intelligence Committee (JIC), Cabinet Secretariat, SECRET, 16 February 1966, *Nanda Papers*, Nehru Memorial Museum and Library (NMML), p. 54.

64. For more on India's approach towards the Tibetan uprising and its secret collaboration with the US see, Anne F Thurston and Gyalo Thondup, *The Noodle Maker of Kalimpong: The Untold Story of My Struggle for Tibet* (London: Penguin, 2015); John Kenneth Knaus, *Orphans of the Cold War: America and the Tibetan Struggle for Survival* (Public Affairs, 1999); Carole McGranahan, *Arrested Histories: Tibet, the CIA, and Memories of a Forgotten War* (Durham, NC: Duke University Press, 2010); Bhasin, *Nehru, Tibet, and China* (2021).

65. GoI, 'Kao to Haksar: SSB and Bangladesh', 3 February 1972, TOP SECRET, *Haksar Papers*, SF 220, III Instalment, NMML, p. 22.
66. Ibid., p. 22.
67. Ibid., p. 23.
68. Ibid., p. 23.
69. Uban, *Phantoms of Chittagong*, pp. 55–61.
70. Dacca to New Delhi, FS from Sengupta, TOP SECRET (Cipher Telegram), *R&AW*, 14 March 1971, *Haksar Papers*, 3rd Instalment, SF 90(a), NMML, pp. 2–3.
71. Interview 30.
72. GoI, 'Annual Report for 1958 from Karachi', *MEA*, SECRET, 1959, 3(10)-RI/59, NAI, p. 34.
73. Ibid., p. 34.
74. 'Humayun Kabir to Nehru', *SWJN*, 2(51), 14 August 1959, p. 634.
75. Ibid., p. 636.
76. Ibid., p. 637.
77. Ibid., p. 634.
78. Ibid., p. 637.
79. Ibid., p. 637.
80. Ibid., p. 638.
81. Ibid., p. 638.
82. 'Nehru to Desai', *SWJN*, 2(64), 3 November 1960, p. 395.
83. 'Humayun Kabir to Nehru', *SWJN*, 2(51), 14 August 1959, pp. 636–637.
84. Ibid., p. 636.
85. 'In the Lok Sabha: Colonel Bhattacharjee's Trial in Pakistan', *SWJN* 2(70), 16 August 1961, p. 541–547. For the Pakistani officer's version, see Mumtaz Malik, 'The Story of Another Kulbhushan Jadhav: A Page from History', *Hilal* (English), 2016: https://www.hilal.gov.pk/eng-article/detail/NDA1.html.
86. Bhattacharya authored his version of events, which match Capt. Mumtaz Malik's. Bhattacharya, 'The Turn of Wheel: A Spiritual Sojourn', *PastConnect*, https://www.pastconnect.net/the-turn-of-wheel-a-spiritual-sojourn/.
87. 'In the Lok Sabha: Colonel Bhattacharjee's Trial in Pakistan', *SWJN*, 2(70), 16 August 1961, pp. 541–547; 'In Rajya Sabha: Bhattacharyya's Espionage Trial in Pakistan', *SWJN*, 2(71), 30 August 1961, pp. 715–718. Indian spy sent to jail', *The Dawn* [50 Years Ago Today], 11 November 2011, https://www.dawn.com/news/672532/indian-spy-sent-to-jail.
88. 'Lok Sabha: Bhattacharya's Conviction in Pakistan', *SWJN*, 2(72), 20 November 1961; the case continued to generate parliamentary interest well into 1963, when a young parliamentarian from the Jana Sangh, Atal Bihari Vajpayee, and senior communist leader Bhupesh Gupta remained interested in knowing how the government was helping Bhattacharya and his family. 'In Lok Sabha: Conviction of Colonel Bhattacharya', *SWJN* 2(81), February–April 1963, pp. 695–698 Bhattacharya was sentenced to eight years in prison but was released after four in 1965.

89. 'Nehru to Chaliha: Closing Pakistan Office in Shillong', *SWJN*, 2(76), 23 April 1962, p. 297.

90. Ibid., p. 297.

91. Ibid., p. 297.

92. Sheikh Mujibur Rahman, *The Unfinished Memoirs* (Dhaka: University Press, 2012) p. xx.

93. Sumon Mahbub, 'Bangabandhu returned home after getting no response from Nehru in 1962: Hasina', *BDNews24*, 10 March 2018: https://bdnews24.com/bangladesh/2018/03/10/bangabandhu-returned-home-after-getting-no-response-from-nehru-in-1962-hasina.

94. Ibid.

95. Ibid.

96. Ibid.

97. Rahman, *The Unfinished Memoirs*, p. xx.

98. 'Nehru to Gundevia: Mujibur Rahman', *SWJN*, 2(76), 16 March 1962, p. 508.

99. Sheikh Hasina ed. *Secret Documents of the Intelligence Branch on the Father of the Nation, Bangladesh: Bangabandhu Sheikh Mujibur Rahman,Vol.VII, 1962–63* (London: Routledge, 2022) p. 425.

100. Sashanka S Banerjee, *India, Mujibur Rahman, Bangladesh Liberation & Pakistan* (self-published memoirs, 2011) pp. 9–10.

101. Ibid., p. 15.

102. Hasina ed. *Secret Documents,Vol 7*, p. 76.

103. 'In the Rajya Sabha: Closure of Rajshahi Office', *SWJN*, 2(84), 12 December 1963, pp. 628–634.

104. Ibid., p. 630.

105. Ibid., p. 630.

106. 'Talk with Chester Bowles', *SWJN*, 2(84), 11 December 1963, pp. 595–596.

107. GoI, 'Annual Reports from Dacca for 1965', *MEA*, SECRET, H1/1011(10)/66-II, 1965, NAI, p. 46.

108. Ibid., p. 63.

109. Ibid., p. 61. The other officers who were changed in 1965, before the war, were B K Sengupta (by B M Lal) as chief visa officer on 8 February 1965, and S K Das (by P K George) as first secretary on 3 September 1965 (he joined after the war). For more on Banerjee see Nitin Gokhale, *RN Kao: Gentleman Spymaster* (New Delhi: Bloomsbury India, 2019). Banerjee's cover-name as 'P N Ojha' is confirmed by former Indian intelligence officials who served on the Bangladesh desk after 1971. Interview 48.

110. Ibid., p. 92.

111. Ibid., p. 92.

112. Garver, *Protracted Contest*, pp. 195–203.

113. Subramaniam, *India's Wars*, p. 322.

114. Underlined as in original. GoI, 'Annual Report for the year 1966 from the Dy. High Commission, Dacca', *MEA*, SECRET, HI/1011/91/6, NAI, p. 4.

115. Ibid., p. 4.

116. GoI, 'Political Reports (other than annual report) from Dacca', *MEA*, SECRET, HI/1012(32)/69, 1969, NAI, p. 10.

117. Hasina ed. *Secret Documents,Vol 9*, p. 333.

118. GoI, 'Monthly political reports (other than annual reports) from Pakistan, Dacca', *MEA*, SECRET, HI/1012(32)67, 1967, NAI, p. 87.

119. 'Six Point Demands: Roadmap for Bangladesh's Emancipations: https://www.albd.org/articles/news/31111/Six-Point-Demands:-Roadmap-For-Bangladesh%E2%80%99s-Emancipation.

120. Hasina ed. *Secret Documents,Vol 7*, p. 247.

121. Bina D'Costa, *Nationbuilding, Gender, and War Crimes in South Asia* (London: Routledge, 2010) pp. 75–143; Zakaria, *1971*, p. 176–200; Salil Tripathi, *The Colonel Who Would Not Repent: The Bangladesh War and its Unquiet Legacy* (New Haven:Yale University Press, 2016)

122. Annual Report for the year 1966 from the Dy. High Commission, Dacca', *MEA*, SECRET, HI/1011/91/6, 1966, NAI, pp. 7–9.

123. Ibid., p. 9.

124. GoI, 'Monthly political reports (other than annual reports) from Pakistan, Dacca', *MEA*, SECRET, HI/1012(32)67, 1967, NAI, p. 83.

125. Annual Report for the year 1966 from the Dy. High Commission, Dacca', *MEA*, SECRET, HI/1011/91/6, 1966, NAI, pp. 5–14.

126. Annual Report for the year 1966 from the Dy. High Commission, Dacca', *MEA*, SECRET, HI/1011/91/6, 1966, NAI, p. 6.

127. GoI, 'Monthly political reports (other than annual reports) from Pakistan, Dacca', *MEA*, SECRET, HI/1012(32)67, 1967, NAI, p. 27.

128. Annual Report for the year 1966 from the Dy. High Commission, Dacca', *MEA*, SECRET, HI/1011/91/6, 1966, NAI, p. 6.

129. GoI, 'Monthly political reports (other than annual reports) from Pakistan, Dacca', *MEA*, SECRET, HI/1012(32)67, 1967, NAI, p. 25.

130. Ibid., p. 25.

131. Ibid., p. 81

132. Ibid., pp. 81–82.

133. Ibid., p. 82.

134. For a history of the Awami League see Shyamali Ghosh, *The Awami League, 1949–1971* (Dhaka: Academic Publishers, 1990).

135. GoI, 'Monthly political reports (other than annual reports) from Pakistan, Dacca', *MEA*, SECRET, HI/1012(32)67, 1967, NAI, p. 95.

136. Ibid., p. 82.

137. GoI, 'Annual Report, Dy. High Commissioner of India, Dacca (East Pakistan), 1968', *MEA*, SECRET, HI/1011(10)/69-II, NAI, p. 8.

138. Interview 31.

139. GoI, 'Monthly political reports (other than annual reports) from Pakistan, Dacca', *MEA*, SECRET, HI/1012(32)67, 1967, NAI, p. 99.

140. Dutt to Kewal Singh, TOP SECRET, 14 June 1974, No.F.29/HC/74, *Subimal Dutt Papers*, SF 74, NMML, p. 24.

141. Ibid., p. 24.

142. Ibid., p. 24.

143. 'Textbook 'incorrectly' describes Agartala Case: Shawkat', *The Daily Star*, 12 June 2010, https://www.thedailystar.net/news-detail-142345; Syed Badrul Ahsan, 'Col. Shawkat Ali, the Agartala Case and our History', *Dhaka Tribune*, 19 November 2020, https://archive.dhakatribune.com/opinion/op-ed/2020/11/19/op-ed-col-shawkat-ali-the-agartala-case-and-our-history.

144. GoI, 'Annual Report, Dy. High Commissioner of India, Dacca (East Pakistan), 1968', *MEA*, SECRET, HI/1011(10)/69-II, NAI, pp. 8–10.

145. Ibid., p. 11.

146. GoI, 'Chronology of Principal Events in Bangla Desh', *MEA*, SECRET, HI/121(1)/71, NAI, p. 21.

147. GoI, 'Political Reports (other than annual report) from Dacca', *MEA*, SECRET, HI/1012(32)/69, 1969, NAI, p. 6.

148. Ibid., p. 6.

149. Ibid., p. 17.

150. Ibid., p. 17.

151. Ayub to Khan, 26 March 1969, https://pakistanspace.tripod.com/archives/69ayub24.htm.

152. GoI, 'Political Reports (other than annual report) from Dacca', *MEA*, SECRET, HI/1012(32)/69, 1969, NAI, pp. 77–78.

153. Ibid., pp. 77–78.

154. Hasina ed. *Secret Documents,Vol 5,* p. 133.

155. Hasina ed. *Secret Documents,Vol 9,* p. 274.

156. GoI, 'Political Reports (other than annual report) from Dacca', *MEA*, SECRET, HI/1012(32)/69, 1969, NAI, pp. 125–127.

157. S Biswas; P Daly, '"Cyclone not above politics": East Pakistan, disaster politics, and the 1970 Bhola Cyclone', *Modern Asian Studies*, 55(4), 2021, pp. 1382–1410.

158. Willem van Schendel, *A History of Bangladesh* (Cambridge: Cambridge University Press, 2009), pp. 123–125.

159. GOI, Additional Secretary R&AW to Cabinet Secretary, TOP SECRET, *Cabinet Secretariat*, 14 January 1971, *Haksar Papers*, 3rd installment, SF 220, NMML, pp. 162–188.

160. Ibid., p. 268.

161. Ibid., p. 268.

162. GoI, Haksar to Gandhi, *Prime Minister's Secretariat*, TOP SECRET, 5 January 1971, *Haksar Papers*, 3rd Installment, SF 163, NMML, p. 249.

163. Ibid., p. 249.

164. GoI, 'Kao to Haksar: SSB and Bangladesh', 3 February 1972, TOP SECRET, *Haksar* Papers, 3rd Instalment, SF 220, NMML, p. 22.

165. Rehman Sobhan, *Untranquil Recollections: The Years of Fulfilment* (New Delhi: Sage Publishers, 2016), pp. 347, 360.

166. Quoted in Jairam Ramesh, *Intertwined Lives: PN Haksar & Indira Gandhi* (New Delhi: Simon & Schuster, 2018), p. 207.

167. P N Dhar, *Indira Gandhi, the 'Emergency', and Indian Democracy* (New Delhi: Oxford University Press, 2000) p. 168.

168. GoI, Haksar to Cabinet Secretary, Prime Minister's Secretariat, TOP SECRET, *Haksar Papers*, 3rd Installment, SF 165, NMML, pp. 48–49.

169. GoI, Haksar to Dhar, 7 April 1971, TOP SECRET, *Haksar Papers*, 3rd Installment, SF 165, NMML, pp. 93–94.

170. Ibid., pp. 93–94.

171. GoI, 'Record of PM's Conversation with Mr. Gromyko, Soviet Foreign Minister', *Prime Minister's Secretariat*, TOP SECRET, 9 August 1971, *Haksar Papers*, NMML, pp. 43–45.

172. GoI, Haksar to Dhar, 7 April 1971, TOP SECRET, *Haksar Papers*, 3rd Installment, SF 165, NMML, pp. 93–94.

173. Ibid., pp. 93–94.

174. GoI, Dhar to Haksar: Most immediate, 15 April 1971, TOP SECRET, *Haksar Papers*, 3rd Installment, SF 165, NMML, pp. 95–97.

175. GoI, Dhar to Haksar, 18 4 1971, TOP SECRET, MOS/AMB/461/71, *Haksar Papers*, 3rd Installment, SF 89, NMML, p. 29.

176. Ibid., p. 30.

177. Ibid., p. 30.

178. GoI, 'Situation in Bengal', *Intelligence Bureau*, MHA, SECRET, 15 February 1970 11/91/71G&Q, NAI, pp. 6–10.

179. GoI, Dhar to Haksar, 18 April 1971, TOP SECRET, MOS/AMB/461/71, *Haksar Papers*, 3rd Installment, SF89, NMML, p. 33.

180. Sobhan, *Untranquil Recollections: The Years of Fulfilment,* p. 370.

181. GoI, Dhar to Haksar, 18 April 1971, TOP SECRET, MOS/AMB/461/71, *Haksar Papers*, 3rd Installment, SF89, NMML, p. 33.

182. GoI, Subrahmanyam to Haksar, 4 April 1971, SECRET, *Haksar Papers*, 3rd Installment, SF276, NMML.

183. Ibid.

184. In this meeting DP emphasised the need for guerilla training for Mukti Bahini cadre, and recommended reading Vietnamese communist General Võ Nguyên Giáp's book on such warfare. He remained in regular contact with Tajuddin and warned him about the opposition against him within the Awami League. Faruq Aziz Khan, *Spring 1971: A Centre Stage Account of Bangladesh War of Liberation* (Dhaka: University Press, 1998) pp. 191–192.

185. GoI, Dhar to Haksar, Undated, TOP SECRET, Haksar Papers, 3rd Installment, SF 89, NMML, p. 6.

186. Ibid., p. 7.

187. Ibid., p. 7.

188. Ibid., p. 8.

189. Ibid., p. 9.

190. Ibid., p. 10.

191. Ibid., p. 11.

192. GoI, Dhar to Haksar, Undated, TOP SECRET, *Haksar Papers*, 3rd installment, SF 89, NMML, p. 11.

193. Ibid. Dhar convinced Gandhi of the Maoist threat enough for her to make that a talking point with international interlocutors. Shortly after reading this note, Gandhi informed visiting US Senator Robert Kennedy on 16 August that the threat or pro-China elements taking over the movement was real and that the operations of the Mukti Bahini would expand in East Pakistan regardless of India's help given the situation there. Prime Minister's Secretariat, 'Record of PM's Conversation with Senator Kennedy on 16 August 1971', SECRET, *Haksar Papers*, 3rd instalment, SF 89, NMML, p. 45.

194. Prime Minister's Secretariat, 'Record of PM's Conversation with Mr. Gromyko, Soviet Foreign Minister', TOP SECRET, *Haksar Papers*, 9 August 1971, SF 89, NMML, pp. 43–45.

195. Ibid; Dhar, *Indira Gandhi, the 'Emergency', and Indian Democracy*, p. 168.

196. Interview 33.

197. Sydney H Schanberg, 'He Tells Full Story of Arrest and Detention', *The New York Times*, 18 January 1972: https://www.nytimes.com/1972/01/18/archives/he-tells-full-story-of-arrest-and-detention-sheik-mujib-describes.html.

198. Dacca to New Delhi, Foreign Secretary from Sengupta, TOP SECRET (Cipher Telegram), *R&AW*, 14 March 1971, *Haksar Papers*, 3rd instalment, SF 90(a), NMML, pp. 2–3.

199. Ibid., pp. 2–3.

200. Ibid., pp. 2–3.

201. For more on Mujibnagar government see Dasgupta, *India, and the Bangladesh Liberation War*, pp. 67–80.

202. Interview 32.

203. Dhar, *Indira Gandhi, the 'Emergency', and Indian Democracy*, p. 167.

204. Amit Das Gupta, *Serving India: A Political Biography of Subimal Dutt (1903-1992), India's Longest Serving Foreign Secretary* (New Delhi: Manohar Publishers, 2017) p. 485.

205. S Chattopadhaya: 'A Note on the talks with Maulana Bhashani', Undated (sometime in 1971) *Dutt Papers*, SF 65, NMML, pp. 31–33.

206. Ibid., p. 33.

207. Dhar, *Indira Gandhi, the 'Emergency', and Indian Democracy*, p. 167.

208. Ibid., p. 167.

209. Chattopadhaya: 'A Note on the talks with Maulana Bhashani', p. 32.

210. Dasgupta, *India, and the Bangladesh Liberation War*, p. 72.

211. Dhar, *Indira Gandhi, the 'Emergency', and Indian Democracy*, pp. 167–168.

212. Senior Awami League leaders such as Khondkar Mushtaq (who was appointed foreign minister in the cabinet), Mansoor Ali, and Qamruzzaman were unhappy with this turn of events. Sobhan, *Untranquil Recollections: The Years of Fulfilment*, pp. 365–366.

213. Khan, *Spring 1971*, p. 178.

214. Uban, *Phantoms of Chittagong*, p. 110.

215. GoI, Dhar to Haksar, Undated, TOP SECRET, *Haksar Papers*, 3rd installment, SF 89, NMML, p. 14.

216. Uban, *Phantoms of Chittagong*, p. 33.
217. Ibid., p. 34.
218. Ibid., p. 34.
219. Ibid., p. 34.
220. Gokhale, *RN Kao*, p. 175.
221. The occurrence of this meeting is corroborated by Tajuddin's 2iC who fought along with Tajuddin. But the meeting was not intended to oust Mujib. Khan, *Spring 1971*, pp. 53–54.
222. Gokhale, *RN Kao*, p. 175.
223. Uban, *Phantoms of Chittagong*, p. 31.
224. Interview 32; Khan, *Spring 1971*, p. 52.
225. Sobhan, *Untranquil Recollections: The Years of Fulfilment*, pp. 364–366.
226. Ibid.
227. Khan, *Spring 1971*, pp. 52–53.
228. On Mujib Uban, *Phantoms of Chittagong*, pp. 35–37.
229. Quoted in Khan, *Spring 1971*, p. 52.
230. Ibid., pp. 53–54.
231. Anthony Mascarenhas, *Bangladesh: A Legacy of Blood* (London: Hodder & Stoughton, 1986), p. 37.
232. Interview 32.
233. Ibid.
234. Dutt to FS, TOP SECRET, 23/02/1974, *Dutt Papers*, SF 74, p. 46.
235. GoI, 'Notes from Shri GS Misra (Cabinet Secretariat) on Bangladesh, received from Secy. K R Narayanan', *MEA*, TOP SECRET, 1976, PP(JS)414/75, *A K Damodaran Papers*, NAI, pp. 30–31.
236. Singh, *The Naxalite Movement in India*, pp. 5–24.
237. Punny Kabir, 'Shib Narayan Das: The flag redesign was pre-planned', *Dhaka Tribune*, 12 December 2013: https://archive.dhakatribune.com/uncategorized/2013/12/12/shib-narayan-das-the-flag-redesign-was-pre-planned.
238. Myoe, *In the Name of Pauk-Phaw,* pp. 181–185.
239. 'Spring Thunder Over India', *People's Daily*, Communist Party of China, 7 July 1967: https://www.marxists.org/subject/china/documents/peoples-daily/1967/07/05.htm.
240. Julia Lovell, *Maoism: A Global History* (London: Bodley Head, 2019) Chapter 10; B Paul, *The First Naxal: An Authorised Biography of Kanu Sanyal* (New Delhi: Sage Publishers, 2019).
241. Interview 34.
242. Ibid.
243. Interview 35.
244. Interviews 33, 35, 36, 37, 38, and 40.
245. Rajiv Bhatia, *India-Myanmar Relations: Changing Contours* (New Delhi: Routledge, 2016), p. 96.
246. GoI, 'Political Reports etc. (other than annual) from Rangoon', *MEA*, SECRET, HI/1012(12)72, 1972, NAI, pp. 3–4.

554555

6. SONS OF THE SOIL

1. BK Nehru to KC Pant, SECRET, 08/10/1970, NMML, *Braj Kumar Nehru (BKN) Papers*, SF19, NMML.
2. AL Dias Lt. Governor of Tripura to Indira Gandhi, SECRET, D.O. No. 18/LG/RN/70, 30 September 1970, *Haksar Papers*, 3rd instalment, SF160, Nehru Memorial Museum and Library (NMML), p. 172.
3. Sanjib Baruah, 'Nationalizing Space: Cosmetic Federalism and the Politics of Development in Northeast India', *Development and Change*, 34(5), 2003, pp. 923–924.
4. Ibid., pp. 915–917.
5. Ibid., p. 924; Gulshan Sachdeva, *Economy of the North-East: Policy, Present, Conditions, and Future Possibilities* (New Delhi: Konark Publishers, 2000).
6. Interview 24.
7. Haksar and Hongray, *Kuknalim*, pp. 42–154.
8. Nitin Gokhale, 'A life roughed-out in the jungle', *Tehelka*, 1 October 2005.
9. Zoya Hasan, *Congress After Indira: Policy, Power, Political Change (1984–2009)* (New Delhi: Oxford University Press, 2012) p. 5.
10. GoI, 'Note for the Cabinet Committee on Political Affairs: 'Reorganisation of north-eastern region—common governor', *MHA*, SECRET, 13 July 1971, National Archives of India (NAI), p. 2.
11. Ibid., p. 3.
12. Braj Kumar Nehru to T N Kaul, SECRET, GA-67/69, 11 September 1969, *Braj Kumar Nehru (BKN) Papers*, SF21, p. 34.
13. GoI, 'Note for the Cabinet Committee on Political Affairs: 'Reorganisation of north-eastern region—common governor', *MHA*, SECRET, 13 July 1971, NAI, p. 4.
14. GoI, 'Broadcast by Shri B.K. Nehru, Governor of Nagaland, on Republic Day 26.1.1971', *BKN Papers*, SF21, NMML, pp. 97–98.
15. Ibid., p. 98.
16. GoI, 'Note for the Cabinet Committee on Political Affairs: 'Reorganisation of north-eastern region—common governor', *MHA*, SECRET, 13 July 1971, NAI, pp. 6–8.
17. Ibid., p. 7.
18. BKN to Chavan, SECRET, 1 September 1969, No.GA-66/69, *BKN Papers*, pp. 27–28.
19. GoI, 'Note for the Cabinet Committee on Political Affairs: 'Reorganisation of north-eastern region—common governor', *MHA*, SECRET, 13 July 1971, NAI, p. 4.
20. Ibid., p. 4.
21. BKN to Chavan, SECRET, 1 September 1969, No.GA-66/69, *BKN Papers*, SF21, NMML, p. 27.
22. Ibid., pp. 27–28.
23. Ibid., p. 28.

24. Ibid., p. 28.

25. Ibid., p. 28.

26. Ibid., p. 28.

27. BKN to K. C. Pant, 8 Oct. 1970, *BKN Papers*, SF19, p. 34.

28. BKN to Swaran Singh, SECRET, 21 July 1969, *BKN Papers*, SF21, pp. 1–2.

29. BKN to Dinesh Singh, SECRET, 23 July 1969, *BKN Papers*, SF21, pp. 17–18.

30. BKN to Dinesh Singh, SECRET, 12 April 1970, *BKN Papers*, SF21, pp. 38–42.

31. BKN to Dinesh Singh, TOP SECRET, 13 August 1969, *BKN Papers*, SF21, pp. 25–26.

32. Ibid., p. 25.

33. BKN to Dinesh Singh, SECRET, 14 April 1969, *BKN Papers*, SF 21, p. 3.

34. Ibid., p. 4.

35. GoI, 'Interrogation—Dusoi Chakesang', *Ministry of Defence (MoD)*, Army Headquarters, DDMI (A), SECRET, 26 April 1969, NAI, p. 6.

36. Ibid., p. 11.

37. Ibid., p. 14.

38. Ibid., p. 14.

39. Ibid., p. 14.

40. Ibid., p. 15.

41. Ibid., p. 15.

42. Ibid., p. 7.

43. Ibid., p. 6.

44. BKN to Giri, SECRET, 5 September 1969, *BKN Papers*, SF 21, p. 29.

45. Ibid., p. 30.

46. Ibid., p. 32.

47. GoI, 'Desirability or Otherwise of Declaring the MNF as Unlawful', *MHA-Intelligence Bureau*, SECRET, 20 March 1974, 920(d)/HS/74, NAI, p. 112.

48. Ibid., p. 112.

49. LP Singh to BKN, SECRET, 12 April 1976, *BKN Papers*, SF 33, pp. 80–81.

50. Singh to BKN, SECRET, 5 June 1976, *BKN Papers*, SF 39, p. 2.

51. 'Visit of a delegation of Naga ex-underground and Nagaland Peace Committee to London to meet Phizo—A Background Note', *MHA*, SECRET, 21 January 1977, *BKN Papers*, SF 39, p. 23.

52. GoI, 'Tribal Affairs: Paris—a Centre of contact and coordination of Indian tribal insurgents', SECRET, *MHA-Intelligence Bureau*, 21 October 1971, D.2266-NII/71, NAI, p. 73.

53. Ibid., p. 73.

54. GoI, 'Tribal Affairs: Nagaland—Phizo', *MHA-Intelligence Bureau*, SECRET, 1432-DS(Unclear)/71, NAI, p. 54.

55. Ibid., p. 54.

56. GoI, 'Naga Affairs', *MHA-Intelligence Bureau*, SECRET, 4 December 1970, 3/TRIBE(0)/70(8)II-188, NAI, p. 33.

57. Singh to BKN, SECRET, 12 April 1976, *BKN Papers*, SF 33, NMML, pp. 80–81.

58. BKN to Singh, PERSONAL & SECRET, 18 July 1976, *BKN Papers*, SF 39, p. 6.

59. BKN to Singh, SECRET, 2 September 1976, *BKN Papers*, SF 39, pp. 11–13.

60. Ibid., p. 13.

61. Intelligence Note, SECRET, *BKN Papers*, SF 39, p. 26.

62. Nakro, Ramyo, & Yallay to Gandhi, 21 February 1977, *BKN Papers*, SF 39, p. 41.

63. New Delhi to London, TOP SECRET, 7 February 1977, *BKN Papers*, SF 39, pp. 38–39.

64. Ibid., p. 39.

65. 'Visit of Naga Delegates to London', TOP SECRET, *BKN Papers*, SF 39, pp. 38–42.

66. BKN to K Brahmananda Reddi, TOP SECRET, 17 March 1977, *BKN Papers*, SF 39, p. 51.

67. Uban, *Phantoms of Chittagong*, pp. 45–47.

68. Nibedon, *Mizoram*, p. 174.

69. GoI 'Note from the Government of Mizoram for declaring the underground Mizo National Front an unlawful association', *MHA*, SECRET, 102(76)/73-NE, 15 March 1974, NAI, p. 32.

70. Ibid., p. 32.

71. Dutt to Haksar, TOP SECRET, 14 December 1972, *Dutt Papers*, p. 23.

72. Ibid., p. 23.

73. Ibid., p. 23.

74. *MHA*, SECRET, 102(76)/73-NE, 15 March 1974, p. 175.

75. Ibid., p. 184.

76. Ibid., p. 184.

77. Interview 4.

78. GoI, 'Proposal of Mizoram administration to declare 'MNF/MNA' etc. as unlawful associates under the Unlawful Activities (Prevention) Act 1967', *MHA*, SECRET, 22 March 1974, 102(76)/73-NE, NAI, pp. 1–3.

79. GoI, Chief Secretary-Aizawl to Ashoke Sen, *MHA*, SECRET, 17/10/1973, 102(76)/73-NE, NAI, pp. 11–12.

80. Ibid., p. 12.

81. Ibid., pp. 13, 16.

82. Ibid., p. 14.

83. GoI, 'Record note of discussion with Army Commander held in Raj Niwas on 11th March, 1974', *MHA*, TOP SECRET, NAI, pp. 27–31.

84. GoI, 'Note from the Government of Mizoram for declaring the underground Mizo National Front an Unlawful Association', *MHA*, SECRET, 102(76)/73-NE, 15 March 1974, NAI, pp. 32–40.

85. GoI, 'Mizoram: Desirability or otherwise of declaring the MNF as unlawful', *MHA-Intelligence Bureau*, SECRET, 20 March 1974, 102(76)/73-NE, p. 110.

86. Ibid., p. 110.

87. Ibid., pp. 111–112.

88. Nibedon, *Mizoram*, p. 207.

89. Quoted in ibid, p. 209.

90. Quoted in ibid, p. 209.

91. Ibid., p. 210.
92. Text of the 1976 agreement: ibid, pp. 263–264.
93. Ibid., pp. 217–219.
94. Quoted in ibid., p. 219.
95. GoI, 'Note for the Political Affairs Committee of the Cabinet', *MHA*, SECRET, 6 July 1979, NAI, p. 5.
96. GoI, Lt. Governor-Mizoram to Home Minister, *MHA*, SECRET-IMMEDIATE, 3 July 1979, NAI, p. 2.
97. GoI, 'Wireless Message: New Delhi to Aizawl', *MHA*, SECRET-CRASH, 8 August 1979, No.14014/12/79, NAI, p. 32.
98. GoI, 'Note for the Political Affairs Committee of the Cabinet', p. 4.
99. GoI, 'Notice by the MNF', Appendix AA, *MHA*, NAI, p. 200.
100. GoI, 'Details of financial assistance given by China to Biakvela gang', *MHA*, SECRET, Appendix 'L', NAI, p. 89. Biakvela received SMGs (40), SMG ammunition (18,000 rounds), SARs (108), SAR's ammunition (32,400 rounds), recoilless guns (8), RL's ammunition (240 shells), hand grenades (154), and W/T sets with batteries (3).
101. GoI, 'Details of financial assistance given by China to Demkhoseik's gang', *MHA*, SECRET, Appendix 'K', NAI, p. 85. The ammunition included SMGs (32), Pistol M-20s (12), Rocket Launchers M-40 (4), rockets (78), stick grenades (24), SMG ammunition (28,614 rounds), pistol ammunition (350 rounds), magazines for SMGs (96), radio transmitters and receivers (3). One *tola* is 11.66 grams.
102. GoI, 'Announcement of MNF Hd. Qrs.', *MHA*, SECRET, Appendix 'M', NAI, pp. 90–93.
103. Ibid., p. 91.
104. GoI, 'Chakmas to Jagjivan Ram', *MHA*, 6230/DM/71, 15 November 1971, NAI.
105. GoI, 'The present situation and future trends in Burma', *MEA*, SECRET, 7 May 1983, NAI, p. 22.
106. Interview 50.
107. Nibedon, *Mizoram*, pp. 188–195.
108. 'Bangladesh warns Burma', *Bangkok Post*, 28 April 1978.
109. Quoted in 'Dragon King', *AsiaWeek*, 19 May 1978.
110. Text of Agreement: https://dataspace.princeton.edu/bitstream/88435/dsp01th83kz538/1/1978%20Repatriation%20Agreement.pdf.
111. GoB, Indira Gandhi to Ne Win, 17 April 1973, SECRET, Myanmar National Archives (MNA).
112. GoI, 'The present situation and future trens in Burma', MEA, SECRET, 7 May 1983, NAI, p. 20.
113. Makiko Kimura, *The Nellie Massacre of 1983: Agency of the Rioters* (New Delhi: Sage Publishers, 2013), Introduction.
114. Ibid., p. 1. Horrors of the pogrom, still shaping Assamese politics, are captured in a powerful documentary by Subasri Krishnan called *What the Fields Remember*. Debesh Banerjee, 'The Killing Fields', *Indian Express*, 27 July 2015, https://indianexpress.com/article/lifestyle/the-killing-fields/.

115. E N Rammohan, *Insurgent Frontiers: Essays from the Troubled Northeast* (New Delhi: India Research Press, 2005) p. 31.

116. BKN to Giri, SECRET, F-4/70, 6 July 1970, *BKN Papers*, SF 21, NMML, pp. 45–46.

117. Ibid., p. 46.

118. Ibid., p. 46.

119. Baruah, *India Against Itself*, p. 115.

120. Pisharoty, *Assam*, pp. 47–48.

121. Ibid., p. 48.

122. Ibid., p. 52.

123. For details of the Jana Sangh in Assam, see Rajat Sethi and Shubhrastha, *The Last Battle of Saraighat: The Story of the BJP's Rise in the North-East* (New Delhi: Penguin India, 2017).

124. Mrinal Talukdar, *Postcolonial Assam (1947–2019)* (Guwahati: NTF Publishers, 2019) pp.105–146.

125. Pisharoty, 'Cop and Class', *The Hindu*.

126. Ibid.

127. Ibid.

128. Pisharoty, *Assam*, p. 91.

129. Sanjoy Hazarika, 'Mrs. Gandhi, on a tour of Assam, blames 'agitators' for massacre', *NYT*, 22 February 1983: https://www.nytimes.com/1983/02/22/world/mrs-gandhi-on-a-tour-of-assam-blames-agitators-for-massacre.html.

130. Ibid.

131. Quoted in Ipsita Chakravarty, 'Why was Assam's Nellie massacre of 1983 not prevented, despite intimations of violence?', *Scroll.in*, 18 February 2017, https://scroll.in/article/829682/why-was-assams-nellie-massacre-of-1983-not-prevented-despite-intimations-of-violence.

132. Malini Bhattacharjee, 'Tracing the Emergence and Consolidation of Hindutva in Assam', *Economic and Political Weekly*, 51(16), 16 April 2016, p. 83

133. Ibid., p. 85

134. Shekhar Gupta, *Assam: A Divided Valley* (New Delhi: Vikas Publishers, 1984), pp. 122–123.

135. GoI, 'Discussion on the Illegal Migrants (Determination …) Bill', *LSD*, 15 December 1983, pp. 355–356.

136. Ibid., p. 364.

137. Bhattacharjee, 'Tracing the Emergence and Consolidation of Hindutva in Assam', pp. 84–85.

138. Pisharoty, *Assam*, pp. 114–115.

139. Ibid., pp. 117–120.

140. For details on the relationship between the Assam Movement leaders and the Attackers in the Nellie incident, see Kimura, *The Nellie Massacre of 1983*, pp. 77–81.

141. Pisharoty, *Assam*, p. 116.

142. Ibid., pp. 122–125.

143. Ibid., p. 124.

144. Nani Gopal Mahanta, *Confronting the State: ULFA's Quest for Sovereignty* (New Delhi: Sage Publishers, 2013) Chapters 1 and 2.

145. Pisharoty, *Assam*, p. 147.

146. Ibid., pp. 126–127.

147. Ibid.; Rajeev Bhattacharya, 'NDFB chief gets life imprisonment in 2008 Assam blasts case: Tracing Ranjan Daimary's journey to achieve "sovereignty"', *Firstpost*, 31 January 2019: https://www.firstpost.com/india/ndfb-chief-gets-life-imprisonment-in-2008-assam-blasts-case-tracing-ranjan-daimarys-journey-to-achieve-sovereignty-6000731.html.

148. Baruah, *India Against Itself*, pp. 174–175.

148. Bhattacharya, 'NDFB chief gets life imprisonment in 2008 Assam blasts case', *Firstpost.*

150. Jogendra K. Das, 'The Bodoland Movement in Local and National Perspectives', *The Indian Journal of Political Science*, 55(4), October–December 1994, pp. 417–426.

151. Bismee Taskin, 'What is the Karbi insurgency, its violent past & how it could impact coming Assam elections', *The Print*, 25 February 2021.

152. Ali, *The Fearful State*, p. 163.

153. GoI, 'Separatist Tendency amongst non-Naga Tribals of Manipur and their Unification Movement', *MHA*, SECRET, 18/2/69-SC(Pt), 9 July 1971, NAI, p. 2.

154. Ibid., p. 3.

155. Ibid., p. 7.

156. See T Haokip, 'Essays on Kuki-Naga Conflict: A Review', *Strategic Analysis*, 37(2), 2013, pp. 251–259.

157. Bhonsle, *Mother, Where's My Country?*, pp. 34–78.

158. Interview 24.

159. Interviews 27, 48, and 49.

160. Interview 24.

161. Kanglei Yawol Kanna Lup: South Asia Terrorism Portal (SATP): https://www.satp.org/satporgtp/countries/india/states/manipur/terrorist_outfits/kykl.htm.

162. Ramesh Menon, 'Mizoram: Rebel rousing', *India Today*, 30 September 1988: https://www.indiatoday.in/magazine/indiascope/story/19880930-mizoram-comes-under-president-rule-797758-1988-09-29.

163. Ibid.

164. Ibid.

7. LOSING THE PEACE

1. GoI, 'Notes from Shri GS Misra (Cabinet Secretariat) on Bangladesh, received from Secy. KR Narayanan', *MEA*, TOP SECRET, 1976, PP(JS)414/75, *Damodaran Papers*, National Archives of India (NAI), p. 46.

2. C Dasgupta Interview: 'Did India Really Lost the Peace After Winning the 1971 war?', *The Wire*, 20 November 2021: https://www.youtube.com/watch?v=1Uov9sybmms.

3. Christopher Clary, *The Difficult Politics of Peace: Rivalry in Modern South Asia* (New York: Oxford University Press, 2022).

4. USG, 'Bangladesh: Six Months of Independence', Intelligence Memorandum, SECRET, *Directorate of Central Intelligence*, 27 June 1972, CIA, FOIA, p. 9.

5. The issue of who must be credited for liberation—India or the people of Bangladesh, and if the latter, then who and for what—still animates Bangladeshi politics today. Interviews 31, 31, and 44.

6. Naomi Hossain, *The Aid Lab: Understanding Bangladesh's Unexpected Success* (New York: Oxford University Press, 2017); Amartya Sen, *Poverty and Famines: An Essay on Entitlement and Deprivation* (Oxford: Oxford University Press, 1981).

7. United States Government (USG), 'Intelligence Alert Memorandum: Bangladesh', SECRET, 8 November 1975, *Central Intelligence Agency (CIA)*, Freedom of Information Act Electronic Reading Room (FOIA).

8. William Borders, 'India's Top Aide in Dacca Wounded in Ambush by 6', *The New York Times*, 27 November 1975: https://www.nytimes.com/1975/11/27/archives/indias-top-aide-in-dacca-wounded-in-ambush-by-6.html

9. GoI, 'Military coup in Bangladesh on 15.08.1975: Question of our recognition to the new government and subsequent developments', *MEA*, SECRET, 4/4/PP/JS/75, NAI, p.2; For more see B Z Khasru, *The Bangladesh Military Coup and the CIA Link* (New Delhi: Rupa Publishers, 2014); Lawrence Lifschultz, *Bangladesh: The Unfinished Revolution* (London: Zed Books, 1979).

10. Pupul Jayakar, *Indira Gandhi: A Biography* (New Delhi: Penguin, 1979) p. 220.

11. Christophe Jaffrelot and Pratinav Anil, *India's First Dictatorship: The Emergency, 1975–77* (New Delhi: HarperCollins India, 2021), p. 310.

12. Interview 42.

13. Ali Asif Shawon, 'RAW Chief advised Fazilatunnesa Mujib to leave Dhanmondi residence', *Dhaka Tribune*, 5 August 2021, https://archive.dhakatribune.com/bangladesh/2021/08/05/raw-chief-advised-fazilatunnesa-mujib-to-leave-dhanmondi-residence.

14. Raman, *The Kaoboys of R&AW*, pp. 52–53.

15. For more on economic disparity between East and West Pakistan see, Rounaq Jahan, *Pakistan: Failure in National Integration* (Dhaka: University Press Ltd., 1995).

16. Talukder Maniruzzaman, 'Bangladesh in 1975: The Fall of the Mujib Regime and its Aftermath', *Asian Survey*, 16(2), Feb. 1976, pp. 119–129.

17. GOI, 'Reasons Leading to the coup', SECRET, 4/4/PP/JS/75, pp. 100–102.

18. Interview 40; For more see Hossain, *The Aid Lab*, pp. 90–110.

19. Hossain, *The Aid Lab*, p. 106.

20. 'An Unfashionable Tragedy', John Pilger: http://johnpilger.com/videos/an-unfashionable-tragedy.

21. Hossain, *The Aid Lab*, p. 94.

22. GoI, 'Contingency Plan to Deal with Influx from Bangladesh', SECRET, *MHA*, PP(JS)4(4)/75, p. 55.

23. Ibid., p. 55.

24. Blaine C Richardson, 'Bangladesh Food Aid: PL480 Title I and Title III', Aid Project Impact Evaluation Paper No. 54, *US Agency for International Development*, May 1996: https://pdf.usaid.gov/pdf_docs/pnabe974.pdf.

25. Das Gupta, *Serving India,* p. 500.

26. Sen, *Poverty and Famines*, p. 136.

27. Ibid., p. 501.

28. Interview 38.

29. Gupta, *Serving India*, pp. 499–500.

30. Interviews 31 and 38.

31. GoI, 'Economic Cooperation with Bangladesh', *Prime Minister's Office*, 31 December 1971, CONFIDENTIAL, 37(448)/71-PMS, NAI, pp. 1–5.

32. Ibid., pp. 5–6.

33. GoI, 'Trade Agreement between India and Bangladesh signed in Dacca on 5-7-1973', *MEA*, CONFIDENTIAL, 18 August 1973, NAI, pp. 4–5.

34. GoI, 'Economic Cooperation with Bangladesh', *MEA*, SECRET, 26 September 1974, p. 2.

35. Hossain, *The Aid Lab*, pp. 98–114.

36. Ibid., pp. 106–107.

37. India was negotiating the rupee debt question for the PL480 scheme with the US during this period. GoI, 'Papers reg. PL480 Funds', *MEA*, Unclassified, 1973, WII/205/13/73, NAI, pp. 1–12.

38. GoI, 'Economic Cooperation with Bangladesh', SECRET, 26 September 1974, pp. 3–4.

39. USG, 'Indian View of Flood Situation in Bangladesh', LTD. OFFICIAL USE, *Wikileaks*, 1974NEWDE11152_b, 22/08/1974: https://wikileaks.org/plusd/cables/1974NEWDE11152_b.html.

40. GoI, 'Reasons Leading to the coup', SECRET, 4/4/PP/JS/75, p. 100.

41. Ibid., p. 100.

42. GoI, 'Political Report etc. (other than annual) from Dacca', *MEA*, SECRET, HI/1012(32)/75, 1975, p. 3.

43. GoI, 'Annual Reports from Dacca/Chittagong-1974', *MEA*, SECRET, HI/1011(10)/75-II, NAI, p. 12.

44. Sen, *Poverty and Famines*, pp. 135–137.

45. Interviews 40 and 43.

46. GoI, 'Reasons Leading to the coup', SECRET, 4/4/PP/JS/75, p. 100.

47. GoI, 'Annual Reports from Dacca/Chittagong-1974', *MEA*, SECRET, HI/1011(10)/75-II, 07/01/1975, NAI, p. 16.

48. Gupta, *Serving India,* p. 485.

49. Ibid., p. 485.

50. GoI, 'Note on developing trends in the internal situation and foreign relations of Bangladesh', High Commission of India, Dacca, TOP SECRET, 10 January 1974, *Dutt Papers,* Nehru Memorial Museum and Library (NMML), p. 20.

51. Gupta, *Serving India*, p. 501.

52. Ibid., p. 476.

53. Quoted in ibid., p. 476.

54. Josy Joseph, 'Truth lost? Most military records of Bangladesh war missing', *Times of India*, 9 May 2010: https://timesofindia.indiatimes.com/india/truth-lost-most-military-records-of-bangladesh-war-missing/articleshow/5907855.cms.

55. Interview 38.

56. GoI, 'Reasons Leading to the coup', SECRET, 4/4/PP/JS/75, p. 100.

57. GoI, 'Annual Political Report from Dacca/Chittagong—1974', SECRET, p. 28.

58. Dutt to Haksar, TOP SECRET, 14 December 1972, *Dutt Papers*, p. 9–13; GoI, 'Reasons Leading to the coup', SECRET, 4/4/PP/JS/75, p. 101.

59. Dutt to Singh, TOP SECRET, 23 March 1973, *Dutt Papers*, p. 36–39; Dutt to FS, 'Record of a talk with Mr. Chittaranjan Suttar, M.P. on June 13, 1973', TOP SECRET, *Dutt Papers,* SF 67, p. 111.

60. GoI, 'Annual Report from Dacca/Chittagong', *MEA*, SECRET, 28 March 1974, HI/1011(10)74, NAI, p. 13.

61. Dutt to Haksar, TOP SECRET, 14 December 1972, *Dutt Papers*, p. 22.

62. Dacca to New Delhi, 'Summary of record of Finance Minister Tajuddin Ahmed's talk with the Indian High Commissioner at Dacca on 22.12.1972', TOP SECRET, *Haksar Papers*, 3rd instalment, SF 87, NMML, pp. 136–138.

63. Dutt to Haksar, TOP SECRET, 23 December 1972, *Haksar Papers*, 3rd instalment, SF 88, F.29/HC/72, NMML, p. 139.

64. GoI, 'Military coup in Bangladesh', SECRET, 4/4/PP/JS/75, p. 4.

65. S Mahmud Ali, *Understanding Bangladesh* (London: Hurst Publishers, 2009) pp. 55–100.

66. C Dasgupta to KPS Menon, 'Activities of extremist (Maoist) groups in Bangladesh', TOP SECRET, DAC/POL/103/14/72, 29 January 1974, *Dutt Papers*, p. 33.

67. Ibid., p. 33.

68. GoI, 'Reasons Leading to the coup', *MEA*, SECRET, 4/4/PP/JS/75, p. 100.

69. Ibid., p. 103.

70. Ibid., p. 104.

71. Ibid., p. 104.

72. Interview 35.

73. Quoted in Gupta, *Serving India*, p. 474.

74. Ibid., p. 474.

75. Ibid., pp. 478–481.

76. Dutt to FS, 'A Note on a talk with Mr. Abdul Ghaffar Chaudhury, Editor, JANAPAD, on 11.6.1974', TOP SECRET, *Dutt Papers*, p. 88.

77. Ibid., p. 88.

78. GoI, 'Political Situation in Bangladesh as on 6th Jan '73', HCI-Dacca, TOP SECRET, *Dutt Papers*, SF 67, p. 20.
79. Ibid., p. 21.
80. GoI, 'Annual Reports from Dacca/Chittagong—1974', SECRET, p. 18.
81. 'Note on developing trends in the internal situation and foreign relations of Bangladesh', TOP SECRET, 10 January 1974, *Dutt Paper*, p. 23.
82. GoI, 'Annual Reports from Dacca/Chittagong—1974', SECRET, p. 20.
83. Dutt to Haksar, TOP SECRET, 14 December 1972, No.F.29/HC/72, *Dutt Papers*, p. 23.
84. Dutt to Kewal Singh, TOP SECRET, 14 June 1974, No.F.29/HC/74, *Dutt Papers*, SF74, NMML, p. 24.
85. Dutt to Haksar, TOP SECRET, 12 September 1972, *Dutt Papers*, SF 65, p. 7.
86. Raman, *The Kaoboys of R&AW*, p. 53.
87. Khasru, *The Bangladesh Military Coup*, p. 226–260; Lifschultz, *Bangladesh*, pp.132–139.
88. GoI, 'Reasons Leading to the coup', SECRET, 4/4/PP/JS/75, p. 101.
89. Ibid., p. 103.
90. Ibid., p. 103.
91. Ibid., p. 103.
92. Ibid., p. 104.
93. Ibid., p. 103.
94. Ibid., p. 105.
95. Ibid., p. 92.
96. Ibid., p. 114.
97. GoI, 'BHC calls FS on 19/08/1975', SECRET, 4/4/PP/JS/75, pp. 95–96.
98. Ibid., pp. 95–96.
99. Ibid., 'Military coup in Bangladesh', SECRET, 4/4/PP/JS/75, p. 92.
100. Ibid., 'Reasons Leading to the coup', SECRET, 4/4/PP/JS/75, p. 115.
101. Ibid., p. 115.
102. Ibid., pp. 115–116.
103. Ibid., p. 116.
104. GoI, 'DHC J N Dixit on Bangladesh', TOP SECRET, PP(JS)4(4)/75, p. 46.
105. Ibid., p. 46.
106. USG, 'Bangladesh Coup', New Delhi to Washington D.C., 1975NEWDE11059, 16 August 1975, CONFIDENTIAL, United States National Archives and Records Administration (NARA).
107. USG, 'Intelligence Alert Memorandum: Bangladesh', SECRET, *CIA*, 8 November 1975, p. 2.
108. GoI, 'MHA: Contingency Plan to Deal with Influx from Bangladesh', SECRET, PP(JS)4(4)/75, pp. 52–61, p. 57.
109. USG, 'Intelligence Alert Memorandum: Bangladesh', SECRET, *CIA*, 8 November 1975, p. 3.
110. Ibid., p. 3.
111. GoI, 'MHA: Contingency Plan to Deal with Influx from Bangladesh', SECRET, PP(JS)4(4)/75, pp. 52–61.

112. Ibid., pp. 52–61.
113. USG, 'Indo-Bangladesh Relations', SECRET, *Wikileaks*, 1975NEWDE14274_b, 25 October 1975: https://wikileaks.org/plusd/cables/1975NEWDE14274_b. html.
114. USG, 'Intelligence Alert Memorandum: Bangladesh', 8 November 1975, p. 2.
115. USG, 'Indian Military Capabilities for Intervention in Bangladesh', *Interagency Intelligence Memorandum*, SECRET, DCI/NIO 2494/75, 26 November 1975, FOIA, p. 3.
116. Ibid., p. 3.
117. GoI, 'Agartala to New Delhi', SECRET, 4/4/PP/JS/75, p. 35.
118. Ibid., p. 35.
119. GoI, 'Das to Ajmani', TOP SECRET, 27/08/1975, 4/4/PP/JS/75, pp. 52–53.
120. Ibid., pp. 52–53.
121. Ibid., pp. 52–53.
122. Ibid., pp. 52–53.
123. 'Political Situation in Bangladesh as on 6th Jan '73', TOP SECRET, *Dutt Papers*, p. 206.
124. GoI, 'Military Coup in Bangladesh', SECRET, 4/4/PP/JS/75, p. 118.
125. Ibid., p. 119.
126. Ibid., p. 119.
127. Ibid., p. 119.
128. Ibid., p. 119.
129. Ibid., p. 119.
130. Ibid., p. 119.
131. Ibid., p. 4–5.
132. GoI, 'Das to Ajmani', TOP SECRET, 27 August 1975, 4/4/PP/JS/75, p. 49.
133. Ibid, p. 49.
134. GoI, 'Military Coup in Bangladesh', SECRET, 4/4/PP/JS/75, p. 5.
135. GoI, 'Das to Ajmani', TOP SECRET, 27 August 1975, 4/4/PP/JS/75, p. 52.
136. GoI, 'Agartala to New Delhi', SECRET, 4/4/PP/JS/75, p. 35.
137. Ibid., p. 47.
138. Ibid., p. 48.
139. Ibid., p. 47.
140. GoI, 'Sen to Singh', SECRET, 4 September 1975, 4/4/PP/JS/75, p. 78.
141. Ibid., p. 78.
142. Ibid., p. 78.
143. GoI, 'Peking to New Delhi', SECRET, 27 August 1975, 4/4/PP/JS/75, p. 67.
144. GoI, 'Riyadh to New Delhi', SECRET, 21 August 1975, 4/4/PP/JS/75, p. 60.
145. Ibid., pp. 60–62.
146. GoI, 'Dacca to New Delhi', RESTRICTED, 27 August 1975, 4/4/PP/JS/75, p. 21.
147. Ibid., pp. 23–24.
148. Ibid., pp. 23–24.

149. Ibid., p. 24.
150. Capitals as in original. GoI, 'Agartala to New Delhi', SECRET, 28 August 1975, 4/4/PP/JS/75, p. 41.
151. Ibid., p. 41.
152. Ibid., p. 35.
153. Ibid., p. 45.
154. GoI, 'Suntook to Narang', SECRET, 2 January 1976, PP(JS)4(4)/75, pp. 2–4.
155. Ibid., pp. 2–4.
156. Ibid., pp. 2–4.
157. Interview 48; GoI, 'The Bangladesh situation as seen by a Leftist press correspondent in Calcutta', TOP SECRET, PP(JS)4(4)/75, p. 36; Mahfuz Ullah, *President Zia of Bangladesh: A Political Biography* (Dhaka: Adorn Publication, 2016), p. 47–48. According to a former Indian intelligence office who worked with Suttar, he was known as the 'fat-man' and was very close to Kao and other R&AW officers until his death in New Delhi in November 2002.
158. GoI, 'Suntook to Narang', SECRET, 2 January 1976, PP(JS)4(4)/75, p. 3.
159. GoI, 'Agartala to New Delhi', SECRET, 30 August 1975, 4/4/PP/JS/75, p. 47.
160. Ibid., p. 47.
161. GoI, 'Das to Ajmani', TOP SECRET, 27 August 1975, 4/4/PP/JS/75, p. 52.
162. Ibid., p. 52.
163. GoI, 'FS on Bangladesh', SECRET, 4/4/PP/JS/75, p. 122.
164. Ibid., p. 126.
165. Ibid., p. 125.
166. Ibid., p. 125.
167. Ibid., p. 126.
168. Ibid., p. 127.
169. Ibid., p. 126.
170. USG, 'Indo-Bangladesh Relations, Farakka; Border incidents and the Majors', CONFIDENTIAL, 1976NEWDE06216_b, *Wikileaks*, 28 April 1976: https://wikileaks.org/plusd/cables/1976NEWDE06216_b.html.
171. GoI, 'FS on Bangladesh', SECRET, 4/4/PP/JS/75, p. 126.
172. Ibid., p. 126.
173. Ibid., p. 127.
174. Ibid., p. 127.
175. GoI, 'Das to Ajmani', TOP SECRET, 27 August 1975, 4/4/PP/JS/75, p. 52.
176. Interview 47.
177. GoI, 'Damodaran on Bangladesh', TOP SECRET, 23 December 1975, PP(JS)4(4)/75, pp. 27–28.
178. GoI, 'The Bangladesh situation as seen by a Leftist press correspondent in Calcutta', TOP SECRET, PP(JS)4(4)/75, p. 32.
179. Ibid., pp. 32–34.
180. Ibid., p. 34.
181. GoI, 'Political reports etc. (other than annual) from Dacca' SECRET, HI/1012(32)/75, p. 10.

182. GoI, 'The Bangladesh situation as seen by a Leftist press correspondent in Calcutta', TOP SECRET, PP(JS)4(4)/75, p. 34.

183. Ibid., p. 34.

184. William Borders, 'India's Top Aide in Dacca Wounded in Ambush by 6', *The New York Times*, 27 November 1975: https://www.nytimes.com/1975/11/27/archives/indias-top-aide-in-dacca-wounded-in-ambush-by-6.html.

185. GoI, 'Damodaran on Bangladesh', TOP SECRET, 23/12/1975, PP(JS)4(4)/75, p. 28.

186. HMG, 'Relations between Bangladesh and India', *Foreign & Commonwealth Office (FCO)*, SECRET, FCO37/1566, 10 December 1975, UK National Archives, p. 2.

187. USG, 'Indo-Bangladesh Relations', SECRET, *Wikileaks*, 1975NEWDE1427_b, 25 October 1975: https://wikileaks.org/plusd/cables/1975NEWDE14274_b.html.

188. USG, 'Indian Assessment of Bangladesh Developments', SECRET, *Wikileaks*, 1975NEWDE143838_b, 7 November 1975: https://wikileaks.org/plusd/cables/1975NEWDE14838_b.html.

189. USG, 'Intelligence Alert Memorandum: Bangladesh', SECRET, 08/11/1975, pp. 3–4.

190. GoI, 'Damodaran on Bangladesh', TOP SECRET, 23 December 1975, PP(JS)4(4)/75, p. 27.

191. Ibid., p. 27.

192. Ibid., p. 27.

193. Interview 19.

194. Ali, *Understanding Bangladesh*, pp. 137–142.

195. Ullah, *President Zia*, pp. 102–153.

196. 19-point programme: https://bnpmduk.org/19-points/.

197. Interview 37.

198. GOI, 'Chattopadhyay to Ajmani', TOP SECRET, 10 October 1975, PP(JS)4(4)/75, pp. 23–25.

199. Interview 41.

200. USG, 'General Jacob sees Situation worsening in Bangladesh', Calcutta to Washington, D.C., CONFIDENTIAL, *Wikileaks*, 22 December 1975, 1975CALCUT03019_b: https://wikileaks.org/plusd/cables/1975CALCUT-03019_b.html.

201. USG, 'Arms Policy Towards Bangladesh', Washington, D.C., to Dacca, SECRET, *Wikileaks*, 11 October 1976, 1976STATE252346_b: https://wikileaks.org/plusd/cables/1976STATE252346_b.html.

202. GoI, 'Damodaran on Bangladesh', TOP SECRET, 23 December 1975, PP(JS)4(4)/75, p. 27.

203. GoI, 'For a new policy orientation towards Bangladesh', CONFIDENTIAL, PP(JS)4(4)/75, p. 79.

204. Ibid., p. 80.

205. Ibid., p. 80.

206. Ibid., p. 80.

207. Ibid., p. 80.

208. Ibid., p. 81.

209. Ibid., pp. 81–82.

210. Ibid., p. 82.

211. Ibid., p. 82.

212. Ibid., p. 82.

213. Ibid., p. 83.

214. Ibid., p. 82.

215. 'Record of a talk with Mr. Chittaranjan Suttar, M.P. on June 13, 1973', TOP SECRET, *Dutt Papers*, pp. 111–113.

216. Dutt to FS, TOP SECRET, 27 June 1973, *Dutt Papers*, SF 67, p. 119.

217. Ibid., p. 119.

218. Ibid., p. 119.

219. GoI, 'For a new policy orientation towards Bangladesh', CONFIDENTIAL, PP(JS)4(4)/75, p. 86.

220. Ibid., p. 83.

221. Ibid., p. 85.

222. Ibid., pp. 84–88.

223. Ibid., p. 85.

224. GoI, 'Suntook to Narang', SECRET, PP(JS)4(4)/75, pp. 2–15.

225. GoI, 'Activities of Pakistani missions in Bangla Desh and Measures to Counteract them', TOP SECRET, PP(JS)4(4)/75, p. 18.

226. Ibid., p. 18.

227. Ibid., pp. 18–19.

228. Ibid., p. 19.

229. Nibedon, *Mizoram*, pp. 175–176.

230. GoI, 'Activities of Pakistani missions in Bangla Desh and Measures to Counteract them', TOP SECRET, PP(JS)4(4)/75, p. 20.

231. Ibid., p. 21.

232. Ibid., p. 21.

233. Ibid. Even in Pakistan, the security situation worsened, with R&AW actively supporting Baloch and Pashtun dissidents through Afghanistan. For more on this, see Avinash Paliwal, *My Enemy's Enemy: India in Afghanistan from the Soviet Invasion to the US Withdrawal* (New York: Oxford University Press, 2017).

234. Interviews 45 and 48.

235. GoI, 'Activities of Pakistani missions in Bangla Desh and Measures to Counteract them', TOP SECRET, PP(JS)4(4)/75, p. 21.

236. Samar Sen, India's high commissioner in Dacca, authored a similar assessment in December 1975, shortly after being wounded in a targeted attack against him in Dacca. 'The country is going through a series of adjustments with shifting loyalties, emerging personalities, and many foreign influences at work', noted Sen. GOI, 'Dacca to New Delhi', SECRET, PP(JS)4(4)/75, p. 38.

237. Ullah, *President Zia*, pp. 47–48.

238. USG, 'Indians Profess they are calm and cool about Bangladesh', SECRET, 1976NEWDE11732_b, *Wikileaks*, 10 August 1976: https://wikileaks.org/plusd/cables/1976NEWDE11732_b.html.

239. USG, 'Alleged Indian Activities against Bangladesh', SECRET, 19766DACCA04054_b, *Wikileaks*, 9 August 1976: https://wikileaks.org/plusd/cables/1976DACCA04054_b.html.

240. GoI, 'Settlement of Chakma Refugees', *MHA*, SECRET, 13024/5/73AP, 24/04/1980, NAI, pp. 8–15.

241. USG, 'Alleged Indian Activities against Bangladesh', SECRET, 19766DACCA04054_b.

242. Ibid.

243. Ullah, *President Zia*, p. 48.

244. Bhaumik, *Troubled Frontiers*, pp. 165–166.

245. Ibid., pp. 165–166.

246. Ullah, *President Zia*, p. 47.

247. Interview 48.

248. GoI, 'Farakka', *MEA*, SECRET, HI/103(9)176, 5 October 1976, pp. 2–4.

249. Ibid., pp. 5–8.

250. Quoted in Ullah, *President Zia*, p. 49.

251. Raman, *The Kaoboys of R&AW*, pp. 54–61.

252. 'Bangladesh says it has put down an armed coup', *The New York Times*, 2 October 1977, https://www.nytimes.com/1977/10/02/archives/bangladesh-says-it-has-put-down-an-armed-coup-59-freed-by-hijackers.html.

253. NMJ, 'Murder in Dacca: Ziaur Rahman's Second Round', *Economic & Political Weekly*, 13(12), 25 March 1978, pp. 551–558.

254. Text of Agreement: https://treaties.un.org/doc/Publication/UNTS/Volume%201066/volume-1066-I-16210-English.pdf.

255. Ullah, *President Zia*, p. 301.

256. 'Bangladesh says 561 military men hanged after 1977 cop attempt', *United Press of India*, 24 May 1988, https://www.upi.com/Archives/1988/05/24/Bangladesh-says-561-military-men-hanged-after-1977-coup-attempt/5405580449600/.

257. India: Bangladesh President Ziaur Rahman arrives in India on major international tour, 1977, *British Pathe*: https://www.britishpathe.com/video/VLVADR0F594UJX0U3QF9BS6PXW2C4-INDIA-BANGLADESH-PRESIDENT-ZIAUR-RAHMAN-ARRIVES-IN-INDIA-ON/query/Rahman.

258. Quoted in Ullah, *President Zia*, p. 298.

259. Ibid., p. 300.

260. Ibid., pp. 321–322.

261. GoI, 'Minister of External Affairs P. V. Narasimha Rao's Speech on the Demands for Grants 1981-82', *LSD*, 3 April 1981, FAR 1981.

262. Ibid.

263. 'Kazi Anwarul Huque, Minister of Power, Water Resources and Flood Control, Government of the People's Republic of Bangladesh, on Review Meeting of the Ganges Waters Agreement in New Delhi', 7-9 January 1981, FAR 1981.

264. GoI, 'Minister of External Affairs P. V. Narasimha Rao's Speech on the Demands for Grants 1981-82', *LSD*, 3 April 1981, FAR 1981.

265. GoI, 'Monthly record of events from Dacca, 1981', *MEA*, SECRET, FIII/1012(23)/81, NAI, p. 63.

266. GoI, 'Note on 'Coup in Bangladesh' prepared by Cabinet Secretariat', *MEA*, SECRET, FIII/103(11)/82, *Damodaran Papers*, NAI, p. 5.

267. Ibid., p. 5.

268. Ibid., p. 5.

269. Ibid., p. 5.

270. Ibid., p. 5.

271. 'Statement by the Minister of External Affairs, Shri P. V. Narasimha Rao, in both the Houses of Parliament on the situation in Bangladesh:', 25 March 1982, FAR 1982.

272. GoI, 'Indo-Bangladesh Joint Press Statement', *MEA*, 23 May 1982, FAR.

273. GoI, 'Joint Press Release issued after the 22nd meeting of the Indo-Bangladesh Joint Rivers Commission', *MEA*, 27- 31/081982, FAR.

274. GoI, 'Prime Minister Indira Gandhi's Speech at Dinner for Lt. Gen. Ershad Following is the text of the speech by the Prime Minister, Smt. Indira Gandhi, at the dinner she hosted in honour of Lt. Gen. H. M. Ershad, President of the Council of Ministers of Bangladesh, in New Delhi', *MEA*, 6 October 1982, FAR.

275. 'Text of Bangladesh President's Speech', MEA, 6 October 1982, FAR, p. 248.

276. Interview 47.

277. Interview 48.

278. Ibid.

279. Ibid.

280. GoI, 'Coup in Bangladesh', SECRET, FIII/103(11)/82, p. 5.

281. Ibid., p. 1.

282. Ibid., p. 2.

283. GoI, 'Monthly record of events from Dacca, 1981', *MEA*, SECRET, FIII/1012(23)/81, NAI, p. 166.

284. GoI, 'Coup in Bangladesh', SECRET, FIII/103(11)/82, p. 3.

285. Ibid., p. 3.

286. 'Full Transcript of Bangladesh PM Sheikh Hasina's interview with ANI', *Asia News International,* 4 September 2022: https://www.aninews.in/news/national/general-news/full-transcript-of-bangladesh-pm-sheikh-hasinas-interview-with-ani20220904131433/.

287. GoI, 'Monthly record of events from Dacca, 1981', p. 81.

288. Ibid., p. 69.

289. Ibid., p. 163.

290. Ibid., pp. 81–82.

291. GoI, 'New Moore Island: Proposal for effective and safe movement of BSF troops during Monsoon', *MHA*, 1981, VI-12020/7/81-GSQ, SECRET, NAI, pp. 4–5.

292. Ibid., pp. 4–5.

293. Interview 46.

294. Interview 30.
295. Interview 48.
296. GoI, 'Shri P. V. Narasimha Rao in Rajya Sabha on Mar 04, 1982, on the recent incident in Dacca involving the Indian High Commissioner and Bangladesh security personnel', *MEA*, 4 March 2981, FAR; 'March 2, 1982: Forty Years Ago: Indira on Opposition', *Indian Express*: https://indianexpress.com/article/opinion/editorials/march-2-1982-forty-years-ago-indira-on-opposition-7796585/.

8. ENABLING DEMOCRACY

1. GoI, 'Official Spokesman's Statements', MEA, 10 September 1988: http://mealib.nic.in/?pdf2576?000
2. Congress won 404 of 514 seats; 1985 Election Results: https://www.elections.in/parliamentary-constituencies/1985-election-results.html.
3. For more, see, Hasan, *Congress After Indira*, p.1-95; Atul Kohli, 'India's Democracy Under Rajiv Gandhi, 1985–1989', in Atul Kohli ed. *India's Democracy: An Analysis of Changing State-Society Relations* (Princeton, NJ: Princeton University Press, 1990).
4. N Manoharan, 'Brothers, Not Friends: India-Sri Lanka Relations', *South Asian Survey*, 18(2), 2011, pp. 225-238.
5. Amar N. Ram ed. *Two Decades of India's Look East Policy: Partnership for Peace, Progress, and Prosperity* (New Delhi: Indian Council of World Affairs, 2012).
6. Preet Malik, *My Myanmar Years: A Diplomat's Account of India's Relations with the Region* (New Delhi: Sage Publishers, 2015) p. 61.
7. Quoted in Maung Maung, *The 1988 Uprising in Burma* (Yale University Press, 2000) pp. 255–56.
8. GoI, 'Annual Reports etc. from Rangoon', *MEA*, SECRET, HI/1011/(11)/77-I, National Archives of India (NAI), 1976, p. 7.
9. Ibid., p. 7.
10. GoI, 'Annual Reports etc. from E.I. Rangoon for 1977', *MEA*, SECRET, HI/1011/11/78-I, NAI, 1978, p. 22.
11. Ibid., p. 23.
12. GoI, 'The present situation and future trends in Burma', *MEA*, SECRET, 7 May 1983, NAI, p. 20.
13. Ibid., p. 21.
14. This is based on the MEA's Foreign Affairs Record: https://mealib.nic.in/?2588?000.
15. TP Sreenivasan, *Words,Words,Words: Adventures in Diplomacy* (New Delhi: Longman, 2011) p. 60.
16. Interview 52.
17. Ibid.
18. Ibid.
19. Ibid.
20. Myoe, *In the Name of Pauk-Phaw,* pp. 100–102.

21. 'Shri Khurshed Alam Khan's intervention in the debate in the Lok Sabha on demands for grants of the Ministry of External Affairs and reply by the Prime Minister, Shri Rajiv Gandhi', *MEA*, 9-10 April 1985, FAR.
22. 'Shri K. R. Narayanan, Minister of State in the Ministry of External Affairs in the debate on the demands for grants 1986-87, in the Lok Sabha on Mar 21, 1986, and reply to the debate, by Shri B. R. Bhagat, *MEA*, 24 March 1986, FAR.
23. Ibid.
24. 'Joint press release on the Maritime Boundary Delimitation Agreement between Burma and India in Rangoon', *MEA*, 23 December 1986, FAR.
25. 'Shri Rajiv Gandhi's message on the occasion of the presentation of manuscripts of Gen. Mahabandoola to the Burmese President, Mr. San Yu in Rangoon', *MEA*, 15 December 1987, FAR.
26. Malik, *My Myanmar Years,* pp. 75–76.
27. 'Indo-Burmese Trade Talks', *MEA*, 8 February 1988, FAR.
28. Based on the 1985 dollar-rupee exchange rate of US$1=INR12.37.
29. GoI, 'Indo-Burma Trade Talks Conclude', *MEA*, 8 February 1988: https://mealib.nic.in/?pdf2576?000.
30. 'Strengthening of bilateral cultural relations between India and Burma', *MEA*, 5 April 1988, FAR.
31. GOI, Official Spokesman's Statements, *MEA*, 10 September 1988, FAR, https://mealib.nic.in/?pdf2576?000.
32. Interview 53.
33. Ibid.
34. Ibid.
35. Ibid.
36. 'Official Spokesman', *MEA*, 5 October 1988, FAR.
37. Interview 55.
38. GoI, 'Meeting of the Consultative Committee of Parliament attached to MFA', *MEA*, 5 December 1988, FAR.
39. Interview 1.
40. Ibid.
41. Ibid.
42. Ibid.
43. Ibid.
44. Christina Fink, *Living Silence in Burma: Surviving Under the Military Rule* (London: Zed Books, 2009).
45. James J Lum Dau, *An autobiography of my life experience in the service of KIO-KIA revolutionary movement* (Yunnan: Kachin Research Society Publication, 2015) pp. 200–201.
46. Ibid., p. 202.
47. Naphaw Kaw Mai, *Maran Brang Seng: A Biography* (unpublished) p. 272. Compiled by Brang Seng's wife, this diary offers rare insight into the KIO leader's official and personal life. This material was accessed through and translated from Kachin to English by the Kachinland Research Centre (KRC) in Myitkyina, Myanmar.

48. Interviews 7, 8, and 22; Kaw Mai, *Maran Brang Seng*, p. 325; Lum Dau, *An Autobiography*, pp. 200–201.
49. Lum Dau, *An autobiography of my life*, p. 144.
50. Brang Seng despatched a KIO officer to Arunachal with four jade stones (weighing over 700kgs) and ten imperial jade stones (weighing over 1,000kgs) to explore demand. Six KIO officers were allowed to study at Indian universities. Kaw Mai, *Maran Brang Seng*, p. 263.
51. Though the Nagas enjoyed a relationship with the KIO since the 1960s, the ULFA developed a partnership only in 1987. GoI, National Investigation Agency Charge-Sheet, NIA Case Number: RC-04/2013/NIA-GUW, 2017 (main accused: Paresh Baruah, SS Commander-in-Chief of ULFA—I).
52. Kaw Mai, *Maran Brang Seng*, p. 225–229; Lum Dau, *An autobiography*, p. 146.
53. Kaw Mai, *Maran Brang Seng*, p. 263. This was a huge shift, for in November 1989, Lum Dau visited the ageing patriarch of the Naga movement, A Z Phizo, in London and reaffirmed the KIO's commitment towards the Naga cause, Lum Dau, *An autobiography*, p. 145.
54. The NSCN-IM cadre left after a proper farewell ceremony where Brang Seng gifted them ten rifles including the Heckler and Koch G3 and G4 types, as well as a Bren gun. Kaw Mai, *Maran Brang Seng*, p. 287.
55. Ibid., p. 263.
56. Ahmed, Farzand. 'Various army operations launched against ULFA', *India Today*, 15 October 1991, https://www.indiatoday.in/magazine/special-report/story/19911015-various-army-operations-launched-against-ulfa-814916-1991-10-15.
57. Martin Smith and Larry Jagan, 'Maran Brang Seng: In His Own Words' *Burma Debate*, 1 (3), Dec 1994/Jan 1995, p. 17.
58. Kaw Mai, *Maran Brang Seng*, p. 272.
59. Lintner, *The Rise and Fall of the Communist Party of Burma*, pp. 34–46.
60. Less than a week before his meeting with the Indian prime minister, Brang Seng received reports that the KIO's 4th brigade, stationed in Shan state, broke away in face of Tatmadaw offensives and entered peace talks. The splinter group rebranded itself as the Kachin Defense Army and became a pro-Tatmadaw border guard force with stakes in Tatmadaw-controlled businesses involved in licit and illicit cross-border trade. This was the second such shock to the KIO. In 1989, the disintegration of the CPB triggered an already splintered group to sign a ceasefire with the Tatmadaw within Kachin state. After having split from the KIO in 1968, this group rebranded itself as the New Democratic Army-Kachin (NDA-K), and from 1989, under the Tatmadaw's patronage, became a well-armed local rival of the KIO. Kaw Mai, *Maran Brang Seng*, p. 272; Nicholas Farrelly, 'Ceasing Ceasefire? Kachin Politics Beyond the Stalemate', in Nick Cheesman, Monique Skidmore, & Trevor Wilson eds. Myanmar's Transition: Openings, Obstacles, and Opportunities (Singapore: ISEAS Publishing, 2012) pp. 52–71; Vanda Felbab-Brown, 'Organized Crime, Illicit Economies, Civil Violence, & International Order: More Complex Than You Think', *Daedalus*,

146 (4), October 2017, pp. 98–111; Callahan, *Making Enemies*, pp. 42–45; Brenner, *Rebel Politics*, p. 78.

61. Interview 2; Subir Bhaumik, *Troubled Periphery: Crisis of India's North East* (New Delhi: Sage Publishers, 2006) p. 175; Brenner, *Rebel Politics*, p. 78.

62. Kaw Mai, *Maran Brang Seng*, p. 289.

63. No Than Kap, *Ram Hrang Ruat In*, 42; The KIO agreed to train 82 CNF cadre in 1990 over a period of two years.

64. Interview 8.

65. Ibid.

66. Ibid.

67. Kap, *Ram Hrang Ruat In*, pp. 63–65.

68. Interview 8.

69. Kap, *Ram Hramg Ruat In*, p. 50.

70. Ibid., p. 50.

71. Ibid., p. 50.

72. Ibid., p. 50.

73. Ibid., pp. 82–89.

74. Interview 38.

75. Interview 36.

76. GoI, 'Reply by Prime Minister Shri Rajiv Gandhi during Debate in the Lok Sabha on Demands for Grants of the Ministry of External Affairs', 9-10 April 1985, FAR.

77. GoI, 'Prime Minister Indira Gandhi's Speech at Dinner for Lt. Gen. Ershad', *MEA*, 6 October 1982, FAR.

78. GoI, 'Indo-Bangladesh Ministerial Level Meeting', *MEA*, 22 November 1985, FAR.

79. GoI, 'Minister of External Affairs, in the Lok Sabha in connection with debate on demands of grants of the MEA', 23 April 1987, FAR.

80. GoI, 'Approach paper on India, Nepal, and Bangladesh: Approach to Water Resource Development—Note Circulated by Ministry of Water Resources Development', *MHA*, SECRET, CF-3269333, 6 August 1987, NAI, p. 11.

81. Interview 38.

82. Ibid.

83. Ibid.

84. GoI, 'Training to Tribal Extremists from Tripura in Bangladesh', *Lok Sabha Questions (LSQ)*, 15 December 1983, pp. 115–116.

85. GoI, 'Re Decision of Bangladesh government to Sell Properties of Indians in Bangladesh', *LSQ*, Written Answers, 15 December 1983, pp. 291–292.

86. GoI, 'Clearance of the Claims of Indians from Bangladesh Regarding their Property', *LSQ*, 10 August 1984, pp. 10–15.

87. GOI, 'Smuggling on Indo-Bangladesh and parts of Indo-Burma border', *MHA*, SECRET, VI.12015/2/S1-GsQ, 5 April 1983, NAI, p. 144.

88. Raman, *Kaoboys of R&AW*, p. 191.

89. GoI, 'Barbed wire fencing along Indo-Bangladesh Border', *LSQ*, Written Answers, 4 December 1985, pp. 117–118.

90. GoI, 'Resistance by Bangladesh for Erection of Fence', *LSQ*, 10 April 1985, p. 20.
91. Ibid., p. 21.
92. Ibid., p. 21.
93. Ibid., p. 22.
94. GoI, 'Fencing along Indo-Bangla Border', *LSQ*, 07/08/1987, pp. 219–220.
95. Ibid., pp. 219–220.
96. GoI, 'Chakma refugees', *LSQ*, 22 March 1990, p. 267.
97. GoI, 'Material for Finance Minister's speech for 1991-92 budget', *MHA*, CONFIDENTIAL, 1/3/91-NE-II, 6 February 1991, NAI, p. 7.
98. GoI, 'Demonstration in Front of Bangladesh Visa Office in Agartala', *LSQ*, 3 May 1990, pp. 283–284.
99. Krishnan Srinivasan, *The Jamdani Revolution: Politics, Personalities, and Civil Society in Bangladesh 1989–1992* (New Delhi: Har-Anand Publishers, 2008) p. 234.
100. Srinivasan, *The Jamdani Revolution,* p. 264.
101. Interview 38.
102. Ibid.
103. Interview 20.
104. GoI, 'Statement: Official Spokesman', *MEA*, 1 January 1988, FAR.
105. Srinivasan, *The Jamdani Revolution,* p. 121.
106. Ibid., p. 123.
107. GoI, 'Press Release: Annual Report of Ministry of Defence', *MOD*, 17 April 1989, FAR.
108. Srinivasan, *The Jamdani Revolution,* p. 232.
109. Ibid., p. 232.
110. GoI, 'Statement: Official Spokesman', *MEA*, 28 November 1990, FAR.
111. Ibid.
112. Srinivasan, *The Jamdani Revolution,* p. 240.
113. Interview 38.
114. Ibid.
115. Srinivasan, *The Jamdani Revolution,* p. 241.
116. GoI, 'Statement: Official Spokesman', *MEA*, 5 December 1990, FAR 1990.
117. Srinivasan, *The Jamdani Revolution,* p. 316.
118. A S Dulat, *A Life in the Shadows: A Memoir* (New Delhi: HarperCollins India, 2022) p. 82.
119. Srinivasan, *The Jamdani Revolution,* p. 267.
120. Ibid., p. 260.
121. Ibid., p. 268.
122. Ibid., p. 264.
123. Interview 47.
124. Interview 46.
125. GoI, 'Statement: Official Spokesman', *MEA*, 28 February 1991, FAR.
126. GoI, 'Statement: Official Spokesman', *MEA*, 7 March 1991, FAR.
127. Srinivasan, *The Jamdani Revolution,* p. 271.
128. Ibid., p. 271.

129. Ibid., p. 273.
130. Ibid., p. 274.
131. Barbara Crossette, 'General's Widow Wins Bangladesh Vote', *New York Times*, 1 March 1991. https://www.nytimes.com/1991/03/01/world/general-s-widow-wins-bangladesh-vote.html.
132. Years later, senior BNP leaders accused R&AW for orchestrating Zia-ur-Rahman's assassination but didn't offer any evidence. 'Rizvi: RAW was behind Zia's death', *Dhaka Tribune*, 16 March 2017: https://www.dhakatribune.com/bangladesh/politics/2017/03/16/rizvi-raw-behind-zias-death; interviews 19 and 20.
133. Khaleda Zia appointed Wahidul Haque as DG-NSI in 1991. He would later be convicted on charges of war crimes during the 1971 war. 'War Crimes in 1971: Former NSI chief's trial next month', *Daily Star*, 17 October 2019.
134. GoI, National Investigation Agency Charge-Sheet, 26/03/2011 (prime accused: Anthony Shimray, Self-Styled Commander-in-Chief of the Naga Army), pp. 6–17.
135. Ibid., pp. 6–17.
136. Ibid., pp. 6–17.
137. Ibid., pp. 6–17.
138. Interview 54.
139. GoI, 'Official Statement: Consultative Committee Meeting', *MEA*, 17 December 1991, FAR.
140. Ibid.
141. Interview 52.
142. Interview 54.
143. Interview 1.
144. GoI, 'Statement: Official Spokesman', *MEA*, 5 December 1988, FAR.
145. GoI, 'Talks with Myanmar Regarding insurgent activity', *LSQ*, 5 September 1991, pp. 63–64.
146. Sreeradha Datta, 'Bangladesh's Relations with China and India: A Comparative Study', *Strategic Analysis*, 32(5), 2008, pp. 755–772.
147. Ibid., p. 762.

9. HARD LOOK EAST

1. GoI, 'Message from the External Affairs Minister to Her Excellency Sheikh Hasina Wajed, Prime Minister of Bangladesh', *MEA*, 25 June 1996.
2. Vinay Sitapati, *Half-Lion: How Narasimha Transformed India* (New Delhi: Penguin Viking, 2016).
3. 'Bangladesh Parliament Passes Resolution on Ayodhya', *MEA*, 22 January 1993.
4. Mahadevan, 'Crossing the Line', pp. 3–7.
5. Vanda Felbab-Brown, 'The Political Economy of Illegal Domains in India and China', *The International Lawyer*, 43(4), Winter 2009, pp. 1411–1428; Renaud Egreteau, 'Instability at the Gate: India's Troubled Northeast and its External

Connections', *CSH Occasional Paper No. 16*, (New Delhi: Centre de Sciences Humaines, 2006).

6. Vaishnav, *When Crime Pays*, pp. 13–23.
7. Balachandran, 'The Rao Breakthrough', *Indian Express*, 20 August 2015.
8. Lakhan Mehrotra, 'India's Look East Policy: Its Origin and Development', *Indian Foreign Affairs Journal*, 7(1), January-March 2012, p. 76.
9. Bhatia, *India-Myanmar Relations*, p. 101.
10. Interview 52.
11. Ibid.
12. Interview 10.
13. Malik, *My MyanmarYears,* pp. 63–64.
14. Ibid., pp. 66–67.
15. Ibid., p. 79.
16. Ibid., p. 79.
17. Interview 9.
18. Interview 55.
19. Malik, *My MyanmarYears*, p. 92.
20. Ibid., p. 69.
21. Ibid., p. 93.
22. Ibid., p. 93.
23. The Zokhawthar-Rikhawdar (Mizoram) crossing opened shortly after.
24. GoI, 'Visit of the Deputy Foreign Minister of Myanmar to India', *MEA*, 21 January 1994, FAR.
25. GoI, 'Second Indo-Myanmar National Level Meeting', *MEA*, 16 August 1995, FAR.
26. Interview 52.
27. Interview 4.
28. Interview 21.
29. Ibid.
30. Interview 52.
31. Interview 58.
32. Ibid.
33. Ibid.
34. Ibid.
35. Kanishk Kanodia, 'Are India's oil investments in Myanmar an act of support to its military?', *Quartz*, 23 March 2022, https://qz.com/india/2144291/is-india-supporting-myanmar-military-through-oil-investments.
36. Interviews 59, 62.
37. C Christine Fair and Seth Oldmixon, 'Think Again: Islamism and Militancy in Bangladesh', *The National Interest*, 13 August 2015, https://nationalinterest.org/feature/think-again-islamism-militancy-bangladesh-13567.
38. Srinivasan, *Jamdani Revolution*, pp. 316–317.
39. Ibid., p. 317.
40. Ibid., pp. 317–318.

41. Ibid., p. 322.
42. Ibid., p. 322.
43. Ibid., p. 322.
44. GoI, 'Statement on Tin Bigha', *LSQ*, 26 March 1992, FAR.
45. Srinivasan, *Jamdani Revolution*, p. 338.
46. GoI, 'Banquet in Honour of Bangladesh Premier—Prime Minister's Speech', *MEA*, 26 May 1992, FAR, p. 173.
47. GoI, 'Visit of Begum Khaleda Zia of Bangladesh', *MEA*, 22 May 1992, FAR.
48. Soutik Biswas, 'Chakma refugees fear renewed 'inhuman torture' on return to Bangladesh', *India Today*, 15 July 1993, https://www.indiatoday.in/magazine/indiascope/story/19930715-chakma-refugees-fear-renewed-inhuman-torture-on-return-to-bangladesh-811312-1993-07-14.
49. GoI, 'IRCON bags new road projects in Bangladesh', *MEA*, 1 February 1993, FAR.
50. GoI, 'Indo-Bangladesh Cooperation in Railway Transit Sector', *MEA*, 10 May 1993, FAR.
51. GoI, 'Bangladesh Foreign Minister's Visit to India', *MEA*, 12 June 1993, FAR, p. 189.
52. Srinivasan, *Jamdani Revolution*, p. 257.
53. GoI, 'Communal Incidents Affecting Indians in Pakistan and Bangladesh', *MEA*, 15 December 1992, FAR.
54. Ibid.
55. GoI, 'Move to organise a march to Ayodhya by some Bangladeshis', *MEA*, 4 January 1993, FAR.
56. GoI, 'Bangladesh Parliament Passes Resolution on Ayodhya', *MEA*, 22 January 1993, FAR.
57. Ibid.
58. GoI, 'Official Statement: Bangladesh', *MEA*, 8 October 1993, FAR.
59. GoI, 'Resolution Re. Repatriation of Illegal Immigrants', *LSD*, 8 March 1996, pp. 295–96.
60. Ibid., pp. 297–302.
61. Ibid., pp. 295–296.
62. GoI, 'Formation of a Caretaker Government in Bangladesh', *MEA*, 3 April 1996, FAR.
63. GoI, 'Message from the External Affairs Minister to Her Excellency Sheikh Hasina Wajed, Prime Minister of Bangladesh', *MEA*, 25 June 1996.
64. GoI, 'Transit Facilities through Bangladesh', *LSQ*, Written Answers, 22 July 1996, p. 91.
65. GoI, 'Dawki Amabil Transborder Trade Route', *LSQ*, Written Answers, 22 July 1996, p. 34.
66. Brenner, *Rebel Politics*, p. 78; James Lum Dau was KIO's deputy chief of foreign affairs and played a central role in the KIO Central Committee's (CC) decision-making. He helped convince Brang Seng and the KIO-CC to sign the ceasefire agreement in 1994. Relevant sections of his autobiography were translated by the Kachinland Research Centre and Hkanhpa Sadan.

67. Soe Myint, *Burma File: A Question of Democracy* (New Delhi: India Research Press, 2003) p. 290.
68. Ibid., p. 291.
69. Interview 8.
70. Ibid.; Myint, *Burma File*, 291.
71. Myint, *Burma File*, 291.
72. Ibid., 348–9.
73. Interview 7.
74. Nandita Haksar, *Rogue Agent: How India's Military Intelligence Betrayed the Burmese Resistance* (New Delhi: Penguin, 2009) p. 41.
75. Ibid., p. 42.
76. Ibid., p. 42.
77. Bhaumik, *Troubled Frontiers*, pp. 176–7.
78. Ibid.; the Coco Island issue was not a serious one at this point in time as per Indian defence officials (Interview 21).
79. Saw Tun, 'Personal Diary', *India-Myanmar Papers (NUPA)*, International Institute of Social History (IISH), Amsterdam, February 2018. Translated from Arakanese and Burmese to English by Kyaw Minn Htin (SOAS).
80. Ibid.
81. Interview 7; Haksar, *Rogue Agent*, p. 160–84; Bhaumik, 'Guns, drugs, and rebels', 2005.
82. Interview 56.
83. Haksar, *Rogue Agent*, p. 141.
84. Ibid., pp. 122–42.
85. Interview 14.
86. Interview 7.
87. Interview 25.
88. Nitin Gokhale, 'George Catches a Chill', *Outlook India*, 17 April 2000, https://www.outlookindia.com/magazine/story/george-catches-a-chill/209239.
89. Frances Harrison, 'Bangladesh Peace Treaty Signed', *BBC News*, 2 December 1997: http://news.bbc.co.uk/1/hi/despatches/36256.stm.
90. Interview 20.
91. GoI, 'Statement by Prime Minister: Signing of Ganga Water Treaty with Bangladesh', *LS Committee Reports*, 12 December 1996, pp. 253–258.
92. Ibid., p. 257.
93. Bangladesh, Parliamentary Chamber: Jatiya Sangsad, Elections 1996: http://archive.ipu.org/parline-e/reports/arc/2023_96.htm.
94. Interview 38.
95. Ruben Banerjee, 'Back to Strife', *India Today*, 6 October 1997, https://www.indiatoday.in/magazine/neighbours/story/19971006-bangladesh-prime-minister-sheikh-hasina-fails-to-deliver-on-economic-front-oppositions-step-up-political-offensive-830663-1997-10-05.
96. Ibid.
97. Interview 45.

98. Ibid.
99. Ibid.
100. GoI, National Investigation Agency Charge-Sheet, 26 March 2011 (prime accused: Anthony Shimray, Self-Styled Commander-in-Chief of the Naga Army) pp. 6–17.
101. 'Anup Chetia sent back after 18 yrs', *The Daily Star*, 12 November 2015: https://www.thedailystar.net/frontpage/anup-chetia-sent-india-after-18-yrs-171148.
102. Interview 45.
103. Ibid.
104. GoI, 'Extradition of Anup Chetia, General Secretary ULFA', *MEA*, 30 June 1998, FAR.
105. GoI, 'Discussion Under Rule 193: Recent Developments Affecting India's Foreign Policy', *LSD*, 3 August 1998, pp. 75–76.
106. Interview 60.
107. GoI, 'Trade with Neighbouring Countries', *LSQ*, Written Answers, 9 May 1997, pp. 243–244.
108. GoI, 'Stronger Economic Ties with SAARC Countries', *LSQ*, Written Answers, 4 March 1999, p. 1061.
109. GoI, 'Transportation of Goods', *LSQ*, Written Answers, 4 March 1999, p. 1050.
110. GoI, 'Talks with Bangladesh', *LSQ*, Written Answers, 4 March 1999, p. 1060.
111. GoI, 'Resolution Re: Illegal Immigrants', *LSD*, 28 February 1997, pp. 236–252.
112. Ibid., p. 243.
113. Ibid., p. 257.
114. Ibid., p. 257.
115. GoI, 'Private Member's Resolution', *LSD*, 9 May 1997, p. 319.
116. Ibid., p. 319.
117. Ibid., p. 321.
118. Udayan Namboodiri, Sayanatan Chakravarty, Avirook Sen, 'Shiv Sena-BJP govt launches operation in Mumbai to push illegal Bangladeshi migrants back', *India Today*, 10 August 1998, https://www.indiatoday.in/magazine/nation/story/19980810-shiv-sena-bjp-govt-launches-operation-in-mumbai-to-push-illegal-bangladeshi-immigrants-back-826862-1998-06-09.
119. Ibid.
120. GoI, 'Discussion Under Rule 193: Deportation of certain people by Maharashtra Government', *LSD*, 3 August 1998, pp. 139–140.
121. Ibid., p. 140.
122. Celia W. Dugger, '16 Indian Soldiers Are Victims in Bangladesh Border Skirmish', *NYT*, 26 April 2001, https://www.nytimes.com/2001/04/26/world/16-indian-soldiers-are-victims-in-bangladesh-border-skirmish.html.
123. GoI, 'Regarding recent incidents at India-Bangladesh border', *LSD*, 23 April 2001.
124. Ibid.
125. Ibid.
126. Balachandran, 'The Rao Breakthrough', 20 August 2015.

127. Interview 4.
128. Ibid.
129. Ibid.
130. Ibid.
131. GoI, Nehru to Pandit, 24 June 1960, Pvt. & Confidential, *VLP Papers*, File No. 61, Nehru Memorial Museum and Library (NMML), pp. 304–305.
132. Interviews 14, 59.
133. Interview 4.
134. Balachandran, 'The Rao Breakthrough', 20 August 2015.
135. Ibid.
136. Shalaka Thakur & Rajesh Venugopal, 'Parallel Governance and political order in contested territory: Evidence from the Indo-Naga ceasefire', *Asian Security*, 15(3), 2019, p. 293.
137. GoI, 'Smuggling of Heroin', *LSQ*, Written Answers, 28 February 1997, p. 111.
138. Other routes included (ibid., p. 112)
   (a) Mandalay-Tiddim-Behiang-Singhat-Churachadpur-Imphal,
   (b) Mandalay-Tiddim-Champhai-Aizawl-Silcher-Gauhati-Calcutta,
   (c) Layshi-Meluri (Nagaland)-Jessami-Kohima,
   (d) Singkaling   Hkamti/Homalin/Tamanthi-Noklak-Tuensang-Mokokchung-Dimapur
   (e) Kalemyo-Champhai-Aizawl,
   (f) Paletwa-Alikadam (Bangladesh)-Cox's Bazar/Chittagong,
   (g) Pamsat (Myanmar)-Tusom   Christian-Tusumkhullen-Kharasom-Ukhrul/Jessami-Kohima-Tuensang-Mokokchung-Jorhat,
   (h) Kultuk (Myanmar)-Chassad-Kamjong-Jessami-Dimapur via Kohima,
   (i) Kultuk (Myanmar)-Chassad-Kamjong-Imphal-Silchar/Dimapur,
   (j) Kalemyo (Myanmar)-Malcham-Joupi-Chakpikarong-Sengnu-Kakching-Imphal,
   (k) Kalemyo-Jangdung-Sajiktampak-Singhew-Chakpikarong-Sengna-Imphal/Churachandpur
139. Malik, *My Myanmar Years*, p. 93.
140. S Mangi Singh, 'Understanding Conflict: An Insight into the Factors responsible for the Kuki-Naga Clashes in Manipur during the 1990s', *The Indian Journal of Political Science*, 70(2), April–June, 2009, pp. 495–508.
141. Full Text, NDPS Act 1985: https://legislative.gov.in/sites/default/files/A1985-61.pdf.
142. GoI, 'Calling Attention to a matter of urgent public importance', 7 August 1985, *LSD*, p. 274.
143. Ibid., p. 274.
144. GoI, 'Narcotic Drugs and Pyschotropic Substances (Amendment) Bill', *LSD*, 16 December 1988, p. 43.
145. Ibid., p. 112.
146. GoI, 'Smuggling of Gold and Heroin', *LSQ*, 19 March 1993, pp. 197–198.
147. Ibid., pp. 197–198.

148. GoI, Annual Report 2002, *Narcotics Control Bureau* (NCB), p. 2; GoI, Annual Report 2020, *NCB*, p. 21.
149. UNODC, Drug Prices: https://dataunodc.un.org/dp-drug-prices.
150. Calculated using the GoI, 'Month Wise and State Wise Details of Seizures of Drugs Since Jan 2018 to May 2023, *NCB*: https://narcoticsindia.nic.in/index.php#About-section.
151. UNODC, Drug Prices: https://dataunodc.un.org/dp-drug-prices.
152. Interview 26.
153. Interview 24.
154. Interview 61.
155. Ibid.
156. Interviews 26, 27.
157. Kishalay Bhattacharjee, 'Colonel arrested for smuggling Gold: Extortion by Armed Forces isn't New in the North East', *The Wire*, 6 May 2016: https://thewire.in/security/colonel-arrested-for-smuggling-gold-extortion-by-armed-forces-isnt-new-in-the-north-east.
158. Interview 61.
159. Ibid.
160. Raghu Karnad and Grace Jajo, 'Confessions of a killer policeman', *The Guardian*, 21 July 2016, https://www.theguardian.com/world/2016/jul/21/confessions-of-a-killer-policeman-india-manipur; Kishalay Bhattacharjee, *Blood on my Hands: Confessions of Staged Encounters* (New Delhi: HarperCollins India, 2015).
161. Sunil Narula, 'More importance Has Been Attached to The Prize To Suu Kyi than Bilateral Relations: Interview with U Wynn Lwin', *Outlook India*, 27 December 1995: https://www.outlookindia.com/magazine/story/more-importance-has-been-attached-to-the-prize-to-suu-kyii-than-bilateral-rela/200484.
162. Arafatul Islam, 'Bangladesh's "staged" elections', *DW*, 31/12/2018: https://www.dw.com/en/has-bangladeshs-ruling-party-won-a-managed-election/a-46907035

10. 'TERMITES'

1. Devjyot Ghoshal, 'Amit Shah vows to throw illegal immigrants into Bay of Bengal', *Reuters*, 12 April 2019: https://www.reuters.com/article/india-election-speech-idUSKCN1RO1YD.
2. Devjyot Ghoshal, 'Amit Shah vows to throw illegal immigrants into Bay of Bengal', *Reuters*, 12/04/2019: https://www.reuters.com/article/india-election-speech-idUSKCN1RO1YD
3. Interview 64.
4. Ibid.
5. B Raman, 'Behind the Mutiny', *Outlook India*, 1 March 2009: https://www.outlookindia.com/website/story/behind-the-mutiny/239842.
6. Nirupama Subramaniam, 'After 2009 Bangladesh mutiny, India rallied support for Hasina', *The Hindu*, 27 March 2011.

7. Ibid.

8. Rahul Singh, 'IAF on stand-by, ready to help Bangladesh', *Hindustan Times*, 2 March 2009, https://www.hindustantimes.com/delhi/iaf-on-stand-by-ready-to-help-bangladesh/story-APlOKNxML0MIG9qiQRR0dP.html.

9. Raman, 'Behind the Mutiny', *Outlook India*.

10. Ibid.

11. Interview 18.

12. Ibid.

13. Randeep Ramesh, 'Former Bangladesh PM arrested in corruption crackdown', *The Guardian*, 16 July 2007, https://www.theguardian.com/world/2007/jul/16/bangladesh.

14. Interview 63. Gen. (r) Moeen Uddin was unavailable for interview.

15. Interview 3.

16. Raman, 'Behind the Mutiny', *Outlook India*.

17. Interview 17.

18. Ibid.

19. Interview 18.

20. Interview 63.

21. Julfikar Ali Manik, 'BDR mutiny over as tanks roll in', *The Daily Star*, 27 February 2009: https://www.thedailystar.net/news-detail-77643.

22. Interview 18.

23. Ibid.

24. Subramaniam, 'After 2009 Bangladesh mutiny, India rallied support for Hasina', *The Hindu*.

25. Joseph Allchin: 'The strange case of Salauddin Quader Chowdhury and his plot against India from Bangladesh', Scroll.in, 22 October 2019, https://scroll.in/article/941202/the-strange-case-of-salauddin-quader-chowdhury-and-his-plot-against-india-from-bangladesh.

26. USG, 'Mutiny Investigation Continue, FBI Arrives, Politicians Return to Partisanhsip', CONFIDENTIAL, *Wikileaks*, 09DHAKA254_a 9 March 2009: https://wikileaks.org/plusd/cables/09DHAKA254_a.html.

27. Ibid.

28. Annual Report 2001, *MEA*, p. 3.

29. Interview 45.

30. 'Post-Election Violence in Bangladesh Kills 3', *NYT*, 4 October 2001: https://www.nytimes.com/2001/10/04/international/asia/postelection-violence-in-bangladesh-kills-3.html.

31. Interview 18.

32. Ibid.

33. Ibid.

34. Interview 45.

35. Ibid.

36. Interview 42.

37. Ibid.

38. Interview 18.

39. Raman, 'Behind the Mutiny', *Outlook India*.

40. GoI, 'Discussion regarding situation arising out of bomb blasts in various parts of North-Eastern States with particular reference to Assam', LSD, 15 December 2008.

41. Ibid.

42. Pranab Mukherjee, *The CoalitionYears, 1996–2012* (New Delhi: Rupa Publications, 2017).

43. Mohiuddin Ahmad, *Ek Igaaro: Bangladesh 2007–2008* (Dhaka, 2019) p. 387.

44. Interview 3.

45. Interview 18.

46. Interview 15.

47. GoI, 'Talks with Militants', *Lok Sabha Questions*, 4 December 2001. https://archive.pib.gov.in/archive/releases98/lyr2001/rdec2001/04122001/r0412200110.html.

48. 'Chronology of cease-fire between NSCN-IM and Union Government', SATP: https://www.satp.org/satporgtp/countries/india/states/nagaland/data_sheets/Chronologynscnim.htm.

49. GoI, 'Talks with Militants', *Lok Sabha Questions*, 4 December 2001.

50. Interview 24; Wasbir Hussain, 'Bodo Liberation Tigers signs accord in Delhi, ends revolt in western Assam', *India Today*, 24 February 2003: https://www.indiatoday.in/magazine/indiascope/story/20030224-bodo-liberation-tigers-signs-accord-in-delhi-ends-revolt-in-western-assam-793308-2003-02-23.

51. Interview 15.

52. Ibid.

53. 'Than makes "historic" visit', *Times of India*, 24 October 2004: https://timesofindia.indiatimes.com/india/Than-makes-historic-visit/articleshow/897720.cms?mobile=no.

54. Interview 22.

55. Ibid.

56. Ibid.

57. Interview 15.

58. 'Rice names "outposts of tyranny"', *BBC News*, 19 January 2005, http://news.bbc.co.uk/2/hi/americas/4186241.stm.

59. Interview 15.

60. Shyam Saran, 'Re-Engaging the Neighbouhood: A Personal Perspective on India's Look East Policy.' In Two Decades of India's Look East Policy: Partnership for Peace, Progress, and Prosperity, ed. by Amar N. Ram, xx-xx. New Delhi: ICWA, 2012.

61. Thant Myint U, *The Hidden History of Burma: A Crisis of Race and Capitalism* (US: W.W. Horton & Co., 2020).

62. Interview 44.

63. Myint U, *The Hidden History of Burma,* Introduction.

64. Quoted in Thomas Fuller, 'Extremism Rises Among Myanmar Buddhists', *The New York Times*, 20 June 2013: https://www.nytimes.com/2013/06/21/world/asia/extremism-rises-among-myanmar-buddhists-wary-of-muslim-minority.html.
65. Interview 62.
66. Interview 12.
67. Interview 5.
68. Interview 6.
69. Ibid.
70. Ibid.
71. Yuka Kobayashi, Josephine King, 'Myanmar's strategy in the China-Myanmar Economic Corridor: a failure in hedging?', *International Affairs*, 98(3), May 2022, pp. 1013–1032.
72. Johannes Plagemann, 'Small states and competing connectivity strategies: what explains Bangladesh's success in relations with Asia's major powers?', *The Pacific Review*, 35 (4), pp. 736–764.
73. 'Metro rail project: 3 deals inked with Chinese, Thai firms', *The Daily Star*, 17 September 2017, https://www.thedailystar.net/city/dhaka-metro-rail-project-bangladesh-government-signs-3-deals-with-chinese-thai-firms-1463485.
74. Interview 22.
75. Interview 51.
76. 'Tata group strengthens presence in Myanmar', *Business Standard*, 22 September 2016, https://www.business-standard.com/article/pti-stories/tata-group-strengthens-presence-in-myanmar-116092200966_1.html.
77. Interview 51.
78. Ben Smee & Emanuel Stoakes, 'Adani deal with Myanmar military-linked company raises human rights alarm', *The Guardian*, 13. May 2019, https://www.theguardian.com/business/2019/may/14/adani-deal-with-myanmar-military-linked-company-raises-human-rights-alarm.
79. Interview 51.
80. Sujan Dutta, 'India and Myanmar quietly open up their border for villagers and trade', *The Print*, 25 October 2018, https://theprint.in/diplomacy/india-and-myanmar-quietly-open-up-their-border-for-villagers-and-trade/139877/.
81. Constantino Xavier & Riya Sinha, 'How India Budgets to Become a Leading Power', *Centre for Social and Economic Progress* (CSEP), 8 February 2023, https://csep.org/blog/how-india-budgets-to-become-a-leading-power/.
82. Pieter D. Wezeman, Alexandra Kuimova, & Siemon T. Wezeman, 'Trends in International Arms Transfers, 2021', *SIPRI Fact Sheet*, March 2022, p. 10.
83. Interview 11.
84. Shishir Gupta, 'India renews pitch to build Stilwell Road', *Hindustan Times*, 27 May 2012: https://www.hindustantimes.com/delhi/india-renews-pitch-to-build-stilwell-road/story-wbdrtfrTTqiMPa9Z88Nr4H.html.
85. Interview 24.

415

86. Alka Jain, 'India, Bangladesh to soon start talks for free trade pact', *Live Mint*, 23 December 2022, https://www.livemint.com/news/india/india-bangladesh-to-soon-start-talks-for-free-trade-pact-details-here-11671764046997.html.

87. Plagemann, 'Small states and competing connectivity strategies', p. 745.

88. Ibid., p. 745.

89. Ibid., p. 745.

90. Ibid., p. 745.

91. Ibid., p. 745.

92. 'Tata Group calls off $3bn investment plan in Bangladesh', *Economic Times*, 1 August 2008, https://economictimes.indiatimes.com/news/company/corporate-trends/tata-group-calls-off-3-bn-investment-plan-in-bangladesh/articleshow/3311897.cms.

93. Serajul Islam Quadir, 'Bangladesh unable to guarantee gas supply to Tata', *Reuters*, 11 May 2008, https://www.reuters.com/article/bangladesh-energy-tata-idUKDHA21788820080511.

94. Ravi Nair, 'Is Bangladesh's electricity contract with Adani legally void?', *Adani Watch*, 9 February 2023, https://www.adaniwatch.org/is_bangladesh_s_electricity_contract_with_adani_legally_void.

95. Emran Hossain, 'Adani hides info for higher capacity charge', *New Age*, 12 February 2023.

96. 'Did Modi pressure Hasina to accept Adani deal?', *The Daily Star*, 15 February 2023, https://www.thedailystar.net/news/asia/india/news/did-modi-pressure-hasina-accept-adani-deal-3248186.

97. 'No renegotiation in power agreement with Bangladesh: Adani', *Prothom Alo*, 9 February 2023, https://en.prothomalo.com/bangladesh/utt70m8nkj.

98. Manoj Kumar, 'Japan proposes industrial hub in Bangladesh with supply chains to India', *Reuters*, 11 April 2023, https://www.reuters.com/markets/emerging/japan-proposes-industrial-hub-bangladesh-with-supply-chains-india-2023-04-11/.

99. 'Myanmar army and Arakan Army agree temporary truce in Rakhine State', *The Irrawaddy*, 28 November 2022: https://www.irrawaddy.com/news/war-against-the-junta/myanmar-military-and-arakan-army-agree-temporary-truce-in-rakhine-state.html.

100. Interview 13.

101. Ibid.

102. Interview 49.

103. Interviews 3, 15, 16, and 17.

104. Interview 24.

105. Interview 39.

106. Sandip Roy, '#56InchRocks turns into 50 Shades of Red: PM Modi's Obama moment unravels in Myanmar', *FirstPost*, 13/06/2015: https://www.firstpost.com/politics/56inchrocks-becomes-50-shades-of-red-modis-obama-moment-unravels-in-myanmar-2292678.html

107. Interview 16.

108. Ibid.
109. Interview 57.
110. Interview 13.
111. Ibid.
112. Interview 16.
113. Longkumer, *The Greater India Experiment,* pp. 140–153.
114. Interview 23.
115. Interview 28.
116. Ibid.
117. Interview 20.
118. Ibid.
119. Ibid.
120. Interview 17.
121. 'Operation *Insaniyat*: India to send relief to Bangladesh to help with Rohingya influx', India Today, 14 September 2017: https://www.indiatoday.in/world/story/india-sends-humanitarian-relief-to-bangladesh-rohingya-muslims-influx-un-myanmar-1044417-2017-09-14.
122. Interview 13.
123. Interview 51.
124. Ibid.
125. Krishna N. Das, Sanjeev Miglani, 'India says to deport all Rohingya regardless of U.N. registration', *Reuters*, 14 August 2017, https://www.reuters.com/article/us-myanmar-rohingya-india-idUSKCN1AU0UC.
126. Rajeev Bhattacharyya, 'Why are Rohingya Refugees Returning From India to Bangladesh?', *The Diplomat*, 3 June 2022, https://thediplomat.com/2022/06/why-are-rohingya-refugees-returning-from-india-to-bangladesh/.
127. Ipsita Chakravarty, 'On Rohingya refugees, AAP competes with the BJP in communal rhetoric', *Scroll.in*, 19 August 2022, https://scroll.in/article/1030794/on-rohingya-refugees-aap-competes-with-the-bjp-in-communal-rhetoric.
128. Rifat Fareed, 'It's a nightmare, every day': Rohingya in India live in fear', *Al Jazeera*, 25 August 2022, https://www.aljazeera.com/news/2022/8/25/its-a-nightmare-every-day-crackdown-on-rohingyas-in-india.
129. GoI, 'Reports from the Military Attache, Embassy of India, Rangoon', *MEA*, SECRET, 1-4/55-BC(B), National Archives of India (NAI), 1955, p. 130.
130. GoI, 'Reports (other than annual) from Burma', *MEA*, SECRET, 6(12)-Ref-9/58, NAI, 1959, p. 51.
131. GoI, 'Monthly reports (other than annual reports) from Burma (Rangoon)', *MEA*, SECRET, HI/1012(12)/68, NAI, 1968, p. 57.
132. GoI, 'Annual reports etc. from Rangoon, 1976', MEA, SECRET, HI/011/(11)/77-I, NAI, p. 8.
133. Ibid.
134. 'Anup Chetia sent back after 18 yrs', *The Daily Star*, 12 November 2015: https://www.thedailystar.net/frontpage/anup-chetia-sent-india-after-18-yrs-171148.

135. Interview 42.
136. 'Don't understand why': Bangladesh PM on India's amended citizenship law', *Hindustan Times*, 28 August 2020: https://www.hindustantimes.com/india-news/don-t-understand-why-india-did-it-bangladesh-pm-sheikh-hasina-on-caa/story-fQZrFuSs0yy9OWz0KWY2AK.html.
137. Interview 20.
138. Devjyot Ghoshal, 'Amit Shah vows to throw illegal immigrants into Bay of Bengal', *Reuters*, 12 April 2019.
139. Navine Murshid, *India's Bangladesh Problem: The Marginalization of Bengali Muslims in Neoliberal India* (Cambridge: Cambridge University Press, 2023).
140. Rajeev Bhattacharya, 'In Assam, Hindutva Group's "Training Camp" Teaches Combat, Small Arms', *The Quint*, 8 August 2022, https://www.thequint.com/news/india/in-assam-hindutva-group-conducts-training-camp-for-combat-small-arms#read-more.
141. Ibid.
142. Unnati Sharma, '"Madrasas should disappear, Muslims originally Hindus": Assam CM Himanta Biswas Sarma at RSS event', *The Print*, 23 May 2022: https://theprint.in/india/madrasas-should-disappear-muslims-originally-hindus-assam-cm-himanta-biswa-sarma-at-rss-event/966865/.
143. Rittick Sharma, 'Assam: RSS-Affiliate Demands Removal of Christians From ST List', *TheWire*, 7 February 2023, https://thewire.in/politics/assam-rss-affiliate-removal-christians-st-list.
144. Ibid.
145. 'BJP-MNF joint legislator party stake claim to form govt in Mizoram', *Hindustan Times*, 30 November 2022, https://www.hindustantimes.com/cities/others/bjpmnf-joint-legislator-party-stake-claim-to-form-govt-in-mizoram-101669793786462.html.
146. Alice Yhoshü, 'Peace talks halted after RSS objection: NSCN-IM', *Hindustan Times*, 27 July 2022, https://www.hindustantimes.com/india-news/peace-talks-halted-after-rss-objectionnscnim-101658861538082.html.
147. Ibid.
148. Interview 24.
149. Ibid.
150. Ibid.
151. Ibid.
152. Ibid.
153. Sadiq Naqvi, 'Khango Konyak-led faction of NSCN(K) agrees to join peace talks', *Hindustan Times*, 12 January 2019, https://www.hindustantimes.com/india-news/khango-konyak-led-faction-of-nscn-k-agrees-to-join-naga-peace-talks/story-OtIeWwRuz40FOftVrNTGuL.html.
154. Chit Min Tun, 'Tatmadaw Occupies NSCN-K Headquarter', *The Irrawaddy*, 1 February 2019, https://www.irrawaddy.com/news/tatmadaw-occupies-nscn-k-headquarters.html.
155. Interview 43.

156. John Reed and Benjamin Parkin, 'Gautam Adani's ties with India's Narendra Modi spur scrutiny of overseas deals', *Financial Times*, 23/02/2023: https://www.ft.com/content/38ff5ff6-aebe-46ae-bb97-c8071818b55d

EPILOGUE: GROUNDSWELL

1. 'NIA arrest suspect in transnational conspiracy in Manipur', *Hindustan Times*, 30 September 2023: https://www.hindustantimes.com/india-news/nia-arrests-suspect-in-transnational-conspiracy-in-manipur-101696083956724.html.
2. Vijaita Singh, 'Free Movement Regime to end at Myanmar border', *The Hindu*, 2 January 2024, https://www.thehindu.com/news/national/centre-set-to-scrap-free-movement-regime-with-myanmar-people-in-border-areas-will-require-visas/article67698536.ece.
3. 'Meitei group sets peace terms for Manipur Chief Minister, MLAs', *The Hindu*, 24 January 2024, https://www.thehindu.com/news/national/other-states/manipur-group-sets-peace-terms-for-cm-mlas/article67772535.ece.
4. 'Myanmar Junta chief admits to rising resistance pressure', *The Irrawaddy*, 16 February 2023, https://www.irrawaddy.com/news/burma/myanmar-junta-chief-admits-to-rising-resistance-pressure.html.
5. Avinash Paliwal, 'Could Myanmar Come Apart?', *Foreign Affairs*, 24 January 2024, https://www.foreignaffairs.com/burma-myanmar/could-myanmar-come-apart.
6. 'Myanmar Coup leader admits not in full control of country', *The Irrawaddy*, 4 June 2021, https://www.irrawaddy.com/news/burma/myanmar-coup-leader-admits-not-in-full-control-of-country.html.
7. 'Myanmar president: country at risk of breaking apart due to clashes', Reuters, 9 November 2023, https://www.reuters.com/world/asia-pacific/myanmar-president-country-risk-breaking-apart-due-border-violence-2023-11-09/.
8. Interview 6.
9. Dipanjan Roy Chaudhury, 'India monitors Chinese infrastructure on Coco Islands', *The Economic Times*, 15 April 2023, https://economictimes.indiatimes.com/news/defence/india-monitors-chinese-infrastructure-on-coco-islands/articleshow/99522043.cms.
10. Sushila Sahay, 'Ground Report: Myanmar Refugees in Mizoram Camps are a picture of resilience', *The Wire*, 15 November 2022: https://thewire.in/rights/ground-report-myanmar-refugees-in-mizoram-camps-are-a-picture-of-resilience.
11. Angshuman Choudhury, 'Blurred Lines: Mizoram's uncertain efforts to provide sanctuary to Chin refugees', *The Caravan*, 31 March 2023: https://caravanmagazine.in/conflict/mizoram-uncertain-efforts-sanctuary-chin-refugees.
12. Jayanata Kalita, 'Indian rebels now brothers in arms with Myanmar military', *The Irrawaddy*, 27 January 2022: https://www.irrawaddy.com/opinion/guest-column/indian-rebels-now-brothers-in-arms-with-myanmar-military.html.

13. Poulomi Ghosh, 'Assam Rifles Commanding Officer, wife, son, 3 soldiers killed in terrorist attack in Manipur', *Hindustan Times*, 13 November 2021: https://www.hindustantimes.com/india-news/terrorists-attack-convoy-of-assam-rifles-unit-commanding-officer-in-manipur-101636793971653.html.

14. 'Myanmar Opium Survey 2022: Cultivation, Production, and Implications', United Nations Office on Drugs and Crime, January 2023: https://www.unodc.org/roseap/uploads/documents/Publications/2023/Myanmar_Opium_Survey_2022.pdf.

15. Angshuman Choudhury, 'Is the Myanmar junta facilitating opium cultivation near the Indian border?', *Barbed Wires*, 1 February 2023, https://barbedwires.substack.com/p/is-the-myanmar-junta-facilitating.

16. C Christine Fair, 'Bangladesh in 2019: Hasina Consolidates One-Woman Rule', *Asian Survey*, 60(1), 2020, pp. 189–195.

17. 'Bangladesh: Four killed as protests erupt in Chittagong on day of Modi's visit', *Scroll.in*, 26 March 2021, https://scroll.in/latest/990685/bangladesh-four-killed-as-protests-erupt-in-chittagong-on-day-of-modis-visit.

18. '17 killed, 500 injured in anti-Modi protests: Hefazat', *New Age*, 28 March 2021: https://www.newagebd.net/article/133880/17-killed-500-injured-in-anti-modi-protests-hefazat.

19. On popular support for militant Islamists in Bangladesh see C Christine Fair and Parina Patel, 'Support for Domestic Islamist Terrorism in Bangladesh: Insights from a novel survey', *Politics and Religion*, 2022, pp. 1–27.

20. 'Forex reserve slips below $21 billion', *The Daily Star*, 19 October 2023, https://www.thedailystar.net/business/news/forex-reserve-slips-below-21-billion-3447646.

21. 'IMF's $4.7bn Bangladesh loan not a cure-all, analysts say', *Nikkei Asia*, 2 February 2023, https://asia.nikkei.com/Economy/IMF-s-4.7bn-Bangladesh-loan-not-a-cure-all-analysts-say.

22. Golam Mortoza, 'Islami Bank's loan scams were not unknown to policymakers', *The Daily Star*, 6 December 2022, https://www.thedailystar.net/business/economy/news/islami-banks-loan-scams-were-not-unknown-policymakers-3188411.

23. 'Corruption at Rooppur Nuclear Power Plant: SC stays contractor's bail order', *The Daily Star*, 1 July 2020, https://www.thedailystar.net/rooppur-nuclear-power-plant-corruption-sc-stays-contractor-bail-order-1923401.

24. World Bank Statement on Padma Bridge, 29 June 2012: https://www.worldbank.org/en/news/press-release/2012/06/29/world-bank-statement-padma-bridge.

25. 'Bangladesh ramps up its persecution of Muhammad Yunus', *The Economist*, 13 October 2022, https://www.economist.com/asia/2022/10/13/bangladesh-ramps-up-its-persecution-of-muhammad-yunus.

26. Interview 36.

27. 'Chinese envoy visits Teesta Barrage', *Dhaka Tribune*, 9 October 2022, https://www.dhakatribune.com/bangladesh/2022/10/09/chinese-envoy-visits-teesta-barrage.

28. Jauman Naw, Emily Fishbein, and Ronja Pilgaard, 'Weapons, power and money': How rare earth mining in Kachin enriches a Tatmadaw ally', *Frontier Myanmar*, 3 August 2021, https://www.frontiermyanmar.net/en/weapons-power-and-money-how-rare-earth-mining-in-kachin-enriches-a-tatmadaw-ally/.

29. 'Assam: First Batch of 'Foreigners' Shifted to Matia Detention Centre', *The Wire*, 30 January 2023, https://thewire.in/government/assam-first-batch-of-foreigners-shifted-to-matia-detention-centre.

30. 'Centre's approval required to introduce NRC in Manipur: CM Biren Singh', *The Hindu*, 1 April 2023: https://www.thehindu.com/news/national/other-states/centres-approval-required-to-introduce-nrc-in-manipur-cm-biren-singh/article66686718.ece.

31. 'AFSPA lifted from more areas in Northeast states', Indian Express, 26 March 2023: https://indianexpress.com/article/india/modi-govt-decides-to-reduce-disturbed-areas-under-afspa-in-northeast-amit-shah-8518556/; Tora Agarwala, 'Nagaland civilian killings: MoD denies sanction to prosecute 30 Armymen', *Indian Express*, 14 April 2023: https://indianexpress.com/article/north-east-india/nagaland/nagaland-civilian-killings-mod-denies-sanction-to-prosecute-30-armymen-8555344/.

32. 'Mizoram Assembly adopts resolution opposing any move to implement Uniform Civil Code', *The Hindu*, 14 February 2023, https://www.thehindu.com/news/national/other-states/mizoram-assembly-adopts-resolution-opposing-any-move-to-implement-uniform-civil-code/article66508696.ece.

33. Devesh Kumar, 'Will disintegrate country': Mizoram Assembly adopts resolution against Uniform Civil Code, *Live Mint*, 14 February 2023, https://www.livemint.com/news/india/will-disintegrate-country-mizoram-assembly-adopts-resolution-against-uniform-civil-code-11676380970437.html.

34. 'Mehbooba Mufti placed under house arrest', Times of India, 21 August 2022, https://timesofindia.indiatimes.com/india/mehbooba-mufti-placed-under-house-arrest/articleshow/93689076.cms.

35. Karan Thapar, 'Nagas Will Never Join Indian Union nor Accept India's Constitution: NSCN (I-M) Chief', *The Wire*, 16 October 2020, https://thewire.in/politics/exclusive-nagas-indian-constitution-thuingaleng-muivah-nscn-im.

36. Rajeev Bhattacharyya, 'Why Did Bangladesh's Kuki Chin Flee to India's Northeast?', *The Diplomat*, 21 February 2023, https://thediplomat.com/2023/02/why-did-bangladeshs-kuki-chin-flee-to-indias-northeast/.

37. Shaikh Azizur Rahman, 'India Crackdown Forces Rohingya Refugees to go Underground, Flee to Bangladesh', *VOA*, 7 June 2022, https://www.voanews.com/a/india-crackdown-forces-rohingya-refugees-to-go-underground-flee-to-bangladesh/6606459.html.

38. Riya Sinha, 'Roll East: A Proposal for India-Myanmar-Thailand Railway Connectivity', *Centre for Social and Economic Progress*, 14 February 2023, https://csep.org/reports/roll-east-a-proposal-for-india-myanmar-thailand-railway-connectivity/.

39. Sushant Singh, 'The Challenge of a Two-Front War: India's China-Pakistan Dilemma', *Stimson Centre*, 19 April 2021, https://www.stimson.org/2021/the-challenge-of-a-two-front-war-indias-china-pakistan-dilemma/.

40. GoI, National Investigation Agency Charge-Sheet, 26 March 2011 (prime accused: Anthony Shimray, Self-Styled Commander-in-Chief of the Naga Army), pp. 4–6.

BIBLIOGRAPHY

Private Papers: PN Haksar, BK Nehru, Gulzarilal Nanda, Jawaharlal Nehru, Vijaya Lakshmi Pandit, AK Damodaran, Bishnuram Medhi, VK Krishna Menon, JP Narayan, N Gopalaswamy Ayyenger, Brang Seng (KIO), Saw Tun (AA), NK Rustomji, Subimal Dutt.

Archives:

1. National Archives of India, New Delhi, India: Ministries of External Affairs, Home Affairs (including Intelligence Bureau), Defence, Cabinet Secretariat (including R&AW).
2. Nehru Memorial Museum and Library, New Delhi, India: Private papers (see above)
3. Nagaland State Archives, Kohima, India
4. Mizoram State Archives, Aizawl, India
5. Assam State Archives, Guwahati, India
6. International Institute of Social History, Amsterdam, Netherlands
7. Woodrow Wilson International Centre for Scholars, Washington, DC. US: Cold War Project
8. National Archives of the United Kingdom, London, UK: Foreign & Commonwealth Office, Prime Minister's Secretariat
9. Myanmar National Archives (via Wilson Centre)
10. Wikileaks
11. Foreign Relations of the United States (FRUS) & Central Intelligence Agency (CIA) online libraries

Secondary sources:

A K M Ahsan Ullah, 'Rohingya Crisis in Myanmar: Seeking Justice for the "Stateless"', *Journal of Contemporary Criminal Justice*, 32 (3), 2016, pp. 285–301

A K M Ahsan Ullah, 'Rohingya Refugees to Bangladesh: Historical Exclusions and Contemporary Marginalisation', *Journal of Immigrant and Refugee Studies*, 9 (2), 2011, pp. 139–161

A S Bhasin, *Nehru, Tibet, and China* (New Delhi: India Viking, 2021)

A S Dulat, *A Life in the Shadows: A Memoir* (New Delhi: HarperCollins India, 2022)

Alyssa Ayres, *Speaking Like a State: Language and Nationalism in Pakistan* (Cambridge: Cambridge University Press, 2009)

Amar N. Ram ed. *Two Decades of India's Look East Policy: Partnership for Peace, Progress, and Prosperity* (New Delhi: Indian Council of World Affairs, 2012)

Amartya Sen, *Poverty and Famines: An Essay on Entitlement and Deprivation* (Oxford: Oxford University Press, 1981)

Amit Das Gupta, *Serving India: A Political Biography of Subimal Dutt (1903–1992), India's Longest Serving Foreign Secretary* (New Delhi: Manohar Publishers, 2017)

Anam Zakaria, *1971: A People's History from Bangladesh, Pakistan, and India* (London: Vintage, 2019)

Anubha Bhonsle, *Mother, Where's My Country?: Looking for Light in the Darkness of Manipur* (New Delhi: Speaking Tiger Publishers, 2016)

Andrew B. Liu, *Tea War: A History of Capitalism in China and India* (Yale: Yale University Press, 2020)

Andrew Selth, 'Burma's Mythical Isle', *Australia Quarterly*, 80 (6), November-December 2008, pp. 24–40

Angshuman Choudhury, 'Blurred Lines: Mizoram's uncertain efforts to provide sanctuary to Chin refugees', *The Caravan*, March 2023

Anne F Thurston and Gyalo Thondup, *The Noodle Maker of Kalimpong: The Untold Story of My Struggle for Tibet* (London: Penguin, 2015)

Antara Datta, *Refugees and Borders in South Asia: The Great Exodus of 1971* (London: Routledge, 2013)

Anthony Mascarenhas, *Bangladesh: A Legacy of Blood* (London: Hodder & Stoughton, 1986)

Anwesha Roy, *Making Peace, Making Riots: Communalism and Communal Violence, Bengal 1940–1947* (Cambridge: Cambridge University Press, 2018)

Anwesha Sengupta, 'Breaking Up: Dividing Assets between India and Pakistan in times of partition', *The Indian Economic and Social History Review*, 51 (4), 2014, pp. 529–548

Anwesha Sengupta, 'Unthreading Partition: The Politics of Jute Sharing between Two Bengals', *Economic and Political Weekly*, 53(4), January 27, 2018, pp. 43–49

Arjun Subramaniam, *India's Wars: A Military History, 1947-1971* (New Delhi: HarperCollins India, 2017)

Arupjyoti Saikia, *The Quest for Modern Assam: A History, 1942-2000* (New Delhi: Penguin India, 2023)

Arzan Tarapore, 'Defence without deterrence: India's strategy in the 1965 war', *Journal of Strategic Studies*, 2019, pp. 1–30

Ashfaque Hossain, 'The Making and Unmaking of Assam-Bengal Borders and the Sylhet Referendum', *Modern Asian Studies*, 47 (1), 2013, pp. 250–287

BIBLIOGRAPHY

Ashwini Bhatnagar, *The Lotus Years: Political Life in India in the Time of Rajiv Gandhi* (New Delhi: Hachette India, 2019)

Atul Kohli ed. *India's Democracy: An Analysis of Changing State-Society Relations* (Princeton, NJ: Princeton University Press, 1990)

Avinash Paliwal, 'A Cat's Paw of Indian Reactionaries? Strategic Rivalry and Domestic Politics at the India-China-Myanmar Trijunction', *Asian Security*, 16(1), 2020, pp. 10–11

Avinash Paliwal, 'Colonial Sinews of Postcolonial Espionage—India and the Making of Ghana's External Intelligence Agency, 1958-61', *The International History Review*, 44(4), 2022, pp. 914–934

Avinash Paliwal, *My Enemy's Enemy: India in Afghanistan from the Soviet Invasion to the US Withdrawal* (New York: Oxford University Press, 2017)

Avinash Paliwal, 'Politics, Strategy, and State Responses to Conflict Generated Migration', *Journal of Global Security Studies,* 7(1), 2022

Avinash Paliwal and Paul Staniland, 'Strategy, Secrecy, and External Support for Insurgent Groups', *International Studies Quarterly, 67(1)*, March 2023

Aye Chan, 'The Development of a Muslim Enclave in Arakan (Rakhine) State of Burma (Myanmar)', *SOAS Bulletin of Burma Research*, 3 (2), Autumn 2005, pp. 396–420

Ayesha Jalal, *The Sole Spokesman: Jinnah, the Muslim League, and the Demand for Pakistan* (Cambridge: Cambridge University Press, 1994)

B Pakem, *India-Burma Relations* (New Delhi: Omsons Publishers, 1992)

B Paul, T*he First Naxal: An Authorised Biography of Kanu Sanyal* (New Delhi: Sage Publishers, 2019)

B Raman, *The Kaoboys of R&AW: Down Memory Lane* (New Delhi: Lancer Publishers, 2009)

B K Bhattacharyya, 'A Separate Assam Hills State: What Does it Mean?', *Economic and Political Weekly*, 2(9), March 1967

B Z Khasru, *The Bangladesh Military Coup and the CIA link* (New Delhi: Rupa Publishers, 2014)

Barbara Harriss-White & Lucia Michelutti eds. *The Wild East: Criminal Political Economies in South Asia* (London: UCL Press, 2019)

Berenice Guyot-Réchard, 'Tangled Lands: Burma and India's unfinished separation, 1937-1948', *Journal of Asian Studies*, 80 (2), May 2021, pp. 293–315

Berenice Guyot-Réchard, 'When Legions Thunder Past: The Second World War and India's Northeastern Frontier', *War in History*, 25(3), 2018, pp. 328–360

Bertie R. Pearn, *The Indian in Burma* (Le Play House Press, 1946)

Bertil Lintner, *Great Game East: India, China, and the Struggle for Asia's Most Volatile Frontier* (New Delhi: HarperCollins India, 2016)

Bertil Lintner, *The Rise and Fall of the Communist Party of Burma (CPB)* (Ithaca: Cornell Southeast Asia Program, 1991)

Bina D'Costa, *Nationbuilding, Gender, and War Crimes in South Asia* (London: Routledge, 2010)

Binalakshmi Nepram, *South Asia's Fractured Frontier: Armed Conflict, Narcotics, and Smalls Arms Proliferation in India's Northeast* (New Delhi: Mittal Publishers, 2002)

Blaine C Richardson, 'Bangladesh Food Aid: PL480 Title I and Title III', Aid Project Impact Evaluation Paper No. 54, *US Agency for International Development*, May 1996

Bruce Riedel, *JFK's Forgotten Crisis: Tibet, the CIA, and the Sino-Indian War* (Washington, D.C.: Brookings Institution Press, 2017)

C Christine Fair, 'Bangladesh in 2019: Hasina Consolidates One-Woman Rule', *Asian Survey*, 60(1), 2020, pp. 189–95

C Christine Fair and Parina Patel, 'Support for Domestic Islamist Terrorism in Bangladesh: Insights from a novel survey', *Politics and Religion*, 2022, pp. 1–27

C G Verghese and R L Thanzawna, *A History of the Mizos-Volume I* (New Delhi: Vikas Publishing House, 1997)

C Nunthara, *Impact of the Introduction of Grouping of Villages in Mizoram* (Delhi: Omsons Publications, 1989)

Camelia Dewan, *Misreading the Bengal Delta: Climate Change, Development, and Livelihoods in Coastal Bangladesh* (Washington, D.C.: University of Washington Press, 2022)

Carole McGranahan, *Arrested Histories: Tibet, the CIA, and Memories of a Forgotten War* (Durham, NC: Duke University Press, 2010)

Christina Fink, *Living Silence in Burma: Surviving Under the Military Rule* (London: Zed Books, 2009)

Chris Bayly and Tim Harper, *Forgotten Armies: Britain's Asian Empire & War with Japan* (London: Penguin, 2005)

Christophe Jaffrelot, *The Hindu Nationalist Movement and Indian Politics: 1925 to the 1990s* (New Delhi: Penguin Books, 1993)

Christophe Jaffrelot and Pratinav Anil, *India's First Dictatorship: The Emergency, 1975–77* (New Delhi: HarperCollins India, 2021)

Christopher Clary, *The Difficult Politics of Peace: Rivalry in Modern South Asia* (New York: Oxford University Press, 2022)

Constantino Xavier, *From Inaction to Intervention: India's Strategic Culture of Regional Involvement (Nepal, Sri Lanka, and Myanmar, 1950s-2000s)*, PhD Thesis, Johns Hopkins University, July 2016

David Brenner, *Rebel Politics: A Political Sociology of Armed Struggle in Myanmar's Borderlands* (Ithaca: Cornell University Press, 2019)

David C Engerman, *The Price of Aid: The Economic Cold War in India* (Cambridge, MA: Harvard University Press, 2018)

David Ludden, 'Spatial Inequity and National Territory: Remapping 1905 in Bengal and Assam', *Modern Asian Studies*, 46(3), 2012, pp. 483–525

David Steinberg, Hongwei Fan, *Modern China-Myanmar Relations: Dilemmas of Mutual Dependence* (Singapore: NIAS Press, 2012)

DeepakMishra, Vandana Upadhyay, & Atul Sarma, *Unfolding Crisis in Assam's Tea Plantations: Employment and Occupational Mobility* (London: Routledge, 2012)

Devesh Kapur and Milan Vaishnav eds. *Costs of Democracy: Political Finance in India* (New Delhi: Oxford University Press, 2018)

Diana S. Kim, *Empires of Vice: The Rise of Opium Prohibition across Southeast Asia* (New Jersey: Princeton University Press, 2020)

BIBLIOGRAPHY

Dolly Kikon, *Living with Oil and Coal: Resource Politics and Militarization in Notheast India* (Washington, D.C.: University of Washington Press, 2019)

E N Rammohan, *Insurgent Frontiers: Essays from the Troubled Northeast* (New Delhi: India Research Press, 2005)

Edith Mirante, *Down the Rat Hole: Adventures Underground on Burma's Frontiers* (Hong Kong: Orchid Press, 2006)

Esther M Tariang, *Glimpses on Political Developments in Meghalaya* (Chennai: Notion Press, 2022)

Farooq Bajwa, *From Kutch to Tashkent: The Indo-Pakistan War of 1965* (London: Hurst Publishers, 2013)

Faruq Aziz Khan, *Spring 1971: A Centre Stage Account of Bangladesh War of Liberation* (Dhaka: University Press, 1998)

Farzana Shaikh, *Making Sense of Pakistan* (London: Hurst Publishers, 2018)

Gavin Young, *Indo-Naga War* (Pennsylvania: American Baptist Historical Society, 1961)

Gulshan Sachdeva, *Economy of the North-East: Policy, Present, Conditions, and Future Possibilities* (New Delhi: Konark Publishers, 2000)

Ian Brown, *Burma's Economy in the Twentieth Century* (Cambridge: Cambridge University Press, 2013)

J R Andrus, *Burmese Economic Life* (Stanford: Stanford University Press, 1948)

J V Hluna and Rini Tochhawng, *The Mizo Uprising: Assam Assembly Debates on the Mizo Movement, 1966–1971* (Newcastle upon Tyne: Cambridge Scholars Publishing, 2012)

Jairam Ramesh, *Intertwined Lives: PN Haksar & Indira Gandhi* (New Delhi: Simon & Schuster, 2018)

James J Lum Dau, *An autobiography of my life experience in the service of KIO-KIA revolutionary movement* (Yunnan: Kachin Research Society Publication, 2015)

Janam Mukherjee, *Hungry Bengal: War, Famine, and the End of Empire* (Oxford: Oxford University Press, 2011)

Jawaharlal Nehru, 'Changing India', *Foreign Affairs*, 41 (3), April 1963, pp. 453–465

Jawaharlal Nehru, *The Discovery of India* (London: Penguin Books, 2004)

Jayeeta Sharma, *Empire's Garden: Assam and the Making of India* (Durham: Duke University Press, 2011)

Jelle Wouters, Tanka Subba eds., *The Routledge Companion to Northeast India* (London: Routledge, 2023)

Jogendra K. Das, 'The Bodoland Movement in Local and National Perspectives', *The Indian Journal of Political Science*, 55(4), Oct.-Dec. 1994, pp. 417–426

Johannes Plagemann, 'Small states and competing connectivity strategies: what explains Bangladesh's success in relations with Asia's major powers?', *The Pacific Review*, 35 (4), pp. 736–764

John Christian, 'Burma Divorces India', *Current History*, 46(1), 1937, pp. 82–86

John Dalvi, *Himalayan Blunder: The Curtain-Raiser to the Sino-Indian War of 1962* (Bombay: Thacker Publishers, 1968)

John Garver, *Protracted Contest: Sino-Indian Rivalry in the Twentieth Century* (Perth: UWA Press, 2002)

John Kenneth Knaus, *Orphans of the Cold War: America and the Tibetan Struggle for Survival* (Public Affairs, 1999)

John Thomas, *Evangelising the Nation: Religion and the Formation of Naga Political Identity* (London: Routledge, 2015)

Joy Pachuau, *Being Mizo: Identity and Belonging in Northeast India* (Oxford: Oxford University Press, 2014)

Joya Chatterji, *The Spoils of Partition: Bengal and India, 1947–1967* (Cambridge: Cambridge University Press, 2007)

Julia Lovell, *Maoism: A Global History* (London: Bodley Head, 2019)

Jurgen Haacke, *Myanmar's Foreign Policy: Domestic Influences and International Implications* (Singapore: IISS Press, 2017)

K M Panikkar, *State and Citizen* (Asia Publishing House, 1960)

K Maudood Elahi, 'Refugees in Dandakaranya', *The International Migration Review*, 15 (1/2), Spring-Summer 1981, pp. 219–225

K S Subramaniam, *State, Policy, and Conflicts in Northeast India* (London: Routledge, 2015)

Kali Prasad Mukhopadhyay, *Partition, Bengal and After: The Great Tragedy of India* (Reference Press, 2007)

Kasia Paprocki, *Threatening Dystopias: The Global Politics of Climate Change Adaptation in Bangladesh* (Ithaca: Cornell University Press, 2021)

Kenneth Conboy and James Morrison, *The CIA's Secret War in Tibet* (Kansas: University of Kansas, 2011)

Kishalay Bhattacharjee, *Blood on my Hands: Confessions of Staged Encounters* (New Delhi: HarperCollins India, 2015)

Krishnan Srinivasan, *The Jamdani Revolution: Politics, Personalities, and Civil Society in Bangladesh 1989–1992* (New Delhi: Har-Anand Publishers, 2008)

Lakhan Mehrotra, 'India's Look East Policy: Its Origin and Development', *Indian Foreign Affairs Journal*, 7(1), January-March 2012

Lalthakima, 'Insurgency in Mizoram: A Study of its Origin, Growth, and Dimension', *PhD Thesis*, Mizoram University, 2008

Lawrence Lifschultz, *Bangladesh: The Unfinished Revolution* (London: Zed Books, 1979)

Layli Uddin, '"Enemy Agents at Work": A Microhistory of the 1954 Adamjee and Karnaphuli riots in East Pakistan', *Modern Asian Studies*, 55 (2), 2021, pp. 629–664

Layli Uddin, 'Red Maulanas: Revisiting Islam and the Left in twentieth-century South Asia', *History Compass*, October 2023

Lydia Walker, 'Decolonization in the 1960s: On Legitimate and Illegitimate Nationalist Claims-making', *Past & Present*, 242(1), Feb. 2019, pp. 227–264

M S Golwalkar, *Bunch of Thoughts* (Bangalore: Sahitya Sindhu Prakashan)

Madhav Khosla, *India's Founding Moment: The Constitution of a Most Surprising Democracy* (Cambridge, MA: Harvard University Press, 2020)

Mahfuz Ullah, *President Zia of Bangladesh: A Political Biography* (Dhaka: Adorn Publication, 2016)

Makiko Kimura, *The Nellie Massacre of 1983: Agency of the Rioters* (New Delhi: Sage Publishers, 2013)

Malini Bhattacharjee, 'Tracing the Emergence and Consolidation of Hindutva in Assam', *Economic and Political Weekly*, 51(16), 2016

Malini Sur, *Jungle Passports: Fences, Mobility, and Citizenship at the Northeast India-Bangladesh Border* (Pennsylvania: University of Pennsylvania Press, 2021)

Mandy Sadan, *Being and Becoming Kachin: Histories Beyond the State in the Borderlands of Burma* (Oxford: Oxford University Press, 2013)

Mandy Sadan ed., *War and Peace in the Borderlands of Myanmar: The Kachin Ceasefire 1994–2011* (Singapore: NIAS Press, 2016)

Manu Bhagavan, *The Peacemakers: India and the Quest for One World* (New Delhi: HarperCollins India, 2012)

Mariam Mufti, Sahar Shafqat, Niloufer Siddiqui eds. *Pakistan's Political Parties: Surviving between Dictatorship and Democracy* (Washington, DC: Georgetown University Press, 2020)

Martin Bayly, Elisabeth Leake, Avinash Paliwal, and Pallavi Raghavan eds. 'The Limits of Decolonisation in India's International Thought and Practice: An Introduction', *The International History Review*, 44(4), 2022

Martin Smith, *Burma: Insurgency and the Politics of Ethnicity* (New York: Zed Books, 1999)

Martin Smith and Larry Jagan, 'Maran Brang Seng: In His Own Words' *Burma Debate*, 1 (3), Dec 1994/Jan 1995

Mary Callahan, *Making Enemies: War and State Building in Burma* (Ithaca: Cornell University Press, 2005)

Matthew Browser, 'Partners in Empire? Co-colonialism and the Rise of Anti-Indian Nationalism in Burma, 1930-1938', *The Journal of Imperial and Commonwealth History*, 49 (1), 2021, pp. 118–147

Matthew J Walton, *Buddhism and the Political: Organisation and Participation in the Theravada Moral Universe* (London: Hurst Publishers, 2019)

Matthew J Walton, 'Ethnicity, Conflict, and History in Burma: The Myths of Panglong', *Asian Survey*, 48 (6), 2008, pp. 889–910

Maung Aung Myoe, *In the name of Pauk-Phaw: Myanmar's China Policy Since 1948* (Singapore: ISEAS Publications, 2011)

Maung Maung, *The 1988 Uprising in Burma* (Yale University Press, 2000)

Md. Mahbubar Rahman and Willem van Schendel, 'I am not a Refugee': Rethinking Partition Migration', *Modern Asian Studies*, 37 (3), July 2003, pp. 551–584

Melissa Crouch ed. *Islam and the State in Myanmar: Muslim-Buddhist Relations and the Politics of Belonging* (New York: Oxford University Press, 2016)

Michael Charney, *A History of Modern Burma* (Cambridge: Cambridge University Press, 2009)

Milan Vaishnav, *When Crime Pays: Money and Muscle in Indian Politics* (New Haven: Yale University Press, 2017)

Mohiuddin Ahmad, *Ek Igaaro: Bangladesh 2007-2008* (Dhaka, 2019)

Monirul Hussain, *The Assam Movement: Class, Ideology, and Identity* (New Delhi: Manak Publishers, 1993)

Monirul Hussain, 'State, Identity Movements, and Internal Displacement in the North East', *Economic and Political Weekly*, 35(51), December 16–22, 2000, pp. 4519–4523

BIBLIOGRAPHY

Mrinal Talukdar, *Postcolonial Assam (1947–2019)* (Guwahati: NTF Publishers, 2019)

Mushirul Hasan, 'Memories of a Fragmented Nation: Rewriting the Histories of India's Partition', *Economic and Political Weekly*, October 10-16, 1998, 33 (41), pp. 2662–2668

N Manoharan, 'Brothers, Not Friends: India-Sri Lanka Relations', *South Asian Survey*, 18(2), 2011, pp. 225–238

Nalini R Chakravarti, *The Indian Minority in Burma: The rise and decline of an immigrant community* (London: Oxford University Press, 1971)

Namrata Goswami, *The Naga Ethnic Movement for a Separate Homeland* (New Delhi: Oxford University Press, 2020)

Nandini Sundar, 'Interning Insurgent Populations: The Buried Histories of Indian Democracy', *Economic and Political Weekly*, 46(6), 2011

Nandita Haksar, *Rogue Agent: How India's Military Intelligence Betrayed the Burmese Resistance* (New Delhi: Penguin, 2009)

Nandita Haksar and Sebastian M Hongray, *Kuknalim, Naga Armed Resistance: Testimonies of Leaders, Pastors, Healers, and Soldiers* (New Delhi: Speaking Tiger, 2019)

Nani Gopal Mahanta, *Confronting the State: ULFA's Quest for Sovereignty* (New Delhi: Sage Publishers, 2013)

Naomi Hossain, *The Aid Lab: Understanding Bangladesh's Unexpected Success* (New York: Oxford University Press, 2017)

Naphaw Kaw Mai, *Maran Brang Seng: A Biography* (unpublished)

Navine Murshid, *India's Bangladesh Problem: The Marginalization of Bengali Muslims in Neoliberal India* (Cambridge: Cambridge University Press, 2023)

Neeti Nair, *Hurt Sentiments: Secularism and Belonging in South Asia* (Cambridge, MA: Harvard University Press, 2023)

Nick Cheesman, Monique Skidmore, & Trevor Wilson eds. *Myanmar's Transition: Openings, Obstacles, and Opportunities* (Singapore: ISEAS Publishing, 2012)

Nirmal Nibedon, *Mizoram: The Dagger Brigade* (New Delhi: Lancer Publishers, 1980)

Nitin Verma ed. *Coolies of Capitalism: Assam Tea and the Making of Coolie Labour* (Oldenbourg: De Gruyter, 2018)

Omkar Goswami, 'Sahibs, Babus, and Banias: Changes in Industrial Control in Eastern India', *The Journal of Asian Studies*, 48 (2), May 1989, pp. 289–309

P N Dhar, *Indira Gandhi, the 'Emergency', and Indian Democracy* (New Delhi: Oxford University Press, 2000)

P N Khera, *Operation Vijay: The Liberation of Goa and Other Portuguese Colonies in India, 1961* (New Delhi: Ministry of Defence of India, 1974)

Pallavi Raghavan, *Animosity at Bay: An Alternative History of the India-Pakistan Relationship, 1947–1952* (London: Hurst, 2020)

Paul McGarr, *The Cold War in South Asia: Britain, the United States, and the Indian Subcontinent, 1945–1965* (Cambridge: Cambridge University Press, 2013)

Pia Oberoi, *Exile and Belonging: Refugees and State Policy in South Asia* (New Delhi: Oxford University Press, 2006)

Pierre-Arnaud Chouvy, *Opium: Uncovering the Politics of Poppy* (London: I B Tauris, 2009)

Pieter Steyn, *Zapuphizo: Voice of the Nagas* (Abingdon: Routledge, 2002)

Pradeep K Chibber and Rahul Verma, *Ideology, and Identity: The Changing Party Systems of India* (New York: Oxford University Press, 2018)

Pranab Mukherjee, *The Coalition Years, 1996–2012* (New Delhi: Rupa Publications, 2017)

Pratap Bhanu Mehta, *The Burden of Democracy* (New Delhi: Penguin Random House India, 2017)

Preet Malik, *My Myanmar Years: A Diplomat's Account of India's Relations with the Region* (New Delhi: Sage Publishers, 2015)

Prem Mahadevan, 'Crossing the Line: Geopolitics and Criminality at the India-Myanmar Border', *Global Initiative against Transnational Organized Crime Research Report*, November 2020, pp.19–21

Pupul Jayakar, *Indira Gandhi: A Biography* (New Delhi: Penguin, 1979)

R K Yadav, *Mission R&AW* (New Delhi: Manas Publishers, 2014)

R N Prasad ed. *Autonomy Movements in Mizoram* (New Delhi: Vikas Publishers, 1994)

Rajashree Mazumder, '"I don't envy you": Mixed marriages and immigration debates in the 1920s and 1930s Rangoon, Burma', *The Indian Economic and Social History Review*, 51 (4), 2014, pp. 497–527

Rajashree Mazumder, 'Illegal Border Crossers and Unruly Citizens: Burma-Pakistan-Indian borderlands from the nineteenth to the mid-twentieth centuries', *Modern Asian Studies*, 53 (4), July 2019, p. 1173

Rajat Sethi and Shubhrastha, *The Last Battle of Saraighat: The Story of the BJP's Rise in the North-East* (New Delhi: Penguin India, 2017)

Rajeev Bhattacharya, *Rendezvous with Rebels: Journey to Meet India's Most Wanted Men* (New Delhi: HarperCollins India, 2014)

Rajiv Bhatia, *India-Myanmar Relations: Changing Contours* (New Delhi: Routledge, 2016)

Rakhee Bhattacharjee, *Development Disparities in Northeast India*, (New Delhi: Cambridge University Press, 2011)

Raphaelle Khan and Taylor C Sherman, 'India and overseas Indians in Ceylon and Burma, 1946-1965: Experiments in post-imperial sovereignty', *Modern Asian Studies*, 56(46), 2021, pp. 1153–1182

Rasul Baksh Rais, *China and Pakistan: A political Analysis of Mutual Relations* (Lahore: Progressive Publishers, 1977)

Reeju Ray, *Placing the Frontier in British North-East India: Law, Custom, and Knowledge* (New Delhi: Oxford University Press, 2023)

Rehman Sobhan, *Untranquil Recollections: The Years of Fulfilment* (New Delhi: Sage Publishers, 2016)

Renaud Egreteau, 'Burmese Indians in contemporary Burma: heritage, influence, and perceptions since 1988', *Asian Ethnicity*, 12(1), 2011

Renaud Egreteau, 'Instability at the Gate: India's Troubled Northeast and its External Connections', *CSH Occasional Paper No. 16*, (New Delhi: Centre de Sciences Humaines, 2006)

Ria Kapoor, *Making Refugees in India* (Oxford: Oxford University Press, 2021)

Richard Kozicki, *India and Burma, 1937–1957: A Study in International Relations* (unpublished PhD thesis, University of Pennsylvania, 1959)

Richard Sisson and Leo E. Rose, *War and Secession: Pakistan, India, and the Creation of Bangladesh* (California: University of California Press, 1991)

Robert L Solomon, *Saya San Rebellion* (Washington, D.C,: Rand Corporation, 1969)

Robert McMahon, *The Cold War on the Periphery: The United States, India, and Pakistan* (New York: Columbia University Press, 1996)

Robert H. Taylor, 'The Burmese Communist Movement and Its Indian Connection: Formation and Factionalism', *Journal of Southeast Asian Studies*, 14 (1), March 1983, pp. 95–108

Robert H. Taylor, *General Ne Win: A Political Biography* (Singapore: ISEAS Press, 2015)

Romila Thapar, *Somnatha: The Many Voices of a History* (London: Verso Books, 2005)

Rounaq Jahan, *Pakistan: Failure in National Integration* (Dhaka: University Press Ltd., 1995)

Rudra Chaudhuri, *Forged in Crisis: India and the United States since 1947* (London: Hurst Publishers, 2014)

Rudra Chaudhuri, 'The Making of an All Weather Friendship, Pakistan, China, and the History of a Border Agreement: 1949-1963', *The International History Review*, 40(1), 2018, pp. 41–64

S Biswas; P Daly, '"Cyclone not above politics": East Pakistan, disaster politics, and the 1970 Bhola Cyclone', *Modern Asian Studies*, 55(4), 2021, pp. 1382–1410

S Mahmud Ali, *Understanding Bangladesh* (London: Hurst Publishers, 2009)

S Mangi Singh, 'Understanding Conflict: An Insight into the Factors responsible for the Kuki-Naga Clashes in Manipur during the 1990s', *The Indian Journal of Political Science*, 70(2), April–June, 2009, pp. 495–508

S S Madalgi, 'Hunger in Rural India: 1960–61 to 1964–65', *Economic & Political Weekly*, 3(1/2), Jan. 1968, pp. 61–68

S S Uban, *Phantoms of Chittagong: The 'Fifth Army' in Bangladesh* (New Delhi: Allied Publishers, 1985)

Saadia Toor, *The State of Islam: Culture and Cold War Politics in Pakistan* (Chicago, US: Pluto Press, 2011)

Sahana Ghosh, *A Thousand Tiny Cuts: Mobility and Security across the Bangladesh-India Borderlands* (California: University of California Press, 2023)

Sajal Nag, 'Nehru and the Nagas: Minority Nationalism and the Post-Colonial State', *Economic and Political Weekly*, 44 (49), December 5-11, 2009

Sajal Nag, 'Tribals, Famine, Rats, State and the Nation', *Economic and Political Weekly*, 36(12), March 2001

Salil Tripathi, *The Colonel Who Would Not Repent: The Bangladesh War and its Unquiet Legacy* (New Haven: Yale University Press, 2016

Samrat Choudhury, *Northeast India: A Political History* (London: Hurst Publishers, 2023)

Sangeeta B. Pisharoty, *Assam: The Accord, The Discord* (New Delhi: Penguin India, 2019)

Sanjay Barbora, *Homeland Insecurities: Autonomy, Conflict, and Migration in Assam* (Oxford: Oxford University Press, 2022)

Sanjib Baruah, *In the Name of the Nation: India and its Northeast* (Stanford: Stanford University Press, 2020)

Sanjib Baruah, 'Nationalizing Space: Cosmetic Federalism and the Politics of Development in Northeast India', *Development and Change*, 34(5), 2003, pp. 923–924

Sanjoy Hazarika, *Strangers No More: New Narratives from India's Northeast* (New Delhi: Aleph Books, 2018)

Sashanka S Banerjee, *India, Mujibur Rahman, Bangladesh Liberation & Pakistan* (self-published memoirs, 2011)

Semanti Ghosh, *Different Nationalisms: Bengal, 1905–1947* (New Delhi: Oxford University Press, 2017)

Shalaka Thakur & Rajesh Venugopal, 'Parallel Governance and political order in contested territory: Evidence from the Indo-Naga ceasefire', *Asian Security*, 15(3), 2019

Sheikh Hasina ed. *Secret Documents of the Intelligence Branch on the Father of the Nation, Bangladesh: Bangabandhu Sheikh Mujibur Rahman, Vol. VII, 1962–63* (London: Routledge, 2022)

Sheikh Mujibur Rahman, *The Unfinished Memoirs* (Dhaka: University Press, 2012)

Shekhar Gupta, *Assam: A Divided Valley* (New Delhi: Vikas Publishers, 1984)

Shyamali Ghosh, *The Awami League, 1949-1971* (Dhaka: Academic Publishers, 1990)

Soe Myint, *Burma File: A Question of Democracy* (New Delhi: India Research Press, 2003)

Sreeradha Datta, *Act East Policy and Northeast India* (New Delhi: Vitasta Publishers, 2021)

Sreeradha Datta, 'Bangladesh's Relations with China and India: A Comparative Study', *Strategic Analysis*, 32(5), 2008, pp. 755–772

Srinath Raghavan, *India's War: The Making of Modern South Asia, 1939–1945* (London: Allen Lane, 2016)

Srinath Raghavan, 'Sino-Indian Boundary Dispute, 1948–60: A Reappraisal', *Economic and Political Weekly*, 41(36), September 9-15, 2006, pp. 3882–3892

Subir Bhaumik, *Insurgent Crossfire: North-East India* (New Delhi: Lancer Publishers, 1996)

Subir Bhaumik, *Troubled Periphery: Crisis of India's North East* (New Delhi: Sage Publishers, 2006)

Sufia M Uddin, *Constructing Bangladesh: Religion, Ethnicity, and Language in an Islamic Nation* (Chapel Hill, NC: UNC Press, 2006)

Sumathi Ramaswamy, *Passions of the Tongue: Language Devotion in Tamil India, 1891–1970* (LA: University of California Press, 1997)

Sunil Khilnani, *The Idea of India* (New York: Farrar, Straus, & Giroux, 1997)

T P Sreenivasan, *Words, Words, Words: Adventures in Diplomacy* (New Delhi: Longman, 2011)

Talukder Maniruzzaman, 'Bangladesh in 1975: The Fall of the Mujib Regime and its Aftermath', *Asian Survey*, 16(2), Feb. 1976, pp. 119–129

Tanvi Madan, *Fateful Triangle: How China Shaped US-India Relations During the Cold War* (Washington, D.C.: Brookings Institution Press, 2020)

Tara Kartha, *Tools of Terror: Light Weapons and India's Security* (New Delhi: IDSA, 1999)

Tariq Omar Ali, *A Local History of Global Capitalism: Jute and Peasant Life in the Bengal Delta* (New Jersey: Princeton University Press, 2018)

Ted Svensson, *Production of Postcolonial India and Pakistan: Meaning of Partition* (London: Routledge, 2013)

Thant Myint U, *The Hidden History of Burma: A Crisis of Race and Capitalism* (US: W.W. Horton & Co., 2020)

Thant Myint U, *The Making of Modern Burma* (Cambridge: Cambridge University Press, 2001)

Thant Myint-U, *The River of Lost Footsteps: A Personal History of Burma* (London: Faber & Faber, 2008)

Thongkholal Haokip, 'Essays on Kuki-Naga Conflict: A Review', *Strategic Analysis*, 37(2), 2013, pp. 251–259

Thongkholal Haokip, *India's Look East Policy and the Northeast* (New Delhi: Sage Publishers, 2015)

U Nu, *U Nu: Saturday's Son* (New Haven: Yale University Press, 1975)

Uditi Sen, *Citizen Refugee: Forging the Indian Nation After Partition* (Cambridge: Cambridge University Press, 2018)

Uma Shankar Singh; *Burma and India, 1948–1962: A Study in the Foreign Policies of Burma and India, and Burma's Policies Towards India* (Oxford: IB&H Publishers, 1979)

Vanda Felbab-Brown, 'Organized Crime, Illicit Economies, Civil Violence, & International Order: More Complex Than You Think', *Daedalus*, 146 (4), October 2017, pp. 98–111

Vanda Felbab-Brown, 'The Political Economy of Illegal Domains in India and China', *The International Lawyer*, 43(4), Winter 2009, pp. 1411–1428

Vazira Fazila-Yaccobali Zamindar, *The Long Partition and the Making of Modern South Asia: Refugees, Boundaries, Histories* (New York: Columbia University Press, 2010)

Vinay Sitapati, *Half-Lion: How Narasimha Transformed India* (New Delhi: Penguin Viking, 2016)

Vivek Chadha ed. *Armed Forces Special Powers Act: The Debate* (New Delhi: Manohar Parrikar Institute for Defence Studies and Analyses, 2012)

Wayne Wilcox, 'The Economic Consequences of Partition: India and Pakistan', *Journal of International Affairs*, 18(2), 1964, pp. 188–197

Willem van Schendel, *A History of Bangladesh* (Cambridge: Cambridge University Press, 2009)

Willem van Schendel, 'A War Within a War: Mizo Rebels and the Bangladesh Liberation Struggle', *Modern Asian Studies*, 50 (1), 2015, pp. 75–117

William Johnstone, *Burma's Foreign Policy: A Study in Neutralism* (Cambridge: Harvard University Press, 1963)

Yuimirin Kapai, 'Spatial Organisation of Northeast Inia: Colonial Politics, Power Structure, and Hills-Plains Relationship', *Indian Historical Review*, 47(1), 2020, pp. 150–169

Yuka Kobayashi, Josephine King, 'Myanmar's strategy in the China-Myanmar Economic Corridor: a failure in hedging?', *International Affairs*, 98(3), May 2022, pp. 1013–1032

Zoya Hasan, *Congress After Indira: Policy, Power, Political Change (1984–2009)* (New Delhi: Oxford University Press, 2012)

INDEX

7th Amendment Bill, 242
9/11, 281
22nd East Bengal Regiment, 215–16
22nd Light Infantry Divisions, 234
26/11 Mumbai attacks, 283, 288, 292
77th Light Infantry Divisions, 234
'8888' movement, 227–32, 234

Aam Aadmi Party, 306
AASU. *See* All Assam Student's Union (AASU)
Abdullah, Sheikh, 166
Acharya, B K, 44, 47–9
'Act East' policy, 2–3, 17, 285, 297–309, 326
Adamjee Jute mills, 50
Adani group, 285, 298–9, 301, 315–16, 321
Adani Power Jharkhand Ltd., 316
Adani, Gautam, 298
Afghanistan, 282, 292
  Soviet invasion of, 216
AFSPA. *See* Armed Forces Special Powers (Assam and Manipur) Act (AFSPA)

Agartala Conspiracy Case (1968), 132, 139, 140
Agartala, 69, 132, 139, 203, 242, 286, 291
  Chakmas, 238–45
AGP. *See* Asom Gana Parishad (AGP)
Ahmad, Tofael, 201
Ahmed, Fakhruddin Ali, 124, 291, 292
Ahmed, Gen. Moeen Uddin, 287–8
Ahmed, Khandkar Moshtaque, 189
Ahmed, Prof. Muzaffar, 137
Ahmed, Tajuddin, 119, 148, 193–4
aikia, 177–8, 184
Aizawl, 97, 99, 101, 103, 173, 184, 234, 236, 311
Ajmani, Jagdish, 198, 206–7, 208
'Akhand Bharat Diwas', 31
'Akhand Hindustan' agenda, 26
Akyab (Sittwe), 110
Al Badar, 209
Alam Khan, Serajul, 132, 149
Albania, 163
'Alee Command', 246, 269
Ali, Fakhruddin, 292

Ali, Mansur, 206
Ali, Nasim, 206
Ali, Shawkat, 139–40
Alikadam, 246
All Assam Gana Sangram Parishad, 175
All Assam Student's Union (AASU), 123, 157, 175, 177
All Bodo Students Union, 180
All India Hindu Mahasabha, 119
All India Radio (AIR), 120, 130, 203, 257
All Myanmar Hindu Central Council, 304
All Party Hill Leaders Conference, 106
All-India Service, 158
ALP, 302
Ambani, Dhirubhai, 45
Ambani, Mukesh, 301
America, 48
Amin, Noorul, 44
Anam, Mahfuz, 210
Ananda Bazar Patrika (newspaper), 195–6
Andaman and Nicobar Islands, 9, 41–2
Andaman Sea, 258
Andhra Pradesh, 73, 190
Angami Nagas, 61
Angami, Lt. Gen. Mowu, 67, 86, 163
Angamis, 60, 63
Angarpota enclaves, 261
Anglo-Burmese war III (1885), 7–8
ANLF. *See* Arakan National Liberation Front (ANLF)
anti-Assamese sentiment, 64
anticolonialism, 8, 9–11
anti-Dacca Muslim Bangla Movement, 165

Anti-Fascist People's Freedom League (AFPFL), 71, 86
anti-Indian riot, 9
anti-Karachi sentiment, 67
Anti-Muslim massacres, 9, 25, 121
Ao, Longri, 88
Ao, P Shilu, 87–8
Aos, 63
Arakan 'Mujahids', 32–3
Arakan Army (AA), 266, 301, 319
Arakan Independence Army, 165
Arakan National Liberation Front (ANLF), 98, 103, 165
Arakan ranges, 9, 12, 13, 101, 165, 172, 306
Arakan Rohingya National Organisation, 172
Arakan Rohingya Salvation Army (ARSA), 295, 296, 306
Arakan-based groups, 276
Arakanese Buddhists, 13
Arakanese Muslim (Rohingya), 13, 166–7, 198, 233, 236, 262, 266, 281, 285, 315
    anti-Rohingya crackdown, 295–6
    Rohingya crisis, 305–7
    Shillong accord, 165–73
Arakanese rebels, 269–70
Aref Ahmed, Kazi, 132, 149
Armed Forces (Special Powers) Act (1958), 18
Armed Forces Special Powers (Assam and Manipur) Act (AFSPA), 18, 54, 56, 80–1, 100, 112, 156–7, 161, 182, 259, 324
    imposition of, 58–67
'armed revolution', 205
Article 244A, 18
Article 371(A), 18

Article V (1951), 10
Arunachal Pradesh, 18, 79, 214, 236, 264, 292, 299, 314, 327
Asom Gana Parishad (AGP), 178–9, 180, 272–3
Assam Accord, 157
Assam agitation, 241
Assam Cabinets, 33
Assam Congress, 98
'Assam Movement' (1979–85), 123
Assam Regiment, 55
Assam Reorganisation Bill, 160
Assam Rifles' camp, 33, 62, 241, 265, 279, 327
Assam, 7, 12, 16–21, 25–30, 32, 79, 84, 87, 112, 118–19, 157–60, 200, 215, 223, 236, 240–1, 253, 292, 308, 310
   AFSPA, imposition of, 58–67
   anti-foreigner movement, 15
   armed support, 35–42
   BJP in, 309
   boundary demarcations, 105–11
   China-Burma-India trijunction, 89–96
   cross-border migration and movements, 179–83
   illegal migrants, 324
   language agitation, 42–52
   migration, 173–9
   Mizoram independence, 96–105
   Nehru-Noon agreement, 67–71
   religious disputes, 120–7
   Shillong accord, 165–73
Assamese nationalisms, 14
Assamese rebels, 266
Assamese, 31
Assistant High Commissioner (AHC) (Pakistan), 98, 134

Association of Southeast Asian Nations (ASEAN), 259–60
Astor, David, 70–1
Aung Min, 297, 303
Aung San, 11–12, 39–40
Aung Tun Thet, 298, 305
Australia, 2
Awami League (AL), 6, 44, 118–19, 127–9, 134, 137–42, 195, 206, 209–11, 214, 219–20, 226, 242–3, 269, 292, 308
   mutiny, 287–9
Ayodhya, 262–3

Ba Swe, 71, 92
Babri Masjid, 29, 243, 254–5, 262, 281
Baites, 97, 103, 106, 181
Bajoria, Bajoria, 45
Baksal, 192, 201
Balachandran, V, 259, 274–5
Balanced Trade Payments Arrangement (BTPA), 191–2
Balochistan, 140
Bandarkata border, 214
Bandung conference (1955), 41
Banerjee, Mamata, 264, 309
Banerjee, PN, 134, 139, 150, 197
Bangabandhu. See Mujibur Rahman, Sheikh
'Bangabhaban', 189
Bangabhumi movement, 215
Bangkok, 167, 231, 246, 275
   troops, 200–9
'Bangla Bhai', 291
Bangladesh Krishak Sramik Awami League (Baksal), 190
Bangladesh Liberation Front (BLF), 132–3
Bangladesh liberation war (1971), 15, 100, 222

Bangladesh Nationalist Party
(BNP), 172–3, 209–10, 216,
219, 220–1, 226, 242–5, 250,
281, 292, 322
anti-India nationalism, 268–74
Bangladesh, ties, 245–9
'Look East Policy', 256–64
Bangladesh Power Development
Board, 301
Bangladesh refugee crisis (1971),
15
Bangladesh Rifles (BDR), 205,
241, 274
mutiny, 287–92
Bangladesh, 2, 3–6, 9, 19, 20, 22,
157, 158, 184–5, 198, 228,
231, 253–4, 275, 283, 316
'Act East' policy, 297–309
anti-India nationalism, 268–74
anti-MNF, 165
'Bangabandhu', birth of,
135–43
Chakmas, 238–45
cross-border migration and
movements, 14–17, 179–83
drug smuggling, 274–80
economy and famine, 189–200
intra-party friction, 209–17
language agitation, 42–52
'Look East Policy', 256–64
mutiny, 287–92
Rajiv's outreach, 225–6
Shillong, road to, 158–65
ties, 245–9
See also Hasina, Sheikh
Bangladeshi Hindus, 263, 272, 281
Bangladeshi Muslim, 264
migrants, 285
Bangladesh-Myanmar border, 246
Bangur, Mungeeram, 45
Barua, Hem, 125–6

Baruah, Paresh, 156, 276, 290,
309–10
Baruah, Sanjib, 279
Basu, Chitta, 240
Battalion of the Parachute
Regiment, 285
Bawm communities, 326
Bay of Bengal Initiative for Multi-
Sectoral Technical and Economic
Cooperation (BIMSTEC), 260,
271
Bay of Bengal, 9, 41–2, 258, 260,
266, 309
BDR mutiny, 208
BDR revolt (2009), 284
BDR. See Bangladesh Rifles (BDR)
BDR-HQ, 287
Beihai port, 327
Beijing, 3–4, 20, 226, 235, 255,
257, 266, 297–300, 322, 326–7
Bangladesh, ties, 245–9
Beirut, 167
Belonia railway, 110
Belt and Road Initiative (BRI),
284, 298, 300
Bengal famine (1943), 28, 52
Bengali Hindus, 47, 49
Bengali Muslims, 43, 46, 119,
173–4, 305–6, 309
religious disputes, 120–7
Bengali-Assamese linguistic divide,
12
Bengali-Pashtun leadership, 118
Berlin Wall, 226
Bethel, 246, 270
Bharatiya Jana Sangh, 31, 144, 175,
310, 314
Bharatiya Janata Party (BJP), 2,
182, 260–1, 272–3, 301, 306–
9, 314–16, 323–4, 325, 328
migration, 173–9

Bhashani, Maulana, 44, 50, 145, 192, 193, 324

Bhattacharya, Lt. Col. Gunnindra Lal, 131

Bhave, Vinoba, 121–2

Bhindrawale, 180

Bhola, 289

Bhutan, 102, 139, 142, 143, 180, 275, 276, 300

Bhutto, Zulfiqar Ali, 102, 136, 166–7, 197, 203, 213

Biakchhunga, 171

Bihar, 121, 129, 190

Birla, G.D., 45

BIST-EC (Economic Connectivity), 271

BJP. See Bharatiya Janata Party (BJP)

BNP. See Bangladesh Nationalist Party (BNP)

BNP-Jamaat alliance, 283, 284

Bodh Gaya, 315

Bodo areas, 7

Bodo communities, 157, 179

'Bodo Liberation Tigers (BLT) Saffron Revolution', 292–7

Bodo Security Force, 180

Bodo Territorial Council, 293

Bogra, 216

Bombay, 69

Borbora, Golap, 175

Border Security Force (BSF), 200, 214, 220, 241, 274

boundary agreement (1961) (China), 109

Brahmanbaria, 203, 204

Brahmaputra river, 239

Brang Seng, 234–6, 248, 265

Britain, 9, 10, 66

British Indian Army, 55

Buddhism, 77, 315

Buddhist Chakmas, 171, 272

Buddhist monks, 292–3

Buddhist nationalism, 91, 281, 295, 324

Buddhist Sangha, 315

Buddhist Women Special Marriage and Succession Bill, 9

Burma Citizenship Act (1982), 229

Burma Domicile Bill (1937), 9

Burma Land Nationalization Act (1954), 40

Burma Legislative Council, 8

Burma, 3, 5, 20, 64, 81, 167, 180, 184–5, 246–7, 278, 323
army, 27
boundary demarcations, 105–11
boundary dispute, 74–9
Burmese economy, 71–4
communism in, 31–3
darmed support, 35–42
India and Burma relationship, 6, 233–7
India, separation from, 7–14
and India's policy line, 227–32
Japanese invasion, 9
Mizoram independence, 96–105
Nagaland as a state, 85–9
Nehru-Noon agreement, 67–71
Rajiv's outreach, 225–6

Burma-Bangladesh agreement (1978), 173

Burma-India-China trijunction, 65

Burmanisation of Labour Bill, 9

Burmese communists, 32

Burmese Hindus, 319

Burmese Indian community, 37

Burmese Indians, 26, 34, 228–9, 233
China-Burma-India trijunction, 89–96

Burmese intelligence, 98

Burmese Naga Hills District, 109
Burmese Naga rebels, 102, 257
Burmese rebel territory, 237
Buthidaung township, 13
Buthidaung, 32

CAA-NRC, 308–9, 311, 314, 325
Cachar district, 33, 64, 67, 174
Cairo, 51
Calcutta port, 217, 268
Calcutta, 12, 14, 25, 29, 31, 36,
    100, 120, 169, 211, 230, 236
    religious disputes, 120–7
    Six-Point Movement, 127–35
    troops, 200–9
Callahan, James, 50
Carrott, J, 60
'Cassim', 307
ceasefire agreement (1964), 85, 97
Central Board of Revenue, 37
Central Intelligence Agency (CIA),
    19
Central Public Works Department
    (CPWD), 241
Ceylon, 28, 144
Chagla, M C, 108
Chakesang, 'Lt. Gen.' Dusoi, 161
Chakma accord, 269
Chakma communities, 166
Chakma insurgency, 268
Chakma migrants, 122, 169, 214,
    231, 238–45, 242, 262
    anti-Chakma sentiment, 170
Chakma movement, 242
Chakravarty, Pinak Ranjan, 286,
    288, 292
Chaliha, Bimala Prasad, 88,
    159–60, 174
Champhai district, 99, 103, 234,
    236
Chandigarh, 69

Charbatia airbase, 127
Chatterjee, N C, 121, 125
Chatterjee, Somnath, 240
Chattra League, 149, 197, 202
Chaudhury, Abu Syed, 202
Chavan, Shankarrao B., 241
Chen Yi, 102
Chetia, Anup, 270, 276, 307–8,
    309
Chhattisgarh, 80
Chiang Mai, 167, 231, 234
Chidambaram, P., 292
Chief of Defence Staff, 202
Chin Hills, 9, 98, 104
Chin insurgents groups, 302
Chin migrants, 312
Chin National Front (CNF),
    236–7, 248, 265, 266, 302, 319
Chin rebels, 226
Chin state, 96
Chin, 10, 32, 54, 181, 233, 236–7,
    318–20, 326
China war, 125
China, 1, 3–4, 10, 20, 21, 42, 57,
    80, 119, 144, 155, 157, 164,
    187, 221, 222, 228, 235, 268,
    281, 283, 284, 300, 302, 304,
    310, 318, 322, 323, 326–7
    Bangladesh, economy and
        famine, 189–200
    Bangladesh, ties, 245–9
    boundary demarcations, 105–11
    boundary dispute, 74–9
    Burmese economy, 71–4
    China-Burma-India trijunction,
        89–96
    communist victory in, 31–2
    cross-border migration and
        movements, 179–83
    Cultural Revolution, 153
    expanding strategy, 255

Mizoram independence, 96–105
Myanmar's reliance, 294
Nagaland as a state, 85–9
Rajiv's outreach, 226
religious disputes, 120–7
'Saffron Revolution', 292–7
Shillong accord, 165–73
Six-Point Movement, 127–35
troops, 200–9
US intervention, 83–4
China–Burma–India trijunction, 109
China-Myanmar Economic Corridor, 298
Chins, 32
Chittagong Cantonment, 103
Chittagong city, 246
Chittagong Hill Tracts (CHT), 78, 122, 205
Chittagong port, 110, 289
Chittagong Urea Fertilizer Co. Ltd., 290
Chittagong, 13, 86, 103, 110, 111, 165–6, 172, 213, 244, 249, 268, 271, 290, 320, 323, 327
Chopra, 124–5
Chou Enlai, 76, 91, 100, 104
   China-Burma-India trijunction, 89–96
Choudhury, Sourja Kumar, 131–2, 133–4
Chowdhury, Salahuddin Quader, 289–90
Christianity, 304, 310, 311
Christians, 32, 315, 325
CHT accord, 246, 268, 269, 270, 290, 326
Chumbi Valley, 103
Churachandpur, 181
CIA flights, 127
CIA, 147, 198, 208

'C-in-C', 67
Circuit House, 217
Citizenship (Amendments) Act (2020), 281, 308
Citizenship Act (1955), 124
The Citizenship Act, 157
Citizenship Amendment Act (CAA), 309–10
CNF. See Chin National Front (CNF)
CNN news, 289
Coal Board, 213
Cochran, 201
Coco Islands, 41–2, 230, 258, 260, 266, 319
COIN duties, 327
Colombo, 231
Comilla, 131
communal riot (1964), 211
communalism, 12, 91, 273
communism, 7, 31
Communist International (Comintern), 32
Communist Party of Burma (CPB), 33, 34, 81, 210, 228, 235, 248
Communist Party of India (CPI), 33, 145
Communist Party of India (Marxist) CPI(M), 101, 240, 273
Communist Party, 50, 130
Congress. See Indian National Congress,
Cooch Behar, 67
cordon sanitaire, 26–7
Council Muslim League, 137, 209
COVID-19, 308
Cox, 13, 246
CPB. See Communist Party of Burma (CPB)
CPI(M). See Communist Party of India (Marxist) CPI(M)

CPI. *See* Communist Party of India (CPI)
CPWD. *See* Central Public Works Department (CPWD)
Cultural Revolution, 21, 99, 100, 103
Cyclone Bhola, 142
Czech, 37

Dacca Central Jail, 199, 207
Dacca, 32, 43, 45, 55, 78, 102, 120, 122, 126–7, 172, 189, 195, 200–8, 218–20, 222
    Mizoram independence, 96–105
    Mujib-Tajuddin split, 147–52
    Naxalite movement, 143–7
    Nehru-Noon agreement, 67–71
    Six-Point Movement, 127–35
Dahagram, 84, 126, 261
Daily Ittefaq (newspaper), 133, 201, 245
Daily Star (newspaper), 210
Dakota airplane, 36
Dakota DC-3, 86
Dalai Lama, 75, 77, 327
Dalim, Maj. Shariful Haque, 189, 199–201, 207
Damodaran, A K, 198–9
Dandakaranya camps, 120
'Dandakaranya Project', 67–8
Das, A K, 201, 203–5, 208
Das, Dr. Surinder, 236
Dasgupta, Chandrashekhar, 194–5
Datta, Sreeradha, 249
Daultana, Mian Mumtaz Mohammad, 137–8
Dawki Tamabil border, 264
Dayal, Rajeshwar, 75, 76
Dehradun, 215
    Haflong, 215
Delhi-Jakarta relations, 99

Demagiri, 110
Democratic Action Committee, 140
Democratic Alliance of Burma (DAB), 235
'democratic deviation', 318
Deng Xiaoping, 229
Desai, Morarji, 172, 215, 220
DGFI. *See* Directorate General of Forces Intelligence (DGFI)
Dhaka grenade attack (2004), 290
Dhaka metro rail project, 298
Dhaka, 5, 21, 22, 25, 67, 233, 238–43, 263, 269, 281, 284, 315
    anti-India nationalism, 268–74
    Bangladesh, ties, 245–9
    'Look East Policy', 256–64
    Rajiv's outreach, 225–6
    'Saffron Revolution', 292–7
Dhaka-Shanti Bahini accord (1997), 266
Dhakeshwari, 208
Dhanbad, 177
Dhanmondi, 189
Dhar, Manoranjan, 204
Dhar, Prithvi Nath, 149
Dhubri, 148, 310
DIB, 133, 171
Dima Hasao districts, 7
Dimapur-Kohima-Imphal road, 64
Diphu Pass, 92, 109
Director General of Ansars, 45
'Director of Intelligence', 67
Director of the Asian Affairs Department, 104
Directorate General of Forces Intelligence (DGFI), 238, 240, 245, 246, 269
Dixit, Jyotindra Nath, 192, 195–6, 199, 206, 257–8, 277

Doklam standoff (2017), 327
Doulatram, Jairamdas, 60, 61
Doval, Ajit K., 171
DP, 193, 195, 210
Dumdum airport, 236
Dutt, Subimal, 139, 193, 195–6, 198, 211–12

East Bengal, 14, 29–30, 32, 34
  'Act East' policy, 297–309
  'Bangabandhu', birth of, 135–43
  cross-border migration and movements, 14–17, 179–83
  drug smuggling, 274–80
  economy and famine, 189–200
  Hindu minorities, 31
  intra-party friction, 209–17
  language agitation, 42–52
  'Look East Policy', 256–64
  mutiny, 287–92
  Rajiv's outreach, 225–6
  Shillong, road to, 158–65
  ties, 245–9
East Delhi, 235
East Dinajpur, 124
East Khasi Hills, 274
East Pakistan Awami League (EPAL), 119
East Pakistan Rifles (EPR), 119, 120
East Pakistan, 13, 21, 34, 111
  'Act East' policy, 297–309
  anti-Hindu violence, 117–19
  armed support, 35–42
  'Bangabandhu', birth of, 135–43
  boundary demarcations, 105–11
  China-Burma-India trijunction, 89–96
  cross-border migration and movements, 14–17, 179–83

  drug smuggling, 274–80
  economy and famine, 189–200
  intra-party friction, 209–17
  language agitation, 42–52
  'Look East Policy', 256–64
  Mizoram independence, 96–105
  Mujib-Tajuddin split, 147–52
  mutiny, 287–92
  Naxalite movement, 143–7
  Nehru-Noon agreement, 67–71
  Rajiv's outreach, 225–6
  religious disputes, 120–7
  Shillong, road to, 158–65
  ties, 245–9
East Pakistan-India border, 75
Eastern Command, 100
Egypt, 216
  boundary dispute, 74–9
EPAL, 138
EPR soldiers, 151
Ershad, Maj. Gen., 189, 200, 202, 217–20, 226, 238–9, 242, 249, 250
  anti-India nationalism, 268–74
'euphemism for war', 26
Europe, 275
European Union (EU), 294, 315

famine (1943), 6
famine (1974), 190
Farakka agreement, 216
Farakka barrage issue, 141, 263
Farland, Joseph, 147–8
Farraka, 198–9, 239
Fauj, Mukti, 144
'February Accord', 169
'Federal Government of Nagaland (FGN)', 68, 88–9, 164
Fenny, 110
Fernandes, George, 248, 267
Financial Times (newspaper), 176

First Anglo-Burman War (1825), 230

First India Round Table Conference, 8

Light Infantry Divisions, 234

Forward Bloc, 240

'Forward Policy', 78

'fostered ethnicization', 10

France, 163, 274

Free Movement Regime (FMR), 299, 317

Friendship, Cooperation and Peace, Treaty of, 188

Friendship, Treaty of, 10

Gaddafi, Muammar, 307

Galwan clash (2020), 327

Ganabhaban, 201, 286

'Ganakantha' (newspaper), 197

Ganatantra Dal, 50

Gandhi, Indira, 52, 81, 96, 100, 108–11, 123, 126, 183–5, 189, 195, 227–8, 238, 247, 275, 324
  'Act East' policy, 297–309
  anti-Hindu violence, 117–19
  armed support, 35–42
  'Bangabandhu', birth of, 135–43
  boundary demarcations, 105–11
  Chakmas, 238–45
  China-Burma-India trijunction, 89–96
  cross-border migration and movements, 14–17, 179–83
  drug smuggling, 274–80
  economy and famine, 189–200
  intra-party friction, 209–17
  language agitation, 42–52
  'Look East Policy', 256–64
  migration, 173–9
  Mizoram independence, 96–105

Mujib-Tajuddin split, 147–52

mutiny, 287–92

Naxalite movement, 143–7

Nehru-Noon agreement, 67–71

Rajiv's outreach, 225–6

Rangoon visit, 95

religious disputes, 120–7

Shillong accord, 165–73

Shillong, road to, 158–65

ties, 245–9

Gandhi, Mohandas Karamchand, 29

Gandhi, Rajiv, 6, 21, 177–8, 183–4, 225–6, 238–9, 244, 246–7, 249, 250, 275, 280
  assassination, 227
  Burma and India's policy line, 227–32
  on drug smuggling, 274–80
  'Look East Policy', 256–64
  See also 'Look East Policy'

Gandhi, Sonia, 274

Ganga river, 141, 216–17, 220, 262, 263

Ganga Water Treaty, 255, 263, 268

Ganga-Brahmaputra link, 215

gaon-burras (village elders), 17

Garo, 63, 64

General Officer Commanding (GOC), 62, 100

Geneva, 59, 168

Germany, 20, 220

Ghana, 112

Ghosh, Col. Sailendra C, 133–4

'Ghoshal thesis', 33

Ghoshal, Hamendra Nath, 33

Ghulam Mohammad, Bakshi, 48

'Gilbertarian', 51

Gilgit Baltistan, 74

Gill, Kanwar Pal Singh, 175–6

Global War on Terrorism, 281–2, 284, 292
Goa, 78
Goalpara, 174
Goalphokar, 124–5
GOC-Chittagong, 242
Godda project, 301, 316
Goenka, Badridas, 45
'Golden Bird', 258–9, 265, 276
Golden Crescent, 278
Golden Triangle, 17, 22, 167, 185, 255, 277, 278, 319
Goncalves, Eric, 94
Gono Bahini, 215
Gono Forum, 244–5
Gonsalves, Eric, 79
Gopalganj, 120
Goran area, 269
Goshen, 246, 270
Government of India Act formalised (1935), 9
Gowda, H.D. Deve, 268, 270, 275
'Great Calcutta Killings', 12
Great Depression, 8–9
Great Hall, 100
'great indignation', 13
Grewal, 265, 266–7
Gromyko, Andrei, 147
Guerilla Warfare Training Centre, 164
Guidaillu, Rani, 106
Gujarat, 316
Gujral, 260
Gulmohar Park, 169
Gundevia, Y.D., 122, 132
Gupta, Bhupesh, 145
Gupta, Girish, 232
Gupta, Indrajit, 270
Gupta, Shekhar, 176–7
Gurjal, 264
Gurung, Lt. Gen. (r) Shakti, 267

Guwahati, 159, 291–2, 309, 310

Hajong communities, 122, 166, 169, 241
Haksar, Nandita, 267
Haksar, P N, 108, 142–3
Haldia-Calcutta port, 215
Hamstrung, 269
Haq, A K Fazlul, 44, 48–50
Haque, Fazlul, 129
Hardinge bridge, 193
Harkat-ul-Jihad-al Islami Bangladesh (HuJI-B), 261, 288–9
'hartal', 49
Hasina, Sheikh, 132, 220–1, 238, 242–5, 250, 254, 255, 266–7, 281–3, 316–18, 326
    'Act East' policy, 297–309
    anti-India nationalism, 268–74
    counter religious radicalism, 284–5
    general elections, 320–2
    mutiny, 287–92
    Rajiv's outreach, 225–6
    'Saffron Revolution', 292–7
Hassan Mahmood, Iqbal, 147
Hazratbal, 122
Hefazat-e-Islam, 308, 320
Hekmatyar, Gulbuddin, 236
Herojit, Thounaojam, 280
Hills District, 61
Hindenburg Research, 301
Hindu Mahasabha, 26, 121, 125
Hindu nationalism, 14, 22, 31, 304
Hindu right, 11
Hindu youth, 310
Hinduism, 315
Hindu-Muslim riots, 12
Hindus, 12, 29, 34, 43, 118, 120–1, 211, 304
    cross-border businesses, 45–6

Nehru's diplomacy, 29–30
religious disputes, 120–7
Hindustan Times (newspapaer), 164
Hindutva, 284, 304–5, 314, 320, 323–4
Hizb-ut-Tahrir, 291
Hmar, 97
Home Guard, 97
'Hongkin Government', 60
Hossain, Brig. Gen. Mahmud, 287
Hossain, Dr. Kamal, 150, 193–4, 221
Hôtel de Crillon, 274
Hotel Sonnenberg, 70
HuJI-B, 291
Hunza, 74
Hussain, Touhid, 287
Hussain, Zakir, 129
Hydari, Akbar, 58
Hyderabad, 306

IB report (1971), 181
IB. *See* Intelligence Bureau (IB)
IG-BSF, 242
IHC, 221
Illegal Migrants (Determination and Tribunals) Act (IMDT) (1983), 177, 272
Immigrants (Expulsion from Assam) Act, 26
Imphal Valley, 1, 157, 181, 277, 291, 311, 324
Indemnity Ordinance, 210
India-Myanmar-Thailand highway, 298
India Today (newspaper), 273
India, Constitution of, 26, 80, 168, 184
India, Government of, 236
India-Bangladesh border, 272

India-Bangladesh Economic Community, 191
India-Burma Boundary Agreement (1967), 21
India-East Pakistan border, 120
Indian Air Force (IAF), 86–7, 200, 236
Indian Air Force MI-8 helicopters, 244
Indian Airlines office, 262
Indian army, 18, 62
Indian constitution, 18
Indian Express (newspaper), 245
Indian High Commission, 47, 262
Indian Muslims, 29, 30, 53, 121, 273
Indian National Congress, 26, 32, 45, 48–9, 29, 126, 155–6, 166, 171, 172, 179–82, 184, 233, 240, 244, 250, 264, 311
anti-India nationalism, 268–74
on drug smuggling, 274–80
migration, 173–9
Indian Naxalites, 187
Indian Ocean Region (IOR), 266, 315
Indian Railway Construction Co. (IRCON), 262, 271
Indian rebels, 237
Indian Red Cross, 192
Indian Trading Corporation, 39
Indian troops, 90
Indian Union Muslim League (IUML), 272–3
'Indians Go Home', 8
India-Pakistan war (1965), 84, 95
Indonesia, 108
Institute for Defence Studies and Analyses, 145
Intelligence Bureau (IB), 32, 33–4, 37, 46, 64, 102–3, 112, 121–2, 127, 131–4, 168, 170, 233–6

'Intelligence Wing', 106

International Crimes Tribunal, 307

International Institute of Social History in Amsterdam, 19

International Monetary Fund, 321–2

Inter-Services Intelligence (ISI), 37, 68, 78, 98, 102, 104–5, 133, 140, 166, 213, 236, 264

IOR. *See* Indian Ocean Region (IOR)

Iraq, 282

Irrawaddy, 302

Isak Chishi Swu, 156–7, 276

ISI Liaison Officer, 164

Islam, 304, 310

Islam, Amirul, 148

Islam, Syed Nazrul, 194

Islami Andolan Bangladesh, 320

Islamic conservatism, 11

Islampur police station, 124–5

Islampur, 200

Ittefaq (newspaper), 205

Jacob, Lt. Gen. Jack F R, 199, 200, 209–10

Jaguar Land Rover, 298

Jaintia hills, 63, 64, 106

Jalil, Md. Abdul, 192–3, 208

Jamaat-e-Islami, 137, 209, 273, 281, 288–9, 291, 292, 307, 308

Jamaat-ul-Mujahideen Bangladesh (JMB), 291

Jamir, S C, 160

Jammu and Kashmir, 48, 122, 141–2, 310–11, 325

Jammu, 306

Jamuna River Bridge construction, 262

Janajati Dharma-Sanskriti Suraksha Manch, 310

Janapad, 196

Janata Dal, 189, 216

Japan International Cooperation Agency, 300

Japan, 2, 10, 254, 300

Japanese troops, 13

Jasimuddin, 261

Jasokie, 65

Jasokie, John Bosco, 60–1

Jatiya Chhatra League, 204

Jatiya Party, 226, 242, 243, 322

Jatiya Rakkhi Bahini (National Defence Force JRB), 151, 194–5, 201, 204–5, 207, 211

Jatiya Samajtantrik Dal (JSD), 192–3, 197, 207–8, 211, 213, 215

Jatiya, 245

'Jericho', 97

Jessore border, 45, 131, 289

Jethmalani, Ram, 177

Jews, 295

Jharkhand, 177, 301

Jinnah, Mohammad Ali, 11, 13, 43–4

Jiribam, 181

'Joi Aai Axom' ('Glory to Mother Assam'), 174

Joint Boundary Commission, 109

Joint Intelligence Committee (JIC), 106–7

Joint Rivers Commission, 216–17, 218

Jordon, 270

Jorhat, 286

Joshi, D S, 107–8

JS (Bangladesh), 198

junta, 226, 228–9, 230, 237, 247–8, 254, 255, 267, 277, 282, 303, 317–18, 324, 326

Buddhist monks protest, 292–3

Burma and India's policy line, 227–32

India and Burma relationship, 233–7

'Look East Policy', 256–64

'Saffron Revolution', 292–7

K Yhome, 314

Kabir, Humayun, 129–30

Kabul channel, 166–7, 184

Kabul, 166

Kacharis, 33

Kachin Independence Army, 77

Kachin Independence Organisation (KIO), 77, 94, 101–4, 185, 226–7, 230–7, 246, 248, 265–6, 275–6, 296–7
illicit trade, 323

Kachin insurgency, 81

Kachin insurgents groups, 302

Kachin rebellion, 72, 297, 302

Kachin state, 10, 13, 32, 39, 54, 94, 101, 103, 104, 127, 164, 226, 245, 247, 302
illicit trade, 323

Kader Bahinis, 205, 213, 214–15

Kaito, 78, 98

Kaladan Multi-Modal Transit Transport Project, 267, 298

Kaladan project, 271

Kalaikunda, 286

Kangleipak Communist Party (KCP), 157

Kanoria, Radha Kissen, 45

Kao, Rameshwar Nath, 112, 120, 127, 142–4, 150, 189

Kaptai, 103

Karachi, 12–13, 32, 41, 43, 51–2, 102, 110, 166
boundary dispute, 74–9

Karbi Anglong district, 7, 179, 180

Karbi Anglong movement, 157

Karbi Anglong People's Conference, 180

Karbi communities, 180

Karen National Defence Organisation (KNDO), 38

Karen National Union (KNU), 38–9

Karen rebellion, 6, 20, 32, 35–6, 72
armed support, 35–42

Karenni, 54

Karim, Tariq, 242–3, 268–9, 305, 308

Karimganj riots (1968), 176

Karnaphuli Paper, 50

Karnaphuli river, 56, 70, 96, 103, 110

Kashmir insurgency, 180

Kashmir war (1948), 53

Kashmir, 21, 43, 49, 74–6, 80, 81, 86, 89, 99, 102, 118, 136, 142, 166, 187, 222, 253
'Bangabandhu', birth of, 135–43
boundary demarcations, 105–11
India-Pakistan war, 95
language agitation, 42–52
Nehru-Noon agreement, 67–71
religious disputes, 120–7
US intervention, 83–4
war, 25–6

Kashmiri flag, 325

Katari, R D, 108

Kathmandu, 163

Katju, K.N., 62

Kaul, T N, 58–9, 63, 66, 160

KCP, 182

Keishing, Rishang, 62

Keivom, Lalthlamuong, 232, 233, 248

Kennedy, 77–8

Kenya, 64
Kerala, 32, 73
Kerhuo, Kenneth, 88, 163
Khaleda, 226
Khalifas, 150–1
Khaliquzzaman, Chaudhry, 52
Khalistan movement, 180
Khalistani militants, 236
Khan, Badshah, 48–9
Khan, Col. Fatah, 78
Khan, Gen. Yahya, 141
Khan, General Ayub, 20, 50, 55–7,
    75, 80–1, 99, 104, 118, 122,
    125–7, 137–41
    boundary dispute, 74–9
    Burmese economy, 71–4
    Nagaland as a state, 85–9
    Nehru and, 83–4
    Nehru-Noon agreement, 67–71
    Six-Point Movement, 127–35
Khan, Inayatullah, 207
Khan, Liaquat Ali, 26, 43
Khan, Lt. Gen. Tikka, 148
Khan, Maj. Gen. Akbar, 78
Khan, Serajul Alam, 208
Khan, Zafrullah, 51
Khanna, Rajinder, 231
Khaplang (NSCN-K), 276
Khaplang, Shagwang S, 157, 165,
    274, 313
Khasi hills, 63, 64, 106
Khin Nyunt, 257, 265, 267
Khowai border, 203
Khulna, 14, 29, 45, 122
KIO ceasefire (1994), 293
Kipgens, 181
KNU, 302
Kochar, Maj. Gen. R K, 62
Kohima, 59, 64, 161
Kokang, 318
Kolkata, 309

Konkalion, 87
Konyak, 313
Kuki areas, 327
Kuki armed groups, 317
Kuki communities, 1, 7, 33, 97,
    106, 181, 324
Kuki National Front, 181–2
Kuomintang, 41, 75, 93
Kyi Thein, Brig. Gen., 294, 298

Ladakh, 89, 103
Lahore Resolution (1940), 44
laikunda Air Force Station, 286
Lal Singh, Sachindra ('Sachin-da'),
    132
Laldenga, Mizo rebel leader, 21,
    96–8, 104, 163, 165–70, 173,
    184, 213, 234
    Mizoram independence, 96–105
Lalnunmawia, 98
Lalthangliana, 100
land boundary agreement (1974),
    261
land nationalisation (1954), 90
Land Reforms Commission, 75
Landfall Island, 266
Laos-Myanmar-Thailand, 17
Lawngtlai, 110
Layshi, 87
Left Front, 273
Legislative Assembly of Nagaland,
    18
Lhasa uprising, 75
Liaison Committee, 163
Liberation Front, 149
Line of Actual Control, 327
Liu Shaoqi, 102
Lohit Frontier Division, 109
London, 8, 88, 165, 197–8
'Look East Policy' (LEP), 228,
    254–5, 256–64, 280, 297

Lower Burma, 32
Lum Dau, Col. James, 234, 236
Lunglei district, 99
Lushai hills, 9, 32, 84, 96, 97

'Ma Ma Operation', 98
Machiavellian architect, 189
Madhya Pradesh, 73
Madras, 73
Maha Bandoola, 230
Mahana, 294
Mahanta, Prafulla Kumar, 175, 179
Maharashtra, 273
Mahmuam, 103
Mahmud Chowdhury, Amir
    Khasru, 209
Maintenance of Internal Security
    Act, 169
Maitre, R M, 133
Malaya, 64, 66
Malda, 121
Malik, Capt. Mumtaz, 131
Malik, Gen. V.P., 276
Malik, Preet, 257
Mandalay, 35, 75, 295
Manekshaw, Lt. Gen. Sam, 100
'Manhattan', 166
Mani, R S, 86, 91, 93
Manipur Rifles, 97
Manipur, 7, 9, 18, 34, 65, 87, 101,
    106, 155–7, 231–2, 265, 278,
    311–13
    'Act East' policy, 297–309
    BJP in, 309
    'buffer zone', 1–2
    cross-border migration and
        movements, 179–83
    illegal migrants, 324
    Manipuri militants, 259
    migration, 173–9
    Mizoram independence, 96–105

Nehru-Noon agreement, 67–71
    Shillong, road to, 158–65
Manju, Anwar Hossain, 201,
    205–7
Manzoor, Maj. Gen. Md. Abul, 219
Manzur, Brig. M A, 200
Mao, 32, 77, 101
    death, 229
Mara Autonomous District Council
    (MADC), 311
Maran Brang Seng, 231
Maritime Boundary Delimitation
    Agreement, 230
Martial law, 130
Marxist-Leninist jargon, 34
'master theoretician', 33
Matarbari port, 300, 301
Mathai, Ranjan, 229, 247, 256,
    259–60
Mathur, A., 269, 270, 289, 290
Matikhrü massacre, 86
Mau Tam, 96–7
Maung Aye, Vice Sr. Gen., 260,
    276
Maung, Sr. Gen. Saw, 233
Maungdaw township, 13, 32
'Mayer Kanna' movement, 216
McMahon Line, 10, 76–7
MEA, 34, 40, 42, 46, 63, 66,
    107–8, 118, 131, 160, 198,
    201, 206, 210, 228–9, 245
    'Look East Policy', 256–64
Medhi, Bishnuram, 61, 62, 63
Meghalaya, 7, 18, 64, 155–6, 159,
    200, 241, 27, 311
    BJP in, 309
Meghalaya-Tangail/Mymensigh,
    214
Meitei communities, 1, 14, 97,
    101, 181, 311, 317, 327
Meitei-Naga divide, 311

Memorandum of Settlement, 157

Menon, Krishna, 41

Menon, Shivshankar, 286, 288–9, 293, 302–3

'Maj. Menon' (K Sankaran Nair, future R&AW chief), 139

Mia, Manik, 133, 137

Michael Scott, Reverend, 70–1

Middle East, 51

migrant crisis (1950), 6

military coup (2021), 16

Min Aung Hlaing, Sr. Gen., 283, 296, 297, 303–4, 318

Minister of Commerce, 209

Ministry of Home Affairs (MHA), 159

Ministry of Rehabilitation, 67

'Minus-Two' formula, 291

Mirza, Iskander, 50–1, 52, 54, 68, 71

Mishra, Brajesh, 289

'Mishra' Lt. Col., 139

Mizo Army Chief, 171

Mizo District, 109

Mizo Hills District, 98, 110

Mizo insurgency (1966), 5, 15, 84–5, 96

Mizo National Front (MNF), 97–8, 99, 100, 103, 105, 106, 157, 166–71, 181, 184, 234, 240, 309, 311

Mizo People's Conference (MPC), 166, 171

Mizo rebellion, 3, 21, 97, 222, 236

Mizo Union, 166, 168

Mizo–Chin alliance, 106

Mizoram accord, 181, 184, 234

Mizoram National Famine Front (MNFF)
Mizoram independence, 96–105

Mizoram Peace Accord, 173

Mizoram Pradesh Congress, 168

Mizoram, 19, 56, 97, 103, 166, 170–1, 184, 200, 231, 236, 259, 264–5, 309–12, 315, 319
BJP in, 309
boundary demarcations, 105–11
independence, 96–104

Modi, Narendra, 2, 297–8, 301, 303, 304, 312–16, 320

Moeen, 291, 292

Mohammadpur, 270

Mollah, Abdul Quader, 307

Mon, 54

Moni, 201–2

Montague-Chelmsford reforms, 8

Morarjee, Sumati, 191

Moreh, 17, 105, 255

Moreh-Tamu border, 255, 258, 277

Moscow, 144, 190

Mosharraf, Brig. Gen. Khaled, 207

Moshtaque, 198–9, 201–4, 219, 221
intra-party friction, 209–17

Mountbatten, Louis, 26

Mufti, Mehbooba, 325

Muivah, Thuingaleng, 101, 156–7, 163–5, 274–6, 312–13

Mujahid Party, 306–7

'Mujib Bahini 2.0', 149–51, 206, 210

'Mujib' Rahman, Sheikh Mujibur '. See Mujibur Rahman, Sheikh

Mujibnagar government, 143

Mujib-Tajuddin split, 151–2

Mujibur Rahman, Sheikh, 21, 44, 49–50 113, 119, 126, 128–9, 175, 190, 204, 221–2, 261, 269
assassination, 189, 257
Bangladesh, economy and famine, 189–200
Mujib-Tajuddin split, 147–52

Naxalite movement, 143–7
Six-Point Movement, 127–35
Mukharji, Deb, 209, 292
Mukherjee, Pranab, 220, 286
Mukherjee, Syama Prasad, 29, 30–1, 43
Mukhopadhaya, Gautam, 303–4
Mukti Bahini, 119–20, 127–8, 147, 150, 194
'Mukti Dibas' (Liberation Day), 137
Mukti Fauj, 149–50
Mullik, Bhola Nath, 32, 60
Muslim Bangla Radio, 165–6
Muslim Chamber of Commerce of Chittagong, 13
Muslim League, 27, 43, 46, 49
Muslims, 12, 13, 25, 31, 266, 272, 315, 325
communal riots, 211–12
Myanmar coup (2021), 2
Myanmar Investment Commission, 298
Myanmar National Archives (MNA), 19
Myanmar, 1, 3–5, 15, 19–22, 236, 246, 253–4, 275, 281, 283, 292–3, 296, 302, 315, 318, 323–4
'Act East' policy, 297–309
anti-India nationalism, 268–74
Bangladesh, ties, 245–9
cross-border movements, 14–17
India's policy, 254
'Look East Policy', 256–64
Myanmar's Defence Services Academy, 302
Myitkyina District, 36, 39, 109, 296
Myitsone Dam, 302

Mymensingh, 98–9, 122, 148, 214
Mymensingh-Tangail region, 204–5

Naf river, 13
Naga Army, 67
'Naga card', 80
Naga communities, 160
Naga Federal Government, 168
Naga Hills Districts, 6, 63
Naga Hills-Tuensang Area (NHTA), 66–7, 77
'Naga Home Guard', 61
Naga movement, 5, 18, 54, 275
Naga National Council (NNC), 21, 55, 58–9, 60, 65, 156
Naga National Political Groups (NNPG), 313
Naga Peace Committee (NPC), 163, 164–6
Naga People's Convention (NPC), 87–8
Naga rebels, 3, 9, 10, 14, 15, 17, 21, 40, 41, 98, 235, 256, 266, 274–5
drug smuggling, 274–80
Nehru-Noon agreement, 67–71
'Saffron Revolution', 292–7
Naga Self-Administered Zone of Sagaing, 313
Naga-Akbar Hydari Accord (1947), 58
Nagaland Baptist church, 88
Nagaland Peace Talks, 88
Nagaland, 18–19, 56, 156, 166, 184, 231, 256, 264, 276, 311–13, 324
AFSPA, imposition of, 58–67
BJP in, 309
cross-border migration and movements, 179–83

drug smuggling, 274–80
migration, 173–9
Naga insurgency, 80–1
Nehru-Noon agreement, 67–71
Shillong, road to, 158–65
as a state, 85–9
Nagaon district, 174
Naidu, Padmaja, 123
Nambiar, Vijay, 296, 318
Nanda, Gulzarilal, 105–6
Nandy, Bibhuti Bhushan, 231, 235
Nanking Military Academy, 102
Nanyun township, 313
Narayan, Jayprakash (JP), 88–9, 161–3
Narayanganj, 50, 122
Narcotics Control Bureau (NCB), 19, 233, 260, 277
drug smuggling, 274–80
Nasrallah Khan, Nawab, 138
Nasser, Gamal, 78
'Nath Babu'. See Ojha, P N
National Archives of India, 19
National Awami Party (Bhashani) (NAP-B), 137, 147, 192
National Awami Party (NAP), 137–9
National Awami Party-Muzaffar (NAP-M), 137, 145, 210
National Bank of Pakistan, 14
National Defence College, 217
National Democratic Front of Bodoland (NDFB), 180, 259, 263
National Democratic Front, 137
National Investigation Agency, 246, 317
National League for Democracy (NLD), 227, 248, 254
National Liberation Front of Tripura (NLFT), 157, 181

National Register of Citizens (NRC), 25, 123, 124, 272, 308, 314
National Security Advisor, 171
National Security Council (NSC), 219–20
National Security Intelligence (NSI), 246
National Socialist Council of Nagaland (NSCN), 156, 165, 231
National Socialist Council of Nagaland-Isak Muivah (NSCN-IM), 182, 184–5, 235, 237, 245–6, 249–50, 256, 259, 262–3, 269, 285, 312–14, 325, 327
drug smuggling, 274–80
Nagas, 324
'Saffron Revolution', 292–7
National United Party of Arakan (NUPA), 263, 265, 266, 267
National Unity Government (NUG), 315
Nationwide Ceasefire Agreement (NCA), 265, 297, 302, 318
Naxal uprising (1967), 112
Naxalbari movement, 15, 81
Naxalite uprising (1967), 144–7
Naypyidaw, 5, 284–5, 296–9, 301, 303, 305, 313, 318–20
Nazi Germany, 295
Nazimuddin, Khawaja, 43–4, 51
Nazrul Islam, Kazi, 261
Nazrul Islam, Syed, 148
NDC, 218
Ne Win, General, 20–1, 35, 38–9, 57–9, 107–8, 172–4, 185, 227, 233, 247, 249, 255
boundary dispute, 74–9

Burma and India's policy line, 227–32
Burmese economy, 71–4
China-Burma-India trijunction, 89–96
India and Burma relationship, 233–7
Rajiv's outreach, 225–6
NEC Bill, 158, 160, 163, 174
Nehru Award of International Understanding (1995), 254, 258, 260, 276
Nehru Memorial Museum and Library (NMML), 19
Nehru, Braj Kumar, 174
Shillong, road to, 158–65
Nehru, Jawaharlal, 11, 25–6, 28, 47, 54, 59, 61, 67, 130, 315
AFSPA, imposition of, 58–67
armed support, 35–42
Ayub and, 83–4
'Bangabandhu', birth of, 135–43
boundary demarcations, 105–11
boundary dispute, 74–9
Burmese economy, 71–4
China-Burma-India trijunction, 89–96
death, 84, 88
diplomacy, 29–30
language agitation, 42–52
Nagaland as a state, 85–9
Nehru-Noon agreement, 67–71
Phizo, meetings with, 275
religious disputes, 120–7
Six-Point Movement, 127–35
Nehru-Liaquat Pact (1950), 16, 20, 27, 28, 42–3, 53–4, 118, 175, 310, 323
Nehru-Noon agreement, 67–71, 120

Nehru-Nu visit, 57, 59
Nehruvian secularism, 14
Nellie massacre (1983), 123, 241
Nellie, 173–9
Neogy, Kshitish C, 30
Nepal, 213, 239, 300
boundary dispute, 74–9
Netherlands, 20
New Delhi, 1, 2, 5, 6, 13, 18, 31, 84–5, 111–12
armed support, 35–42
Brang Seng arrival, 234–5
Burma, communism in, 31–3
cross-border movements, 14–17
See also Bangladesh; Burma; China; Manipur; Nehru, Jawaharlal; Nepal; West Pakistan
New Moore Island, 220
New York Times (newspaper), 50, 176, 245–6
New York, 301
NHTA. See Naga Hills-Tuensang Area (NHTA)
Nine-Point Agreement (1947), 38
Niwas, Ram, 304
Nixon, Richard, 229
Nizam-e-Islam, 137, 209
NLD. See National League for Democracy (NLD)
NNC. See Naga National Council (NNC)
No Than Kap, 236–7, 265
Noakhali riots, 12, 121, 203
Non-Aligned Movement, 215
Noon, Firoz Khan, 67
north Andaman, 266
North Cachar Hills, 33, 63, 157, 180
North Eastern Council (1972), 18

North-East Council (NEC) Act,
112, 156
North-East Frontier Agency
(NEFA), 74, 85
northern Rakhine, 233
Northwest Frontier Province
(NWFP), 140
NPC. *See* Naga Peace Committee
(NPC)
NRC. *See* National Register of
Citizens (NRC)
NSCN split (1988), 276
NSCN. *See* National Socialist
Council of Nagaland (NSCN)
NSCN-K
'Saffron Revolution', 292–7
Nu, 27, 60, 71, 76–7, 87, 233
armed support, 35–42
boundary dispute, 74–9
China-Burma-India trijunction,
89–96
NUG. *See* National Unity
Government (NUG)
NUPA. *See* National United Party
of Arakan (NUPA)
Nurul Islam, 172

Obama, Barack, 294
Observer (newspaper), 71
Oil and Natural Gas Ltd. Videsh
(ONGC), 260
Ojha, P N. *See* Banerjee, P N
'open door' policy, 229
Operation (1027), 318
Operation Bajrang, 183, 235
'Operation Chin Hills', 104, 105
Operation Gibraltar, 84
Operation Golden Bird, 263, 270
Operation Grand Slam, 84
Operation Insaniyat (humanity),
305

Operation Jericho, 99, 105
'Operation Jim', 78
Operation Jordon, 246
Operation Leech, 267
Operation Ma Ma, 104
Operation Rhino, 183, 236
Operation Searchlight, 136–7,
144, 147, 190
Operations Bajrang, 184
Operations Rhino, 184
Orissa, 67, 73, 121, 264
Osmany, Gen. MAG, 193, 202

Padma Bridge, 190, 321
Paites, 97, 103, 106, 181
Pakistan Awami League, 138
Pakistan Democratic Movement
(PDM), 137–8
Pakistan International Airlines, 102
Pakistan, 3–4, 6, 10, 11–14, 16,
20–1, 29, 80, 84, 85, 221, 222,
292, 323
armed support, 35–42
Bangladesh, economy and
famine, 189–200
boundary dispute, 74–9
Burmese economy, 71–4
cross-border migration and
movements, 179–83
Nagaland as a state, 85–9
Nehru's diplomacy, 29–30
Nehru-Noon agreement,
67–71
Shillong accord, 165–73
troops, 200–9
Pakistan's Bengali language
movement (1952), 43
Pakistani Deputy High
Commissioner (DHC), 121,
135, 139
Pakistani flag, 32

455

Pakistani Hindus, 46, 121–2
Pakistani intelligence, 55
Pakistani Muslims, 122, 124, 306
Pakistani Santhals, 121
Pandara Road, 220
Panglong conference (1947), 12, 295
Pant, Govind Ballabh, 62
Parbatya Chattagram Jana Samhati Samiti (PCJSS), 205, 242
Paris, 163, 164, 256, 274, 276
Parthasarthy, G, 260
Parva, 266
Parwa, 234
Patel, Sardar Vallabhbhai, 26–7, 53, 312, 327
    Burma, communism in, 31–3
    Nehru's diplomacy, 29–30
Patkai, 9
Patwary, Shameem Haider, 322
Payra, 300
'Treaty of Peace and Friendship', 53
'Peace Mission', 88
Peace-Talks Creation Group, 296
Pegu (Bago), 35
Peking, 74, 76–7, 91, 92–3, 101, 104, 107, 147, 203
Pensat, 87
People's Liberation Army (PLA), 65, 101, 105
    boundary dispute, 74–9
People's Liberation Army of Manipur (PLA-M), 157, 182, 319
People's Relief Committee, 130
People's Revolutionary Party of Kangleipak (PREPAK), 157
Peru, 205
Peshawar, 236
Lee, Peter, 168

Phizo, Zapu, 55–6, 81, 88, 156, 161–3, 184
    AFSPA, imposition of, 58–67
    Nagaland as a state, 85–9
    Nehru's meetings, 275
    Nehru-Noon agreement, 67–71
    Shillong, road to, 158–65
Phukan, Bhrigu, 175
Pilger, John, 190
'Pilkhana', 287–8
Pillai, Gopal Krishna, 18, 182, 279–80, 299, 302, 312–13
Pioneer (newspaper), 274
PL480 programme, 190, 191
PLA. See People's Liberation Army (PLA)
Place de la Concorde, 274
Policy Planning Committee, 195
Praja Socialist Party, 125
Prasad Dhar, Durga (DP), 143–7
Prasad, Rajendra, 31
PREPAK, 182
Presidential Advisory Group, 219
Prevention of Infiltration into India of Pakistani Nationals (PIP), 123–4
Preventive Detention Act (PDA), 59
'Project PIP', 124, 174
Public Security Act (PSA), 132
Public Service Commission, 158
Punjab, 11, 12, 25, 49, 52, 180, 236, 253, 324
    Six-Point Movement, 127–35
Purr, 86
'Purvanchal Hindu Sammelan', 176
Pyinmana, 33

'Quad', 2
Quetta, 147

'Quit Mizoram Order', 170

R&AW. *See* Research & Analysis
    Wing (R&AW)
R&AW-KIO channel, 234
Raghavan, 117, 128
Rahman, Lt. Gen. (r) Mahfuzur,
    287, 305
Rahman, Maj. Gen. Khaliur, 202
Rahman, Maj. Gen. Ziaur, 202
Rahman, Tarique, 289–90, 322
Rajiv-Longowal accord (1985),
    180
Rajkhowa, Arabinda, 156
Rajshahi border, 120
Rajshahi, 69, 121, 122, 127, 131,
    133
Rajshahi-born CPI(M), 177
Rakhine Buddhists, 172, 266
Rakhine coast, 260
Rakhine insurgents, 246
Rakhine state, 54, 98, 266, 298,
    299, 301, 305, 318–19
Rakkhi Bahini, 201
Ram Janmabhoomi movement, 29
Ram Mandir issue, 310–11, 314
Ramcharit Manas, 29
Ramna Gurudwara, 208
Rangamati, 99
Rangoon Water Supply Project,
    228
Rangoon, 8, 12–13, 27–8, 32–5,
    104, 111, 166, 172–3, 223,
    228–9, 231, 237
    armed support, 35–42
    'Bangabandhu', birth of,
        135–43
    boundary demarcations, 105–11
    boundary dispute, 74–9
    Burmese economy, 71–4
    and India's policy line, 227–32

Mizoram independence, 96–105
Naga rebels, 230
Nagaland as a state, 85–9
Nehru-Noon agreement, 67–71
Rajiv's outreach, 226
Rangpur, 205
Rann of Kutch, 84, 126
Rao, P.V. Narasimha, 216–18, 228,
    248–9, 253–6, 274–5, 277
    'Look East Policy', 256–64
    drug smuggling, 274–80
Rao, Rajeshwar, 145
Raschid, Abdul, 307
Rashtriya Bajrang Dal, 310
Ravi, RN, 313
Rawalpindi, 166, 236
Rawat, R.S., 264
Ray, A K, 135
Razzak, Abdur, 132, 149
Red Fort, 189
the 'Red Maulana', 44
Reddy, Sanjiva, 216
Registration of Foreigners Bill, 9
Reliance groups, 285, 301
Reliance Power, 301
Reliance, 45
Representative Office of Kachin
    Affairs, 235
Research & Analysis Wing
    (R&AW), 112, 128, 142,
    143–4, 150, 167, 169–70,
    189, 197, 200–7, 211–15, 219,
    23–3, 248, 255, 274
    Chakmas, 238–45
    drug smuggling, 274–80
    'Look East Policy', 256–64
    Mujib-Tajuddin split, 147–52
    Naxalite movement, 143–7
    Shillong, road to, 158–65
Restoration Council of Shan State,
    302

Rhodesia, 145
Rijiju, Kiren, 292, 306
Riyadh, 203
Rizvi, Gowher, 127, 221
Rohingya. *See* Arakanese Muslim
　(Rohingya)
Roopur nuclear power plant, 300
Roy, Arun K., 177
Roy, Bidhan Chandra, 47
RSS *pracharak*, 304
RSS, 29, 32, 53, 177, 285, 310,
　312–14
　AFSPA, imposition of, 58–67
　vs. Nagas, 324
Ruma Bazaar, 103
Russel, Sheikh, 189
Russia, 308
Rustomji, N K, 58–9
Rwanda, 295

S Alam group, 321
SAARC summit, 230, 255, 257,
　262, 271
Saathi, Col. (partner), 265
Saffron Revolution (2007–08),
　285, 292–7
Sagaing Division, 60
Saikia, Hiteshwar, 175
Sailo, Brig. T, 166, 169–73, 236–7
Sajek Valley, 103
Sakhrie, T, 59–60, 60–1
　assassination, 61
Samad, Abdus, 193
Sanatan Dharma Swayamsevak
　Sangh (SDSS), 304
Sandhu, Maj. Kamaldeep Singh,
　285–6
Santhal community, 121
Saran, Pankaj, 290, 291, 308
Sarkar, Maj. Gen. B N, 193
Sarma, Himanta Biswa, 309–11

Sashastra Seema Bal. *See* Special
　Service Bureau (SSB)
Sattar, Abdus, 219–20
Saudi Arabia, 203
Saw Maung, 250, 257
Saya San, 8
SBPP, 148–9
Schedule Tribe (ST), 310
Scindia Steam Navigation Co. Ltd.,
　36, 191
Scott, Michael, 88–9
Second Five Year Plan, 65
Sema, Kaito, 85–6, 78
Semas, 63
Sen, Amartya, 192
Sen, Prafulla, 121, 124–5
Sen, Samar, 198, 201, 208
Senior Assamese Muslim Congress,
　124
'sepoy mutiny', 207
SFF. *See* Special Frontier Force
　(SFF),
Shah, Amit, 2, 238, 242, 244, 269,
　309
Shah, Fakhir Lallan, 261
Shahbag movement (2013), 307
Shan state, 13, 54, 75, 318
Shanti Bahini, 171, 181, 205, 214,
　226, 242, 255, 256, 262, 268,
　214
Shastri, Lal Bahadur, 81, 95–6, 99,
　122
Shaukat Ali, Mir, 219
Shekhar, Chandra, 235
Shekhawat, Bhairon Singh, 304
Shersabadia Muslims, 124
Shillong accord, 21, 156, 163,
　165–73, 184
Shillong, 60, 98, 131, 168, 264
　road to, 158–65
　Shillong mission, 133

Shillong-Silchar road, 33
Shimray, Anthony, 269, 270, 275–6
Shiromani Akali Dal, 171, 180
Shiv Sena, 273–4
Shiv Sena-BJP alliance, 273
Shrinagesh, SM, 62–4
Shwe gas, 260
Shwe, Sr. Gen. Than, 233
Siddique ul-Islam, 291
Siddique, Kader 'Tiger', 204–5
Sikder, Siraj, 194
Sikh insurgency, 180
Sikhs, 12, 29
Sikkim, 7, 102
    BJP in, 309
Sikkim, Dewan of, 58
Siliguri, 16
Simla Agreement, 187
Sindh, 140
Singapore, 321
Singaporean banks, 298
Singh, Irabat, 34, 182
Singh, Jaswant, 272–4
Singh, Kewal, 198
Singh, Lallan Prasad, 163, 164, 175
Singh, Manmohan, 300
Singh, Swaran, 105
Singha, Capt. Anand, 86
Sinhalese communities, 180
Sino-Burmese boundary agreement, 77, 91
Sino-Burmese boundary, 92
Sino–Burmese relations, 108
Sino-Indian boundary dispute, 42
Sino-Indian relations, 5, 89
Sino-Indian war (1962), 84, 136
Sittwe crosses, 319
Sittwe port, 267, 271, 299, 323
Sitwundan, 38
Six-Point Movement, 127–35

SLORC. See State Law and Order Restoration Council (SLORC)
Sobhan, Rehman, 149
socialism, 31–2
Socialist Party, 38
Soe Thane, 294, 295, 297
Somnath temple, 31
Somra (in Burma), 87
Sonadia port, 298, 300
'SOS', 286
South Africa, 145
South Asia, 262, 322
South Asian Preferential Trade Agreement, 262
South Block, 59–60
South Talpatti, 220
Southeast Asia, 4, 16–17, 225–6, 228
Southeast Asian Treaty Organisation, 41
Soviet-Afghan war, 219
Spanish civil war, 146
Special Economic Zones, 229
Special Frontier Force (SFF), 105, 127–8, 149, 165, 200
Special Service Bureau (SSB), 127–8, 200
Sri Lanka, 153, 227, 231, 260, 271
Sri Lankan civil war, 288
Sri Lankan constitution, 227
Sri Lankan Tamils, 180
    Sri Lankan Tamil assassin, 250
Srinivasan, Krishnan, 242–5, 260–1
St. Martin's Island, 290
'Stable AFPFL', 71
State Law and Order Restoration Council (SLORC), 233, 247, 255
State Minister for Power, 147
State of Nagaland Act, 87

State Sangha Maha Nayaka
  Committee, 294
State Trading Corporation of India,
  211, 213
Statesman (newspaper), 195–6
Stillwell (Ledo), 39
Stilwell Road, 299
Subrahmanyam, K, 145
Suhrawardy, Huseyn Shaheed,
  43–4, 50, 68, 136
  death, 134
Sukarno, 99
Sundarban coast, 166, 198, 220
Suntook, N Framji, 212–15
Supreme Court of India, 29
Suttar, Chittaranjan, 205, 211–12,
  214, 215
Suu Kyi, Aung San, 226–7, 231–2,
  247, 249, 254–60, 276, 281,
  302–5, 318
  'Saffron Revolution', 292–7
Swadhin Bangla Biplobi Parishad
  (SBPP, or Free Bangla
  Revolutionary Council), 131–2,
  208
Swell, George Gilbert, 230
Swu, Isak Chishi, 163–5, 274–5,
  276, 312–13
Sylhet district, 12, 45, 55, 67, 78,
  122, 214, 264
Sylhet referendum (1947), 31

Ta Ga, 313
Ta'ang, 54
Table Island, 41
Tagore, Rabindranath, 49, 261
Taiwan, 76
Tajuddin, 129, 150–1, 199–200
  Mujib-Tajuddin split, 147–52
  Naxalite movement, 143–7
  troops, 200–9

Talu Pass, 109
Talukdar, Mrs., 220
Tamenglong, 181
Tamil Nadu, 180
Tamil, 40, 227, 231
Tamu, 17
Tamu-Moreh crossing, 277
Tangkhuls, 63, 312, 313
Tarique, 291
Tashkent agreement (1966), 84
Tashkent Declaration, 102
Tata Consultancy Services, 298
Tata International, 298, 301
Tata Motors, 294, 298, 301
Tata Power, 298
Tatas, 300–1
Tatmadaw, 71, 104, 161, 165,
  230–5, 248, 255–9, 263, 265,
  276, 313
  Rajiv's outreach, 225–6
Tawang, 103
Tedim (in Burma), 103, 104
Teera, 87
Teesta, 322
Tejgaon airport, 286
Ten-chung, 101
Tenggol, Arambai, 317
'termites', 285, 309–14
Thailand, 4, 20, 167, 168, 185,
  231, 260, 271
Thakur, Shalaka, 277
Than Kap, 265
Than Shwe, 250, 255–8, 265, 271,
  281, 293, 315
Than Than Nu (Nu's daughter),
  233, 257
Thant Kyaw, 303
Thein Sein, 294–6, 301–3
Three Brotherhood Alliance, 318
Tiananmen Square massacre
  (1989), 226, 247

Tibet, 4, 75, 80, 92, 103
Tibetan Mustang Resistance Force, 105, 127
Tibet-Yunnan-Burma border, 65
Times of India (newspaper), 62, 195–6
Tin Bigha corridor, 126, 261
Tin Hlaing, Col., 258–9
Tirana, 163
Tirap Frontier Division, 109
Titan, 298
Tito, Joseph Broz, 220
Tiwari, Narayan Dutt, 239
Tokyo, 300, 301
TP Tewary Commission Report, 176
Trinamool Congress, 309
Tripura National Volunteers (TNV), 240
Tripura, 7, 12, 18, 25, 34, 70, 110, 122, 155–8, 171, 200, 204, 240–1, 263–4
    BJP in, 309
    Chakmas, 238–45
    cross-border migration and movements, 179–83
    language agitation, 42–52
Tuensang Frontier, 59, 61–5, 106, 160
Tukergram, 120
Tutsis, 295
Tweet (X), 2
'Two China' policy, 76
'Two Track' approach, 254
Two-Nation theory, 11

U Nu. *See* Nu
UAPA. *See* Unlawful Activities (Prevention) Act 1967 (UAPA)
Uban, Maj. Gen. Sujan Singh, 149
Ukhrul, 106

Ukraine, 308, 320–1
UN resolution, 75
UN Secretary General, 296
Unfashionable Tragedy, The (documentary), 190
Uniform Civil Code (UCC), 311, 325
Union Enterprise for Humanitarian, Resettlement, and Development, 305
Union of Soviet Socialist Republics (USSR), 147
United Front, 43, 48–50, 69, 101
    language agitation, 42–52
United Kingdom (UK), 20, 197
United Liberation Front of Asom (ULFA), 156, 183–5, 235–7, 245–50, 262
United Liberation Front of Assam-Independent (ULFA-I), 21, 259, 270, 275–6, 290, 309, 327
    drug smuggling, 274–80
United National Liberation Front (UNLF), 157
United Nations (UN), 41, 68
United Nations General Assembly (UNGA), 263
United Nations High Commissioner for Refugees, 306
United Nations Industrial Development Organisation, 216
United Nations Office on Drugs and Crimes (UNODC), 278–9, 319
    drug smuggling, 274–80
United Progressive Alliance (UPA) government, 298
United States, 2, 13, 41, 69, 75, 85–6, 105, 127, 214, 221, 281–4, 288–9, 315

Bangladesh, economy and
    famine, 189–200
United Wa State Party, 302
Unlawful Activities (Prevention)
    Act 1967 (UAPA), 156, 167–8,
    170
Upper Burma, 36
Urdu, 113
US diplomats, 210
US intelligence, 105
US Secretary of State Condoleezza
    Rice (2005), 294
Uttar Pradesh Hindu Mahasabha,
    29
Uttar Pradesh, 129

Vairengte, 265
Vaishnava Hindus, 311
Vajpayee, Atal Bihari, 216
Vancheng, 103
Vanlalngaia, 103
Venugopal, Rajesh, 277
Verghese, Boobli G, 110–11
Verma, AN, 257–8, 274–5
Vijayanagar, 236
Village Defence Parties, 215
Vishwa Hindu Parishad, 176, 310
'Volunteer Force (V-Force)', 13

Wa state, 65
Walong, 103
War Council, 149
Washington, D.C., 158, 190, 200,
    210
Water and Power Consultancy
    Services (India) (WAPCOS),
    228
West Bengal, 12, 25–30, 33, 40,
    118–121, 177, 199–200, 241,
    264, 273, 286, 309
    'Act East' policy, 297–309

'Bangabandhu', birth of, 135–43
Chakmas, 238–45
cross-border migration and
    movements, 14–17, 179–83
drug smuggling, 274–80
economy and famine, 189–200
intra-party friction, 209–17
language agitation, 42–52
'Look East Policy', 256–64
mutiny, 287–92
Rajiv's outreach, 225–6
religious disputes, 120–7
Shillong, road to, 158–65
ties, 245–9
West Dinajpur, 124–5
West Pakistan, 6, 190
    'Act East' policy, 297–309
    'Bangabandhu', birth of,
        135–43
    Chakmas, 238–45
    cross-border migration and
        movements, 14–17, 179–83
    drug smuggling, 274–80
    economy and famine, 189–200
    intra-party friction, 209–17
    language agitation, 42–52
    'Look East Policy', 256–64
    Rajiv's outreach, 225–6
    Shillong, road to, 158–65
    ties, 245–9
    mutiny, 287–92
'White Flag', 103
White-band People's Volunteer
    Organisation, 34
Wilson Center, 19
Wirathu, Ashin, 295
World Bank, 321
World War II, 10, 61–2
Wungau camp, 236
Wynn Lwin, 247, 259, 281

Xi Jinping, 297, 300
Xinjiang, 76

Yahya, 143, 148
Yangon port, 299, 316
Yangon, 254, 256–8, 263–7, 281, 284, 295, 303, 316
Ye Guong, 230
Yebaw Ba Tin. *See* Ghoshal, Hamendra Nath
Youth League, 50
Yunnan province, 4, 164, 229, 298
Yunus, Dr Muhammad, 321–2

Zamindar, Vazira, 12
Zau Seng, 77
Zeliangrong communities, 311
Zeliangrong Nagas, 106
Zemi Nagas, 33

Zia International Airport, 286
Zia, Khaleda, 22, 216, 219, 238–46, 255, 261, 271, 281, 322
    Chakma movement, 242
    'Look East Policy', 256–64
    troops, 200–9
Zia-ul-Haq, 236
Zia-ur-Rahman, Maj. Gen., 21, 171–4, 188, 196, 202, 207–10, 218, 222, 238, 244, 249, 281
    intra-party friction, 209–17
Zin Yaw, 302
Zion, 246, 270
Zo Reunification Organisation, 236
Zo Revolutionary Army, 181–2
Zo-Kuki community, 101, 181
Zoramthanga, 166, 168, 184, 311–12
Zurich, 70, 275